FEMINIST JUDGMENTS: REWRITTEN EMPLOYMENT DISCRIMINATION OPINIONS

How would feminist perspectives and analytical methods change the interpretation of employment discrimination law? Would the conscious use of feminist perspectives make a difference? This volume shows the difference feminist analysis can make to the interpretation of employment discrimination statutes. This book brings together a group of scholars and lawyers to rewrite fifteen employment discrimination decisions in which a feminist analysis would have changed the outcome or the courts' reasoning. It demonstrates that use of feminist perspectives and methodologies, if adopted by the courts, would have made a significant difference in employment discrimination law, leading to a fairer and more egalitarian workplace, and a more prosperous society.

Ann C. McGinley is William S. Boyd Professor of Law and Co-Director of the Workplace Law Program at Boyd School of Law, University of Nevada, Las Vegas. She writes about the intersection of race, gender, masculinities, and employment discrimination law. Author of *Masculinity at Work: Employment Discrimination through a Different Lens* (2016) and coeditor of *Masculinities and the Law: A Multidimensional Approach* (2012), McGinley applies masculinities theory to advocate new interpretations of employment law.

Nicole Buonocore Porter is Professor of Law at University of Toledo College of Law. She writes about the employment rights of women and individuals with disabilities, concentrating on exploring ways that the law can avoid marginalizing both groups of employees. She is the coauthor of two casebooks and one treatise. In 2018, she won a university-wide award for outstanding researcher.

Feminist Judgments Series Editors

Bridget J. Crawford
Elisabeth Haub School of Law at Pace University

Kathryn M. Stanchi
University of Nevada, Las Vegas, William S. Boyd School of Law

Linda L. Berger
University of Nevada, Las Vegas, William S. Boyd School of Law

Advisory Panel for Feminist Judgments Series

Kathryn Abrams, Herma Hill Kay Distinguished Professor of Law, University of California, Berkeley, School of Law

Katharine T. Bartlett, A. Kenneth Pye Professor Emerita of Law, Duke University School of Law

Mary Anne Case, Arnold I. Shure Professor of Law, The University of Chicago Law School

Margaret E. Johnson, Professor of Law, University of Baltimore School of Law

Sonia Katyal, Chancellor's Professor of Law, University of California, Berkeley, School of Law

Nancy Leong, Professor of Law, University of Denver Sturm College of Law

Rachel Moran, Michael J. Connell Distinguished Professor of Law and Dean Emerita, UCLA School of Law

Angela Onwuachi-Willig, Dean and Professor of Law, Boston University School of Law

Nancy D. Polikoff, Professor of Law, American University Washington College of Law

Daniel B. Rodriguez, Dean and Harold Washington Professor, Northwestern University School of Law

Susan Deller Ross, Professor of Law, Georgetown University Law Center

Verna L. Williams, Dean and Nippert Professor of Law, University of Cincinnati College of Law

Feminist Judgments: Rewritten Employment Discrimination Opinions

Edited by

ANN C. MCGINLEY

University of Nevada, Las Vegas, William S. Boyd School of Law

NICOLE BUONOCORE PORTER

University of Toledo College of Law

CAMBRIDGE
UNIVERSITY PRESS

University Printing House, Cambridge CB2 8BS, United Kingdom

One Liberty Plaza, 20th Floor, New York, NY 10006, USA

477 Williamstown Road, Port Melbourne, VIC 3207, Australia

314–321, 3rd Floor, Plot 3, Splendor Forum, Jasola District Centre,
New Delhi – 110025, India

79 Anson Road, #06–04/06, Singapore 079906

Cambridge University Press is part of the University of Cambridge.

It furthers the University's mission by disseminating knowledge in the pursuit of
education, learning, and research at the highest international levels of excellence.

www.cambridge.org
Information on this title: www.cambridge.org/9781108493178
DOI: 10.1017/9781108694643

© Cambridge University Press 2020

This publication is in copyright. Subject to statutory exception
and to the provisions of relevant collective licensing agreements,
no reproduction of any part may take place without the written
permission of Cambridge University Press.

First published 2020

A catalogue record for this publication is available from the British Library.

Library of Congress Cataloging-in-Publication Data
NAMES: McGinley, Ann C., editor. | Porter, Nicole Buonocore, editor.
TITLE: Feminist judgments : rewritten employment discrimination opinions/ edited by Ann
C. McGinley, William S. Boyd School of Law at UNLV [and] Nicole Buonocore Porter,
University of Toledo College of Law
DESCRIPTION: Cambridge, United Kingdom ; New York, NY, USA : Cambridge University
Press, 2020. | Series: Feminist judgment series | Includes index.
IDENTIFIERS: LCCN 2020013353 (print) | LCCN 2020013354 (ebook) | ISBN 9781108493178
(hardback) | ISBN 9781108694643 (ebook)
SUBJECTS: LCSH: Sex discrimination in employment – Law and legislation – United
States – Cases. | Feminist jurisprudence – United States.
CLASSIFICATION: LCC KF3467 .F46 2020 (print) | LCC KF3467 (ebook) | DDC 344.7301/4133–
dc23
LC record available at https://lccn.loc.gov/2020013353
LC ebook record available at https://lccn.loc.gov/2020013354

ISBN 978-1-108-49317-8 Hardback
ISBN 978-1-108-71740-3 Paperback

Cambridge University Press has no responsibility for the persistence or accuracy of
URLs for external or third-party internet websites referred to in this publication
and does not guarantee that any content on such websites is, or will remain,
accurate or appropriate.

For my mother, Mary McGinley, who loved life, lived more than a century, and gave those around her unconditional love –ACM

For the most important females in my life: my mom, Annette, and my three daughters, Kayla, Elise, and Ava –NBP

Contents

Advisory Panel for Feminist Judgments: Rewritten Employment Discrimination Opinions	*page* xii
Notes on Contributors	xiv
Preface	xxiii
Acknowledgments	xxv

1	**Introduction**	1
	Ann C. McGinley and Nicole Buonocore Porter	
2	**Supreme Court and Gender Narratives**	30
	Desert Palace, Inc. v. Costa, 539 U.S. 90 (2003)	43
	Commentary: *Naomi M. Mann*	
	Judgment: *Anne E. Mullins*	
3	**Pregnancy Discrimination**	58
	International Union, UAW v. Johnson Controls,	
	Inc., 499 U.S. 187 (1991)	68
	Commentary: *Wynter P. Allen*	
	Judgment: *Marcia L. McCormick*	
	Young v. United Parcel Services, Inc.,	
	135 S.Ct. 1338 (2015)	87
	Commentary: *Bradley A. Areheart*	
	Judgment: *Deborah A. Widiss*	
4	**Intersectional Approaches to Appearances**	119
	Jespersen v. Harrah's Operating Co., 444 F.3d 1104	
	(9th Cir. 2006) (en banc)	128

ix

Commentary: *Roxana S. Bell*
Judgment: *Angela Onwuachi-Willig and JoAnne Sweeny*

**Equal Employment Opportunity Commission v.
Catastrophe Management Solutions, 852 F.3d 1018
(11th Cir. 2016)**   146
Commentary: *Jasbir (Jesse) Kaur Bawa*
Judgment: *D. Wendy Greene*

Webb v. City of Philadelphia, 562 F.3d 256 (3d Cir. 2009)   180
Commentary: *Sahar F. Aziz*
Judgment: *Valorie K. Vojdik*

5   Harassment Because of Sex   215
**Meritor Savings Bank, FSB v. Vinson, 477 U.S. 57
(1986) (opinion reproduced from *Feminist Judgments*)**   227
Commentary: *Trina Jones*
Judgment: *Angela Onwuachi-Willig*

**Oncale v. Sundowner Offshore Services, Inc., 523
U.S. 75 (1998) (opinion reproduced from *Feminist
Judgments*)**   245
Commentary: *Nancy E. Dowd*
Judgment: *Ann C. McGinley*

6   Sexual Orientation and Gender Identity Discrimination
as Sex Discrimination   266
**Etsitty v. Utah Transit Authority, 502 F.3d 1215
(10th Cir. 2007)**   278
Commentary: *Pamela A. Wilkins*
Judgment: *Catherine Jean Archibald*

**Hively v. Ivy Tech Community College, 853 F.3d 339
(7th Cir. 2017) (en banc)**   301
Commentary: *Danielle D. Weatherby*
Judgment: *Ryan H. Nelson*

7   Systemic Claims and Gender: Proving Disparate
Treatment and Impact   334
**American Federation of State, County, and Municipal
Employees, AFL-CIO (AFSCME) v. State of Washington,
770 F.2d 1401 (9th Cir. 1985)**   344

Commentary: *Stephanie Bornstein*
Judgment: *Teresa Godwin Phelps*

Equal Employment Opportunity Commission v. Sears, Roebuck & Co., 839 F.2d 302 (7th Cir. 1988)   361
Commentary: *Maria L. Ontiveros*
Judgment: *Leticia M. Saucedo*

Ricci v. DeStefano, 557 U.S. 557 (2009)   383
Commentary: *Rebecca K. Lee*
Judgment: *Marley S. Weiss*

Wal-Mart Stores, Inc. v. Dukes et al., 564 U.S. 338 (2011)   430
Commentary: *Charles A. Sullivan*
Judgment: *Tristin K. Green*

8   **Retaliation**   462
Clark County School District v. Breeden, 532 U.S. 268 (2001)   462
Commentary: *Rebecca Hanner White*
Judgment: *Michael Z. Green*

Index   486

Advisory Panel for *Feminist Judgments: Rewritten Employment Discrimination Opinions*

Sahar Aziz, Professor of Law and Chancellor's Social Justice Scholar, Rutgers Law School

Mary Ann Case, Arnold I. Shure Professor of Law, University of Chicago Law School

Frank Rudy Cooper, William S. Boyd Professor of Law and Director of the Program on Race, Gender, and Policing, University of Nevada, Las Vegas, William S. Boyd School of Law

Tristin Green, Professor of Law, Associate Dean for Faculty Scholarship and Dean's Circle Scholar, University of San Francisco School of Law

D. Wendy Greene, Professor of Law, Drexel University Thomas R. Kline School of Law

Lynne Henderson, Emerita Professor of Law, University of Nevada, Las Vegas, William S. Boyd School of Law

Marcia McCormick, Associate Dean for Academic Affairs and Professor of Law and Women's and Gender Studies, Saint Louis University School of Law

Angela Onwuachi-Willig, Dean and Professor of Law, Boston University School of Law

Gowri Ramachandran, Professor of Law, Southwestern Law School

Vicki Schultz, Ford Foundation Professor of Law and Social Sciences, Yale Law School

Elaine Shoben, Emerita Judge Jack and Lulu Lehman Professor of Law, University of Nevada, Las Vegas, William S. Boyd School of Law

Advisory Panel

Charles Sullivan, Professor of Law and Senior Associate Dean for Finance and Faculty, Seton Hall University School of Law

Michael Waterstone, Fritz B. Burns Dean and Professor of Law, Loyola Law School and Senior Vice President, Loyola Marymount University

Notes on Contributors

Wynter P. Allen is a partner with Alden Law Group and a Commissioner on the D.C. Commission on Human Rights. Ms. Allen was also the chair of the D.C. Public Employee Relations Board from 2011 until 2013. Ms. Allen has spoken on various topics relating to labor and employment for the International Brotherhood of Teamsters Women's Conference, International Conference of Teamster Lawyers, Federal Workplace Conference, the National Employment Lawyers Association, the American Federation of Labor and Congress of Industrial Organizations (AFL–CIO) Lawyers Coordinating Committee (LCC) Conference, and the American Bar Association. She served as an adjunct professor for the Elon Law School Externship Program and Howard University School of Law.

Catherine Jean Archibald is an associate professor of law at University of Detroit Mercy School of Law. Prior to joining Detroit Mercy Law, she worked for several years as a litigation associate at international law firm Dewey & LeBoeuf LLP in New York City. Her scholarship on transgender rights has been published in some of the nation's top law reviews, including the *Duke Journal of Gender Law & Policy* and the *UMKC Law Review*.

Bradley A. Areheart is an associate professor at the University of Tennessee College of Law. He writes about antidiscrimination theory, disability rights, genetic discrimination, social movements, and equality of opportunity. His scholarship has been published in, among other places, the *Yale Law Journal*, *Michigan Law Review*, and *University of Chicago Law Review*.

Sahar F. Aziz is a professor of law and Chancellor's Social Justice Scholar at Rutgers University Law School, where she researches and teaches on national security, civil rights law, and Middle East law. Professor Aziz is the founding director of the Center for Security, Race and Rights, and serves on the US Institute for Peace RESOLVE Network Research Advisory Council.

Jasbir (Jesse) Kaur Bawa is an assistant professor of lawyering skills at Howard University School of Law. She specializes in teaching legal writing and appellate advocacy through a civil rights lens, including employment discrimination issues. She has also taught a course in racial profiling across communities of color. She received her B.A. from McMaster University in Hamilton, Ontario, Canada. She received her J.D. from Howard University School of Law.

Roxana S. Bell is a professor of law at the University of Detroit Mercy School of Law, where she teaches civil procedure and legal communication. Prior to becoming a law professor, Bell practiced labor and employment law at a large law firm in Indianapolis. She focused her practice on management-side defense and general employment and workplace policies. Bell researches and writes in the area of antidiscrimination law.

Stephanie Bornstein is an associate professor of law at the University of Florida Levin College of Law, where she teaches and writes in the areas of employment and labor law, antidiscrimination law, and civil procedure. She served previously as a visiting assistant professor at the University of California, Hastings College of Law, Deputy Director of UC Hastings' Center for WorkLife Law, and a staff attorney at national public interest law center Equal Rights Advocates. Bornstein received her bachelor's degree *magna cum laude* from Harvard University and her law degree from the University of California, Berkeley, School of Law.

Nancy E. Dowd is a professor and David Levin Chair in Family Law at the University of Florida Fredric Levin College of Law. She is Emeritus Director of the Center on Children and Families. She writes in the areas of constitutional law, family law, juvenile justice, feminist and masculinities theory, critical race theory, civil rights, children's rights, and social justice. Her most recent book is *Reimagining Equality: A New Deal for Children of Color* (2018).

Michael Z. Green is a professor of law and Director of the Workplace Law Program at Texas A&M University School of Law. Professor Green's scholarship focuses on workplace disputes, with an emphasis on race and sex, as well as alternatives to the court resolution process. He teaches employment discrimination law, and he has published dozens of law review articles and several book chapters on the subject. He is also the coauthor for two pending employment discrimination books. An elected Fellow of the College of Labor and Employment Lawyers and a member of the American Law Institute, he thanks Texas A&M University School of Law 2019 graduate Spencer Mainka for her thoughtful research and dedicated edits that added tremendous value to this completed chapter.

Tristin K. Green is a professor of law at the University of San Francisco School of Law. She specializes in laws affecting race- and sex-based inequality, especially employment discrimination law. She brings to her scholarship a background in journalism and sociology, and an interest in human relations and in the ways in which laws and contexts shape those relations. She is the author of *Discrimination Laundering: The Rise of Organizational Innocence and the Crisis of Equal Opportunity Law* (2017).

D. Wendy Greene is one of the nation's leading legal experts on "grooming codes discrimination" in workplaces and schools. Internationally recognized for her legal scholarship and public advocacy on this civil rights issue, Greene's efforts have generated a global public awareness campaign, #FreeTheHair, alongside legal protections at municipal, state, and federal levels, including the CROWN Acts: the first pieces of legislation in US history to clarify that the discrimination African descendants encounter on the basis of natural hairstyles constitutes race discrimination. Professor Greene's legal theories were also instrumental to the litigation and adjudication of *Equal Employment Opportunity Commission v. Catastrophe Management Solutions*.

Trina Jones is Jerome M. Culp Professor of Law at Duke University School of Law. Her scholarly research and writing focuses on racial and socioeconomic inequality. She is a leading legal expert on skin color discrimination, or colorism. Before joining Duke's faculty, she practiced law at Wilmer, Cutler, and Pickering (now Wilmer Hale) in Washington, D.C. From 2008 to 2011, she was a founding faculty member at the University of California, Irvine, School of Law, where she created and directed the Center on Law, Equality and Race. Professor Jones received her undergraduate degree from Cornell University and her J.D., with honors, from the University of Michigan Law School.

Rebecca K. Lee is an associate professor of law at Thomas Jefferson School of Law. She is an expert in the areas of employment discrimination, employment law, affirmative action, and leadership. She has written on the relationship between diversity and antidiscrimination objectives, the importance of orga-nizational leadership in achieving substantive equality, empathy in judicial decision-making, the constitutionality and relevance of affirmative action, and sexual harassment. Professor Lee has previously served as a chair of the

Notes on Contributors xvii

Association of American Law Schools (AALS) Section on Labor Relations and Employment Law. She is a board member of the Conference of Asian Pacific American Law Faculty and also the Western Law Professors of Color.

Naomi M. Mann is an associate clinical professor at Boston University School of Law. She is a founder and director of the Access to Justice Clinic, which tackles the intersections of the legal system with multiple systemic barriers to equity and justice. She dedicates her chapter in loving memory to her mentor Alexis Anderson.

Marcia L. McCormick is a professor of law and women's and gender studies at Saint Louis University and currently Associate Dean for Academic Affairs for the Saint Louis University Law School. She regularly teaches a variety of labor and employment law courses, along with constitutional law courses and criminal law. She has also taught civil rights and seminars on civil rights history and gender or sexuality and the law. Her research has focused on the law and social policy related to the workplace and federal courts.

Ann C. McGinley is William S. Boyd Professor of Law and a co-director of the Workplace Law Program at the University of Nevada, Las Vegas, Boyd School of Law. An internationally recognized scholar on employment discrimination, employment law, masculinities theory, and disability law, McGinley has published more than sixty law review articles and book chapters, and a handful of books. Her most recent book is *Masculinity at Work: Employment Discrimination Law Through a Different Lens* (2016). McGinley has presented her research at Yale, Harvard, Boston, Duke, and Stanford Universities and the University of Chicago in the United States, as well as in Chile, Spain, Italy, Israel, Germany, and Denmark.

Anne E. Mullins is an associate professor at Stetson University College of Law and a scholar of rhetoric in judicial writing. Before entering academia, she practiced law at Susman Godfrey LLP in Houston, Texas. Professor Mullins clerked for the Honorable Jacques L. Wiener (Fifth Circuit) and the Honorable Sarah S. Vance (E.D. La.). She earned her J.D., with honors, from the University of Chicago Law School and her A.B. in women's studies from Dartmouth College. Professor Mullins is especially grateful to Jessica Fenton for her advice and feedback on this opinion, and to Kelley Thompson for her research assistance.

Ryan H. Nelson is a lecturer at Boston University School of Law and a former adjunct professor of law at New York Law School. Previously, he served as in-house employment counsel for a Fortune 50 company and as an attorney at one of the nation's largest labor and employment law firms. He received

xviii   *Notes on Contributors*

LL.M. from Harvard Law School; his J.D., *cum laude*, from Yeshiva University's Benjamin N. Cardozo School of Law; and his B.S.B.A. with a major in economics from the University of Florida. He would like to thank Ann C. McGinley and Nicole Buonocore Porter for their invaluable mentorship throughout this project.

Maria L. Ontiveros is a professor of law and a co-director of the Labor and Employment Law Program at the University of San Francisco School of Law. She holds an A.B. from University of California, Berkeley, a J.D. from Harvard Law School, an M.I.L.R. from Cornell University, and a J.S.D. from Stanford Law School. Her research focuses on organizing immigrant workers, workplace harassment of women of color, and modern-day applications of the Thirteenth Amendment. She is coauthor of the bestselling *Employment Discrimination Casebook* and a member of the U.A.W. Public Review Board.

Angela Onwuachi-Willig is Dean and a professor of law at Boston University. Prior to becoming Dean, she served as Chancellor's Professor of Law at University of California, Berkeley. She is author of *According to Our Hearts:* Rhinelander v. Rhinelander *and the Law of the Multiracial Family* (2013). Her articles have appeared in leading law journals such as the *Yale Law Journal, Virginia Law Review,* and *California Law Review*. She is a past chair of the AALS Employment Discrimination Section and the AALS Minority Groups Section. Before joining the academy, she practiced labor and employment law at Jones Day-Cleveland and Foley Hoag-Boston.

Teresa Godwin Phelps is Emerita Professor of Law at American University's Washington College of Law, where she taught and directed the Legal Rhetoric Program from 2006 to 2019. Prior to 2006, she taught and directed the Legal Writing Program at Notre Dame Law School. She has written extensively in legal rhetoric, law and literature, women's rights, human rights, and narrative and the law, including her book *Shattered Voices: Language, Violence, and the Work of Truth Commissions* (2004).

Nicole Buonocore Porter is a professor of law at the University of Toledo College of Law, where she teaches employment discrimination, disability law, feminist legal theory, contracts, and criminal law. She is a nationally known expert in disability law, and her research interests focus on the employment rights of women and individuals with disabilities. Porter has published (or has forthcoming) more than thirty-five law review articles and four books since she began her academic career in 2004. She has been a visiting professor of law at the University of Denver Sturm College of Law and University of Iowa College of Law. Prior to academia, Porter graduated from Michigan Law

School, *magna cum laude*, clerked for the Honorable James L. Ryan on the US Court of Appeals for the Sixth Circuit, and practiced employment law for a large firm and then as in-house counsel for a manufacturing company.

Leticia M. Saucedo is a professor of law at University of California Davis School of Law. She is an expert in employment, labor, and immigration law, and she teaches immigration law, employment law, labor law, and torts at Davis. Professor Saucedo's research focuses on the impact of employment and labor laws on conditions in low-wage workplaces. Her law review articles have appeared in *Washington University Law Review*, *Notre Dame Law Review*, *North Carolina Law Review*, the *Ohio State Law Journal*, *Buffalo Law Review*, and *Richmond Law Review*, among others.

Charles A. Sullivan has been a professor of law at Seton Hall Law School since 1978, where he has held the Catania Chair and served as Associate Dean, Director of the Rodino Law Library, and Associate Dean for Finance and Faculty. A renowned scholar in employment discrimination law and elected member of the American Law Institute, Dean Sullivan has published many books and law review articles, including *Employment Discrimination: Law and Practice* (2019), *Cases and Materials on Employment Discrimination* (2020), *Employment Law: Private Ordering and Its Limitation* (2019), and *Cases and Materials on Employment Law* (2001).

JoAnne Sweeny is a professor of law at the University of Louisville, Louis D. Brandeis School of Law. She obtained her Ph.D. at Queen Mary, University of London and her J.D. at the University of Southern California. Before returning to academia, she was an employment litigator in Los Angeles. Her current scholarship focuses on the intersection of feminist jurisprudence and freedom of expression. She is also a Fulbright Scholar, which allowed her to research comparative #MeToo movements in Finland and several other European countries.

Valorie K. Vojdik is Waller Lansden Distinguished Professor of Law at the University of Tennessee College of Law, where she teaches civil rights, gender and the law, civil procedure, and federal courts. Her recent scholarship focuses on feminist jurisprudence, masculinities theory, international women's rights, and gender violence. She is a member of the Tennessee State Advisory Committee to the US Commission on Civil Rights. She has litigated numerous cases involving sex discrimination and civil rights, and was lead counsel to Shannon Faulkner, who successfully challenged the males-only admission policy of the Citadel in South Carolina.

xx   *Notes on Contributors*

Danielle D. Weatherby is an associate professor of law at the University of Arkansas School of Law, where she teaches employment discrimination, education law, and legal research and writing. Her scholarship, which focuses on the intersection between religious exercise and antidiscrimination law, First Amendment jurisprudence and its impact on student speech, and education law, has been published in some of the nation's top law journals, and she is regularly interviewed by local, state, and national media for her expertise. She offers special thanks to Professor Brian Gallini and her colleagues for their support, and to Jessica Guarino for her research assistance.

Marley S. Weiss is a professor of law at University of Maryland Carey School of Law, where she has been teaching since 1984. She has also taught in Budapest, Hungary, at Eötvös Loránd University Faculty of Law and at the Central European University. She previously practiced labor and employment law for ten years at the International Union, UAW. She received her B.A. from Barnard College and her J.D. from Harvard Law School. Her academic research focuses on international and comparative labor law and antidiscrimination law, as well as labor-related aspects of transnational integration.

Rebecca Hanner White is Dean and J. Alton Hosch Emerita Professor of Law at the University of Georgia School of Law and served as Dean of the Law School from 2003 to 2015. Previously, she served as Associate Provost and Associate Vice President of Academic Affairs. She specializes in the areas of labor law, employment discrimination, employment law, and labor arbitration. White's scholarship includes numerous articles and books on employment discrimination and labor law. In 2000, White received the Josiah Meigs Award, University of Georgia's highest honor for teaching excellence.

Deborah A. Widiss is a professor of law and Associate Dean for Research and Faculty Affairs at Indiana University Maurer School of Law. Her research focuses on employment law, family law, and the legislative process. She has received several awards for her scholarship, including the Outstanding Scholarly Paper Award from the Association of American Law Schools. Professor Widiss is frequently consulted as an expert by the media, and she has been quoted in the *New York Times*, the *Chicago Tribune*, and the *Washington Post*. She received a J.D. and a B.A. from Yale University.

Pamela A. Wilkins is an associate professor of law at the University of Detroit Mercy School of Law, where she teaches legal writing, torts, criminal law and procedure, and feminist legal theory. Her scholarship has focused principally on the death penalty and on gender and the law. Professor Wilkins would like to thank Professor Catherine Archibald, who wrote the feminist judgment for *Etsitty*, and Professors Ann C. McGinley and Nicole Buonocore Porter for their outstanding and collegial work shepherding this volume to publication.

Preface

Could feminist perspectives and methods change the shape of employment discrimination law? To answer this question, we assembled a group of scholars and lawyers to use feminist perspectives and methodology to rewrite significant employment discrimination cases from the US Courts of Appeals and the US Supreme Court.

This volume, like all of the books in Cambridge University Press's Feminist Judgments series, demonstrates that judges with feminist viewpoints could have changed the law and the reasoning underlying the law, based on the precedent and other legal sources in effect at the time of the original decision. It demonstrates that use of feminist approaches can assure a more accurate and fair resolution of employment discrimination disputes – a resolution that more closely mirrors the purposes of the employment discrimination statutes.

In essence, employment discrimination laws were enacted to protect the most vulnerable workers – those who are less powerful because of their age, race, color, sex, gender identity and expression, sexual orientation, national origin, disability, and religion – from discriminatory hiring, working conditions, promotions, and discharges. But unfortunately, the law has developed in ways that make it difficult for vulnerable workers who have suffered discrimination to prevail in their claims. Some of these reasons entail the complexity and difficulty of proving employment discrimination. Others include a focus on the intent of the individual decision-maker rather than the systemic policies and practices that affect vulnerable workers more harshly than others. Finally, judges' reliance on their own "common sense" and refusal to accept expert testimony that explains why employers act as they do also contributes to the law's stymied development.

Together, the opinions and commentaries in this volume illustrate the importance of diversity on the bench so that judges do not approach their work with a uniform worldview influenced by the same set of preconceptions and privileges. For judges, lawyers, legislators, students, and members of the general public, reading these opinions helps to expose the ways in which judges – and, in turn, the development of the law – are subtly influenced by preconceptions, existing power hierarchies, prevailing social norms, and "conventional" wisdom. This book demonstrates that employment discrimination law is not neutral, but rather shaped by the society that produces it and the judges who apply it. At the same time, this book offers the hope that employment discrimination law can be reformed to be an instrument of greater justice and equality for all people. One possible way of doing this is for Congress to step in and overrule some of the more egregious decisions by the federal bench. Another is to increase diversity on the bench and so shift perspectives and understanding among the federal judges. And another is for state legislatures to continue to enact broad-based employment discrimination laws and for state judges to interpret those laws in ways that expand the protections of vulnerable workers beyond the limited protections that the federal laws afford today.

Acknowledgments

Ann C. McGinley would like to thank Jeff Stempel, her husband and colleague, for his enduring support, both emotional and intellectual, during this long process and Dean Dan Hamilton for supporting the project by hosting a workshop at the University of Nevada, Las Vegas (UNLV), gathering the book contributors in preparation for the writing of this volume. She would also like to thank David McClure and the Wiener-Rogers Law Library at UNLV, Boyd School of Law, for his consistently excellent research support. Finally, she thanks Nicole for her outstanding hard work, intelligent approach, and careful, prompt editing.

Nicole Buonocore Porter would like to thank her husband and colleague, Bryan Lammon, for his never-ending patience and encouragement during this book project (especially considering her frequent technical questions). She would also like to thank Ann for asking her to join this project and for her amazing work ethic.

Both editors would like to thank the original editors of the Feminist Judgments Project, Kathryn Stanchi, Linda Berger, and Bridget Crawford, for trusting them with this book and for their support. The volume editors would also like to thank the wonderful opinion and commentary authors for their superb work on this project and for tolerating the editors' several rounds of edits.

1

Introduction

ANN C. MCGINLEY AND NICOLE BUONOCORE PORTER

Equal pay, equal work, and equal working conditions for women and all other subordinated groups are crucial to their ability to live productive lives in our society. Historically, cultural and legal structures defined roles for women with reference to men (particularly white, heterosexual, gender-conforming men). Men were deemed the heads of families with responsibility to earn the family's income, and women served as caretakers of the family. These gender-based roles and sex stereotypes still dominate our culture today; as a result, many women, those men who fail to live up to male stereotypes, and other gender-nonconforming individuals suffer discrimination in hiring and terms and conditions of employment. Moreover, those with intersectional identities, such as racial minority, LGBTQ+, older, and disabled individuals, have even greater hurdles to jump.

Federal statutes such as the Equal Pay Act of 1963 and Title VII of the Civil Rights Act of 1964 were enacted to assure workplace gender equality, but, as we shall see, changing cultural norms is not simple, and many court decisions that may appear neutral failed to achieve the ideal of equal working conditions for all. This failure highlights the importance of interpreting law through a feminist lens so that all members of the community may achieve workplace success. Feminist perspectives and those offered by masculinities and critical race theorists provide important tools with which to consider workplace law and its approach to equality at work. This book seeks to offer an alternative view of what the law could have been had judges interpreting the law consciously engaged with these tools.

BACKGROUND

This book is a volume in the Feminist Judgments series. The first book of the series, *Feminist Judgments: Rewritten Opinions of the Supreme Court*, was

2   *Introduction*

edited by Kathryn M. Stanchi, Linda L. Berger, and Bridget J. Crawford. The volume included twenty-five rewritten US Supreme Court opinions that were originally decided between 1873 and 2015 and commentaries on each rewritten decision.[1] The contributors rewriting the opinions used feminist methodologies, perspectives, and theories to decide the cases. The editors of the original volume were inspired by the UK Feminist Judgments project, which also influenced a number of other feminist judgments projects dealing with law in Canada, Ireland, Australia, and New Zealand.[2]

An important goal of the editors of that original US volume was to "uncover that what passes for neutral law making and objective legal reasoning is often bound up in traditional assumptions and power hierarchies."[3] The editors posited that using feminist approaches widened the lens through which law is created. In our view, the original volume successfully demonstrates that "systemic inequalities are not intrinsic to law, but rather may be rooted in the subjective (and often unconscious) beliefs and assumptions of the decision makers."[4]

Because of the success of the original US book, Cambridge University Press has contracted with a number of editors to publish additional volumes that rewrite US opinions from the Supreme and lower federal courts and from state courts that deal with specific doctrinal areas of the law. This volume on rewritten employment discrimination cases is part of this series.

This book includes fifteen rewritten opinions from the US federal courts, accompanied by fifteen commentaries. Two of the rewritten opinions – *Meritor Savings Bank v. Vinson* and *Oncale v. Sundowner, Inc.* – are published "as is" from the original book, but with new commentaries to keep the analysis fresh. The commentaries accompanying those cases in the original book, *Feminist Judgments*, are excellent, but it has been four years since its publication, and we believed that new commentaries would capture important changes that have occurred since then. The other thirteen rewritten opinions included in this volume are entirely original, as are their accompanying commentaries.

Goals

We decided early on that we wanted this book to accomplish two major goals. First, in keeping with the original, this volume would be a compilation of

---

[1] FEMINIST JUDGMENTS: REWRITTEN OPINIONS OF THE UNITED STATES SUPREME COURT (Kathryn M. Stanchi, Linda L. Berger, & Bridget J. Crawford eds., 2016).

[2] *Id.* at 6–7.

[3] *Id.* at 4.

[4] *Id.* at 5.

Introduction

rewritten opinions in employment discrimination law that would be grounded in feminist theories, perspectives, and methodologies; it would challenge the supposed objectivity and neutrality of current employment discrimination law. Second, this volume differs from the original *Feminist Judgments* because we aimed to create a collection of employment discrimination opinions that would be internally consistent. In other words, our second goal was to create a volume that would demonstrate a potential (but untaken) path for the body of employment discrimination law had the courts considered feminist theories and perspectives when they decided the cases. Our hope was to create a volume that, when read in its entirety, would demonstrate that employment discrimination law would be significantly more protective of the rights of employees if the courts had used feminist theories and perspectives. By the same token, we did not want to sacrifice the power of individual cases or our authors' creative decisions to that goal of internal consistency. This approach resulted, in some instances, in a tension when it came to selecting the cases for inclusion and the writing and editing of the opinions. Creating a body of only fifteen cases that were to be internally consistent was an extremely tricky endeavor, especially considering the rules established for all volumes in the Feminist Judgments series – but it was one worth undertaking.

Under the rules of the original volume, which were also applicable to this book, authors of the rewritten opinions were limited to using only those materials that were available at the time of the original opinion. Besides the records of the original cases, authors consulted scholarly or other relevant materials only if those sources had already been published at the time the original cases were decided. Given this rule and our goals, our approach was often to select the earliest cases possible to obviate the need to rewrite many of the cases decided later. In essence, had the earlier cases in a particular area been decided as rewritten, those later cases that answered questions raised in the earlier cases would never have come before the courts. With the goal of internal consistency in mind, one other rule created some limitations: a rule forbidding opinion authors from citing other rewritten opinions in the book. This meant that our authors did not have the benefit of building on the rewritten opinions of cases originally decided earlier than their own. Had they been able to do so, we may have achieved even more internal consistency.

Although the authors of the rewritten opinions were limited to citing materials available at the time of the original opinions, the authors of the commentaries were subject to no such limitation. This freedom permitted commentary authors to explain the original opinions, comment on the restrictions to which the authors of the rewritten opinions were subject, detail how the rewritten opinion would have changed the law in that particular area, and

Introduction

explain which subsequent opinions would have been avoided had the law been decided as in the rewritten opinion.

Given our goals, case selection was key. We wanted to rewrite opinions that would allow for interesting analyses and would generate the greatest potential impact not only for women, but also for all workers who suffer the effects of discrimination in the workplace. Unlike the original book, this volume is not limited to US Supreme Court cases, but we wanted the cases we included to have an impact. We therefore selected decisions of the US Supreme Court and federal courts of appeals that we believed would best fit with our goals. Because we hoped to create an internally consistent body of law, we limited our authors to rewriting majority opinions only, but we did not limit our case selection to those decisions that we sought to reverse. Instead, we selected cases with holdings that we believed were consistent with feminist perspectives if we thought that the opinions themselves could have more forcefully furthered feminist goals (i.e., *Oncale*; *Desert Palace*; *Johnson Controls*; *Young*; *Hively*; *Meritor Savings Bank*).

We also wanted to include a broad variety of cases that demonstrated different deficiencies: procedural (i.e., *Ricci*; *Wal-Mart*) and substantive (i.e., *Young*; *Hively*; *AFSME*; *Meritor*; *Sears*); a failure to adopt a feminist process, such as a refusal to describe the facts when the courts found them to be too explicit (i.e., *Oncale*; *Etsitty*; *Desert Palace*); a failure to recognize a potential conflict in legal rights (i.e., *Breeden*; *Johnson Controls*); and a failure to explain potential intersectional harms (i.e., *Meritor*; *Webb*; *Jespersen*; *Catastrophe Management*).

Employment discrimination law as it stands today is extraordinarily complicated, with various theories of recovery (e.g., individual disparate treatment and disparate impact), proof methodologies for both individual cases and class actions, burgeoning gender-based theories (e.g., sex stereotyping, harassment, and the rights of LGBTQ+ individuals), a number of statutes dealing with many protected classes (i.e., the Equal Pay Act of 1963, Title VII of the Civil Rights Act of 1964, the Age Discrimination in Employment Act of 1967, and the Americans with Disabilities Act of 1990), a concern with implicit and explicit biases, a general refusal to engage in intersectional analysis, and three major forms of violating the various statutes (discrimination, harassment, and retaliation). To comprehensively rewrite employment discrimination law, we would have had to rewrite many more than fifteen opinions. Given our numerical constraint, we chose those opinions that would result in the most representative range of cases and deal with many of the fundamental questions in the law today.[5]

---

[5] *See* the next section for an explanation of why we chose not to rewrite certain key cases or address other areas of employment discrimination law.

Introduction

We leave to the readers to decide whether we have accomplished these goals.

Process: Case Selection and Editing

Our first task was to recruit an Advisory Board that would help us to select the cases for the volume.[6] The Advisory Board comprises a cross-section of well-known scholars in employment discrimination, gender law, and feminist theory.[7] We, the editors of this volume, separately compiled a list of potential cases to rewrite, and we asked our Advisory Board to do the same. When the lists were aggregated, we had more than ninety cases. We narrowed that list to approximately thirty cases that would serve the purposes of the book. At that point, we sent the revised list to the Advisory Board, with questions (e.g., Would you select Case A or Case B for the purposes of rewriting a disparate impact case? A class action case? A case that illustrates appearance discrimination?) and asked the Advisory Board members for their comments. With the help of their replies, we narrowed our list to twenty cases. Finally, we considered how we might group the cases, established those groups, and eliminated five more cases from the list.

We had our fifteen cases.[8]

Our next step was to select authors for the rewritten opinions and the commentaries. It was important to the editors of the original *Feminist Judgments* book that the opinion and commentary authors should represent a broad, diverse group of individuals from the legal academy. We share that value and were convinced that if we were going to produce the best volume possible, we needed to recruit a very diverse group not only from the legal academy (and all aspects of it), but also from practice. We instituted a broad search by putting out a call for authors and asking applicants to note their first, second, and third choices for opinions or commentaries. We received a large number of applications and selected nearly all authors from among those applications, but we also recruited directly some authors whom we thought were particularly qualified to rewrite certain opinions, based on their expertise in certain areas. The result was impressive: we ended up with an extremely diverse group of men and women, junior and senior professors, practitioners and scholars, spanning diverse races, religions, and sexual

---

[6] The editors of the original *Feminist Judgments* book were extremely helpful throughout the entire process described in this section.

[7] The members of the Advisory Board and their credentials are listed in the preliminary pages of this book.

[8] This entire selection process took many months to complete.

6   *Introduction*

orientations. Among those who are in the legal academy, we have chaired professors, and full, associate, assistant, clinical, and legal writing professors, from a total of twenty-five different law schools. Many of our authors and commentators have published in the area of feminist theory, masculinities theory, employment discrimination, and/or employment law – including books, law review articles, and other scholarly publications. Some are experts in legal writing – specifically, law and rhetoric. Others are practitioners or academics who previously practiced law and who have served in various professional leadership roles. This diversity, we believe, is one of the great strengths of this volume.

After submitting our volume proposal to the original editors and Cambridge University Press, we conducted a workshop at University of Nevada, Las Vegas, Boyd School of Law, in April 2018. At the workshop, which was attended by nearly two-thirds of the opinion and commentary authors, we discussed feminist theory and different possible approaches to rewriting the case opinions and writing the accompanying commentaries. We also discussed employment discrimination law as it currently stands. We then asked opinion authors to submit their first drafts by August 2018, and we sent them on to the commentary authors, so that they could begin working on the commentaries.

While each of us took the lead for half of the opinions and commentaries, we both edited all of the opinions and commentaries, reviewing each at least four times. Our goal was to allow as much freedom to the authors and commentators as possible, while keeping the quality of the opinions and commentaries consistent in theory, doctrine, and writing. Some authors made decisions that one or both of us did not agree with, but all of the authors' decisions, we believe, are rational and justifiable.

Potential Uses of This Volume

We envision this volume being used to teach law courses in a number of ways, including as a stand-alone text or as a supplement in an employment discrimination law course, a course on feminist theory and law, or a seminar on judicial writing from a feminist perspective. Its purpose would be to teach students alternative ways of thinking of the case law and to challenge their acceptance of the supposed neutrality and objectivity of federal courts' decisions in important cases. One of the editors (Ann) plans to use this volume in a seminar titled "Employment Discrimination Law, Feminism, and Judicial Writing". She plans to ask all seminar students to read original opinions and rewritten opinions and commentaries, and then to discuss how the substance changed when viewed through a feminist lens. In the second half of the

Introduction

seminar, students will each rewrite one opinion that has not previously been rewritten and will write a commentary on another student's rewritten opinion.

Researchers should find this volume, as a whole, useful in examining how feminist employment discrimination scholars believe the law in the area could have developed if the courts had applied feminist methodologies, perspectives, and theories. Researchers can also consider how the opinion authors and commentators interpret the original cases, how the opinions could have originally been written, and the effect that such a rewrite would have on the individual case and the entire body of employment discrimination law.

Practicing lawyers and judges can use this volume to reconsider how to frame their arguments and opinions. Moreover, state court judges who are not bound by federal antidiscrimination laws when interpreting their own state antidiscrimination laws may find this volume useful in avoiding the errors that harm the most vulnerable employees among us.

SUMMARY OF REWRITTEN OPINIONS

Chapter 2, "Supreme Court and Gender Narratives," contains one case: *Desert Palace, Inc. v. Costa*.[9] The original case decided by the Supreme Court was a victory for the plaintiff, who argued that, when proving a mixed-motives case under the 1991 Amendments to Title VII, she need not limit her case to direct evidence. Like other civil plaintiffs, the Court held, Title VII plaintiffs may use direct or circumstantial evidence, or a combination of both. The original opinion, however, reported the facts in a very brief and "neutral" manner without taking into account the evidence before the jury. The feminist judgment – authored by Anne Mullins, with a commentary by Naomi Mann – corrects this omission by detailing the egregious facts in the case that shed light on the gendered treatment suffered by the plaintiff. This treatment included repetitive severely hostile behaviors by her coworkers and differential treatment by her supervisors. Mullins' rewritten opinion gives the reader a significantly different view of the case from that presented in the original opinion. Mullins demonstrates that the feminist method of storytelling illuminates how the facts occurred in the real world and creates a counterbalance to the presumably "neutral" and "objective" view presented by the Court.

Chapter 3, "Pregnancy Discrimination," deals with an issue that affects many, if not most, women: pregnancy or the ability to become pregnant. In *International Union, UAW v. Johnson Controls*,[10] the Court held that the

---

[9] 539 U.S. 90 (2003).
[10] 499 U.S. 187 (1991).

8   Introduction

employer's fetal protection policy that broadly excluded fertile women, but not men, from jobs working with lead was sex discrimination under Title VII and could not be justified by the Bona Fide Occupational Qualification (BFOQ) defense. Because of the breadth of the policy, which excluded nearly all women absent proof of sterilization, this case was a victory not only for pregnant women, but also for all women working at the company. Nonetheless, the original opinion failed to focus on the stories of hardships of individual women who would be excluded from work, ignored evidence that men's offspring can also suffer harm from excess exposure to lead, and failed to suggest that workplaces with toxic substances should clean up and/or provide personal protective equipment to the extent feasible rather than exclude employees from valuable jobs. The rewritten opinion by Marcia McCormick, with a commentary by Wynter Allen, uses feminist emphasis on narrative to tell the stories of three of the individual plaintiffs: two women and one man. It details the economic and personal hardships suffered by the plaintiffs, and it explains that, in 1979, 100,000 women were excluded from jobs as a result of fetal protection policies, the majority in male-dominated positions. The rewritten opinion disavows the stereotypes furthered by the policy that all women are potential mothers for nearly their entire working lives and concludes that the policy lets employers avoid their duty to eliminate workplace health hazards. While the rewritten opinion does not change the holding, it places emphasis on the importance of avoiding gender-based and sex stereotypes and on furthering healthy workplaces for all employees.

Young v. United Parcel Service, Inc.[11] deals more directly with pregnancy. In the original case, the Court held that a pregnant employee can establish that an employer's refusal to make accommodations for her pregnancy violates the Pregnancy Discrimination Act of 1978 by demonstrating that the employer accommodates a large percentage of nonpregnant workers while failing to accommodate a large percentage of pregnant workers. Although this was seen as a positive step for pregnant women, the Court's convoluted analysis generated a great deal of criticism. The feminist judgment, rewritten by Deborah Widiss, with a commentary by Bradley Areheart, takes a much more straightforward approach. Widiss holds that when an employer provides accommodations for employees with physical restrictions that are similar to those of the pregnant plaintiff, the employer must provide those same accommodations to the pregnant employee. Widiss highlights the history of discrimination against pregnant women, which has proven to be a significant cause of women's subordination in the workplace. This subordination occurs because many

---

[11] 135 S.Ct. 1338 (2015).

Introduction

women have been forced to quit when their employers refused to provide them with simple accommodations that would allow the employees to remain employed while pregnant.

The first case in Chapter 4, "Intersectional Approaches to Appearances," is *Jespersen v. Harrah's Operating Co.*[12] In that case, the Ninth Circuit held that the employer's firing of a female bartender for failing to comply with a sex-specific grooming policy, which included a comprehensive makeup requirement for female employees, did not constitute sex discrimination based on the unequal burdens on women or unlawful sex stereotyping. The rewritten opinion is coauthored by Angela Onwuachi-Willig and JoAnne Sweeny, with a commentary written by Roxana Bell. The opinion coauthors expose the harm caused by allowing employers to have sex-specific grooming policies generally and makeup mandates specifically. They hold that the unequal burdens test should be jettisoned and propose instead that *any* sex-specific grooming policy would violate Title VII. They also hold, in the alternative, that even if the unequal burdens test were to apply, the makeup policy, which has no corollary in time or money spent for men, poses an unequal burden on the female employees of the casino. Finally, the authors hold that requiring women to wear makeup (and refusing to allow men to wear makeup) is sex stereotyping that violates Title VII. Although the plaintiff was a white woman who was not challenging the casino's sex-specific hair requirements, the coauthors sprinkle some intersectional dicta throughout the rewritten opinion, exposing how the casino's hair mandates could discriminate based on both sex and race.

EEOC v. Catastrophe Management Solutions[13] deals more directly with race and hair. In the original case, the court held that it was not race discrimination for the employer to refuse to hire a black woman because she wore her hair in locs, stating that Title VII was meant to prohibit only discrimination based on "immutable characteristics," and the wearing of locs is not immutable. The rewritten opinion by Wendy Greene, with a commentary by Jesse Bawa, holds that the refusal to hire black women because they wear their hair in locs is race discrimination under Title VII. The rewritten opinion first explores the lengthy and tragic history of hair discrimination against black women. The opinion then eliminates the immutability requirement, confirming that discrimination against cultural practices associated with race constitutes race discrimination. In so holding, the rewritten opinion also explores the intersectional nature of the discrimination against black women.

---

[12] 444 F.3d 1104 (9th Cir. 2006) (en banc).
[13] 852 F.3d 1018 (11th Cir. 2016).

10   *Introduction*

The last case in this chapter is *Webb v. City of Philadelphia*.[14] In the original opinion, the Third Circuit upheld the lower court's grant of summary judgment to the City. The plaintiff, a Muslim female police officer, alleged illegal sex and religious discrimination because the City denied her an accommodation to wear a religious headscarf with her uniform, even though male police officers who are Muslim had been accommodated and permitted to wear beards. The court agreed with the City's argument that the requested accommodation would impose an undue burden on the defendant. Valorie Vojdik's rewritten opinion, with a commentary by Sahar Aziz, focuses on the intersectional harm based on the plaintiff's sex, combined with her religion, and overturns the lower court's grant of summary judgment, concluding that the defendant's argument that permitting the plaintiff to wear a headscarf tucked into her uniform shirt collar would destroy the *esprit de corps* of the police force is specious. According to the rewritten opinion, the defendant offered no evidence of harm at all, much less evidence of undue burden.

Chapter 5, "Harassment Because of Sex," contains two cases that are republished (with permission) from the original *Feminist Judgments* book, with new commentaries. In *Meritor Savings Bank, FSB v. Vinson*,[15] the Supreme Court held for the first time that an employer is liable to an employee for a sexually hostile work environment created by a supervisor even absent economic harm to the employee if the behavior is severe or pervasive. The employer's liability is not automatic, but depends on agency principles. In the rewritten opinion, Angela Onwuachi-Willig, with a new commentary by Trina Jones, focuses on the hidden race issues in the case. Unlike the original opinion, the rewritten opinion explains that the black female plaintiff was especially vulnerable because of her youth and the fact that the harasser, a bank vice president and branch manager, was a well-respected man in the black community, who repeatedly assaulted her at work. Importantly, the rewritten opinion establishes a new, less stringent test for proving a hostile work environment and holds that an employer is strictly liable for injuries caused by such an environment created by a supervisor.[16] By making employers strictly liable, the rewritten opinion would have effectively eliminated a number of subsequent lower court cases and two Supreme Court cases, *Burlington Industries, Inc. v Ellerth*[17] and *Faragher v. City of Boca*

---

[14] 562 F.3d 256 (3d Cir. 2009).

[15] 477 U.S. 57 (1986).

[16] The rewritten opinion left untouched the "negligence" standard that courts apply when the harasser is a coworker or a third party, where an employer is liable if it knew or should have known about the harassment and failed to take appropriate remedial action.

[17] 524 U.S. 742 (1998).

Introduction

Raton,[18] which created an affirmative defense for employers in the case of a supervisor's harassment of a subordinate where there is no tangible employment action. The rewritten opinion also would have avoided *Vance v. Ball State University*,[19] which narrowed the definition of "supervisor" and thereby limited employer liability.

In *Oncale v. Sundowner Services*,[20] the Supreme Court held that plaintiffs may sue their employers for workplace harassment perpetrated by an individual of the same sex as the victim. While this opinion's holding is consistent with feminist perspectives, Justice Scalia, the author of the original opinion, openly refused to relate the egregious facts of sexual harassment that the plaintiff had allegedly suffered. Moreover, lower courts have often interpreted *Oncale* to hold that harassment that occurs between individuals of the same sex was not "because of sex." These courts see *Oncale* as furthering the distinction between illegal harassment based on the victim's failure to conform to sex stereotypes and legal harassment based on the victim's sexual orientation. Ann McGinley's rewritten opinion, with a new commentary by Nancy Dowd, employs feminist storytelling techniques to demonstrate the harm of harassment suffered by the male plaintiff at the hands of his coworkers. The rewritten opinion also explains that harassment by men of other men often occurs because of societal pressures on men to prove their masculinity to one another and to police the boundaries of sex and sexuality presented by other men at work. McGinley's opinion holds that discrimination based on sexual orientation, gender expression, and gender identity are all forbidden by Title VII.[21] Moreover, the rewritten opinion shifts the burden to the defendant to prove that the harassment did not occur because of sex once the plaintiff demonstrates that the behavior itself was sexual or gendered in nature.

The first case in Chapter 6, "Sexual Orientation and Gender Identity Discrimination as Sex Discrimination," is *Etsitty v. Utah Transit Authority*.[22]

---

[18] 524 U.S. 775 (1998).

[19] 570 U.S. 421 (2013).

[20] 523 U.S. 75 (1998).

[21] This case is an example of the tension we confronted between our two goals, as we described earlier. Because the rewritten opinion stated that discrimination based on sexual orientation and gender identity and expression is illegal and fits within the definition of discrimination because of "sex" in Title VII, we could have accomplished our goal of creating law that would consistently further feminist values by choosing not to rewrite other opinions dealing with these issues. We concluded, however, that a deep analysis of the subject was necessary in cases that directly addressed the issue of protection for sexual orientation and transgender status under Title VII. Thus we opted to rewrite both *Hively* and *Etsitty* rather than to rely on the analysis in *Oncale*, where the issue was not raised directly. Of course, had *Oncale* been decided as the rewritten opinion was, it is unlikely that *Hively* and *Etsitty* would have been litigated.

[22] 502 F.3d 1215 (10th Cir. 2007).

In *Etsitty*, the Tenth Circuit held that a bus company did not violate Title VII when it fired a transgender woman bus driver with (to quote the Court) "male genitalia" for using public women's restrooms along her bus route. The court, like other courts before it, concluded that discrimination based on transgender status does not violate Title VII's prohibition of discrimination "because of sex" and that, even if it did, the plaintiff was fired because of bathroom use, not discrimination. The rewritten opinion by Catherine Archibald, with a commentary by Pamela Wilkins, reverses course, finding that the employer's behavior violated both Title VII and the Equal Protection Clause of the Fourteenth Amendment to the US Constitution. The rewritten opinion concludes that discrimination based on transgender status violates Title VII because it is discrimination based on an individual's genitalia or presumed genitalia. In the alternative, the rewritten opinion holds that the plaintiff's sex is a motivating factor when an employer discriminates based on transgender status. Archibald also concludes that discriminating against individuals based on the bathroom they use has an illegal disparate impact on transgender persons. Finally, the rewritten opinion also adds dicta concluding that single-sex bathrooms violate both Title VII and the Equal Protection Clause.

Hively v. Ivy Tech Community College[23] addresses discrimination based on sexual orientation. The original opinion has a positive outcome for feminist theorists, where the Seventh Circuit held that sexual orientation discrimination is sex discrimination under Title VII, creating a circuit split that, at the time of writing, is expected to be resolved in 2020 by the Supreme Court.[24] The rewritten opinion, authored by Ryan Nelson, arrives at the same conclusion as the original decision, but the rewritten opinion has a very different feel than the original opinion. First, as commentary author Danielle Weatherby describes, Nelson pays "homage to the LGBTQ+ experience, offering a more humanistic lens through which to view the legal question posed by *Hively*." In his rewritten opinion, Nelson relies on several legal theories and arguments to support the conclusion that discrimination based on sexual orientation *is* sex discrimination under Title VII, including but-for causation, sex stereotyping, sex-plus, associational discrimination (which Nelson calls

---

[23] 853 F.3d 339 (7th Cir. 2017) (en banc).

[24] In October 2019, the Supreme Court heard oral argument on three cases dealing with whether discrimination based on sexual orientation and gender identity is illegal under Title VII. *See Zarda v. Altitude Express, Inc.*, 883 F.3d 100, 112 (2d Cir. 2018) (en banc) (sexual orientation), *cert. granted* 139 S.Ct.1599 (2019); *Bostock v. Clayton County Bd. Commissioners*, 723 Fed. Appx. 964 (11th Cir. 2018) (sexual orientation), *cert. granted* 139 S.Ct. 1599 (2019); *EEOC v. R.G. & G.R. Harris Funeral Homes*, 884 F.3d 560 (6th Cir. 2018) (gender identity), *cert. granted* 139 S. Ct. 1599 (2019). At the time of our final edit, these cases have not yet been decided by the Supreme Court.

Introduction

"relationship discrimination"), and a unique use of the motivating factor provision in Title VII.

The first case in Chapter 7, "Systemic Claims and Gender: Proving Disparate Treatment and Impact," is *AFSCME v. State of Washington*.[25] *AFSCME* is widely known to be the case that sounded the death knell for the comparable worth theory. The Ninth Circuit held that the plaintiffs' class claim of pay discrimination failed under both disparate treatment and disparate impact theories. The feminist judgment, written by Teresa Phelps, with a commentary by Stephanie Bornstein, arrives at a diametrically opposite conclusion. The feminist judgment exposes the implicit bias in the market forces that caused the pay disparities and uses narrative to tell the real-life stories of the women whose pay was substantially lower despite their performance in positions of equal value as male-dominated positions. As commentary author Stephanie Bornstein highlights, if this 1985 case had been decided as written in the feminist judgment, it could have ameliorated the substantial gender pay gap that persists in the United States.

EEOC v. Sears, Roebuck & Co.[26] is a systemic disparate treatment case. The original opinion upheld the lower court's finding of no sex discrimination despite the plaintiff's unrefuted statistics that demonstrated a statistically significant difference in the hiring of men and women into commission sales jobs, which paid more and had more prestige than the noncommission sales jobs. The court reached this conclusion by crediting the employer's defense that women were not interested in the commission sales jobs and that this lack of interest was a complete defense to the claim despite the overwhelming statistics. The rewritten opinion by Leticia Saucedo, with a commentary by Maria Ontiveros, chastises the lower court for its blind acceptance of expert testimony that attempted to rebut the statistics. The expert testimony in question identified a lack of interest on the part of female applicants and employees in making more money and taking greater risks as required by the commission sales job. Saucedo's opinion characterizes this testimony as sex stereotyping. It holds that courts may not use gender-based and sex stereotypes to rebut a plaintiff's strong statistical evidence by plaintiffs in pattern or practice cases. This conclusion was especially important in *Sears* because the statistics in this case had taken interest and experience into account, and there was other expert testimony that explained that the employer played an important role in creating (men's) or discouraging (women's) interest in the commission sales jobs.

---

[25] 770 F.2d 1401 (9th Cir. 1985).
[26] 839 F.2d 302 (7th Cir. 1988).

Introduction

Ricci v. DeStefano[27] is the only case in this chapter that is not about sex, per se, but because this case, as originally decided, will likely have a devastating effect on sex- and gender-based discrimination cases using the disparate impact method of proof, we have included it in the volume. Disparate impact cases, unlike disparate treatment cases, do not require proof of intentional discrimination; rather, disparate impact plaintiffs prevail if they prove that the employer's policy or practice creates an adverse disparate impact on the hiring or promotion of members of a protected group, and if the employer fails to prove that the policy is job-related and consistent with business necessity. Plaintiffs have serious difficulties proving intentional discrimination because employers are clearly aware of the antidiscrimination statutes and hide their motives, make decisions based on implicit bias, and/or unintentionally set up systems in their organizations that harm employees because of their gender. Given this reality, a disparate impact cause of action has the potential to reach a much broader array of organizational behaviors than the disparate treatment model, which is based on a showing of intentional discrimination.

Ricci is an especially important case for large employers who use standardized tests and for explaining how the disparate impact and disparate treatment theories should interact. In the original opinion, the Court held that the City of New Haven had engaged in intentional race discrimination when it refused to use the results of a promotional exam for firefighters that had a disparate impact on African American and Latinx candidates. The Court held that an employer could defend the intentional discrimination that arose from refusing to certify the test results only if it had a "strong basis in evidence" to believe that it *would have been liable* under the disparate impact theory. In other words, it was insufficient for the department to defend its actions by proving that the policy in question had a disparate impact on a protected group, which the *Ricci* promotion exams clearly had; defendants also had to prove that a strong basis in evidence existed that its defenses would fail. And the Court held, as a matter of law, that the employer did not have a strong basis in evidence to believe that it would have lost a disparate impact challenge if the test results had been certified. The rewritten opinion, authored by Marley Weiss, with a commentary by Rebecca Lee, reverses course. Weiss adopts a new standard: an employer attempting to avoid disparate impact liability is required only to show that it had an actual belief that it would suffer liability for disparate impact and that this belief was reasonable at the time it made the decision. Because this is a reverse discrimination claim, Weiss also places the

---

[27] 557 U.S. 557 (2009).

Introduction 15

burden on the nonminority plaintiffs to prove the lack of an actual and reasonable belief that certifying the test results would have resulted in disparate impact liability. Unlike the original *Ricci* opinion, Weiss's rewritten opinion focuses on the importance of continuing the viability of both disparate treatment and disparate impact causes of action. Moreover, the rewritten opinion carefully avoids future potential conflicts between disparate impact claims and the Equal Protection Clause.

Most significantly, the rewritten opinion emphasizes the strength and importance of disparate impact – a cause of action that is crucial to equal treatment in the workplace for women. In fact, the New Haven Fire Department, the primary defendant in *Ricci*, had a history of hiring a vast majority of white men. Even in 2010, women represented only approximately 4 percent of that Department and 3.7 percent of fire departments nationwide.[28] Indeed, the fact that any female firefighters exist is largely a result of Title VII disparate impact litigation.[29] Weiss explains that, in addition to the significant racial impact of the exam results, the employer could not have proven that this outdated, mostly pen-and-paper test was job-related and consistent with business necessity. She also emphasizes the several alternatives that were available to the City that would have had a less discriminatory effect. This analysis would apply equally to lawsuits brought by female litigants.

The last opinion in this chapter is the famous class action case, *Wal-Mart Stores, Inc. v. Dukes*,[30] which held that the lower court improperly certified a class of approximately 1.5 million women who alleged they suffered sex discrimination in employment at Wal-Mart. The Court focused on the "commonality" requirement under Federal Rule of Civil Procedure 23(a) and concluded that, absent a policy to discriminate against women, the plaintiffs could not prove commonality in this case. Concluding that there was an insufficient showing of commonality, the Court rejected the plaintiffs' statistics, anecdotal evidence of discrimination, and the plaintiffs' expert's social framework evidence, which explained that the implicit bias of managers likely permitted the discriminatory conditions to prevail. Tristin Green's rewritten

---

[28] *See* Ann C. McGinley, Ricci v. DeStefano: A *Masculinities Theory Analysis*, 33 Harv. J.L. & Gender 581, 594 (2010). A recent study estimates that there are approximately 40,000 female firefighters missing from fire departments across the country. This disparity is likely to be the result of discrimination. *See id.* (citing Denise R. Hulett *et al.*, A National Report Card on Women in Firefighting 2 (Apr. 2008), www.womeninfire.org/wp-content/uploads/2014/07/35827WSP.pdf).

[29] *See, e.g.*, McGinley, *supra* note 28, at 593 (describing the disparate impact litigation against the New York City fire department that took place in the late 1970s and early 1980s).

[30] 564 U.S. 338 (2011).

16   *Introduction*

opinion, with a commentary by Charles Sullivan, holds that the plaintiffs can properly prove commonality by means of statistics and expert testimony. Green's opinion also holds that a showing of intent is not necessary when the statistics demonstrate discriminatory outcomes and the employer fails to rectify the problem.[31]

Chapter 8, "Retaliation," features *Clark County School District v. Breeden*,[32] where the Court held that the plaintiff's retaliation claim under Title VII fails because no reasonable person could believe that a single incident of harassment violated Title VII. The rewritten opinion, authored by Michael Green, with commentary by Rebecca Hanner White, retains the reasonable belief rule, but applies it in a remarkably broad way. Exposing the bias many women suffer in the workplace as a result of microaggressions and using the perspective of a reasonable person in the plaintiff's shoes, Green holds that even a single incident of harassment is sufficient to constitute a reasonable belief that the plaintiff is experiencing actionable harassment. This holding is consistent with the incentives set up under Supreme Court jurisprudence that encourage employees to complain about harassment early lest they lose their harassment claim.[33] The rewritten opinion also broadens the causation element in retaliation cases in two ways. First, it refuses to set a bright-line rule for the passage of time between the protected activity and the adverse employment action. Second, it allows mixed-motive causation rather than but-for causation, which would have made retaliation claims easier to win and eliminated *Univ. Tex. S.W. Medical Center v. Nassar*,[34] where the Court held that plaintiffs had to prove that retaliation was a but-for cause of the adverse employment action.

---

[31] This definition of systemic discrimination that does not require proof of intent may conflict with the rewritten opinion in *Ricci v. DeStefano*, which appears to require proof of purpose for taking the action to sue for systemic intentional discrimination.

[32] 532 U.S. 268 (2001).

[33] Given that the rewritten opinion in *Meritor Savings Bank, FSB v. Vinson* holds that employers are strictly liable for their supervisors' illegal harassment of employees, and there is no opportunity for employers to prove an affirmative defense, this issue may not be as stark as it is today because, without the *Faragher* and *Ellerth* opinions, employers will not have the possibility of raising an affirmative defense. Thus employers may not have created policies that require employees to report harassment as soon as it takes place. Professor Lauren Edelman, however, has noted that employers began to require reporting of harassment even before *Faragher* and *Ellerth* were decided. *See* Lauren B. Edelman, Working Law: Courts, Corporations, and Symbolic Civil Rights 11–12 (2016). As noted earlier, the negligence standard would continue to apply to coworker and customer harassment; thus there would still be an incentive for employers to want to know about harassment early, so that they will not be found negligent for failing to remedy it.

[34] 570 U.S. 338 (2013).

IMPLICATIONS

This part addresses two topics. First, we discuss the implications of the body of rewritten opinions. How would the law have changed for the better? Which subsequent cases would not have existed? How would the careers (and lives) of subordinated employees have improved under our rewritten body of cases? How would the rewritten cases affect the job opportunities of LGBTQ+ or gender-nonconforming persons? Or of racial, religious, and ethnic minorities? Second, we discuss the road not taken. Which seminal or well-known cases did we choose *not* to rewrite, and why? More importantly, are there areas within employment discrimination law that we wished we could have fixed, but did not?

A New Body of Law

If all of the rewritten cases had replaced the original ones, what would employment discrimination law look like? And, more broadly, what effect would this body of law have had on US workplaces?

Relating Women's (and Men's) Stories

At a minimum, the body of rewritten cases demonstrates the power of the stories told by women and gender-nonconforming men. Feminist legal theory has long emphasized the importance of narrative – of telling women's stories. Many of the authors of the rewritten opinions have used the feminist tool of narrative to share the stories of the victims. Anne Mullins' artful narrative in *Desert Palace* is perhaps the most memorable, but many of our other authors dug deep into the records of the cases to tell the stories of the victims – stories that the courts (and especially the Supreme Court) had ignored.[35]

Strengthening Litigation Tools

More concretely, the new body of law would give plaintiffs and their lawyers tools with which to challenge all kinds of discrimination, using class actions, comparable worth theory, a revitalized systemic disparate treatment, and disparate impact. Employment discrimination law contains all of these legal tools and theories of discrimination that ostensibly protect victims of discrimination, but courts (including the Supreme Court) have made it very difficult to successfully challenge discrimination, especially (but not only) class-based

---

[35] Ann McGinley's description of the facts in the rewritten *Oncale* case is one notable example.

18 *Introduction*

discrimination.[36] The rewritten cases of *AFSCME*, *Sears*, *Ricci*, and *Wal-Mart* would give victims much more ammunition in fighting that discrimination.

Guaranteeing Diversity through Less Appearance Regulation

American workplaces would "look" more diverse under our rewritten body of cases. By this, we mean that employers' overregulation of appearances would hopefully cease to exist. Employers would still have the right to require that employees have good hygiene and professional appearances commensurate with the working environment, but sex-specific hair and makeup requirements would disappear,[37] as would racially discriminatory bans on certain hairstyles. Religious minorities would be free to don their religious garb or to follow the appearance-based requirements of their faiths without penalty. We use the word "hopefully" because all three of our appearance-based cases are appellate cases (*Jespersen*, *Catastrophe Management*, and *Webb*) and not Supreme Court cases. Thus it is an open question whether the rewritten opinions would have taken hold in other circuits or survived a challenge in the Supreme Court.

Eliminating the "Double Bind"

Many of the opinions exposed the "double bind" experienced by women in the workplace. Most prominently, we see this in the pregnancy context, and the rewritten *Young* opinion exposes the double bind of pregnancy whereby, for decades, women have been made to choose between their livelihoods and having a family. The double bind experienced by Crystal Etsitty, a transgender woman who was fired for using the women's restrooms even though she identified as and was presenting as a woman, is exposed, as is the double bind that Darlene Jespersen experienced when fired for her failure to wear makeup that made her feel uncomfortable and without dignity at work.

---

[36] *See generally* Sandra F. Sperino & Suja A. Thomas, Unequal: How America's Courts Undermine Discrimination Law (2017) (explaining how the courts have, in essence, deradicalized the law).

[37] The rewritten law might also mean that sex-specific uniform requirements would also be unlawful. Although one of us (Ann) is comfortable with that result because she is concerned about uniform requirements for gender-nonconforming workers, the other (Nicole) is not. Nicole is worried that gender-neutral uniforms would most likely be based on typical men's bodies, and, as a petite woman, Nicole thinks wearing uniforms designed around male bodies would be quite horrible.

Introduction   19

Recognizing LGBTQ+ Rights

After our rewritten body of cases, US workplaces would also have been friendlier and more welcoming places for LGBTQ+ employees. As rewritten, *Etsitty* would make it unlawful to discriminate based on transgender status, and rewritten *Hively* would make it unlawful for employers to discriminate against employees based on their sexual orientation. More broadly, rewritten *Oncale* prohibits same-sex harassment based on the victim's failure to live up to gender-based or sex stereotypes, the perpetrator's sexual interest in the victims, and the sexual orientation and gender identity of the victim.[38] Of course, the Supreme Court could eviscerate all of this real (*Hively*,[39] *Zarda*,[40] and *R.G. & G.R. Harris Funeral Homes*[41]) and imagined (rewritten *Etsitty* and *Hively*) progress when it decides a trio of cases during the October 2019– June 2020 term that interrogate whether Title VII prohibits discrimination based on sexual orientation and/or gender identity.[42]

Preventing and Remedying Sex- and Gender-Based Harassment

Not surprisingly, a huge focus of Title VII (especially recently[43]) has been on sex-based harassment. Although we are not naive enough to believe that these rewritten opinions would have ended harassment itself, we do believe that if

---

[38] *See supra* note 21 for a description of our decision to rewrite *Etsitty* and *Hively*.

[39] 853 F.3d 339 (7th Cir. 2017) (en banc) (holding that sexual orientation discrimination is sex discrimination under Title VII).

[40] *Zarda v. Altitude Express, Inc.*, 883 F.3d 100 (2d Cir. 2018) (holding that sexual orientation discrimination is sex discrimination under Title VII), *cert. granted* 139 S.Ct. 1599 (2019).

[41] *EEOC v. R.G. & G.R. Harris Funeral Homes, Inc.*, 884 F.3d 560 (6th Cir. 2018) (holding that discrimination against a transgender employee is sex discrimination under Title VII), *cert. granted* 139 S.Ct. 1599 (2019).

[42] *See Bostock v. Clayton County Bd. Commissioners*, 723 Fed. Appx. 964 (11th Cir. 2018) (holding that discrimination based on sexual orientation is not prohibited by the sex discrimination provision of Title VII), *cert. granted* 139 S.Ct. 1599 (2019); *Altitude Express, Inc. v. Zarda*, *supra* note 40; *R.G. & G.R. Harris Funeral Homes v. EEOC*, *supra* note 41. Consolidated cases *Bostock* and *Zarda* ask whether Title VII's prohibition on discrimination "because of sex" covers discrimination because of sexual orientation. *Harris Funeral Homes* asks whether the prohibition covers discrimination based on gender identity. At time of our final edit, the Supreme Court has not yet decided these cases.

[43] The #MeToo movement, which was originally founded by Tarana Burke in 2006, went viral after actor Alyssa Milano borrowed the term and posted it online in 2017. The reaction was explosive: women all over the world declared "#MeToo," meaning that they too had been victims of sexual harassment or assault. Articles published by the *New York Times* and the *New Yorker* describing multiple women who had accused movie producer Harvey Weinstein of sexual violence had prompted Alyssa Milano's post. *See* Ann C. McGinley, *The Masculinity Motivation*, STAN. L. REV. ONLINE (June 2018), www.stanfordlawreview.org/online/the-masculinity-motivation/, at nn. 1–4 and accompanying text.

Meritor and Oncale had been decided as rewritten, victims of harassment would now more easily and successfully be able to sue their employers, and this would hopefully have led employers to take the goal of eradicating harassment more seriously. Most significantly, the rewritten Meritor decision would make employers automatically liable for harassment by supervisors. This would mean that neither Burlington Industries, Inc. v. Ellerth[44] nor Faragher v. City of Boca Raton[45] would have been decided. These cases allowed employers to assert an affirmative defense in situations where a supervisor harasses an employee and there is no tangible employment action such as a firing, failure to promote, demotion, etc. The affirmative defense has been accepted unthinkingly in many subsequent cases, with lower courts holding that employees acted unreasonably as a matter of law in failing to report harassment to the employer, even though the employer has the burden of persuasion on the issue.[46] This, combined with a tendency even before Ellerth and Faragher were decided for human resources (HR) departments in large companies to create policies and practices that do not really work to prevent harassment, has created a perception of fairness, and, according to Professor Lauren Edelman, has resulted in the courts' deference to symbolic (but ineffective) structures such as training and policies in the workplace.[47] Actually, however, these structures have not prevented sex- and gender-based harassment; rather, they have led to "bulletproofing" of the employer's workforce.[48] In other words, these structures serve to prevent or decrease liability, but have not decreased illegal harassment.[49]

Taking Intersectional Approaches to Avoiding Discrimination

Rewritten opinions in this volume also emphasize the importance of considering intersectional discrimination and the history of discrimination against

[44] 524 U.S. 742 (1998).

[45] 524 U.S. 775 (1998).

[46] See Anne Lawton, Operating in an Empirical Vacuum: The Ellerth and Faragher Affirmative Defense, 13 COLUM. J. GENDER & L. 197 (2004) (arguing that the courts unreasonably grant the defendants' affirmative defense even in the absence of proof that the behavior that the victim engaged in was unreasonable).

[47] See Edelman, supra note 33, at 11–12 (naming this judicial deference to corporate symbolic structures as "legal endogeneity").

[48] Susan Bisom-Rapp, Bulletproofing the Workplace: Symbol and Substance in Employment Discrimination Law Practice, 26 FLA. ST. U. L. REV. 959 (1999); Susan Bisom-Rapp, Sexual Harassment Training Must Change: The Case for Legal Incentives for Transformative Education and Prevention, 71 STAN. L. REV. ONLINE 62 (2018), www.stanfordlawreview.org/online/sex-harassment-training-must-change-the-case-for-legal-incentives-for-transformative-education-and-prevention/.

[49] Bisom-Rapp, Bulletproofing, supra note 48; Bisom-Rapp, Sexual Harassment Training, supra note 48.

women of color. As rewritten, *Meritor*, *Jespersen*, and *Catastrophe Management* all address the intersection of gender and race discrimination, while rewritten *Webb* addresses the intersection of sex and religion. These cases would have educated judges on the importance of recognizing intersectional claims. Such education may have avoided the gaps that judges leave when they do not take intersectional claims seriously.[50]

Recognizing Implicit Bias and Stereotypes That Cause Discrimination

Probably the most notable accomplishment of the rewritten opinions is combating implicit bias and stereotypes in the workplace. Virtually every rewritten opinion exposed the way in which stereotypes about gender, race, and/or religion have negatively affected the workplace environment for women and/or racial and gender minorities. Exposing these stereotypes and refusing to allow the law to further the use of stereotypes is perhaps one of the greatest contributions of the rewritten body of cases.[51]

Specific Changes to the Law That the Rewritten Opinions Would Have Made

Besides these nuanced approaches and changes, the rewritten opinions in this volume would have effected many specific and tangible changes to employment discrimination law had they been the original opinions (and, if the rewritten opinions are lower court decisions, had these opinions been adopted by the Supreme Court).

- *Ellerth*,[52] *Faragher*,[53] *Vance*,[54] and *Nassar*[55] would not have been decided at all.

---

[50] For a description of intersectional claims, see Kimberlé Crenshaw, *Demarginalizing the Intersection of Race and Sex: A Black Feminist Critique of Antidiscrimination Doctrine, Feminist Theory and Antiracist Politics*, 1989 U. Chi. Legal F. 139 (explaining that black women have different injuries and additional potential claims than their white female and black male counterparts).

[51] For a collection of research on how implicit bias affects employers' decision-making processes and a recommendation of how it should be dealt with in antidiscrimination law, see Ann C. McGinley, Masculinity at Work: Employment Discrimination through a Different Lens 140–48, 212–14 (2016); *see also* Ann C. McGinley, ¡Viva la Evolución! *Recognizing Unconscious Motive in Title VII*, 9 Cornell J. L. Pub. Pol'y 415, 434–46 (2000) (collecting scientific studies).

[52] *See supra* note 44.

[53] *See supra* note 45.

[54] *See supra* note 19.

[55] *See supra* note 34.

- There would be a new standard for liability in sex-based, gender-based, or other illegal harassment. Employers would be strictly liable, and there would be no affirmative defense for employers in harassment cases where the harasser is a supervisor.[56]
- The immutable/mutable distinction in dress code, hair, and appearances decisions would no longer exist, and race and sex discrimination would be expanded to include discrimination based on dress and appearances.
- Discrimination based on sexual orientation, gender identity, and gender expression would be illegal sex discrimination occurring "because of sex."
- There would be a new clear standard for systemic disparate treatment cases that would hold employers responsible for systemic discrimination that exists in their workplaces. In other words, statistics demonstrating disparities in hiring, compensation, or promotions, combined with the employers' failure and/or refusal to fix differentials, would be sufficient to prove systemic discrimination. Courts would not be permitted to accept expert testimony based on gender-based and sex stereotypes to justify the differentials.
- A new standard would exist for judging employer behavior that seeks to avoid a disparate impact. Unlike the Court's original opinion in *Ricci*, which decimated disparate impact theory and made it virtually impossible for employers to eliminate the effects of the biased results of examinations, employers would be free to remedy a significant disparate impact caused by examinations, and disparate impact liability would remain on equal footing with disparate treatment liability.[57]

---

[56] Because the harassment cases that are rewritten here do not deal with customer and coworker harassment against the plaintiff, there is no rewritten case that sets up the standard for employer liability for harassment of employees by customers, coworkers, and other third parties. We assume that the negligence standard that is currently in use would be sufficient to protect employees, but rewritten *Meritor* announces a broad definition of "supervisor" that contradicts the US Supreme Court's decision in *Vance* and would mean more employees would be considered supervisors, where strict liability would attach.

[57] There is a potential conflict between the systemic disparate treatment standards in rewritten *Wal-Mart* and rewritten *Ricci*. Rewritten *Wal-Mart*, consistent with the theory of structural discrimination, concludes that an employer's awareness that its decision-making processes have resulted in disparate results for men and women should make the employer liable for the disparate results even in the absence of an individual intent. Rewritten *Ricci* concludes, in contrast, that, in a systemic disparate treatment case, the plaintiffs must prove an intent to discriminate (i.e., a purpose or reason for adopting the decision-making process was to discriminate against a protected group).

Introduction

- Retaliation claims would use the "reasonable good faith" standard in determining whether the plaintiff has a legitimate claim. In the situation where the plaintiff complains about only one or few instances of discriminatory behavior and the employer retaliates against the plaintiff for speaking out, the employer's retaliation would be illegal if the behavior reported would, if repeated, culminate in an actionable claim.

The Road Not Taken

There are several important employment discrimination opinions that we chose *not* to rewrite. One of them is *Price Waterhouse v. Hopkins*.[58] The reason was simply that the *Price Waterhouse* case had already been rewritten in the original *Feminist Judgments* volume. We could not get permission to reprint it for our volume, and we did not think it would be appropriate to include a different version of it. Thus the rewritten *Price Waterhouse* opinion published there would stand alongside our rewritten body of cases.[59] Of course, mixed-motive liability under the Civil Rights Act of 1991 would also still exist (and the rewritten *Desert Palace* addresses mixed-motive liability).[60] We have to hope that *Price Waterhouse* is still standing after the Supreme Court decides the three cases pending regarding gender identity and sexual orientation.[61]

One staple of employment discrimination law that we did not choose to rewrite is *McDonnell Douglas Corp. v. Green*,[62] which, as most readers know, is the case that first established the burden-shifting framework for Title VII disparate treatment cases.[63] As many scholars have discussed, many plaintiffs are unable to get past the prima facie stage of the burden-shifting framework, even though it was not meant to be an onerous burden.[64] Many scholars predicted that, after *Desert Palace*,[65] *McDonnell Douglas* would be dead,[66]

---

[58] 490 U.S. 228 (1988).

[59] *See* Martha Chamallas, *Price Waterhouse v. Hopkins*, in Stanchi *et al.*, *supra* note 1, at 345.

[60] 42 U.S.C. §2000e-2(m).

[61] *See supra* note 24.

[62] 411 U.S. 792 (1973).

[63] *Id.* at 802–05.

[64] *See, e.g.*, Sandra F. Sperino, *Rethinking Discrimination Law*, 110 MICH. L. REV. 69, 87–88 (2011) ("Even in cases where plaintiffs present evidence that they might have been treated differently because of a protected trait, courts use the *McDonnell Douglas* framework to find no cognizable claim").

[65] 539 U.S. 90 (2003).

[66] *See, e.g.*, Michael J. Zimmer, *The New Discrimination Law:* Price Waterhouse *Is Dead, Whither* McDonnell Douglas?, 53 EMORY L.J. 1887, 1939–40 (2004) (suggesting that *McDonnell Douglas* will have little value after *Desert Palace*); William R. Corbett,

24   *Introduction*

but, as we have seen, that has not proven to be the case.[67] At the outset of this project, we imagined that a rewrite of *Desert Palace* might address *McDonnell Douglas*,[68] and we believed that *Desert Palace* was the better case to rewrite – in part because it dealt directly with sex discrimination, but also because it is a story with facts that needed to be told.

The use of the *McDonnell Douglas* burden-shifting framework is so pervasive that it has even spilled over into the Americans with Disabilities Act of 1990 (ADA), which is a major employment discrimination statute that it is not directly addressed in this book.[69] The ADA is mentioned briefly in the rewritten *Young* case in relation to the fact that pregnancy might be considered a disability under the broadened definition of "disability" in the ADA Amendments Act of 2008 (ADAAA). Part of the reason we chose not to address the ADA is that there was not one case (especially not a Supreme Court case) that could have been rewritten in such a way that it would have dramatically changed the status of the law (other than the negative Supreme Court cases on the definition of disability,[70] which were superseded by the ADAAA[71]). All volumes in the Feminist Judgments series are limited to no more than fifteen opinions, and so we had to make tough decisions. Both of us wish we could have included a disability law case because not only is the ADA still not

---

McDonnell Douglas, 1972–2003: *May You Rest in Peace?*, 6 U. PA. LAB. & EMP. L. 199, 219 (2003); Jeffrey A. Van Detta, *"Le Roi Est Mort; Vive Le Roi!" An Essay on the Quiet Demise of* McDonnell Douglas *and the Transformation of Every Title VII Case after* Desert Palace, Inc. v. Costa *into a "Mixed-Motives" Case*, 52 DRAKE L. REV. 71, 76 (2003).

[67] For a comprehensive analysis of *McDonnell Douglas, see* Sandra Sperino, MCDONNELL DOUGLAS: THE MOST IMPORTANT CASE IN EMPLOYMENT DISCRIMINATION LAW (2018).

[68] For a comprehensive analysis of how *Desert Palace* may have weakened *McDonnell Douglas* by encouraging, in most individual employment discrimination cases, the use of the mixed-motives approach rather than the complicated burden shifting approach of *McDonnell Douglas*, see Zimmer, *supra* note 66, at 1891 (positing that "a new, uniform proof structure will evolve from *Desert Palace* and that the approach established in § 703 (m) will apply to almost all individual discrimination cases"). It appears, however, some fifteen years after Professor Zimmer published this article, that *McDonnell Douglas* is still very much alive.

[69] This is especially surprising given that both of us are experts in the area. We are both coauthors of competing disability law casebooks. *See* Laura Rothstein & Ann C. McGinley, DISABILITY LAW: CASES, PROBLEMS (6th ed. 2017); Stephen F. Befort & Nicole Buonocore Porter, DISABILITY LAW: CASES AND MATERIALS (2017). Nicole also frequently publishes scholarship about the ADA.

[70] We are, of course, referring to the *Sutton* trilogy of cases, which held that, when determining whether someone is disabled, courts should look at the person in their mitigated state, considering any measures they use to ameliorate the effects of their disability. *See generally*, Nicole Buonocore Porter, *The New ADA Backlash*, 82 TENN. L. REV. 1, 9–10 (2014) (discussing the *Sutton*-trilogy of cases); *see also* Toyota Motor Manufacturing v. Williams, 534 U.S. 184 (2002) (narrowly construing the definition of "substantially limits" in the definition of disability).

[71] Porter, *supra* note 70, at 14–17 (discussing the Amendments and their effect on the definition of disability).

Introduction

a plaintiff-friendly statute,[72] but also research demonstrates that women with disabilities are often treated worse than men with disabilities, creating intersectional disadvantages for women with disabilities.[73]

Neither did we choose to rewrite *Gross v. FBL Financial Services, Inc.*,[74] which held that plaintiffs suing under the Age Discrimination in Employment Act of 1967 (ADEA) cannot proceed under a mixed-motive theory and instead must establish that their age was a but-for cause of the adverse employment action.[75] Ideally, we wished we had room to include a rewritten *Gross*, in part because the inability to bring mixed-motive cases under the ADEA means that older women will have a much harder time establishing intersectional sex-plus-age claims.[76] Moreover, studies demonstrate "robust evidence" of age discrimination against older women.[77]

Another important case that we did not include that has harmed employees who work for religious organizations is *Hosanna-Tabor Evangelical Lutheran Church & School v. EEOC.*[78] The Court in *Hosanna-Tabor* held that the "ministerial exception" prohibited a cause of action for discrimination and retaliation under the ADA by a teacher in a Lutheran school.[79] The ministerial exception, which has its roots in the First Amendment to the US Constitution, protects religious organizations from governmental intrusion and prohibits plaintiffs who are deemed "ministers" from bringing suits against their religious employers under the antidiscrimination statutes. The Court defines "minister" in an extraordinarily broad manner – to include any employee whose job involves getting out the message of the employer – and the exemption applies against "ministers" in religious organizations even when the

---

[72] *See* Nicole Buonocore Porter, *Explaining "Not Disabled" Cases 10 Years after the ADAAA: A Story of Ignorance, Incompetence, and Possibly Animus*, 26 GEO. J. ON POVERTY L. & POL'Y 383 (2019) (discussing more than 200 cases where courts erroneously held that plaintiffs were not disabled).

[73] *See, e.g.*, Michelle A. Travis, *Gendering Disability to Enable Disability Rights Law*, 105 CALIF. L. REV. 837 (2017); *see also* Nicole Buonocore Porter, *Mothers with Disabilities*, 33 BERKELEY J. GENDER L. & JUST. 75 (2018).

[74] 557 U.S. 167 (2009).

[75] *Id.* at 176–78.

[76] *See, e.g.*, Marc Chase McAllister, *Extending the Sex-Plus Discrimination Doctrine to Age Discrimination Claims Involving Multiple Discriminatory Motives*, 60 B.C. L. REV. 469, 493–97 (2019) (demonstrating that the majority of courts have held that age-plus claims are not valid under the ADEA); *see also* Nicole Buonocore Porter, *Sex Plus Age Discrimination: Protecting Older Women Workers*, 81 DENV. U. L. REV. 79 (2003).

[77] *See, e.g.*, McAllister, *supra* note 76, at 503–04 (citing studies); *see also* Susan Bisom-Rapp & Malcolm Sargeant, LIFETIME DISADVANTAGE, DISCRIMINATION AND THE GENDERED WORKFORCE (2016).

[78] 565 U.S. 171 (2012).

[79] *Id.*

26   *Introduction*

subject of the lawsuit is not related to religious belief or doctrine.[80] In other words, harassment, discrimination, and retaliation based on race, color, sex, gender, religion, age, national origin, and disability are not compensable against a religious employer in a large majority of cases after *Hosanna-Tabor*.[81]

Finally, we would have loved to rewrite *Gilmer v. Interstate/Johnson Lane Corp.*[82] and its progeny, which hold that the Federal Arbitration Act (FAA)[83] applies to individual employment contracts in discrimination claims.[84] Before *Gilmer*, an employment discrimination plaintiff was not required to arbitrate a statutory civil rights claim.[85] In *Gilmer*, an age discrimination case brought under the ADEA, the Court held that the FAA requires an employee, who contractually agrees before the dispute arises, to arbitrate all upcoming employment disputes rather than go to court.[86] Given the unequal bargaining power between employers and employees, the unilateral imposition of mandatory arbitration provisions upon employees by employers, the lack of arbitrator specialty in discrimination law, the failure to require that the substantive law be properly applied in arbitrations, and the very rare opportunity to appeal an arbitration award, this decision and its progeny literally deprived thousands of employees (many of them women alleging sexual harassment) of their days in court.[87] Moreover, since *Gilmer*,

---

[80] *See* Leslie C. Griffin, A *Word of Warning from a Woman: Arbitrary, Categorical, and Hidden Religious Exemptions Threaten LGBT Rights*, 7 ALA. CIV. RIGHTS & CIV. LIBERTIES L. REV. 97, 116 (2015) (describing how Catholic schools have fired gay and lesbian employees precipitously for having children out of wedlock even though they are legally married).

[81] *Id.* at 113–16. Thanks to Professor Griffin for her input on this section.

[82] 500 U.S. 20 (1991).

[83] 29 U.S.C. §621, *et seq.*

[84] *Gilmer*, technically, is not an employment case. The clause was imposed by the stock exchange, not by the employer. The issue of whether the section 1 employment exclusion in the Federal Arbitration Act broadly excludes employees from the Act's coverage was resolved later, in *Circuit City Stores v. Adams*, 532 U.S. 105 (2001) (holding that the employment exclusion applies narrowly to employees in transportation). For a view that section 1 excludes all employees, not merely transportation workers, *see* Jeffrey W. Stempel, *Reconsidering the Employment Contract Exclusion in Section 1 of the Federal Arbitration Act: Correcting the Judiciary's Failure of Statutory Vision*, 1991 J. DISP. RESOL. 259, 263 (criticizing the view that the exclusion was narrow in scope). Thanks to Professor Sternlight for her input on this section.

[85] *Alexander v. Gardner-Denver Co.*, 415 U.S. 36 (1974).

[86] *Gilmer*, 500 U.S. at 35.

[87] *See, e.g.,* Jean R. Sternlight, *Mandatory Arbitration Stymies Progress towards Justice in Employment Law: Where To, #MeToo*, 54 HARV. C.R.-C.L. L. REV. 155 (2019); Alexander J. S. Colvin, *The Growing Use of Mandatory Arbitration: Access to the Courts in Now Barred for More Than 60 Million American Workers*, ECON. POLICY INST. (Sep. 27, 2017), www.epi.org /publication/the-growing-use-of-mandatory-arbitration/ (reporting that 56 percent of nonunion employees in the study were subject to mandatory arbitration provisions).

Introduction 27

the Court has continuously expanded its holding. It has even upheld waivers of class actions in arbitration.[88] Additionally, courts have upheld arbitration clauses that appear in employee handbooks and others appearing in small print in employment contracts that employees sign unwittingly or not at all.[89]

Since the #MeToo movement, the Court's arbitration jurisprudence has become an important gender issue because mandatory predispute arbitration clauses have prevented victims from suing their employers in open court. Not only are many of these individuals receiving only partial or no justice, but also the secret proceedings have hindered the courts' ability to develop the law as societal norms change. Empirical evidence demonstrates that plaintiffs in employment discrimination cases generally fare worse in arbitration than in a trial in court.[90]

As a result of pressure placed by the #MeToo movement to legislatively overrule the Court's interpretation of the FAA that deprives harassment victims of recourse, a number of federal bills specifically dealing with forced arbitration of sex- and gender-based harassment suits have been introduced with significant support, but to date none has passed into law.[91]

Obviously, there are other cases and areas of the law that we could not address in this book. The cases described in this section are those that are perhaps the most prominent: the cases and areas where the absence of feminist rewrites will be most missed.

---

[88] *See American Express v. Italian Colors Restaurant,* 570 U.S. 228 (2013) (concluding that arbitration clauses can impose class action waivers even when doing so effectively precluded relief); *Epic Systems v. Lewis,* 138 S.Ct. 1612 (2018) (permitting companies to use mandatory arbitration clauses to forbid class action by employees).

[89] For a discussion of the expansion of the courts' interpretation of the Federal Arbitration Act to eliminate workers' rights to trial both in federal and state court actions, *see* Sternlight, *supra* note 87, at 172, 173–76.

[90] *See generally,* Alexander J. S. Colvin, *An Empirical Study of Employment Arbitration: Case Outcomes and Processes,* 8 J. EMPIRICAL LEG. STUDS. 1, 6 (2011). One example is that of Fox News former cohost of *The Five,* Andrea Tantaros, who evidently spent more than $1 million in arbitration to no avail and is currently challenging her arbitration under New York's new provision barring mandatory predispute arbitration of sexual harassment employment disputes. Eriq Gardner, *Former Fox Star Tests Anti-Arbitration Rule for Sexual Harassment Claims,* HOLLYWOOD REPORTER (July 16, 2019), www.hollywoodreporter.com/thr-esq/fox-news-star-tests-anti-arbitration-rule-sexual-harassment-claims-1224537.

[91] Sternlight, *supra* note 87, at 206–07; *see also* Alexia Fernández Campbell, *Democrats Want to Ban Mandatory Arbitration at Work. Republicans Are Listening,* VOX (Apr. 3, 2019), www .vox.com/2019/4/3/18292168/forced-arbitration-senate-bill-hearing (noting that while many bills have been introduced and Republicans seem less opposed to these bans recently, none of the bills mentioned in the article have passed).

28   *Introduction*

The Future of Employment Discrimination Law

This book presents a hopeful outlook in suggesting that using feminist perspectives, theories, and methods would improve the effectiveness of federal employment discrimination law; implicit in its goal is the belief that we may be able to nudge the law to be more protective of women, men, and gender-nonconforming individuals and less tolerant of gender-based discrimination, harassment, and retaliation. But, realistically, we understand the direction that the federal courts (and their interpretation of federal law) is going. Given that President Trump has successfully appointed Justices who make the majority on the Supreme Court more conservative and that Senate Majority Leader Mitch McConnell has successfully pushed through dozens of Trump judges on the lower federal courts, the chances are good that the federal antidiscrimination law will become more conservative and less protective of plaintiffs in the years to come.

One potential solution is to encourage state legislatures to improve the protection provided by state antidiscrimination laws. Another is to appoint (or elect), in more liberal states, state court judges who will interpret the state antidiscrimination law liberally. While this volume deals exclusively with federal law, the rewritten opinions and commentaries may provide examples and analysis that help state court judges to assure that their state antidiscrimination laws deliver greater protection than that provided by federal law. We encourage state court judges to seriously consider the perspectives, methodologies, and theories offered in this volume in their own judgments.

CONCLUSION

This volume demonstrates that use of feminist perspectives and methodologies, if adopted by the courts, would have made a significant difference in employment discrimination law. Not only would individual opinions have changed, but also large portions of the law would have been more open to equality in employment for persons regardless of sex or gender, sexual orientation, race, national origin and religion. This, we believe, would have created a fairer, more egalitarian, and even more prosperous society.

We both found this project to be deeply rewarding. Conceptualizing a reimagined body of employment discrimination law was challenging, but it was also fun and exciting. Working with our talented authors was (for the most part) a labor of love. Each opinion and commentary exposed us to something new: either some interesting fact about the case that was not widely

Introduction 29

known, or a new theory or idea that made us think about the law in a new way. We hope that our authors found the editing process helpful, but it is certainly possible that we derived more value from it than they did. We hope that readers of this book enjoy thinking about how employment discrimination law (and workplaces) might be improved if judges were willing to evaluate facts and legal doctrine from a variety of feminist perspectives.

2

Supreme Court and Gender Narratives

Commentary on *Desert Palace v. Costa*

NAOMI M. MANN

INTRODUCTION

In *Desert Palace v. Costa*,[1] the female plaintiff, a warehouse worker and heavy equipment operator, sued the defendant, doing business as Caesar's Palace Hotel and Casino, for firing her after she got into an altercation with a male employee who was not disciplined as severely as she was. The Supreme Court held that, under section 703(m) of Title VII of the Civil Rights Act of 1964,[2] plaintiffs do not need to "present direct evidence of discrimination in order to obtain a mixed-motive [jury instruction]."[3] This holding was undoubtedly correct as a matter of statutory construction. But while the opinion is elegant in its simplicity, its failure to address the serious facts that led to Catharina Costa's lawsuit contributes to a systemic failure to openly address and redress the experiences of victims of gender discrimination. The feminist judgment, authored by Professor Anne Mullins, writing as Justice Mullins, corrects that error by providing a powerful narrative of the discrimination, harassment, and retaliation suffered by Ms. Costa.

THE ORIGINAL OPINION

After the Court issued its plurality opinion in *Price Waterhouse v. Hopkins*[4] in 1989, with its multiple concurrences and unclear majority consensus, courts splintered on how to handle mixed-motive disparate treatment cases – cases where the employer's actions are motivated by both legitimate and impermissible

---

[1] *Desert Palace, Inc. v. Costa*, 539 U.S. 90 (2003).
[2] Section 703(m), 42 U.S.C. §2000e-2(m).
[3] *Desert Palace*, 539 U.S. at 92.
[4] 490 U.S. 228 (1989).

Desert Palace, Inc. v. Costa

(or discriminatory) reasons.[5] Under the *McDonnell Douglas*[6] burden-shifting framework, as it stood before *Price Waterhouse* was decided, the question was whether discrimination was the one true reason motivating the employer, and if it was, the employer was liable for discrimination. *Price Waterhouse* allowed for a more nuanced analysis, permitting plaintiffs to prevail in the messier, yet more true to real-life mixed-motive cases where plaintiffs can prove that, in spite of the existence of nondiscriminatory reasons for how their employer treated them, gender played a substantial factor in the contested treatment.[7] Once a plaintiff met this standard, the burden then shifted to the defendant to prove that it would have made the same decision absent the impermissible consideration of the plaintiff's gender. If it met this burden, the defendant would avoid liability.

Given that *Price Waterhouse* was a plurality opinion, without a clear majority consensus, some courts began reading the opinion within the narrower confines of the two concurrences. Of importance for *Desert Palace* is that Justice O'Connor's concurrence required direct evidence that gender was a substantial factor in the employer's decision in order to shift the burden to the employer. Circuit courts consequently split on the issue of whether direct evidence was necessary to shift the burden to employers as per Justice O'Connor's concurrence or whether circumstantial evidence could also be used to prove that the discriminatory motive was a substantial factor in the decision-making.[8]

Congress amended Title VII in 1991, partly in response to the developing circuit split.[9] The 1991 Act included two provisions on mixed-motive cases. First, Congress codified the mixed-motive approach, stating that a plaintiff can prove illegal discrimination by demonstrating that "sex ... was a *motivating* factor for [the] employment practice, even though other factors also motivated

---

[5.] "Since the Supreme Court's opinion in *Price Waterhouse v. Hopkins*, the judicial system has been rife with confusion over the correct evidentiary standard to apply in 'mixed-motive' cases of employment discrimination." Michael Abbott, *A Swing and a Miss: The U.S. Supreme Court's Attempt to Resolve the Confusion over the Proper Evidentiary Burden for Employment Discrimination Litigation* in Costa v. Desert Palace, 30 J. OF CORP. L. 573, 573 (2005).

[6.] *McDonnell Douglas Corp. v. Green*, 411 U.S. 792 (1973).

[7.] While the *Price Waterhouse* plurality opinion advocated a "motivating factor" test, the majority did not agree with this, and thus the higher standard of "substantial factor" used in Justice O'Connor's concurrence became the de facto test until the 1991 amendments to Title VII, which uses the "motivating factor" test. *Price Waterhouse*, 490 U.S. at 244, 276.

[8.] *Desert Palace*, 539 U.S. at 95 ("Since the passage of the 1991 Act, the Courts of Appeals have divided over whether a plaintiff must prove by direct evidence that an impermissible consideration was a "motivating factor" in an adverse employment action").

[9.] *Id.*

32 Desert Palace, Inc. v. Costa

the practice."[10] Once this standard is met, the defendant is liable. Second, the 1991 Act provided employers with a partial affirmative defense that would limit the remedies available to the plaintiff if the employer could prove that it "would have taken the same action in the absence of the impermissible motivating factor."[11] Left unaddressed, however, was the question of what type of evidence plaintiffs needed to produce in order to meet their burden of proving that discrimination was a motivating factor.

The original *Desert Palace* opinion answered this evidentiary question by holding that the plaintiff could use direct *or* circumstantial evidence to prove disparate treatment based on gender. The opinion uses a classic statutory interpretation method, with the focus squarely on the text of the legislation and Congress's intent when modifying Title VII.[12] The Court concluded that, because the revised statutory text did not explicitly limit the plaintiff's proof in Title VII mixed-motive cases to direct evidence, Ms. Costa's claim should be treated as a traditional civil case, which may be proven by direct and/or circumstantial evidence. After all, the Court reasoned, when Congress wants to impose a higher evidentiary burden, it does so explicitly; its failure to do so in the 1991 amendments to Title VII was determinative.[13] In defense of circumstantial evidence, the Court noted that it is not inherently less reliable; it can sometimes be "more certain, satisfying and persuasive," and it is admissible even to prove guilt in criminal cases.[14]

Desert Palace is usually considered a victory for Title VII plaintiffs because of its holding that plaintiffs can use both direct and circumstantial evidence when proving disparate treatment. By allowing circumstantial evidence, not only did the ruling place Title VII disparate treatment plaintiffs on equal footing with other civil plaintiffs, but it also removed a serious evidentiary barrier to plaintiffs' discrimination cases, given that direct evidence of discriminatory animus is rare.[15] A feminist analysis nevertheless provides several important critiques of the original opinion.

First, the statute, rather than the plaintiff's narrative or the gender discrimination that she suffered, is the focus of the original case. Ms. Costa and her experience are relegated to the background, not appearing until page four of the opinion. While Justice Thomas provides the reader with a snapshot of

[10] 42 U.S.C.A. §2000e-2(m) (emphasis added).
[11] 42 U.S.C.A. §2000e-5(g)(2)B).
[12] *Desert Palace*, 539 U.S. at 98–99.
[13] *Id.* at 99.
[14] *Id.* at 100 (citing *Rogers v. Missouri Pacific R. Co.*, 352 U.S. 500, 508 n.17 (1957)).
[15] Suzanne Goldberg, *Discrimination by Comparison*, 120 YALE L.J. 728, 731 and n.1 at 731 (2011) ("[P]utative discriminators rarely admit discriminatory intent . . . no sensible employer would admit that it based a decision on one of the prohibited classifications").

some of Ms. Costa's specific factual claims, he shortens them considerably, and he removes the detail and context that demonstrate how severe the discrimination and harassment was. By contrast, the Ninth Circuit fills the first two pages of its opinion with the "egregious" acts of discrimination that Ms. Costa faced as a "trailblazer" in her industry.[16] The facts described by the Ninth Circuit and the Supreme Court are so different that they could be from two separate cases. This sanitization of the facts is reminiscent of the Court's original opinion in *Oncale v. Sundowner Offshore Services*,[17] which asserts "brevity and dignity" as reasons to skirt the troubling and explicit facts of the discrimination in that case.[18]

In addition to reporting the facts at arm's length, the Court presented itself as a neutral reporter when it actually recounted the facts from the employer's perspective. The Court's factual recitation uses neither the word "victim" nor the word "discrimination." Ms. Costa's claims (which were proven at trial, justified an award of punitive damages, and were upheld by the Ninth Circuit) are minimized and reported in a dry and impersonal manner. The incident where a coworker physically assaulted Ms. Costa, leaving bruises, is described as her having been "involved in a physical altercation."[19] As noted below, the Court's narrow lens has multiple important consequences for Title VII plaintiffs and the legal system's ability to adequately understand, evaluate, and address sex discrimination in the employment context.

Second, the Court does not question why the direct evidence requirement arose and why it was, and still is, problematic for Title VII plaintiffs. Why were victims of discrimination subjected to higher evidentiary standards than the typical civil plaintiff? Why did most courts of appeal continue to impose this higher evidentiary standard even after Congress amended Title VII without including a direct evidence requirement? In ducking this issue, the Court ignores the long history of the legal system's failure to believe victims of discrimination and of imposing, whether overtly in law[20] or implicitly through reluctance to believe victims, higher proof requirements for victims to prevail.[21] Coupled with the sparse facts about what happened, the original

---

[16] *Costa v. Desert Palace, Inc.*, 299 F.3d 838, 844–47 (9th Cir. 2002).

[17] 523 U.S. 75 (1998).

[18] *Id.* at 77.

[19] *Desert Palace*, 539 U.S. at 95.

[20] Michelle Anderson, *Campus Sexual Assault Adjudication and Resistance to Reform*, 125 YALE L.J. 1940 (2016) (detailing the history of additional burdens that female sexual assault victims have historically had to meet).

[21] Although Title VII case law asserts that victims have the same burdens of proof as in other cases, women face hurdles to being credited when they allege discrimination. *Compare Swierkiewicz v. Sorema*, 534 U.S. 506 (2002) (no need for Title VII plaintiffs to plead with more particularity

34   Desert Palace, Inc. v. Costa

opinion does little to explain why the direct evidence requirement runs counter to Title VII's purposes and goals.[22]

Third, the opinion rejects any consideration of the stereotype arguments that were advanced by the plaintiff and addressed in the court below.[23] This is especially striking given that the Court is positioning *Desert Palace* as a case that answers one of the major questions left open in *Price Waterhouse*, itself a landmark case for the consideration of stereotypes in gender discrimination jurisprudence. Stereotypes, and the biases that they raise, are a critical part of discrimination and should be addressed where they are present to effectuate Title VII's goals.[24]

THE FEMINIST JUDGMENT

Mullins places Ms. Costa and her story front and center in the opinion. This case is about Ms. Costa and gender discrimination first, and the employer's explanations and the doctrines of statutory interpretation second. Through this broader focus, important new themes emerge.

First, through the more complete narrative, the discrimination is laid bare: harsh, unrelenting, and clearly aimed at Ms. Costa because she is a woman. We are told specifics of the discrimination, including Ms. Costa's reprimand for allegedly "provoking" a coworker into calling her a "fucking cunt" and her employer's telling her that a male coworker (and not Costa) deserved overtime opportunities because he had a family to support. This narrative sharply contrasts with the Court's original opinion, which describes very briefly a plaintiff who has had trouble with management and coworkers that resulted in a number of disciplinary sanctions.[25] By contrast, Mullins uses the facts to provide a road map of why and how the employer's actions were discriminatory.

Why does this matter? It matters because the original opinion, by examining the facts both at a distance from the victim and from the employer's perspective, ignored both the lived experience and the human cost of discrimination.

than others) *with* Kathy Mack, *Continuing Barriers to Women's Credibility: A Feminist Perspective on the Proof Process*, 4 Crim. L. Forum 327 (1993).

[22.] Mark R. Bandsuch, *Ten Troubles with Title VII and Trait Discrimination, Plus One Simple Solution (A Totality of the Circumstances Framework)*, 37 Capital U. L. Rev. 965 (2009) (detailing concerns about how a direct evidence requirement limits Title VII's applicability).

[23.] *Costa*, 299 F.3d at 845–46.

[24.] *See generally* Stan Malos, *Overt Stereotype Biases and Discrimination in the Workplace: Why Haven't We Fixed This by Now?*, 27 Emp. Resp. & Rights J. 271 (2015); *see also* Amy Horton, *Of Supervision, Centerfolds, and Censorship: Sexual Harassment, the First Amendment, and the Contours of Title VII*, 46 U. Miami L. Rev. 403, 426 (1991).

[25.] *Desert Palace*, 539 U.S. at 95–96.

Mullins cautions that the Court should not use its power to sanitize discrimination, even if tackling such sensitive topics is uncomfortable. The impersonal tone of the original opinion is not neutral at all. By presenting the facts from the employer's perspective behind a facade of neutrality, the opinion diminishes Ms. Costa's discriminatory treatment. While the facts were proven at trial and rarely awarded punitive damages were imposed, the Court still treated both sides' claims as equally credible. In so doing, the Court ignored that Ms. Costa had to work every day with supervisors who actively discriminated against her and coworkers who actively harassed and assaulted her. By suffering attacks from above and below, Ms. Costa experienced a burdensome daily work life that was not faced by her male coworkers.

By contrast, Mullins' approach draws the reader into the lived experience of Ms. Costa and the treatment that she endured. Without the vicarious experience of Ms. Costa's challenges, those without direct experience of discrimination of this kind can more easily maintain emotional and cognitive distance, allowing themselves to ignore the impact of discriminatory behavior on the victim and on society. It is critical to break this distance. Even in the era of #MeToo, when victims' voices appear more prominent, the details of victims' stories are frequently silenced and/or devalued, thereby making it less likely that the legal system and the public will understand, value, and properly address the victim's experiences.[26] The rewritten opinion highlights the victim's story and explains how her treatment was discriminatory and why the legal system must address it. In so doing, it emphasizes that the court system will give these experiences weight and due credibility. With this larger context explained, subtler forms of discrimination – such as Ms. Costa's being the only warehouse worker kicked out of the break room, even if the supervisor was correct that she had work to do – are more readily understood. When courts detail discriminatory treatment, whether or not it involves unseemly or emotional facts (and especially if it does), the courts' statements help to educate the public and push the judicial system, as well as employers, to act to effectuate the purposes of Title VII.

Mullins also broadens our understanding of victims of discrimination. The rewritten opinion is clear: Title VII does not protect only plaintiffs with easy narratives. In the rewritten opinion's more nuanced retelling, a more complete portrait of Ms. Costa emerges. On the one hand, we are told that she did

---

[26.] *See What Changed after Blasey Ford, Kavanagh Hearing?*, CNN: Opinion (Sep. 28, 2018), www-m.cnn.com/2018/09/27/opinions/kavanaugh-blasey-ford-testimony-roundup/index.html?r=https%3A%2F%2Fwww.google.com%2F; Anna North, *The #MeToo Movement and Its Evolution, Explained*, Vox (Oct. 11, 2018), www.vox.com/identities/2018/10/9/17933746/metoo-movement-metoo-brett-kavanaugh-weinstein.

good work, managers could rely on her, she got along with colleagues, and she served her coworkers as their union steward. On the other hand, we are told that she had multiple conflicts with coworkers and supervisors, could be tardy, and may not have been an easy coworker to get along with. Ms. Costa was not a perfect employee and colleague.[27] However, as Mullins reminds us, Costa's personality is not the legal issue; rather, the legal issue is that she was treated differently from male coworkers and held to different or higher standards. Mullins reminds us that Title VII protects qualified individuals from discrimination on prohibited grounds, whether or not they are perfect or even likeable. It is critical that judges, lawyers, jurors, and the general public understand that victims of discrimination are complex, just like everyone else, and that their complexity is not a reason to deny them protection under Title VII.

The rewritten opinion also includes a troubling fact. While Ms. Costa was herself discriminated against on the basis of gender, on one occasion she was disciplined for allegedly making a "vulgar ethnic remark." This is important because it illustrates the complexity of discrimination in the workplace. Just as Ms. Costa's female supervisor was capable of discriminating against Ms. Costa even though they were both women, so too are victims of sex discrimination capable of engaging in racial discrimination.[28] Ms. Costa was suspended for thirty days for allegedly making this remark – a comment that was apparently frequent in that workplace. Her discipline was much harsher than that received by others who made similar remarks. Caesar's Palace should take racial discrimination seriously regardless of the identity of the discriminator. A feminist court should address and acknowledge the intersectionality and complexity of the set of facts and the individuals involved.

The broader narrative also holds the employer accountable for its discrimination. The original opinion sanitized the employer's actions. The reader of the original opinion could easily develop the impression that this case was about a Caesar's Palace that steadily reprimanded a difficult employee, who then alleged discrimination. This impression is light-years from the Caesar's Palace that permitted its supervisors to actively and repeatedly discriminate against a female employee. The original opinion's neutral approach protected Caesar's Palace from the costs of its discrimination. If the Court does not acknowledge and describe the discrimination that existed, then the employer

---

[27] *Costa*, 299 F.3d at 844–46.

[28] Kimberlé Crenshaw, *Demarginalizing the Intersection of Race and Sex: A Black Feminist Critique of Antidiscrimination Doctrine, Feminist Theory, and Antiracist Politics*, 1989 U. Chi. Legal Forum 139; Mariana Ortega, *Being Lovingly, Knowingly Ignorant: White Feminism and Women of Color*, 2 Hypatia (Jan. 9, 2009).

can escape the inevitable public scrutiny and consequences that a fuller and more accurate factual summary could provoke.[29] The Court plays a powerful role in bringing victims' narratives forward and in exposing the structural inequalities that underlie victims' experiences.[30] As Mullins explains, where courts do not shine a light on discrimination, they do not fully exercise their obligation to meet Title VII's purpose to protect employees from unlawful discrimination.

Second, Mullins' opinion confronts the inherent bias in the higher evidentiary standard that Caesar's Palace advocated and many circuit courts were then using.[31] Requiring direct evidence is, in essence, telling the victim that she is somehow less credible than other civil plaintiffs – that direct proof is needed if we are to believe her story of discrimination. In the past, this bias has been enshrined in the law in areas such as rape corroboration requirements, wherein a woman needed a witness in order to prevail in a rape case.[32] As the #MeToo movement has highlighted, victims of gender discrimination often do not report for fear that they will not be believed.[33] A direct evidence requirement itself sends a powerful message to victims of gender discrimination that their testimony alone is not enough to prevail. It also sends the message that, by contrast, the employer is considered more credible per se. After all, in the precedent that the Court considered, the employer is not limited to direct evidence in making out its affirmative defense;[34] it may use both circumstantial and direct evidence. Victims of gender discrimination could thus reasonably conclude that the cards were stacked against them.

When discrimination victims believe that they will not be given a fair opportunity in court, they are less willing to seek court protection.[35] If these

---

[29] *See, e.g.,* Emily Steel & Michael S. Schmidt, *Bill O'Reilly Thrives at Fox News, Even as Harassment Settlements Add Up,* N.Y. TIMES (Apr. 1, 2017), www.nytimes.com/2017/04/01/business/media/bill-oreilly-sexual-harassment-fox-news.html.

[30] *See* Margaret Johnson, *Feminist Judgments & #MeToo,* 94 NOTRE DAME L. REV. ONLINE 51, 52 (2018) (discussing the role that authoritative storytellers play in constructing the narratives that are prioritized and given space).

[31] *See supra* note 5 and accompanying text.

[32] *The Rape Corroboration Requirement: Repeal Not Reform,* 81 YALE L.J. 1365 (1972).

[33] Jacey Fortin, *#WhyIDidntReport: Survivors of Sexual Assault Share Their Stories after Trump Tweet,* N.Y. TIMES (Sep. 23, 2018), www.nytimes.com/2018/09/23/us/why-i-didnt-report-assault-stories.html.

[34] *Desert Palace,* 539 U.S. at 101.

[35] Nicole Buonocore Porter, *Ending Harassment by Starting with Retaliation,* 71 STANFORD L. REV. ONLINE 49 (2018); Stefanie K. Johnson *et al., Why We Fail to Report Sexual Harassment,* HARVARD BUS. REV. (Oct. 4, 2016), *available at* https://hbr.org/2016/10/why-we-fail-to-report-sexual-harassment; Alexia Fernández Campbell, *How the Legal System Fails Victims of Sexual Harassment,* VOX (Dec. 11, 2017), www.vox.com/policy-and-politics/2017/12/11/16685778/sexual-harassment-federal-courts.

38   Desert Palace, Inc. v. Costa

victims do not seek remedies in court, Title VII rights go unprotected, and employers are not held accountable. Not holding employers accountable fosters continued gender discrimination, leaves existing discrimination and narratives in place,[36] and allows the courts to abdicate their role in addressing workplace discrimination. Mullins' feminist opinion explicitly refuses to allow the courts to further this dynamic.

Mullins thus proceeds to link the purposes of Title VII and the appropriate evidentiary burdens in mixed-motive cases. Given that evidentiary rules aim to ensure accurate and just results, a direct evidence requirement is not appropriate because it captures merely a slice of discrimination, leaving out both those employers who harbor overt animus, but are able to hide it, and those employers who, affected by implicit bias, act in a discriminatory manner. Mullins clarifies the evidentiary standard to reaffirm that Title VII protects all individuals who are discriminated against on the basis of protected categories, not only those who are discriminated against in a manner provable by direct evidence.

In so doing, the rewritten opinion matches the evidentiary burdens more closely with the reality of how gender discrimination works on the ground. By 1992, when *Desert Palace* was originally decided by the federal district court, the Anita Hill sexual harassment allegations were fresh in the public's mind.[37] Employers were becoming more sophisticated about not using direct language tying their decisions to gender, often necessitating the use of circumstantial evidence for plaintiffs to prevail.[38] As a result, the direct evidence requirement was out of step with how discrimination was occurring and was addressing only a fraction of what Title VII was intended to cover.[39] The rewritten opinion realigns the evidentiary rules to hold liable those employers with discriminatory

---

[36.] *See* Johnson, *supra* note 30, at 51 (describing the #MeToo movement narratives as "shift[ing] power structures").

[37.] "It was a live morality play. A state of war between men and women. In the course of three days – Friday, Saturday and Sunday, Oct. 11, 12 and 13 – an issue called 'sexual harassment' got outed in America." Paul Hendrickson, *The Thomas-Hill Witnesses, One Year Later*, WASHINGTON POST (Oct. 12, 1992), www.washingtonpost.com/archive/lifestyle/1992/10/12/the-thomas-hill-witnesses-one-year-later/fd104d3a-6d7d-4783-b21d-bd637d6b4f61/.

[38.] Ann C. McGinley, *Credulous Courts and the Tortured Trilogy: The Improper Use of Summary Judgment*, 34 B. C. L. REV. 203, 214 (1993) ("As defendants become increasingly sophisticated about the law, [direct] admissions occur very rarely. Plaintiffs therefore normally use circumstantial evidence to prove their Title VII and ADEA cases.").

[39.] Horton, *supra* note 24, at 426 ("Race discrimination cases parallel sexual harassment cases . . . In each, litigants first attacked employers' overt denials of employment to minorities or women based upon race or sex. Later it became necessary, to further the goals of Title VII, to attack the more subtle means of discrimination that kept minorities and women out of certain workplaces or positions.").

Desert Palace, Inc. v. Costa

animus who are sophisticated enough to avoid direct expressions of gender-based discrimination.

Gender discrimination is not a fixed concept that remains static over time. Just as some employers were moving from more overt discrimination to subtler forms of discrimination, social scientists were expanding our understanding of how discrimination works.[40] Courts are often slow to recognize new paradigms for long-standing problems and thus can become out of step with the harms they attempt to address. Implicit bias is a key illustration of this point. Scientific research demonstrates that much discrimination plays out subconsciously: many employers are affected by bias and stereotypes, often in complex ways of which they are not even aware.[41] The original opinion does not address the implicit bias dynamic, which is a powerful cause of gender discrimination and would not be redressed by a direct evidence requirement.

By contrast, in addition to reframing the applicable evidentiary rules, the Mullins' Court places an affirmative burden on courts to stay up to date with scientific understanding of discrimination and bias in order to recognize how gender discrimination occurs in practice and to effectuate Title VII. Here, this means recognizing that scientific research shows that implicit bias exists and acknowledging that discrimination expressed overtly and intentionally is only a slice of what discrimination can look like. Allowing circumstantial evidence is therefore about much more than the dry statutory interpretation reflected in the original opinion. It is explicitly about enabling the courts to effectuate Title VII by reflecting reality on the ground and by incentivizing employers, through the threat of liability for Title VII violations, to root out their discriminatory practices, whether overt and intentional or not.

Third, the rewritten opinion addresses the role of stereotyping.[42] The original opinion embraces the stereotype of Ms. Costa as the difficult woman by framing the case as one where an employee with a disciplinary record got into an argument with a coworker and then sued for gender discrimination after she was fired. The more complete facts in the rewritten opinion challenge this narrative, indicating that Ms. Costa was working in

---

[40] See Anthony Greenwald & Mahzarin Banaji, *Implicit Social Cognition: Attitudes, Self-Esteem, and Stereotypes*, 102 PSYCH. REV. 15, 19 (1995); *see also* Sarah A. DeCosse, *Simply Unbelievable: Reasonable Women and Hostile Environment Sexual Harassment*, 10 L. & INEQ. 285 (1992). For an overview of studies on implicit bias through the 2000s, *see* Sendhil Mllainathan, *Racial Bias, Even When We Have Good Intentions*, N.Y. TIMES (Jan. 3, 2015), www.nytimes.com/2015/01/04/upshot/the-measuring-sticks-of-racial-bias-.html.

[41] Ann C. McGinley, ¡Viva la Evolucion! Recognizing Unconscious Motive in Title VII, 9 CORNELL J. L. & PUB. POL'Y 415, 434–36 (2000); Jerry Kang et al., *Implicit Bias in the Courtroom*, 59 UCLA L. REV. 1124, 1172 (2012).

[42] For an analysis of sex stereotyping as disparate treatment, *see* Ann C. McGinley, *Masculinities at Work*, 83 ORE. L. REV. 359, 384–89 (2004).

a hypermasculine[43] environment and was thus perceived as difficult simply because she was a woman. Under masculinities theory, she was punished first for being female in a male-identified job and second for acting in a nonfeminine (or masculine) manner.[44]

Stereotypes harmed Ms. Costa in multiple ways. She was explicitly sanctioned for not acting feminine enough. When she complained that a co-worker had called her a "fucking cunt," she was disciplined for provoking her co-worker into using that word. In essence, because she acted like one, she deserved to be called one. We also know that after she complained about abusive treatment by a male employee, Costa was disciplined. Why? For not being feminine, in that she was accused of being rude to the male employee. In both instances, because Costa stepped out of line and did not conform to the stereotype of how a woman should act, the message was that she deserved the (discriminatory) treatment that she received.

Ms. Costa was also disciplined differently for engaging in the same conduct as her male colleagues. When Ms. Costa was late, she was disciplined, whereas the men were often given overtime to make up their lost hours. When Ms. Costa had to miss work for medical reasons, she was disciplined, whereas the men were again given overtime instead. While the men were permitted to swear and lose their tempers, Ms. Costa was frequently admonished and even suspended for the same behavior. The message was clear: Ms. Costa was not wanted in this masculine workplace.

These stereotypes worked in a complex way when it came to a female supervisor's stalking of Ms. Costa. When Ms. Costa complained to her manager about the stalking, the manager mocked her for thinking that a woman was dangerous to her. Even some of Ms. Costa's male coworkers described the supervisor's behavior as stalking, but management was not interested in exploring the possibility. It could be because they viewed Ms. Costa as an aggressor since she did not fit female stereotypes, or perhaps they did not think that one woman could threaten a second woman, especially when they perceived that second woman to be acting like a man. Either way, the result was that Ms. Costa was denied protection from stalking at her workplace because she was a woman who did not act how a woman was supposed to act.[45]

[43.] For a discussion of hypermasculinity in blue-collar workplaces, *see* Ann C. McGinley, MASCULINITY AT WORK: EMPLOYMENT DISCRIMINATION THROUGH A DIFFERENT LENS 24–27 (2016).

[44.] *See* McGinley, *supra* note 42, at 364 (detailing how cultural norms of how men and women should act intersect with the structural practices of workplace discrimination); Greenwald & Banaji, *supra* note 40, at 15–17, 19.

[45.] Leigh Goodmark, *When Is a Battered Woman Not a Battered Woman? When She Fights Back*, 20 YALE J. OF L. & FEM. 75 (2008) (detailing how battered women who do not fit the stereotype

The event that precipitated her firing illustrates the bind created by the stereotypes that imprisoned Ms. Costa. She was physically assaulted by a male coworker, who trapped her in an elevator. Her testimony about what happened remained consistent over time, and the jury credited it. A third-party witness saw her assailant push her into the elevator, and there was documented bruising consistent with Costa's report of the incident. By contrast, Costa's male coworker changed critical facts of his story and offered no corroborating evidence for his allegation that Costa attacked him first. The employer nonetheless decided to punish them both. In order to do so, her employer discredited the indicia of reliability in Ms. Costa's story, while crediting the male coworker's story despite indicia of its falsity. It is hard to fathom how and why this happened without stereotyping. Given that Ms. Costa did not act sufficiently "feminine," she was not deemed deserving of protection from physical aggression by a male colleague.[46] As a woman who was intruding into a masculine space, she was also deemed per se less credible; even where her story was consistent and corroborated, it was not valued.

By punishing both Ms. Costa and her assailant, the employer did not treat them equally. This decision to punish them both was not neutral because they were not similarly situated. Ms. Costa had a longer disciplinary record precisely because she was a woman doing a man's job who was treated and disciplined differently than her male colleagues.[47] Given that Ms. Costa had this longer disciplinary history, her employment was terminated, while the male coworker was suspended for five days. *But for* her gender, Costa would not have had that disciplinary record, and *but for* that record and gender bias, she would not have been fired while her male colleague was merely disciplined.

THE IMPLICATIONS OF THE REWRITTEN OPINION

If it had been law, the rewritten opinion would have had a significant impact on future Title VII gender discrimination cases both within the court system itself and in society at large.

Mullins' narrative approach would have helped to transform the dominant narrative of sexual harassment. The Court has a powerful voice and

---

of the passive, white victim face hurdles in gaining protection, especially when they have fought back against their abusers).

[46.] *Id.*

[47.] This conclusion was drawn at both the trial and appellate levels. *See Costa*, 299 F.3d at 845–47 ("At trial, the evidence showed a pattern of disparate treatment favoring male co-workers over plaintiff in the application of disciplinary standards ... "; on appeal the court found "Costa presented extensive evidence that she received harsher discipline than the men").

a structural role in shaping and prioritizing legal and popular conceptions,[48] and it could have played an integral role in advancing understanding about sexual harassment at the time of *Desert Palace*. As the #MeToo and Time's Up movements have shown, disrupting the power structure allows new voices to be heard and discrimination to be exposed.[49] Where courts explain why and how conduct and biases operate as discrimination, they educate the public, employees, and employers about what is prohibited under Title VII.

If courts were required to educate themselves about implicit bias and to address its repercussions, we would have a clearer understanding of discrimination, and much more discrimination could be rooted out.[50] As the #MeToo movement has shown, many employers rarely affirmatively address gender discrimination without some outside pressure, and the issue of sexual harassment remains far too often in the shadows.[51] The rewritten opinion would have provided clearer guidance to employers about their legal obligations to curtail sex discrimination in the workplace, extending to all forms of bias, not only obvious direct bias, and they would have had to act affirmatively to address the issues.

If the original opinion had called on the courts to recognize the role that they can play in furthering the reduction of bias, it would have likely enabled many more plaintiffs to proceed with their cases.[52] For example, while evidence rules exist to maximize fairness, judges are given great deference on appeals of their evidentiary rulings. Many cases are decided on the basis of evidentiary rulings alone. Where judges allow their own implicit biases to affect their rulings, such as with the decision to import an evidentiary standard requiring direct evidence only, plaintiffs' cases suffer, and gender discrimination is neither addressed nor punished.[53] Justice Mullins would have involved the courts in a process of self-education to minimize the effect of future implicit bias on the judiciary itself.

[48.] Ralph Lerner, *The Supreme Court as Republican Schoolmaster*, 1967 S.CT. REV. 127.

[49.] *See* Johnson, *supra* note 30, at 52 (discussing the role that authoritative storytellers play in constructing the narratives that are prioritized and given space).

[50.] Nancy Gertner & Melissa Hart, *Implicit Bias in Employment Discrimination Litigation, in* IMPLICIT RACIAL BIAS ACROSS THE LAW 80–95 (Justin D. Levinson & Robert J. Smith eds., 2012) (arguing that judges are affected by implicit bias, which, in turn, affects decisions in Title VII cases).

[51.] Charisse Jones, *#MeToo One Year Later: Cosby, Moonves Fall, Sex Harassment Fight at Work Far from Over*, USA TODAY (Oct. 4, 2018), www.usatoday.com/story/money/2018/10/04/metoo-workplace-sexual-harassment-laws-policies-progress/1378191002/.

[52.] *See* Gertner & Hart, *supra* note 50, at 80–95; *see also* McGinley, *supra* note 43, at 199–214 (explaining that courts should not use their common sense in determining whether human behavior reflects implicit and explicit biases, but should admit expert evidence on the topic).

[53.] Kang *et al.*, *supra* note 41, at 1172; *see also* McGinley, *supra* note 42, at 378–96.

Although the original opinion provided sex discrimination plaintiffs with a "win" in allowing circumstantial evidence in Title VII cases, it fell far short of its potential to address sex discrimination, especially within such a ripe cultural moment. The feminist perspective would have undoubtedly made an impact on Title VII, and society at large, if it had been utilized by the Court.

Desert Palace, Inc. v. Costa,
539 U.S. 90 (2003)

JUSTICE ANNE E. MULLINS DELIVERED THE OPINION OF THE COURT.

Catharina Costa sued Caesar's Palace for firing her after she was assaulted by a male coworker. Her story is complex; the legal issue it raises is not. Does Title VII of the Civil Rights Act of 1964 require a plaintiff to advance direct evidence of discrimination to get a mixed-motive jury instruction? The Court holds that it does not.

I BACKGROUND

In February 1987, Catharina Costa was hired by Caesar's Palace as a heavy equipment operator in the warehouse. Costa operated forklifts and pallet jacks to move food and drinks. Costa was the first woman in the job. In fact, she was the only woman in the job during her tenure of more than seven years with Caesar's.

Costa did her job successfully. Her supervisors described her work as "good" to "[e]xcellent." They "knew when she was out there, the job would get done." She also served as union steward for the International Brotherhood of Teamsters Local 995. In that role, she developed a reputation for being an effective advocate for her fellow Teamsters.

Although she was good at her job, her relationships at work were more of a mixed bag. Some said she "got along with most people" and "had few arguments"; others called her "strong-willed," "opinionated," and "confrontational." They also regularly used sex-based slurs to refer to her.

Ultimately, Costa experienced problems with coworkers and management. Initially, she kept her head down and did her work. But Costa eventually realized that the reason for at least some of her problems was that she is a woman. For example, Caesar's had an official protocol in place for the assignment of overtime hours. Caesar's didn't follow its own protocol in practice, and Costa was repeatedly excluded from overtime assignments in favor of her male coworkers. By 1991, her fourth year on the job, Costa began to fight back. She would no longer tolerate unequal treatment in an environment riddled with sex- and gender-based insults. In April 1991, Costa filed a formal grievance in an attempt to be treated equally to the men in the distribution of overtime assignments. A subsequent review of overtime assigned to eight workers substantiated Costa's claim. Of the 99.5 hours of overtime in one period, Costa received only 2. This wasn't the only time Costa fought for overtime; it was just the first. As detailed further below, Costa had to grieve repeatedly for equitable assignment of overtime during her employment and until her termination in 1994.

In August 1991, a coworker called Costa a "fucking cunt." Warehouse workers frequently used rough language, including vulgar ethnic remarks and profanity. Even so, to Costa's mind, "fucking cunt" went too far. As a result, Costa wrote a letter to management to express her concern. Caesar's agreed that the language was unacceptable, but it sanctioned Costa with a three-day suspension. For what? Engaging in a verbal confrontation that provoked her colleague to the use of such language. (In other words, Costa was asking for it by acting the part.)

The next month, in September 1991, Costa arrived to work one minute late. Her supervisor issued her a written reprimand. A review of the timesheets for that period revealed that a male coworker had failed to clock in for two days in a row. He received no disciplinary action.

In December 1991, Costa called ahead to let her supervisor know she would be late for work. When her coworkers did the same, they were given additional hours to make up the lost time. Not Costa. Instead of getting hours, Costa got disciplined.

Things didn't get any better in 1992. On April 5 of that year, Costa was late again, and she was disciplined again. And a review of the same timesheets showed multiple coworkers knocking off early with no resulting disciplinary action. The next month, Costa missed work to have a tumor surgically removed. The vice president of human resources (HR) had granted Costa medical leave for the procedure and recovery. When her coworkers missed work for medical reasons, they were assigned overtime to make up the hours. Not Costa. Instead, her supervisor suspended her for missing work. Costa had to file a formal grievance to have her suspension voided.

In the summer of 1992, Costa made a vulgar ethnic remark and was suspended for thirty days – what, at the time, may have been the harshest suspension meted out by Caesar's ever. As noted already, this type of rough language was commonplace in the warehouse. The men used vulgar ethnic remarks and profanity regularly with impunity. Not Costa. Ultimately, Costa grieved her suspension, the case went to arbitration, and the suspension was eventually overturned.

Later that fall, another Caesar's employee visited the warehouse for supplies. In the process, he was abusive to Costa. Costa did not respond to him; instead, she reported the incident to her supervisor and asked him to intercede. Costa's complaint, like so many before, was futile, and it came at a price. Costa's supervisor chastised her for being rude. When Costa objected to her supervisor's response, her supervisor disciplined her again.

Nevertheless, she persisted.

In October 1992, the same supervisor suspended Costa for recklessly endangering a fellow employee with an electric cart. Costa grieved the suspension. The resulting investigation revealed that Costa's supervisor had lied in his report. Incidentally, Caesar's declined to share this finding with Costa, who found out about it only years later.

The same month, Costa attempted to eat her lunch in the receiving office. The receiving office was officially off-limits to warehouse employees, but supervisors looked the other way when Costa's male coworkers used it to eat, socialize, and read the newspaper. On this particular day, the weather was cold, and Costa joined her male coworkers inside at lunchtime. A supervisor subsequently entered the office and singled Costa out, asking, "Don't you have work to do?" Costa was thrown out, while her male coworkers remained inside. Costa complained, but to no avail.

In 1993, things took a turn for the worse. Caesar's hired Karen Hallett as an assistant manager. In Hallett's own words, she "was going to be on [Costa's] every move" because she intended to "get rid of that bitch." Hallett regularly followed Costa into the freezer or produce box; when she wasn't on Costa's heels, she was seen peeking around corners to spy on Costa. Costa's coworkers testified that Hallett singled Costa out for particularly intense scrutiny – scrutiny so intense that they characterized it as "stalking." Costa brought Hallett's actions to the attention of the labor relations manager. Instead of making things right, the manager made fun of Costa, minimizing her concerns and sarcastically suggesting that she "go file a police report."

Meanwhile, Costa was still fighting for equitable assignment of overtime. In September 1993, two-and-a-half years after she filed her first grievance for overtime, she filed another one. Weeks later, Costa's supervisor backfilled her disciplinary record for having been late nine times in the previous nine months. Costa had been under a doctor's care at the time, but her supervisor refused to consider doctor's notes justifying the late arrivals. During the same period, a coworker missed several full workdays with no note. Instead of disciplinary action, however, he got additional hours to make up the lost time. When Costa raised the disparity with HR, the HR representative pointed out that the male employee "has a family to support."

In the interest of painting a fuller picture, Caesar's did not always let the male employees skate when they missed work. One male employee testified that Karen Hallett disciplined him during the same period for missing work without a note, and in the process she *apologized* to him. She explained that "she had to give it to me because she was beating Catharina to death with it, you know, she was giving Catharina a lot of warnings so she had to give me one."

In March 1994, Hallett generated a list of employees who had declined overtime in the last six months. She listed Costa as refusing an offer of overtime on March 17. That Costa was out of the country on vacation that day puts the lie to Hallett's representation. Nevertheless, Caesar's offered Costa overtime more frequently after March 1994. The terms on which Caesar's offered the overtime, however, reveals that these offers were disingenuous. To this end, Caesar's offered Costa overtime just minutes before she clocked out for the day, making it nearly impossible for her to accept. Her male coworkers, in comparison, were offered overtime in the morning, enabling them to adjust their personal sche-dules and accept the assignments.

Again, Costa grieved. This time, Caesar's promised to (finally) end its practice of inequitably assigning overtime. Costa's years-long battle for over-time appeared to end in victory. Unfortunately for Costa, however, victory was illusory: Caesar's never followed through.

By May 1994, Costa had had enough. The environment at Caesar's "made my life miserable ... I knew I was being treated differently because I was a woman." She was an "outcast," whose "word meant nothing." Costa filed a complaint with the Nevada Equal Rights Commission and the federal Equal Employment Opportunity Commission, alleging sexual harassment and sex discrimination.

Less than four months later, on August 15, 1994, Costa was fired. Caesar's says that it terminated Costa for engaging in a physical altercation with a male coworker. The record suggests that the underlying altercation went something like this: Costa's coworker thought she made a false report about him taking unauthorized breaks. As a result, he trapped Costa in an elevator and slammed her against the wall. Costa went directly to Hallett and reported the incident in detail. Hallett assured Costa she would investigate. Satisfied with Hallett's assurance, Costa returned to work, only to have her coworker "come at" her again.

Desert Palace, Inc. v. Costa 47

In the ensuing investigation, Costa's account of the incident never changed. Indeed, Costa's version of events was corroborated by photographs showing extensive bruising on her upper arm and testimony from a bystander who saw the coworker trap Costa in the elevator. The coworker, however, didn't report the incident. When confronted, he initially said nothing happened. He then changed his story over the course of the investigation, claiming in the end that Costa was the one who hit him. He advanced no physical evidence or testimony to corroborate his version of events.

The Caesar's official responsible for investigating the dispute couldn't figure out whom to believe. As a result, he punished both employees. The male employee got a five-day suspension; Costa got fired. Caesar's justified Costa's harsher punishment because her disciplinary record – inflated by her employer's discriminatory treatment – was worse than that of her coworker.

On January 4, 1996, Costa sued Caesar's for sexual harassment, sex discrimination, and retaliation. Her sexual harassment and retaliation claims were dismissed,[54] and the case went to trial on the sex discrimination claim. After deliberations, the jury determined that Caesar's subjected Costa to "egregious" sex discrimination. Therefore, given that sex was at least a "motivating factor" in Costa's termination, the jury awarded her $264,377.74 in back pay and compensatory damages. Because the discrimination Costa suffered was found to be "egregious," the jury awarded Costa an additional $100,000 in punitive damages.

II ANALYSIS

A A *Simple Case of Statutory Interpretation*

The legal issue in this case is whether Costa was entitled to a mixed-motive instruction under Title VII, as amended in 1991. A mixed-motive instruction permits a jury to find a defendant liable if it determines, as the jury did here, that the defendant's actions were motivated by both legitimate and

---

[54] By reporting the procedural posture in which the case went to trial, the Court is not suggesting, implicitly or otherwise, that Costa did not suffer sexual harassment or retaliation. Those questions are not before the Court. However, it is exceedingly difficult to imagine circumstances such as these not amounting to sexual harassment, at a minimum. Such a determination could make sense on this record only if one were to confuse the meaning of the modifier "sexual" in "sexual harassment." "Sexual" means on the basis of sex and not simply relating to intercourse. Nothing in Title VII's language requires sexual advances or similar activity to qualify as sexual harassment under the law. See *McKinney v. Dole*, 765 F.2d 1129, 1138 (D.C. Cir. 1985) (rejecting the argument that harassment requires "sexual advances or of other incidents with clearly sexual overtones").

discriminatory reasons. Despite the evidence she presented at trial, Caesar's contends that Costa was not entitled to a mixed-motive instruction because she failed to advance direct evidence of discrimination. As Caesar's counsel's questioning at trial reveals, Caesar's interpretation of Title VII requires a plaintiff in a mixed-motive case to, for example, provide eyewitness testimony that one of her supervisors specifically stated that she received harsher treatment "because she's a *woman*," or fulfill every trial lawyer's dream and get an explicit admission on the stand ("Ok! I did it! And I did it because she's a *woman*!").

At its heart, this is a case of statutory interpretation. As such, the starting point is the text of the statute. *See Connecticut Nat. Bank v. Germain*, 503 U.S. 249, 253–54 (1992). And when the words of the statute are unambiguous, the "judicial inquiry is complete." *Id.* at 254 (quoting *Rubin v. United States*, 449 U.S. 424, 430 (1981)). This is one of those cases.

Title VII makes unlawful any employment practice for which "the complaining party demonstrates that ... sex ... was a motivating factor ... even though other factors also motivated the practice." 42 U.S.C. §2000e–2(m). When a plaintiff demonstrates that sex was a motivating factor, the burden shifts to her employer. Her employer can advance a limited affirmative defense to restrict the available remedies. To prevail on its affirmative defense, the employer must "demonstrate that [it] would have taken the same action in the absence of the impermissible motivating factor." 42 U.S.C. §2000e–5(g)(2)(B).

Section 2000e–2(m) unambiguously states that a plaintiff need only "demonstrat[e]" that an employer used a forbidden consideration with respect to "any employment practice." On its face, the statute does not mention, much less require, that a plaintiff advance direct evidence or make any other type of heightened showing. In other words, the text of Title VII is clear and unambiguous: there is no direct evidence requirement for a plaintiff in a mixed-motive case. The judicial inquiry is complete.

But even if the Court's inquiry were to extend beyond the language of section 2000e–2(m), other provisions in the statute confirm the Court's reading. To this end, Congress explicitly defined the term "demonstrates" in the 1991 Act, confirming that there is no special evidentiary requirement. The definition requires that the plaintiff "mee[t] the burdens of production and persuasion." 42 U.S.C. §2000e(m). The default burdens of production and persuasion for a plaintiff are to prove her case by a preponderance of the evidence, using direct evidence, circumstantial evidence, or a combination of the two. Congress's definition of "demonstrate" does not create any special requirement that plaintiffs present direct evidence. Moreover, Caesar's fails to advance any accompanying legislative history to suggest that Congress included a direct evidence requirement in section 2000e(m). As such, the only reasonable conclusion is that the default evidentiary rules apply.[55] Congress's failure to include an explicit direct evidence requirement for mixed-motive cases is particularly significant within the broader context of Title 42. Congress is unequivocal when departing from the default evidentiary standards and imposing heightened proof requirements. Title 42 is no exception. *See, e.g.,* 8 U.S.C. §1158(a)(2)(B) (requiring asylum seekers to "demonstrate … by clear and convincing evidence" that they filed their application for asylum within one year of arrival in the United States); 42 U.S.C. §5851(b)(3)(D) (prohibiting relief in retaliation cases involving whistleblowers under the Atomic Energy Act of 1954 when the employer can "demonstrat[e] by clear and convincing evidence that it would have taken the same unfavorable personnel action" despite the whistleblowing).

Title VII's text and the broader context in which it appears confirm that the Court should follow the default evidentiary rules for civil cases in mixed-motive cases: the plaintiff must prove her case by a preponderance of the evidence, and she may do so with "direct or circumstantial evidence." *Postal Service Bd. of Governors v. Aikens,* 460 U.S. 711, 714 n. 3 (1983).

In addition to the statutory text and context, the purpose of Title VII in combination with the purpose of evidentiary burdens further confirms the Court's conclusion. Title VII protects employees from unlawful discrimination and ensures equal opportunity for economic advancement. When employers engage in unlawful discrimination, Title VII gives employees recourse. The purpose of evidentiary burdens is to help courts and juries to reach the right result, most of the time. Permitting Title VII mixed-motive plaintiffs to prove their cases through circumstantial evidence advances both of these goals. As the Court acknowledged in *Reeves v. Sanderson Plumbing Products, Inc.,* 530 U.S. 133 (2000), for example, evidence that a defendant's explanation for an employment practice is "unworthy of credence" is "one form of circumstantial evidence that is probative of intentional discrimination." *Id.* at 147. And, as Costa's case reveals, circumstantial evidence can

---

[55.] The Court notes that the same definition of "demonstrates" applies equally to defendants. Title VII provides defendants the opportunity to "demonstrate" their affirmative defense to an allegation of discrimination. 42 U.S.C. §2000e-5(g)(2)(b). The only fair reading of this language is to permit defendants to prove their case with direct evidence, circumstantial evidence, or a combination of the two. The word "demonstrate" imports no heightened burden on defendants. To read the same word in the same statute with the same definition in dramatically different ways runs afoul of basic statutory interpretation. Moreover, it defies common sense to do so in this situation, where we are being asked to interpret "demonstrates" in a way that imposes a higher burden on the party more likely to be hindered by informational asymmetry.

50 Desert Palace, Inc. v. Costa

provide a jury with overwhelming proof of discrimination – discrimination so invidious as to be characterized as "egregious."

Indeed, the extent to which a direct evidence requirement would undermine the legislative intent of Title VII stands out in bold relief when we consider the particular circumstances this case presents. One of the primary purposes of Title VII was to ensure women's integration into fields traditionally reserved for men. *See, e.g.,* H. R. Rep. No. 92–238, at 4–5 (1971) ("[W]omen are placed in the less challenging, the less responsible and the less remunerative positions on the basis of their sex alone. Such blatantly disparate treatment is particularly objectionable in view of the fact that Title VII has specifically prohibited sex discrimination since its enactment in 1964."), reprinted in 1972 U.S.C.C.A.N. 2137, 2140. Research reveals that women like Costa – the only woman in a traditionally man's job – are more likely than most to endure hostility and harassment on the job. *See, e.g.,* U.S. Merit Sys. Protection Bd., SEXUAL HARASSMENT IN THE FEDERAL GOVERNMENT: AN UPDATE 20 (1988); U.S. Merit Sys. Protection Bd., SEXUAL HARASSMENT IN THE FEDERAL WORKPLACE: IS IT A PROBLEM? 51–52 (1981). Notably, "[n]ot all the men in a work environment – nor even the majority – need to participate" in the discriminatory activity to create a hostile workplace. Vicki Schultz, *Reconceptualizing Sexual Harassment*, 107 YALE L.J. 1683, 1759 (1998). And, as Karen Hallett's participation in the events leading to this case reveals, women too can be active participants in discrimination on the basis of sex against other women.

Ultimately, for this Court to require direct evidence would create absurd incentives and produce absurd results. From the employee's standpoint, a direct evidence requirement provides recourse to only a subset of victims of unlawful discrimination. Specifically, in a direct evidence world, Title VII redresses discrimination only when a plaintiff's employer harbors overt sex-based animus and is too stupid to hide it; Title VII looks the other way when a plaintiff's employer is ignorant enough to harbor animus, but smart enough to cover its tracks.

Similarly excluded are plaintiffs whose employers don't possess overt sex-based animus, but nevertheless import bias and stereotype into their employment practices in subtle and complex ways. It is now generally accepted among scientific researchers that gender bias frequently operates at an unconscious level. Ann C. McGinley, *¡Viva la Evolución! Recognizing Unconscious Motive in Title VII*, 9 CORNELL J. L. & PUB. POL'Y 415, 434–46 (2000) (collecting scientific studies); *cf. Fernandes v. Costa Bros. Masonry, Inc.*, 199 F.3d 572, 580 (1st Cir. 1999) (observing that "discrimination tends more and more to operate in subtle ways, [so] direct evidence is relatively rare"); *Ostrowski v. Atlantic*

Mut. Ins. Cos., 968 F.2d 171, 182 (2d Cir. 1992) (noting that " 'direct' evidence as to a mental state is usually impossible to obtain"). The risks posed by unconscious bias cannot be overstated. Cognitive and social psychologists have amassed mounting evidence that unconscious bias impacts any number of behaviors – and what is particularly troubling is that people are frequently totally unaware of their bias, and they are therefore unaware of the behaviors that result from it. *See* Anthony G. Greenwald *et al.*, *Measuring Individual Differences in Implicit Cognition: The Implicit Association Test*, 74 J. Pers. Soc. Psychol. 1464 (1998) (revealing implicit biases among people who were avowedly unprejudiced); *see also* Gary Blasi, *Advocacy against the Stereotype: Lessons from Cognitive and Social Psychology*, 49 U.C.L.A. L. Rev. 1241, 1246–55 (2002) (collecting scientific studies); Anthony G. Greenwald & Mahzarin R. Banaji, *Implicit Social Cognition: Attitudes, Self-Esteem, and Stereotypes*, 102 Psych. Rev. 4 (1995) (review of empirical studies revealing and exploring unconscious bias). Specific to our focus on the workplace here, unconscious bias leads employers to, among other things, devalue employees from marginalized groups and impose implicit prototypes rooted in stereotype against which all employees are measured. Martha Chamallas, *Deepening the Legal Understanding of Bias: On Devaluation and Biased Prototypes*, 74 S. Cal. L. Rev. 747, 755 (2001).

Significantly, nothing in the statute requires conscious intent to discriminate on the basis of sex; plain old cause and effect is what matters. If discrimination happens because of sex, it is what it is: sex discrimination. Ultimately, the scientific research revealing unconscious bias has serious implications for jurisprudence that limits recourse to cases of explicit stereotyping alone. *See id.* at 750–51 (observing that the "current legal disapproval of gender stereotyping is insufficient, for example, to challenge the use of policies based on implicit male norms without some further showing of hostility or animus against women").

In sum, the effect on the employee in all of the above-described scenarios – unlawful discrimination leading to a negative employment outcome – is the same. Nothing in Title VII suggests that Congress intended to distinguish between these types of victims of discrimination, providing recourse to one and not to the others. Indeed, such distinctions are absurd given Title VII's purpose – and particularly so given the increasingly subtle and unconscious ways in which discrimination creeps into the workplace.

But there's more. A direct evidence requirement not only thwarts the purpose of Title VII and the employee protections it put into place. It also puts employers in a bizarre position by creating absurd incentives. Among employers that harbor overt animus, a direct evidence requirement could

52   Desert Palace, Inc. v. Costa

reduce Title VII to incentivize only more strategic discriminatory behavior. Where employers are unaware of bias in their practices, the direct evidence requirement rewards their ignorance and provides no incentive to create workplaces free from bias. Nothing in Title VII suggests that Congress intended to deter some employers who discriminate, but not others, on the basis of how they practice their discrimination. The deterrence goal of Title VII reaches discrimination however practiced, period. Concomitantly, the normative effect of Title VII is to incentivize good behavior on the part of all employers by creating an affirmative duty to maintain workplaces free from discrimination. This affirmative duty includes, among other things, evaluating whether facially neutral policies nevertheless import bias and stereotype into the workplace.

In the end, a direct evidence requirement places a thumb on the scales of justice for employers by holding employees to a higher standard.[56] In the absence of statutory text that compels it or legislative history that supports it, a higher standard is "not only unhelpful, it is baffling." *Tyler v. Bethlehem Steel Corp.*, 958 F.2d 1176, 1184 (2d Cir. 1992). Courts routinely instruct juries that "the law makes no distinction between the weight to be given to either direct or circumstantial evidence." Edward J. Devitt & Charles B. Blackmar, FEDERAL JURY PRACTICE & INSTRUCTIONS §15.02, at 441–42 (3d ed. 1977). The reason for treating circumstantial and direct evidence alike is both clear and deep-rooted: "Circumstantial evidence is not only sufficient, but may also be more certain, satisfying and persuasive than direct evidence." *Rogers v. Missouri Pacific R. Co.*, 352 U.S. 500, 508 n. 17 (1957). Indeed, the Court has never questioned the sufficiency of circumstantial evidence in criminal cases, where the burden of proof is much higher: beyond a reasonable doubt. *See Holland v. U.S.*, 348 U.S. 121, 140 (1954) (observing that circumstantial evidence is "intrinsically no different from testimonial evidence"). We send criminal defendants in capital cases to their deaths on the basis of circumstantial evidence alone. Neither Caesar's nor its *amici* can point to any other circumstance in which the Court has required a litigant to advance direct evidence absent an affirmative directive in the statutory language. Tr. of Oral Arg. 13.

Against this backdrop, the Court is deeply concerned with the implicit suggestion that the direct evidence requirement here makes: plaintiffs in mixed-motive cases are simply not to be believed – poignantly reproducing Costa's own lived experience that "[her] word mean[s] nothing" and immortalizing it with the hand of the law. This the Court will not do.

[56.] The Court acknowledges the irony of holding plaintiffs to a higher standard in the context of a case like this, in which the plaintiff is before the Court precisely because she has been held to a higher or different standard in the workplace – and unfairly so.

B How Did We Get Here?

If this is a simple case of statutory interpretation, how did it reach the highest court in the land? The answer to that question is a bit more complicated, and it begins with the Court's decision in *Price Waterhouse v. Hopkins*, 490 U.S 228 (1989). At that time, Title VII made it unlawful for an employer "to discriminate against any individual ... because of such individual's race, color, religion, sex, or national origin." 78 Stat. 255, 42 U.S.C. §2000e–2(a)(1). In *Hopkins*, the issue was whether an employment decision is made "because of" sex when there is evidence that the decision was the result of mixed motives, some legitimate and some discriminatory. The Court held that, under section 2000e–2(a)(1), an employer could "avoid a finding of liability ... by proving that it would have made the same decision even if it had not allowed gender to play such a role." *Price Waterhouse*, 490 U.S. at 244; *see also id.* at 261 (White, J., concurring); *id.* at 261 (O'Connor, J., concurring).

The devil, of course, was in the details. The Court split as to just how a plaintiff could prove her case. The plurality did not "suggest a limitation on the possible ways of proving that [gender] stereotyping played a motivating role in an employment decision." *Id.* at 251–52. Instead, the plurality would have simply held that "when a plaintiff ... proves that her gender played a motivating part in an employment decision, the defendant may avoid a finding of liability only by proving by a preponderance of the evidence that it would have made the same decision even if it had not taken the plaintiff's gender into account." *Id.* at 258.

Justices White and O'Connor concurred in the judgment, but they each wrote separately to express different interpretations of the burdens of proof and persuasion in mixed-motive cases. Justice White would have shifted the burden to the employer only when a plaintiff "show[ed] that the unlawful motive was a *substantial* factor in the adverse employment action." *Id.* at 259. Justice O'Connor would have gone a step further, requiring the plaintiff to "show by direct evidence that an illegitimate criterion was a substantial factor in the decision" to shift the burden of proof on causation to the employer. *Id.*

In 1991, two years after *Hopkins*, Congress amended Title VII to its present form, "in large part [as] a response to a series of decisions of this Court." *Landgraf v. USI Film Products*, 511 U.S. 244, 250 (1994). In particular, section 107 of the 1991 Act "respond[ed]" to *Hopkins* by "setting forth standards applicable in 'mixed motive' cases" in two new statutory provisions. *Id.* at 251. As laid out *supra* section II.A, the first of the new provisions declares unlawful any employment practice motivated even in part by sex. 42 U.S.C. §2000e–2(m) (providing that "an unlawful employment practice is established when the complaining party demonstrates that race, color, religion, sex, or national origin was a motivating factor for any employment practice, even though other factors also motivated the practice"). At the same time, Congress provided employers who would have taken the same action in the absence of discrimination a limited affirmative defense. As noted earlier, that affirmative defense restricts the remedies available to the plaintiff while still holding the employer liable for discrimination. 42 U.S.C. §2000e–5(g)(2)(B). In enacting the 1991 amendments, Congress sent a powerful message to employers: they cannot escape liability for any amount of unlawful discrimination in their employment practices.

Significant to this case, when Congress amended Title VII in 1991, it was well aware of the Court's splintered decision in *Hopkins*. The opinions plainly reveal that the members of the Court had vastly differing approaches to how a mixed-motive plaintiff should prove her case. On one end of the spectrum, four justices prescribed no restrictions to how a plaintiff should prove her case; on the other, Justice O'Connor required direct evidence. It was against this backdrop that Congress amended Title VII. In so doing, Congress declined to include Justice O'Connor's direct evidence requirement. In the absence of Congress's explicit endorsement, the default evidentiary rules apply.

Caesar's argues that the weight of authority from the appellate courts is heavily in its favor. Caesar's is not wrong. Until the Ninth Circuit's *en banc* opinion in this case, almost every circuit court of appeals to have encountered a mixed-motive case since 1991 has held the plaintiff to a direct evidence standard. Caesar's points the Court to several examples. *See Fernandes v. Costa Bros. Masonry, Inc.*, 199 F.3d 572, 580 (1st Cir. 1999) (requiring "direct evidence of discriminatory animus" for plaintiffs to proceed under a mixed-motive analysis); *Fields v. New York State Office of Mental Retardation and Developmental Disabilities*, 115 F.3d 116, 122 (2d Cir. 1997) (requiring either "direct evidence of discrimination" or "circumstantial evidence that is 'tied directly to the alleged discriminatory animus' [citation omitted]"); *Watson v. Southwestern Pa. Transp. Auth.*, 207 F.3d 207, 215 (3d Cir. 2000) (observing that only plaintiffs who " 'demonstrate ... ' with 'sufficient direct' evidence that an impermissible factor was a motivating factor" may proceed under a mixed-motive analysis, quoting *Price Waterhouse*, 490 U.S. at 275 (O'Connor, J., concurring)); *Wagner v. Dillard Dep't. Stores, Inc.*, 17 Fed. Appx. 141, 148 (4th Cir. 2001) (requiring "direct evidence that decisionmakers placed substantial negative reliance on an illegitimate criterion," quoting *Price Waterhouse*, 490 U.S. at 277 (O'Connor, J., concurring)); *Sreeram v. Louisiana State Medical Center-Shreveport, et al.*, 188 F.3d 314, 321 (5th Cir. 1999) (opining that when there was insufficient evidence to support an inference of discrimination, the plaintiff did not produce the direct evidence necessary for a mixed-motive analysis); *Laderach v. U-Haul of Northwestern Ohio, et al.*, 207 F.3d 825, 829 (6th Cir. 2000) (explaining that "[o]nce there is credible direct evidence, the burden of persuasion shifts to the defendant to show that it would have terminated the plaintiffs employment had it not been motivated by discrimination"); *Plair v. E.J. Brach & Sons, Inc.*, 105 F.3d 343, 347 (7th Cir. 1997) (requiring direct evidence to proceed under a mixed-motive analysis); *Gagnon v. Sprint Corp.*, 284 F.3d 839, 847 (8th Cir. 2002) (explaining that the plaintiff can proceed under a mixed-motive analysis if he adduces direct evidence that discrimination was a motivating factor in the adverse action); *Shorter v. ICG Holdings, Inc.*, 188 F.3d 1204, 1208 n. 4 (10th Cir. 1999) (explaining that a "mixed-motive analysis" applies only when plaintiff has established "direct evidence" of discrimination); *Carter v. Three Springs Residential Treatment*, 132 F.3d 635, 641–42 (11th Cir. 1998) (determining that there was insufficient direct evidence to trigger the mixed-motive analysis.).

Of course, as Caesar's concedes, the "direct evidence" requirement has varying meaning both across and within the circuit courts of appeals. *See Febres v. Challenger Caribbean Corp.*, 214 F.3d 57, 60 (1st Cir. 2000) (observing that "the courts of appeals are in some disarray as to what constitutes direct evidence sufficient to provoke a mixed-motive instruction"); *Fernandes*, 199 F.3d at 581–83 (collecting cases and characterizing the different approaches to "direct evidence"). Indeed, some courts count circumstantial evidence as "direct evidence" when deciding whether to use a mixed-motive framework. *Fernandes*, 199 F.3d at 582 (citing *Taylor v. Virginia Union Univ.*, 193 F.3d 219, 231–32 (4th Cir. 1999); *Thomas v. Natl. Football League Players Ass'n*, 131 F.3d 198, 204 (D.C. Cir. 1997)).

All of this is to say that, against this legal landscape, the litigation strategy that Caesar's pursued was not beyond reason.

In contrast, the persistence of Justice O'Connor's direct evidence requirement among the courts of appeals is disturbing. Not only does Title VII's amended language reject it, but also reasonable minds could differ – as they do here – on whether Justice O'Connor's concurrence provides the controlling holding from *Hopkins*.[57] The courts of appeals had to surmount significant obstacles to graft a direct evidence requirement onto Title VII, as amended in 1991.

To be clear, the Court is not suggesting that the courts of appeals consciously discriminated by holding plaintiffs in mixed-motive cases to

---

[57.] The Court need not determine which *Hopkins* opinion actually controls because the language of the 1991 amendments renders such a determination unnecessary.

a higher standard. But the pattern that emerges from their holdings, given the state of the law and growing scientific knowledge of how bias operates, requires comment from the Court. To faithfully execute our duties as an objective body that interprets and applies the law, we must educate ourselves on the nature of bias. This is the only way of ensuring that we don't unknowingly perpetuate bias and stereotype or – worse – give it the blessing of the law. Knowing what we do now, if we stick our heads in the sand, we become a powerful tool of bias instead of the refuge that we hold ourselves out to be.

Clinging to the direct evidence requirement in mixed-motive cases is one way in which we have (unwittingly) become such a tool. The requirement restricts recourse to only a portion of employees subjected to unlawful discrimination, it offers cover to employers consciously acting upon animus, and it provides little incentive to well-meaning employers to examine their practices and create workplaces free from bias and stereotype. Such a reality underscores Audre Lorde's words from so many years ago – still relevant today – that "the master's tools will never dismantle the master's house. They may allow us to temporarily beat him at his own game, but they will never enable us to bring about genuine change."Audre Lorde, Sister Outsider: Essays and Speeches 120 (1984).

The courts will not be the master's tools. Congress intended Title VII to bring about genuine change, and it amended Title VII in 1991 to better effectuate that intent. The Court will honor Congress's intent and the words Congress used to express it.

III CONCLUSION

For these reasons, the Court holds that Title VII does not require plaintiffs to advance direct evidence of discrimination to prevail. Indeed, such a requirement would render illusory Title VII's promise to promote equal opportunity for economic advancement. Nobody is perfect, and Catharina Costa is no different. She showed up late sometimes. She experienced conflict with supervisors and coworkers. What's different about Costa is that Caesar's treated her differently from her male coworkers by holding her to different standards some of the time and higher standards other times. As a result, Costa's disciplinary record looked much different than it would have looked had Costa been a man. And so, at the end of the altercation, Costa's coworker was out for five days; Costa was out of a job. This is the essence of discrimination.

Because direct evidence of discrimination is not required in mixed-motive cases, the court of appeals correctly concluded that the district court did not abuse its discretion in giving a mixed-motive instruction to the jury.

* * *

The judgment of the court of appeals is affirmed.

It is so ordered.

3

Pregnancy Discrimination

Commentary on *International Union, UAW v. Johnson Controls, Inc.*

WYNTER P. ALLEN

INTRODUCTION

There once was an era when employers issued discriminatory fetal protection policies that made decisions for female employees regarding their own reproductive health. Exclusionary policies that hindered female employment had severe financial impacts on women and their families.[1] No person should have to choose between having a family and having a job. No employer should make decisions about their employees' reproductive health or the health of a fetus.

This commentary analyzes *International Union, UAW v. Johnson Controls, Inc.*,[2] which held that Title VII of the Civil Rights Act of 1964 forbids fetal protection policies that limit presumably fertile women's employment opportunities. Johnson Controls' fetal protection policies prohibited fertile women from working in particular jobs, the employer aiming to protect these women's potential future fetuses. Fertile men were not covered by these policies. As a result, only fertile men, not fertile women, were given a choice as to whether they wished to risk their reproductive health.[3] This commentary will also analyze the rewritten feminist opinion by Professor Marcia McCormick, writing as Justice McCormick, which addresses crucial issues that the original Supreme Court decision ignored or did not fully explore.

THE ORIGINAL OPINION

Johnson Controls concerned an employer's sex-based fetal protection policy.[4] The crux of the case was whether an employer can exclude a fertile female

---

[1] S. Rep. No. 331, 95th Cong. 2d Sess. 6 (1978).
[2] *See International Union, UAW v. Johnson Controls, Inc.*, 499 U.S. 187 (1991).
[3] *Id.* at 197.
[4] *Id.* at 192–94.

International Union, UAW v. Johnson Controls, Inc.   59

employee from certain jobs because of the employer's concerns for the health of any fetus that the employee may conceive.[5] The Supreme Court invalidated Johnson Controls' fetal protection policy and held that:

> Fertile women, as far as appears in the record, participate in the manufacture of batteries as efficiently as anyone else. Johnson Controls' professed moral and ethical concerns about the welfare of the next generation do not suffice to establish a BFOQ [bona fide occupational qualification] of female sterility. Decisions about the welfare of future children must be left to the parents who conceive, bear, support, and raise them rather than to the employers who hire those parents. Congress has mandated this choice through Title VII, as amended by the PDA [Pregnancy Discrimination Act of 1978]. Johnson Controls has attempted to exclude women because of their reproductive capacity. Title VII and the PDA simply do not allow a woman's dismissal because of her failure to submit to sterilization.[6]

Background

Johnson Controls manufactured batteries in a process that exposed its employees to lead. The manufacturing process included health risks such as the risk of harm to a fetus carried by a female employee.[7] Before 1964, Johnson Controls did not employ women in battery-manufacturing jobs.[8] In 1977, Johnson Controls issued a policy that required women who wished to be considered for employment to sign a statement that they had been advised of the risks involved in having a child while exposed to lead.[9] Johnson Controls' 1977 policy did not exclude women capable of childbearing from lead exposure.[10] Johnson Controls' policy at the time stated:

> [P]rotection of the health of the unborn child is the immediate and direct responsibility of the prospective parents. While the medical profession and the company can support them in the exercise of this responsibility, it cannot assume it for them without simultaneously infringing their rights as persons. ... Since not all women who can become mothers wish to become mothers (or will become mothers), it would appear to be illegal discrimination to treat all who are capable of pregnancy as though they will become pregnant.[11]

---

[5] *Id.* at 190.
[6] *Id.* at 188–89.
[7] *Id.* at 190; 29 C.F.R. §1910 (1987); *see also* 43 Fed. Reg. 52960; 43 Fed. Reg. 52966.
[8] *See Johnson Controls*, 499 U.S. at 190.
[9] *Id.*
[10] *Id.*
[11] *Id.* at 191.

60 International Union, UAW v. Johnson Controls, Inc.

Between 1979 and 1983, eight female employees became pregnant while their blood lead was at critical levels for workers planning to have a family, as determined by the Occupational Safety Health Administration (OSHA).[12] In response, in 1982, Johnson Controls issued a revised policy barring all women, except those whose infertility was medically documented, from jobs that would or could expose them to lead levels that exceeded the OSHA standard, as well as from jobs from which they could be promoted or "bumped" into the barred jobs.[13] The revised policy set forth: "[I]t is [Johnson Controls'] policy that women who are pregnant or who are capable of bearing children will not be placed into jobs involving lead exposure or which could expose them to lead through the exercise of job bidding, bumping, transfer or promotion rights."[14]

Employees filed a class action challenging the policy. Among the individual plaintiffs were Mary Craig, Elsie Nason, and Donald Penney. Craig had chosen to be sterilized to avoid losing her job. Nason, a fifty-year-old woman, suffered a loss in compensation when Johnson Controls transferred her out of a job where she was exposed to lead. Johnson Controls denied Penney's request for a leave of absence for the purpose of lowering his lead level to prepare for becoming a father.[15] The district court granted summary judgment in favor of Johnson Controls, stating that the policy was gender-neutral and that the defendant had met its burden under the business necessity defense that courts applied in fetal protection cases.[16]

The court of appeals affirmed the grant of summary judgment, agreeing with the district court that the fetal protection policy was facially neutral, and that therefore the proper standard for evaluating the policy was the business necessity defense. The court further held that even if the proper standard were the bona fide occupational qualification (BFOQ) analysis, which applies to facially discriminatory rules, Johnson Controls was still entitled to summary judgment.[17] The court of appeals determined that "industrial safety is part of the essence of [the] respondent's business, that the fetal protection policy is reasonably necessary to further that concern," and that " 'more is at stake' than simply an individual woman's decision to weigh and accept the risks of employment."[18]

[12.] *Id.* at 192; *see also* 29 C.F.R. §1910.1025 (1990).
[13.] *See Johnson Controls*, 499 U.S. at 192.
[14.] *Id.*
[15.] *Id.*
[16.] *Id.* at 193.
[17.] *Id.* at 194.
[18.] *Id.* at 195.

International Union, UAW v. Johnson Controls, Inc. 61

Supreme Court Analysis

Johnson Controls argued that its exclusion of female applicants from manufacturing jobs involving lead was justified because its intent was the broader, good-faith purpose of protecting at-risk third parties (the women's potential unborn children) per the so-called safety exception set out in *Dothard v. Rawlinson*,[19] and, in light of this policy, it argued that being a man or a nonfertile woman was a BFOQ for these jobs.[20]

Johnson Controls' Policy Was Facially Discriminatory

Johnson Controls first argued that its policy was facially neutral; therefore, it had to meet only the easier "business necessity" test that applies to such policies rather than the more difficult BFOQ test that applies to policies that are facially discriminatory.[21] Rejecting Johnson Controls' argument, the Supreme Court began its analysis by stating: "The bias in Johnson Controls' policy is obvious. Fertile men, but not fertile women, are given a choice as to whether they wish to risk their reproductive health for a particular job."[22] The Court also reasoned that:

> Johnson Controls' policy classified on the basis of gender and childbearing capacity, rather than fertility alone. [The] Respondent does not seek to protect the unconceived children of all of its employees. Despite evidence in the record about the debilitating effect of lead exposure on the male reproductive system, Johnson Controls is concerned only with the harms that may befall the unborn offspring of its female employees.[23]

Johnson Controls' policy was discriminatory on its face (and therefore not gender-neutral) because it required only female employees to produce proof that they were not capable of reproducing.[24] Given that this was a facially

---

[19.] *Id.* at 202–04. In *Dothard*, the Alabama state penitentiary rejected a female applicant for the position of correctional counselor (prison guard). *See Dothard v. Rawlinson*, 433 U.S. 321 (1977). The applicant challenged the employer's bona fide occupational qualification (BFOQ) excluding female guards from "contact areas" within maximum-security men's prisons. *Id.* at 331–36. The Court characterized the Alabama prison environment as having "rampant violence" and a "jungle atmosphere." *Id.* at 334. The prison did not segregate the prisoners by level of dangerousness. *Id.* at 335. The Court reasoned that a woman's ability to maintain order in a maximum-security men's prison in Alabama would be "directly reduced by her womanhood." *Id.* The Court therefore held that being a man was a BFOQ for the prison guard job. *Id.* at 336–37.

[20.] *Johnson Controls*, 499 U.S. at 197.

[21.] *Id.* at 197–98.

[22.] *Id.*

[23.] *Id.* at 198.

[24.] *Id.*

62   International Union, UAW v. Johnson Controls, Inc.

discriminatory policy, Johnson Controls could not use the business necessity defense and would have to prove instead that female infertility was a BFOQ.

The Court reasoned that Johnson Controls' 1982 policy violated the PDA because it explicitly relied on potential for pregnancy as a reason for excluding women from certain positions. The policy violated Title VII and the PDA because the policy did not apply to the reproductive capacity of male employees in the same way as it applied to that of female employees.[25] The Court held that "Johnson Controls' fetal protection policy is sex discrimination forbidden under Title VII unless [the] respondent can establish that sex is a 'bona fide occupational qualification.' "[26]

Johnson Controls' Policy Was Not Protected by the BFOQ Safety Defense

The Supreme Court next addressed whether Johnson Controls' fetal protection policy was one of those certain instances where sex discrimination is "reasonably necessary" to the "normal operation" of the particular business or enterprise.[27] Johnson Controls argued that its fetal protection policy adhered to the safety exception of the BFOQ defense.

The safety exception is limited to instances in which the employee's sex or pregnancy actually interferes with the employee's ability to perform the job.[28] Johnson Controls had to show that the "essence" or "central mission" of its business would be undermined if it did not bar all potentially pregnant women from jobs that would expose them to lead.[29] Johnson Controls also had to demonstrate that not being pregnant related to an employee's ability to do the job and was reasonably necessary to ensure the continued operation of the business.[30]

The Court's precedent regarding the safety exception was fully analyzed in cases regarding female prison guards and flight attendants. In *Dothard v. Rawlinson*, the Court allowed the employer to hire only male guards in contact areas of maximum-security male penitentiaries because "more was at stake than the 'individual woman's decision to weigh and accept the risks of employment.' "[31] The Court held that an employee's sex was a BFOQ because the employment of a female guard would create real safety risks to others if

[25.] *Id.*
[26.] *Id.*
[27.] *Id.* at 200–01.
[28.] *Id.* at 204.
[29.] *Id.* at 202–04.
[30.] *Id.*
[31.] *Id.* at 202 (quoting *Dothard*, 433 U.S. at 335).

International Union, UAW v. Johnson Controls, Inc.   63

violence were to break out because the guard was a woman.[32] Thus the Supreme Court in *Dothard* affirmed that sex discrimination was tolerated because sex was related to the guard's ability to maintain prison security. The Court in *Johnson Controls* favorably cited lower courts' approval of airlines' layoffs of pregnant flight attendants at different points during the first five months of pregnancy because these layoff policies were necessary to ensure the safety of the passengers.[33]

Johnson Controls' argument failed because "the unconceived fetuses of Johnson Controls' female employees ... are neither customers nor third parties whose safety is essential to the business of battery manufacturing."[34] Finally, the Court reasoned that "[n]o one can disregard the possibility of injury to future children; the BFOQ, however, is not so broad that it transforms this deep social concern into an essential aspect of battery making."[35]

The Court also reminded Johnson Controls that:

> The PDA's amendment to Title VII contains a BFOQ standard of its own: Unless pregnant employees differ from others "in their ability or inability to work," they must be "treated the same" as other employees "for all employment-related purposes." 42 U.S.C. § 2000e(k). This language clearly sets forth Congress' remedy for discrimination on the basis of pregnancy and potential

---

[32.] In *Dothard*, the Court failed to recognize the danger that all guards face in Alabama prisons. Instead, the opinion relied upon a presumption that female guards would generate sexual assaults. In his dissent, Justice Marshall wrote:

> [T]his rationale regrettably perpetuates one of the most insidious of the told myths about women that women, wittingly or not, are seductive sexual objects. The effect of the decision, made I am sure with the best of intentions, is to punish women because their very presence might provoke sexual assaults. It is women who are made to pay the price in lost job opportunities for the threat of depraved conduct by prison inmates.
>
> *Dothard*, 433 U.S. at 345.

[33.] *See Johnson Controls*, 499 U.S. at 202; *see also Harriss v. Pan Am. World Airways, Inc.*, 649 F.2d 670 (9th Cir. 1980) (holding that the policy requiring commencement of leave upon pregnancy was justified by its safety considerations); *Burwell v. Eastern Air Lines, Inc.*, 633 F.2d 361 (4th Cir. 1980) (stating that the airline's mandatory pregnancy leave policy for flight attendants after the thirteenth week of pregnancy was legitimately established as a business necessity to enhance the safety of passengers); *Condit v. United Air Lines, Inc.*, 558 F.2d 1176 (4th Cir. 1977) (holding that the airline's maternity leave policy constituted a BFOQ because pregnancy could incapacitate flight attendants in ways that might threaten the safety of the operation of aircraft); *In re National Airlines, Inc.*, 434 F.Supp. 249 (S.D. Fla.1977) (striking down an employment policy requiring a flight attendant's removal from her position immediately upon discovery of her pregnancy, but agreeing that pregnant flight attendants pose a threat to passenger safety; the airlines could not mandate maternity leave before thirteen weeks, but could allow individual evaluation between thirteen and twenty weeks).

[34.] *Johnson Controls*, 499 U.S. at 203.

[35.] *Id.* at 203–04.

64 International Union, UAW v. Johnson Controls, Inc.

pregnancy. Women who are either pregnant or potentially pregnant must be treated like others "similar in their ability ... to work." *Id.* In other words, women as capable of doing their jobs as their male counterparts may not be forced to choose between having a child and having a job.[36]

The Court in *Johnson Controls* held that Title VII prohibits employers from discriminating against women because of their capacity to become pregnant unless their reproductive potential prevents them from performing the duties of their jobs.[37]

THE FEMINIST JUDGMENT

Professor Marcia McCormick, writing as Justice McCormick, pens a decision that differs from the original opinion in that she uses the feminist move of narrative to recognize and explain the practical effects of a fetal protection policy on society – specifically, the cost of such a policy to women and their children. Excluding women from well-paying jobs with health insurance benefits negatively affects the family. McCormick reasons, "Women who do not receive adequate prenatal care are more likely to give birth to low-birthweight babies who have a high probability of experiencing development problems." Additionally, McCormick condemns Johnson Controls' policy because it completely ignored the danger of lead to men's reproductive health. McCormick's use of the personal stories of employees affected by the fetal protection policies highlights that the fetal protection policies had negative effects. Toxic work environments harm the reproductive potential of all employees. The fetus-centered focus of the original decision, which addressed only half of the reproductive equation, missed the mark legally and pragmatically.

In contrast, McCormick presents a human-first analysis, reminding employers that toxins in the workplace affect the fertility of all employees and that focusing only on the role of women in childbearing ignores harms to mens' reproductive health. This conclusion does not detract from McCormick's emphasis on the Hobson's choice faced by many pregnant women in workplaces with toxic environments. In fact, it reinforces her feminist focus because shifting the calculus to a humanist one serves to protect employees and their offspring from the consequences when employees are forced to choose between their children and their jobs. Characterizing the issue as a human problem, rather than a woman's problem, should garner much

[36.] *Id.* at 204.
[37.] *Id.* at 187–89.

more support for a resolution that does not require an individual to choose between job and children. Recognizing that nearly all workers are in the same position, workplaces have an incentive to reduce or eliminate toxins to the maximum extent possible. This is good for all workers, for their children, and for their ability to protect their jobs.

The original decision, however, implicitly maintained a paradigm whereby women are the only parties responsible for the health of offspring and men are responsible only for financially supporting those women. In the rewritten opinion, McCormick highlights the plights of not only Craig and Nason, but also Penney, the male plaintiff. Johnson Controls could have avoided this litigation if it had focused on the safety of all employees rather than excluding only potentially fertile women from the workplace.

Analysis of the Impact of the Fetal Protection Policy on Women and Families

As McCormick highlights, "At the most basic level, these policies would not serve to protect future children and would further perpetuate sex-based inequality in the United States ... In 1979, fetal protection policies closed at least 100,000 jobs to women." Further, McCormick explains that exclusionary fetal protection policies usually existed only in workplaces with male-dominated jobs even though female-dominated jobs may involve similar risks of exposure. This suggests that the underlying motives for the policies may not be as benign as claimed: any policies that assist in keeping women out of the workforce altogether and out of jobs dominated by men inherently counter the purpose of both Title VII and the PDA.

The PDA's Senate Report noted that:

> [P]erhaps the most important effect of the PDA is to prohibit employer policies which forced women who became pregnant to stop working regardless of their ability to continue ... as the history of sex discrimination shows, such policies have long-term effects upon the careers of women and account in large part for the fact that women remain in low-paying dead-end jobs.[38]

The history and effect of such policies were addressed in statements by House and Senate members, as well as in testimony before the committees considering the legislation. These statements emphasized the economic hardship faced by women and their families when discrimination based on pregnancy and related medical conditions occurs in the workplace. By enacting the PDA, Congress rejected policies that often resulted from and reinforced antiquated

---

[38.] S. Rep. No. 331, 95th Cong. 2d. Sess. 6 (1978).

beliefs about pregnancy. Congress also rejected the outdated attitudes that viewed pregnancy as inconsistent with the full participation of women in the economic system and perpetuated women's second-class status in the workplace.[39] By focusing on the difficulties women have faced in breaking into male-dominated workplaces, McCormick's decision reinforces the original intent and goal of this legislation.

Although fetal protection policies are not now as common as they once were, the issue of the choice between a healthy pregnancy and working is still an unfortunate dilemma for many women.[40] Women who have jobs that might result in harm to them and/or their fetuses during pregnancy are now protected in twenty-three states, the District of Columbia, and four cities by laws requiring employers to provide reasonable accommodations to pregnant workers.[41] The options available to some pregnant women in the workforce aim to lessen the burden of having to choose between healthy pregnancies and

---

[39.] *See Carney v. Martin Luther Home, Inc.*, 824 F.2d 643, 646–47 (8th Cir. 1987).

[40.] *See, e.g.,* Jessica Silver-Greenberg & Natalie Kitroeff, *Miscarrying at Work: The Physical Toll of Pregnancy Discrimination*, N.Y. TIMES (Oct. 21, 2018), www.nytimes.com/interactive/2018/10/21/business/pregnancy-discrimination-miscarriages.html; Jessica Silver-Greenberg & Natalie Kitroeff, *Pregnancy Discrimination Is Rampant Inside America's Biggest Companies*, N.Y. TIMES (June 15, 2018), www.nytimes.com/interactive/2018/06/15/business/pregnancy-discrimination.html.

[41.] Alaska Stat. §39.20.520 (2013); Cal. Code Regs. tit.2, §11049 (2013); Cal. Gov't Code §§12945, 12926 (West 2012); 2016 Colo. Legis. Serv. Ch. 207 (to be codified at Colo. Rev. Stat. §§24-34-401, 24-34-402.3); Colo. Rev. Stat. §24-34-401 (2016); Conn. Gen. Stat. §§46a-60(a)(7), 46a-51 (2011); Del. Code tit. 19, §§710, 711, 716 (2014); Protecting Pregnant Workers Fairness Act of 2014, D.C. Act. 20–458 (2014); Haw. Code R. §12–46-107 (1990); 775 Ill. Comp. Stat. 5/2–101, 102 (2014); La. Rev. Stat. §§23:342, 23–341 (1997); Md. Code, State Gov't §§20–609, 20–601 (2013); H. 3680, 109th Leg., Reg. Sess. (Mass. 2017) (to be codified at Mass. Gen. Laws ch. 151B, §4(1E) (2017)); Mass. Gen. Laws ch. 151B, §1 (2017); Minn. Stat. §§181.940, 181.9414, 181.9436 (2014); Neb. Rev. Stat. §§48–1107.01(2), 48–1107.02(1)(e) (2015); Neb. Rev. Stat. §48–1121 (2015); Neb. Rev. Stat. §48–1102 (2015); S.B. 253, 79th Leg., Reg. Sess. (Nev. 2017) (to be codified at Nev. Rev. Stat. §§613.335 *et seq.* (2017)); N.J. Stat. §10:5–12(s) (2013); N.J. Admin. Code §13:8–1.2 (2006); N.J. Stat. Ann. §10:5–5 (2010); 2015 N.Y. Sess. Laws Ch. 369 (to be codified at N.Y. Exec. Law §§292, 296); N.Y. Comp. Codes R. & Regs. tit. 9, §§466.1(a), (b) (2015); N.Y. Exec. Law §§292(5), (6) (2015); N.D. Cent. Code §14–02.4–03(2) (2015); N.D. Cent. Code §§14–02.4–02(8), (7) (2015); R.I. Gen. Laws §§28–5-7.4(a)(1), (3), (2), (4) (2015); R.I. Gen. Laws §§28–5-6(8)(i), (7) (2015); S.C. Code Ann. §1–13-80(A) (2018); 30 S.C. Code Ann. §1–13-30(e); Tex. Loc. Gov't Code §180.004 (2001); 2016 Utah Laws Ch. 330 (to be codified at Utah Code §§34A-5–106(1)(g), (7)); Utah Code §§34A-5–102(i), (h) (2015); H. 136, 2017–2018 Leg., Reg. Sess. (Vt. 2017) (to be codified at 21 V.S.A. §495k (2017)); 21 V.S.A. §495d(1) (2017); S. B. 5835, 2017–2018 Leg. Reg. Sess. (Wash. 2017) (to be codified at 43.70 RCW (2017)); W. Va. Code §§5-11b-1, *et seq.* (2014); W. Va. Code §5–11-3(d) (1998); Central Falls, R.I. Code §12–5 (2014); N.Y. City Admin. Code §8–107(22)(a) (2015); N.Y. City Admin. Code §8–107(22)(b) (2015); N.Y. City Admin. Code §8–102(5) (2015); Philadelphia, Pa., Code §9–1128 (2014); Philadelphia, Pa., Code §9–1102 (2014); Providence, R.I., Code §§16–57(c)(1)(g), (b)(1)(c), (c)(1)(f) (2015); Providence, R.I., Code §16–84 (2015); Providence, R.I., Code §§16–54(h), (g) (2015); and Local Laws, June 2018.

International Union, UAW v. Johnson Controls, Inc.   67

their jobs. Although many states are moving in the right direction to accommodate pregnant employees, however, the statutes do not address some of the underlying issues presented in *Johnson Controls*. For example, many of the state laws address pregnant women or women who have recently given birth. None of the statutes appears to require employers to provide safe workplaces for all of its employees prior to pregnancy.[42]

Disregard of Safety Concerns for the Entire Workforce

McCormick's decision also highlights that Johnson Controls' policy failed to consider establishing a workplace free of reproductive hazards for all of its employees and not only its female employees. The OSHA regulations on which Johnson Controls partially relied developed mandatory protections that could effectively minimize any risk to the fetus. McCormick opines, "[C]ommon workplace toxins can cause harm that creates heritable effects in any individual ... If employers are really concerned about the health of future generations, a laudable goal, then the most sound fetal protection policies will apply to all employees." In the instant case, Johnson Controls could have avoided litigation and provided its workforce with an environment that effectively minimized the risk if it had adhered to the law, considered its entire workforce, and left to each individual employee the choice about how to safeguard their own reproductive health.[43] If Johnson Controls were truly concerned about the health of its employees, it could have followed the OSHA guidelines, which included medical surveillance to minimize employee exposure to lead by utilizing periodic blood sampling, medical evaluations, annual examinations, blood testing, temporary medical removal for workers, and time limitations on workers' exposure to lead.[44] Furthermore, Johnson Controls could have lessened its employees' exposure to toxins by providing appropriate respiratory protection equipment and/or protective clothing.[45] Johnson Controls could have used various tools in its quest to protect its female workforce other than discriminatory policies.

---

[42] For example, an Alaska statute requires a transfer of a pregnant public employee to a less strenuous or hazardous position upon the employee's request. However, that statute does not appear to apply to women prior to pregnancy and/or anyone attempting to start a family. Alaska Stat. 39.20.520. In Maryland, employers must explore possible reasonable accommodations for an employee's pregnancy if an employee requests a transfer to a less strenuous or less hazardous position as a reasonable accommodation. Md. Code, State Gov't 20–609. The Maryland statute is another example of a state assisting pregnant employees, but with a measure that does not appear to apply to anyone planning to start a family wanting to be transferred to a less hazardous position as a reasonable accommodation.

[43] *See* 29 C.F.R. §1910.1025 Appx. C (1979).

[44] See 29 C.F.R. §1910.1025(j).

[45] See 29 C.F.R. §1910.1025(g).

68 International Union, UAW v. Johnson Controls, Inc.

CONCLUSION

No fetal protection policy cases have made it to the Supreme Court since *Johnson Controls*, but lower federal courts and state courts have dealt with the issue on numerous occasions.[46] In the recent fetal protection policy cases, the courts have failed to explain in depth the everyday practical effects that families face as a result of these unlawful exclusionary policies. The courts' analysis should explain the difficult choices that women face because many must still choose between their jobs and protecting their fetuses. Such analysis would help to reinforce the purpose of the forty-year-old PDA and the fifty-four-year-old Title VII: to give women and men equal footing in employment in the United States.

International Union, UAW v. Johnson Controls, Inc., 499 U.S. 187 (1991)

JUSTICE MARCIA L. MCCORMICK DELIVERED THE OPINION OF THE COURT.

Mary Craig earned good money with good benefits, necessary and sufficient to support her family, working for Johnson Controls. When the company adopted a policy excluding potentially fertile women from well-paying positions to protect potential fetuses from lead exposure, she chose to undergo sterilization surgery in order to avoid losing her job. Elsie Nason, a fifty-year-old divorcee, was involuntarily transferred into a lower-paying job because her original position exposed her to lead, and, at her age, sterilization surgery was more risky. In her new position, Nason had to put up with "smutty comments" from men about her having a period at her age. At the same time, Donald Penney

---

[46.] *See, e.g., Everts v. Sushi Brokers LLC*, 247 F.Supp.3d 1075 (D. Ariz. 2017) (holding that a restaurant's policy of reassigning pregnant wait staff to a lower-paying position discriminated against pregnant women and was not excused by a BFOQ); *Davis and Collins v. Lockheed Martin Corp.*, No. 1:06-cv-1338-ODE, 2008 WL 11333524 (N.D. Ga. Mar. 28, 2008) (holding that Lockheed's fetal protection policy was facially discriminatory because it placed blanket restrictions on pregnant women); *EEOC v. Catholic Healthcare West d/b/a Northridge Hosp. Med. Ctr.*, 530 F.Supp.2d 1096, 1102 (C.D. Cal. 2008) (holding that the employer violated the PDA by maintaining a "facially discriminatory policy" stating that "pregnant personnel shall not partake in any fluoroscopy or portable procedures during her term," even though, as all parties agreed, radiation exposure would be below allowable limits for pregnant women); *Peralta v. Chromium Plating & Polishing Corp.*, No. 1:99-CV-3996, 2000 WL 34633645 (E.D. N.Y. Sep. 15, 2000) (granting summary judgment for the plaintiff because the employer's justifications for forbidding the pregnant plaintiff from working without a doctor's note – concerns over her health, possible danger to her unborn child, and possible future tort liability – were inadequate under *Johnson Controls*).

wasn't even given a choice to avoid exposure when he was denied a request for a leave of absence for the purpose of lowering his lead level because he intended to become a father. These three, along with five more individuals and the unions that represent the workers in nine Johnson Controls plants, brought this cause of action, challenging the fetal protection policy.

Johnson Controls argues that its fetal protection policy presumptively excluding nearly all women from a broad range of jobs is essential to protect the potential fetuses of those women and thus is not a violation of the sex discrimination prohibition in Title VII of the Civil Rights Act of 1964. However, an employer concerned about employees' occupational health may not exclude potentially fertile women from employment opportunities and neglect to guard against dangers to fertile men instead of ensuring a workplace free of reproductive hazards for all of its workers. While exposure to toxic chemicals in the workplace may raise legitimate safety concerns about developing fetuses, an employer may not, consistent with Title VII, craft its policies to protect potential fetuses of female employees while ignoring the same or similar risks to potential fetuses of the partners of male employees. In other words, employers cannot half-solve a health problem by creating a discrimination problem.

I JOHNSON CONTROLS' POLICY

The respondent, Johnson Controls, Inc., manufactures batteries, which include the element lead as a primary ingredient. Occupational exposure to lead entails health risks to workers, including not only the risk of harm to any fetus carried by a pregnant employee, but also risks to those who live with workers and who may be exposed to lead contamination that travels with those workers, on their clothes, on their skin, or in their bones, tissues, and bodily fluids when they go home.

Before the Civil Rights Act of 1964 became law, Johnson Controls did not employ any women in battery-manufacturing jobs. In June 1977, however, it announced its first official policy concerning its employment of women in lead-exposure work:

> [P]rotection of the health of the unborn child is the immediate and direct responsibility of the prospective parents. While the medical profession and the company can support them in the exercise of this responsibility, it cannot assume it for them without simultaneously infringing their rights as persons.
> ... Since not all women who can become mothers wish to become mothers (or will become mothers), it would appear to be illegal discrimination to treat all who are capable of pregnancy as though they will become pregnant.

70   International Union, UAW v. Johnson Controls, Inc.

Consistent with that view, Johnson Controls "stopped short of excluding women capable of bearing children from lead exposure," but emphasized that a woman who expected to have a child should not choose a job in which she would have such exposure. The company also required a woman who wished to be considered for employment to sign a statement that she had been advised of the risk of having a child while she was exposed to lead. The statement informed such a woman that although there was evidence "that women exposed to lead have a higher rate of [miscarriage]," this evidence was "not as clear ... as the relationship between cigarette smoking and cancer." But it was, "medically speaking, just good sense not to run that risk if you want children and do not want to expose the unborn child to risk, however small."

In 1978, the Occupational Health and Safety Administration (OSHA), acting pursuant to its statutory authority to "promulgate any ... occupational ... health standard" under 29 U.S.C. §655, announced its Final Standard for Occupational Exposure to Lead. 29 C.F.R. §1916.1025 (1987). When it was considering that standard, OSHA studied the possible effect on fetuses carried by pregnant workers to determine whether the risk justified excluding women entirely from at least certain lead-exposed positions. 43 Fed. Reg. 52960. "No topic was covered in greater depth or from more vantage points than the subject of women in the lead industry." *Id.* On the basis of its close analysis, OSHA concluded that "there is no basis whatsoever for the claim that women of childbearing age should be excluded from the workplace in order to protect the fetus or the course of pregnancy." 43 Fed. Reg. 52966; *see also, e.g.,* 43 Fed. Reg. 54398.

OSHA further found evidence that elevated blood lead levels damaged men's reproductive health. Lead-exposed men suffered serious harm to their spermatogenesis, including malformed sperm, decreased mobility of sperm, and decreased number of sperm. Older studies found alarmingly high rates of spontaneous abortion, stillbirth, and birth defects in the pregnancies of women married to lead-exposed workers, and other studies found chromosomal abnormalities among lead-exposed male workers. Thus, "because of the demonstrated adverse effects of lead on reproductive function in both the male and female as well as the risk of genetic damage of lead on both the ovum and sperm, OSHA recommends a 30 microgram 100 g maximum permissible blood level in both males and females who wish to bear children." 29 C.F.R. Pt 1910, at 833–34 (1987).

To protect all workers and their offspring, OSHA established a series of mandatory protections that, taken together, "should effectively minimize any risk to the fetus and newborn child." 43 Fed. Reg. 52966. Those protections, based upon the recognition that workers who are planning families should

International Union, UAW v. Johnson Controls, Inc. 71

have blood lead levels below 30 micrograms per deciliter, included: (1) periodic biological and air testing; (2) medical surveillance and consultation concerning the effects of lead on reproduction, including fertility testing and the right to review by several physicians; (3) educational and training provisions, so that "workers are fully informed of the potential hazards from exposure to lead on their reproductive ability, during pregnancy and following birth"; (4) the right of workers planning families to use respirators for increased protection; and, (5) where workers are planning families and reduction of blood lead levels is medically indicated, the possibility of temporary removal from lead-exposed jobs, with wage protection and assured possibility of return to the lead-exposed position for up to eighteen months. 29 CFR §1910.125 (k)(ii).

Johnson Controls' own experts acknowledged the efficacy of these measures, generally, and the risk to potential fetuses in the households of male workers where these measures were not adopted. As explained by Jean Beaudoin, Manager of Health, Safety and Environmental Control for the Battery Division of Johnson Controls, Inc., good hygiene and the use of respirators can significantly minimize blood lead levels. App. at 156, 164. In fact, as Dr. Fishburn – an assistant clinical professor at the University of Wisconsin, certified in occupational health – stated, without good hygiene, family members of male workers, including fetuses, could be exposed to unsafe lead levels.

After OSHA's studies and regulatory guidance, over a five-year period eight employees at Johnson Controls became pregnant while they had blood levels over 30 micrograms per deciliter. As a result, in 1982, the company responded by announcing a broad exclusion of women from jobs that exposed them to lead: "[I]t is [Johnson Controls'] policy that women who are pregnant or who are capable of bearing children will not be placed into jobs involving lead exposure or which could expose them to lead through the exercise of job bidding, bumping, transfer or promotion rights."

The policy presumed fertility for all women. It defined "women . . . capable of bearing children" as "[a]ll women except those whose inability to bear children is medically documented." It further stated that an unacceptable work station was one where, "over the past year," any employee had recorded a blood lead level of more than 30 micrograms per deciliter or the work site had yielded an air sample containing a lead level higher than 30 micrograms per cubic meter. And because women could not even be placed in positions that would allow them to bid, bump, transfer, or be promoted into an unacceptable work station, women were effectively excluded from almost all of the jobs in the plants.

72 International Union, UAW v. Johnson Controls, Inc.

II PROCEEDINGS BELOW

In April 1984, the petitioners, including the individual plaintiffs named above, filed a class action in the US District Court for the Eastern District of Wisconsin, challenging Johnson Controls' fetal protection policy as sex discrimination that violated Title VII of the Civil Rights Act of 1964, as amended. 42 U.S.C. §2000e *et seq.* Upon stipulation of the parties, the district court certified a class consisting of "all past, present and future production and maintenance employees" in United Auto Workers (UAW) bargaining units at nine of Johnson Controls' plants "who have been and continue to be affected by [the employer's] Fetal Protection Policy implemented in 1982."

The district court granted summary judgment for defendant-respondent Johnson Controls. 680 F.Supp. 309 (E.D. Wis. 1988). Acknowledging that Johnson Controls' policy made out a prima facie case of disparate treatment "because the fetal protection policy excludes women from positions which men are not excluded from," the district court rather inexplicably concluded that the policy was nonetheless neutral because a woman might not realize that she was pregnant and might not realize "the severe risk of harm that may occur if [the fetus is] exposed to lead." *Id.* at 314, 316. Applying a three-part business necessity defense derived from fetal protection cases in the Courts of Appeals for the Fourth and Eleventh Circuits, the district court concluded that while "there is a disagreement among the experts regarding the effect of lead on the fetus," the hazard to the fetus through exposure to lead was established by "a considerable body of opinion," that although "[e]xpert opinion has been provided which holds that lead also affects the reproductive abilities of men and women ... [and] that these effects are as great as the effects of exposure of the fetus ... a great body of experts are of the opinion that the fetus is more vulnerable to levels of lead that would not affect adults," and that petitioners had "failed to establish that there is an acceptable alternative policy which would protect the fetus." *Id.* at 315–16. The court stated that, in view of this disposition of the business necessity defense, it did not "have to undertake a bona fide occupational qualification's [*sic*] ('BFOQ') analysis." *Id.* at 316 n.5.

The Court of Appeals for the Seventh Circuit heard the case, and, before the panel opinion was issued, a majority of the members of the court voted to hear the case *en banc*. Ultimately, the Seventh Circuit affirmed the summary judgment by a seven-to-four vote. 886 F.2d 871 (1989). The majority held that because fetal protection policies recognized that men and women were not similarly situated when it comes to their reproductive roles, they had more in common with disparate impact claims than with disparate treatment claims. That, plus this Court's emphasis that the proof structures that have been

International Union, UAW v. Johnson Controls, Inc.

developed should not be inflexibly applied, led the court of appeals to hold that the proper standard for evaluating the fetal protection policy was the defense of business necessity, that Johnson Controls was entitled to summary judgment under that defense, and that even if the proper standard were a BFOQ, Johnson Controls was still entitled to summary judgment.

The court of appeals first reviewed fetal protection opinions from the Eleventh and Fourth Circuits. *Id.* at 883–85; *see Hayes v. Shelby Mem. Hosp.*, 726 F.2d 1543 (11th Cir. 1984); *Wright v. Olin Corp.*, 697 F.2d 1172 (4th Cir. 1982). Those opinions established the three-step business necessity inquiry: whether there is a substantial health risk to the fetus; whether transmission of the hazard to the fetus occurs only through women; and whether there is a less discriminatory alternative equally capable of preventing the health hazard to the fetus. 886 F.2d at 885. The court of appeals agreed with the Eleventh and Fourth Circuits that "the components of the business necessity defense the courts of appeals and the EEOC [Equal Employment Opportunity Commission] have utilized in fetal protection cases balance the interests of the employer, the employee and the unborn child in a manner consistent with Title VII." *Id.* at 886. The court further noted that, under *Wards Cove Packing Co. v. Atonio*, 490 U.S. 642 (1989), the burden of persuasion remained on the plaintiff in challenging a business necessity defense, and – unlike the Fourth and Eleventh Circuits – it thus imposed the burden on the plaintiffs for all three steps. 886 F.2d at 887–93.

Applying this business necessity defense, the court of appeals ruled that Johnson Controls should prevail. Specifically, the court concluded that there was no genuine issue of material fact about the substantial health-risk factor because the parties agreed that there was a substantial risk to a fetus from lead exposure. *Id.* at 888–89. The court also concluded that, unlike the evidence of risk to the fetus from the mother's exposure, the evidence of risk from the father's exposure that petitioners presented "is, at best, speculative and unconvincing." *Id.* at 889. Finally, the court found that petitioners had waived the issue of less discriminatory alternatives by not adequately presenting it. *Id.* at 890–93.

Having concluded that the business necessity defense was the appropriate framework and that Johnson Controls satisfied that standard, the court proceeded to discuss the BFOQ defense and concluded that Johnson Controls met that test too. *Id.* at 893–94. The *en banc* majority ruled that industrial safety is part of the essence of the respondent's business and that the fetal protection policy is reasonably necessary to further that concern. Quoting *Dothard v. Rawlinson*, 433 U.S. 321, 335 (1977), the majority emphasized that, in view of the goal of protecting the unborn, "more is at stake" than simply an

74   International Union, UAW v. Johnson Controls, Inc.

individual woman's decision to weigh and accept the risks of employment. 886 F.2d at 898.

Judges Cudahy and Posner dissented, and they would have reversed the judgment and remanded the case for trial. Both would have held that the only defense available was the BFOQ defense. Both also would have further held that the employer's concerns about the effects of its practices on third parties could make sex a BFOQ "reasonably necessary to the normal operation" of a business, but that the defendant had to prove this. *Id.* at 901, 902 & n.1, 904, 906.

Judge Easterbrook, also in dissent and joined by Judge Flaum, agreed with Judges Cudahy and Posner that the only defense available to Johnson Controls was the BFOQ defense. He concluded, however, that the BFOQ defense could not prevail because the respondent's stated concern for the health of the unborn was irrelevant to the operation of its business under the BFOQ defense. He also viewed the employer's concern as irrelevant to a woman's ability or inability to work under the Pregnancy Discrimination Act's amendment to Title VII. 42 U.S.C. §2000e(k). Judge Easterbrook also stressed what he considered the excessive breadth of Johnson Controls' fetal protection policy. It applied to all women (except those with medical proof of incapacity to bear children), although most women in an industrial labor force do not become pregnant, most of those who do become pregnant will have blood lead levels under 30 micrograms per deciliter, and most of those who become pregnant with levels exceeding that figure will bear children unaffected by the exposure. 886 F.2d at 912–13. "Concerns about a tiny minority of women cannot set the standard by which all are judged." *Id.* at 913.

With its ruling, the Seventh Circuit became the first court of appeals to hold that a fetal protection policy directed exclusively at women could qualify as a BFOQ. We granted *certiorari* to resolve the obvious conflict between the Fourth, Seventh, and Eleventh Circuits on this issue, and to address the important and difficult question of whether an employer, seeking to protect potential fetuses, may discriminate against women based solely on their ability to become pregnant.[47] 494 U.S. 1055 (1990),

---

[47.] Since our grant of *certiorari*, the Sixth Circuit has reversed a District Court's summary judgment for an employer that had excluded fertile female employees from foundry jobs involving exposure to specified concentrations of airborne lead. *See Grant v. Gen. Motors Corp.*, 908 F.2d 1303 (1990). The court said: "We agree with the view of the dissenters in Johnson Controls that fetal protection policies perforce amount to overt sex discrimination, which cannot logically be recast as disparate impact and cannot be countenanced without proof that [female] infertility is a BFOQ ... [The] plaintiff ... has alleged a claim of overt discrimination that her employer may justify only through the BFOQ defense." *Id.* at 1310. In *Johnson Controls, Inc. v. Fair Emp. & Housing Comm'n*, 267 Cal. Rptr. 158 (Ct. App. 1990), the court held the respondent's fetal protection policy invalid under California's fair employment law.

International Union, UAW v. Johnson Controls, Inc.   75

III BFOQ IS THE APPROPRIATE STANDARD

The bias in Johnson Controls' policy is obvious: fertile women may not risk their reproductive health for a particular job – nor even be placed in jobs that, at some undetermined future point, might lead to a job that might jeopardize their reproductive health – while fertile men may not avoid either the present or potential future risk. Section 703(a) of the Civil Rights Act of 1964, as amended, prohibits sex-based classifications in terms and conditions of employment, in hiring and discharging decisions, and in other employment decisions that adversely affect an employee's status. 42 U.S.C. §2000e-2(a). The respondent's fetal protection policy explicitly discriminates on the basis of sex. The policy excludes women with childbearing capacity from jobs remotely connected with lead-exposed jobs and fails to give men the opportunity to avoid lead-exposed jobs; it thus creates a facial classification based on sex. The respondent assumes as much in its brief before this Court.

Nevertheless, the courts of appeals that have considered this issue assumed that sex-specific fetal protection policies do not involve facial discrimination. *UAW*, 886 F.2d at 886–87; *Hayes*, 726 F.2d at 1547; *Wright*, 697 F.2d at 1190. These courts analyzed the policies as though they were facially neutral and had only a discriminatory effect upon the employment opportunities of women because the asserted reason for the sex-based exclusion (protecting women's unconceived offspring) was ostensibly benign. That assumption was incorrect.

First, Johnson Controls' policy classifies on the basis of sex and childbearing capacity rather than fertility alone. The respondent does not seek to protect the unconceived children of all of its employees. Despite evidence in the record about the debilitating effect of lead exposure on men's reproductive capacity and unborn offspring, Johnson Controls is concerned only with the harms that may befall the unborn offspring of its female employees. In fact, it appears that Johnson Controls would have lost in the Eleventh Circuit under *Hayes* because its policy does not "effectively and equally protec[t] the offspring of all employees." 726 F.2d at 1548. This Court faced a conceptually similar situation in *Phillips v. Martin Marietta Corp.*, 400 U.S. 542 (1971) and found sex discrimination because the policy established "one hiring policy for women and another for men – each having pre-school-age children." *Id.* at 544. Johnson Controls' policy is facially discriminatory because it requires only a female employee to prove that she is not capable of reproducing.

Our conclusion is bolstered by the Pregnancy Discrimination Act of 1978 (PDA), in which Congress explicitly provided that, for the purposes of Title

VII, discrimination "on the basis of sex" includes discrimination "because of or on the basis of pregnancy, childbirth, or related medical conditions." 42 U.S.C. §2000e(k); *Newport News Shipbuilding & Dry Dock Co. v. EEOC*, 462 U.S. 669, 684 (1983). In its use of the words "capable of bearing children" in its 1982 policy statement as the criterion for exclusion, Johnson Controls explicitly classifies employees on the basis of their potential for pregnancy. Under the PDA, such a classification must be regarded, for Title VII purposes, in the same light as explicit sex discrimination. Respondent has chosen to treat all of its female employees as potentially pregnant and to limit opportunities only for potentially pregnant employees; that choice evinces discrimination on the basis of sex.

Moreover, the absence of antifemale animus or other malevolent motive does not convert a facially discriminatory policy into a neutral policy with a discriminatory effect. Explicit facial discrimination is disparate treatment; it does not depend on why the employer discriminates, but rather on the explicit terms of the discrimination. In *Martin Marietta*, the motives underlying the employer's express exclusion of women did not alter the intentionally discriminatory character of the policy nor did the arguably benign motives lead to consideration of a business necessity defense. 400 U.S. 542 (1971). The question in that case was whether the discrimination in question could be justified under section 703(e) as a BFOQ. The beneficence of an employer's purpose does not undermine the conclusion that an explicit gender-based policy is sex discrimination under section 703(a) and thus may be defended only as a BFOQ.

The enforcement policy of the EEOC accords with this conclusion. On January 24, 1990, the EEOC issued policy guidance in the light of the Seventh Circuit's decision in the present case. The document noted: "For the plaintiff to bear the burden of proof in a case in which there is direct evidence of a facially discriminatory policy is wholly inconsistent with settled Title VII law." The Commission concluded: "[W]e now think BFOQ is the better approach."

In sum, Johnson Controls' policy "does not pass the simple test of whether the evidence shows 'treatment of a person in a manner which but for that person's sex would be different.'" *Los Angeles Dep't of Water & Power v. Manhart*, 435 U.S. 702, 711 (1978) (quoting *Developments in the Law, Employment Discrimination and Title VII of the Civil Rights Act of 1964*, 84 HARV. L. REV. 1109, 1170 (1971)). We hold that Johnson Controls' fetal protection policy is sex discrimination forbidden under Title VII unless the respondent can establish that sex is a "bona fide occupational qualification."

IV THE BFOQ DEFENSE AND THIRD-PARTY SAFETY

Under section 703(e)(1) of Title VII, an employer may discriminate on the basis of "religion, sex, or national origin in those certain instances where religion, sex, or national origin is a bona fide occupational qualification reasonably necessary to the normal operation of that particular business or enterprise." 42 U.S.C. §2000e-2(e)(1). We therefore turn to the question of whether Johnson Controls' fetal protection policy is one of those "certain instances" that come within the BFOQ exception.

The BFOQ defense is written narrowly, and this Court has read it narrowly. *See, e.g., Dothard*, 433 U.S. at 332–37; *Trans World Airlines, Inc. v. Thurston*, 469 U.S. 111, 122–25 (1985). We have read just as narrowly the BFOQ language of section 4(f) of the Age Discrimination in Employment Act of 1967 (ADEA), as amended, which tracks the BFOQ provision in Title VII. 29 U.S.C. §623(f) (1); *see Western Air Lines, Inc. v. Criswell*, 472 U.S. 400 (1985). Our emphasis on the restrictive scope of the BFOQ defense is grounded in both the language and the legislative history of section 703.

The wording of the BFOQ defense contains several terms of restriction that indicate that the exception reaches only special situations. The statute thus limits the situations in which discrimination is permissible to "certain instances" where sex discrimination is "reasonably necessary" to the "normal operation" of the "particular" business. Each one of these terms – certain, normal, particular – prevents the use of general subjective standards and favors an objective, verifiable requirement. But the most telling term is "occupational"; this indicates that these objective, verifiable requirements must concern job-related skills and aptitudes.

The majority in the Seventh Circuit, along with Judges Cudahy and Posner, essentially defined "occupational" as meaning related to a job. Accepting such a framing would make any discriminatory requirement imposed by an employer "job-related" simply because the employer has chosen to make the requirement a condition of employment. In effect, that would allow sterility to be an occupational qualification for women because Johnson Controls has chosen to require it. This reading of "occupational" renders the word mere surplusage. "Qualification" by itself would encompass an employer's idiosyncratic requirements. By modifying "qualification" with "occupational," Congress narrowed the term to qualifications that affect an employee's ability to perform the tasks necessary to do the job.

Johnson Controls argues that its fetal protection policy falls within the so-called safety exception to the BFOQ. Our cases have stressed that discrimination on the basis of sex because of safety concerns is allowed only in narrow circumstances. In *Dothard v. Rawlinson*, this Court indicated that danger to a woman herself does not justify discrimination. 433 U.S. at 335. In that case, we allowed the employer to hire only male guards in contact areas of maximum-security men's penitentiaries only because more was at stake than the "individual woman's decision to weigh and accept the risks of employment." *Id.* The majority found sex to be a BFOQ because it concluded that the presence of a woman in those particular highly dangerous men's prison facilities would create real risks of safety to other inmates if violence were to break out because the guard was a woman. Sex discrimination was tolerated because, under this rationale, sex was related to the guard's ability to do the job of maintaining prison security. We required in *Dothard* a high correlation between sex and ability to perform job functions, and we refused to allow employers to use sex as a proxy for strength even if it might be a fairly accurate one.

Since *Dothard*, our jurisprudence has further refined the inquiry into an employer's justifications for sex-based classifications. We have recognized that employers are not free to act on gender-based stereotypes, even if, in the aggregate, those stereotypes are statistically accurate. *City of Los Angeles Dep't of Water & Power v. Manhart*, 435 U.S. 702 (1978) (prohibiting sex-based differentials in pension contributions or benefits even though women tend to have longer lifespans than men). We have also recognized that employers who act based on sex stereotypes engage in unlawful sex discrimination. *Price Waterhouse v. Hopkins*, 490 U.S. 228 (1989). Given these developments, if *Dothard* were to come before us today, it is doubtful we would reach the conclusion that the prison conditions at issue made sex a BFOQ. To justify its decision, the majority relied on commonly held views and stereotypes about women's invitations to sexual assault, about women's soft-heartedness and emotional response to manipulation, and about women's lack of physical strength. *Dothard*, 433 U.S. at 342–47 (Marshall, J., dissenting). To avoid falling into the same kind of stereotyping trap, we must caution the lower courts that the core holding of *Dothard* – that safety of third parties can, in some circumstances, make sex a BFOQ – must be read exceedingly narrowly.

Moreover, fetuses have generally not been considered third parties for the purpose of the safety BFOQ exceptions. For example, some courts have approved airlines' layoffs of pregnant flight attendants at different points during the first five months of pregnancy on the ground that the employer's policy was necessary to ensure the safety of passengers. *See Harriss v. Pan Am. World Airways, Inc.*, 649 F.2d 670 (9th Cir. 1980); *Burwell v. Eastern Air Lines, Inc.*, 633 F.2d 361 (4th Cir. 1980); *Condit v. United Air Lines, Inc.*, 558 F.2d 1176

International Union, UAW v. Johnson Controls, Inc.   79

(4th Cir. 1977); *In re Nat'l Airlines, Inc.*, 434 F.Supp. 249 (S.D. Fla. 1977). In two of these cases, the courts pointedly indicated that fetal, as opposed to passenger, safety was best left to the pregnant employee. *Burwell*, 633 F.2d at 371; *Nat'l Airlines*, 434 F.Supp. at 259.

In fact, those third parties must be closely linked to the business's product or service. We considered safety to third parties in *Western Airlines, Inc. v. Criswell* in the context of the ADEA. We focused upon "the nature of the flight engineer's tasks" and the "actual capabilities of persons over age 60" in relation to those tasks. *Criswell*, 472 U.S. at 406. Our safety concerns were not independent of the individual's ability to perform the assigned tasks, but rather involved the possibility that, because of age-connected debility, a flight engineer might not properly assist the pilot and might thereby cause a safety emergency. Furthermore, although we considered the safety of third parties in *Dothard* and *Criswell*, those third parties were indispensable to the particular business at issue. In *Dothard*, the third parties were the inmates; in *Criswell*, the third parties were the passengers on the plane. We stressed that, to qualify as a BFOQ, a job qualification must relate to the *essence*, or to the "central mission of the employer's business." *Dothard*, 433 U.S. at 333; *Criswell*, 472 U.S. at 413.

This is not to say that Johnson Controls is free to ignore the occupational dangers to its employees' reproductive health. These dangers simply do not justify discrimination on the basis of sex. Ruling otherwise would improperly expand what is now the very narrow BFOQ defense. Third-party safety considerations properly entered into the BFOQ analysis in *Dothard* and *Criswell* because they went to the core of the employees' job performance. Moreover, that performance involved the central purpose of the enterprise. *Dothard*, 433 U.S. at 335 ("The essence of a correctional counselor's job is to maintain prison security"); *Criswell*, 472 U.S. at 413 (the central mission of the airline's business was the safe transportation of its passengers). The unconceived fetuses of Johnson Controls' female employees, however, are neither customers nor third parties whose safety is essential to the business of battery manufacturing. No one can disregard the possibility of injury to future children; the BFOQ, however, is not so broad that it transforms this deep social concern into an essential aspect of battery making.

To do so would repeat the errors that led to Title VII's prohibition on sex discrimination and the enactment of the PDA in the first place. Stereotypes of women as primarily mothers and caregivers have long played a role in justifying their exclusion from the workplace or limitations on them there. *See, e.g., Muller v. Oregon*, 208 U.S. 412, 421 (1908) (upholding protective labor legislation "to preserve the strength and vigor of the race"). The assumption that women's employment and wage-earning are not essential to their well-being or to the well-being of future generations has worked to keep women economically dependent, resulting in protective legislation that has kept them from "male" jobs, depressed wages in female-dominated jobs, and limited women's earning capacity. Alice Kessler-Harris, OUT TO WORK 180, 184–85, 190, 193–94 (1982); Nancy S. Barrett, *Obstacles to Economic Parity for Women*, 72 AM. ECON. REV. 160 (1982); Elisabeth M. Landes, *The Effect of State Maximum-Hours Laws on the Employment of Women* in 1920, 88 J. POL. ECON. 476 (1980).

Additional stereotypes or similar generalizations are reflected in the lower courts' opinions. They assume that all fertile women are likely to become pregnant, that healthy pregnancies depend exclusively upon women, that pregnant women are weaker or more fragile than men, and that women are less capable of ethical decision-making about issues related to their fertility or pregnancy. These stereotypes and others transform what appear to be neutral concerns about workers or families into vehicles for discrimination against women. *See* Madeline Morris, *Stereotypic Alchemy: Transformative Stereotypes and Antidiscrimination Law*, 7 YALE L. & POL'Y REV. 251 (1989). Moreover, when women do not conform to stereotypes, for example the stereotype that women will or should sacrifice their own health or well-being for their potential children or fetuses in the face of any risk at all, they may be pressured to "voluntarily" withdraw or, if that does not work, be fired. *See* Kathryn M. Bartol, *Female Managers and Quality of Working Life: The Impact of Sex-Role Stereotypes*, 3 J. OCC. BEHAVIOR 205, 216–17 (1980).

To avoid the malign influence of such stereotypes, our case law makes clear that the safety exception is limited to instances in which the employee's sex or pregnancy actually interferes with the employee's ability to perform the job. This approach is consistent with the language of the BFOQ provision itself, for it suggests that permissible distinctions based on sex must relate to ability to perform the duties of the job. Johnson Controls suggests, however, that we expand the exception to allow fetal protection policies that mandate particular standards for pregnant or fertile women, but not fertile men. We decline to do so. Such an expansion contradicts not only the language of the BFOQ and the narrowness of its exception, but also the plain language and history of the PDA.

The PDA's amendment to Title VII contains a BFOQ standard of its own: unless pregnant employees differ from others "in their ability or inability to work," they must be "treated the same" as other employees "for all employment-related purposes." 42 U.S.C. §2000e(k). This language clearly sets forth Congress's remedy for discrimination on the basis of pregnancy and potential pregnancy. Women who are either pregnant or potentially pregnant must be

International Union, UAW v. Johnson Controls, Inc. 81

treated like others "similar in their ability … to work." *Id.* In other words, women as capable of doing their jobs as their male counterparts may not be forced to choose between having a child and having a job.

The legislative history confirms what the language of the PDA compels. Both the House and Senate reports accompanying the legislation indicate that this statutory standard was chosen to protect female workers from being treated differently from other employees simply because of their capacity to bear children. *See* Amending Title VII, Civil Rights Act of 1964, S. Rep. No. 95–331, at 4–6 (1977):

> Under this bill, the treatment of pregnant women in covered employment must focus not on their condition alone but on the actual effects of that condition on their ability to work. Pregnant women who are able to work must be permitted to work on the same conditions as other employees.
>
> […]
>
> … [U]nder this bill, employers will no longer be permitted to force women who become pregnant to stop working regardless of their ability to continue.

See also Prohibition of Sex Discrimination Based on Pregnancy, H.R. Rep. No. 95–948, at 3–6 (1978), 1978 U.S.C.C.A.N. 4749.

This history counsels against expanding the BFOQ to allow fetal protection policies. The Senate report quoted above states that employers may not require a pregnant woman to stop working at any time during her pregnancy unless she is unable to do her work. Employment late in pregnancy often imposes risks on the unborn child, but Congress indicated that the employer may take into account only the woman's ability to get her job done. *See* Wendy Chavkin, *Walking a Tightrope: Pregnancy, Parenting, and Work, in* Double Exposure: Women's Health Hazards on the Job and at Home 196, 196–202 (Wendy Chavkin ed., 1984); Mary E. Becker, *From* Muller v. Oregon *to Fetal Vulnerability Policies*, 53 U. Chi. L. Rev. 1219, 1255–56 (1986). With the PDA, Congress made clear that the decision to become pregnant or to work while being either pregnant or capable of becoming pregnant was reserved for each individual woman to make for herself.

We conclude that the language of both the BFOQ provision and the PDA, which amended it, as well as the legislative history and the case law, prohibit an employer from discriminating against a woman because of her capacity to become pregnant unless her reproductive potential prevents her from performing the duties of her job. We reiterate our holdings in *Criswell* and *Dothard* that an employer must direct its concerns about a woman's ability to perform her job safely and efficiently to those aspects of the woman's job-related activities that fall within the "essence" of the particular business, and

82   International Union, UAW v. Johnson Controls, Inc.

we add that those concerns cannot be based on stereotypes about what women are like or ought to be like. If we were "beyond the day when an employer could evaluate employees by assuming or insisting that they matched the stereotype associated with their group" in 1989 when we decided *Price Waterhouse*, we are well beyond it now. 490 U.S. at 251.

V THE APPLICATION OF THE BFOQ DEFENSE

We have no difficulty concluding that Johnson Controls cannot establish a BFOQ. Fertile women, as far as appears in the record, participate in the manufacture of batteries as efficiently as anyone else. Johnson Controls' professed moral and ethical concerns about the welfare of the next generation do not suffice to establish a BFOQ of female sterility. The scope and focus of the ban undermine this assertion. Johnson Controls bars women even from lead-free environments if there is any chance it could promote them from those environments into ones with lead exposure, and it bars women up to the age of seventy when there is no more than a biblical chance of pregnancy. The ban also ignores any danger to the next generation posed by men's exposure. Employers have a duty to safeguard workers' safety under OSHA, and that duty extends to protecting workers' reproductive health. But Title VII prohibits employers from making decisions about workers' reproductive health based only on the sex of those workers. In that context, decisions about the welfare of future children must be left to the parents who conceive, bear, support, and raise them rather than to the employers who hire those parents. Johnson Controls has attempted to exclude women because of their reproductive capacity. Title VII and the PDA simply do not allow a woman's dismissal because of her failure to submit to sterilization.

Neither can concerns about the welfare of the next generation be considered a part of the "essence" of Johnson Controls' business. Judge Easterbrook, in this case, pertinently observed: "It is word play to say that 'the job' at Johnson [Controls] is to make batteries without risk to fetuses in the same way 'the job' at Western Air Lines is to fly planes without crashing." 886 F.2d at 913.

Johnson Controls argues that it must exclude all fertile women because it is impossible to tell which women will become pregnant while working with lead. This argument is somewhat academic in light of our conclusion that the company may not exclude fertile women at all; it perhaps is worth noting, however, that Johnson Controls has shown no "factual basis for believing that all or substantially all women would be unable to perform safely and efficiently the duties of the job involved." *Weeks v. Southern Bell Tel. & Tel. Co.*, 408 F.2d 228, 235 (5th Cir. 1969), *quoted with approval in Dothard*, 433 U.S. at 333. Even on this

International Union, UAW v. Johnson Controls, Inc.   83

sparse record, it is apparent that Johnson Controls is concerned about only a small minority of women. Of the eight pregnancies reported among the female employees, it has not been shown that any of the babies have been affected by lead exposure. The record does not reveal the birth rate for Johnson Controls' female workers, but national statistics show that approximately 9 percent of all fertile women become pregnant each year. The birth rate drops to 1 percent for blue-collar workers over the age of thirty. *See* Becker, *supra*, at 1233. Johnson Controls' fear of prenatal injury, no matter how sincere, does not begin to show that substantially all of its fertile women employees are incapable of doing their jobs.

VI THE LARGER CONTEXT

Although our consideration of this issue necessarily arises in the context of a case involving a single employer, our interpretation of Title VII must be made in the context of Congress's goal in enacting that legislation. Legislation is aimed at creating rules of general applicability, usually to large numbers of people to be regulated by that legislation. Thus, when Congress enacted Title VII, it was concerned with the employment practices across the economy. Accordingly, we must consider the result across the economy if employers were allowed to employ sex-specific fetal protection policies. At the most basic level, these policies would not serve to protect future children and would further perpetuate sex-based inequality in the United States: "That women may and do become pregnant is the most significant single factor used to justify the countless laws and practices that have disadvantaged women for centuries." Katherine T. Bartlett, *Pregnancy and the Constitution: The Uniqueness Trap*, 62 Cal. L. Rev. 1532, 1532 (1974). Treating all, or nearly all, women as potentially pregnant and uniquely vulnerable to injury is just the kind of stereotype that this Court has repeatedly rejected in a variety of contexts.

In 1979, fetal protection policies closed at least 100,000 jobs to women. Bill Richards, *Faceoff on Hazardous Jobs: Women's Rights, Fetus Safety*, Wash. Post A6 (Nov. 3, 1979). There is no reason to think that this number is smaller today, especially given the fact that Johnson Controls adopted its policy in 1982. And these jobs, like the ones at Johnson Controls, are fairly well-paying and with good benefits. Excluding women from good jobs will only perpetuate labor market segregation and sex-based inequality.

Furthermore, exclusion of women from one hazardous job is no guarantee of protection for their offspring. Even if a woman were able to obtain another job, there is no guarantee that job would not pose a hazard. Across US workplaces, exclusionary fetal protection policies have been adopted most often in male-dominated jobs even though female-dominated jobs have similar risks of exposure. Becker, *supra*, at 1238–39; Wendy W. Williams, *Firing the Woman to Protect the Fetus: The Reconciliation of Fetal Protection with Employment Opportunity Goals under Title VII*, 69 GEO. L.J. 641, 649 (1981). In male-dominated blue-collar jobs especially, women tend to be viewed in stereotypical ways and not given the same chances to work as men. *See* Barbara F. Reskin & Irene Padavic, *Supervisors as Gatekeepers: Male Supervisors' Response to Women's Integration in Plant Jobs*, 35 SOC. PROBS. 536 (1988). Moreover, another job is unlikely to pay as well or provide the same level of benefits, especially in smaller industrial towns, where a single plant might be the only source of well-paying jobs. In fact, women's wages are below men's in almost every employment category, and female-headed households are four times as likely as two-earner or male-headed households to live in poverty. Bureau of the Census, US Dep't of Commerce, STATISTICAL ABSTRACT OF THE UNITED STATES 406–07 (109th ed. 1989); Women's Research & Educ. Inst., THE AMERICAN WOMAN 1990–1991 376 (Sara E. Rix ed., 1990).

Lower income itself poses risks to women's offspring. Poverty and inadequate prenatal care are linked with premature birth and low birthweight, which in turn are linked to higher infant mortality. David Rush, *Socioeconomic Status and Perinatal Outcome*, *in* PERINATAL INTENSIVE CARE 14, 16–18 (Silvio Aladjem & Audrey K. Brown eds. 1977); Donald B. Binsacca *et al.*, *Factors Associated with Low Birth Weight in an Inner City Population: The Role of Financial Problems*, 77 AM. J. PUB. HEALTH 505 (1987). Children living in poverty are at risk, especially in urban areas, where the self-help of growing one's own food is unavailable, and the problems of poverty are multiplied by the concentration of low-income individuals in one geographic location. *See generally* Mark Alan Hughes, POVERTY IN CITIES (1989); William Julius Wilson, THE TRULY DISADVANTAGED: THE INNER CITY, THE UNDERCLASS, AND PUBLIC POLICY (1987); Richard P. Nathan & Charles F. Adams, Jr., *Four Perspectives on Urban Hardship*, 104 POL. SCI. Q. 483, 492–95 (1989). For those women who are unable to find another job, welfare provides a safety net for pregnant women and women with small children, but government support provides only subsistence living. It also comes with increased scrutiny of and judgment against women's fertility, morality, and conduct. Phyllis J. Day, *Sex-Role Stereotypes and Public Assistance*, 53 SOC. SERV. REV. 106 (1979). Further, both the woman and her children are more likely to suffer malnutrition when they rely on only subsistence-level support. Additionally, the offspring of these women are likely to face more hazards than if their mothers worked in well-paying jobs. Children living in poor neighborhoods are more likely to be exposed to crime, toxic chemicals such as lead paint, and pollution.

See, e.g., Nat'l Ctr. for Children in Poverty, Sch. of Pub. Health, Columbia Univ., FIVE MILLION CHILDREN: A STATISTICAL PROFILE OF OUR POOREST YOUNG CITIZENS 51, 54 (1990).

These jobs pay well, and the health insurance benefits that they provide might be even more important. These benefits give women access to good prenatal care and good care during childbirth, both of which are "especially important from the child's point of view." Becker, *supra*, at 1230. Women who do not receive adequate prenatal care are more likely to give birth to low-birthweight babies who have a high probability of experiencing developmental problems. Thus children are likely to face significantly greater risks as a result of maternal unemployment. Rush, *supra*; Binsacca *et al.*, *supra*.

Permitting employers to simply focus their policies on excluding women has two additional negative impacts: letting employers off the hook when it comes to workplace safety generally and allowing employers to ignore dangers to men's health. Allowing employers to exclude women may permit employers to ignore the harms that workplace toxin exposure causes *all* employees. Maureen Paul *et al.*, *Corporate Response to Reproductive Hazards in the Workplace: Results of the Family, Work, and Health Survey*, 16 AM. J. INDUS. MED. 267 (1989) (finding that all but one company that excluded classes of employees from jobs with reproductive hazards excluded only women despite reproductive risk to all employees). Moreover, the risks ignored might not only be risks to reproductive health. For example, the US Environmental Protection Agency has documented effects on the cardiovascular system of adult men at levels near those set by Johnson Controls for fertile women. 50 Fed. Reg. 9401 (1985); Environmental Protection Agency, COSTS AND BENEFITS OF REDUCING LEAD IN GASOLINE: FINAL REGULATORY IMPACT ANALYSIS V-45 (1985).

Excluding women is likely to appear significantly less expensive than minimizing exposure to toxins for all workers. In a perfect world, an employer would be able to take account of the costs of losing out on female talent, and the cost–benefit analysis might show that exclusionary policies are more costly even at the individual firm level. However, because women have often been historically excluded from these jobs and because lost talent might be easier to quantify on a much broader scale, individual employers are unlikely to consider that lost talent a cost. Men in the aggregate, for example, lose nearly twice as many workdays per year as women as a result of accidents or injuries and have more disability weeks from any cause (including pregnancy) than women. Melvin H. Rudov & Nancy Santangelo, HEALTH STATUS OF MINORITIES AND LOW INCOME GROUPS, Office of Health Resources

Opportunity, US Dep't of Health, Educ. & Welfare, Pub. No. 79–627, 155 (1979); Metropolitan Life Ins. Co., STATISTICAL BULLETIN 9 (1981). As a result, female employees may be more productive and less costly, but in any workplace that employs few women, this aggregate effect may not be visible. Thus any single employer's cost-benefit analysis will likely come out the same way: in favor of the exclusion of women. That women workers are perceived to be more expensive is precisely the justification that has been used for excluding or paying them less in the past. *See City of Los Angeles Dep't of Water and Power v. Manhart*, 435 U.S. 702 (1978). Because it will nearly always look less expensive to exclude women, employers may then underestimate the benefits of reducing toxic exposure in comparison with the costs of doing so. The end result is a workplace that is less safe than it could be.

Allowing employers to simply exclude women also permits them to continue to ignore potential hazards to men's reproductive health and the reproductive health of the household members of male workers. There may be some workplace toxins that pose a danger only to the fetuses of pregnant women, but none has yet been identified; rather, common workplace toxins can cause harm that creates heritable effects in any individual. Becker, *supra*, at 1237; Williams, *supra*, at 658–60. Causation, though, is hard to trace, and employers and scientists tend to assume that birth defects are caused by something connected with the woman carrying the offspring. In fact, despite evidence that many workplace toxins cause mutagenic effects – damaged germ cells – in men, the effects of such exposure have rarely been studied. Williams, *supra*, at 661. If employers are really concerned about the health of future generations, a laudable goal, then the most sound fetal protection policies will apply to all employees.

VII CONCLUSION

Our holding today that Title VII, as so amended, forbids sex-specific fetal protection policies is neither remarkable nor unprecedented. Concern for a woman's existing or potential offspring has historically been the excuse for denying women equal employment opportunities. *See, e.g., Muller v. Oregon*, 208 U.S. 412 (1908) (upholding statutory limits on work hours for women, only because the health of future children depended on healthy mothers). In the PDA, Congress prohibited discrimination on the basis of a woman's ability to become pregnant. We do no more than hold that the PDA means what it says.

It is no more appropriate for the courts than it is for individual employers to decide whether a woman's reproductive role is more important to herself and

Young v. United Parcel Services, Inc. 87

her family than her economic role or whether a man's economic role is more important to himself and his family than his reproductive role. Congress has reserved this choice for workers themselves.

* * *

The judgment of the court of appeals is reversed, and the case is remanded for further proceedings consistent with this opinion.

It is so ordered.

Commentary on *Young v. United Parcel Services, Inc.*

BRADLEY A. AREHEART

INTRODUCTION

The treatment of pregnancy in the workplace has long been a perplexing issue for both legislatures and courts. Should we treat pregnant employees *similarly* to other workers by simply ensuring nondiscrimination on the basis of pregnancy? Or should we treat pregnant workers *differently* from other workers by paying special attention to the needs of pregnant employees to ensure equality of opportunity? These questions map onto seemingly intractable debates regarding what women in the workplace need to achieve equality of opportunity; such theoretical divides include sameness versus difference, special treatment versus equal treatment, and formal equality versus substantive equality. Regardless of the theoretical frame, the quintessential issue is whether we should treat women – and, in this particular context, pregnant workers – similarly to or differently from men to achieve equality. In *Young v. United Parcel Services, Inc.*,[48] the Court dealt with these difficult questions.

Historically, legislatures and courts sought to protect pregnant workers by treating them differently. They limited the number of hours pregnant women could work, prohibited them from working night shifts, and excluded them altogether from hazardous occupations.[49] This led women's rights advocates to decry such laws and insist, in essence, that women should be treated the same as men in the workplace.[50] Congress responded by passing the Pregnancy

---

[48] 135 S.Ct. 1338 (2015).

[49] Brief for American Civil Liberties Union *et al.* as *amici curiae, California Fed. Sav. & Loan Ass'n v. Guerra*, 479 U.S. 272 (No-85–494) 1986 WL 728369, at *12–13.

[50] *See* Mary Becker, *The Sixties Shift to Formal Equality and the Courts: An Argument for Pragmatism and Politics*, 40 WM. & MARY L. REV. 209, 210 (1998) (describing how, by 1970, the vast majority of feminists were "on the formal equality bandwagon").

Discrimination Act of 1978 (PDA).[51] The statute has two main clauses. The first clause redefines "sex" under Title VII of the Civil Rights Act of 1964 to include pregnancy, childbirth, or related medical conditions. This definitional expansion was necessary because, prior to the PDA, employers who discriminated against pregnant workers could prevail by claiming that their decision was not based on a male/female distinction, but instead based on the analytically separate fact of an employee's pregnancy.[52] The PDA set straight the record that an employer cannot use pregnancy as a reason not to hire or promote someone; to do so is discrimination based on sex.

The second clause provides that "women affected by pregnancy, childbirth, or related medical conditions shall be treated the same for all employment-related purposes ... as other persons not so affected but similar in their ability or inability to work."[53] This clause means that an employer cannot deny benefits to pregnant employees who are "similar in their ability or inability to work" to "other persons" receiving such benefits. For example, if an employer provides workers with health insurance or short-term disability benefits, it would be discrimination for an employer to exclude pregnancy from the coverage of such policies. But to whom exactly is a pregnant worker similarly situated? The statute clearly gives pregnant workers "equal" or "negative" rights to be let alone, but it does not textually ensure any positive treatment, such as the guarantee of accommodations to people with disabilities found in the Americans with Disabilities Act of 1990 (ADA).[54] Instead, any positive rights under the PDA, such as accommodations for pregnant workers, must flow from a comparative assessment.

Over time, employers have developed a variety of policies and practices under which they accommodate workers. Some of these policies have grown out of legal requirements, such as light-duty work for those who have a disability under the ADA. Others have been driven by policy concerns, such as light-duty work for those who are injured on the job. Such policies are neutral as to sex and generally have not been seen as facilitating unequal treatment vis-à-vis pregnant workers. Indeed, every federal circuit court that considered pregnancy-neutral policies prior to *Young* held that they do not

---

[51] Pregnancy Discrimination Act, Pub. L. No. 95–555, 92 Stat. 2076 (1978) (codified at 42 U.S.C. §2000e).

[52] *See General Electric Co. v. Gilbert*, 429 U.S. 125, 145–46 (1976) (holding that the exclusion of pregnancy from a disability policy was not discrimination on the basis of "sex").

[53] 42 U.S.C. §2000e(k).

[54] Pub. L. 101–336, 104 Stat. 327 (1990) (codified as amended at 42 USC §12101 *et seq.*); 42 U.S.C. §12111(9)(B).

Young v. United Parcel Services, Inc.

violate the PDA.[55] Such courts held that an employee who was accommodated pursuant to a pregnancy-neutral rule or law was not an appropriate comparator, since the relevant rule kept the employee who was accommodated from being similarly situated to the pregnant worker.[56]

Moreover, the ADA's regulations have historically excluded pregnancy from coverage,[57] with courts following suit based on the rationale that pregnancy itself is "healthy" and not the result of a physiological disorder of any type.[58] However, in light of the large number of women in the workforce and the documented toll the denial of accommodations may take on pregnant workers,[59] scholars and activists have argued for a legislatively guaranteed right to reasonable workplace accommodations. The most prominent recommendations have included broader statutory interpretations of the PDA or ADA, or a stand-alone federal statute that would provide pregnant women with a general right to workplace accommodations.[60]

In short, the treatment of pregnant workers illustrates the thorny "dilemma of difference" that Professor Martha Minow eloquently depicted in the late twentieth century.[61] People everywhere are different from one another, but

---

[55] *See, e.g., Troupe v. May Dep't Stores Co.*, 20 F.3d 734, 738 (7th Cir. 1994); *Serednyj v. Beverly Healthcare, LLC*, 656 F.3d 540, 548–49 (7th Cir. 2011); *Reeves v. Swift Transp. Co.*, 446 F.3d 637, 641 (6th Cir. 2006); *Spivey v. Beverly Enters., Inc.*, 196 F.3d 1309, 1312–13 (11th Cir. 1999); *Urbano v. Cont'l Airlines, Inc.*, 138 F.3d 204, 207–08 (5th Cir. 1998).

[56] *See Serednyj*, 656 F.3d at 551–52 (finding that employees who were accommodated pursuant to "pregnancy-blind" policies were not appropriate comparators).

[57] 29 C.F.R. pt. 1630, app. §1630.2(h) ("[C]onditions, such as pregnancy, that are not the result of a physiological disorder are also not impairments. However, a pregnancy-related impairment that substantially limits a major life activity is a disability under the first prong of the definition.").

[58] *See, e.g., Young v. United Parcel Serv., Inc.*, 707 F.3d 437, 440 (4th Cir. 2013) (citing with approval *Wenzlaff v. NationsBank*, 940 F.Supp. 889, 890 (D. Md. 1996) ("With near unanimity, federal courts have held that pregnancy is not a 'disability' under the ADA"), *vacated* 135 S.Ct. 1338 (2015).

[59] *See, e.g.*, Jessica Silver-Greenberg & Natalie Kitroeff, *Miscarrying at Work: The Physical Toll of Pregnancy Discrimination*, N.Y. Times (Oct. 21, 2018), www.nytimes.com/interactive/2018/10/21/business/pregnancy-discrimination-miscarriages.html.

[60] *See* Bradley A. Areheart, *Accommodating Pregnancy*, 67 Ala. L. Rev. 1125, 1128–29, 1139–41 (2016) (detailing such proposals). *See also* the federal bipartisan bill pending in Congress at time of writing, Pregnant Workers Fairness Act, S. 1101, 114th Cong. (2017); H.R. 2417, 115th Cong. (2017). Approximately half of the states have passed laws, varying both in scope and focus, which are designed to ensure reasonable accommodations for pregnant employees. Areheart, *supra*, at 1129 n.12; National Partnership for Women & Families, Reasonable Accommodations for Pregnant Workers: State and Local Laws (June 2018), www .nationalpartnership.org/research-library/workplace-fairness/pregnancy-discrimination/reason able-accommodations-for-pregnant-workers-state-laws.pdf.

[61] Martha Minow, Making All the Difference: Inclusion, Exclusion, and American Law (1990).

90 Young v. United Parcel Services, Inc.

that observation does not tell us whether to treat them differently. Minow singled out pregnant workers in particular and asked whether accommodating them might "undermine equality by treating them differently."[62] Accordingly, one could see a possible entitlement to pregnancy accommodations as treatment that is different from that of men (and hence "special" treatment) or as treatment that is similar to how other groups are sometimes treated, such as people with disabilities or those injured on the job (and hence "equal" treatment). It depends on one's frame of reference.

THE ORIGINAL OPINION

Any right to accommodation under the PDA has historically been about pregnant employees' right not to arbitrarily be treated worse than others because of their pregnancy. But *Young v. United Parcel Services, Inc.* asked whether the rights of pregnant workers should be understood more broadly. In *Young*, UPS had a policy of providing accommodations to three categories of employees: (1) employees injured on the job; (2) employees with "a permanent impairment cognizable" under the ADA; and (3) employees who lost their Department of Transportation (DOT) certification to drive a commercial motor vehicle.[63] Peggy Young sought a light-duty accommodation when her pregnancy resulted in a lifting restriction.[64] UPS refused because she did not fit into any of the three categories.[65] Young sued, alleging that UPS had violated the PDA by failing to provide her with the same accommodations it provided to other nonpregnant employees who fell within one of the three categories and who were similar in their relative ability to work.[66] The issue was whether Young could argue that workers who are accommodated pursuant to pregnancy-neutral laws and policies are "similar [to pregnant women] in their ability or inability to work." In particular, should pregnant workers, who are similar in their relative ability to work to persons with disabilities (or employees who were injured on the job or who lost their DOT certification), have a right to accommodation just as these other groups of workers have a right to accommodation?

The heart of the dispute in *Young* thus lies in the meaning of the PDA's second clause. It is clear enough from the first clause that pregnancy

[62.] *Id.* at 12; *see also* Areheart, *supra* note 61 (arguing that gender-asymmetrical rights, such as those that could be codified under the Pregnant Workers Fairness Act, may have expressive harms for women's opportunities in the workplace).

[63.] *Young v. United Parcel Serv., Inc.*, 707 F.3d 437, 439–40 (4th Cir. 2013).

[64.] *Id.* at 440–41.

[65.] *Id.*

[66.] *Young v. United Parcel Serv., Inc.*, 2011 WL 665321, at *8–9 (D. Md. Feb. 14, 2011).

discrimination is sex discrimination. The question is what, if anything, the second clause adds. Young's argument before the Supreme Court was that the second clause had to be something more than just an illustration of the first clause's principle; otherwise, the second clause would be superfluous.[67] Young argued that, where an employer accommodates some workers pursuant to a rule or policy, it must provide similar accommodations to all pregnant workers with comparable physical limitations.[68] In contrast, UPS argued that the second clause merely gave application to the PDA's redefinition of "sex."[69] UPS also argued that Young's position would mandate special treatment for pregnancy and grant it "most-favored nation" status by entitling pregnancy to better treatment than any other basis under Title VII.[70]

The Court said that neither UPS's nor Young's position was correct.[71] UPS's stance was wrong because it rendered the second clause of the PDA superfluous.[72] Young's argument was also misguided because such an interpretation would undercut disparate treatment law, which generally allows for differential treatment of protected class members so long as there is a legitimate, nondiscriminatory reason for doing so.[73] Instead, the Court reached a compromise between the poles of what Young and UPS sought – an interpretation that was different from that advocated by either party.[74] It said that the role of pregnancy-neutral policies that accommodate some employees, but not pregnant ones, is that they can help to prove pretext under the *McDonnell Douglas* burden-shifting framework.[75] In particular, "the plaintiff may reach a jury on this issue by providing sufficient evidence that the employer's policies impose a significant burden on pregnant workers, and that the employer's 'legitimate, nondiscriminatory' reasons are not sufficiently strong."[76]

One might naturally wonder under what conditions an employer's policy imposes "a significant burden" on pregnant employees. The Court gives one example: a plaintiff "can create a genuine issue of material fact as to whether a significant burden exists by providing evidence that the employer accommodates a large percentage of non-pregnant workers while failing to

[67] Petitioner's Brief at 23–24; *Young*, 135 S.Ct. 1338 (No. 12-1226), 2014 WL 4441528, at *23–24.
[68] *Id.* at 20, 2014 WL 4441528, at *20.
[69] *Id.* at 27, 2014 WL 5464086, at *27 (citing *Newport News Shipbuilding & Dry Dock Co. v. EEOC*, 462 U.S. 669, 678 n.14 (1983)).
[70] *Id.* at 13, 2014 WL 5465086, at *13.
[71] *Young*, 135 S.Ct. at 1349.
[72] *Id.* at 1352.
[73] *Id.* at 1350.
[74] *Id.* at 1353.
[75] *See id.* at 1354–55 (explaining how such proof would fit into the *McDonnell Douglas* scheme).
[76] *Id.* at 1354.

92   Young v. United Parcel Services, Inc.

accommodate a large percentage of pregnant workers."[77] In the same vein, Justice Stephen Breyer pleads: "[W]hy, when [UPS] accommodated so many, could it not accommodate pregnant women as well?"[78] But how many non-pregnant workers must be accommodated before it triggers a violation of the PDA? Said differently, at what point does the refusal to provide accommodations for a pregnant employee constitute pretext? After all, the Court clearly acknowledges that an employer can implement policies that sometimes harm members of a protected class "as long as the employer has a legitimate, nondiscriminatory, nonpretextual reason for doing so."[79] And how would one go about proving the burden? Must a plaintiff identify specific nonpregnant workers who have been accommodated, or is it enough to show that the *scope* of nonpregnant workers an employer could reasonably accommodate through certain policies is large or broad? It is unclear under *Young* how a company might reasonably implement a policy that accommodates some employees, but not pregnant ones, and still comply with the PDA.

One might also inquire what it means for a reason to be "sufficiently strong"? Here, the Court gives two negative examples. It says that a legitimate nondiscriminatory reason "normally cannot consist simply of a claim that it is more expensive or less convenient to add pregnant women to the category of those ('similar in their ability or inability to work') whom the employer accommodates."[80] The Court explained that the employer in *General Electric Co. v. Gilbert*[81] could likely have made just such a claim, yet Congress overruled that decision.[82] But what constitutes a legitimate reason for not accommodating pregnant workers if we exclude cost and difficulty? The majority opinion provides no direct answers to this question. However, Justice Samuel Alito, in his concurring opinion, intimates that compliance with another law (such as the ADA) or avoiding workers' compensation payments (by accommodating those injured on the job) may be neutral, legitimate reasons to accommodate nonpregnant employees and not pregnant ones.[83] While many questions remain unanswered, one clear upshot of *Young* is that it is now risky – in a way that it previously was not – to have a pregnancy-neutral policy that accommodates many other employees.

---

[77] *Id.*
[78] *Id.* at 1355.
[79] *Id.* at 1350.
[80] *Id.* at 1354.
[81] 429 U.S. 125 (1976).
[82] *Id.*
[83] *Id.* at 1360 (Alito, J., concurring).

THE FEMINIST JUDGMENT

Young and UPS set up a binary dispute centered on the meaning of the second clause's phrase, "other persons." The fundamental issue was whether to treat pregnancy-neutral rules and policies as outliers – such that those who benefit under such rules and policies are not appropriate comparators – or whether to treat any accommodations received under such rules as the minimum benefits to which pregnant employees are entitled. Professor Deborah Widiss, writing as Justice Widiss, authors her opinion in a way that is anchored in this same frame and would fully validate Young's arguments on appeal.[84] Widiss finds that "other persons" simply means other persons with comparable work-related limitations who are accommodated – regardless of *why* they are accommodated. In other words, pregnant employees should be treated as well as the most favorably treated employees with similar work-related abilities or deficiencies. So, for example, if employees with illnesses or injuries that would constitute disabilities under the ADA are accommodated, then pregnant workers with comparable work-related limitations must also be accommodated.

Widiss concludes that the history of the statute, as well as current sociological realities, compel this interpretation. She first chronicles how women's earnings are now far more essential than they were at the time the PDA passed. She also observes that the United States – in contrast to most other developed countries – has failed to provide the accommodations or leave that pregnant employees often need to remain productive members of the workforce. Separately, she observes that allowing employers to provide a legitimate, nondiscriminatory reason for denying benefits to pregnant employees does not fit with the history or legislative purpose of the PDA. In particular, the PDA was passed to overrule *Gilbert* – a case where cost-based concerns were held to be a nondiscriminatory rationale for not extending benefits to pregnant employees. Finally, she returns to the "larger purpose of the law," which she characterizes as "expanding pregnant women's opportunity." If there is ambiguity regarding which of two statutory constructions is correct, she notes that this larger purpose provides important guidance. It is for these reasons, taken cumulatively, that she concludes pregnant workers ought to be compared to

---

[84] Professor Widiss's opinion draws on arguments she made more fully in law review articles published before and after the decision in the actual *Young* case. *See generally* Deborah A. Widiss, Gilbert *Redux: The Interaction of the Pregnancy Discrimination Act and the Amended Americans with Disabilities Act*, 46 U.C. Davis L. Rev. 961 (2013); Deborah A. Widiss, *The Interaction of the Pregnancy Discrimination Act and the Americans with Disabilities Act after* Young v. UPS, 50 U.C. Davis L. Rev. 1423 (2017).

94   Young v. United Parcel Services, Inc.

any others who have been accommodated – and without allowance for the employer to try to justify the differential treatment.

Widiss also engages the possible argument that her interpretation might confer "most-favored nation" status on pregnant employees. She decides instead that it would merely confer status "equal" to other employees. It would indeed confer equal status to those accommodated (in the *Young* case, people with disabilities, those injured on the job, or those who lost DOT certification), but it would also confer preferential treatment compared to any employees with similar physical limits who are not so accommodated pursuant to a rule or policy (in this case, those who were injured outside of work or not deemed as having a disability under the ADA). So Widiss's interpretation of the PDA would ensure better treatment than some – a point she acknowledges when she writes that some nonpregnant workers with similar limitations would be "less favored" – and the same treatment as some others.[85]

Widiss's opinion would change the law dramatically. Previously, pregnancy-neutral accommodation rules were held *not* to violate the PDA. The *Young* case held that pregnancy-neutral rules *may* violate the PDA if the justifications for such rules are shown not to be sufficiently strong and the rules would impose a significant burden on pregnant workers. Widiss's opinion would go further by holding that pregnancy-neutral accommodation rules that accommodate people with physical limitations that are comparable to those of pregnant workers *always* violate the PDA. Such an opinion would be nearly tantamount to giving pregnant workers an affirmative right to workplace accommodations. Under Widiss's opinion, one would still need to secure such a right through a comparison of some sort, but most employers would likely accommodate (or be required to accommodate) at least some workers on a basis that is not specific to pregnancy.[86]

Widiss's opinion would also make the law stronger than other employment discrimination laws through her interpretation that the text should trump the strictures of the *McDonnell Douglas* burden-shifting framework for disparate treatment. Under most employment discrimination laws, an employer can

[85.] As is always the case when one thinks about equal or preferential treatment, the question is: equal or preferential to whom?

[86.] Widiss writes that "[a] plaintiff may make the requisite showing through evidence that the employer has provided the requested accommodation or that the employer would clearly be required to provide the requested accommodation pursuant to its policies or other applicable laws." This seems to indicate a comparison either to an accommodation the employer has actually extended or to an accommodation the employer would hypothetically be required to provide, if requested, under policy or law.

defend itself against a claim of intentional discrimination by proffering any nonpretextual, nondiscriminatory reason.[87] The *Young* Court circumscribed that general rule by finding that cost and convenience will "normally" not suffice as reasons. But Widiss's opinion would exempt PDA accommodation claims altogether from these burden-shifting standards by no longer allowing employers to defend themselves against a discrimination claim by arguing that they had a legitimate, nondiscriminatory reason for rules that accommodate some employees, but not pregnant ones.

Of course, the degree to which Widiss's opinion would sweep may depend on how pregnancy is ultimately treated under the ADA Amendments Act of 2008 (ADAAA). Prior to the ADAAA, pregnancy was consistently excluded from coverage. Both the ADA's regulations and courts found that pregnancy must be categorically excluded from the ADA's ambit based on the rationale that pregnancy is "normal," "healthy," and not the result of a physiological disorder.[88] But the ADAAA lowered the bar for proving "disability," dramatically enlarging the scope of the protected class.[89] Since then, scholars and commentators have observed that pregnant employees should now have a much more viable claim under the ADA for workplace accommodations.[90] Widiss underscores these views in her opinion, and if such views were to ultimately become established law, then enlargement of the PDA's scope may be of less consequence for securing pregnancy accommodations.[91]

[87.] Even under the ADA – a statute that expressly provides a right to "reasonable accommodation" – an employer can defend itself against a "failure to accommodate" claim by showing the accommodation is not "reasonable" or would constitute an "undue hardship."

[88.] Areheart, *supra* note 61, at 1134.

[89.] Kevin Barry, *Toward Universalism: What the ADA Amendments Act of 2008 Can and Can't Do for Disability Rights*, 31 Berkeley J. Emp. & Lab. L. 203 (2010); Michelle A. Travis, *Impairment as Protected Status: A New Universality for Disability Rights*, 46 Ga. L. Rev. 937 (2012). As an example of this lowered bar, the Appendix to the ADAAA's implementing regulations provides that "if an individual has a back impairment that results in a 20-pound lifting restriction that lasts for several months, he is substantially limited in the major life activity of lifting, and therefore covered under the first prong of the definition of disability." 29 C.F.R. §1630, App. at §1630.2(j)(1)(viii).

[90.] *See, e.g.*, Jeannette Cox, *Pregnancy as "Disability" and the Amended Americans with Disabilities Act*, 53 B.C. L. Rev. 443 (2012) (arguing that the ADAAA's expansion "to include many short-term and relatively minor physical limitations sweeps aside many standard objections to characterizing pregnancy as an ADA disability").

[91.] There is another way in which the sweep of Widiss's opinion may be more limited than apparent. After *Young*, law firms and commentators around the country began to recommend, as best practice, that employers prophylactically act to accommodate pregnant workers. If companies have already modified their practices, then stronger doctrine might have less practical consequence than expected.

96 Young v. United Parcel Services, Inc.

CONCLUSION

The dispute in *Young* concretized some of the long-standing theoretical fissures in feminism, such as sameness versus difference and special treatment versus equal treatment. In particular, should pregnant workers be treated *equally* or *specially* when compared to those with similar physical deficiencies whom the employer does not accommodate? The *Young* case gave us an answer that did not satisfy many – certainly not employers who wanted a clear rule or female workers who wanted a guarantee of workplace accommodations. Widiss's opinion might satisfy those who yearn for a more accommodating workplace, but worry those concerned about the expressive effects of gender-asymmetrical protections in the workplace.[92] The enduring question for scholars and activists is what methods will best achieve equality for female workers, while prompting the fewest unintended – and perhaps negative – consequences. The answer, as with many things, remains to be seen.

Young v. United Parcel Services, Inc., 135 S.Ct. 1338 (2015)

JUSTICE DEBORAH A. WIDISS DELIVERED THE OPINION OF THE COURT.

This case concerns the ability of women to work safely through a pregnancy – a question of pressing importance for many women. Pregnancy, and maternal functions more generally, were once widely used as a justification to deny women employment opportunities. However, for more than thirty-five years, the Pregnancy Discrimination Act of 1978 (PDA) has specified that it is illegal to discriminate against employees on the basis of pregnancy and that employees affected by pregnancy must be treated the "same" as other employees who have comparable limitations. 42 U.S.C. §2000e(k). Petitioner Peggy Young was forced to take unpaid leave for the entire duration of her pregnancy, even though her employer, United Parcel Services, Inc. (UPS), routinely accommodated many other employees with health conditions that caused lifting

---

[92] For example, I have argued elsewhere that gender-asymmetrical rights, such as those that could be codified under the Pregnant Workers Fairness Act or those that could be provided interpretively under the PDA or ADA, may have expressive harms for women's opportunities in the workplace. Areheart, *supra* note 61; *see also* Nicole Buonocore Porter, *Mutual Marginalization: Individuals with Disabilities and Workers with Caregiving Responsibilities*, 66 Fla. L. Rev. 1099, 1111–15 (2014) (exploring systematically how coworkers become resentful when employers allow some employees to "deviate from the normal workplace rules or give them any other kind of special treatment").

restrictions like Young's. The court of appeals affirmed a grant of summary judgment in favor of the employer. Because we conclude that the undisputed facts establish that UPS's failure to accommodate Young violates the applicable language of the PDA, we vacate that court's judgment and remand for further proceedings.

I FACTUAL BACKGROUND

Given that the district court granted summary judgment to UPS, we must construe all contested factors in the light most favorable to Young. In most respects, however, the facts are undisputed, with the differences between the parties turning on their interpretation of the relevant statutory language.

In late July 2006, after two unsuccessful attempts at *in vitro* fertilization (IVF), petitioner Peggy Young took an unpaid leave of absence from her job at respondent UPS prior to undergoing a third round of IVF. *See Young v. UPS*, 707 F.3d 437, 440 (4th Cir. 2013). At that point, Young had worked for UPS for more than six years. The IVF was successful. Shortly after learning that she was, in fact, pregnant, Young met with her medical provider. Her doctor indicated that she would be able to go back to work, but that, given her prior history of pregnancy loss, she should avoid lifting more than 20 pounds during the first twenty weeks of her pregnancy and that she should not lift more than 10 pounds thereafter. *Id.*

Young worked as an "air driver" for UPS. This position required her to go to the airport early in the morning to pick up letters and packages that had been flown into her region and then to deliver them to their intended recipients. *Id.* Although UPS's list of essential job functions for the air driver position indicated that drivers had to be able to lift packages weighing up to 70 pounds, most packages on Young's route were far lighter. This is not surprising given that UPS's pricing scheme made shipping heavy packages via air quite expensive. In fact, on average, only two of the seventy-eight deliveries Young made each week exceeded 20 pounds. JA 642–45.

In September 2006, while still on unpaid leave, Young gave her supervisor and UPS's occupational health manager a note from her health provider, which included the recommendation that Young should avoid lifting objects that weighed more than 20 pounds. By October 2006, in her third month of pregnancy, Young indicated to her supervisor that she was ready to return to work. She did not ask for a different position or specific accommodation. She did not believe that any formal accommodation was necessary, because Young shared the route with a senior driver who was willing to take responsibility for delivering the heavier packages. JA 658–59.

98   Young v. United Parcel Services, Inc.

Nonetheless, the company's occupational health manager refused to permit Young to return to her job, and she also refused to transfer Young to a different position. *Young*, 707 F.3d at 441. In November 2006, Young spoke to UPS's division manager, Myron Williams, about her desire to return to work. He allegedly "told her she was 'too much of a liability' while pregnant and that she 'could not come back into the [facility in which she worked] until [she] was no longer pregnant.'" Pet. App. 8a. Williams denies that he made this statement, but, given the procedural posture of this case, we must accept it as true. In any event, this factual dispute is immaterial to our resolution of the case.

UPS routinely accommodated other employees with health conditions that interfered with work, including conditions that caused lifting restrictions like Young's. Specifically, UPS provided accommodations for three different classes of workers: employees who were injured on the job; employees who had conditions that qualified as disabilities under the Americans with Disabilities Act of 1990 (ADA); and employees who had lost their Department of Transportation (DOT) licenses, which could be revoked on the basis of a wide range of health conditions, as well as other factors, such as convictions for driving while intoxicated. *Young*, 707 F.3d at 439–40. UPS contended that it denied accommodations to all employees who did not fit within one of these three categories. However, a shop steward testified that, "[t]o the best of [her] knowledge, the *only* light duty requested restrictions that became an issue" in her workplace "were with women who were pregnant." JA 504 (emphasis added).[93]

As a result of UPS's refusal to permit Young to do her regular job or to transfer her to an alternative position, Young was required to remain on unpaid leave for the entire duration of her pregnancy. Partway through this period, she lost the medical insurance that was provided through her job at UPS. Young ultimately returned to her job at UPS two months after the birth of her child. At that point, she had been forced to live without her salary from the company for approximately eleven months – a situation that caused significant financial stress for her family. Pet. App. at 43a-44a.

Young timely filed a charge with the Equal Employment Opportunity Commission (EEOC), alleging that UPS's refusal to permit her to work and denial of accommodation violated Title VII of the Civil Rights Act of 1964, as

---

[93] At oral argument, there was extensive discussion of how many (if any) employees other than pregnant employees were denied accommodations. Since the district court granted summary judgment to the respondent, there was never the opportunity for a trial to resolve this factual question. However, it is undisputed that, pursuant to the policies described in the text, UPS routinely accommodated employees with lifting limitations that were similar to Young's. Under the interpretation of the statute that we adopt, this is sufficient to demonstrate that UPS's refusal to provide comparable accommodations to Young was unlawful.

amended by the PDA. Her initial charge also included allegations of race and disability discrimination that she is no longer pursuing. After receiving a right to sue letter from the EEOC, Young timely filed suit in the district court. The district court granted summary judgment in favor of UPS. *Young v. UPS*, 2011 WL 665321 (D. Md. Feb. 14, 2011). Young appealed, and the Fourth Circuit affirmed. *Young*, 707 F.3d at 439. We granted *certiorari*, and we now reverse and remand.

II PREGNANT WOMEN'S NEEDS FOR WORKPLACE ACCOMMODATIONS

As the numerous *amicus* briefs submitted in this case make clear, Young's situation is, sadly, far from unusual. The once-common assumption that pregnant women do not need to work because they can (or at least should) be supported by their partners is patently unrealistic. In the United States today, 41 percent of births are to unmarried women. US Dep't of Health & Human Servs., BIRTHS, FINAL DATA FOR 2009 (2011). Working wives provide, on average, 37 percent of their families' total income, and more than one-third of wives outearn their husbands. Bureau of Labor Statistics, Dep't of Labor, WOMEN IN THE LABOR FORCE: A DATABOOK tbls. 24 and 25 (2011). Women's earnings are particularly crucial for poor and working-class women. In families in the lowest quintile of income distribution, 70 percent of working wives earn as much as or more than their husbands. *See* Sarah Jane Glynn, *The New Breadwinners: 2010 Update*, CENTER FOR AMERICAN PROGRESS 3 (Apr. 2012), https://cdn .americanprogress.org/wp-content/uploads/issues/2012/04/pdf/breadwinners.pdf.

Given the centrality of women's earnings to most families, it is not surprising that most pregnant women, like Young, seek to work throughout much or all of a pregnancy. US Census Bureau, US Dep't of Commerce, MATERNITY LEAVE AND EMPLOYMENT PATTERNS OF FIRST-TIME MOTHERS 1961–2008 6 (Oct. 2011), www.census.gov/prod/2011pubs/p70-128.pdf (82 percent of first-time mothers who gave birth 2006–08 worked during the last month of their pregnancy). Pregnancy discrimination, however, remains alarmingly common. While it is clearly illegal for them to do so, employers routinely fire women when they announce a pregnancy or when the pregnancy becomes visibly obvious; this is particularly prevalent in low-wage workplaces. *See, e.g.*, Stephanie Bornstein, POOR, PREGNANT, AND FIRED (2011), https://worklifelaw.org/publications/ PoorPregnantAndFired.pdf. Studies and case law confirm that pregnant women also face subtler bias, such as being judged to be less competent or committed than other employees. *See, e.g.*, Stephen Benard *et al.*, *Cognitive Bias and the Motherhood Penalty*, 59 HASTINGS L.J. 1359, 1368–72 (2008)

100 Young v. United Parcel Services, Inc.

(collecting and discussing lab experiments and other studies that demonstrate that pregnant women are routinely undervalued as compared to other employees with equivalent qualifications).

This case concerns the distinct, but related, set of challenges that often occur when pregnant women ask to have changes made at work to promote their health or comfort. Notably, many women can work safely through a pregnancy without any need for accommodations at work. However, depending on the pregnancy and the nature of the job, pregnancy can, like other health conditions, sometimes interfere with work responsibilities. Pregnant women may be advised by their health providers to drink water regularly or to eat frequent snacks, or to avoid long periods of standing or heavy lifting. *See* Br. of Healthcare Providers, National Partnership for Women and Families, and Other Organizations Concerned with Maternal and Infant Health as *Amici Curiae* in Support of Petitioner, *Young v. UPS*, 135 S.Ct. 1338 (2015).

Many women with professional jobs can easily comply with such suggestions without seeking any form of workplace "accommodation" (or even conceptualizing such changes as an accommodation). But women who are employed in work environments that are more strictly controlled may need to seek formal permission for even minor modifications such as extra restroom breaks or permission to carry a bottle of water or snacks. *See, e.g., Wiseman v. Wal-Mart Stores*, No. 08–1244, EFM, 2009 WL 1617669 (D. Kan. June 9, 2009) (pregnant employee fired for carrying a water bottle, as recommended by her doctor to address urinary and bladder infections). Women in physically demanding jobs may need to be relieved from certain aspects of their regular responsibilities. Such requests are routinely denied, placing pregnant women in the extraordinarily difficult position of needing to choose between earning income and promoting a healthy pregnancy. *See, e.g.*, Br. of the American Civil Liberties Union and A Better Balance, *et al.*, as *Amici Curiae* in Support of Petitioner at 17–21, *Young v. UPS*, 135 S.Ct. 1338 (2015) (providing examples of women denied workplace accommodations). A review of case law suggests that it is particularly common for employers to refuse to make accommodations in jobs, like Young's, that are typically male-dominated. *See* Br. of Law Profs. and Women's and Civil Rights Orgs. as *Amici Curiae* in Support of Petitioner at 33–36, *Young v. UPS*, 135 S. Ct. 1338 (2015).

It is not unusual for women to be, like Young, required to take unpaid leave when requests for such accommodations are denied. This places significant financial hardship on families. Over 70 percent of American households cannot pay their normal expenses if a wage-earner is unable to work for six months because of a health condition. *See* Stephen Mitchell, *Testimony to ERISA Advisory Council* (June 2012), summarized in *Managing Disability*

Risks in an Environment of Individual Responsibility (Dep't of Labor, Report to Hon. Hilda L. Solis). Because many Americans live paycheck to paycheck, this includes a sizeable share of Americans who would be typically considered "middle class." *See* Annamaria Lusardi *et al.*, FINANCIALLY FRAGILE HOUSEHOLDS: EVIDENCE AND IMPLICATIONS (2011), www.brookings.edu/wp-content/uploads/2011/03/2011a_bpea_lusardi.pdf.

The real-world impacts of such losses are made clear in the stories submitted to this Court. For example, Armanda Legros was sent home from her job as a manager at an armored truck company when she was six-and-a-half months pregnant because she had asked to avoid heavy lifting. She shared that she was "scared every time [she] looked in her empty fridge" that she would not be able to feed her older son and newborn baby. *See* Br. of ACLU and ABB at 17. Natasha Jackson, forced to take leave from her job at a Rent-A-Center when she asked to avoid occasional heavy lifting, described how loss of her income, shortly after she and her husband had made a down payment on a house, ultimately meant that they were forced out of the contract. *Id.* at 18.

Moreover, although Young was placed on long-term unpaid leave, and she was ultimately able to return to her job at UPS, many other workers in her position would lose their job entirely. In the United States, the primary federal law addressing leave from work for medical conditions is the Family and Medical Leave Act of 1993 (FMLA). The FMLA applies only to workplaces with at least fifty employees and to workers who meet relatively stringent longevity and hour requirements; collectively, these provisions exclude about half of the American workforce. Family and Leave Act Regulations; A Report on the Department of Labor's Request for Information, 72 Fed. Reb. 35550, 35622 (2007). Even employees who are eligible under the Act may take only twelve weeks of leave per year, and this leave is unpaid. Although this leave may be used to address an employee's own serious health condition or to care for a new baby, leaves are cumulative. This means that if an employee uses twelve weeks of leave because of medical needs during her pregnancy, she will have exhausted her total leave allotment for the year and will not be able to take additional FMLA leave to care for a newborn child.

The financial and emotional costs of being forced out of a job or placed on unpaid leave *during* a pregnancy are compounded by American law's failure to provide paid leave or other dedicated income supports to new mothers. Notably, the United States is the only developed country in the world that fails to guarantee paid maternity leave. *See* Human Rights Watch, FAILING ITS FAMILIES: LACK OF PAID LEAVE AND WORK-FAMILY SUPPORTS IN THE U.S. 33 (Feb. 23, 2011), www.hrw.org/report/2011/02/23/failing-its-families/lack-paid-leave-and-work-family-supports-us. Many countries provide paid time off to new

102   Young v. United Parcel Services, Inc.

fathers, as well – something the United States also fails to do. *See id.* Addressing the denial of accommodations in cases like Young's is an essential element of realizing the PDA's larger objective of making it possible for women to work productively through a pregnancy and helping women and their families to maintain economic security as they start families.

III THE PREGNANCY DISCRIMINATION ACT'S STATUTORY MANDATE

This case arises under Title VII of the Civil Rights Act of 1964, as amended by the PDA. As discussed more fully below, Congress enacted the PDA to make clear that discrimination on the basis of pregnancy is unlawful and to overturn this Court's earlier decision to the contrary. As in any case of statutory interpretation, we begin with the text of the statute. The PDA provides:

> The terms "because of sex" or "on the basis of sex" include, but are not limited to, because of or on the basis of pregnancy, childbirth, or related medical conditions; and women affected by pregnancy, childbirth, or related medical conditions shall be treated the same for all employment-related purposes, including the receipt of benefits under fringe benefit programs, as other persons not so affected but similar in their ability or inability to work.   42 U.S.C. §2000e(k).

We note, at the outset, that although the entirety of the PDA is found within Title VII's definitional sections, only the first clause is worded like a typical definition in that it clarifies the meaning of a term whose operative significance obtains meaning when it is inserted in the statute's more general substantive mandates. The second clause, following the semicolon, is linguistically distinct. It includes its own affirmative mandate: women affected by pregnancy "shall" be treated the same as relevantly similar nonpregnant employees.

The case calls for us to elucidate the relationship between these two clauses. In doing so, we recognize the general rule of statutory construction that, when possible, a statute ought to be construed so that no clause is rendered "superfluous, void, or insignificant." *TRW Inc. v. Andrews*, 534 U.S. 19, 31 (2001) (internal quotations omitted). Additionally, as described more fully *infra* section IV, the PDA was enacted to supersede our decision in *General Electric Co. v. Gilbert*, 429 U.S. 125 (1976), which had held that pregnancy discrimination was not a form of sex discrimination. "When Congress amended Title VII in 1978, it unambiguously expressed its disapproval of both the holding and the reasoning of the Court in the *Gilbert* decision."

Newport News Shipbuilding & Dry Dock Co. v. EEOC, 462 U.S. 669, 678 (1983). Thus the interpretation that we give the language should be such that, if applied to a case like *Gilbert*, the result would be different than it was in *Gilbert*.

With those threshold assumptions in place, we first address – and reject – the approach taken below. The lower courts understood the question to be whether Young could prove UPS's refusal to provide her accommodations was motivated by animus or hostility against her because of her pregnancy. Reasoning that Young had failed to identify direct evidence that the relevant decision-maker was biased and noting that the policies according to which UPS provided accommodations did not explicitly reference pregnancy, the lower courts applied the burden-shifting process we first articulated in *McDonnell Douglas v. Green*, 411 U.S. 792 (1973).[94] Although there were some differences in their analysis, both lower courts focused on the reasons *why* UPS accommodated other employees, rather than assessing the functional ability or inability of the employees who received accommodations, and concluded that none of the other classes of employees were relevantly "similar" to the petitioner. See *Young*, 707 F.3d at 450; 2000 WL 665321, at *14. Lower courts in other circuits have used a similar approach, either holding that employees injured on the job or accommodated pursuant to the ADA were not comparators at all, or that so long as a "pregnancy-blind" policy was applied on an even-handed basis and was not adopted as a pretext for excluding pregnant employees, it is permissible. See *Serednyj v. Beverly Healthcare, LLC*, 656 F.3d 540, 548–49 (7th Cir.2011); *Reeves v. Swift Transp.Co.*, 446 F.3d 637, 641 (6th Cir.2006); *Spivey v. Beverly Enter., Inc.*, 196 F.3d 1309, 1312–13 (11th Cir.1999); *Urbano v. Cont'l Airlines, Inc.*, 138 F.3d 204, 207–08 (5th Cir.1998) (all applying similar reasoning). The respondent likewise urges this interpretation, saying that

---

[94] The lower courts also suggested that there were two, and only two, avenues of proof through which this showing could be made: "direct" evidence showing that her pregnancy motivated the adverse action or *McDonnell Douglas* burden-shifting. *Young*, 707 F.3d at 226 ("Applying the usual Title VII analytical construct for sex discrimination claims, we first consider whether Young has shown any direct evidence of discrimination. In the absence of that, we apply the familiar burden shifting framework articulated in *McDonnell Douglas* and subsequent cases."); *Young*, 2011 WL at *9 ("Young may avoid summary judgment via the two alternative avenues of proof available to all discrimination plaintiffs"). This is incorrect. Although this is not an appropriate vehicle to explore fully the proof structure that should be applied to disparate treatment cases that do not involve the PDA's same-treatment language, Title VII's statutory language makes no distinction between so-called direct and circumstantial evidence. See *Desert Palace, Inc. v. Costa*, 539 U.S. 90, 99–101 (2003) (holding that a violation of 42 U.S. C. §2000e-2(m) may be proven with any kind of evidence). Additionally, *McDonnell Douglas* offers a helpful way of organizing evidence in many cases, but ultimately what matters is whether a plaintiff can satisfy the requisite *statutory* standard.

104 Young v. United Parcel Services, Inc.

the second clause does no more than "clarify" the PDA's baseline rules regarding evenhanded treatment of pregnancy. Resp. Br. at 27.

In other words, courts have approached claims concerning the denial of accommodations to pregnant employees like any other "disparate treatment" claim, such that an employer's convincing showing that the challenged action was based on a legitimate nondiscriminatory rationale is an adequate defense.[95] The problem with this approach is that it makes the second clause of the PDA entirely superfluous. The PDA's first clause, in conjunction with Title VII's more general prohibition on discriminatory actions, is already sufficient to make clear that adverse actions based on animus or bias against pregnant employees is unlawful. *See* 42 U.S.C. §2000e-2(a). Moreover, this approach ignores the clear import of the plain language of the second clause: a mandate that employees affected by pregnancy "shall be treated the same" as other employees who are "similar in their ability or inability to work." This standard instructs courts to consider only the ability or inability of employees, not the reasons why an employer might choose to accommodate certain conditions and not others, or the source of the relevant health condition. This makes sense. An employer's failure to treat pregnancy and related health conditions as favorably as other health conditions that cause comparable limitations necessarily disadvantages women. The PDA provides that such differential treatment is *by definition* a form of prohibited discrimination on the basis of sex. The employer's justification for the differential treatment is irrelevant.

Clarifying that PDA accommodation claims do not require a showing of discriminatory bias, however, does not fully resolve the issue in this case. There are still two groups of employees who may be arguably "similar" in their "inability to work" to Young: employees with lifting restrictions accommodated pursuant to UPS's various policies (i.e., employees with lifting restrictions as a result of on-the-job injuries, impairments that qualify as disabilities under the ADA, or conditions that result in the loss of a DOT license) and employees with lifting restrictions who are *not* accommodated pursuant to any of these policies. It is not clear from the statutory language

[95.] The petitioner's initial complaint did not include a claim that the respondent's policies were unlawful because of their disparate impact on women, and the district court denied the petitioner's subsequent request to amend the complaint to add in a disparate impact claim. *Young*, 707 F.3d at 442. Accordingly, we offer no opinion on whether the petitioner's policies violate Title VII's disparate impact provisions. *Cf. Germain v. Cnty. of Suffolk*, No. 07-CV -2523, 2009 WL 1514513, at *4 (E.D.N.Y. May 29, 2009) (concluding that the plaintiffs could proceed with a disparate impact claim challenging a policy of providing light-duty positions to employees with workplace injuries while refusing to provide light-duty to pregnant employees).

alone which group of employees provides the appropriate comparison in Young's case.

Where the proper interpretation of statutory language is ambiguous or open to two interpretations, we consider whether the history that gave rise to the provision and the statute's overall purpose can assist in determining which interpretation should be applied. We also consider any regulations or guidance promulgated by an agency with expertise enforcing the relevant statute. *See Chevron, USA v. NRDC*, 467 U.S. 837 (1984); *Skidmore v. Swift & Co.*, 323 U.S. 134, 140 (1944). In this instance, consideration of the statute's history and larger purpose and the EEOC's guidance both support Young's interpretation.

IV THE HISTORY AND PURPOSE OF THE PREGNANCY DISCRIMINATION ACT

Because the circumstances that gave rise to the PDA have significance for the resolution of this case, we review this history in some detail. Before 1964, when Title VII was enacted, it was common to fire female employees when they announced a pregnancy or when a pregnancy began to show. *See, e.g.*, Dorothy Sue Cobble, THE OTHER WOMEN'S MOVEMENT: WORKPLACE JUSTICE AND SOCIAL RIGHTS IN MODERN AMERICA 186–87 (2004). Employment policies that provided support for employees' medical needs also routinely treated pregnancy less favorably than other health conditions. For example, employer-provided health insurance often excluded costs associated with pregnancy and childbirth, and employers that provided disability benefits for short-term health conditions that interfered with work often refused to provide benefits for pregnancy-related absences. *Id.* at 127–29; Elizabeth Duncan Koontz, *Childbirth and Child Rearing Leave: Job-Related Benefits*, 17 N.Y. L. FORUM 480, 491 (1971). State policies made the same distinction. At that time, five states required employers to provide short-term disability insurance; four of these states excluded benefits for pregnancy entirely, and one provided less extensive benefits for pregnancy than other health conditions. *Id.* at 485. Private and public policies were structured this way because women were typically considered marginal workers who were expected to leave paid employment upon the birth of a child.

When Title VII became effective, women who were fired or forced to take unpaid leave because of their pregnancy, or denied benefits when pregnancy impacted their ability to work, began to bring lawsuits alleging that these practices were a form of sex discrimination. They claimed that these practices violated Title VII and, where applicable, constitutional guarantees of equality. In 1972, the Equal Employment Opportunity Commission (EEOC), the

106 Young v. United Parcel Services, Inc.

agency charged with implementing Title VII, released formal guidelines on sex discrimination. The guidelines indicated that terminating employees because of pregnancy, or treating pregnancy less well than other short-term disabilities under health, disability, or sick leave plans, were both forms of discrimination on the basis of sex. 29 C.F.R. §1604.10, as printed in 37 Fed. Reg. 6837 (Apr. 5, 1972). The courts of appeals unanimously agreed. *See General Electric Co. v. Gilbert*, 429 U.S. 125, 147 (1976) (Brennan, J., dissenting) (collecting cases).

When the question reached the Supreme Court, however, we took a different approach. In *General Electric Co. v. Gilbert*, a class of female employees alleged that GE's short-term disability policy, which provided benefits for almost all health conditions that interfered with work other than pregnancy, violated Title VII. Relying on the reasoning in an earlier constitutional case, we held that GE's policy was permissible. We reasoned that the plan did not discriminate on the basis of sex, because it divided employees into two categories, "pregnant persons" and "non-pregnant persons," and the latter group included both men and women. *Gilbert*, 429 U.S. at 135 (quoting *Geduldig v. Aiello*, 417 U.S. 484, 495–96 n.20 (1974)). We also rejected arguments that the specific exclusion of pregnancy benefits – benefits that obviously would be claimed only by women – was a form of "invidious" discrimination by suggesting that pregnancy was "significantly different from the typical covered disease or disability" in that it is "not a disease at all." *Gilbert*, 429 U.S. at 136 (internal quotations omitted). In light of this putative distinction, the majority accepted the district court's finding that GE had adopted the policy because of its concern over increased costs, not any animus against employing pregnant women. This Court then concluded that such cost-based concerns were a legitimate nondiscriminatory rationale and thus permissible. *See id.*

Three Justices dissented. Justices Brennan and Marshall argued that the EEOC's regulations on point should be given deference, and they noted additionally that the disability policy was emblematic of "a history of General Electric practices that have served to undercut the employment opportunities of women who become pregnant while employed." *Id.* at 149 (Brennan, J., dissenting). Justice Stevens, in a separate dissent, reasoned simply that, by placing pregnancy in a "class by itself," the plan discriminated against women, characterizing the capacity to become pregnant as the primary distinction between women and men. *Id.* at 161–62 (Stevens, J., dissenting).

Within days of the decision in *Gilbert*, lawyers and activists began to organize to lobby Congress to supersede it. This coalition ultimately included more than 200 organizations, including advocacy organizations specifically committed to advancing women's rights, the broader civil rights community, labor unions, and several pro-life organizations that were concerned that the discrimination permitted by *Gilbert* would spur women to seek abortions rather than risk the loss of a job because of pregnancy. *See* Kevin S. Schwartz, *Equalizing Pregnancy: The Birth of a Super Statute* 63–67 (May 7, 2005), http://digitalcommons.law.yale.edu/ylsspps_papers/41/. In the decades since the PDA was enacted, abortion rights has become an increasingly polarizing issue; nonetheless, pro-life and pro-choice groups have likewise come together in this case to support Young. *See* Br. of Twenty-Three Pro-Life Organizations and the Judicial Education Project as *Amici Curiae* in Support of Petitioner at 1, *Young v. UPS*, 135 S.Ct. 1338 (2015); Br. of the American Civil Liberties Union and A Better Balance, *et al.*, as *Amici Curiae* in Support of Petitioner, *Young v. UPS*, 135 S.Ct. 1338 (2015).

Members of Congress heard testimony regarding the crucial contribution that working women made to their families' financial health and the negative consequences of employment policies that provided less protection to pregnancy than other health conditions. Based on this testimony, the Senate committee considering the bill concluded that "[w]orking women have become a major part of this country's workforce ... [and] most women work out of hard economic necessity." S. Rep. No. 95–331, at 9 (1977) (internal quotations omitted); *see also, e.g.*, Staff of S. Comm. on Labor & Hum. Res., *Legislative History of the Pregnancy Discrimination Act of 1973*, at 12 (statement of Sen. Hawkins) ("Seventy percent of all women who work are either the sole wage earner or married to men who make under $7000 a year. Their income is essential to support themselves and their families."). By explicitly rejecting *Gilbert*'s conclusion that pregnancy discrimination was not sex discrimination and by specifying that pregnant employees must be treated the "same" as other employees with similar limitations, Congress sought to protect women's ability to work through their pregnancies. "The Reports, debates, and hearings make abundantly clear that Congress intended the PDA to provide relief for working women and to end discrimination against pregnant workers." *California Fed'l Sav. & Loan Assoc. v. Guerra*, 479 U.S. 272, 285–86 (1987).

The legislative history also establishes that members of Congress understood that the rule established by the PDA – that employees who are limited in their ability to work by pregnancy must receive at least as much support as employees who are limited in their ability to work by other health conditions – would impose additional costs on employers. Indeed, much of the opposition to the bill focused on the "cost of including pregnancy in health and disability plans." *Cal. Fed.*, 479 U.S. at 286; *see also id.* n.21 (citing S. Rep. No. 95–331, p. 9 (1977) (discussing the cost objections)). Although the committees that considered the bill rejected some industry projections of costs as unduly inflated, they accepted the Department of Labor's conclusion that enacting the bill would impose approximately $190 million of additional expenses related to disability payments and also additional expenses related to health insurance benefits. *See* S. Rep. No. 95–331, at 10–11; H.R. Rep. No. 95–948, at 10. The bills ultimately passed both houses with broad bipartisan support. *See Legislative History of the Pregnancy Discrimination Act of 1973*, at 136 (reporting the Senate vote as seventy-five in support, eleven opposed, and fourteen not voting); *id.* at 187 (reporting the House vote as 376 in support, 43 opposed, and 13 not voting). Differences between the bills, relating to coverage of costs associated with abortion, were resolved by a conference committee and then approved by voice votes in each chamber. *Id.* at 205, 209.

Very shortly after the PDA was enacted, we recognized that Congress's intent in passing the bill was to "unambiguously express" its disapproval of *Gilbert* and to overturn "both the holding and the reasoning" of the decision in that case. *Newport News Shipbuilding & Dry Dock Co. v. EEOC*, 462 U.S. 669, 678 (1983). We have emphasized that the first and second clauses of the PDA do distinct work in this respect. *See Cal. Fed.*, 479 U.S. at 285 (characterizing the first clause as reflecting Congress's disapproval of the reasoning in *Gilbert* and the second clause as intended to "overrule the holding in *Gilbert* and illustrate how discrimination against pregnancy is to be remedied"). Indeed, this history helps to confirm the correctness of our holding today that the employer's intent is irrelevant when assessing its failure to treat employees affected by pregnancy "the same" as others with comparable limitations. As described above, in *Gilbert*, a majority of the Court accepted GE's contention that its refusal to provide disability benefits to pregnant employees was based on legitimate concerns regarding costs, rather than any invidious animus. Accordingly, if we were to accept the respondent's contention that, to succeed in a PDA case, an employee must establish bias, the PDA would fail to lead to a different result in the *Gilbert* case itself. This interpretation cannot be correct.

We have also previously recognized that our interpretation of the PDA should be informed by the larger purpose of the law. Our decision in *California Federal Savings and Loan Ass'n v. Guerra*, 479 U.S. 272 (1987), is particularly instructive. In that case, we were asked to determine whether a California statute that mandated that employers provide maternity leave for the period of disability related to pregnancy and childbirth conflicted with the PDA. The employer in the case, CalFed, and other *amici* representing business interests argued that the state statute could not be enforced because California law did not require comparable leave for employees with other

Young v. United Parcel Services, Inc.   109

disabilities. We rejected this contention, noting that the PDA's underlying objective was expanding pregnant women's opportunity: " 'The entire thrust ... behind this legislation [the PDA] is to guarantee women the basic right to participate fully and equally in the workforce, without denying them the fundamental right to full participation in family life.' 123 Cong. Rec. 29658 (1977)." *Cal. Fed.*, 479 U.S. at 288 (quoting Senator Williams, a sponsor of the Act). Recognizing that the PDA and the California statute both sought to expand equal employment opportunity, we held that the California statute was enforceable. *Id.* at 288–91.

Finally, we note that, in considering the bill, congressional leaders understood that pregnancy discrimination both reflected and perpetuated stereotypical assumptions regarding traditional gender roles. As the Senate committee report explained, "[T]he assumption that women will become pregnant and leave the labor market is at the core of the sex stereotyping resulting in unfavorable disparate treatment of women in the workplace," and accordingly the failure to address pregnancy discrimination would "undermine the central purpose of the sex discrimination prohibitions of Title VII." S. Rep. No. 95–331, at 3; *see also* H.R. Rep. No. 95–948, at 3 ("[T]he assumption that women who will become pregnant and leave the labor force leads to the view of women as marginal workers, and [it] is at the root of the discriminatory practices which keep women in low-paying and dead-end jobs."). By stating explicitly that pregnant employees are to be judged based on their *actual* abilities and inabilities, rather than based on assumptions regarding their commitment to work, the PDA's "same" treatment language is intended to combat such stereotypes. As such, it advances Title VII's more general commitment to ending discrimination on the basis of sex. *Cf. Nevada Dep't of Human Res. v. Hibbs*, 538 U.S. 721, 736 (2003) (recognizing that providing parental leave to both male and female employees is an appropriate mechanism to address sex discrimination because stereotypes that women have primary responsibility for domestic responsibilities create a "self-fulfilling cycle of discrimination that forced women to continue to assume the role of primary family caregiver, and fostered employers' stereotypical views about women's commitment to work and their value as employees").

V THE EQUAL EMPLOYMENT OPPORTUNITY COMMISSION'S
INTERPRETATION OF THE PREGNANCY DISCRIMINATION ACT

When statutory language is ambiguous, we also routinely consider agency interpretations of the relevant language. Although we typically do not afford the EEOC's substantive interpretations of Title VII full *Chevron* deference, we have long recognized that they may merit weight under the standard first enunciated in *Skidmore v. Swift*, 323 U.S. 134, 140 (1944). *See, e.g., Federal Exp. Corp. v. Holowecki*, 552 U.S. 389, 399 (2008) (internal quotations omitted) (asserting that the EEOC's policy statements reflect "a body of experience and informed judgment to which courts and litigants may properly resort for guidance" and that they are entitled to a "measure of respect" under the *Skidmore* standard). Under that standard, we assess the "thoroughness evident in [the agency's] considerations, the validity of its reasoning, its consistency with earlier and later pronouncements, and all those factors which give it the power to persuade." *Skidmore*, 323 U.S. at 140; *see also United States v. Mead Corp.*, 533 U.S. 218, 227–39 (2001) (discussing *Skidmore* deference in detail).

In the pregnancy discrimination context, there is a long history regarding the Court's willingness to defer to the agency's interpretation of the law. As noted earlier, in our decision in *Gilbert*, we refused to follow the EEOC's guidance relating to pregnancy on the grounds that the formal guidance conflicted with some opinion letters issued prior to its release. *See Gilbert*, 429 U.S. 125, 142–43 (1976). In dissent, Justices Brennan and Marshall argued that majority's approach was flawed in that it penalized the agency for having taken time to properly consider the appropriate interpretation of the statute. *Id.* at 157–58 (Brennan, J., dissenting). The congressional committees that drafted the PDA specifically endorsed the EEOC's prior interpretation of the Act. S. Rep. No. 95–948, at 2 ("In the committee's view these [EEOC] guidelines rightly implemented the Congress' intent in barring sex discrimination the 1964 [A]ct"); H.R. Rep. No. 95–948, at 2 (similar). While this prior history is not dispositive of the deference we should afford the EEOC's interpretations in this case, we believe it suggests that we should at least carefully consider the agency's interpretation of the statute.

The EEOC's most detailed discussion of the specific question posed by this case is found in guidance the agency published in July 2014. *See EEOC Pregnancy Guidance*, 2 EEOC Compliance Manual §626-I(A)(5) (2014).[96] In that guidance, the EEOC states that "[a]n employer may not refuse to treat a pregnant worker the same as other employees who are similar in their ability or inability to work by relying on a policy that makes distinctions based on the source of an employee's limitations (e.g., a policy providing light duty only to workers injured on the job)." *Id.* This duty of equal treatment applies to "providing modified tasks, alternative assignments, leave, or fringe benefits." *Id.* The guidance also explains that the "burden shifting analysis set out in

---

[96.] [*Editors' note*: The EEOC's Pregnancy Guidance has since been revised to reflect the Supreme Court's holding in the actual *Young* decision.]

Young v. United Parcel Services, Inc.   111

McDonnell Douglas Corp. v. Green [is not necessary] ... to establish a violation of the PDA" where there is evidence that the employer has provided accommodations to other employees with limitations like those experienced by a pregnant employee.

The 2014 guidance expands upon prior statements, in that it is more explicit that the source or cause of a health condition is irrelevant to the analysis under the PDA, but it is consistent with the agency's long-standing interpretation of the statutory language. Shortly after the PDA was enacted, the EEOC reaffirmed its earlier position that Title VII required that disabilities related to pregnancy be treated the same as any other temporary disabilities. At that time, the EEOC issued an explanatory "Questions and Answers" (Q&A) document that was published as an appendix to the pre-existing regulation. One question asks whether an employer has to provide an "alternative job" if an employee "for pregnancy related reasons ... is unable to perform the functions of her job." 44 Fed. Reg. 23804 (Apr. 20, 1979), codified at 29 C.F.R. Pt. 1604 App. qu. 5. The EEOC's answer was that the employer is "required to treat an employee temporarily unable to perform the functions of her job in the same manner as it treats other temporarily disabled employees, whether by providing modified tasks, alternative assignments, disability leaves, leaves without pay, etc." *Id.* Although this answer does not specify that a policy that limited such accommodations to those with on-the-job injuries would be unlawful, it makes no reference to the reason why an employer might relieve other employees of such responsibilities, suggesting that the agency believed the reason was irrelevant.

The 1979 Q&A document likewise makes clear that employers located in states with laws requiring payment of short-term disability benefits would need to provide comparable benefits to employees who were unable to work because of pregnancy or childbirth. *See id.* at qu. 19. At the time, employers would probably have asserted – truthfully, in many cases – that their failure to provide such benefits was not the result of any animus against pregnant employees, but rather reflected a desire to save money by providing the minimum benefits required by the applicable laws. In that respect, it parallels arguments made by the respondent UPS in this case that its failure to provide accommodations to pregnant employees, while doing so for employees with conditions that qualify as disabilities under the ADA, does not reflect any animus against pregnant employees, but rather merely a desire to do the minimum required by the applicable laws. However, the EEOC's long-standing guidance suggests such intent-based analysis is irrelevant, even when benefits are provided to comply with other statutory mandates.

112   Young v. United Parcel Services, Inc.

It is unsurprising that – in light of the lower courts' decisions in this case and lower court decisions in other similar cases challenging employers' claims that limiting light-duty positions to those with on-the-job injuries was permissible – the EEOC would take the opportunity in its 2014 guidance to clarify and amplify its earlier statements on point. Agencies are well positioned to identify issues where statutory language, regulations, or prior guidance is ambiguous enough that litigation ensues, and it is helpful to both courts and regulated entities when they provide clarification to address any such confusion. Such clarifications should not be deemed to reduce the weight we afford to interpretations promulgated by the agency, at least so long as (as is true in this case) the clarification provided is consistent with the agency's prior statements. In other words, we should not characterize such clarifications as evidence of "inconsistency" that diminishes the likelihood that we would defer to the interpretation under the factors set forth in *Skidmore* and its progeny. That approach would have a perverse effect; agencies might fear that taking steps to clarify a prior position would be grounds for rejecting the agency's position entirely.

Likewise, we deem the fact that the 2014 guidance was issued shortly after we granted *certiorari* in this case to be of little significance. We afford deference to well-supported agency interpretations because the agency has a depth of experience and expertise that we lack. That expertise does not disappear simply because we grant *certiorari* in a case. In fact, the agency's perspective can be particularly helpful at that point, because its position is informed by consideration of multiple cases in an area, whereas our analysis necessarily focuses on the case actually pending before us. This is why we often (as we did in this case) solicit the government's input when we are resolving cases that call for statutory interpretation. If guidance issued by an agency subsequent to a grant of *certiorari* were to take a position that was dramatically different from an agency's prior position, such guidance might appropriately be discounted by the Court. That, however, is not the case here. Indeed, in its *amicus* brief submitted in this case, the Solicitor General advocates that we adopt the EEOC's interpretation and notes that the "Commission's recent guidance is consistent with its longstanding and reasonable interpretation of the PDA." Br. for the United States as *Amicus Curiae* in Support of Petitioner at 27, *Young v. UPS*, 135 S.Ct. 1338 (2015).

The respondent, however, contends that the EEOC's most recent guidance and the Solicitor General's endorsement of that interpretation should be rejected on the ground that they fail to conform to the position that "the government" has taken in earlier cases brought against the US Postal Service, which has had a policy that is substantially similar to UPS's. *See* Resp. Br. at

15–18. As a general matter, we have long held that litigation positions may be afforded less deference than agency regulations or guidance. *See, e.g., Bowen v. Georgetown University Hospital*, 488 U.S. 204, 212–13 (1988) (asserting that "[d]eference to what appears to be nothing more than an agency's convenient litigating position would be entirely inappropriate," and distinguishing between litigation positions and interpretations that are articulated in regulations, rulings, or administrative practice); *Investment Co. Institute v. Camp*, 401 U.S. 617, 628 (1971) ("Congress has delegated to the administrative official and not to appellate counsel the responsibility for elaborating and enforcing statutory commands.").

Beyond these general concerns with the appropriate level of deference to afford to litigation positions, this case highlights a particular tension that arises in the employment field because the "government," writ large, plays multiple roles. The EEOC, a government agency, was created by Congress specifically to interpret and enforce antidiscrimination laws. The federal government is also an exceptionally large employer. As an employer, the government may be sued by its employees for allegedly improper actions. There are difficult questions – which we need not resolve here – about the precise scope of government lawyers' ethical duty to "zealously represent" their client. We simply observe that, when faced with a claim that the postal service's policies regarding light duty violated the PDA, it is unsurprising that the lawyers in the regional US attorneys' offices charged with defending the Postal Service (as well as the Postal Service's own attorney) would cite existing circuit court precedent suggesting that the Postal Service's policies were lawful.[97] This has little, if any, bearing on our assessment of the appropriateness of deferring to the EEOC's guidance – a deference that is premised on the EEOC's particular expertise and its charge to enforce antidiscrimination laws.

In summary, applying the *Skidmore* factors, we find the EEOC's reasoning in its recent guidance concerning pregnancy discrimination to have been thorough and complete, as well as consistent with the agency's earlier guidance. We conclude that it is a reasonable interpretation of the statutory language, as the statutory language asserts that pregnant employees must be treated "the same" as others with similar limitations. It also accords with the statute's underlying purpose of ensuring that women who are pregnant can continue to work and expanding economic opportunity for women more generally. We further note that the Solicitor General, joined by counsel by the EEOC, filed an *amicus* brief urging that we adopt this position and

---

[97.] This is particularly true because, prior to the explicit clarification included in the 2014 guidance, there was at least some level of ambiguity in the EEOC's guidance on the point.

114   Young v. United Parcel Services, Inc.

explaining that it is consistent with the EEOC's earlier explications of the statutory language. Although some of the government's civil defense lawyers have taken a different position in prior litigation in the lower courts, this inconsistency only minimally, if at all, reduces the extent to which we consider the agency's interpretation to be a persuasive indication of the appropriate interpretation of the statute.

VI THE PREGNANCY DISCRIMINATION ACT MANDATES LEVELING UP

The history and purpose of the PDA, as well as the guidance issued by the agency charged with enforcing our antidiscrimination laws, makes resolution of this case straightforward. In a case such as this, where an employer accommodates some employees with limitations like those caused by pregnancy, but refuses accommodation to some other employees with limitations like those caused by pregnancy, the PDA mandates that the pregnant employee be compared to the former group, not the latter. This interpretation promotes the PDA's larger purpose of expanding employment opportunities for pregnant women and combating stereotypical assumptions that women's primary responsibilities are centered on the home or family life. It also accords with the interpretation of the statute promulgated by the EEOC.

It is true that, under this interpretation, it is possible that pregnant employees will receive more support from their employers than will employees with other health conditions that are not work-related and which also do not qualify as disabilities under the ADA. However, this is entirely consistent with our prior interpretations of the statute. Almost thirty years ago, we held that "Congress intended the PDA to be a floor beneath which pregnancy disability benefits may not drop – not a ceiling above which they may not rise." *Cal. Fed.*, 479 U.S. at 285 (internal quotation marks omitted). Accordingly, as noted above, we approved a state statute that mandated that employers provide women with maternity leave, even though comparable leaves were not afforded to disabilities generally, since both statutes were intended to improve equal employment opportunity for pregnant women. Given this history, it is unremarkable to conclude now, as we do, that the PDA requires that pregnant employees receive supports that *are* provided to employees with other disabilities, even if some additional employees with different health needs do not receive such benefits.

The lower court in this case, lower courts in similar cases, and several Justices at oral argument expressed concern, however, that the interpretation we adopt improperly affords pregnant employees "preferential" treatment or, more derisively, a "most-favored nation" status. *See, e.g., Young v. UPS*, 707 F.3d 437, 446 (4th Cir. 2013) (asserting that the petitioner's argument "posits that the PDA ... compel[s] employers to grant pregnant employees a 'most favored nation' status ... regardless of whether such status was available to the universe – male and female – of nonpregnant employees"); *Reeves v. Swift Transp. Co.*, 446 F.3d 637, 642 (6th Cir. 2006) (rejecting the plaintiff's challenge to light-duty policy limited to on-the-job injuries as asking for "preferential treatment"); *Urbano v. Continental Airlines*, 138 F.3d 204, 208 (5th Cir. 1998) (same). We find this contention puzzling. The entire premise of the PDA's "same treatment" clause is that pregnant women are being compared to *other employees with similar limitations*. The interpretation we adopt treats pregnant employees as an "equally favored nation," not a "most-favored nation," albeit recognizing that some employees with other health conditions may indeed be *less* favored.

We call attention to this rhetoric to interrogate the implicit baseline it assumes regarding the appropriate comparison for pregnant employees. As the *amici* law professors and women's and civil rights organizations suggest, the contention that equal treatment of pregnant employees is actually preferential treatment "reinstates the very stereotypes about work and pregnancy that the [PDA] was designed to eradicate," in that it reflects courts' intuitions that accommodating male workers is part of the ordinary costs of business, but costs related to pregnancy are "extra" costs that employers should not have to bear. Br. of Law Profs. and Women's and Civil Rights Orgs. as *Amici Curiae* in Support of Petitioner at 21, *Young v. UPS*, 135 S.Ct. 1338 (2015). Moreover, to the extent that UPS, or any other employer, wants to avoid providing benefits to pregnant employees that are not provided to all employees, it can, of course, choose – as a matter of company policy – to provide comparable support to all employees with health conditions that impact work. *Cf. Cal. Fed.*, 479 U.S. at 291 (pointing out that California's maternity leave statute "does not compel ... employers to treat pregnant workers *better* than other disabled employees," because employers could choose to provide comparable leave to other employees with health conditions that temporarily interfere with work).

Recent amendments to the ADA may mitigate this issue in any event. *See* ADA Amendments Act of 2008 (ADAAA), Pub. L. No. 110–325, 122 Stat. 3553 (2008). The ADAAA rejects prior judicial interpretations of the standard for determining what impairments qualify as a disability as unduly stringent and clarifies that an impairment that substantially limits any of a broad range of major life activities, specifically including "walking, standing, lifting, [and] bending," may qualify. 42 U.S.C. §12102(2). The EEOC's implementing regulations indicate that temporary disabilities can meet this standard. 29

C.F.R. §1630.2(j)(ix). Because this case arose before the effective date of the ADAAA and because Young is no longer pursuing a claim under the ADA, we have no cause to address how the amended statute should apply in the context of pregnancy. However, commentators have advanced the contention that pregnancy-related conditions – and perhaps even "normal" pregnancies that cause such limitations – could qualify as disabilities under the ADAAA. *See* Jeannette Cox, *Pregnancy as Disability and the Amended Americans with Disabilities Act*, 53 B.C. L. REV. 443 (2012); Joan C. Williams *et al.*, *A Sip of Cool Water*, 32 YALE L. & POL'Y REV. 97 (2013). Lower courts have agreed. *See, e.g.*, *McKellips v. Franciscan Health Sys.*, No. C-13-5096 MJP, 2013 WL 1991103, at *4 (W.D. Wash. May 13, 2013) (holding that severe pelvic pain caused by pregnancy could qualify as a disability); *Alexander v. Trilogy Health Servs.*, No 1:11-CV-295, 2012 WL 5268701, at *11–12 (granting summary judgment in favor of a plaintiff where the employer failed to accommodate pregnancy-related hypertension).

The enactment of the ADAAA is important to our analysis for a different reason. The respondent, and the lower courts in this case, suggested that employees accommodated pursuant to the ADA were categorically unavailable as comparators in PDA cases, on the ground that an employer's need to comply with the ADA was a "pregnancy-blind" and unbiased justification for differential treatment. Under the interpretation of the PDA that we announce today, such defenses are clearly inapposite, because intent is irrelevant. However, we think that the expansion of support for disabilities under the ADA and the ADAAA helps to elucidate *why* our interpretation is correct and in accordance with the history and purpose of the PDA. There is no question that if an employer voluntarily accommodates an individual with a limitation like that caused by pregnancy, such as an employee with a back injury that causes a temporary lifting restriction, the PDA mandates comparable support for pregnant employees. *See, e.g.*, *Ensley-Gaines v. Runyon*, 100 F.3d 1220, 1223 (6th Cir. 1996) (evidence that a defendant provided "light duty" to employees with off-the-job injuries, but denied "light duty" to a pregnant employee was sufficient to preclude summary judgment on a PDA claim). Prior to the enactment of the ADAAA, it is unlikely that an individual with a temporary limitation of this sort would have been deemed to have a qualifying disability. Without prejudging the specific meaning of language in the ADAAA, it is undisputable that the amended statutory language broadens the scope of what constitutes qualifying disabilities, and thus, going forward, it is more likely that employers will be required to provide accommodations for such conditions. Accordingly, if ADA-accommodated employees were categorically off-limits as comparators for PDA claims, the expansion of support for other disabilities would have the perverse effect of *decreasing* the level of support for pregnant employees by reducing the pool of potential comparators.

This interpretation would undermine the entire structure of the PDA. As described *supra* section IV, the PDA was enacted to ensure that pregnancy would be treated as well as other health conditions that caused similar limitations. This was true whether employer support for such health conditions was pursuant to statutory mandates (such as the state statutes existing at the time the PDA was enacted, which required employers to provide short-term disability benefits) or the employer's own assessment that employees should receive health-related benefits such as health insurance, light duty, or leave. The architects of the PDA adopted a comparative mandate quite purposefully, as they were concerned that requiring "special" privileges for pregnancy would increase *ex ante* discrimination against pregnant employees specifically, or women of childbearing age more generally. The premise, however, was that when employers chose, or governments mandated, to provide support for other health conditions, the PDA would ensure that pregnancy would receive the same level of support. *See, e.g.*, H.R. No. 95–948, at 5 ("This bill would require that women disabled by pregnancy ... be provided the same benefits as those provided other disabled workers. This would include temporary and long-term disability insurance, sick leave, and other forms of employee benefit programs."); *id.* at 11 (discussing then-existing state laws requiring benefits for short-term disabilities).

The ADA and the ADAAA have since expanded support for employees with health conditions that cause limitations like those caused by pregnancy. The PDA is intended, as its plain language suggests, to ensure that pregnancy receives at least the same level of support. This is true whether or not Congress considered this interaction when it enacted the ADA or the ADAAA: "The well-settled presumption [is] that Congress understands the state of existing law when it legislates." *Bowen v. Massachusetts*, 487 U.S. 879, 898 (1988). "The courts are not at liberty to pick and choose among congressional enactments, and when two statutes are capable of co-existence, it is the duty of the courts, absent a clearly expressed congressional intention to the contrary, to regard each as effective." *Morton v. Mancari*, 417 U.S. 535, 551 (1974).

Accordingly, we hold that when an employer provides accommodations for health conditions that cause limitations like those caused by pregnancy – whether to comply with the ADA, as a response to workers' compensation statutes, in conformity with a collective bargaining agreement, or simply as a matter of employer discretion, pursuant to a policy or on an ad hoc basis – the

PDA mandates that comparable accommodations be provided to pregnant employees. This is required even if some other employees with health conditions that cause similar limitations do not receive the same support.[98] A plaintiff may make the requisite showing through evidence that the employer has provided the requested accommodation or that the employer would clearly be required to provide the requested accommodation pursuant to its policies or other applicable laws.

This approach does not mean that all accommodations that might benefit a pregnant woman are required; the touchstone is how the employer treats employees with similar abilities or inabilities. Evidence that an employer provides the relevant support in response to other kinds of health needs demonstrates that the requested accommodation is reasonably feasible. The comparative approach adopted by the PDA is important. By focusing on the extent to which employers have already committed to providing comparable accommodations, it ensures that the assessment of whether it is "worth it" to provide support for a pregnant employee will not be infected by the still-pervasive belief that pregnant women are less capable and less committed than other employees. Indeed, by facilitating and encouraging the possibility of women working productively through a pregnancy, the PDA's same-treatment language, properly interpreted, can help to counter such stereotypes more generally and thus better achieve the PDA's larger purpose. Women, like men, should be able to start a family without jeopardizing their employment.

* * *

For these reasons, we vacate the judgment of the Fourth Circuit and remand the case for further proceedings consistent with this opinion.

It is so ordered.

[98.] Our holding does not mean that all special benefits an employer might provide to individual employees, or some classes of employees, must be extended to pregnant employees. The statute indicates that the appropriate standard is employees who are "similar in their ability or inability to work" to employees affected by "pregnancy, childbirth, or related medical conditions." 42 U.S.C. §2000e(k). This language most naturally invites a comparison to employees with medical conditions other than pregnancy that cause limitations like those experienced by a pregnant employee. When an employer chooses to extend benefits on the basis of a factor that is disconnected from the ability or inability to work – such as benefits premised on seniority – the second clause of the PDA is inapplicable, although the first clause and the more general prohibition on discriminatory treatment means that pregnant employees must be treated equivalently to nonpregnant employees under the relevant policy. We are confident that, in most instances, it will be relatively easy to determine whether supports or benefits are connected to an inability to work that is "similar" to the limitations experienced by pregnant employees. To the extent that there is ambiguity in the statutory language, we will address that in a future case.

4

Intersectional Approaches to Appearances

Commentary on *Jespersen v. Harrah's Operating Co.*

ROXANA S. BELL

INTRODUCTION

In *Jespersen v. Harrah's Operating Co.*, the US Court of Appeals for the Ninth Circuit, sitting *en banc*, held that an employer's sex-differentiated appearance and grooming policy complied with Title VII of the Civil Rights Act of 1964 because it imposed equal burdens on men and women and did not violate Title VII's prohibition of sex stereotyping.[1] The feminist judgment of Dean Angela Onwuachi-Willig and Professor JoAnne Sweeny, writing as Judges Onwuachi-Willig and Sweeny, ultimately reaches a dramatically different conclusion: one based largely on their rejection of two analytical frameworks that problematically reinforce a gender binary.

The facts of this layered case are deceivingly straightforward. Darlene Jespersen had worked for nearly twenty years as a bartender at Harrah's Casino in Reno, Nevada, when the company adopted a new "Personal Best" grooming policy that required all employees with customer contact to adhere to sex-specific appearance standards. For women, these standards included "clear, white, pink, or red color" nail polish, "teased, curled, or styled" hair that must be "worn down at all times, no exceptions," and a full face of makeup, including face powder, blush, mascara, and lip color.[2] Although the company had previously encouraged its servers to wear makeup, the "Personal Best" program marked the first time the company made wearing makeup mandatory. Jespersen found the new policy both demeaning and distracting to her job performance; she did not believe that she could continue to perform her job duties confidently while being forced to wear makeup. She explained her objection to the policy in an op-ed she wrote for the *Reno Gazette*: "I had to become a sex object . . . Although it had nothing to do

---

[1] *Jespersen v. Harrah's Operating Co., Inc. (Jespersen III)*, 444 F.3d 1104, 1113 (9th Cir. 2006) (en banc).
[2] *Id.* at 1107.

120   Jespersen v. Harrah's Operating Co.

with mixing drinks and handling customers, keeping my job became more and more about meeting Harrah's extreme and outdated idea of what a woman should look like."[3] Jespersen refused to comply with the makeup requirement, and Harrah's subsequently gave her thirty days to apply for a different position without customer contact. After thirty days passed, Jespersen had not done so, and Harrah's fired her.

Initially, this case appears to involve a classic catch-22, known in feminist legal theory as a double bind:[4] Jespersen faced the impossible choice of being degraded (and consequently disadvantaged at performing her job) or being fired. However, as the Ninth Circuit's original *en banc* opinion demonstrates, the impossibility of that choice may seem open to debate in a male-centric society that routinely expects women to conform to certain beauty standards to appear professional.[5] Upon a closer look, Jespersen's case exposes the reductive inadequacy of the Ninth Circuit's prevailing test regarding the legality of sex-differentiated grooming policies – namely, whether the policy imposes an equal burden on male and female workers. The case also highlights a glaring loophole in the Ninth Circuit's existing interpretation of sex stereotyping: specifically, its failure to recognize that an employee need not prove that she faced an impossible choice in order to avail herself of the sex-stereotyping protections of Title VII.

Although the original Ninth Circuit *en banc* opinion affirmed the trial court's grant of summary judgment for Harrah's, Onwuachi-Willig and Sweeny's feminist judgment reverses and remands the trial court's decision. These judgments differ with respect to not only the outcome, but also the analytical frameworks under which Harrah's summary judgment motion is considered, as well as the specific evidence in the record that each of the judgments deems material or immaterial.

THE ORIGINAL OPINION

In the original opinion, an *en banc* panel of the Ninth Circuit split seven to four in affirming the trial court's grant of summary judgment to Harrah's on

---

[3] Darlene Jespersen, *Opinion: Case Is About Civil Rights and Sex Bias*, RENO GAZETTE-J. 11A (Feb. 5, 2004).

[4] Martha Chamallas, INTRODUCTION TO FEMINIST LEGAL THEORY 10 (3d ed. 2013) (describing double binds as "situations in which options are reduced to a very few and all of them expose one to penalty, censure, or deprivation"); *see also Price Waterhouse v. Hopkins*, 490 U.S. 228, 251 (1989) ("An employer who objects to aggressiveness in women but whose positions require this trait places women in an intolerable and impermissible catch 22: out of a job if they behave aggressively and out of a job if they do not. Title VII lifts women out of this bind.").

[5] *See* Jessica Bennett, *The Beauty Advantage: How Looks Affect Your Work, Your Career, Your Life*, NEWSWEEK (July 19, 2010), www.newsweek.com/beauty-advantage-how-looks-affect-your-work-your-career-your-life-74313.

Jespersen's sex discrimination claims.[6] The opinion followed an initial three-judge panel decision affirming the same.[7] In the first line of its *en banc* opinion, the Ninth Circuit explained that it intended to use Jespersen's case "to reaffirm [its] circuit law concerning appearance and grooming standards [and] clarify [its] evolving law of sex stereotyping claims."[8] Presumably, the Ninth Circuit saw the need for clarification in light of the differing grounds on which the trial court and the three-judge panel found in favor of Harrah's.[9] First, the trial court found that Harrah's policy could not possibly violate Title VII because it did not discriminate against her based on the "immutable characteristics" of her sex.[10] The trial court's opinion never defines the terms "mutable" and "immutable" (indeed, no clear definition exists), but it implies that the readily manipulated characteristics implicated by Harrah's policy (e.g., cutting/styling hair and applying/removing makeup) involve mutable characteristics.[11] It further held that Jespersen could not allege a sex-stereotyping claim, as recognized by the US Supreme Court in *Price Waterhouse v. Hopkins*,[12] because "the Ninth Circuit expressly excepted grooming and appearance standards from the confines of the *Price Waterhouse* rule."[13] On appeal, the three-judge panel disagreed with the trial court's reasoning, holding instead that *Price Waterhouse* could apply to grooming policies, but only if the employee suffered sexual harassment for not complying with the policy.[14]

On rehearing *en banc*, the Ninth Circuit was curiously silent about the mutable/immutable distinction on which the trial court relied,[15] but it did clarify that grooming policies may indeed be the subject of *Price Waterhouse* sex-stereotyping claims regardless of whether the employee suffered harassment for failure to conform.[16] The court then considered Jespersen's claims of sex discrimination under two theories: (a) that the grooming policy imposed

---

[6] See *Jespersen III*, 444 F.3d at 1108, 1113–14.

[7] See *Jespersen v. Harrah's Operating Co., Inc.* (*Jespersen II*), 392 F.3d 1076, 1083 (9th Cir. 2004).

[8] *Jespersen III*, 444 F.3d at 1105.

[9] See generally *Jespersen II*, 392 F.3d at 1080–83; *Jespersen v. Harrah's Operating Co.* (*Jespersen I*), 280 F.Supp.2d 1189, 1191–94 (D. Nev. Oct. 22, 2002).

[10] *Jespersen I*, 280 F.Supp.2d at 1192 ("[S]ex-differentiated regulation of dress, cosmetic or grooming practice, which do not discriminate on the basis of immutable characteristics or intrude upon a person's fundamental rights, do not fall within the purview of Title VII").

[11] See *id.* at 1193 ("[T]he makeup requirement involves a mutable characteristic").

[12] 490 U.S. 228 (1989).

[13] *Jespersen I*, 280 F.Supp.2d at 1193 (citing *Nichols v. Azteca Restaurant Enterprises, Inc.*, 256 F.3d 864 (9th Cir. 2001)).

[14] *Jespersen II*, 392 F.3d at 1082–83.

[15] See *Jespersen III*, 444 F.3d at 1106 (summarizing the reasoning of the trial court and three-judge panel).

[16] *Id.*

122 Jespersen v. Harrah's Operating Co.

unequal burdens on women and men; and (b) that the grooming policy required Jespersen to conform to sex stereotypes.[17] Ultimately, for the reasons that follow, the court found both theories unavailing in Jespersen's case.[18]

The Equal Burdens Test

First, the court rejected Jespersen's unequal burdens argument, finding that Jespersen failed to establish that Harrah's grooming policy was more burdensome for women than for men.[19] Under the Ninth Circuit's equal burdens test, employers may differentiate between men and women in appearance and grooming policies as long as the policy does not create a "significantly greater burden of compliance" for one sex than for another.[20] In reaching its decision, the court relied on precedent in *Gerdom v. Cont'l Airlines, Inc.*[21] and *Frank v. United Airlines, Inc.*,[22] both of which held that an airline violates Title VII by having strict weight requirements for female flight attendants and either lax or no weight requirements for men.[23] The court emphasized the "facially unequal" nature of the airlines' weight policies and characterized Harrah's grooming policy as "stand[ing] in marked contrast" to those policies because its sex-differentiated grooming requirements are "not more onerous for one gender than the other."[24] Instead, the court found that Harrah's grooming standards "appropriately differentiate between the genders" and reiterated its position that "not every differentiation between the sexes creates [an unequal burden]."[25]

Having concluded that the policy was not facially unequal, the court then considered whether Jespersen had created a triable issue as to whether Harrah's policy placed a greater burden on women than men.[26] In finding that she had not done so, the court pointed to a lack of evidence of the relative cost and time required to comply with the grooming requirements.[27] Specifically, the court criticized Jespersen's failure to submit any evidence of the time and cost associated with female makeup and male haircuts, and it sharply refused Jespersen's request that it take judicial notice of the fact that "it costs more money and takes more time for a woman to comply with the makeup

---

[17] *Id.* at 1106.
[18] *Id.*
[19] *Id.* at 1111.
[20] *Id.* at 1110 (internal quotation omitted).
[21] 692 F.2d 602 (9th Cir. 1982).
[22] 216 F.3d 845 (9th Cir. 2000).
[23] *Jespersen III*, 444 F.3d at 1109–10.
[24] *Id.* at 1109.
[25] *Id.* at 1110.
[26] *Id.*
[27] *Id.*

Jespersen v. Harrah's Operating Co.

requirement than it takes for a man to comply with the requirement that he keep his hair short ..."[28] One of the dissenting judges acknowledged that the record "might have been tidier" if Jespersen had introduced evidence of the time and cost associated with the makeup requirement, but he nevertheless disagreed with the majority on whether the court should have granted her request for judicial notice of those "incontrovertible facts," wryly remarking that "Harrah's policy requires women to apply face powder, blush, mascara and lipstick. You don't need an expert witness to figure out that such items don't grow on trees."[29]

The problems with the majority's unequal burdens analysis extend beyond the court's willful blindness to the cost of makeup products and the daily time and labor associated with applying (and reapplying) those products. Even if one overlooks the false equivalence the court creates between the female makeup requirement and male haircut requirement (which ignores the requirement that women must tease, curl, or style their hair[30]), there is a deeper problem rooted in the equal burdens test itself. A framework that condones sex-differentiated grooming requirements (so long as they are equally burdensome to males and females) is inherently problematic because it perpetuates both a reductive gender binary[31] and the accompanying power structure historically favoring men. The court's characterization of Harrah's policy as one "aimed at creating a professional and very similar look for all [bartenders]" is highly telling. As one of the dissenting judges explains, "The inescapable message is ... that women's faces are incomplete, unattractive, or unprofessional without full makeup."[32] Indeed, the court's unequal burdens analysis unwittingly brings to light the inherent sexism of any test that allows employers to impose sex-differentiated requirements that are unrelated to any bona fide occupational qualification (BFOQ),[33] but rather are born of sex stereotypes repackaged as social norms.

---

[28] *Id.*

[29] *Id.* at 1117 (Kozinski, J., dissenting).

[30] As one of the dissenting judges aptly noted, "Every requirement that forces men to spend time or money on their appearance has a corresponding requirement that is as, or more, burdensome for women: short hair v. teased, curled, or styled hair; clean trimmed nails v. nail length and color requirements; black leather shoes v. black leather shoes. The requirement that women spend time and money applying full facial makeup has no corresponding requirement for men, making the overall policy more burdensome for the former than for the latter." *Id.* (Kozinski, J., dissenting) (internal citation and quotation marks omitted).

[31] *See* Amy Harmon, *M, F or X? Added Option Makes States Rethink Nature of Gender*, N.Y. TIMES (May 29, 2019), www.nytimes.com/2019/05/29/us/nonbinary-drivers-licenses.html.

[32] *Jespersen III*, 444 F.3d at 1116 (Kozinski, J., dissenting).

[33] Title VII provides employers a defense to claims of discrimination when "sex ... is a bona fide occupation qualification [BFOQ] reasonably necessary to the normal operation of that particular business or enterprise." 42 U.S.C. §2000e-2(e)(1). The US Supreme Court has long held that the BFOQ defense is an "extremely narrow exception." *Dothard v. Rawlinson*, 433 U.S. 321,

124   Jespersen v. Harrah's Operating Co.

Sex Stereotyping

Next, the court disposed of Jespersen's *Price Waterhouse* claim in short order by holding that there is no evidence "to indicate that [Harrah's] policy was adopted to make women bartenders conform to a commonly-accepted stereotypical image of what women should wear."[34] The court noted in quick succession that Harrah's policy did not "tend ... to stereotype women as sex objects" or subject Jespersen to sexual harassment.[35] The court then summarily held that Jespersen's claim must fail because she had presented evidence only of her "own *subjective* reaction to the makeup requirement."[36] Discounting Jespersen's testimony that she felt degraded, humiliated, and unable to perform her job when forced to wear a full face of makeup, the court opined instead that Harrah's policy did not require anything "that would *objectively* impede a woman's ability to do the job."[37]

The court's dismissive approach to Jespersen's deposition testimony is as disappointing as it is confounding. By suggesting that Jespersen's discomfort and refusal to wear foundation, blush, mascara, and lip color is somehow idiosyncratic and unreasonable,[38] the court again perpetuated the feminine/masculine paradigm and constructed reality from a position of male dominance and power. Indeed, the court seemed blind to the possibility that requiring female bartenders to appear stereotypically "feminine" supported the subordination of women to men, particularly if other female bartenders did not share Jespersen's objections to wearing makeup.[39]

THE FEMINIST JUDGMENT AND ITS IMPLICATIONS

Onwuachi-Willig and Sweeny's rewritten *Jespersen* opinion differs from the Ninth Circuit's *en banc* opinion in several meaningful respects. First, and perhaps most notably, the feminist authors reject both of the problematic

---

    334 (1977); *see also Int'l Union, UAW v. Johnson Controls, Inc.*, 499 U.S. 187, 201–03 (1991) (limiting the BFOQ defense to instances in which sex-based differentiation either preserves the central mission of the employer's business or ensures the safe and efficient performance of job duties).

[34] *Jespersen III*, 444 F.3d at 1112.

[35] *Id.*

[36] *Id.* at 1108 (emphasis added).

[37] *Id.* at 1112 (emphasis added).

[38] *See id.* at 1113 ("[T]he touchstone is reasonableness").

[39] *See* Deborah L. Rhode, *The Subtle Side of Sexism*, 16 COLUM. J. GENDER & L. 613, 633 (2007) (discussing the psychological and cultural pressures associated with appearance-related sex discrimination and remarking that "[s]exism often enlists individuals in their own subordination").

frameworks under which the trial court and the three-judge panel previously decided Jespersen's disparate treatment claims: specifically, the mutable/immutable distinction and the equal burdens test. They also reject the notion that sex-specific "social norms" are somehow distinct from sex stereotypes, and they unequivocally condemn both as impermissible justifications for grooming standards that cannot meet the BFOQ test. Finally, they acknowledge the double bind into which Harrah's placed Jespersen, and they afford proper weight to Jespersen's deposition testimony regarding how wearing makeup negatively affected her job performance.

The feminist authors' discussion of the mutable/immutable distinction provides the clarity that the Ninth Circuit promised in its opening line, but ultimately failed to deliver. Whereas the original opinion left unclear whether the trial court properly relied on the mutable/immutable distinction in deciding that makeup and hairstyle requirements did not constitute sexual stereotyping, the feminist authors' rewritten opinion unambiguously denounces the mutable/immutable analytical framework as untenable. By pointing out the socially constructed nature of race and gender, the feminist authors expose the mutable/immutable distinction as not only too vague to be consistently applied, but also harmful to society, because it advances the inaccurate narrative that race and gender are sharply defined, scientific categories, rather than fluid, socially constructed characteristics.

Likewise, the feminist authors' unequal burdens analysis provides clarity that the original opinion lacks – specifically, regarding the respective burdens ascribable to men and women employed by Harrah's and whether Jespersen's personal objection to wearing makeup is relevant to the analysis. Whereas the original opinion is dismissive of the time, money, and psychological costs to Harrah's female employees, the rewritten opinion takes judicial notice of the time and expense associated with wearing makeup, and it fully credits Jespersen's deposition testimony detailing the degradation, objectification, and humiliation that Harrah's policy caused her. Although the feminist judgment ultimately rejects the equal burdens test as problematic because of the false gender binary that it perpetuates, the opinion nevertheless acknowledges that Jespersen's claim should have survived summary judgment under such a test.

With the equal burdens test eliminated, the feminist authors then consider whether the Harrah's sex-differentiated standards are grounded in the BFOQ defense. They make short work of concluding that that they are not – particularly in light of Jespersen's many years of successful bartending with an "unmade face." Finally, the feminist authors address Jespersen's claim under a theory of sex stereotyping and find that her claim clearly survives Harrah's summary judgment motion. Specifically, they point out that there is no practical difference between social norms and sex stereotypes, and they expressly hold that the Supreme Court's decision in *Price Waterhouse* extends to gender-specific dress codes and appearance standards.

Other highlights from the feminist authors' rewritten opinion include their:

- provision of concrete examples demonstrating the shortcomings of the mutable/immutable framework;
- recognition that Harrah's policy places a higher burden on women of color – particularly black women – who face higher prices for makeup and must alter the natural state of their hair to comply with Harrah's styling requirements;
- highlighting of the long-standing precedent that a customer's preference for an employee's appearance is not a BFOQ unless sexual desire is an essential part of the employer's business;
- rejection of the reasoning of older Title VII cases that permitted sex-differentiated grooming standards based on so-called social norms, which are actually oppressive and outdated beauty standards; and
- reframing of *Jespersen*'s sex-stereotyping analysis as a straightforward question of whether a man would have been terminated for refusing to wear makeup.

Ultimately, the feminist authors reverse and remand the decision of the trial court, finding that Harrah's was not entitled to summary judgment on Jespersen's claims.

The implications of the Ninth Circuit's *en banc* decision in *Jespersen* have been far-reaching. Most notably, in 2008, a similar case involving casino workers arose in New Jersey when a group of twenty-one then-current or former cocktail servers of the Borgata Hotel Casino and Spa in Atlantic City (referred to by the company as "Borgata Babes") sued the casino for sex discrimination and harassment, alleging that the female servers were held to strict weight standards and harassed over weight gained as a result of pregnancy or medical conditions. The trial court initially dismissed the plaintiffs' claims in 2013, using a rationale similar to that of the Ninth Circuit in *Jespersen*. In 2015, the New Jersey appellate court affirmed only the trial court's dismissal of the sex discrimination claims. The sexual harassment claims were then remanded to the trial court, only to be dismissed again the following year. In May 2019, the New Jersey appeals court held unequivocally that the remaining five plaintiffs may finally proceed to trial on their sexual harassment claims, causing one editorialist to muse, "Given how much societal awareness of and

Jespersen v. Harrah's Operating Co.

sensitivity to sexual harassment has increased since 2015, Borgata may wish that it had let the lawsuit proceed then."[40]

It is a valid point. In the last few years, the tide of public sentiment has shifted sharply against the objectification and degradation of women. During the 2015 entertainment awards season, actor Reese Witherspoon criticized the pageantry of red-carpet awards, using an Instagram post to point out the sexism that red-carpet reporters display by interviewing male celebrities mostly about their work and female celebrities mostly about their outfits.[41] Using the social media hashtag #AskHerMore, Witherspoon urged journalists to elicit more meaningful dialogue with women about their professional talents, rather than only their appearance. As the entertainment industry became more mindful of respecting women as professionals, other industries followed suit. Shortly on the heels of the #AskHerMore campaign, even the American Bar Association revisited its stance on sexual discrimination, strengthening the language of its Model Rules of Professional Conduct to expressly forbid "demeaning verbal or physical conduct . . . of a sexual nature."[42]

Accompanying this shift in the tide regarding women's objectification and degradation has been a growing rejection of male- and European-centric notions of beauty informing standards of professional dress and grooming. In July 2019, California became the first state to protect its citizens against discrimination based on black natural hairstyles. State Bill 188, known as the CROWN Act (Creating a Respectful and Open Workplace for Natural Hair), was signed into law following several highly publicized incidents involving dreadlocks, braids, twists, cornrows, and other hairstyles.[43] Most memorably, in December 2018, a high school wrestling referee deemed a black varsity student's dreadlocks in violation of an unnamed rule and gave him the choice of either cutting his hair off ringside or forfeiting the match. Footage of a school official haphazardly lopping off the student's dreadlocks soon went viral and was followed by a public outcry against the racial bias shown by the referee. State Senator Holly Mitchell, who authored the bill, told the *Los*

---

[40] *Opinion: Borgata May Wish It Had Let Lawsuit by Some "Babes" Proceed*, THE PRESS OF ATLANTIC CITY (May 24, 2019), www.pressofatlanticcity.com/opinion/editorials/borgata-may-wish-it-had-let-lawsuit-by-some-babes/article_2403649b-f228-5bfb-b20c-d88fc3bea8a7.html.

[41] Charlotte Alter, *Oscars 2015: Reese Witherspoon Asks Media to #AskHerMore on Red Carpet*, TIME (Feb. 23, 2015), https://time.com/3718008/enums.

[42] American Bar Association, MODEL RULES PROF'L CONDUCT R. 8.4, comment 3 (2016). *See also* Elizabeth Olson, *Goodbye to "Honeys" in Court, by Vote of American Bar Association*, N.Y. TIMES (Aug. 9, 2016), www.nytimes.com/2016/08/10/business/dealbook/aba-prohibits-sexual-harassment-joining-many-state-bars.html.

[43] Marco della Cava, *Dreadlocks, Cornrows, and Other Natural Styles Protected under California Law*, USA TODAY (July 3, 2019), www.usatoday.com/story/news/nation/2019/07/03/california-first-state-ban-hair-discrimination-crown-act/1643833001.

128   Jespersen v. Harrah's Operating Co.

Angeles Times that the bill was intended both to "dispel myths about black hair, its texture, and the black hair experience, and to challenge what constitutes 'professionalism' in the workplace."[44] At the time the CROWN Act was signed into law, lawmakers in New York and New Jersey had introduced similar statewide bills, and New York City had already adopted a local anti-discrimination measure to the same effect. However, even ardent supporters of these protective measures are nevertheless dismayed that people should need legal protections for their natural appearance. Tiffany Dena Loftin, youth and college director of the National Association for the Advancement of Colored People, told USA Today, "I'm not going to say we shouldn't have a law that allows us to wear our hair the way it naturally is, but it's also sad that in 2019, we have to have one in the first place."[45]

Fifteen years earlier, Jespersen expressed a nearly identical sentiment in her 2004 op-ed in the *Reno Gazette Journal*: "The men who worked by my side did not conceal their faces. Harrah's considers them professional when they look like themselves."[46] Although progress has come slowly since then, the tide continues to shift toward a redefinition of professionalism in ways that do not strip individuals of their identity or dignity. Still, one has to wonder whether such progress would have come sooner had the Ninth Circuit handed down a judgment in the *Jespersen* case more like the feminist judgment written by Onwuachi-Willig and Sweeny.

Jespersen v. Harrah's Operating Co.,
444 F.3d 1104 (9th Cir. 2006) (en banc)

JUDGES ANGELA ONWUACHI-WILLIG AND JOANNE SWEENY DELIVERED THE OPINION OF THE COURT (ON REHEARING EN BANC).

This case concerns the termination of a female casino employee, Darlene Jespersen, based solely on her refusal to comply with her employer's gendered appearance and grooming policy. The policy required that female employees wear a specific kind and style of makeup and wear their hair down and teased, curled, or styled, while it forbade male employees from wearing any makeup,

---

[44] Phil Willon & Alexa Diaz, *California Becomes First State to Ban Discrimination Based on One's Natural Hair*, L.A. TIMES (July 5, 2019), www.latimes.com/local/lanow/la-pol-ca-natural-hair-discrimination-bill-20190703-story.html.

[45] della Cava, *supra* note 43.

[46] Jespersen, *supra* note 3.

having long hair, and wearing nail polish. Jespersen was discharged for refusing to wear makeup on the job, and she subsequently brought a sex discrimination claim under Title VII of the Civil Rights Act of 1964, alleging that the makeup requirement was discriminatory against women because it (1) imposed a greater burden on female employees than male employees, and (2) forced women to conform to a restrictive gender stereotype as a condition of employment.

The district court granted summary judgment in favor of the employer, reasoning that the makeup policy was reasonable, restricted men and women, and therefore did not violate Title VII. A three-judge panel affirmed the district court's opinion, with the majority holding that Jespersen had failed to show that Harrah's grooming policy affected men and women unequally and that a sex-stereotyping claim could survive only if the grooming standards amounted to sexual harassment. *Jespersen v. Harrah's Operating Co.*, 444 F.3d 1104 (9th Cir. 2004). We disagree with the original panel and reverse the district court's ruling on both the disparate treatment and sex-stereotyping grounds.

I BACKGROUND

Darlene Jespersen began working at Harrah's Casino in Reno, Nevada, in 1979, as a dishwasher. Excerpts of Record (ER) 114. Through hard work and great skill, Jespersen was promoted to a bartender position in 1980 – a position she held for over twenty years. ER 114. As a bartender, Jespersen was a favorite among regulars, who consistently praised her warm demeanor and her bartending abilities. Jespersen's supervisors also had nothing but praise for her exceptional work and made no suggestions on how she could improve her job performance. ER 135–36, 169–98.

Like most of its employees, bartenders at Harrah's are required to wear uniforms. The bartenders' uniform consists of black pants and white shirts, bow ties, and nonskid black shoes. In the 1980s, Harrah's instituted a makeup requirement for its female employees and sent them to a "makeup consultant" in furtherance of that requirement. ER 118–20. Jespersen tried to comply with the requirement and started wearing makeup at work, but she found the experience degrading and humiliating. Jespersen Dep. 137:1–138:10; ER 121. She felt "naked," "exposed," and "degraded" wearing makeup. Jespersen Dep. 137:1–138:10, 138:18–23; ER 121. It also made her feel sexualized and objectified by the men around her. Because of her discomfort, Jespersen felt unable to properly do her job, which requires concentration and a friendly disposition. After two weeks, Jespersen stopped wearing makeup, with no objection from her employer. Jespersen Dep. 139:12–19; ER 121–22. Until the year 2000, when

130 Jespersen v. Harrah's Operating Co.

Harrah's implemented the Beverage Department Image Transformation, or "Personal Best," program, which, among other things, redefined appearance standards, Harrah's never tried to enforce its existing makeup requirement for Jespersen or any other employee. Throughout this entire period, Jespersen was consistently evaluated as meeting or exceeding expectations, and her appearance was always deemed acceptable. ER 121–22. Indeed, in 1985, her supervisor scored her as "highly effective" in all areas, including appearance. ER 129–30. Similarly, in 1988, her supervisor not only indicated that her "attitude [was] very positive & *exceptional*" and that "she [was] an asset to [the] dept," but also asserted that she did not need to improve in any areas. ER 136. Jespersen's work was so good that, in 1996, her supervisor nominated her for a special award because of her "outstanding" job performance. ER 185.

In 2000, Harrah's adopted the "Personal Best" program's appearance standards, which imposed different grooming requirements on men and women. ER 19–20. Specifically, the standards required women to wear their hair "down at all times" and "teased, curled, or styled every day [they worked]," while it prohibited men from wearing their hair below their shirt collars and from donning ponytails.[47] Brand Standard Appearance and Grooming, Exhibit E, ER 79–80. The grooming policy allowed women to wear clear, white, pink, or red color nail polish and nails of "no exotic ... length" and with "no exotic art," while requiring men to have neatly trimmed fingernails and forbidding men from wearing all but clear nail polish. *Id.* Most importantly for this lawsuit, the policy required female employees to wear four types of makeup – foundation or face powder, blush, mascara, and lipstick – while it prohibited male employees from wearing any makeup. *Id.* Women were required to do more than simply wear these four items of makeup on their faces; they had to wear their hair and makeup in the fashion individually proposed for them by an image consultant. The "Personal Best" program required employees to meet with an image consultant, who provided each female employee with a makeover. After their makeover, employees then had two photos taken of them looking their "Personal Best" – one of their faces and one full-body – and female employees were expected to replicate the makeup in that photo each day at work. Brand Standard Appearance and Grooming, ER 80.

---

[47] The appellees' version of the "Personal Best" policy states that women can wear their hair up or down, but that, if up, it must be completely off the neck and face: no ponytails, braids, or wisps of hair may escape. The ends also have to be "finished, curled and/or pinned under." ER 35, 79–80. Women are prohibited from styling their hair in "[p]onytails, multiple ponytails, regular braids, buns, and hair worn half-up/half-down." *Id.* It is unclear how hair can be worn up unless it is in a ponytail, braid, or bun.

The "Personal Best" program has few grooming rules that are identical for men and women. For example, one common grooming rule was that neither men nor women could wear "faddish hairstyles or unnatural colors," although neither "faddish" nor "unnatural" was defined. Brand Standard Appearance and Grooming, Exhibit E, ER 79–80. In addition, both men and women had to wear shoes that were "solid black leather or leather type with rubber (non-skid) soles." *Id.* Finally, both men and women had to wear jewelry, if issued, could not wear large chokers, chains, or bracelets, and had to "maintain their Personal Best image portrayed at the time of hire." *Id.*

Remembering the prior makeup policy and the negative effects it had on her job performance and mental health, Jespersen refused to comply with the "Personal Best" makeup policy and continued performing her duties without makeup. Jespersen Dep. 78:6–12; ER 115. Harrah's ultimately terminated Jespersen solely for her refusal to wear makeup. ER 20, 35–36, 88, 115–17.

Jespersen filed suit in district court under Title VII and related state law claims. The district court ultimately granted summary judgment in favor of Harrah's Casino, and Jespersen appealed to this Court. A three-judge panel affirmed the district court's opinion on December 28, 2004. On May 13, 2005, this Court voted to rehear this case *en banc*.

The issues on appeal are twofold:

(1) whether the district court erred in granting summary judgment in favor of Harrah's on the ground that Harrah's makeup policy does not constitute disparate treatment under Title VII; and

(2) whether the district court erred in granting summary judgment in favor of Harrah's on the ground that Harrah's makeup policy does not violate Title VII under a sex-stereotyping theory.

II STANDARD OF REVIEW

The standard of review in this case is *de novo*, with no deference to the district court's opinion. Because this case comes to us on a motion for summary judgment, if there is a dispute of fact, it must be resolved in favor of the nonmoving party, Jespersen. Fed. R. Civ. Pro. 56(c); *Villiarimo v. Aloha Island Air, Inc.*, 281 F.3d 1054, 1061 (9th Cir. 2002). In addition, as noted by the Supreme Court, "[c]redibility determinations, the weighing of the evidence, and the drawing of legitimate inferences from the facts are jury functions, not those of a judge, whether he is ruling on a motion for summary judgment or for a directed verdict. The evidence of the non-movant is to be believed, and all

132 Jespersen v. Harrah's Operating Co.

justifiable inferences are to be drawn in his favor." *Anderson v. Liberty Lobby, Inc.*, 477 U.S. 242, 255 (1986).

III TITLE VII: DISPARATE TREATMENT

Jespersen argues that Harrah's appearance policy – particularly its makeup requirement (which applies only to women) – discriminates against women because it contains sex-differentiated requirements that impose an unequal burden on women, and it requires women to conform to detrimental sex stereotypes.

Harrah's has advanced two arguments in support of its grooming policy. First, it argues that the sex-differentiated requirements under its policy are not unlawful because they regulate mutable, not immutable, characteristics and are based on accepted social norms, and they are equally burdensome for men and women. Second, Harrah's contends that the sex-stereotyping prohibitions articulated in *Price Waterhouse v. Hopkins*, 490 U.S. 228 (1989), do not apply in cases where a policy imposes equal burdens on men and women. We reject both of these arguments and reverse the district court's grant of summary judgment in favor of Harrah's. More specifically, we disagree with Harrah's argument that its policy does not discriminate against women because its sex-differentiated requirements are rooted in accepted social norms and impose no greater burden on women than on men. This Court also agrees with Jespersen that Harrah's grooming policy constitutes disparate treatment under a sex-stereotyping theory.

A Equal Burdens

Harrah's contends that its grooming policy is not discriminatory because it imposes no greater burden on women than it does on men. Under Title VII, employers generally cannot use a facially discriminatory policy unless doing so satisfies the narrow bona fide occupational qualification (BFOQ) defense. *Int'l Union v. Johnson Controls, Inc.*, 499 U.S. 187, 201 (1991). In grooming code cases, however, this Court has previously held that gender-differentiated dress code policies are generally permissible under Title VII if they are "reasonable" because they affect "mutable characteristics," which can be easily changed by the plaintiff. *See, e.g., Baker v. California Land Title Co.*, 507 F.2d 895, 897–98 (9th Cir. 1974) (upholding a policy whereby an employer regulated hair, which was considered to be a mutable characteristic); *see also Tavora v. N.Y. Mercantile Exch.*, 101 F.3d 907, 908 (2d Cir. 1996) (requiring short hair on men, but not women); *Brown v. D.C. Transit Sys., Inc.*, 523 F.2d

Jespersen v. Harrah's Operating Co. 133

725, 728 (D.C. Cir. 1975) (restricting facial hair for men). Additionally, according to *Baker* and *Frank*, there is no Title VII violation so long as the sex-differentiated "appearance standard . . . imposes different but essentially equal burdens on men and women." *Frank v. United Airlines, Inc.*, 216 F.3d 845, 854 (9th Cir. 2000) (holding a policy unlawful because it imposed unequal burdens with respect to weight requirements for men and women); *see also Baker*, 507 F.2d at 896–98.

To determine whether Harrah's grooming policy discriminates against women, as well as the propriety of the arguments made by Harrah's in defense of its policy, we deem it necessary to reconsider our decisions in *Baker* and *Frank*. In *Baker*, we held that Title VII's provisions prohibiting discrimination on the basis of race, sex, color, and national origin apply only to conduct related to immutable characteristics and not to "personal modes of dress or cosmetic effects," such as how one dresses or wears her hair. *Baker*, 507 F.2d at 897. In *Frank*, we held that appearance standards that impose "different but essentially equal burdens on men and women" do not constitute disparate treatment and thus do not have to be justified by a BFOQ. *Frank*, 216 F.3d at 854–55.

Today, we reject both of these rules. Instead, we hold that the application of Title VII in grooming code cases does not turn on the mutability/immutability distinction. We also hold that:

(1) the application of Title VII in grooming code cases does not turn on the mutability/immutability distinction; and
(2) the equal burdens test is no longer valid because it reinforces a gender binary, and it unnecessarily and impermissibly excludes and discriminates against gender-nonconforming individuals and any other individuals who do not fit what society has traditionally deemed the normative ideal of femininity and masculinity.

1 Rejecting the Mutability/Immutability Distinction

Contrary to what *Baker* held, Title VII prohibits discrimination on the basis of race, sex, color, and national origin whether or not the characteristic in question is deemed "mutable" or "immutable." Making distinctions on the applicability of Title VII based on mutability or immutability is harmful because it relies on the inaccurate notion that characteristics such as race and gender are static categories determined only by fixed physical characteristics, and it fails to acknowledge the more fluid nature of race and gender, both of which are social constructs. *See* Maxine Baca Zinn & Bonnie Thornton Dill, *Theorizing*

Difference from Multiracial Feminism, 22 FEMINIST STUDS. 321, 321, 324 (1996); see generally Leslie Espinoza & Angela P. Harris, Embracing the Tar-Baby: LatCrit Theory and the Sticky Mess of Race, 10 LA RAZA L.J. 499 (1997). The socially constructed nature of race, gender, and other characteristics makes it impossible to develop a coherent framework for employers, employees, and courts to use in determining whether a characteristic is mutable or immutable. For instance, is the tightly coiled hair that most black people have a mutable or immutable characteristic? Technically, the texture and structure of the curls in a black person's naturally grown Afro could be changed with extreme heat through the use of a hot comb or relaxers made out of a dangerous and burning chemical called lye, but that does not mean that such hair is a mutable characteristic. See Tracey Owens Patton, Hey Girl, Am I More Than My Hair? African American Women and Their Struggles with Beauty, Body Image, and Hair, 18 NWSA J. 24, 29 (2006) (discussing how black women have used hot combs and relaxers to straighten their hair); Maude Johnson, Caring for African American Hair, 34 VIEW 169, 169 (2003) (noting that "[e]ven the best relaxers are chemically based"); cf. Paulette M. Caldwell, A Hair Piece: Perspectives on the Intersection of Race and Gender, 1991 DUKE L.J. 365, 365, 369. Thus not only do we reject the idea that race and gender are static characteristics, untouched and unshaped by social, historical, and other factors, but we also reject the immutable/mutable distinction upon which it rests and the idea that characteristics such as hair can neatly fall into either category.

Additionally, the mutable/immutable distinction is problematic because it minimizes the psychological impact these discriminatory policies can have by telling a plaintiff to simply conform because she physically can do so. The more appropriate question to be asked and answered in grooming code discrimination cases is not whether an employee can change the characteristic(s) or identity factor(s) in question, but instead whether the employee should be required to do so. The fact that something can easily be changed has no relationship to its importance to an individual's identity and self-esteem, as Jespersen herself proves. Although it is true that many women wear makeup and often derive pleasure and self-esteem from doing so, Jespersen did not. In fact, wearing makeup made her feel "naked" and objectified. Choosing to wear makeup was therefore not a real choice for Jespersen at all.[48] Even though Jespersen technically could have chosen to

---

[48] It is true that Ms. Jespersen cannot present evidence that wearing makeup led to her being harassed on the job because she never complied with the "Personal Best" policy. However, Title VII does not require that a woman follow a policy she believes will lead to her objectification just to prove to her employer (or a court) that the policy constitutes sex-based discrimination. That is not her burden to carry.

comply with the "Personal Best" program, doing so would have sublimated her own identity and self-esteem; as important, it would have hurt her job performance, which, prior to the enforcement of the makeup requirement, had always been above average to outstanding. Title VII does not require her to make such a (false) choice.[49] Accordingly, we now hold that the mutability of the characteristics governed by the "Personal Best" program – here, Jespersen's own face and how she presented herself to the world – is not a relevant consideration under Title VII.

Moreover, as the facts in *Frank* reveal, the "mutable/immutable" distinction is hardly a clear one. Indeed, courts have failed to consistently apply it from case to case. For example, in *Frank*, we struck down gendered weight restrictions for flight attendants, even though weight is technically changeable. *Frank*, 216 F.3d at 855. Similarly, the Seventh Circuit found a dress code in violation of Title VII in another case because, combined with the defendant's openly stated discriminatory intent, the policy required women to wear a uniform, but allowed men to simply wear their own business attire. *Carroll v. Talman Fed. Sav. & Loan Ass'n of Chicago*, 604 F.2d 1028, 1032–33 (7th Cir. 1979). The clothes one wears, however, are clearly changeable. Such inconsistent applications demonstrate precisely why the mutability/immutability distinction is untenable.

Indeed, one need only look at the facts of this case to recognize how nonsensical the mutable/immutable distinction is and to see that it does not align well with the intent of Title VII. In this case, Jespersen, a female bartender, was fired for behavior that her male colleagues also engaged in: not wearing makeup. Yet only she, the female bartender, lost her job. Although it is true that Jespersen could have changed her appearance, including her hair, makeup, and clothes, requiring her to do so based on her gender flies in the face of Title VII's purpose, which is to proscribe all policies that treat employees differently on the basis of sex without proving that the

---

[49] Jespersen's other purported "choice" – to apply for another position that did not require her to comply with the "Personal Best" policy – is another false choice. This Court notes that Harrah's did not indicate which jobs Jespersen could apply for, and we therefore have no way of knowing if they were of similar pay or stature. The fact that they were hidden from public eye (thus not requiring compliance with the "Personal Best" policy) suggests that they were not as desirable in part because they were likely not tipped positions. Second, even if some of the posted positions were as prestigious or desirable as a bartending job, Jespersen should not have been required to quit a job she loved and was very good at, something that provided her with self-esteem and meaning, to conform to Harrah's makeup policy. Quitting her bartending job and taking another was not a real choice for Jespersen, and Harrah's is being disingenuous to suggest that it was. The only way of upholding the makeup policy for women is for Harrah's to prove that wearing makeup is a bona fide occupational qualification (BFOQ) for women to do the job of bartender. Obviously, as we will discuss, Harrah's is unable to carry this burden.

136   Jespersen v. Harrah's Operating Co.

requirement is reasonably necessary to the performance of the job. Essentially, declaring appearance requirements "mutable" and therefore beyond Title VII's purview entirely misses the point.

2 Rejecting the Gender Binary in the Equal Burdens Test

In addition to rejecting the mutability/immutability distinction, we also reject the equal burdens test. The test unnecessarily and impermissibly excludes and discriminates against gender-nonconforming individuals by reinforcing the gender binary of male and female. It also discriminates against any and all individuals who do not fall within what society has traditionally deemed the normative ideal of femininity and masculinity. For this reason, we hold that sex-differentiated grooming codes violate Title VII unless the employer can establish the BFOQ affirmative defense.

a WHY THE GENDER BINARY IS HARMFUL AND DISCRIMINATORY.   We find the equal burdens test to be particularly problematic because it rests on the fiction that there are only two sexes: men and women. *See* Laura Hermer, *Paradigms Revised: Intersex Children, Bioethics & the Law*, 11 ANNALS HEALTH L. 195, 195 (2002). The gender binary therefore erases the presence of currently gender-nonconforming individuals, particularly those whose body parts do not correspond with widely held societal beliefs about how someone with such body parts should behave and feel. Sara R. Benson, *Hacking the Gender Binary Myth: Recognizing Fundamental Rights for the Intersexed*, 12 CARDOZO J.L. & GENDER 31, 58 (2005) (arguing for a fundamental right to gender identity). Even worse, it also marks such individuals as deviant. The equal burdens test also raises the question of how one could even determine which sex-specific requirements apply to gender-nonconforming individuals. The lack of any meaningful and reliable answer to this question will almost certainly result in the diminution of and discrimination against gender-nonconforming employees such as transgender employees.

Equally problematic, the test permits employers to enforce sex-based expectations and stereotypes in the workplace – even if they have no relation to job performance – simply because they conform to widely held views about gender performance in society. The Supreme Court denounced employer decisions that are grounded in an expectation of conformity with gendered expectations of femininity and masculinity that have nothing to do with job performance in *Price Waterhouse*. In that case, the Court determined that a female plaintiff had shown proof of an accounting firm's impermissible and improper use of gender stereotypes in denying her partnership in the firm.

Several partners involved in the ultimate decision-making described the female plaintiff – also the associate who brought in the most money for the firm – as a woman who needed "a course at charm school." And her mentor, "the partner responsible for informing[her] of the factors which caused her candidacy to be placed on hold, indicated that her 'professional' problems would be solved if she would 'walk more femininely, talk more femininely, wear make-up, have her hair styled, and wear jewelry.' " *Price Waterhouse*, 490 U.S. at 256 (1989) (plurality opinion).

Much like *Price Waterhouse*, this case presents a clear example of the potentially harmful impact of allowing gendered expectations in the workplace that have no connection to job performance. Here, Jespersen, a woman who did not conform to the gendered expectation that women wear makeup to look pretty and presentable, lost her job, which she had consistently performed well for more than twenty years, solely because she did not meet that expectation. More so, Jespersen's inability to conform to her employer's expectations limited her employment options at Harrah's because the makeup requirement applied to all jobs in the public areas of the casino. These positions potentially enable employees to earn more money because customers tip these employees.

As the *amici* brief details, Jespersen's experience was not unique. Other individuals who do not conform to gender norms suffer regularly. Studies have consistently shown, for example, "that transgender people frequently experience negative employment consequences because they have ... characteristics that differ from stereotypical expectations about how men and women should behave and appear." And the San Francisco Human Rights Commission found "that 'the economic hardship imposed on some transgender ... persons due to discrimination in employment and in medical and insurance services frequently forces them to live in poverty or to turn to sex work to survive.' " Brief of The National Center for Lesbian Rights and the Transgender Law Center as *Amici Curiae* in Support of Plaintiff-Appellant, *Jespersen v. Harrah's Operating Co., Inc.*, 2005 WL 1501598, at *5 (June 8, 2005). Furthermore, a study conducted by both the Transgender Law Center and the National Center of Lesbian Rights found that 67 percent of the transgender population in its survey identified "employment discrimination as the issue that concerned them most." *Id.*

b HARRAH'S DOES NOT SATISFY THE BONA FIDE OCCUPATIONAL QUALIFICATION (BFOQ) TEST. Without the equal burdens test to rely on, Harrah's must show that its sex-differentiated standards are rooted in a BFOQ, which Harrah's cannot do. The BFOQ defense is intended to be extremely

138   Jespersen v. Harrah's Operating Co.

narrow. *Dothard v. Rawlinson*, 433 U.S. 321, 334 (1977). *International Union v. Johnson Controls, Inc.* holds that sex-differentiated qualifications satisfy the BFOQ defense only if they relate to the "essence," or the "central mission," of the employer's business purpose and are necessary for performing the employee's job tasks and responsibilities. *Johnson Controls*, 499 U.S. at 201. Moreover, the employer has the burden of proving that, absent the policy requirements, it "had reasonable cause to believe . . . that all or substantially all women would be unable to perform safely and efficiently the duties of the job involved" or that the policy is "generally reasonable" because "it is impossible or highly impractical to deal with women on an individualized basis." *Harriss v. Pan Am. World Airways, Inc.*, 649 F.2d 670, 676 (9th Cir. 1980) (internal quotation marks and citations omitted). Although protecting a company's image may, under some circumstances, satisfy the BFOQ requirement, customer preference for an employee's appearance will generally not fulfill a grooming policy's BFOQ requirement unless sexual desire is an essential part of the employer's business. *Fagan v. National Cash Register Co.*, 481 F.2d 1115, 1124–25 (D.C. Cir. 1973); *Fernandez v. Wynn Oil Co.*, 653 F.2d 1273, 1276–77 (9th Cir. 1981) (citing *Diaz v. Pan Am World Airways, Inc.*, 442 F.2d 385, 389 (5th Cir. 1971)); *see also* Katharine T. Bartlett, *Only Girls Wear Barrettes: Dress and Appearance Standards, Community Norms, and Workplace Equality*, 92 MICH. L. REV. 2541, 2573 (1994).

Here, Harrah's has argued that its "Personal Best" policy is intended to project a good image to customers. However, Harrah's has failed to show why requiring its bartenders to wear makeup affects its image at all. The highly specific policy does more than require its employees to be well-kempt;[50] rather, female employees at Harrah's who are subject to the "Personal Best" policy must wear makeup that corresponds to the specific look a makeup expert chose for them. Moreover, it is unclear why, after twenty years, Harrah's suddenly required Jespersen (and other female bartenders) to do more than have a neat appearance – particularly when Jespersen was a customer favorite despite her "unmade" face. Jespersen herself, then, is the epitome of why the Harrah's makeup policy does not satisfy the BFOQ requirement.[51] Moreover, Harrah's action in not enforcing its own makeup requirement for several years reveals that even Harrah's knew that wearing

---

[50] Indeed, being "well-kempt" seems to apply only to male employees, while female employees are held to stricter standards for their facial appearance.

[51] Harrah's has also failed to show that its policy was "generally reasonable" because it could not deal with its female employees on an individualized basis. Not only has Harrah's not provided any evidence in support of such an argument, but also its existing grooming policy was highly individualized for its female employees already: each female employee was given an individual signature "look."

makeup did not go to the essence of the bartender job and was not necessary to performing tasks and responsibilities of a bartender. For these reasons, we hold that Harrah's has failed to satisfy the BFOQ requirement under the Title VII's disparate treatment analysis.

3 Harrah's Could Not Satisfy the Equal Burdens Test Even If It Did Apply

Even if we were to apply the equal burdens test to the facts of this case, we would still reverse the district court's grant of summary judgment in favor of Harrah's because Harrah's grooming policy places a far greater burden on women than on men. Harrah's has repeatedly argued that the "Personal Best" policy does not violate Title VII because it also burdens men. Below, the district court accepted Harrah's argument and refused to acknowledge that forcing women to wear makeup results in costs in terms of money and time that men do not have to incur. On appeal, Harrah's has argued that Jespersen provided no evidence that wearing makeup costs both time and money. In response, Jespersen has requested that we take judicial notice of these facts.

This Court has long held that judicial notice may be "taken of all matters generally known." *Greeson v. Imperial Irr. Dist.*, 59 F.2d 529, 531 (9th Cir. 1932) (citing *Muller v. Oregon*, 208 U.S. 412 (1908)); *see also United States v. Ritchie*, 342 F.3d 903, 908–09 (9th Cir. 2003) (asserting that courts may take judicial notice of only "adjudicative facts that are not subject to reasonable dispute" and that "[f]acts are indisputable, and thus subject to judicial notice, only if they are either generally known ... or capable of accurate and ready determination by resort to sources whose accuracy cannot be reasonably questioned" (internal quotation marks and citation omitted)). As this Court has explained, "[g]enerally known matters" include geography, population statistics, and "public activities within the common experience of [people] within the jurisdiction, and more especially of public conferences and meetings of members of a community of common interest and wide concern of which the court ought to have known." *Greeson*, 59 F.2d at 531.

We can think of no more obvious fact than that the purchase of cosmetics costs money and that the application of cosmetics takes time. Indeed, this Court has repeatedly taken judicial notice of much more complex economic realities. *See, e.g., Miller v. Fed. Land Bank of Spokane*, 587 F.2d 415, 422 (9th Cir. 1978) (taking judicial notice that application of settlement to mortgage debt would have reduced the interest to be paid because it "is a matter of mathematics"); *Whitman v. Walt Disney Productions, Inc.*, 263 F.2d 229, 230–31 (9th Cir. 1958) (taking judicial notice that "that there are such things

140 Jespersen v. Harrah's Operating Co.

as airplanes and automobiles and motion pictures, and that in their total cost such things represent millions of dollars in value").

Other circuits have done the same. *See, e.g., Adarand Constructors, Inc. v. Slater*, 228 F.3d 1147, 1170 (10th Cir. 2000) (taking judicial notice "of the obvious causal connection between access to capital and ability to implement public works construction projects"); *ADR Tr. Corp. v. Carr*, 13 F.3d 425, 430 (1st Cir. 1993) (taking judicial notice of the fact that commercial real estate commands a lower price when sold at auction during a recession); *Feldman v. Allegheny Airlines, Inc.*, 524 F.2d 384, 390 (2d Cir. 1975) (taking judicial "notice of the facts of life, including the cost of living for those in ... metropolitan areas as Washington, D.C."); *United States v. Ricciardi*, 357 F.2d 91, 97 (2d Cir. 1966) (taking judicial notice of "the obvious and indisputable" fact that "the amount of fuel used in 5,500 apartment buildings is substantial, and has a substantial dollar value").

We are capable of confidently asserting that buying things such as makeup costs money. We do not know how much it would actually cost Jespersen to comply with the specific "Personal Best" look set out for her, but we do know that the makeup was not given to her and that therefore she would have had to spend some amount of money to purchase it. Moreover, we know that the amount of makeup that female employees at Harrah's were expected to apply every day was generally more extensive than the amount of makeup that the average makeup-wearing woman would have to apply, because a Harrah's female employee was expected to wear her "Personal Best" face, which included a minimum of foundation, blush, mascara, and lipstick. Men, meanwhile, would incur no costs in makeup.

In addition to noting that buying things costs money, courts can take judicial notice of the fact that completing a common task takes time. *Cf. Bridgeman v. Ford, Bacon & Davis*, 161 F.2d 962, 965 (8th Cir. 1947) (taking judicial notice of the time it takes to make beds and do other domestic chores). Accordingly, we take judicial notice of the fact that applying makeup takes more time than not doing so. Jespersen was required not only to apply makeup every day she went to work, but also to ensure that it included foundation, blush, mascara, and lipstick, and that the makeup was always visible – particularly her lipstick. Under the "Personal Best" policy, Jespersen would therefore have to repeatedly take time out of her day to ensure that she complied with the policy. Again, this Court does not know exactly how much time these activities would take for Jespersen. However, there were four types of makeup required (foundation, blush, mascara, and lipstick), and Jespersen was required to "match" her "Personal Best" photo, which had been created by a makeup expert. If the average woman spends 5–10 minutes applying her makeup, putting on one's "Personal Best" face would require at least twice as much time, as compared to zero minutes of time spent by men when putting on makeup. These requirements lead this Court to believe that Jespersen would have spent a considerable amount of time in putting on her makeup. Certainly, no matter her skill level or speed, Jespersen would necessarily have had to spend more time putting on makeup than her male counterparts, who did not wear makeup at all.

Finally, because the district court could have taken judicial notice of the fact that purchasing makeup costs money and applying it takes time, this Court can also take judicial notice of these obvious facts. *Nev-Cal Elec. Securities Co. v. Imperial Irr. Dist.*, 85 F.2d 886, 905 (9th Cir. 1936) (internal quotation marks and citation omitted) ("An appellate court can properly take judicial notice of any matter of which the court of original jurisdiction may properly take notice"). We choose to do so rather than to require the plaintiff to produce evidence of something so commonly known. Indeed, it is unclear what evidence she could have produced, particularly since she did not comply with the makeup policy at issue here; she could not have obtained any receipts for makeup she did not purchase.

We also note that, in addition to time and money spent, Jespersen would have suffered psychological costs if she had complied with the "Personal Best" policy and worn makeup. As noted in the Brief of the National Center for Lesbian Rights and the Transgender Law Center, Ms. Jespersen's very identity was impacted by the policy because it attempted to alter the amount of (traditional) femininity she presented to the world. Brief of the National Center for Lesbian Rights and the Transgender Law Center as *Amici Curiae* in Support of Plaintiff-Appellant, 2005 WL 1501598. The psychological effects of wearing makeup were not trivial to Ms. Jespersen; she testified in her deposition that wearing makeup made her feel awkward and unable to perform her job effectively. ER 121.

Moreover, Jespersen also testified that wearing makeup made her feel objectified, and she feared it would make her vulnerable to sexual harassment from her customers and coworkers. Her fears are well-founded. Bars – and particularly bars in casinos – carry dangers for the women who work there. Intoxicated men are more likely to harass women, verbally or physically, especially in a traditionally male-dominated setting like a casino. *See* Ted Gregory, *Sexual Harassment Suits Put Casinos in Spotlight*, CHI. TRIB., 1998 WLNR 6513326 (Aug. 8, 1998). Moreover, casinos typically have their employees play into gender stereotypes, which has been correlated with increased sexual harassment. *See* Tamara Penix Sbraga & William O'Donohue, *Sexual Harassment*, 11 ANNUAL REV. OF SEX RESEARCH 258, 265–66 (2000).

142   Jespersen v. Harrah's Operating Co.

Harrah's argument that the "Personal Best" program overall also negatively impacts men's grooming choices is, first, not relevant to our analysis and, second, actually harmful to Harrah's case. Under Title VII, this Court's sole focus is whether Jespersen was discriminated against because of her sex, which places the focus squarely on Jespersen, how she was treated by her employer, and why. For that reason, as noted by the Second Circuit, "the ultimate issue is the reasons for *the individual plaintiff's* treatment, not the relative treatment of different *groups* within the workplace. As a result, discrimination against one employee cannot be cured, or disproven, solely by favorable, or equitable, treatment of other employees of the same race or sex." *Brown v. Henderson*, 257 F.3d 246, 252 (2d Cir. 2001) (citations omitted and emphasis original) (cited by *Back v. Hastings on Hudson Union Free Sch. Dist.*, 365 F.3d 107, 121–22 (2d Cir. 2004)). Harrah's cannot overcome its treatment of Jespersen by trying to pull focus from her plight, and whether Harrah's hair policy (or any other policy) negatively affected its male employees is a question that will have to wait for another day and a different lawsuit.[52] The sole question for this Court is whether Jespersen would have kept her job if she were a man who refused to wear makeup. The answer, quite clearly, is "yes."

Additionally, although the issue was not specifically raised by Jespersen, Harrah's hair policy is also sex-differentiated and problematic under Title VII. Harrah's and the district court emphasized that male employees were disadvantaged by having to keep their hair short. However, both courts failed to note that although female employees have a choice when it comes to the length of their hair, they were highly restricted in terms of its style. Under the "Personal Best" program, women are required to tease, curl, or style their hair every day. Unlike the men, who had to expend resources only to get their hair cut on a regular basis, women not only had to pay money to get their hair cut, but also had to spend money on the products needed to tease, curl, or style their hair every day, or to have someone else do so for them on a consistent basis. Their male counterparts did not have to incur any such expense. Again, styling products cost money and premium salon services can cost $100–300 per visit. Susan Carpenter, *Real People, High-End Hair; Phenomenal Style Doesn't Have to Break Your Bank, But It Might Test Your Nerves*, L.A. TIMES 32 (Feb. 17, 2005).

For women of color – particularly black women – the costs of complying with Harrah's grooming policy are likely to be even greater because makeup that matches the skin tones of black women is available in far fewer stores than

---

[52] Indeed, if Harrah's entire argument is that its grooming policy was "reasonable," evidence that all employees were negatively affected seems to undermine the entire policy's reasonableness. A negative impact on all employees does not bespeak reasonableness to this Court.

the makeup that matches white women's skin tones. This scarcity usually results in higher prices (given supply and demand) and in higher costs to drive or otherwise travel to the venues. The same applies to hair salons, many of which do not have stylists who can treat and style the tightly coiled hair that most black women wear. Moreover, some of these salons engage in race-based pricing against black women in providing styling services. *See* Lori S. Robinson, *The Politics of Hair*, THE CRISIS 9 (2006) (discussing a lawsuit brought by seven black women against Dillard's department store's beauty salon for charging black women more money for the same listed services, e.g., 50 percent more than white women for a wash-and-set, and noting that even as Dillard's denied "charging African Americans more than Whites as a matter of policy, the company has presented evidence that doing Black hair is more difficult and time-consuming"). More so, the requirement that certain employees wear their hair teased, curled, or styled *and* down at all times essentially mandates that black women with tightly coiled hair (as most black women have) straighten their hair, either through a chemical process or use of a hot comb. Because black women's hair tends to grow out of their heads as tightly coiled, curly hair, if it is to hang down and be teased, styled, or curled, it must be pressed with a hot comb, which can burn a woman's scalp, or relaxed, which also can cause chemical burns to a woman's scalp. Telling a woman to style her hair in a manner that would force her to change the texture and structure of her hair as it grows out of her head is both demeaning and discriminatory. Compliance with Harrah's hair policy would also be more costly for black women, resulting in another discriminatory effect for them as compared to white men and men of color. For instance, in 2003, one researcher found that black women who relaxed or permed their hair spent an average of $800 per year on such treatments as compared to black women who wore their hair in natural styles like Afros, braids, locs, or twists, who spent on average $300 a year. *See* Sybil Dione Rosado, *No Nubian Knots or Nappy Locks: Discussing the Politics of Hair among Women of African Descent in the Diaspora – A Report on Research in Progress*, 11 TRANSFORMING ANTHROPOLOGY 60, 61 (2003). In essence, Harrah's policy, with its requirement that all female employees wear their hair teased, curled, or styled and down at all times, not only imposes an unequal burden of time and costs on all women, but also specifically discriminates against black women. The only way in which it would not be discriminatory is if the "Personal Best" policy were to permit black women to wear their hair in locs, braids, or twists, which the policy does not allow.

Moreover, being forced to style one's hair in a manner that one does not like can cause feelings of low self-esteem, just as Harrah's makeup policy did for

144 Jespersen v. Harrah's Operating Co.

Jespersen. As noted by one legal scholar, "Hair is a big deal," and having "bad hair" has been shown to increase pessimistic thinking, social insecurity, and self-consciousness. Michelle L. Turner, *The Braided Uproar: A Defense of My Sister's Hair and A Contemporary Indictment of* Rogers v. American Airlines, 7 CARDOZO WOMEN'S L.J. 115, 116 (2001). Accordingly, even if this Court were to apply the equal burdens test, Harrah's "Personal Best" policy would still constitute discrimination under Title VII.

B Title VII: Sex Stereotyping

Alternatively, Jespersen's Title VII case should have survived summary judgment based on her sex-stereotyping argument. Sex stereotyping was first articulated by the Supreme Court in *Price Waterhouse*. In that case, a female senior manager was denied partnership at least in part because she did not conform to her male superiors' opinions of how a woman should act and look. *Price Waterhouse*, 490 U.S. at 235. Prior to *Price Waterhouse*, courts were willing to accept "reasonable" sex-differentiated dress codes if they were justified by "commonly accepted social norms." *Carroll*, 604 F.2d at 1032. However, post *Price Waterhouse*, "social norms" should no longer be allowed as a reasonable justification for treating people differently. More specifically, the Sixth Circuit has succinctly stated how *Price Waterhouse* should apply to a makeup requirement: "After *Price Waterhouse*, an employer who discriminates against women because, for instance, they do not wear dresses or makeup, is engaging in sex discrimination because the discrimination would not occur but for the victim's sex." *Smith v. City of Salem, Ohio*, 378 F.3d 566, 574 (6th Cir. 2004) (allowing a sex-stereotyping claim by a transgender woman who was discriminated against and harassed for feminine gender expression at work).

In *Nichols v. Azteca Rest. Enters., Inc.*, this Court recently expanded on *Price Waterhouse* by finding that sex stereotyping can apply to men who do not act in a stereotypically masculine way. 256 F.3d 864, 874–75 (9th Cir. 2001). *Nichols* is an important case for our analysis because, as the district court here noted, *Nichols* explicitly refused to extend sexual stereotyping to dress codes. That is understandable: *Nichols* was not dealing with a dress code and, in dicta, chose to leave that issue for another day. *Id.* at 875 n.7. That day is today.

Relying on older Title VII cases, Harrah's argues that "social norms" are an appropriate reason to have different standards for different genders and that its makeup policy merely reflects those social norms. Women wear makeup, Harrah's asserts, and men do not, so memorializing those norms in an

Jespersen herself provides another perfect example of why "social norms" are an inappropriate justification for treating genders differently. Jespersen was an excellent employee who did not conform to the sexual stereotype that women should wear makeup. Under the "Personal Best" makeup policy, Jespersen was placed in a double bind: Conform to the beauty standards, lose her confidence, and perform poorly (likely leading to her termination); or refuse, continue to do her job well, and be terminated. Jespersen, like Hopkins in *Price Waterhouse*, did her job well in part because she refused to conform to sexual stereotypes. As the Supreme Court made clear in *Price Waterhouse*, Title VII is intended to lift women out of such binds, enabling them to be their authentic selves and to use the very traits that have allowed them to be successful at work, whether or not they are gender-conforming. Here, Jespersen should not be penalized for failing to conform to an oppressive, outdated beauty standard – one that hindered her actual job performance.

employment policy does not violate Title VII.[53] We find that Harrah's "social norms" are merely "sex stereotyping" in disguise. The whole concept of sex stereotyping is punishing a woman (or a man) for failing to conform to what her employer thinks that women (or men) "should" be like. What else is that but relying on the absurd notion that society – and, specifically, employers – can define and place individuals into the narrow, binary categories of man or woman and then dictate whether that individual is acting in what the employers deem to be a sufficiently feminine or masculine manner?

That no court has explicitly dealt with makeup policies under Title VII is of no import to this Court. There is a first time for everything. As we have evolved in our understanding of the insidious ways that sexism can hinder the advancement and well-being of women in the workplace, courts have created new ways of getting at the root of the pernicious problem of sexism in the workplace. *Price Waterhouse* is an excellent example of this evolution: the recognition of sex stereotyping was essential to properly responding to the disparate treatment suffered by the plaintiff in that case. We choose today to rely on *Price Waterhouse* in taking the next logical step: to denounce and reject sex stereotyping in gender-specific dress codes and appearance standards. Accordingly, we find that Harrah's makeup policy violates Title VII's prohibition on making adverse employment decisions against an employee because the employee

---

[53] The district court agreed with Harrah's that its makeup policy follows social norms. However, the district court also found that many men wear makeup in today's society, and many women do not, which throws the social norms argument into question and further underscores how inappropriate a "social norms" justification is in the modern world. *Jespersen v. Harrah's Operating Co.*, 280 F.Supp.2d 1189, 1193 (D. Nev. 2002).

146 EEOC v. Catastrophe Management Solutions

fails to comply with gender stereotypes associated with and expected from her self-identified or assumed group.

Jespersen was a model employee who did her job well. Throughout this case, the onus should have been on Harrah's to justify why it did not engage in sex discrimination by terminating Jespersen's employment simply because she refused to wear makeup. When the focus is returned to where it belongs – Jespersen and her treatment by Harrah's – Harrah's dogmatic adherence to its makeup requirements can be seen only for what it truly is: gender discrimination in the guise of a larger personal appearance policy. Jespersen's humiliation and mistreatment by her employer are unjustifiable and a clear violation of Title VII.

* * *

The decision of the district court is accordingly reversed and remanded.

It is so ordered.

Commentary on *Equal Employment Opportunity Commission v. Catastrophe Management Solutions*

JASBIR (JESSE) KAUR BAWA

INTRODUCTION

Beauty ideals are subjective notions that are based on learned stereotypes established by the white majority in the United States. But if you grow up as a girl of color in America, you can never meet the subjective stereotype of beauty. A young girl cannot completely control the color of her skin, the amount of hair on her face or body, her body size, or the texture of her hair. However, those are traits that potentially subject her to ridicule or bullying since they are often perceived as ugly when they do not fit into the norms as defined by the white majority. Ideals concerning professional appearance work much in the same way. "Professional" appearance for women is a subjective stereotype and is heavily influenced by notions of femininity and beauty derived from the white majority in America. As *EEOC v. Catastrophe Management Solutions*[54] demonstrates, these notions disadvantage many women of color in finding and

---

[54] *EEOC v. Catastrophe Mgmt. Sols.*, 11 F.Supp.3d 1139, 1140 (S.D. Ala. 2014), *aff'd sub nom. Equal Employment Opportunity Comm'n v. Catastrophe Mgmt. Sols.*, 837 F.3d 1156 (11th Cir. 2016), *opinion withdrawn and superseded*, 852 F.3d 1018 (11th Cir. 2016), and *aff'd sub nom. Equal Employment Opportunity Comm'n v. Catastrophe Mgmt. Sols.*, 852 F.3d 1018 (11th Cir. 2016).

retaining employment, since their appearances do not fit into long-held beliefs of what is professional and/or beautiful.

In any Title VII case involving a plaintiff who is a woman of color, it is critically important to appreciate the experiences of being both a woman and of color. Cases are sorely lacking in an analysis of the intersectionality of being both Black and female. Chastity Jones, an African American woman, applied for a job with Catastrophe Management Solutions (CMS).[55] The company's grooming policy stated that "hairstyle should reflect a business/professional image. No excessive hairstyles or unusual colors are acceptable ..."[56] Jones was interviewed, offered a position, and had the offer rescinded when she refused to cut her locs[57] in order to obtain this job with CMS.[58] What does it feel like for a Black woman to have her hair judged and declared ugly at every age and stage of her life in a myriad of settings, including when she tries to find a job? Professor D. Wendy Greene, writing as Justice Greene, provides an in-depth analysis of the experience of being both Black and female and judged on the basis of hair in and out of professional settings.

THE ORIGINAL OPINION

The district court granted the defendant's motion to dismiss, holding that the complaint failed to state a claim for which relief can be granted – namely, that the facts alleged in the complaint did not support a plausible claim of intentional discrimination on the basis of race because "dreadlocks" is a hairstyle, and "Title VII does not protect against discrimination based on traits, even a trait that has sociocultural racial significance."[59]

The district court decided that grooming practices are not protected by Title VII based upon precedent that forms the basis of the immutability doctrine.[60] This precedent is also critical for the Eleventh Circuit opinion as well.

A 1975 Fifth Circuit Court of Appeals decision, *Willingham v. Macon Telephone Publishing Co.*,[61] formed the roots of the immutability doctrine. In that case, a qualified male copy layout artist was refused employment because of his shoulder-length hair. The court held that the employer did not engage in unlawful sex discrimination because:

---

[55] *Id.*

[56] *Id.*

[57] This commentary will refer to dreadlocks as "locs" so as to be consistent with Justice Greene's opinion and not perpetuate any negative connotation associated with the word "dreadlocks."

[58] *Catastrophe Mgmt.*, 11 F.Supp.3d at 1140.

[59] *Id.* at 1144.

[60] *Id.*

[61] 507 F.2d 1084, 1091 (5th Cir. 1975).

Equal employment opportunity may be secured only when employers are barred from discriminating against employees on the basis of immutable characteristics, such as race and national origin ... But a hiring policy that distinguishes on some other ground, such as grooming codes or length of hair, *is related more closely to the employer's choice of how to run his business than to equality of employment opportunity* ... If the employee objects to the grooming code he has the right to reject it by looking elsewhere for employment, or alternatively he may *choose to subordinate his preference* by accepting the code along with the job.[62]

Immutability was also the basis of a 1981 decision in *Rogers v. American Airlines, Inc.*[63] by the Southern District of New York, which the district court in *Catastrophe Management* relied upon. In *Rogers*, the court held that when American Airlines prohibited the cornrow braids of a Black female customer service employee, it did not violate Title VII because braids are not an "immutable characteristic." The plaintiff argued that cornrows have a special significance for Black women reflective of the cultural, historical essence of the Black woman in American society: "There can be little doubt that, if American adopted a policy which foreclosed Black women/all women from wearing hair styled as an 'Afro/bush,' that policy would have very pointedly racial dynamics ..."[64] The court concurred that an employer's grooming policy prohibiting the "Afro/bush" style might offend Title VII because that style implicates an immutable characteristic. It then stated: "[A]n all-braided hairstyle is a different matter. It is not the product of natural hair growth but of artifice. An all-braided hair style is an 'easily changed characteristic,' and, even if socioculturally associated with a particular race or nationality, is not an impermissible basis for distinctions ... by an employer."[65]

The court therefore decided that skin color or an Afro is an immutable racial characteristic, but that cornrow braids were a mutable, easily changeable, stylistic choice and that American Airlines' no-braids policy had "at most a negligible effect on employment opportunity."[66] In her prior works, Professor Greene has argued that *Rogers* became a powerful precedent harmful to Black women since it "accorded employers essentially limitless freedom, authority, and privilege to stigmatize, exclude, and marginalize African descendant women in the workplace because of their hair."[67]

---

[62] *Id.* (emphasis added).

[63] 527 F.Supp. 229 (S.D.N.Y. 1981).

[64] *Id.* at 232 (quoting Plaintiff's Memo. in Opposition to Motion to Dismiss).

[65] *Id.*

[66] *Id.* at 231.

[67] D. Wendy Greene, *Splitting Hairs: The Eleventh Circuit's Take on Workplace Bans against Black Women's Natural Hair in* EEOC v. Catastrophe Management Solutions, 71 U. Miami L. Rev. 987, 1036 (2017).

In the Eleventh Circuit's original opinion in *Catastrophe Management*, the Equal Employment Opportunity Commission (EEOC) argued that locs are a racial characteristic that is physiologically and culturally associated with people of African descent.[68] The court countered with decades of precedent that rejected the argument that Title VII protects hairstyles culturally associated with race.[69]

Notably, this original opinion engaged in a deeper discussion about race and the definition of race. The court observed that Title VII does not define the word "race" nor is there a clear understanding of what race meant at the time that Title VII was enacted.[70] The EEOC's Compliance Manual, which takes an expansive view of race, was not persuasive to the court in *Catastrophe Management* because the manual contravenes the agency's own reliance on prior immutability case law (*Willingham* and *Rogers*) without "a reasoned justification for the shift" in policy away from the immutability doctrine.[71] The court ignored the agency's manual and rejected a more expansive interpretation of Title VII that would eliminate the biological conception of race and include cultural characteristics associated with race because "every court to have considered the issue has rejected the argument that Title VII protects hairstyles culturally associated with race."[72] The court acknowledged in a footnote that, in other federal legislation during the late 1980s, "Congress still thought of 'race,' in at least one context, as including common physical characteristics."[73] The court noted that the request to interpret "race" as culture has not been unanimous – that it is incredibly difficult to know which cultural practices deserve the protections of Title VII and which ones do not. Moreover, it questioned whether cultural characteristics or traits associated with one racial group can be transferred to a different race.[74]

---

[68] *Catastrophe Mgmt.*, 852 F.3d at 1023.

[69] *Id.* at 1032.

[70] *Id.* at 1026.

[71] *Id.* at 1031–32.

[72] *Id.* at 1032–33.

[73] *Id.* at 1028 n.3. ("And in the Geneva Convention Implementation Act of 1987, legislation that post-dated Title VII by about two decades, Congress defined the term 'racial group' as 'a set of individuals whose identity as such is distinctive in terms of physical characteristics or biological descent.' 18 U.S.C. § 1093(6). ... We merely point out that in the late 1980s Congress still thought of 'race,' in at least one context, as including common physical characteristics.").

[74] *Id.* at 1034. The opinion raises:

> ... whether cultural characteristics or traits associated with one racial group can be absorbed or transferred to members of a different racial group. At oral argument, for example, the EEOC asserted that if a white person chose to wear dreadlocks as a sign of racial support for her black colleagues, and the employer applied its dreadlocks ban to that person, she too could assert a race-based disparate treatment claim.

150   EEOC v. Catastrophe Management Solutions

Ultimately, the court did not expressly pick a side, but implicitly did so by continuing to adhere to the current definition of race as including only biological, immutable characteristics. The court further suggested that perhaps Congress should define what race means and/or further define discrimination based upon ethnic traits.[75] This is an interesting suggestion, but one that is unlikely to occur in the contemporary state of affairs given the heightened partisan nature of American politics.

The court relied on *Willingham* to conclude that Title VII shields protected groups with respect to their immutable characteristics, but not their cultural practices.[76] The court recognized that the distinctions between immutable and mutable characteristics of race are difficult lines to draw.[77] According to the court, discrimination on the basis of a Black hairstyle, such as braids or cornrows (a mutable choice), is not prohibited by Title VII, but discrimination on the basis of Black hair texture, such as an Afro (an immutable characteristic), is prohibited by Title VII.[78] The court took a very narrow and restrictive view of race and failed to acknowledge the ramifications of this decision for Black women in their quest for equal employment opportunities or the underlying racism and stereotypes that drive this decision. The feminist opinion rectifies this failure.

THE FEMINIST JUDGMENT

Professor D. Wendy Greene, writing as Justice Greene, abandons the immutability doctrine in favor of an intersectional approach that evaluates the unequal burdens imposed by the grooming policy upon Black women.

Greene examines the district court's reliance on key precedent on the immutability doctrine, which she defines as a "judicially created prerequisite to Title VII race discrimination cases when grooming regulations are at issue." Greene explains that, under the immutability doctrine, the discrimination alleged must be prompted by a trait, present at birth, which is impossible or difficult to change. The trait must be shared or possessed exclusively by all of the individuals who identify as members of a particular racial group. Greene determines that this evidentiary requirement is difficult, if not impossible, to meet. Moreover, Greene concludes, immutability is not rooted in the plain language of Title VII, and its imposition violates the purpose of the law. Greene observes that federal courts, including the courts in this case, in effect

[75] *Id.* at 1035.
[76] *Id.* at 1029–30.
[77] *Id.* at 1030.
[78] *Id.*

allow discrimination on the basis of a Black hairstyle, such as braids or cornrows (a mutable choice), but Title VII prohibits discrimination on the basis of Black hair texture, such as an Afro, (an immutable characteristic).[79] The feminist opinion finds that this distinction makes no sense because the same woman can be protected from employment discrimination under Title VII by wearing one hairstyle (an Afro), but not if she wears a different hairstyle (locs or braids). Afros are perceived as immutable because they are permanent and exclusive to African descendants, whereas locs are not exclusive to African descendants nor are they present at birth. This odd double standard allows private employers to deprive Black women of equal employment opportunities. Greene dismisses the distinction between hair texture and hairstyles as nonsensical and the immutability doctrine as a "legal fiction: a judicial rule that is not based in fact yet treated as such to legitimize zones of protection and inclusion."

As noted in the feminist opinion, immutability as used within the district court's opinion "incentivizes the hyper-regulation of Black women's bodies via their hair and the exclusion of Black women from contemporary workplaces when their hair is not straightened – or, rather, does not conform to a racialized and gendered construction of professionalism, beauty, femininity, acceptability, and womanhood associated with white women." This hyper-regulation of Black women's hair is based upon subjective paternalistic notions of what is deemed appropriate, professional, and attractive, and therefore permissible in the workplace.[80]

Greene describes the social and historical context of the regulation of Black women's hair dating from early slavery until the present day. She views this case through an intersectional lens – an analysis of Black women's experience that is deeper and richer than that found in any of the cases on point and unimaginable in the Eleventh Circuit's original opinion. Greene acknowledges that Black men who sport locs have also been victims of workplace discrimination, but notes that, because Black women are subjected to heightened standards of appearance and grooming, they have had to change their natural hair to conform to what is deemed acceptable or beautiful to be employable. She explains the stigma and hyper-regulation of Black hair in the context of a variety of facets of the life of a Black woman: the *de jure* and *de facto* policies that created racially segregated salons because of the pejorative stigma of Black women's hair; the criticism of Black hair by a Brazilian singer, demonstrating the global policing of Black hair; online disgust at an

---

[79] *Id.*
[80] *Id.* at 1005.

Afro-Brazilian celebrity wearing her hair naturally curly; and the regulation of Black hair among schoolgirls – and even at airport security checkpoints.

Greene observes that when the district court decided Ms. Jones's case, the US Army was under public scrutiny for its grooming policy preventing African American women from wearing locs and twists. Neither the district court's nor the Eleventh Circuit's opinion even mentions this highly relevant change in American tradition. The grooming policy prohibition in both the Army and here is rooted in the biased and pejorative perception that African American hair is unprofessional unless it is straightened. Other communities of color have similarly experienced this grooming policy bias within the Army: notably, visible religious articles of faith such as the Muslim hijab and Sikh turban still require religious exceptions to the requisite grooming policy.[81]

Greene accurately observes that, in the district court and the 1806 Virginia Supreme Court opinion *Hudgins v. Wrights*,[82] both judges "constructed 'woolly' or Afro hair texture as an inheritable marker of Blackness or African ancestry." In both instances, the courts afforded "legal freedom to women who possessed a white skin complexion and straight hair and unbridled, lawful regulation of women's bodies and personhood if they possess a darker skin complexion and 'woolly' or unstraightened hair." This analogy is striking in that the same racialized underpinnings present today existed 200 years ago. There has been little to no evolution in how Black women's hair is perceived in 200 years, and beauty has been and continues to be measured relative to whiteness and straight hair. This is particularly problematic in the employment context, where Black women are deprived of jobs because of their hair.

The feminist opinion demonstrates that employers are insulated from Title VII's requirements by the early dismissal of Title VII cases. The protection of the powerful employer at the expense of the often-powerless employee is troubling to Greene. Employees cannot necessarily find employment elsewhere if they do not conform to a prospective employer's grooming policy, and the original opinion allows for unchecked policies rooted in subjective, assimilationist, and biased ideas of what is "professional." There is almost never a relationship between the grooming policy and the ability to do a job. Not everyone has myriad employment opportunities, and Black women will be further limited as to what jobs will allow them to look like themselves. Courts applying the

---

[81] Meghann Myers, *New Army Policy OKs Soldiers to Wear Hijabs, Turbans and Religious Beards*, ARMY TIMES (Jan. 5, 2017), www.armytimes.com/news/your-army/2017/01/05/new-army-policy-oks-soldiers-to-wear-hijabs-turbans-and-religious-beards/.

[82] 11 Va. (1 Hen. & M.) 133, 133–34 (1806).

immutability doctrine to grooming policies fail to ask questions about whether those in power have legitimate reasons for imposing moralizing judgments on citizens or employees.[83] The employer's power goes virtually unchecked. Greene's opinion highlights that failure by providing the in-depth context of Black women and their hair and examining the intersectional stereotypes and unequal burdens placed upon Black women simply for being Black women.

With regard to intersectional stereotypes, the feminist opinion discusses the seminal Supreme Court case of *Price Waterhouse v. Hopkins*,[84] which held that an employer engages in intentional sex discrimination if it mandates conforming to a gender stereotype as a term or condition of employment. Greene argues that it is plausible that CMS rescinded its job offer to Ms. Jones because she did not comply with and conform to racial and gender norms, as measured by white women and straight hair. Ms. Jones was "contravening an operational standard of white womanhood and thereby presented herself in a way CMS deemed 'too Black.'" Consequently, Greene decides that the EEOC should be permitted to discover whether such racial and gendered stereotyping shaped CMS's actions in violation of Title VII.

Greene, in the feminist opinion, takes judicial notice of the temporal, economic, and emotional burdens on Black women who attempt to comply with a straight-hair mandate, and she permits the EEOC to gather evidence to support this theory of intentional discrimination. As Greene explains, the district court's holding creates an impossible choice for Ms. Jones and other Black women: "Don your natural hair at the risk of (lawfully) being deprived of an employment opportunity," or "[D]on straight hair at the risk of enduring consequential costs to your economic, psychological, physiological, and physical well-being."

While Greene completely rejects the immutability doctrine in her opinion, there is an alternative expanded definition of immutability that could further aid marginalized groups in employment discrimination cases by focusing on dignity instead of changeability. In *Catastrophe Management*, the National Association for the Advancement of Colored People (NAACP) and others as *amici* argued before the Eleventh Circuit that the immutability doctrine counters the moral underpinnings of Title VII, especially since more inclusive alternatives to immutability do exist.[85] In *Obergefell v. Hodges*, the Supreme Court affirmed that the

---

[83] Jessica A. Clarke, *Against Immutability*, 125 YALE L.J. 2, 20 (2015).

[84] 490 U.S. 228 (1989).

[85] Brief of NAACP, Legal Aid Society, Professor D. Wendy Greene and Professor Angela Onwuachi-Willig, in *EEOC v. Catastrophe Management Solutions*, 2016 WL 7173828, at *14 (11th Cir.) (NAACP Brief) (citing *Obergefell v. Hodges*, 135 S.Ct. 2584, 2597 (2015)).

Fourteenth Amendment protects "personal choices central to individual dignity and autonomy, including intimate choices that define identity and beliefs."[86] Thus, in determining who is entitled to Title VII protections, the NAACP explained that an individual should not be forced to make such profound changes that touch upon their individual dignity and identity in order to remain employed or find employment. Instead, the NAACP urged the Eleventh Circuit in *Catastrophe Management* to consider the individual autonomy and dignity of individuals as the Supreme Court did in *Obergefell*. If that is done in the Title VII context, the statute's prohibition against discrimination can reach an employer's discrimination against individuals whose appearance includes identity dimensions of race. The implications of this expanded definition are beyond race; indeed, one's dignity and identity can touch upon all protected classes of Title VII and future aspiring protected classes.[87]

Under new guidelines published by the progressive New York City Commission on Human Rights, discrimination based on hair or hairstyle will now be deemed to be racial discrimination.[88] The guidelines are founded upon the argument that hair is "inherent to one's race and can be closely associated with racial, ethnic, or cultural identities."[89] The law is aimed specifically at providing a remedy for the disparate treatment of Black New Yorkers who have a right to maintain their "natural hair, treated or untreated hairstyles such as locs, cornrows, twists, braids, Bantu knots, fades, Afros, and/or the right to keep hair in an uncut or untrimmed state."[90] The guidelines themselves cited Greene's prior works and the NAACP's *amicus* brief to the Eleventh Circuit.[91] According to the guidelines, prohibiting natural hair or hairstyles associated with Black people is based upon "a widespread and fundamentally racist belief that Black hairstyles are not suited for formal settings, and may be unhygienic, messy, disruptive, or unkempt."[92]

This view that immutability includes an individual's dignity and autonomy rights, as seen in *Obergefell* and in the New York Commission on Human Rights' guidelines, has been applied by lower federal courts in sexual

---

[86] *Id.*

[87] *Id.* at *13.

[88] Stacey Stowe, *New York City to Ban Discrimination Based on Hair*, N.Y. TIMES (Feb. 18, 2019), www.nytimes.com/2019/02/18/style/hair-discrimination-new-york-city.html.

[89] NYC Comm'n on Human Rights, LEGAL ENFORCEMENT GUIDANCE ON RACE DISCRIMINATION ON THE BASIS OF HAIR (Feb. 18, 2019), www.jacksonlewis.com/sites/default/files/docs/NYCHairGuidance.pdf.

[90] *Id.* at 3.

[91] *Id.* at 3 n.15.

[92] *Id.* at 4.

orientation discrimination claims.[93] The Eleventh Circuit's opinion does not address this specific argument. But Greene addresses the notion in the feminist opinion that when a court declares that an Afro is the only hairstyle that signifies a woman as a Black woman, that court is "dictating to Black women which features and experiences inform or define their personhood and self-understanding as a Black or African descended woman in the world." In Greene's view, the rejection of the immutability doctrine, as used in the original opinion, is thus a rejection of "the disempowerment of Black women in workplaces and the dismissal of Black women's experiences within civil rights doctrine and advocacy." The feminist opinion therefore reverses the court below, concluding that the district court dismissed the EEOC's claim prematurely and that the EEOC is entitled to pursue discovery.

THE IMPLICATIONS FOR OTHER COMMUNITIES OF COLOR

The underlying stereotypes that Greene highlights in her opinion also deny equal employment opportunities to other communities of color. Cases have held that grooming policies can regulate facial hair and length of hair, even if doing so implicates cultural or religious practices of some communities of color.[94] For example, orthodox Sikh men and women keep their hair as a sign of devotion to their faith. Men tie their hair in a topknot on top of their head and cover it with a long fabric wrapped into a turban. Some Sikh women do not cut or trim facial hair, defying feminine beauty norms of hairlessness, and often encountering ridicule in public or online spaces.[95] In the context of religious garb, many grooming policies prohibit hats and include Sikh turbans and Muslim hijabs as prohibited items, despite the fact that such items are not subjectively perceived as optional for the devout in those faiths.[96] Prison grooming policies subjugate male inmates who do not cut their hair for religious reasons to solitary confinement. In a particularly egregious example, Rastafarian inmates have been held in solitary confinement for over a decade in Virginia because they refuse, in accordance with their religious beliefs, to

---

[93] NAACP Brief, *supra* note 85, at *14.

[94] *Hussein v. The Waldorf-Astoria*, 134 F.Supp.2d 591, 598 (S.D.N.Y. 2001), *aff'd sub nom. Hussein v. Waldorf Astoria Hotel*, 31 F. App'x 740 (2d Cir. 2002) (harm to reputation, standards, and discipline are undue burden to employer from beard-wearing Muslim employee.) *See also* additional cases cited *infra* note 98.

[95] Rheana Murray, *Sikh Woman Defends Facial Hair with Graceful Response about Religion after Being Mocked on Reddit*, N.Y. DAILY NEWS (Sep. 26, 2012), www.nydailynews.com/news/world/sikh-woman-defends-facial-hair-graceful-response-religion-mocked-reddit-article-1.1168486.

[96] *See, e.g., EEOC v. Abercrombie & Fitch Stores, Inc.*, 135 S.Ct. 2028 (2015).

156 EEOC v. Catastrophe Management Solutions

cut their hair.[97] While this act does not implicate Title VII, the idea is the same: that grooming standards are subjective and subject to pejorative stereotypes about people who do not assimilate into white society – those perceived to be unprofessional, unkempt/unclean, or "other." The stereotypes that women should not have facial hair, or that men should not have long hair, or that adherents of minority religions should not wear religious garb are harmful to people of color attempting to find equal employment and to participate in American society. When grooming policies prohibit long hair on men because it is not a social norm for men in America to wear their hair long, they violate a number of religious or cultural traditions that require men to have long hair or facial hair.[98] Does this mean that, in effect, Title VII protects only those who fit into cultural norms of white society? That cannot be right, since it defies the primary purpose of Title VII: to prevent unequal terms, conditions, and privileges of employment, as Greene notes.

At the time of writing, there are no other Title VII lawsuits that pertain to Black hair that cite this Eleventh Circuit opinion. If the feminist opinion had been the actual opinion of the Eleventh Circuit, other courts would likely factually limit and distinguish this precedential case to avoid scrutinizing the nuanced burdens of each Title VII plaintiff. Sadly, the notion that courts would walk in the shoes of each Title VII plaintiff is revolutionary. This feminist opinion addresses the lack of intersectionality in the original opinion and provides specific insight on the numerous burdens on any Black woman attempting to be perceived as professional. Ending the immutability doctrine is a necessary step to eliminating the subjective and paternalistic shields of professionalism entrenched in white-centric stereotypes of beauty that curtail employment opportunities for Black women.

---

[97] Frank Green, *Rastafarian Inmate Relents on Haircut after Ten Years*, RICHMOND-TIMES DISPATCH (June 8, 2013), www.richmond.com/news/virginia/rastafarian-inmate-relents-on-haircut-after-years/article_f88c584o-ebo5-5cce-b65e-482eoe6fabbe.html.

[98] While religious accommodations do exist, employers can validly refuse such accommodations because of the *de minimis* cost of an undue burden. Some courts have held that deviation from a uniform image is an undue burden. *See, e.g., Webb v. City of Philadelphia*, 562 F.3d 256, 262 (3d Cir. 2009) (finding no Title VII violation against Muslim police officers not permitted to wear religious headscarves); *EEOC v. GEO Grp., Inc.*, 616 F.3d 265 (3d Cir. 2010) (finding no Title VII violation against Muslim prison officials not permitted to wear religious head coverings). Even a restaurant employer has successfully asserted an undue burden (against a Sikh male with long hair and facial hair) that was "based on management's perception and experience" that consumers preferred clean-shaven restaurant employees: "Adverse customer reaction in this market to beards arises from a simple aversion to, or discomfort in dealing with, bearded people; from a concern that beards are unsanitary or conducive to unsanitary conditions ..." *See EEOC v. Sambo's of Georgia, Inc.*, 530 F.Supp. 86, 89 (N.D. Ga. 1981).

Equal Employment Opportunity Commission v. Catastrophe Management Solutions,
852 F.3d 1018 (11th Cir. 2016)

JUDGE D. WENDY GREENE DELIVERED THE OPINION OF THE COURT.

This case presents important substantive and procedural issues for the present and future of federal antidiscrimination law. Substantively, this case raises a question concerning the extent to which Title VII of the Civil Rights Act of 1964 governs discrimination arising out of the enforcement of workplace grooming policies and practices. Specifically, this case presents the following questions:

(1) whether an employer violates Title VII's prohibitions against race discrimination when it enforces a grooming policy to rescind an employment opportunity from a qualified applicant because she is a Black woman who dons dreadlocks and refuses to cut off her hair as a condition of employment;

(2) whether a judicially created rule known as the "immutability doctrine" remains applicable in Title VII race discrimination cases challenging grooming regulations; and

(3) whether the Equal Employment Opportunity Commission (EEOC) presented a "plausible claim" of race discrimination in violation of Title VII and whether, as a result, the district court's dismissal of the agency's complaint pursuant to Federal Rule of Civil Procedure 12(b)(6) was in error.

Before proceeding, it is important to clarify that, for the remainder of this opinion, this Court will refer to locked hairstyles as "dreadlocks" only when it is relaying the specific words of a speaker. This Court itself will refer to dreadlocks as "locs," so as to not perpetuate long-held negative connotations of the former, rooted in the forced migration, trade, and enslavement of Africans and their descendants in the Americas and Caribbean.[99] Additionally, throughout the opinion, this Court will use the terms Black

---

[99] According to Ayana D. Byrd & Lori L. Tharps, HAIR STORY: UNTANGLING THE ROOTS OF BLACK HAIR IN AMERICA 121 (2d ed. 2014):

> The name [dreadlock] derives from the days of the slave trade. When Africans emerged from the slave ships after months spent in conditions adverse to any personal hygiene, Whites would declare the matted hair that had grown out of their kinky unattended locks to be "dreadful". (For that reason, many today wearing the style choose to drop the *a* in *dredloc* to remove all negative connotations.)

158   EEOC v. Catastrophe Management Solutions

and African descendant interchangeably to capture all individuals who identify as African descended, Black, and/or African American.

I FACTUAL BACKGROUND

Catastrophe Management Solutions (CMS) is a for-profit company based in Mobile, Alabama, which provides customer service and administrative support for insurance companies processing insurance claims. App. T-8, Doc. 21–1, at 2. On May 3, 2010, Chastity Jones submitted an online application for a customer service representative position with CMS. *Id.* at 3. As a customer service representative, Ms. Jones would be responsible for responding to inquiries from customers via phone in a call center, alongside other representatives: a role that did not involve face-to-face engagement with customers *Id.* at 3–4. CMS invited Ms. Jones to participate in a group interview, which took place approximately a week after she applied for the position. *Id.* at 4–5. Ms. Jones wore a blue business suit to the interview and her blonde locs in a curly formation also known as "curlilocks."[100] *Id.* at 4. After a successful group interview and an individual interview with a company trainer, CMS offered Ms. Jones the position as a customer service representative, which she accepted. CMS's human resources (HR) manager, Jeannie Wilson, informed all applicants of scheduled lab tests and additional paperwork that needed to be completed before they could assume their positions. *Id.* at 4–5. Ms. Wilson also instructed Ms. Jones and the other new hires to meet with her privately if they had any scheduling conflicts. *Id.* at 5. At no point before or during the interview nor when Ms. Jones was extended the job offer did a CMS representative comment on Ms. Jones' hair or relay that CMS had a written grooming policy in place, which reads as follows: "All personnel are expected to be dressed and groomed in a manner that projects a professional and businesslike image while adhering to company and industry standards and/or guidelines ... [H]airstyles should reflect a business/professional image. No excessive hairstyles or unusual colors are acceptable ..." *Id.* at 3–6.

Pursuant to Ms. Wilson's announcement, Ms. Jones proceeded to reschedule her lab tests due to a conflict. *Id.* at 5. As Ms. Jones prepared to leave this brief meeting with Ms. Wilson, Ms. Wilson asked her, "Are those dreadlocks you are wearing?" *Id.* Ms. Jones answered affirmatively, which prompted Ms. Wilson to explain that she was unable to hire Ms. Jones "with the dreadlocks." *Id.* Ms. Jones sought Ms. Wilson's reasoning for the rescission of the customer service representative position she had proven her ability to perform, which CMS had extended to her, and which she had accepted. *Id.* Ms. Wilson

---

[100] The ends of the locs are manipulated to give a curlier effect than locs that are merely straight.

responded, "[T]hey [i.e., locs] tend to get messy, although I'm not saying yours are, but you know what I'm talking about." *Id.* Ms. Wilson also mentioned that previously, a Black male employee cut off his locs to maintain his employment with CMS. *Id.* Essentially, Ms. Wilson intimated that CMS also expected Ms. Jones to cut off her locs as a condition of employment. *Id.* Ms. Jones refused to cut her hair; in turn, Ms. Wilson rescinded Ms. Jones' offer of employment, despite her demonstrated qualifications, and instructed her to return paperwork provided earlier in the day. *Id.* at 5–6.

II PROCEDURAL HISTORY

Chastity Jones filed a timely charge of discrimination with the EEOC, and the EEOC decided to pursue legal action on behalf of Ms. Jones. The EEOC filed a federal lawsuit, challenging CMS's prohibition against locs as a form of intentional race discrimination in violation of Title VII. 42 U.S.C. §§2000 e-2 (a)(1), 2000e-2(m). CMS sought dismissal of the EEOC's case pursuant to Federal Rule of Civil Procedure 12(b)(6). In deciding whether the EEOC's case should be dismissed, the district court strictly adhered to a judicially created rule – the "immutability doctrine" – articulated by the Fifth Circuit Court of Appeals in 1975 in *Willingham v. Macon Telephone Company.* 507 F.2d 1084 (5th Cir. 1975). In *Willingham*, the Fifth Circuit held that a private employer did not violate Title VII's proscriptions against intentional sex discrimination when it refused to hire a qualified male applicant as a copy artist because his hair was shoulder-length. *Id.* at 1091. The court reasoned that:

> Equal employment opportunity may be secured only when employers are barred from discriminating against employees on the basis of immutable characteristics, such as race and national origin ... But a hiring policy that distinguishes on some other ground, such as grooming codes or length of hair, is related more closely to the employer's choice of how to run his business than to equality of employment opportunity... *Id.* at 1091.

Although the *Willingham* court adopted the immutability doctrine in a Title VII sex discrimination case, several federal courts, like the district court below, have applied this judicially created prerequisite to Title VII race discrimination cases where grooming regulations are at issue. Accordingly, to trigger Title VII's protections against race discrimination, complainants are required to demonstrate that the regulated or proscribed trait, like a Black woman's hair color or, as in this case, a Black woman's naturally locked hair, is an "immutable characteristic." *See Santee v. Windsor Court Hotel*, No. 99-3891, 2000 WL 16100775, at *1 (E.D. La. Oct. 26, 2000). In other words, based upon our synthesis of the cases, the discrimination that the plaintiff suffers must be animated by a trait that either is (1) impossible to change, (2) difficult to change, (3) one with which a person is born, (4) one shared by all individuals who identify as members of a particular racial group, or (5) one that is possessed only by individuals who identify as a member of a particular racial group. *See, e.g., Garcia v. Gloor*, 618 F.2d 264, 269 (5th Cir. 1980) ("Save for religion, the discriminations on which [Title VII] focuses its laser of prohibition are those that are either beyond the victim's power to alter [like one's race or national origin] or that impose a burden on an employee on one of the prohibited bases"); *see also, e.g., EEOC v. Catastrophe Mgmt. Sols.*, 11 F.Supp.3d 1139, 1144 (S.D. Ala. 2014) (concluding that fulfillment of the immutability doctrine in a Title VII race discrimination case requires a complainant to demonstrate that individuals who identify as a members of a particular racial group exclusively possess the proscribed trait). As this Court will explain, this is a difficult, if not impossible, evidentiary requirement that seemingly only Title VII race discrimination plaintiffs must fulfill when challenging workplace grooming codes. Moreover, since the *Willingham* decision, federal appellate courts, including the US Supreme Court, have rejected the immutability doctrine – a doctrine that is not grounded in the plain language of the statute and which, in its effect, engenders violations of Title VII and contravenes the aims of this landmark civil rights law.

Nonetheless, in its application of the immutability doctrine, the district court declared that an Afro is a hair *texture*, which is an immutable racial characteristic of Black or African descended people. While recognizing that Ms. Jones' locs are the result of the unimpeded growth of what the district court appreciated as "Afro hair texture," the court did not similarly deem locs an immutable, racial characteristic. In fact, the court opined: "[A] hairstyle is *not* inevitable and immutable just because it is the reasonable result of hair texture, which is an immutable characteristic." Based upon this reasoning, the court held that Ms. Jones' locs constituted a "mutable, cultural hair*style*." The court further declared that "*no* amount of expert testimony can change the fact that dreadlocks is a hairstyle." The district court dismissed the EEOC's complaint, concluding that the EEOC did not state a plausible claim of intentional race discrimination; rather, CMS's ban on Ms. Jones' locs amounted to discrimination on the basis of a "cultural characteristic" beyond the scope of Title VII's protections. *See id.* at 1142–44 (emphasis added). The district court also denied the EEOC's motion for leave to amend its complaint, declaring that any proposed amendments would be "futile." App. T-4, Doc. 27, at 2. Because the dismissal of the EEOC's case on behalf of Ms. Jones occurred during the preliminary stages of civil litigation – before either party was able to engage in the discovery process – the district court essentially announced that the EEOC (and subsequent Title VII plaintiffs) would never be able to assert allegations or be permitted an opportunity to compile evidence to support a claim of intentional race discrimination when a covered employer bars Black natural hairstyles[101] – even those that are the consequence of their natural hair texture – except in one instance: when an employer prohibits a Black employee from wearing an Afro. The EEOC appealed the district court's decision, and this Court granted the EEOC oral argument.

For nearly four decades, federal courts have reproduced the immutability/mutability and/or racial/cultural distinction in race discrimination cases employed by the courts below. Federal courts' regurgitation of the immutability doctrine has left Black women without legal recourse under our federal antidiscrimination laws when they suffer discrimination for adorning natural hairstyles like locs, braids, and twists. Curiously, however, pursuant to the immutability doctrine, federal courts have carved out statutory protection for Black women when they are discriminated against for donning an Afro. *See, e.g., Rogers v. American Airlines*, 527 F.Supp. 229, 232 (S.D.N.Y. 1981) (opining that "an employer's policy prohibiting the 'Afro/bush' *style* might offend Title VII" (emphasis added)). Notably, a federal appellate court – without applying the immutability doctrine – also deemed Afros a natural *hairstyle* and discrimination against Black women donning Afros to be unlawful race discrimination. *See, e.g., Jenkins v. Blue Cross Blue Mut. Hosp. Ins., Inc.*, 538 F.2d 164, 168 (7th Cir. 1976) (holding that a Black female employee's denial of promotion because, according to her supervisor, she "could never represent [the company] with her Afro" violated Title VII, because the "reference to the Afro *hairstyle* was merely the method by which the plaintiff's supervisor allegedly expressed the employer's racial discrimination" (emphasis added)).

---

[101] "Natural hairstyles" is a term widely used by African descendants to denote hairstyles such as braids, locs, curls, or Afros, which are generally not achieved through chemical relaxants or heat and are conducive to or resemble the growth and texture of many, if not most, African descendants' hair. This Court rejects a judicial distinction between a hair texture and a hairstyle for several reasons. First, in common parlance, the terms "hair texture" and "hairstyle" are interchangeable and overlapping. For example, straight hair is called a hair texture and a hairstyle; so too are Afros, locs, braids, and twists. Furthermore, Afros, like any other hairstyle/hair texture, can be manipulated and changed. We cannot justify basing legal protection upon whether a judge treats a complainant's hair as a texture or a style; it is an illusory prerequisite to protection under federal civil rights laws that defies common sense. Indeed, such a legal distinction does not capture the ways in which Afros and their transfiguration into braids, locs, and twists have been (and are) marked by law and society as both hair textures and hairstyles indicative of African ancestry or a Black racial identity. Lastly, this legal distinction does not reflect how the predominant wearers – those who classify themselves as African descendants – generally denominate these styles as "natural hairstyles" regardless of whether they are the result of unimpeded hair growth, synthetic or natural hair extensions, or synthetic or natural hair wigs.

The district court's attempt to distinguish between a natural hair *texture* and a natural *hairstyle* based upon the immutability doctrine reflects a lack of understanding about Black women's hair and is simply wrong. Moreover, the district court's ruling ensconces an already narrow space in which Black women, like Chastity Jones, can wear their hair the way it inevitably grows or in a style most conducive to their hair texture without risking loss of employment for which they are qualified. In effect, private employers are afforded an unfettered right to deprive Black women who don locs and other natural hairstyles – except Afros – employment and attendant compensation, as well as to impose unequal terms, privileges, and conditions upon them if they are to obtain and maintain employment. The instant Title VII case initiated on behalf of Ms. Jones provides this Court with an important opportunity to appraise this unbalanced and unfortunate state of affairs, which has resulted from a dogged application of the immutability doctrine in intentional race discrimination cases. For these reasons and the reasons that follow, we cannot affirm the district court's ruling.

III THE LEGAL STANDARD

To survive a motion to dismiss under Fed. R. Civ. P. 12(b)(6), a complaint must plead "enough facts to state a claim to relief that is plausible on its face." *Bell Atl. Corp. v. Twombly*, 550 U.S. 544, 570 (2007). Facial plausibility exists "when the plaintiff pleads factual content that allows the court to draw the reasonable inference that the defendant is liable for the misconduct alleged." *Ashcroft v. Iqbal*, 556 U.S. 662, 678 (2009). An inference of a mere possibility of misconduct is not sufficient to support a plausible claim. *Id.* at 679. Yet, when reviewing a motion to dismiss, the court must "assume [the] veracity" of the allegations set forth, draw all "reasonable inference[s]" in the plaintiff's favor, and use its "judicial experience and common sense" to conduct a "context-specific" analysis of the complaint. *Id.* at 678–79.

IV THE REGULATION OF BLACK WOMEN'S HAIR IN CONTEXT

Before delving into the legal analysis, it is important to situate the discrimination that Ms. Jones suffered[102] within the broader historical and social context,

---

[102] Catastrophe Management Solutions did not deny the EEOC's recitation of how its HR manager communicated to Ms. Jones the company's ban on locs and the underlying reasoning. Indeed, CMS defends the HR manager's decision to rescind Ms. Jones' offer of employment because she refused to cut off her hair as a legitimate enforcement of its written grooming policy.

as well as to evaluate the EEOC's claims of racial discrimination through an intersectional lens. *See* Kimberlé Crenshaw, *Demarginalizing the Intersection of Race and Sex: A Black Feminist Critique of Antidiscrimination Doctrine, Feminist Theory, and Antiracist Politics*, 1989 U. CHI. LEGAL F. 139, 147 (calling on courts to apply an intersectional analysis to the discrimination claims of Black women that recognizes the particular experiences that Black women encounter as "Black women – not the sum of race and sex discrimination, but as Black women"). It is true that bans on natural hairstyles are not limited to Black women: the facts of this case illustrate that Black men who don locs are also victims of workplace discrimination. *See, e.g., Eatman v. United Parcel Serv.*, 194 F.Supp.2d 256 (S.D.N.Y. 2002). However, women are generally subjected to heightened appearance and grooming expectations in comparison to men. Workplace regulation of Black women's hair is far more pervasive, and the burdens that Black women endure to conform to management's appearance expectations and desires – as they relate to hair – are appreciably different from the expectations of Black men and other women. Indeed, in one case, an employer restrained a Black woman's ability to wear different hairstyles by requiring her to seek management approval before she changed her hair, but did not impose the same mandates on white women. *See Hollins v. Atl. Co.*, 188 F.3d 652 (6th Cir. 1999). Other employers have directed Black women to change their natural hairstyles until they conform to management's subjective ideals of what was acceptable, beautiful, or natural, while not requiring white female employees to do the same. *See, e.g., Pitts v. Wild Adventures*, 2008 WL 1899306 (M.D. Ga. Apr. 25, 2008). Like CMS, other private employers have stigmatized Black women's braids, locs, and twists as "unclean," "messy," and "unprofessional," and have placed Black women in a humiliating double bind: either cover, alter, or cut off your hair, or be deprived of current or prospective employment. Moreover, Black women's natural hairstyles have also influenced supervisors' perceptions of their job performance, resulting in decreased compensation, discipline, and termination; these negative employment actions Black women suffer are also accompanied by demoralizing and subordinating judgments about their attractiveness, femininity, and the judiciousness of their personal grooming decisions. *See, e.g., id.* at *1 (a Black female employee was terminated from employment after her supervisor instructed her to change her cornrow braids to a "pretty hairstyle" and expressed disapproval when she reported to work donning another natural hairstyle, known as "two-strand twists," because her hair resembled locs).

In her pioneering work, legal scholar Paulette Caldwell offered a poetic, personal narrative that gave a voice to the game of tug-of-war that Black women play with their hair from childhood to adulthood: to relax[103] or "press it"[104]; to wear it straightened or "natural"[105]; to cut or to "grow it long"; to braid or wear it "out"[106]; to "wrap it,"[107] roll it,[108] or plaid it[109]; to put a weave in it or put a wig over it; to twist,[110] braid, or lock it; to color, highlight, or not to color at all. *See generally* Paulette M. Caldwell, *A Hair Piece: Perspectives on the Intersection of Race and Gender*, 1991 DUKE L.J. 365. Black women's deliberations over their hair and the pressures to which they are responding may be shared to a certain extent by all women. However, the confluence of emotional, personal, political, and professional considerations often shaping Black women's deliberations and decisions about their hair is unique to their experience – historically and contemporarily. This experience is informed by sociolegal constructions of race and gender and the attendant racism and sexism out of which a particular negative stigma associated with Black women's unstraightened hair texture was born and intersectional exclusion, subordination, and regulation ensued. Consequently, as Professor Caldwell explains, Black women's deliberative decisions concerning their hair "reflect the search for a survival mechanism in a culture where social, political, and economic choices of racialized individuals and groups are conditioned by the extent to which their physical characteristics, both mutable and immutable, approximate those of the dominant racial group." *Id.* at 383. The magnitude of Professor Caldwell's poignant observation became clearer once I, a member of the federal judiciary, educated myself about the historical and contemporary consequence of hair for African descended women not only in the United States, but also around the world. In 2016 – in an era of universal emancipation – Chastity Jones and countless African descended women are being required to conform to workplace grooming regulations in eerily parallel ways to the African descended women who navigated their freedom and survival in an era of racial slavery.

---

[103] A term used to describe the process of straightening the cuticle and hair shaft of curly hair through chemical relaxants.

[104] A term used to describe the process of straightening the cuticle and hair shaft of curly hair by using a heating agent such as a pressing comb or a flat iron.

[105] A term used to describe wearing one's hair in an Afro, loose curls, braids, locs, twists, or other hairstyle that does not require straightening of the hair cuticle and hair shaft.

[106] A term used to describe wearing one's hair in an Afro or loose curls without straightening it.

[107] A term used to describe the technique of tightly wrapping one's hair or brushing it in a circular pattern to achieve or maintain a straightened style.

[108] A term used to describe the technique of using plastic or foam hair rollers to straighten the hair cuticle while maintaining a sleeker, yet voluminous, curl pattern.

[109] An alternative term for braiding one's hair.

[110] A term used to describe braiding one's hair using two or three strands.

Like individuals possessing a darker skin complexion, legal and social institutions imputed a badge of perpetual servitude upon individuals who possessed a tighter curl pattern, or "woolly," hair texture because they were classified as African or African descendants. In a widely examined freedom suit, three women argued before the Virginia Supreme Court in 1806 that they were wrongfully enslaved because they were the daughter, granddaughter, and great-granddaughter of an indigenous woman named Butterwood Nan. *Hudgins v. Wrights*, 11 Va. (1 Hen. & M.) 133, 133–34 (1806). At the time these women of color sought a judicial declaration of their freedom, the Virginia legislature had already established that one's status – whether free or enslaved – would be determined by the status of one's mother, and the enslavement of indigenous peoples had been abolished. *Id.* at 137. The Virginia Supreme Court pronounced these three women free in part because they possessed a white skin complexion, yet, more importantly, straight, long, black hair, which judges reasoned was evidence of indigenous ancestry and not African ancestry. *Id.* at 139–40. Appreciating the reality of interracial intimacy and what today we might call "multiracialism," the court espoused a persisting belief that, despite one's skin complexion, a "woolly head of hair . . . was so strong an ingredient in the African constitution" that it marked a person as an African descendant and presumptively enslaveable. *Id.* at 139. Alternatively, a person who possessed white skin and hair texture "not woolly or inclining thereto," among other physical characteristics, would be presumed a European descendant and free. *Id.* at 140. Thus a legal presumption of slave status would be imputed upon a person possessing white or fair skin and a hair texture that either appeared "woolly" or had the propensity to become "woolly." Accordingly, scholar Althea Prince reports incidences of lighter-skinned, fugitive slave women who shaved off their hair. Althea Prince, THE POLITICS OF BLACK WOMEN'S HAIR 11 (2009). According to Dr. Prince, "In this way, [African descended women] hoped to be able to pass for white and escape the slave catcher." *Id.* For African descended women, covering, altering, or cutting off one's hair was a pathway of freedom and survival.

Throughout the era of racial slavery, slave traders, slave owners, and overseers fully understood the personal and cultural meaning of hair to Africans and their descendants. Historians Shane White and Graham White explain:

> In African cultures, the grooming and styling of hair have long been important social rituals. Elaborate hair designs, reflecting tribal affiliation, status, sex, age, occupation, and the like, were common, and the cutting, shaving, wrapping, and braiding of hair were centuries-old arts. In part, it was the

texture of African hair that allowed these cultural practices to develop; as the historian John Thornton has observed, "the tightly spiraled hair of Africans makes it possible to design and shape it in many ways impossible for the straighter hair of Europe."

Shane White & Graham White, *Slave Hair and African American Culture in the Eighteenth and Nineteenth Centuries,* 61 J. OF SOUTHERN HIST. 45, 49–50 (1995).

The bodies of Africans and their descendants served as a critical site upon which slave owners, traders, and overseers reinscribed their physical, social, and legal control. Alongside the grotesque practices of shackling and branding, the hair of Africans and African descendants was shorn to cement their legally subjugated status devoid of cultural identity, personal liberty, agency, and autonomy. White and White report that "some eighteenth-century owners did resort to hair cropping, or shaving the head, as a form of punishment – for instance, the young slave Hannah had had 'her Hair ... lately cut in a very irregular Manner, as a Punishment for Offences,' and Peter, a frequent runaway, had been branded 'S on the cheek, and R on the other,' and had had his hair cut entirely off." *Id.* at 49.

As Governor of the Spanish American territories of Louisiana and Florida, Esteban Miró issued in 1786 an "Edict of Good Government," which included a sumptuary law exclusively regulating the hair of African descended women in Louisiana. *See* Virginia M. Gould, *"A Chaos of Iniquity and Discord": Slave and Free Women of Color in Spanish Ports of New Orleans, Mobile, and Pensacola, in* THE DEVIL'S LANE: SEX AND RACE IN THE EARLY SOUTH 237–38 (Catherine Clinton & Michele Gillespie eds., 1997).

Governor Miró concluded that the elaborate ways in which African descended women freely wore their hair engendered physical or sexual attraction from European males, resulting in an ordinate prevalence of intimate relationships between white men and African descended women in the province. *Id.* Governor Miró perceived the freedom with which African descended women wore their hair as a singular threat to a social order that reserved white men's affections as white women's distinctive privilege. To protect white women's social privilege, Miró regulated the bodies of African descended women, ordering them to cover or wrap their hair in cloth. *Id.* Miro's edict, also known as the "Tignon Law," sought to establish a visual demarcation between white and African descended women that would stigmatize African descended women as inferior and unattractive. Notably, in response, enslaved and free women of color adorned colorful and often extravagant headscarves known as tignons, which amplified their beauty and, for some, signified their resistance and empowerment within a sociolegal order aimed at suppressing their personhood, individuality, and freedom. *Id.*

During the eras of racial slavery and universal emancipation, African descended women (and men) applied hot towels, toxic chemicals, hair lotions, and hot irons to temporarily loosen (or "relax") their hair cuticle and shaft in an effort to achieve a straightened hairstyle. For some Black women, straightening one's hair was a simple function of personal choice and aesthetic expression; for others, it reflected a means of achieving economic and social mobility. Ayana Byrd and Lori Tharps explain that, during the early 1900s, African descendants' "hair, having been subjected for nearly three hundred years to both creative and at times damaging experiments in the quest for straightness and 'manageability' was a key element in the construction of [the] New Negro image," and one's "appearance, including hair was the means to a socio-economic end" for many Black men and women. Ayana Byrd & Lori Tharps, HAIR STORY: UNTANGLING THE ROOTS OF BLACK HAIR IN AMERICA 28, 30 (2d ed. 2014). Indeed, "[b]y the early 1900s, straight hair had become the preferred look to signal middle-class status." *Id.* at 30. As the remainder of this opinion illustrates, this state of affairs remains in the twenty-first century.

Moreover, post-emancipation, when Black women were better able to enjoy the services of professional hair stylists, *de facto* practices and *de jure* policies maintained racially segregated hair salons in part because of a pejorative stigmatization of Black women's hair as "kinky," "bad," and "unruly." These negative associations imputed to Black women's hair continue to serve as the basis of exclusion for Black women who attempt to patronize hair salons that exclusively serve a white clientele. *See* Constance Dionne Russell, *Styling Civil Rights: The Effect of § 1981 and the Public Accommodations Act on Black Women's Access to White Stylists and Salons*, 24 HARV. BLACK LETTER L.J. 189, 197–99 (2008).

The negative stigma associated with Black women's natural hair is not limited to the United States; it has been embraced globally and expressed publicly. In October 2015, Afro-Brazilian actress Tais Araújo was subjected to a parallel barrage of dehumanizing epithets after she posted on Facebook a picture in which she donned her naturally curly hair in an Afro-like hairstyle. Social media users called Araújo a gorilla and insinuated that she belonged in a zoo. A social media user referred to Araújo's hair as a Brillo pad and derided, "Lend me your hair[.] I want to wash the dishes." Another commenter highlighted the inextricable role that African descended women's hair plays in the external assessment of their physical attractiveness when that commenter queried: "How can anyone find that hair beautiful?" Indeed, in Brazil, like in the United States, tightly curled or "frizzy hair" is associated with African ancestry and marked as "cabelo ruim," or "bad hair," whereas straight hair is associated with European ancestry and celebrated as "cabelo bom," or "good hair." These racialized and gendered stigmas and privileges linked to women's hair operate in workplace decisions as well. For example, in Brazil, it is common for employers to seek applicants with a "boa aparencia," or a "good appearance." These descriptions often reflect a widely held preference for employees with straight hair and a lighter skin complexion. Consequently, relatively dark-skinned women who don curly or unstraightened hairstyles are castigated as unattractive, unpresentable, and unworthy of employment opportunities.

Beginning in their youth, it is communicated to Black women that wearing their hair freely or freely wearing their natural hair is "wrong" and deserving of policing, punishment, and lack of opportunity. This reality persists into adulthood and reflects a deeply rooted and pervasive phenomenon unique to Black girls and women vis-à-vis their hair: the hyper-regulation of their bodies and agency in private and public spaces. For example, African descended girls in the United States and abroad are deprived of educational opportunities when they adorn natural hairstyles. School administrators have disciplined, suspended, and expelled Black girls who don braids, locs, twists, and Afros, calling their hair "distracting," "unruly," or "unkempt." *See, e.g.,* Clare Kim, *Florida School Threatens to Expel Student over "Natural Hair,"* MSNBC (Nov. 26, 2013), www.msnbc.com/the-last-word-94. In the workplace context, since the 1970s, Black women have opposed prohibitions against their adornment of Afros, synthetic braids, twists, locs, cornrows with beads, straightened blonde hair, locked blonde hair, finger waves, and ponytails. The breadth of employment discrimination litigation elucidates not only the diversity of Black women's hair, but also a hyper-regulation of their bodies and suppression of their agency in the workplace. This hyper-regulation extends to public spaces and begins in childhood: Black women and girls are subjected to physical examinations, unwanted touching, and attendant stigmatization of their natural hair. It is common for Black women to have their natural hairstyles caressed – without their consent – or to be asked by both strangers and acquaintances for permission to touch their hair. These intrusions upon their privacy and bodily integrity can also accompany demeaning commentary. For example, in an article written for *The Conversation,* Professor Hlonipha Mokoena relays one of her earliest memories of suffering humiliation because of her natural hair. At high school, a female classmate would repeatedly touch Mokoena's hair and say in front of onlookers, "Your hair feels like pubic hair." To this, Professor Mokoena felt compelled to respond with a threat of violence, urging her classmate to cease publicly touching and demeaning her hair – and Mokoena herself – in the process. Hlonipha Mokoena, *From Slavery to Colonialism and School Rules: A History of Myths about Black Hair*, THE CONVERSATION (Aug. 31, 2016), http://theconversation.com/from-slavery-to-colonialism-and-school-rules-a-history-of-myths-about-black-hair-64676. Black women's natural hairstyles have been further demeaned at airport security checkpoints as a potential threat to travelers' safety and thereby searched by TSA agents. In 2011, Laura Adiele, a Black woman, reported that a TSA agent at the Seattle, Washington, airport searched her Afro, which she wore in a bun on top of her head (also known as an "Afro puff"). Ms. Adiele expressed that, as the TSA agent touched and scrutinized her hair, she felt that her personal privacy and bodily integrity were being invaded and that she had been specifically targeted because she was a Black woman. *See, e.g.*, Allen Shauffler, *TSA to Woman: "We're Going to Have to Examine Your Hair"* (July 5, 2011), www.sott.net/article/231187-US-TSA-to-Woman-We-re-Going-to-Have-to-Examine-Your-Hair. According to Ms. Adiele, TSA agents were not following a formal policy when they searched her Afro puff, but, noticeably, the agents did not use their discretion to search non-Black women who donned straight hair in buns or ponytails. *Id.*

It is important to note that, as the district court was deciding the case before us, like Ms. Adiele and Ms. Jones, Black servicewomen were being subjected to heightened levels of scrutiny and regulation when adorning natural hairstyles. Like CMS, the US Army prohibited Black women from wearing locs and twists. Maya Rhodan, *U.S. Military Rolls Back Restrictions on Black Hairstyles*, TIME (Aug. 13, 2014), http://time.com/3107647/military-black-hairstyles/. The Army also policed the width of cornrow braids that servicewomen routinely wear, requiring strict uniformity. *Id.* The Army's policy expressly denigrated twists, locs, braids, and Afros – hairstyles that are predominantly worn by Black servicewomen – as "matted and unkempt" hairstyles. *Id.* The US Army mandated heightened surveillance and resulting punishment of Black servicewomen who wore their hair unstraightened – not because of any bearing on their ability to effectively protect our country, but because of a deeply entrenched belief that Black women's hair either in its natural state or worn in a natural hairstyle is inherently or uniquely susceptible to being disheveled, unpresentable, and unattractive. Accordingly, this pejorative stigma did not disqualify all Black women from serving our country, but solely Black women who donned natural hairstyles. The same racialized and gendered stigma that animated this discrimination against Black servicewomen motivated CMS's decision to rescind Chastity Jones' job offer in the instant case – despite all of these women's proven qualifications and abilities.

170 EEOC v. Catastrophe Management Solutions

Like Chastity Jones, Jasmine Jones, a Black female sergeant, opposed the Army's grooming policy because of its racialized nature. Sergeant Jones petitioned the White House and President Barack Obama to urge the Army to reconsider its regulations, because she, along with countless others, deemed the Army's natural hairstyle ban to be racially discriminatory. More than 17,000 people signed the petition. *Id.* Although Sergeant Jones' petition fell short of the 100,000 signatures needed to elicit a response from the White House, lawmakers took up the cause. On behalf of the Black women who were serving in the US Congress, Congresswoman Marcia Fudge, chair of the Congressional Black Caucus, authored a letter to Defense Secretary Chuck Hagel, explaining that the Army's natural hairstyle ban appeared to specifically target Black servicewomen and that it was "offensive and biased" to describe hairstyles they traditionally don as "unkempt" and "matted." *Id.* In response to the negative press the Army's natural hairstyle ban generated, as well as Congresswoman Fudge's public letter criticizing it, Secretary Hagel ordered all military branches to reevaluate their grooming codes. *Id.* In August 2014, the US Army issued new regulations, which: permit two-strand twists and locs; changed "dreadlocks" to "locs"; increased the permissible size of twists and braids; eliminated the spacing requirement for braided hairstyles; and removed the words "unkempt" and "matted," recognizing the offensiveness of such terminology. *Id.* The US Air Force and Navy amended their grooming codes to expressly authorize braided and twisted hairstyles, and to remove derogatory and discriminatory terms; the US Marine Corps has created a "special uniform board" to consider the expansion of permissible hairstyles. *Id.* The military's recent revisions are a positive step toward realizing more equal treatment and inclusion of women of color in the US Armed Forces, as well as disrupting the negative stigma and stereotypes associated with natural hairstyles adorned by countless African descended servicewomen. Today, we have an opportunity to do the same for countless African descendant women currently seeking employment and working in the private and public sector throughout the country.

V LEGAL ANALYSIS

A *The Protections and Purposes of Title VII of the Civil Rights Act of 1964*

At the height of the modern civil rights movement, the US Congress enacted one of the most important pieces of antidiscrimination legislation

EEOC v. Catastrophe Management Solutions

in US history: the Civil Rights Act of 1964. Congress's primary objective in enacting Title VII of the Act was to reduce, if not eliminate, nationwide workplace segregation, subordination, and exclusion from employment opportunities on the basis of race and color. Although Congress expanded the proscriptions against workplace discrimination to include national origin, religion, and sex, its central aim was to cease systemic barriers to African descendants' employability and economic mobility simply because of their racial identity. In so doing, for the first time in American history, Congress compelled private employers to make employment decisions based upon applicants' and employees' abilities and qualifications rather than their racial classification and assumptions related thereto. Specifically, Congress made it unlawful for private employers with fifteen or more employees:

(1) to fail or refuse to hire or to discharge any individual, or otherwise to discriminate against any individual with respect to his compensation, terms, conditions, or privileges of employment, because of such individual's race, color, religion, sex, or national origin; or

(2) to limit, segregate, or classify his employees or applicants for employment in any way which would deprive or tend to deprive any individual of employment opportunities or otherwise adversely affect his status as an employee, because of such individual's race, color, religion, sex, or national origin.

42 U.S.C. §§2000e-2(a)(1)–(2), §§703(a)(1)–(2).

Since its enactment, the US Supreme Court has interpreted Title VII to prohibit intentional discrimination – employment decisions that are consciously motivated by animus, stereotypes, and mere consideration of a protected classification – as well as unintentional discrimination. *See McDonnell Douglas Corp. v. Green*, 411 U.S. 792, 800 (1973) (animus); *Price Waterhouse v. Hopkins*, 490 U.S. 228, 256–58 (1989) (stereotypes); *Ricci v. DeStefano*, 557 U.S. 557, 592–93 (2009) (mere consideration of a protected classification); *Griggs v. Duke Power Co.*, 401 U.S. 424, 431 (1971) (adopting a disparate impact theory of discrimination in Title VII cases to redress "not only overt discrimination but also practices that are fair in form, but discriminatory in operation"). In 1991, Congress codified the disparate impact theory of liability. *See* 42 U.S.C. §2000e-2(k)(1)(A)-(C). In Title VII cases challenging express policies mandating different grooming or dress requirements for men and women, federal courts have treated such mandates – when they impose unequal or unreasonable burdens upon women or men – as intentional sex discrimination. *See, e.g., Jespersen v. Harrah's Operating Co., Inc.,* 444 F.3d 1104, 1110 (9th Cir. 2006) (recognizing undue burdens analysis and discontinuing the application of the immutability doctrine to Title VII intentional discrimination cases where sex-differentiated appearance standards are challenged).

In the case before us, the EEOC contends that CMS's rescission of Ms. Jones' job offer because she refused to cut off her locs constitutes intentional race discrimination. CMS defends this adverse employment decision on the ground that it was enforcing a neutral grooming policy that proscribes "excessive hairstyles" and requires "hairstyles that reflect business/professional image." CMS further argues that the negative enforcement of its grooming policy is beyond the scope of Title VII's prohibitions against racial discrimination because, in 1964, Congress intended to regulate workplace discrimination on the basis of "immutable characteristics." However, the legislative history, plain language of Title VII, and judicial interpretations do not support CMS's proposition. Although not expressly envisioned by Congress in 1964, as previously discussed, natural hairstyle bans are a systemic, intersectional barrier to Black women's employability, economic security, and equality – in the twenty-first century – that Title VII can and should redress. Indeed, CMS's proscription against Ms. Jones' locs reflects pejorative stereotyping on the basis of race and gender and imposes unequal burdens on her as a Black woman, which violates Title VII.

B CMS's Ban on Locs as Intersectional Stereotyping of Black Women

The EEOC explicates that grooming policies barring locs, twists, or braids effectively require Black women to cut off, cover, or alter their hair texture by using straightening agents. Consequently, employers' natural hairstyle bans are the functional equivalent of a "straight hair" mandate or expectation uniquely imposed upon Black women. The EEOC argued that this implicit or explicit term or condition of employment for Black women is informed by a long history of privileging hair texture – namely, straight hair – associated with white women and denigrating Black women's hair texture. Consequently, natural hairstyles are maligned and prohibited because of their negative association with Blackness, whereas straight hairstyles are expected, if not required, as a result of their positive association with whiteness. An employer in turn may not discriminate against all Black women –but, as is seen in this case, an employer may exclusively discriminate against a Black woman who is stereotyped as "too Black" by virtue of her natural hairstyle. Thus Black women are pressured or compelled to wear straight hair. As a result, workplace bans on locs (and other natural hairstyles) impose a racialized and gendered assimilationist appearance norm upon Black women that essentially no other women are expected to fulfill in order to obtain and maintain employment.

In the seminal case, *Price Waterhouse*, the US Supreme Court held that an employer engages in intentional sex discrimination if it mandates conformity with gender stereotypes as a term or condition of employment. In *Price Waterhouse*, despite her superior objective qualifications, Ann Hopkins was denied a promotion to partner at the accounting firm. To increase her chances of promotion, Ann Hopkins was instructed to "walk more femininely, talk more femininely, dress more femininely, wear make-up, have her hair styled, and wear jewelry," and to exhibit a less "aggressive" demeanor. *See Price Waterhouse*, 490 U.S. at 235. In other words, the national accounting firm of Price Waterhouse denied Ann Hopkins a promotion because she did not conform to socially constructed stereotypes of how a woman should behave and look. Accordingly, Ms. Hopkins was not denied partnership simply because she was a woman; she was denied partnership because she was perceived as behaving and presenting herself in a way that was "too masculine," which the Supreme Court held constituted unlawful gender stereotyping.

It is plausible that, in the present case, racialized and gendered stereotyping similarly shaped CMS's decision to deprive Ms. Jones of an employment opportunity for which she was qualified. It could be persuasively argued that CMS rescinded Ms. Jones' job offer not simply because she was Black, but because, as a Black woman, she did not comply with racialized and gendered appearance norms, which privilege straight hair and thereby necessitate conformity with white womanhood. Thus CMS did not deprive Ms. Jones employment simply because she identified as a Black woman, but because Ms. Jones was catalogued as the "wrong kind of Black woman" once the HR manager confirmed that Ms. Jones was donning locs. It is plausible that CMS perceived Ms. Jones as contravening an operational standard of white womanhood by presenting herself in a way CMS deemed "too Black" – parallel to how male partners at Price Waterhouse deemed Ms. Hopkins as "too masculine." Consequently, the EEOC should not be precluded from discovering whether such racialized and gendered stereotyping shaped CMS's implementation and enforcement of its ban on locs to rescind Ms. Jones' offer of employment. Such evidence would establish a violation of Title VII.

It is clear, however, based upon the evidence presented, that CMS's condition of employment was shaped by a widely held pejorative stereotype associated with African descendants' natural hairstyles: they are "unkempt," "unattractive," and "unprofessional."

As noted earlier, Black women's natural hairstyles are often perceived as "unprofessional." Indeed, a recent Google search for "unprofessional hairstyles for women" primarily generated pictures of Black women donning natural hairstyles, whereas a search for "professional styles for women" yielded pictures of white women with straight hair. Leigh Alexander, *Do Google's "Unprofessional Hair" Results Show It Is Racist?*, THE GUARDIAN (Apr. 8, 2016), www.theguardian.com/technology/2016/apr/08/does-google-unprofessional-hair-results-prove-algorithms-racist-. Notably, at no point during the series of interviews with Ms. Jones did a CMS representative express an opinion about Ms. Jones' hair being unprofessional, excessive, or potentially violative of CMS's grooming policy. It was not until Ms. Jones confirmed that she was wearing locs that Jeannie Wilson's perception of Ms. Jones and her hair changed. In fact, Ms. Wilson conveyed to Ms. Jones that she did not find her locs unkempt at the time; instead, Ms. Wilson forecast that Ms. Jones' locs would one day become messy, and therefore she needed to cut off her hair so that CMS would preserve its offer of employment.

By dismissing the EEOC's discrimination claim, the district court foreclosed the EEOC's opportunity to uncover evidence concerning the enforcement of Ms. Wilson's "propensity to have messy hair standard." In other words, was this subjective grooming standard used to justify the exclusive regulation of Black applicants' and employees' natural hair, or were all employees and applicants – regardless of their racial identity – required to cut off or alter their hair if it were perceived that it might eventually become messy? This evidence would undoubtedly substantiate the EEOC's claim of intentional race discrimination. However, it does not seem necessary. At this juncture, based upon CMS's admission, it has instructed only Black applicants donning locs to cut off their hair. Moreover, it is clear that the enforcement of the grooming policy against Ms. Jones not only was cultivated by, but also perpetuates negative stereotypes of Black women's natural hair as "unprofessional," "messy," and "excessive." If we were to adhere to the district court's exacting application of the immutability doctrine, this Court would be willfully ignoring this reality. In the process, this Court would not only sanction the deprivation of employment for which Black women are qualified alongside the economic security, dignity, and mobility derived from meaningful employment, but also endorse the continued operation of long-held pejorative stereotypes associated with Black women's hair in the contemporary workplace.

C CMS's Locs Ban Imposes a "Straight Hair" Mandate and Unequal Burdens upon Black Women

In addition to perpetuating intersectional stereotyping, CMS's ban on locs imposes unequal burdens upon Black women to obtain and maintain their employment. Although the EEOC did not expressly argue that the court should apply the unequal burdens analysis the Ninth Circuit adopted in *Jespersen*, 444 F.3d at 1110, it is clear that the EEOC was urging the district court to consider the different burdens that CMS's locs ban imposes upon Chastity Jones not simply as someone who identifies as a Black person, but specifically as a Black woman. Notably, to date, the unequal burdens analysis has not been applied to intentional race discrimination cases initiated by Black plaintiffs challenging workplace bans on locs, braids, or twists. *Cf. generally* Angela Onwuachi-Willig, *Another Hair Piece: Exploring New Strands of Analysis under Title VII*, 98 Geo. L.J. 1079, 1112–20 (2010) (arguing that courts should allow Black female plaintiffs to put forth evidence of the temporal, economic, and emotional burdens of complying with a straight-hair mandate in comparison to white women). However, it does not prevent this Court from taking judicial notice of this reality at this stage of the litigation and thereby permitting the EEOC to gather evidence to establish this theory of intentional discrimination.

The EEOC explained that Black women often wear natural hairstyles such as Afros, locs, and braids because they are the styles most conducive to their natural hair texture. App. T-8, Doc. 21–1, at 8–9. The EEOC alleged that Black women often apply harsh, chemical relaxants, and/or extreme heat to their hair to achieve straightened hair. Additionally, Black women often don wigs, weaves, and extensions to achieve straight hair. The EEOC alleged that these methods of achieving and maintaining straightened hair are expensive and time-consuming. The Perception Institute has recently published *The "Good Hair" Study* – the first to examine the explicit and implicit biases related to Black women's natural hair – which affirms the EEOC's allegations. Perception Institute, The "Good Hair" Study: Explicit and Implicit Attitudes toward Black Women's Hair (Feb. 2017), https://perception.org /goodhair/results/. The study indicates that Black women reportedly suffer greater levels of anxiety, pressure, and stress in their efforts to comply with formal or informal straight-hair expectations than do white women. *See id.* Also, Black women spend more time and money on professional hairstyling than do white women. *See id.* Because of the expense, time, and consequence of maintaining straightened hair, the Perception Institute's study illuminates a common phenomenon among Black women that also negatively impacts their physical health and well-being. When donning straight hair, many Black women refrain from physical or outdoor activities such as exercising because perspiration or exposure to humidity or water will revert the texture of their hair to its naturally curly state. *See id.*

Additionally, the long-term use of chemical relaxants, heat, wigs, and/or weaves often causes temporary or permanent damage to Black women's hair and scalp. It is common for Black women to suffer through chemical burns as chemical relaxers are applied to their hair and scalp, which are not only excruciatingly painful, but also severely damaging. Black women often endure temporary hair breakage, temporary and permanent balding, and scalp disorders such as traction alopecia as a result of chemical relaxers, as well as wigs, weaves, and extreme heat being applied. Balding, hair loss, and scalp damage naturally engender emotional or psychological harms such as stress, depression, diminished confidence, and a negative body image, alongside additional financial investments to repair the harm. *See* Pamela Madu & Roopal V. Kundu, *Follicular and Scarring Disorders in Skin of Color: Presentation and Management*, 15 AM. J. CLINIC. DERMATOLOGY 307 (2014); Louise Gagnon, *Community Partnerships Connect Hair Loss Patients with Dermatologists*, 36 DERMATOLOGY TIMES 27 (2015). A recent study also reports that there may even be a linkage between Black women's long-term use of chemical relaxants to straighten their hair and their increased likelihood of developing uterine fibroids. *See* Lauren A. Wise *et al.*, *Hair Relaxer Use and Risk of Uterine Leiomyomata in African-American Women*, 175 AM. J. EPIDEMIOLOGY 432 (2012). Therefore, for many Black women, complying with a "straight hair mandate or expectation" – either through chemical relaxants, heat, wigs, or weaves – comes with real costs and burdens of which many employers (and members of the general public) are not aware.

The EEOC offered to present expert witness testimony not only to educate the court about the unequal temporal and economic burdens that Black women endure when barred from wearing locs and other natural hairstyles, but also to establish Title VII liability pursuant to this evidentiary framework. However, as a consequence of its myopic employment of the immutability doctrine, the district court emphatically declared that "no amount of expert testimony can change the fact that dreadlocks is a hairstyle" and thus that CMS's (and other employers') discrimination against locs will never violate Title VII. The district court's holding places Ms. Jones and countless African descended women in a precarious double bind: Don your natural hair at the risk of (lawfully) being deprived of an employment opportunity and attendant compensation; or don straight hair at the risk of enduring consequential costs to your economic, psychological, physiological, and physical well-being.

D The Immutability Doctrine Fosters Discrimination on the Basis of Race and Gender

As previously explained, federal courts have almost uniformly applied the immutability doctrine to Black women's challenges against discrimination suffered because of their natural hairstyles such as locs, twists, and braids on the grounds that these styles are not "immutable, racial characteristics." *See, e.g., Rogers v. American Airlines*, 527 F.Supp. 229 (S.D.N.Y. 1981). Likewise, in the instant case, the district court applied the immutability doctrine to the exclusion of established evidentiary and theoretical frameworks employed in intentional discrimination cases. In so doing, the court suggested that the EEOC could present a viable claim of intentional race discrimination only if it produced evidence that "Blacks are the exclusive wearers of dreadlocks." *Catastrophe Mgmt. Sols.*, 11 F.Supp.3d at 1144. To be clear, there is no hairstyle exclusively worn by African descendants nor are all African descendants born with the same hair texture. Simply, "there are no genetic characteristics possessed by all Whites but not non-Whites." Ian F. Haney Lopez, *The Social Construction of Race: Some Observations on Illusion, Fabrication, and Choice*, 29 HARV. C.R.-C.L. REV. 1, 11–12 (1994). African descendants do not exclusively wear Afros nor are all African descendants born with Afros. However, it appears that this idea influenced or motivated the district court's declaration that an Afro is an "immutable Black hair texture" – or, rather, an inevitable, biological physical feature signifying Blackness or African ancestry. We would be remiss if we were not to note the important correlation between the district court's opinion in this case and the Virginia Supreme Court's opinion in 1806 in *Hudgins v. Wrights*. Despite the expiration of 200 years, the same racialized understandings of hair operated in Ms. Jones' employment discrimination case as in the Wrights' freedom suit, and the parallels in the legal consequences are striking. In both cases, the judges constructed "woolly," or Afro, hair texture as an inheritable marker of Blackness or African ancestry. And, in both cases, the courts rendered legal freedom to women who possessed a white skin complexion and straight hair, yet unbridled, lawful regulation of women's bodies and personhood if they possess a darker skin complexion and "woolly" or unstraightened hair.

By declaring that an Afro is "an immutable Black hair texture" and locs are a mutable, cultural hairstyle, the district court concludes that prohibiting a Black woman from donning the former constitutes intentional race discrimination violative of Title VII, whereas proscribing the latter is beyond the scope of Title VII and is completely lawful. The district court's hairsplitting distinctions between immutable, racial characteristics and mutable, cultural

178 EEOC v. Catastrophe Management Solutions

characteristics superficially narrows the scope of protection against race discrimination under current antidiscrimination laws, which the following examples illustrate.

Imagine that, one day, a Black woman comes to work with her natural hair in a cropped styled likely deemed an Afro. The next day, she arrives at work with her hair locked. Applying the district court's holding, if the employer fires the woman because her hair is in an Afro, she can benefit from Title VII's protections against race discrimination. Yet, at the point she transforms or grows her Afro into locs, braids, or twists, federal protection against race discrimination is no longer available to her. Similarly, it would have been unlawful for CMS to disqualify Ms. Jones from employment for which she was demonstrably qualified if she had worn her natural hair in a cropped, unstraightened hairstyle. However, because Ms. Jones grew her natural hair texture long and locked it, the EEOC's Title VII race discrimination claim on her behalf failed, and CMS's grooming policy and Ms. Jones' rescinded job offer fell within the bounds of lawfulness. All of these instances of discrimination involved the same woman with the same hair. However, one act of discrimination is deemed unlawful and the other is legal; one act of discrimination is deemed remediable and the other, irreparable. We agree with the EEOC's contention that "[t]here is no principled or legal distinction between policies prohibiting Afros and policies prohibiting dreadlocks ... [i]t is thus disingenuous to distinguish between natural hair growth as immutable and natural hairstyles as mutable. They are inextricably linked." The district court's distinction between hair texture and hairstyles is nonsensical, and the immutability doctrine it employs to get to this conclusion is a legal fiction: a judicial rule that is not based in fact, but is treated as such to legitimize zones of protection and inclusion.

Furthermore, it would be imprudent for us to hold that Congress meant only to proscribe discrimination against "immutable characteristics" when the US Supreme Court in *Price Waterhouse* and the Ninth Circuit in *Jespersen* affirmed that allegations of discrimination based upon "immutable" or "unchangeable" characteristics is not a prerequisite to Title VII protection. Applying the district court's heightened application of the immutability doctrine contravenes the plain language of Title VII by perpetuating unequal terms, conditions, and privileges of employment for Black women when they grow their natural hair long or when it simply does not fit into an Afro. The dismissal of the EEOC's case at this early litigation stage effectively insulates covered employers that ban locs and other natural hairstyles – when they are not Afros – from Title VII liability as long they enact written grooming policies requiring "professional" hairstyles. As a result, the district court's decision incentivizes the hyper-regulation of Black women's bodies via their hair and the exclusion of Black women from contemporary workplaces when their hair is not straightened – or, rather, does not conform to a racialized and gendered construction of professionalism, beauty, femininity, acceptability, and womanhood associated with white women. In so doing, the district court's holding and its reasoning aids the suppression of Black women's exercise of freedom, autonomy, and agency over and through their hair, which white women are able to enjoy, and thus preserves Black women's relative vulnerability and subordination in the workplace.

Lastly, it is important to note that Renee Rodgers,[111] the plaintiff in the seminal case *Rogers v. American Airlines* decided in 1981, argued that her cornrow braids, which American Airlines banned, were "historically, a fashion and style adopted by Black women, reflective of cultural, historical essence of Black women in American society." *Rogers*, 527 F.Supp. at 231–32. Similarly, Chastity Jones, via the EEOC, argued that her locked hair is central to her subjective understanding of not only her racial identity, but also, more specifically, her identity as a Black woman. Every time a court propagates the immutability doctrine in discrimination cases like the one before us and erroneously declares that an Afro is the only hairstyle that signifies a woman as a Black woman, we are in essence dictating to Black women which features and experiences inform or define their personhood and self-understanding as Black or African descended women in the world. Judges are supplanting their lived experience with our personal judgments about what *we believe* defines and bears import to them as women and, in particular, as Black women. Therefore, by rejecting the immutability doctrine, this Court will no longer facilitate the disempowerment of Black women in workplaces and the dismissal of Black women's experiences within civil rights doctrine and advocacy.

VI CONCLUSION

For nearly four decades, employment policies banning African descended women's natural hairstyles have been treated as harmless acts of employer prerogative unrelated to race and gender, and as inconsequential to workplace equality and employment opportunity. *See id.* at 232 (holding that since the employer's ban on braided hairstyles did not regulate an immutable characteristic, the grooming policy did not violate federal employment

---

[111] Professor Paulette Caldwell reveals that the accurate spelling of the plaintiff's last name is Rodgers although the official case name spells it as "Rogers." *See* Paulette M. Caldwell, *Intersectional Bias and the Courts: The Story of* Rogers v. American Airlines, *in* RACE LAW STORIES 571, 575 n. 12 (Devon Carbado & Rachel F. Moran eds. 2008).

discrimination laws because it had "at most a negligible effect on employment opportunity" and concerned "a matter of relative low importance in terms of constitutional interests protected by the Fourteenth Amendment and Title VII"). However, situating Ms. Jones' claim within the broader social and legal context explicates that workplace regulation of Black women's natural hairstyles is not merely a function of harmless employer prerogative, but precisely an operation of discrimination at the intersection of race and gender. Natural hair bans constitute a ubiquitous barrier to Black women's employment and professional advancement, and it is not lost on us that, in 2016, Chastity Jones, a Black woman, is imploring the federal judiciary to recognize her right to wear her hair as it naturally grows and to be afforded the equal privilege of performing her job without heightened regulation, retribution, and stigmatization when doing so.

The district court erred in exclusively applying the immutability doctrine to decide the case before us. The district court's application of this legal fiction produces incoherent, unjustifiable, and harmful results. It is also at odds with Title VII's plain language, established evidentiary routes to prove intentional discrimination, and Congress's intent to weed out systemic barriers to employment opportunities, equality, and economic security for African descendants when passing the historic civil rights legislation at issue in this case.

We find that the district court dismissed the EEOC's claim prematurely. The EEOC has stated a plausible claim of intentional race and gender discrimination violative of Title VII of the Civil Rights Act of 1964, and it is entitled to pursue discovery.

* * *

The district court's decision is reversed.

It is so ordered.

<h2 style="text-align:center">Commentary on Webb v. City of Philadelphia</h2>

SAHAR F. AZIZ

<h3 style="text-align:center">INTRODUCTION</h3>

What a difference a judge can make when issues of race, gender, and religious liberty converge in the workplace. The Third Circuit's opinion in *Webb v. City of Philadelphia* brings to the forefront why a judge's understanding of gender and racial hierarchy matters when the employee is a Black woman and

Webb v. City of Philadelphia

her religion is Islam. Two minority identities frequently subjected to outsider stereotyping – Islam and Blackness – intersect with gender in *Webb*.[112]

The Philadelphia Police Department rejected Kimberlie Webb's request to wear a hijab, a religious headscarf worn by Muslim women, because it purportedly imperiled the neutrality, cohesiveness, and *esprit de corp* of the police force. Although Kimberlie Webb did not file a race discrimination claim, her status as an African American cannot be disconnected from the grounds on which the court rejected her religious accommodation claim.[113] Since the arrival of African Muslim slaves in the seventeenth century, Islam has been associated with heathenism and foreignness in the United States.[114] After centuries of violent suppression by Christian slave owners, African Americans returned to openly practicing Islam, first, as members of the Nation of Islam, then as Sunni Muslims. Civil rights Muslim leaders such as Malcolm X and Muhammad Ali symbolized the government's worst fear: African Americans refusing to assimilate into European Christian culture. The historic exclusion of women from law enforcement agencies only reinforces Webb's outsider status.[115] Thus it is no surprise that the court interpreted the police department's policies through the subjective, majoritarian lens of white male Christian normativity.[116]

Because nearly half of all federal district and appellate judges are white men, the judiciary is institutionally ill-equipped to understand the unique forms of discrimination experienced by women of color.[117] Judicial politics research "shows that judges' personal backgrounds, professional experiences,

[112] *Webb v. City of Philadelphia*, 562 F.3d 256 (3d Cir. 2009). *See generally* Sahar F. Aziz, *Coercing Assimilation: The Case of Muslim Women of Color*, 18 J. GENDER RACE & JUST. 1 (2015) (examining the myriad ways in which Muslim women are adversely affected by their intersectional identities and how it impacts their ability to be economically independent through gainful employment).

[113] Jamaal Abdul-Alim, *Kimberlie Webb Believes She Can Work as a Police Officer and Observe Her Religion at the Same Time. Not Everyone Agrees*, PHILADELPHIA WEEKLY (Sep. 17, 2008) (in which a photo shows Kimberlie Webb as an African American woman wearing a hijab).

[114] Edward E. Curtis IV, MUSLIMS IN AMERICA: A SHORT HISTORY (2009).

[115] Michael J. Palmiotto *et al.*, *An Analysis of Discrimination between African American and Women Police Officers: Are There Differences? Similarities?*, 18 CRIM. JUST. STUD. 347, 349–50 (2005).

[116] All three Third Circuit judges presiding in *Webb v. City of Philadelphia* were male; two were White (Anthony J. Scirica and D. Brooks Smith), and one was African American (Theodore McKee). The district judge was also White and male (Harvey Bartle III). Interview with Judge Harvey Bartle, Legal Oral History Project, University of Pennsylvania School of Law, https://scholarship.law.upenn.edu/lohp/4/. None of the judges was Muslim.

[117] *See* Ramzi Kassem, *Implausible Realities: Iqbal's Entrenchment of Majority Group Skepticism towards Discrimination Claims*, 114 PENN ST. L. REV. 1443, 1459 n.66 (2010) (summarizing studies finding that the race and gender of judges affect their exercise of discretion, particularly in antidiscrimination cases).

life experiences, and partisan and ideological loyalties might impact their decision-making."[118] Studies suggest that more gender and racial diversity in the judiciary would result in rulings more favorable to women and minorities, respectively.[119] When gender is a salient factor in a case, one study found that adding a woman to an otherwise all-male appeals panel increases the likelihood that the panel will decide in favor of plaintiffs.[120] And if the case involves sex discrimination or race discrimination, a female judge is more likely to find in favor of the plaintiff than is a male judge; a Black judge is more likely to find in favor of the plaintiff than is a non-Black judge.[121]

According to the Congressional Research Service, 63 percent of federal circuit courts of appeals judges are men, 76 percent are white, and 45 percent are white men.[122] Only 4 percent of federal circuit judges are African American women.[123] Federal district judgeships fare worse in terms of race and gender disparities, with 66 percent of judges men, 81 percent white, and 49 percent white men.[124] No Muslim judges serve on the federal judiciary, and only a few Muslim judges serve on state courts.[125] Couple these skewed demographics

[118] Allison P. Harris & Maya Sen, *Bias and Judging*, 22 ANN. REV. OF POL. SCI. 241 (2019) (noting that although ideology plays the biggest role in predicting judging outcomes, a judge's race and gender affects that judge's ideology).

[119] *Id. See also* Pat K. Chew, *Race, Gender, and Class at a Crossroads: A Survey of Their Intersection in Employment, Economics, and the Law*, 14 J. GENDER RACE & JUST. 359 (2011) (summarizing the studies on the impact of gender and race in judging).

[120] Christina L. Boyd *et al.*, *Untangling the Causal Effects of Sex on Judging*, 54 AMER. J. POL. SCI. 389, 411 (2010).

[121] *Id.* at 406. *See also* Christina L. Boyd, *Representation on the Courts? The Effects of Trial Judges' Sex and Race*, 69 POL. RES. Q. 788, 789 (Dec. 2016) (examining employment discrimination cases brought by the Equal Employment Opportunity Commission in federal district courts).

[122] Of the 179 federal circuit judgeships, only 21 federal circuit judges are African American, 14 are Hispanic, and 5 are Asian American. Barry J. McMillion, *U.S. Circuit and District Court Judges: Profile of Select Characteristics*, CONG. RES. SERV. 4–8 (Aug. 1, 2017), https://fas.org/sgp/crs/misc/R43426.pdf. *See also* Jonathan K. Stubbs, *Demographic History of Federal Judicial Appointments by Sex and Race: 1789–2016*, 26 BERKELEY LA RAZA L.J. 92 (2016) (providing a demographic summary of the federal judiciary by race and gender).

[123] *See* McMillion, *supra* note 122, at 8.

[124] *Id.* at 20.

[125] President Obama's attempt to nominate the first Muslim judge to the federal bench, Abid Riaz Qureshi, ultimately failed. Daniel Victor, *Obama Nominates First Muslim to Be a Federal Judge*, N.Y. TIMES (Sep. 7, 2016), www.nytimes.com/2016/09/08/us/obama-nominates-first-muslim-to-be-a-federal-judge.html; David Smith, *Trump Thinks Muslim Judges Would Be biased against Him – but There Are None*, THE GUARDIAN (Jun. 7, 2016), www.theguardian.com/us-news/2016/jun/07/donald-trump-muslim-judges-barack-obama?CMP=share_btn_tw; S. M., *Donald Trump Is Poised to Paint America's Judiciary Red*, THE ECONOMIST (Jan. 3, 2017), www.economist.com/democracy-in-america/2017/01/03/donald-trump-is-poised-to-paint-americas-judiciary-red. Although there is no data on the number of Muslim judges in state courts, the author was able to identify five sitting and retired state judges

Webb v. City of Philadelphia

with the disproportionately negative media coverage of Muslims as terrorists, foreign, and disloyal,[126] and a courtroom becomes a precarious space for a Black Muslim woman seeking equal opportunity.

Professor Valorie Vojdik, writing as Judge Vojdik, notably starts her feminist judgment by explicitly identifying the plaintiff, Kimberlie Webb, as a Muslim female police officer. In doing so, she puts the reader on notice that this case is about Muslim women, not only Muslims. While Vojdik exposes the original opinion's failure to recognize the gendered nature of Webb's religious accommodation request to wear a hijab, a headscarf worn by Muslim women, she is not able to discuss the importance of Webb's race in her intersectional analysis because Webb did not file a racial discrimination charge, and her lawyer never raised her race in court documents. In a city with a large African American population, being an African American Muslim woman has its own set of intersectional adverse consequences that warrant naming and deconstructing.[127]

That said, the feminist judgment methodically exposes how the Third Circuit's formalism denied Kimberlie Webb her lawful right to practice her faith as a Muslim woman and to stay in her chosen profession – precisely what Title VII of the Civil Rights Act of 1964 aims to prevent.

THE ORIGINAL OPINION

In *Webb v. City of Philadelphia*, the exercise of judicial discretion is ultimately what denied a Black Muslim female police officer her day in court. Kimberlie Webb sought to wear at work the Muslim hijab, which covers the hair, forehead, sides of the head, and neck, tucked inside her police shirt and under her police hat. Her commanding officer denied her request pursuant to

---

who self-identify as Muslim: Judge Carolyn Walker-Diallo (New York); Judge Hassan El-Amin (Maryland, retired); Judge Zakia Mahasa (Maryland); Judge Fatima Al-Amin (Georgia); and Judge David Shaheed (Indiana, retired). *See* Rana Khan, *First Muslim Appointed to Maryland's Highest Court*, THE MUSLIM LINK (Oct. 7, 2011), www.muslimlinkpaper.com/index .php/community-news/community-news/2775-first-muslim-appointed-to-marylands-highest -court.html; *Hon. Carolyn Walker-Diallo '03 Named Supervising Judge of Kings County Civil Court*, NYLS, www.nyls.edu/news-and-events/nyls-news/hon-carolyn-walker-diallo-03-named- supervising-judge-of-kings-county-civil-court/ (*last visited* Mar. 28, 2020); *Zakia Mahasa: Biography*, WISE, www.wisemuslimwomen.org/muslim-woman/zakia-mahasa-2/#ftn1 (*last visited* Mar. 28, 2020).

[126] *See, e.g.*, Brigitte L. Nacos & Oscar Torres-Reyna, FUELING OUR FEARS: STEREOTYPING, MEDIA COVERAGE, AND PUBLIC OPINION OF MUSLIM AMERICANS (2007); Evelyn Alsultany, ARABS AND MUSLIMS IN THE MEDIA: RACE AND REPRESENTATION after 9/11 (2012).

[127] *See* Aminah Beverly McCloud, *African American Islam: A Reflection*, 4 RELIGION COMPASS 538 (2010).

184 Webb v. City of Philadelphia

Philadelphia Police Department Directive 78, which is silent with regard to the wearing of religious clothing.[128] Whether Kimberlie Webb's hijab would impose an undue burden on the police department was the material fact in dispute.[129]

Not all practicing Muslim women wear the hijab, due to differing religious interpretations of whether it is a mandatory Islamic practice.[130] Nevertheless, Webb apparently sincerely believed that Islam required her to cover her hair, which is all she had to prove for the purposes of establishing a basis for a religious accommodation.[131] For the request to be lawfully denied, the police department needed only to show that the religious accommodation imposes more than a *de minimis* cost – an easy threshold for most employers to meet. In this case, the Philadelphia Police Department could not show that any actual harm would result from a Black Muslim woman wearing a headscarf – not even *de minimis* harm. Yet the district judge granted summary judgment for the City, and the Third Circuit affirmed. The judge determined that a reasonable jury could not find in favor of Webb, even though all inferences must be drawn in the light most favorable to Webb.

By failing to adhere to the legal standard applicable to deciding motions for summary judgment, the circuit court validated the police department's bias against Muslim women. The courts accepted the police department's conclusory claim that Webb's hijab would impede its ability to promote uniformity, cohesiveness, cooperation, and *esprit de corps*. Even though Webb was willing to wear a headscarf matching her uniform, tucked behind her ear, under the collar of her uniform, and under a police hat, the courts agreed with the police department that the hijab *per se* was a threat to the police's public safety mission.[132] The very sight of an obviously Black Muslim woman on the police force pushed the limits of formalistic liberal notions of religious tolerance too far.

Consequently, Kimberlie Webb was denied the opportunity to put forth her case before a jury of her peers. In a city where 42 percent of residents are Black and there are established African immigrant Muslim communities, Webb could have proven why her request for an accommodation to wear

---

[128] *Webb v. City of Philadelphia*, 2007 U.S. Dist. Lexis 42727 (E.D. Penn. 2007).

[129] *Webb v. City of Philadelphia*, 562 F.3d 256, 258–59 (3d Cir. 2009).

[130] Katherine Bullock, Rethinking Muslim Women and the Veil: Challenging Historical and Modern Stereotypes (2002).

[131] *EEOC v. Abercrombie & Fitch Stores, Inc.*, 135 S.Ct. 2028, 2032 (2015).

[132] *Webb v. City of Philadelphia*, 2007 U.S. Dist. Lexis 42727 (E.D. Penn. 2007); *Webb v. City of Philadelphia*, 562 F.3d 256, 258–59 (3d Cir. 2009).

a religiously mandated headscarf was not only reasonable, but also consistent with the Philadelphia Police Department's stated diversity goals.[133]

Instead, the district court opinion accepted the police department's narrow interpretation of Directive 78. The Directive set forth the uniform requirements and permitted officers to wear scarves around the neck.[134] Although the policy made no mention of the permissibility of religious clothing or symbols, the police department interpreted the omission as a prohibition of Webb's hijab. When Webb showed up to work on three consecutive days wearing her hijab, she was sent home and threatened with termination should she wear it to work again. On the fourth day, when Webb returned to work with her hair uncovered, she was suspended for thirteen days for the two days when she had worn her hijab. She subsequently filed a charge with the Equal Employment Opportunity Commission (EEOC), alleging religious discrimination, hostile work environment, and retaliation. Webb later added a sex discrimination claim in her court pleadings, which the district court determined was not sufficiently related to her religious discrimination claim to avoid dismissal for failure to exhaust administrative remedies.[135] That Webb did not file a race discrimination claim suggests that her lawyers may not have understood the historical connection between anti-Muslim bias and anti-Black racism.[136] Whether as slaves during the antebellum era or civil rights activists in the twentieth century, Black Muslims were treated as more savage and dangerous than non-Muslim African Americans.[137] As a result, practicing Muslim African Americans are racialized as outsiders in the workplace on account of both their religion and their race.

In affirming the lower court's dismissal of Webb's case on the defendant's motion for summary judgment, the Third Circuit relied on the Supreme Court's rulings in *Kelley v. Johnson*[138] and *Goldman v. Weinberger*,[139] which denied religious accommodation in a police department and the military, respectively. Each case cited the defendants' interests in uniform regulation to promote an image of impartiality, religious neutrality, uniformity, and subordination of personal preferences in favor of the group mission. The Court

---

[133] Steve Patterson, *Philadelphia Police Continue Effort to Create a Diverse Workforce*, CBS PHILLY (Aug. 28, 2015), https://philadelphia.cbslocal.com/2015/08/28/philadelphia-police-diverse/.

[134] *Webb v. City of Philadelphia*, 2007 U.S. Dist. Lexis 42727 (E.D. Penn. 2007).

[135] *Id.*

[136] Khaled Beydoun, *Antebellum Islam*, 58 HOWARD L.J. 141 (2014).

[137] Edward E. Curtis, *The Study of American Muslims: A History, in* THE CAMBRIDGE COMPANION TO AMERICAN ISLAM 76 (2013).

[138] 425 U.S. 238 (1975).

[139] 475 U.S. 503 (1986).

186   Webb v. City of Philadelphia

also cited the Fifth Circuit decision in *Daniels v. City of Arlington*,[140] where a police officer was denied his request to wear a gold cross pinned to his uniform because it impeded the department's desire to create an appearance of neutrality.

Although the Third Circuit recognized that Webb's religious belief in covering her hair was sincere, the court ruled that accommodating that request would impose an undue hardship on the Philadelphia Police Department.[141] It relied solely on the testimony of Commissioner Sylvester Johnson, an African American Muslim man, who stated that an appearance of religious neutrality was crucial for dealing and cooperating with the public.[142] Commissioner Johnson also claimed that strict adherence to the uniform policy promoted the image of the police force as disciplined and impartial.[143] Accepting this reasoning would *per se* exclude practicing Muslim women who wear the hijab, thereby eviscerating Title VII's religious accommodation and sex discrimination provisions.

Other than Commissioner Johnson's opinion, the police department put forth no evidence of actual harm that would incur to the police department were it to permit Webb to wear a matching hijab tucked under her collar, behind her ear, and under her police hat. While a neck scarf is permissible, a Muslim headscarf is not. Webb rightly pointed out that this contradiction falls squarely within the holding of *Fraternal Order of Police Newark Lodge No. 12 v. City of Newark*,[144] requiring that exceptions for secular purposes must also apply to the same practice for religious purposes.[145] The Philadelphia Police Department responded that neck scarves worn for warmth do not implicate the ban under Directive 78 "on clothing or ornamentation that expresses potentially divisive individual differences or viewpoints. The sole treatment of such scarves, as well as similar items such as socks, neckties, undershirts, shoes, sweaters, and boots, is to standardize them, when worn, within certain narrow limits of color or material solely to promote uniformity."[146] In accepting this argument, the court endorsed the defendant's position that uniformity bars identifiably Muslim women on its police force.

The question thus becomes how conjecture, speculation, and conclusory statements are sufficient to deny Webb her day in court. How did the Third Circuit agree with the district court in deciding, as a matter of law, that there

[140] 246 F.3d 500, 506 (5th Cir. 2001).
[141] *Webb v. City of Philadelphia*, 562 F.3d 256, 264 (3d Cir. 2009).
[142] *Id.* at 261.
[143] *Id.*
[144] 170 F.3d 359 (3d Cir. 1999).
[145] *Webb*, 562 F.3d at 262 n.5.
[146] *Webb v. City of Philadelphia*, Case No. 07-3081, Brief of Appellee 38–39 (3d Cir. filed 2/25/08).

Webb v. City of Philadelphia

was no genuine issue as to the material fact of whether a hijab imposes an undue burden on one of America's largest police departments? The feminist opinion demonstrates precisely why the original opinion was a miscarriage of justice with adverse implications for both Muslim women and religious diversity in public workplaces.[147]

THE FEMINIST JUDGMENT

In reversing the grant of defendant's motion for summary judgment, the feminist opinion brings to the forefront two issues overlooked by the original opinion: the inherently gendered facet of Webb's religious accommodation request, and the dominance of Christian normalcy in the interpretation of neutrality and impartiality. By denying Kimberlie Webb her request to wear the hijab, the City forced her to choose between complying with her sincerely held religious belief as a Muslim and continuing her public employment. This outcome contradicts the principles of tolerance and inclusion of religious diversity animating Title VII.

Even though the original opinion noted that a religious accommodation must be granted if a similar request based on secular reasons is granted, it denied Webb's request. In *City of Newark*, African American Muslim male police officers received a religious exemption to the no-beards uniform policy because such exemptions were granted to other officers for medical reasons.[148] Directive 78 explicitly allows the secular practice of wearing of scarves so long as they matched the color of the uniform. Thus Webb's request would have been permissible had it not been based on her Islamic faith. As such, a jury could have found that Directive 78, on which the police department relied to argue undue burden, does not prohibit a hijab merely because it omits it. Most likely, those who drafted the police dress policy in 1975 never considered the hijab because the Philadelphia Police Department had neither Black nor Muslim police officers, much less Black Muslims, on their squads at that time.[149] The original opinion ensured that this legacy would continue to harm Muslim women.

---

[147] Section 701(j) was added by Congress in a 1972 amendment to define religion to "include … all aspects of *religious observance and practice*, as well as belief, unless an employer demonstrates that he is unable to provide reasonable accommodate to an employee's or prospective employee's religious observance or practice without undue hardship on the conduct of the employer's business" (emphasis added). 42 U.S.C §2000e(j).

[148] *See supra* note 144.

[149] David Alan Sklansky, *Not Your Father's Police Department: Making Sense of the New Demographics of Law Enforcement*, 96 J. CRIM. L. & CRIMINOLOGY 1209, 1213–14 (2005–06).

188   Webb v. City of Philadelphia

Judge Vojdik called out this double standard. Not only did the original opinion fail to meaningfully inquire into why a scarf was permissible for secular purposes while a headscarf for religious purposes was unduly burdensome, but it also missed the obvious: a headscarf is worn only by Muslim *women*. The original opinion's failure to understand that sex discrimination arises from Webb's religious discrimination claim evinces a lack of understanding of how intersectionality operates in employment discrimination.

Vojdik insightfully recognizes that "Officer Webb's identity cannot simply be defined in terms of her sex; her identity also includes her religion." When the police department suspended Webb, it engaged in sex discrimination because it denied her the right to accommodation of religion afforded to Muslim men. This was not the first time that the Philadelphia Police Department had discriminated against its female officers. Vojdik points to litigation in the 1970s that required the department to assign female officers to patrol duty, as well as to actively recruit and integrate women.[150] This check-ered history should have put judges on alert that sex discrimination was deeply entrenched in the operation of the Philadelphia Police Department.

Vojdik also notes the objectification of women's bodies in America's broader culture wars. At a time when Islamophobia is on the rise, a Muslim female police officer wearing a hijab symbolizes a threat to Christian dom-inance in America.[151] So when the police department claims that a hijab compromises perceptions of the police department's political neutrality, it is really saying that the police force's presumptively Christian male identity is put into question. Rejecting the headscarf also signifies adoption of stereotypes of Muslim women as lacking agency and strength. Importantly, Vojdik finds that the refusal to accommodate Officer Webb "erases [her] religious identity as a Muslim, while simultaneously reinforcing the identity of the Philadelphia Police Department as male and masculine."

The police department's claims that a Black Muslim woman's hijab threa-tens police cohesiveness and the *esprit de corps* mirrors public prejudice against Muslims in the post-9/11 era. In other words, the visibility of mosques, Muslim women wearing hijabs, Muslim men wearing beards, and immigrants speaking Arabic threaten American safety and Christian identity. The original opinion's message to Webb – and, by extension, all Muslim employees – is

---

[150] *Fifty-Six Women Officers Are the First to Patrol Philadelphia's Streets*, N.Y. TIMES 18 (Sep. 26, 1976); *United States v. Philadelphia*, 499 F.Supp. 1196, 1197 (E.D. Pa. 1980).

[151] Sahar F. Aziz, *Coercive Assimilationism: The Perils of Muslim Women's Identity Performance in the Workplace*, 20 MICH. J. RACE & L. 1 (2014) (discussing the ways in which Muslim women experience coercive assimilation into White Protestant norms pervasive in the workplace).

clear: you must fully assimilate into white Judeo-Christian normativity if you want to be a member of the community. Indeed, Vojdik does not mince words when she states, "The refusal to permit Muslim female officers to wear the headscarf in this post-9/11 world serves to reinforce the identity of the state as Christian, Western, and anti-Muslim."

As a result, the "appearance of neutrality" policy is nothing more than a pretext for excluding practicing Muslims, Hindus, Jews, Sikhs, and other religious minorities from law enforcement agencies. If they fail to hide their religious identities, they are presumed to be incapable of working as impartial professionals. The religious garb brands them as presumptively biased on account of their visibly non-Christian identity. If Webb wants to practice her faith, she has no rightful place within US police and military services – who are the guardians of public safety. The same presumption used to apply to African Americans, who were systematically excluded from police departments.[152] As such, our laws continue to be infected by religious, gender, and racial bias, thereby demonstrating that we have a long way to go in upholding the goals of Title VII.

The irony in the original opinion's reasoning is that the institutions it cites for support – the military and police departments – disagree with the argument put forth by the Philadelphia Police Department. As Judge Vojdik highlights, over the past twenty-five years, the US military and three metropolitan police departments (New York, Los Angeles, and Chicago) have codified accommodation of religious dress in their policies. With a rapidly diversifying population racially and ethnically, police departments are struggling to retain their legitimacy by hiring officers who reflect the demographics of the residents they serve.[153] To earn the trust of their communities, whom they need to report crimes and cooperate in investigations, police departments must demonstrate that they value diversity among their ranks.

In military affairs, both military leadership and Congress support accommodation of religious clothing. Vojdik reveals the City's bad faith argument of undue burden when she cites the US Coast Guard's decision to alter its uniform regulations "to include wearing of religious headgear under certain conditions." The Religious Apparel Requirement Law also explicitly provides

---

[152] Eugene J. Watts, *Black and Blue: Afro-American Police Officers in Twentieth-Century St. Louis*, 7 J. URB. HIST. 131, 138 (1981) (highlighting the use of discriminatory practices against Black candidates by the St. Louis police departments, including application denials and more exacting physical requirements than for their White counterparts).

[153] Jeremy Ashkenas & Haeyoun Park, *The Race Gap in America's Police Departments*, N.Y. TIMES (Apr. 8, 2015), www.nytimes.com/interactive/2014/09/03/us/the-race-gap-in-americas-police-departments.html; Brian A. Reaves, LOCAL POLICE DEPARTMENTS, 2007 14 (Dec. 2010), www.bjs.gov/content/pub/pdf/lpd07.pdf.

that "a member of the armed forces may wear an item of religious apparel while wearing the uniform of the member's armed force," so long as it does not interfere with the member's military duties.[154] If this standard had applied to Kimberlie Webb, she would not have been forced to choose between practicing her religion and keeping her job. Indeed, the Philadelphia Police Department admitted that she could have performed all of her duties while wearing her hijab.[155] It simply did not want a visibly Muslim woman on the squad.

Vojdik points out that the case law cited by the original opinion weakens, rather than supports, the police department's claims of undue hardship. In contrast to the facts here, the cases upholding denials of a religious accommodation did so because employers would have been exposed to criminal liability, health and safety hazards, and violations of collective bargaining agreements.[156] Other cases upholding the undue burden defense explained that the proposed accommodations imposed material burdens that required employers to change work schedules, work duties, or modes of operation.[157] None of these material or legal burdens would have been at stake had Webb's request to wear a hijab been granted.[158]

In contrast to the original opinion's blanket acceptance of Commissioner Johnson's uncorroborated testimony, Vojdik holds the police department to the law's requirement that employers "produce actual, demonstrated hardship to avoid the duty of accommodation." No investigation was conducted to assess the effect of permitting Officer Webb to wear her headscarf nor did

---

[154] 10 U.S.C. §774 (1987).

[155] *Webb v. City of Philadelphia*, 562 F.3d 256, 261 (3d Cir. 2009) (citing the testimony of Commissioner Sylvester Johnson).

[156] *See, e.g.*, *United States v. Board of Education*, 911 F.2d 882 (3d Cir. 1990) (finding hardship where accommodation would violate criminal statute); *Kalsi v. New York City Transit Auth.*, 62 F.Supp.2d 745 (E.D.N.Y. 1998) (concluding that the employer did not violate §701 in discharging an employee who, for religious reasons, refused to wear a hard hat, which was required for safety reasons); *Trans World Airlines, Inc. v. Hardison*, 432 U.S. 63 (1977) (finding religious exemption from working on Saturdays that violate a collective bargaining agreement imposes undue hardship on an employer).

[157] *Mattingly v. Univ. of S. Fla. Bd. of Trs.*, 931 F.Supp.2d 1176, 1185 (M.D. Fla. 2013) (granting a plaintiff's request for shorter shifts imposes an undue burden because an employer must deny shift preferences to other officers and change officers' work schedules); *Beadle v. City of Tampa*, 42 F.3d 633, 638 (11th Cir. 1995) (requiring a police department to grant shift exceptions would result in a greater than *de minimis* cost and constitute an undue burden).

[158] *United States v. Board of Education of Philadelphia*, 911 F.2d 882 (3d Cir. 1990) (denying a Muslim school teacher's request to wear a hijab because it would violate the Religious Garb Statute and expose the school to criminal liability); *Equal Employment Opportunity Commission v. Reads, Inc.*, 759 F.Supp. 1150, 1150 (E.D. Pa. 1991) (denying an employee's request not to work on Saturdays because this accommodation would violate a collective bargaining agreement).

anyone in the Philadelphia Police Department communicate with the other major police departments who have granted such requests, to learn from their experiences. Vojdik concludes that such a blatant failure to make a good faith effort to show undue burden arises from the City of Philadelphia's reliance on "the fears or prejudices of employers or members of the public to relieve it of its Title VII obligation to accommodate religious diversity in the workplace." Should public fears and prejudices against Muslims be the standard for applying religious accommodation law, America's police departments would be far from neutral.[159]

CONCLUSION

By the end of the feminist judgment, it becomes crystal-clear why it matters that a judge understands how patriarchy works in the twenty-first century. Even though the original opinion did not explicitly state that Muslim women should have fewer rights than men, the court's undue deference to the police department and the sole male witness produces the same effect. The already low *de minimis* standard was replaced with a blanket acceptance of a man's word without any requirement that it be corroborated by competent evidence. Had the feminist opinion been the original opinion, we could have avoided the devastating harms that *Webb v. City of Philadelphia* has already imposed and will continue, inevitably, to impose on Muslim women in public service, not to mention government efforts to meaningfully diversify their workforces to reflect the residents they serve. And we would be one step closer to allowing women to both earn a livelihood and preserve their dignity.

Webb v. City of Philadelphia, 562 F.3d 256 (3d Cir. 2009)

JUDGE VALORIE K. VOJDIK DELIVERED THE OPINION OF THE COURT.

Kimberlie Webb, a female Muslim police officer, has filed this suit against the City of Philadelphia, challenging the refusal of the Philadelphia Police Department to grant her request for religious accommodation to allow her to wear a headscarf with her police uniform. Her complaint alleges that, *inter*

---

[159] Forty-one percent of Americans believe that Islam is more likely to encourage violence, and 50 percent say Islam is not part of mainstream American society. *How the U.S. General Public Views Muslims and Islam*, PEW RESEARCH CENTER (July 26, 2017), www.pewforum.org/2017/07/26/how-the-u-s-general-public-views-muslims-and-islam/.

alia, the City discriminated against her under Title VII of the Civil Rights Act of 1964 because of her sex and religion.[160]

The City claims that permitting Officer Webb to wear a headscarf with her uniform would result in an undue hardship. Uniformity of appearance, the City asserts, is essential to unit cohesion, *esprit de corps*, and subordination to hierarchy. Permitting Officer Webb to wear a headscarf, therefore, would impair police effectiveness. The City also argues that Officer Webb failed to exhaust her administrative remedies with respect to her claim of sex discrimination under Title VII.

The district court agreed with the City and granted summary judgment in favor of the City on all of Webb's claims. *See Webb v. City of Philadelphia*, No. 05–5283, 2007 WL 1866763; 2007 U.S. Dist. LEXIS 46872 (E.D. Pa. June 27, 2007). Officer Webb appeals from the decision of the district court granting summary judgment on her claims of religious and sex discrimination under Title VII. We now reverse.

Title VII compels religious tolerance and inclusion of religious diversity in the workplace. Employers must make religious accommodation available to all employees on an equal basis, regardless of their sex. The City has not offered any competent evidence that allowing Webb to wear a headscarf will result in actual harm, let alone undue hardship. The US military and many other police departments permit similar accommodations for religious dress, with no evidence of harm. In fact, while it argues that strict uniformity of appearance is required, the City's uniform policy permits exemptions from its no-beards requirement for Muslim and other men for religious purposes. Because the factual issue of undue hardship remains in dispute, the City is not entitled to summary judgment.

Officer Webb's claim of sex discrimination falls directly within the scope of her religious discrimination claim filed with the Equal Employment Opportunity Commission (EEOC). The City's refusal to allow Officer Webb to wear an item of sex-specific clothing worn only by women inherently raises the issue of whether its policy discriminates on the basis of sex. In its defense, the City relies on Directive 78, its written uniform policy, which provides a religious exemption for male officers, including Muslim men, from its no-beards requirement. The City's uniform policy thus treats men and women differently, granting Muslim men religious accommodation from its

---

[160] Officer Webb's complaint also included claims for violation of Title VII's prohibition on retaliation, which included creation of a hostile work environment, and for violation of Pennsylvania's Religious Freedom Protection Act, 71 Pa. Stat. Ann. §2401. She has not appealed the judgments in favor of the City on those claims.

uniform requirements, but not Muslim women. Officer Webb's claim of sex discrimination must therefore be allowed to proceed.

I FACTS AND PROCEDURAL HISTORY

Kimberlie Webb is a female police officer employed by the City of Philadelphia since 1995. She is also a practicing Muslim. On February 11, 2003, Officer Webb requested in writing permission from her commanding officer, Captain Michael Murphy, to wear a headscarf while in uniform and on duty. She explained that her Islamic religious faith required women to wear a headscarf, also called a khimar or hijab. The headscarf covers the hair and neck. Officer Webb explained in her request that she would wear a scarf underneath her police hat and tucked into her shirt. In all other respects, she would comply with the uniform dress and grooming code adopted by the City of Philadelphia Police Department in 1975, called Directive 78.

Captain Murphy denied her request for accommodation based solely on Directive 78. Deposition of Captain Murphy, Exhibit E to Defendant City of Philadelphia's Motion for Partial Summary Judgment. In denying Webb's request, Captain Murphy did not consider whether or not the City could accommodate her request for religious accommodation without placing an undue burden on the operations of the Philadelphia Police Department. *Id.*

Directive 78 requires all officers to wear the same items of clothing and a police hat. It permits police officers to wear scarves with their uniform. Directive II(E)(5), 78–3. It does not specify or restrict the purposes for which a scarf may be worn, or the manner or form of how it may be worn. *Id.* Directive 78 thus does not prohibit police officers from wearing scarves wrapped around their heads and/or necks in the same manner as that requested by Officer Webb. The only limitation is the color of the scarf: officers may wear black or navy blue scarves, and those holding the rank of captain or above may wear white scarves. *Id.* Nothing in the Directive prohibits officers from wearing scarves for religious purposes.

Contrary to the City's assertion, Directive 78 does not mandate complete uniformity of appearance. The Directive includes sex-specific hair, makeup, and jewelry requirements that are different for female and male officers. Directive III(D), 78–8. For example, it permits female officers to wear their hair longer than male officers. Directive III(D)(1)(a), III(D)(2)(a). The Directive permits female, but not male, officers to wear lipstick, clear nail polish, and jewelry. *See* Directive III(D)(2)(b) and (c). The Directive also prohibits male officers from wearing beards and goatees, except when

194   Webb v. City of Philadelphia

consistent with assignment (e.g., if required for undercover work). Directive III(D)(1)(d).

Although the City claims that officers are prohibited from wearing religious symbols, Directive 78 contains no language to that effect. The only reference to religion appears on page 78–8, where the Directive authorizes religious exceptions for male officers from its otherwise applicable no-beards requirement. The Police Commissioner may authorize a waiver of the no-beards requirement to male employees upon a showing by the employee's religious leader "that the employee practices a religion that requires him to wear a beard." *Id.* The Directive provides for the form of the waiver request and requires the employee to reapply at the end of a twelve-month period, when the waiver expires. The Directive also authorizes a medical exception for male officers if the police medical director advises that the employee has a medical condition that prevents him from shaving. *Id.*

Commissioner Johnson testified that this religious exception to the no-beard rule resulted from *Fraternal Order of Police Lodge No. 12 v. City of Newark*, 170 F.3d 359 (3d Cir. 1999). In that case, Muslim male police officers sued the City of Newark, alleging that the no-beards rule of the Newark Police Department violated their First Amendment rights to exercise their religious faiths. The City of Newark permitted male officers with certain medical conditions to obtain a waiver of its no-beards requirement for nonreligious, or "secular," reasons, but refused to permit Muslim officers a similar accommodation for religious purposes. This Court concluded that Newark's willingness to exempt from the rule some officers for medical reasons, but refusal to exempt other officers for religious reasons, demonstrated bias against religious practice. Johnson testified that the City of Philadelphia subsequently modified its no-beards rule to provide both medical and religious exceptions for male officers, including Muslim men, who are prohibited from shaving or who are required to wear beards. Johnson Affidavit, ¶20.

Directive 78 permits the waiver of its uniform and appearance code for male officers to accommodate their religious beliefs and practice, but does not provide any religious exception for female officers. The City permits Muslim male officers to practice their religious faith and remain on the police force, but has denied Officer Webb, a Muslim female officer, the same opportunity. The City also permits scarves to be worn by all officers for any purpose, but refused to permit Officer Webb, a Muslim female officer, to wear a scarf for religious reasons.

On February 28, 2003, Officer Webb filed *pro se* a charge of discrimination under Title VII of the Civil Rights Act of 1964, 42 U.S.C. §2000e-2(a)(1), with the EEOC and the Pennsylvania Human Rights Commission. She alleged that her religion was Al-Islam and that she had requested permission "to wear a khimar, a Muslim head covering" as a religious accommodation – a rule exemption that the City had denied.

While the EEOC charge was pending, Officer Webb came to work wearing her headscarf on three consecutive days in August 2003, and the Police Department sent her home after she refused to remove it. On August 14, the City warned her that her conduct could lead to disciplinary action, after which she reported to work without a headscarf. The City of Philadelphia later filed disciplinary charges of insubordination against Webb for wearing the headscarf and suspended her without pay for thirteen days.

After receiving a right-to-sue letter from the EEOC on July 8, 2005, Officer Webb timely filed suit on October 5, 2005, against the City of Philadelphia and individual defendants, alleging three causes of action under Title VII, 42 U.S. C. §2000e-2(a)(1) – religious discrimination, "retaliation/hostile work environment," and sex discrimination – and one cause of action under the 2002 Pennsylvania Religious Freedom Protection Act (RFPA).[161] Her complaint seeks declaratory and injunctive relief, as well as actual, compensatory, and punitive damages, and attorney fees and costs. The individual defendants have been dismissed from the suit.

The district court granted summary judgment against Officer Webb on all four claims. *See Webb*, 2007 WL 1866763; 2007 U.S. Dist. LEXIS 46872. It granted summary judgment for the City of Philadelphia on Officer Webb's Title VII claim of religious discrimination, finding that Directive 78 bars the wearing of religious dress or symbols when a police officer is in uniform and has no medical or secular exceptions. The district court concluded that the City established "compelling, nondiscriminatory reasons for Directive 78" and had demonstrated as a matter of law that it would suffer an undue hardship if required to permit Officer Webb to wear a headscarf with her police uniform. With respect to her claim of sex discrimination under Title VII, the district court held that Officer Webb failed to exhaust her administrative remedies and concluded that it lacked subject matter jurisdiction over the claim. The district court also granted summary judgment against Officer Webb on her Title VII claim of retaliatory harassment and held that she failed to meet the statutory notice requirements for her RFPA claim.

Officer Webb appeals only the district court's adverse judgments on the religious discrimination and sex discrimination claims. She also raises on

---

[161] Officer Webb claimed that the City of Philadelphia retaliated against her, which created a hostile work environment – a claim often referred to as "retaliatory harassment."

196   Webb v. City of Philadelphia

appeal constitutional claims arising from the same set of facts alleged in her complaint, which she did not raise in the district court.

The district court had jurisdiction under 28 U.S.C. §§1331 and 1367. We have jurisdiction to hear this appeal under 28 U.S.C. §1291.

II STANDARD OF REVIEW

Our review of a district court's grant of summary judgment is plenary. *Huber v. Taylor*, 469 F.3d 67, 73 (3d Cir. 2006). Summary judgment is appropriate only when "the movant shows that there is no genuine dispute as to any material fact and the movant is entitled to judgment as a matter of law." Fed. R. Civ. P. 56(a). "In considering a motion for summary judgment, a district court may not make credibility determinations or engage in any weighing of the evidence." *Marino v. Indus. Crating Co.*, 358 F.3d 241, 247 (3d Cir. 2004). Rather, "the non-moving party's evidence 'is to be believed and all justifiable inferences are to be drawn in his favor.'" *Id.* (citation omitted). On appeal, this Court "view[s] all evidence and draw[s] all inferences therefrom in the light most favorable to the non-movant, affirming if no reasonable jury could find for the non-movant." *Shelton v. Univ. of Med. and Dentistry of N.J.*, 223 F.3d 220, 224 (3d Cir. 2000). Because the grant of summary judgment was entered against Officer Webb, we view the record in the light most favorable to her.

III RELIGIOUS DISCRIMINATION

Title VII prohibits employers, including the City of Philadelphia, from discriminating against employees on the basis of religion. It makes it an unlawful employment practice for any employer to discharge, discipline, or otherwise discriminate against any individual with respect to that individual's compensation, terms, conditions, or privileges of employment because of that individual's religion. 42 U.S.C. §2000e-2(a)(1).

Title VII also imposes an affirmative duty on employers to reasonably accommodate an employee's religious belief and practice. Section 701(j) of the Act, added by Congress in a 1972 amendment, defined "religion" to include "all aspects of religious observance and practice, as well as belief, unless an employer demonstrates that he is unable to provide reasonable accommodation to an employee's or prospective employee's religious observance or practice without undue hardship on the conduct of the employer's business." 42 U.S.C. §2000e(j); *see also Protos v. Volkswagen of America*, 797 F.2d 129 (3d Cir. 1986). As the Supreme Court held, "The intent and effect of this definition was to make it an unlawful employment practice under Sec. 703 (a)(1) for an employer not to make reasonable accommodations, short of hardship, for the religious practices of his employees and prospective employees." *Trans World Airlines, Inc. v. Hardison*, 432 U.S. 63, 74 (1977).

To establish a prima facie case of religious discrimination under section 2000e(j), an employee must show that she: (1) holds a sincere religious belief that conflicts with a job requirement; (2) informed her employer of the conflict; and (3) was disciplined for failing to comply with the conflicting requirement. *Shelton*, 223 F.3d at 224. Once the employee establishes these elements, the burden shifts to the employer to produce evidence showing either that it made a good faith effort to reasonably accommodate the religious belief or that it cannot reasonably accommodate the employee without incurring undue hardship. *Id.*; *Protos*, 797 F.2d at 133–34.

The US Supreme Court held in *Hardison* that employers must provide religious accommodation even if it requires the employer to modify its work requirements. An employer must provide a religious accommodation unless it can demonstrate that it will suffer more than *de minimis* harm. *Hardison*, 432 U.S. at 84. Undue hardship therefore requires something more than inconvenience or mere hardship. *See Cummins v. Parker Seal Co.*, 516 F.2d 544, 551 (6th Cir. 1975) (rejecting the employer's defense to the employee's request to not work on Saturday Sabbath; neither "mere inconvenience" nor objections of other employees constitute "undue hardship").

Whether or not an employer can reasonably accommodate an employee's religious practice is a question of fact. *Equal Employment Opportunity Commission v. Reads, Inc.*, 759 F.Supp. 1150, 1160 (E.D. Pa. 1991) (citing *Hardison*). *Hardison* is the only case where the Supreme Court has considered the duty to accommodate religious practices under Title VII. In that case, the Court held that the employer, TransWorld Airlines, could refuse to accommodate an employee's request for exemption from working on Saturdays. The employee's religion celebrated Saturday as the Sabbath and prohibited him from working on that day. The employer, however, was bound by a collective bargaining agreement that incorporated a seniority system. The Court found that the employer established undue hardship by showing that it could not accommodate the employee's request without: (1) incurring actual additional costs of substituting other employees for Saturday work; and (2) violating the rights of other employees guaranteed under the collective bargaining agreement. This constituted more than *de minimis* harm, the Supreme Court held, and therefore constituted undue hardship.

To establish its defense of undue hardship, an employer may not rely on hypothetical or speculative claims of harm. *See, e.g., Toledo v. Nobel-Sysco*,

198   Webb v. City of Philadelphia

Inc., 892 F.2d 1481, 1492 (10th Cir. 1989); *Tooley v. Martin Marietta Corp.*, 648 F.2d 1239, 1243 (9th Cir. 1981); *Brown v. General Motors Corp.*, 601 F.2d 956, 961 (8th Cir. 1979). EEOC guidelines provide that "[a] refusal to accommodate is justified *only* when an employer . . . can demonstrate that an undue hardship *would in fact result* from each available alternative method of accommodation." 29 C.F.R. §1605.2(c) (emphasis added). "A mere assumption that many more people, with the same religious practices as the person being accommodated, may also need accommodation is not evidence of undue hardship." 29 C.F.R. §1605.2(c)(1). Rather than defer to an employer's unsupported allegations of possible harm, federal courts have required an employer to produce evidence of actual, demonstrated hardship, such as where accommodation would expose the employer to criminal liability or expose the employee to health or safety hazards. *See, e.g., United States v. Board of Education*, 911 F.2d 882 (3d Cir. 1990) (finding hardship where accommodation would violate criminal statute); *Kalsi v. New York City Transit Auth.*, 62 F.Supp.2d 745 (E.D.N.Y. 1998) (the employer did not violate §701 in discharging an employee who, for religious reasons, refused to wear a hard hat, which was required for safety reasons).

A The City Has Established Neither Good Faith Efforts to Accommodate nor Undue Hardship

The district court held that Officer Webb met her burden of establishing a prima facie case of religious discrimination and failure to accommodate under Title VII. *Webb*, 2007 U.S. Dist. LEXIS 46872 at *3; 2007 WL 1866763. The City does not dispute this determination on appeal: Officer Webb's religious beliefs are sincere; she informed the City of her beliefs and the conflict with the City's uniform code; and the City disciplined her for failing to conform to its requirements. *Id.* The burden thus shifts to the City of Philadelphia to demonstrate that it made good faith efforts to accommodate Webb's belief or that the requested accommodation would in fact result in an undue hardship.

The City concedes that it has not offered Webb a reasonable accommodation. *Id.* Officer Webb's supervisor, Captain Murphy, denied Webb's request because he concluded it conflicted with Directive 78, and he did not consider whether accommodation would result in any harm or hardship. Commissioner of the Philadelphia Police Department, Sylvestor Johnson, admitted that he never considered Officer Webb's request nor conducted any investigation to determine whether accommodation would be feasible or detrimental to the police department. Deposition of Sylvester Johnson, Exhibit F to Defendant

City of Philadelphia's Motion for Partial Summary Judgment (Johnson Dep.), at 30–36. The City now seeks to defend its refusal to allow Officer Webb to wear a headscarf on the ground that it would impose an undue hardship.

The City has not presented evidence sufficient to establish that accommodation would result in undue hardship. The City did not offer any evidence that accommodating Webb's request to wear a headscarf would result in any economic harm, require the City to violate any existing seniority system or collective bargaining agreement, or violate any criminal statute or other applicable law. The City does not claim that wearing a headscarf would interfere with Webb's ability to perform her job duties or expose her to health and safety risks. Instead, the City argues that allowing Webb to wear her headscarf underneath her hat and tucked into her shirt would damage the police department's culture of cooperation, *esprit de corps*, hierarchical structure, and authoritative and neutral image. *Webb*, 2007 U.S. Dist. LEXIS 46872 at *3; 2007 WL 1866763. It alleges that this constitutes "noneconomic" harm that rises to the level of undue hardship.

The City has not offered any evidence that accommodation would result in actual harm (economic or noneconomic), let alone undue hardship. Instead, the City offers only conclusory and uncorroborated testimony about unspecified "noneconomic harm" that might possibly occur. The only testimony proffered by the City to prove "noneconomic" harm was the testimony of Commissioner Sylvester Johnson. Johnson testified that the uniform is intended to promote cooperation among officers, to foster *esprit de corps*, to emphasize the hierarchical nature of the police force, and to portray a sense of authority and neutrality to the public. *See* 6/27/07 Op. at 4–5. In Johnson's opinion, police must maintain political and religious neutrality, and Directive 78 is designed to achieve these goals. *Id.* He further opined that allowing Officer Webb to cover her hair in a manner that identifies her as Muslim would undermine these goals. *Id.*

Commissioner Johnson's testimony is insufficient as a matter of law to provide the necessary factual basis of the City's claim of undue hardship. First, Johnson admits that he did not conduct any investigation to determine the effect of allowing Officer Webb to wear a headscarf with her uniform. Johnson Dep. at 34–36. Johnson admits that he did not reach out to other police departments that have accommodated requests by individual officers to wear religious dress or symbols to learn about their experiences. *See id.* at 13. He instead based his opinion on his experience in the police department, which does not permit officers to wear the headscarf or other religious symbols. Thus he has no personal knowledge of the impact of allowing police officers to wear the headscarf or other religious symbols. *See* Johnson Affidavit, ¶¶8, 9.

Second, Commissioner Johnson's testimony does not offer evidence of actual harm, but instead consists of speculation and conjecture. Johnson states in his affidavit that permitting officers to wear different religious symbols on their uniforms "is likely" to have a polarizing effect on officers and "*possibly*" create division and resentments in the ranks. Johnson Affidavit at ¶11 (emphasis added). He states that he believes that there is "*potential*" for disruption of law enforcement services and that allowing modifications to the uniform "*could*" endanger police officers. *Id.* at ¶12 (emphasis added). Allowing Officer Webb to wear a headscarf, he opines, "*may* leave an impression" on the public that the police department endorses her religious beliefs and "*could*" be construed as favoring religious belief over nonbelief. *Id.* at ¶13 (emphasis added). Rather than establish concrete and actual hardship, Commissioner Johnson's testimony suggests merely the possibility of possible harm.

Neither does Commissioner Johnson identify with any specificity any tangible, actual consequences that would in fact result. For example, he did not explain the type of "disruption" of services that he opines could "potential[ly]" occur. Such vague assertions are insufficient as a matter of law to entitle an employer to ignore the duty to accommodate an employee's religious belief or practice. To hold otherwise would render the requirement of accommodation meaningless.

Even if Johnson's allegations were grounded in fact, as a matter of law the City cannot rely on the fears or prejudices of employees or members of the public to relieve it of its Title VII obligation to accommodate religious diversity in its workforce. Even assuming that some officers might be upset because an employer modifies its workplace rules to meet the religious needs of another employee, the objections and complaints of other employees alone do not constitute undue hardship. *Draper v. U.S. Pipe & Foundry Co.*, 527 F.2d 515 (6th Cir. 1975) (finding the possibility of grumbling by coworkers not enough to constitute undue hardship). Title VII does not permit such resentments or preferences to deny an employee equal employment opportunity. Subjecting Officer Webb to suspension or other forms of discipline, including termination, because of the City's perceptions of other officers' or its citizens' preferences or views, constitutes disparate treatment based on religion in violation of Title VII. *See, e.g.,* EEOC, Compliance Manual on Religious Discrimination §12-II(B) (2008) ("If an employer takes an action based on the discriminatory preferences of others, including co-workers or clients, the employer is unlawfully discriminating"). It is the same as if the City had refused to hire her because other officers objected to her because she is Muslim. It is not a defense under Title VII that customers or coworkers prefer to discriminate. *Id.*; *Diaz v. Pan American World Airways*, 442 F.2d 385 (5th Cir. 1971) (rejecting the argument that customer preferences can justify sex discrimination because "it would be totally anomalous if we were to allow the preferences and prejudices of the customers to determine whether sex discrimination were valid"); *White v. Cmty. Care, Inc.*, No. 07–1507, 2008 U.S. Dist. LEXIS 108444, at *26 (W.D. Pa. Dec. 11, 2008) (citing *Cain v. Hayatt*, 734 F.Supp. 671, 681 (E.D. Pa. 1990) (" 'customer preference has repeatedly been rejected as a justification for discrimination' ")).

The testimony of Commissioner Johnson therefore does not constitute competent evidence of undue hardship sufficient to establish a defense to accommodation. The argument advanced by the City of Philadelphia – that uniformity of appearance is essential to unit cohesion, *esprit de corps*, and subordination to hierarchy, and that the accommodation of different groups will harm or destroy the institution – is a familiar one. Similar claims have been used throughout history to preserve traditionally male or white institutions from the demands for inclusion of women, racial minorities, and LGBTQ+ persons.

The US military, for example, has argued that changing its policies to include these groups will destroy unit cohesion and undermine military effectiveness. These claims have been rooted in fear, not fact. Opponents of women in combat have argued that the presence of women will undermine male bonding and unit cohesion and thereby erode military effectiveness. *See* Valorie K. Vojdik, *Beyond Stereotyping in Equal Protection: Reframing the Exclusion of Women from Combat*, 57 ALA. L. REV. 303, 335 (2005). Numerous studies, however, have concluded that the inclusion of women in previously all-male training and field exercises did not impair unit cohesion or adversely affect the performance of trainees. *Id.* Similar arguments were made against the racial integration of troops during World War II, yet postwar surveys found that unit cohesion did not suffer. *Id.*; Joshua Goldstein, WAR AND GENDER 199 (2001). The military has made "disturbingly similar" arguments to justify the exclusion of gay and lesbian service members. *See Philips v. Perry*, 106 F.3d 1420, 1433 (Fletcher, J., dissenting).

The City of Philadelphia's claim of undue hardship recycles these familiar objections to the inclusion of women and members of minority groups previously excluded from these historically white, male, and Christian institutions. Such speculative claims are not entitled to judicial deference, as the City argues, but rather to heightened scrutiny. The US Supreme Court recognized in *United States v. Virginia* that the argument that women will impede male bonding and unit cohesion is the type of "doomsday prediction" used throughout history to keep women out of all-male institutions. 518 U.S.

515, 542–43 (1996). As Judge K.K. Hall explained, "Unit cohesion is a facile way for the ins to put a patina of rationality on [the military's] efforts to exclude the outs. The concept has been a favorite of those who, through the years, have resisted the irresistible erosion of white male domination of the armed forces." *Thomasson v. Perry*, 80 F.3d 915, 952 (4th Cir. 1996) (Hall, J., dissenting).

The City cannot rely on similar assertions that accommodation of Muslim women like Officer Webb will impair police effectiveness. Its claim of undue hardship is unsupported by competent evidence and based on speculation. As a matter of law, it has not established that it is entitled to summary judgment.

B Judicial Deference Is Unwarranted

Faced with the absence of credible factual evidence in support of its defense, the City nevertheless argues that the court must grant judicial deference to its police uniform regulations, citing *Goldman v. Weinberger*, 457 U.S. 503 (1988) and *Kelley v. Johnson*, 425 U.S. 328 (1976). Neither *Goldman* nor *Kelley* involved claims for religious accommodation or religious discrimination under Title VII. Neither opinion justifies deferring to the City's claims of undue hardship or exempting the City from its duty of reasonable accommodation under Title VII.

In *Goldman*, the Supreme Court rejected a First Amendment challenge brought by a Jewish Air Force chaplain to an Air Force regulation that prohibited him from wearing a yarmulke as part of his official uniform. In upholding the regulation, the Court was careful to limit its analysis to the context of the US military, which the Court clearly distinguished from the civilian world. "The Executive and Legislative branches have charged the military with carrying out the Nation's military policy," the Court explained. "[J]udicial deference ... is at its apogee when legislative action under the congressional authority to raise and support armies and make rules and regulations for their governance is challenged." *Goldman*, 457 U.S. at 507 (citing *Rostker v. Goldberg*, 453 U.S. 57, 70 (1981)).

The deference afforded this nation's military in *Goldman* does not extend to local police departments. The Philadelphia Police Department is a civilian agency, not a military institution, and Officer Webb is a city employee, not a military service member. The department is a municipal agency and has not been delegated authority by the Executive Branch or Congress to carry out the nation's military policy. Like any other civilian employer (and unlike the US military), the City of Philadelphia is subject to the requirements of Title VII. Its claim of undue hardship is not entitled as a matter of law to judicial deference.

Kelley v. Johnson is equally inapplicable. The case did not involve either Title VII or a claim of religious liberty. A male police officer challenged a New York City Police Department regulation restricting the length of men's hair, claiming that it violated his alleged liberty interest in his own personal appearance under the Fourteenth Amendment. *Kelley*, 435 U.S. at 240–41, 248. The Supreme Court rejected his argument, holding that the department's grooming regulation was not "so irrational that it may be branded 'arbitrary,' and therefore a deprivation of [plaintiff's] 'liberty' interest in freedom to choose his own hairstyle." *Id*. Noting that the majority of state and local police are uniformed, the Court held that this choice "may be based" on a desire to make police officers more recognizable to the public or a desire for *esprit de corps*. Either possible rationale, the Court concluded, "is a sufficiently rational justification for the regulations so as to defeat [the officer's] claim based on the liberty guarantee of the Fourteenth Amendment." *Id*. *Kelley* did not involve a religious challenge to a workplace requirement under Title VII nor did it hold, as a matter of law, that police departments were entitled to judicial deference to their workplace regulations.

Recognizing the importance of diversity in our nation's military, Congress adopted the Religious Apparel Amendment in direct response to the decision of the Supreme Court in *Goldman*. 133 Cong. Rec. E 1846 (daily ed. May 11, 1987). Representative Steve Solarz, sponsor of the bill, explained that the bill "would ensure that members of the Armed Forces will not be forced to choose between their sincere religious beliefs and a desire to serve their country." *Id*. Codified in 10 U.S.C. §774(a) and (b), the law provides that "a member of the armed forces may wear an item of religious apparel while wearing the uniform of the member's armed force," provided that the religious item does not "interfere with the performance of the member's military duties" and is "neat and conservative." Representative Solarz rejected the claim that allowing variation in appearance would "threaten uniformity and reduce military cohesion" and impair morale, offering concrete examples of exceptions to uniformity that did not reduce military effectiveness. 133 Cong. Rec. E 1846. The sponsor of a similar bill in the Senate similarly argued that the amendment "would strengthen morale by affirming that the military is a humane and tolerant institution." 133 Cong. Rec. 12,780 at 32 (daily ed. Sep. 22, 1987) (statement of Sen. Lautenberg, bill sponsor).

In requiring the US military to allow military members to wear religious dress, Congress rejected earlier claims by military leaders that absolute uniformity of every aspect of dress was essential to military discipline, *esprit de corps*, and military effectiveness. On January 9, 2007, the US Coast Guard announced that it would alter its uniform regulations "to include wearing religious headgear under certain conditions." US Coast Guard Office of Civil Rights Newsletter, Vol. 2, Number 1, January 2007. Implementing a policy that recognizes and promotes religious diversity of its troops, the Department of Defense has issued a directive that offers a broad range of religious accommodations to US service members, including discretionary provisions for holy day worship, separate or supplemental rations, waivers of immunizations, religious training, and a process for appealing rejected requests to wear religious apparel in uniform. Dept. of Defense Directive, No. 1300.17, Feb. 3, 1998. The Army, the Navy, the Air Force, the Marines, and the Coast Guard thus accommodate religious clothing needs, fostering diversity and inclusion of religious difference. The military also accommodates gender-appropriate grooming and uniform requirements. *See, e.g.*, US Dep't of Air Force, DRESS AND PERSONAL APPEARANCE OF AIR FORCE PERSONNEL, Air Force Instruction 36–2903 (Aug. 2, 2006); US Dep't of the Army, WEAR AND APPEARANCE OF ARMY UNIFORMS AND INSIGNIA, Army Regulation 670–1 (Feb. 3, 2005); Christine L. Williams, GENDER DIFFERENCES AT WORK, WOMEN AND MEN IN NON-TRADITIONAL OCCUPATIONS 4 (1991) (analyzing differences in dress and appearance standards for female Marines).

The factual basis for the grant of judicial deference in *Goldman* and *Kelley*, therefore, has changed dramatically in the intervening twenty-five or thirty years. Since those earlier judicial opinions, police departments likewise have rejected the requirement of absolute uniformity of dress, adopting more flexible policies to permit the accommodation of religious dress in the workplace. Webb has offered evidence that similar policies of accommodation by the Illinois Cook County Sheriff's Department, New York City Department of Corrections, and Metropolitan Police of London allow officers to wear religious headgear. *See* Affidavits of Ali al-Rahman and Larry Grant, Exhibits H and I to Plaintiff's Motion in Opposition to Defendant's Supplemental Motion for Summary Judgment. Police forces in the nation's three largest metropolitan areas (New York, Los Angeles, and Chicago) and in the second-largest county in the country (Cook County, Illinois) have accommodated officers wishing to wear religious garb. *See* Brief in Support of Reversal of *Amici Curiae* American Civil Liberties Union of Pennsylvania, American Civil Liberties Union, Council on American Islamic Relations, *et al.*, at 13–32. Police, correctional, firefighting, emergency response, and security and military organizations around the world have granted accommodations for religious dress without sacrificing the degree of uniformity that those organizations need to be effective. *Id.*

C The City's Defense of "Religious Neutrality" Fails

The City also argues that allowing Officer Webb to wear a headscarf would identify her as a Muslim and thus violate its policy of "neutrality," which strictly prohibits any religious symbols. This policy of "neutrality," the City argues, is entitled to deference under *United States v. Board of Education of Philadelphia*, 911 F.2d 882 (3d Cir. 1990).

The City's reliance on *Board of Education* is misplaced. In that case, this Court upheld the decision of a school board to deny a Muslim schoolteacher's request to permit her to wear a headscarf and long dress. The school district established undue hardship, this Court concluded, because accommodating the teacher's request would cause it to violate Pennsylvania's Religious Garb Statute, enacted in 1895, which prohibited teachers from wearing religious dress in public schools. The Garb Statute also imposed criminal liability upon school directors who, after notice of such violation, failed to comply with the statute. 24 Pa. Stat. Ann., §11–1112. A panel of this Court found that the Board of Education established undue burden because accommodation would expose school administrators to a "substantial risk of criminal prosecution, fines, and expulsion from the profession." *Board of Education*, 911 F.2d at 891.

Regardless of the wisdom of the decision, we do not need to revisit it to decide the issue before us. Directive 78 is not a state statute nor does it reflect the will of the legislature. There is no state law that prohibits the City of Philadelphia from allowing Officer Webb to wear a headscarf or that imposes criminal liability for any such accommodation. Cases involving religious expression and free speech in public schools, moreover, involve unique considerations, given the age and impressionability of children who have not yet reached maturity. *See generally Wisconsin v. Yoder*, 406 U.S. 205 (1972). In reaching its decision in *Board of Education*, this Court recognized that issues surrounding public schools involve the unique context of education. This case does not involve schoolchildren who might be susceptible to undue religious influence, but diverse citizens of a multicultural city who do not require protection from the marketplace of ideas.

The City's defense of "religious neutrality" fundamentally conflicts with the mandate of inclusion under section 701 of Title VII. To assure equality of treatment and therefore religious nondiscrimination, Congress has required employers to reasonably accommodate the religious beliefs of their employees by modifying workplace rules and practices. The goal is to better include members of different faiths, whose religious practices may conflict with rules designed for the religious majority. Congress thus has codified tolerance and inclusion of diversity in the workplace. An employer is neutral with respect to religion when it provides all employees the ability to work, regardless of their religion.

Philadelphia's uniform requirements, however, are consistent with, and conform to, the religious practices of the majority-Christian faith in this nation. In a Christian-majority country or police force, prohibiting the Muslim headscarf may appear neutral – but Philadelphia is a diverse city, as the City concedes, and its citizens belong to multiple religious faiths. To those citizens who are Muslim or Sikh or Orthodox Jews, a uniform that forbids the headscarf or other religious headgear codifies the religious norms of the Christian majority. To Muslims, the uniform is not a neutral symbol, but a Christian symbol that compels women to expose their hair and neck. Consider this: Christian police officers do not need to seek accommodation to practice their religious beliefs. Their religious practice appears as the norm; the headscarf, however, is defined as "different" and in need of accommodation. The appearance of neutrality, then, depends on whose viewpoint is being considered.

While the City claims that its policy is neutral with respect to religion, its failure to accommodate different religious beliefs imposes a tangible burden upon Muslim officers such as Officer Webb, who must choose between abiding by the religious requirements of her faith and continuing her employment with the City. Members of other nonmajoritarian religious groups, such as Sikhs and Orthodox Jewish men, face the same burden. Directive 78 does not require police officers whose religious practices are consistent with its dress and appearance requirements to deny their religious identity as the price of public employment. As a Muslim female officer, however, Officer Webb is denied that benefit. This is not religious neutrality; it is a denial of equal employment opportunity.

At heart, religious accommodation requires willingness to reexamine traditional practices that may appear neutral to the employer or members of the majority religion, but which exclude members of different religious faiths. The inclusion of members of previously excluded groups, such as Officer Webb, requires employers to critically examine the practice and policies developed for a homogenous workforce and to modify them unless undue hardship would result.

Commissioner Johnson's unsupported and speculative allegations of some vague and unspecified harm are insufficient to overcome the duty to accommodate religious belief in the workplace. Claims that the inclusion of difference will harm or destroy an institution are no longer entitled to deference, but are subject to skeptical scrutiny. To permit the City of Philadelphia to avoid accommodating a Muslim female officer by the simple recitation of potential harms that *might* occur would render the obligation to provide religious accommodation illusory. Similar claims, we have learned, are too easily used by traditionally male and/or white institutions to exclude women, persons of color, and members of minority religions who may appear different from members of the majority group. In fact, Directive 78 permits male officers an exception from its no-beards rule for religious and medical reasons, and it allows Muslim men to wear beards for religious reasons, even though they look different from other male officers. There is no evidence in the record that this accommodation of Muslim men has caused any harm or impaired the effectiveness of the police department.

D Genuine Disputes of Fact Preclude Summary Judgment

There are genuine disputes of material fact regarding the City of Philadelphia's claim of undue hardship that preclude summary judgment of Officer Webb's claim of religious discrimination.

First, there is a genuine dispute of material fact as to whether the City of Philadelphia has a policy of "religious neutrality" that prohibits police officers from wearing religious symbols. While Commissioner Johnson testified as to the existence of such a policy, his testimony is contradicted by Directive 78, which does not contain any such prohibition. It is also contradicted by the fact that the Directive permits a religious accommodation for male officers who wear beards. While Commissioner Johnson testified that this is not a religious symbol, the meaning of beards and the public perception of beards are questions of fact for the jury.

Officer Webb also presented testimony that she and another witness, Officer Bilal, had seen uniformed police officers in the Philadelphia Police Department wear various religious symbols with their uniform, including cross pins worn on lapels and symbols of crosses etched on the forehead in observance of Ash Wednesday. Deposition of Officer Rochelle Bilal, Exhibit C to Defendant City of Philadelphia's Motion for Partial Summary Judgment, at 37. The City argues that Officer Webb has failed to identify the names of these officers or the dates when the religious items were worn. This is a motion for summary judgment, however, and those concerns go to the weight of the testimony and the credibility of the witnesses, which are not issues for this Court to decide. Directive 78 also permits all officers to wear scarves without restriction as to purpose or form, which a jury could infer does not prohibit Officer Webb from wearing a headscarf for religious purposes. A jury could reasonably conclude from these facts that the City does not have a policy of prohibiting religious symbols or prohibiting Officer Webb from wearing a headscarf with her uniform for religious purposes.

A jury could also reasonably infer that the City of Philadelphia intentionally discriminated against Officer Webb on the basis of her religion. The record contains evidence that the City tolerates expressions of the Christian faith, while refusing to permit expressions of the Islamic faith. Commissioner Johnson testified that Officer Webb has been the only officer to be disciplined for allegedly wearing religious dress in violation of Directive 78. Johnson Dep. at 38–39. These facts proffered by Officer Webb – that the City permits officers to wear other religious symbols, including Christian symbols such as crosses, and to work without repercussion, while prohibiting Muslim symbols such as the headscarf – support an inference of intentional religious discrimination.

Finally, whether the City would suffer undue hardship by allowing Officer Webb to wear a headscarf is a disputed issue of material fact. The City has offered only the opinion of a single witness, Commissioner Johnson, to testify as to the factual basis of its claim of undue hardship. His testimony was unsupported by factual investigation or research, speculative, and vague as to the existence of any specific harm.

Officer Webb, however, has presented evidence that the US military permits the accommodation of uniform requirements for religious reasons and that other police and correctional departments have modified their policies to permit officers to wear religious headwear. The existence of these policies of accommodation raises the factual question of whether, in fact, accommodating Webb's request to wear a headscarf would result in the alleged harms claimed by the City and Commissioner Johnson. The record also contains evidence that the City permits some men to wear beards, contradicting its claim for the need for strict uniformity of appearance. This raises the question of whether permitting Officer Webb to wear a headscarf would impair the effectiveness of the Philadelphia Police Department. Evidence that the City tolerates other religious symbols, including pins in the shape of a cross worn on uniform lapels and ash crosses worn on the forehead on Ash Wednesday, also raises that same question. Viewing the facts in the light most favorable to the nonmovant, a reasonable jury could conclude that permitting Officer Webb to wear a headscarf would not impair the effectiveness of the Philadelphia Police Department or cause the City more than *de minimis* harm.

For these reasons, we reverse the judgment of the district court granting summary judgment to the City on Officer Webb's religious discrimination claim and remand for further proceedings.

IV SEX DISCRIMINATION

Kimberlie Webb is not only a Muslim police officer, but also a *female* Muslim police officer. Her complaint alleges that the City of Philadelphia intentionally discriminated against her based on not only her religion, but also her sex. Compl. ¶¶38–40. Specifically, she alleges in her complaint that the City accommodated the religious needs of male officers, but failed to accommodate her religious needs as a female officer. Directive 78, by its own terms, permits male officers a religious exception to its uniform and appearance requirement, accommodating the religious beliefs and practice of Muslim male officers. It has refused to extend a similar accommodation to Officer Webb, a Muslim female officer. On its face, the complaint states an actionable claim of sex discrimination under Title VII.

The City claims that the district court lacks subject matter jurisdiction over her sex discrimination claim because Officer Webb failed to exhaust her administrative remedies. It concedes that Webb filed a timely charge of discrimination with the EEOC, but asserts that the charge alleged only religious discrimination and thus that Webb did not satisfy the requirement of exhaustion on her claim of sex discrimination.

The district court, as the City admits, also has jurisdiction to hear additional claims of discrimination that an employee did not include in her charge of discrimination with the EEOC. Under well-established circuit precedent, a district court has jurisdiction to consider other claims that "can reasonably be expected to grow out of the charge of discrimination, including new acts that occur during the pendency of the proceeding." *Ostapowicz v. Johnson Bronze Co.*, 541 F.2d 394, 398–99 (3d Cir. 1976). The City inexplicably asserts that the EEOC would not have discovered the allegations of sex discrimination during the course of its investigation. The City's argument strains credulity, ignoring the plain text of Directive 78 and the gendered nature of the Islamic headscarf.

On its face, Directive 78 treats male and female officers differently. Because the City relies on Directive 78 to establish its defense, any EEOC investigation would have quickly revealed the factual and legal basis of Officer Webb's claim of sex discrimination. By its terms, Directive 78 permits male officers religious accommodations from its no-beards requirement, yet does not provide female officers with any religious accommodation. The City's uniform requirements challenged by Officer Webb therefore also constitute intentional sex discrimination under Title VII. In addition, the headscarf requirement itself is sex-specific and applies only to women in the Islamic faith. While there are multiple interpretations or traditions of Islam, no interpretation requires that men cover their heads or necks. Thus only female officers are harmed by the City's refusal to permit Officer Webb to wear a headscarf. The City, in Directive 78, permits Muslim male officers an exception from its uniform requirements, yet it has refused to permit a Muslim female officer a similar exception. Muslim male officers may continue their employment with the Philadelphia Police Department without violating their religious beliefs, but Muslim female officers, including Officer Webb, cannot.

At heart, the City's argument fundamentally ignores the intersectional nature of the discrimination that Officer Webb has alleged. Officer Webb's identity cannot simply be defined on the basis of sex; her identity also includes her religion, as well as her race, national origin, age, and gender identity. While the City seeks to disentangle her claim of discrimination into two separate claims – religious discrimination, on the one hand, and sex discrimination, on the other hand – they are inherently intertwined.

Title VII prohibits discrimination based upon the intersection of two or more protected bases, such as race and sex. *See, e.g.,* Equal Employment Opportunity Commission, RACE AND COLOR DISCRIMINATION, 2 Compliance Manual §15-IV(C) (Apr. 19, 2006) (EEOC Compliance Manual 2006); *Lam v. University of Hawai'i,* 40 F.3d 1551, 1562 (9th Cir. 1994) (recognizing that discrimination can occur on the basis of two or more protected factors, such as race and sex; in such cases, "the court must determine whether the employer discriminates on the basis of that combination of factors, not just whether it discriminates against people of the same race or of the same sex"); *Jeffries v. Harris County Comty. Action Comm'n,* 615 F.2d 1025, 1032–34 (5th Cir. 1980) ("we hold that when a Title VII plaintiff alleges that an employer discriminates against black females, the fact that black males and white females are not subject to discrimination is irrelevant").

The EEOC's Compliance Manual explicitly recognizes that claims of religious discrimination frequently raise related claims of other forms of discrimination. Equal Employment Opportunity Commission, RELIGIOUS DISCRIMINATION, 2 Compliance Manual §628 (July 22, 2008). The prohibition against discrimination based on religion, for example, may overlap with the prohibition against discrimination based on other factors. *See* EEOC Compliance Manual 2006 at §15-IV(B). For example, both race and religion might be implicated where an employer discriminates against an employee based on her belief in a religion tied to a particular race or ethnicity. *Id.* "The same set of facts," the EEOC Manual instructs, "may raise multiple protected bases of discrimination ..., both because negative stereotypes and biases may be directed at more than one protected basis at a time, and because certain protected bases overlap considerably." *Id.* at 15-IV. A complaint of sex discrimination by a female employee thus can implicate other protected bases of discrimination, such as religion or race. *Id.* Because the EEOC Compliance Manual explicitly recognizes the potential for these intersectional claims of discrimination, "[t]he question is whether any prohibited factors led to an adverse employment action, *alone or combined.*" *Id.* (emphasis added).

In this case, Officer Webb's complaint to the EEOC stated facts that raised two protected bases of discrimination. She challenged the denial of her request to wear the headscarf, a requirement specific to women only. The City's refusal to accommodate in this case discriminates against Officer Webb not only on the basis of her Muslim religious identity, but also on the basis of her sex. As a Muslim officer, she was suspended because of her religion for practicing her faith at work; as a female officer, she was denied the right to accommodation of religion afforded to Muslim men. The fact that Muslim male officers received a religious accommodation does not mean that Officer Webb did not suffer discrimination on the basis of her religious practice. Similarly, the fact that non-Muslim women also could practice their religion does not mean that Officer Webb did not experience discrimination on the basis of her sex.

Discrimination against Muslim women who wear headscarves, unfortunately, is not unusual or uncommon. Post 9/11, our nation has witnessed public expressions of anti-Muslim hostility, harassment, and violence against Muslim Americans. Civil rights complaints filed with one Muslim advocacy group rose from 366 in 2000 to 2,467 in 2006, an increase of 674 percent. Council on American Islamic Relations (CAIR), PRESUMPTION OF GUILT: THE STATUS OF MUSLIM CIVIL RIGHTS IN THE UNITED STATES 8 (2007). Because of their visibility, Muslim women who wear the headscarf face particular exposure to discrimination. *Id.* at 20. Muslim women who wear the headscarf have been harassed, fired from jobs, denied access to public places, and otherwise discriminated against because they wear the headscarf. *Id.* In 2004, the City of Omaha refused to permit Lubna Hussein, a Muslim woman, to enter the area near the city's municipal swimming pool with her children unless she removed her headscarf. Kevin O'Hanlon, *City Settles Suit with Woman Who Was Told to Remove Muslim Garb*, JOURNAL STAR (Feb. 17, 2005), https://journalstar.com/news/state-and-regional/city-settles-suit-with-woman-who-was-told-to-remove/article_485e474e-030c-5752-8888-242ba3494fb1.html. After she sued, the City subsequently settled and agreed to accommodate religious and/ or medical needs. *Id.*

Harassment of Muslim women wearing the headscarf has included physical violence. In the months following 9/11, Muslim women in Chicago "repeatedly reported having their head scarves yanked off or being spit at on the streets." Louise Cainkar & Sunaine Malra, *Targeting Arab/Muslim/South Asian Americans: Criminalization and Cultural Citizenship*, 313 AMERASIA J. 1, 12 (2005). In 2003, a Muslim woman wearing a headscarf was attacked in the parking lot of a K-Mart store in Springfield, Virginia, by a young man who allegedly shouted, "You terrorist pig." *Id.* In another incident in 2006, a Muslim female student at Baylor University reported that a man physically and verbally attacked her while she was walking on campus wearing a headscarf. The assailant pushed, shoved, and kicked her, using racial and anti-Muslim slurs, and forcibly removed her headscarf. *Id.* at 9. She was treated at a local hospital for injuries. *Id.*

Throughout history, women's bodies have served as highly visible symbols of the collective group to which they belong. *See* Nira Yuval-Davis, GENDER AND NATION 23 (1997) (discussing role of gender and gender symbols as symbolic border guards for social collectivities). Social, cultural, and religious groups often regulate the dress and appearance of female members, using women's bodies to symbolically construct and enforce the identity of the larger group. As the embodiment of the larger social, religious, or political collectives to which they belong, women's bodies too often become the targets for attack by outside groups. The headscarf is no exception. In the wake of 9/11, the headscarf is not merely a religious symbol or practice, but a highly contested political symbol within this nation and the global political arena.

Western media has largely interpreted the Muslim headscarf or hijab as a symbol of the forced subordination of women who have no choice but to cover in public. The assumption that women who wear the headscarf lack free choice and agency rests on stereotypes and overly broad generalizations about this particular group of women. *See, e.g.*, Adrien Katherine Wing & Monica Nigh Smith, *Critical Race Feminism Lifts the Veil? Muslim Women, France, and the Headscarf Ban*, 39 U.C. DAVIS L. REV. 743, 747–50, 758–74 (2006). These stereotypes conflict with the gendered expectation that police officers should be assertive, independent, and dominant. The City's refusal to permit female officers to wear headscarves thus reinforces the identity of police officers as male, powerful, and dominant, while excluding those women who are assumed to be weak and submissive. Refusing to permit Officer Webb to wear a headscarf to practice her religion therefore erases Officer Webb's religious identity as a Muslim, while simultaneously reinforcing the identity of the Philadelphia Police Department as male and masculine. The refusal to permit Muslim female officers to wear the headscarf in this post-9/11 world serves to reinforce the identity of the state as Christian, Western, and anti-Muslim. The City of Philadelphia implicitly makes this claim, arguing that the police department must maintain both religious *and* political neutrality.

Officer Webb's charge of discrimination, moreover, raises the issue of the treatment of a female police officer by the Philadelphia Police Department, which has openly discriminated against female officers, refusing to assign them as patrol officers, as recently as 1976. *Fifty-Six Women Officers Are the First to Patrol Philadelphia's Streets*, N.Y. Times 18 (Sep. 26, 1976). The US Attorney General filed a suit against the City in 1974, alleging that the City denied women equal employment opportunities in violation of Title VII. *United States v. Philadelphia*, 499 F.Supp. 1196, 1197 (E.D. Pa. 1980). A consent decree approved by the federal court in 1980 required the City to "cease and desist" from discriminating against women in the Philadelphia Police Department and, *inter alia*, to engage in affirmative action to recruit and integrate women. *Id.* at 1197–98.

Given the history of sex discrimination in the Philadelphia Police Department, it is reasonable to expect that the EEOC would have inquired whether the City's refusal to accommodate a female officer's religious practice was also rooted in, or perpetuated, discrimination on the basis of sex. This is particularly true because the prohibited dress – a headscarf – is worn exclusively by women. The refusal to accommodate thus involves a sex-specific religious practice that, *ipso facto*, applies to women and not men. Merely opening the door to women and racial minorities does not ensure the elimination of discriminatory practices and attitudes in the workplace. Traditionally all-male institutions, such as the Philadelphia Police Department, create and reinforce gender through policies and practices that construct officers as male and celebrate masculinity as their institutional identity. *See* Valorie K. Vojdik, *Gender Outlaws: Challenging Masculinity in Traditionally Male Institutions*, 17 Berkeley Women's L.J. 68 (2002).

For all of these reasons, Officer Webb's EEOC charge of religious discrimination was sufficient to provide notice of her claim of sex discrimination. The requirement of exhaustion is not intended to elevate form over substance or to trap claimants who typically file EEOC complaints *pro se*. Discrimination against a Muslim woman for wearing a headscarf is inherently bound up in regulation of both religion and sex. Officer Webb therefore has demonstrated that she exhausted her claim of sex discrimination against the City, and the City is not entitled to summary judgment on this claim.

V CONSTITUTIONAL CLAIMS

Officer Webb also appeals the district court's denial of her constitutional claims, raised for the first time on this appeal. She alleges that the City's refusal to accommodate her request to wear the headscarf violated her constitutional rights under the First Amendment and the Fourteenth Amendment of the US Constitution. These claims were not raised below, and the district court did not have the opportunity to consider their merits. We therefore decline to address them in this appeal. On remand, however, Officer Webb may seek to amend the complaint to include these constitutional claims, and we see no reason why such amendment would not be permitted.

VI CONCLUSION

For these reasons, we reverse the district court's grant of summary judgment in favor of the City on Webb's claim of religious discrimination (Count I of Complaint) and on her claim of sex discrimination (Count IV of Complaint).

* * *

We remand the case for further proceedings, consistent with our holding.
   It is so ordered.

5

Harassment Because of Sex

Commentary on *Meritor Savings Bank, FSB v. Vinson*

TRINA JONES

BACKGROUND

Harvey Weinstein. Bill Cosby. Bill O'Reilly. Matt Lauer. Charlie Rose. Garrison Keillor. Alex Kozinski. Mario Batali. Russell Simmons. Al Franken. Roy Moore. Louis C.K. These are some of the immensely powerful men who, to varying degrees, have been exposed in recent years for their allegedly harassing and violent treatment of women.[1] Thanks in part to #MeToo and Time's Up,[2] Americans have been reminded of the ubiquitous nature of sexual harassment and sexual assault against women.[3] Yet while some empires have toppled, fueling hope for broader cultural transformation, the national

---

[1] For an extensive listing of men who have been accused of sexual harassment or assault within the last two years and a summary of their alleged acts, see Audrey Carlsen *et al.*, *#MeToo Brought down 201 Powerful Men. Nearly Half of Their Replacements Are Women*, N.Y. TIMES (Oct. 29, 2018), www.nytimes.com/interactive/2018/10/23/us/metoo-replacements.html; Dan Corey, *A Growing List of Men Accused of Sexual Misconduct since Weinstein*, NBC NEWS (Nov. 8, 2017), www.nbcnews.com/storyline/sexual-misconduct/weinstein-here-s-growing-list-men-accused-sexual-misconduct-n816546.

[2] Tarana Burke (a Black woman) founded "me too." in 2006 to help survivors of sexual violence, particularly Black women and girls from low-income communities. As a result of the viral spread of the hashtag #MeToo on social media in October 2017, "me too." has become a global movement against sexual harassment and sexual assault. me too., *History and Vision* (2018), https://metoomvmt.org/about/. Hollywood celebrities founded Time's Up in January 2018 to help women across all industries and all classes fight against sexual violence. Time's Up, *About*, https://timesupnow.org/about/ (*last visited* Mar. 30, 2020).

[3] Although men are also subject to sexual harassment and sexual violence, in this commentary the word "women" references victims because women are disproportionately targeted. Amanda Rossie *et al.*, OUT OF THE SHADOWS: AN ANALYSIS OF SEXUAL HARASSMENT CHARGES FILED BY WORKING WOMEN 2 (2018), https://nwlc-ciw49tixgw5lbab.stackpathdns.com/wp-content/uploads/2018/08/SexualHarassmentReport.pdf; Michael Alison Chandler, *Men Account for Nearly 1 in 5 Complaints of Workplace Sexual Harassment with the EEOC*, WASH. POST (Apr. 8, 2018), www.washingtonpost.com/local/social-issues/men-account-for-nearly-1-in-

216   Meritor Savings Bank, FSB v. Vinson

discourse around sexual harassment and sexual assault remains deeply troubling, revealing the continuing vulnerability and tremendous backlash that victims face. Women who challenge their attackers risk their reputations, their jobs, and their lives. They are accused of lying, of being insane, and of having provoked or invited the sexual misconduct.[4] Even when they are believed, what happens to women is too often ignored or brushed aside in pursuit of "more important" objectives.

All of this was evident in 1991, when the Senate Judiciary Committee considered then Judge Clarence Thomas for appointment to the U.S. Supreme Court. In her book, *Speaking Truth to Power*, Professor Anita Hill writes of the threats of rape, sodomy, and death that she received after her allegations of sexual harassment against Thomas became public.[5] She describes the not-so-subtle suggestion that she was lying and/or engaging in political gamesmanship, noting, "I can't count the number of times since October 1991 that I have been asked, 'Why did you wait ten years to raise charges of sexual harassment against Clarence Thomas?' "[6] Professor Hill recounts, and many readers will recall, the doubting gazes of US senators who asked Professor Hill if she had fantasized about Judge Thomas or had otherwise invited or welcomed his behavior.[7] She writes about those who appeared to be more concerned with appointing Judge Thomas to the Supreme Court than they were with thoroughly investigating his fitness for the job and with understanding what women who experience sexual harassment endure. She observes that the African American community was divided over whether she should have spoken or remained silent – over whether it was preferable to "air the dirty laundry" of sexism within the African American community or to sacrifice gender justice in the quest for racial equity.[8]

Perhaps Shakespeare was correct when he wrote *"the past is prologue."*[9] Twenty-seven years after the Hill-Thomas hearings, Dr. Christine Blasey Ford received similar backlash when her allegations of sexual assault against then

---

5-complaints-of-workplace-sexual-harassment-with-the-eeoc/2018/04/08/4f7a2572-3372-11e8-94fa-32d48460b955_story.html?noredirect=on&utm_term=.c37f5ba8a18e.

[4] *See infra* notes 6, 7, 11–14 and accompanying text; *see, e.g.*, Sam Levin, *Women Accusing Trump of Sexual Harassment Are Lying, Says White House*, THE GUARDIAN (Oct. 28, 2017), www .theguardian.com/us-news/2017/oct/27/donald-trump-sexual-harassment-claims-women-lying -white-house; Johnny Edwards & Jennifer Peebles, *Her Sexual Harassment Complaint Led to a Fight for Her Reputation*, ATLANTA JOURNAL-CONSTITUTION (Oct. 27, 2018).

[5] Anita Hill, SPEAKING TRUTH TO POWER 129, 270 (1997).

[6] Some people accused Hill of conspiring to prevent Thomas's appointment, when in fact she wanted to keep her story private. *Id.* at 270.

[7] *Id.* at 181–82, 198.

[8] *Id.* at 199–200, 257.

[9] William Shakespeare, THE TEMPEST Act II, Scene 1.

Meritor Savings Bank, FSB v. Vinson

Judge Brett Kavanaugh became public. During her testimony before the Senate Judiciary Committee, Dr. Ford described the hate mail and death threats that forced her to hire a security detail and to leave her family home.[10] Like Hill's, Dr. Ford's credibility was repeatedly questioned and attacked.[11] Some commentators claimed that Dr. Ford was part of a left-wing conspiracy to thwart Kavanaugh's appointment, suggesting that Dr. Ford either made up the allegations or brought them forward only to assist with Kavanaugh's defeat.[12] Indeed, in a press conference the day before Dr. Ford's testimony, US President Donald Trump repeatedly asked why Dr. Ford waited thirty-six years to report the assault.[13] Later that same week, at a political rally, President Trump mocked Dr. Ford's "I don't know" responses to questions posed during the hearing.[14] As was the case with Professor Hill, some thought that even if Kavanaugh had assaulted Dr. Ford, Kavanaugh should nonetheless be appointed to the Supreme Court to ensure a conservative majority. In other words, sexual harassment could be excused for partisan advantage. In this respect, one notes Senator McConnell's insistence to "plow right through" and move to confirm Kavanaugh as quickly as possible – even if "plowing

---

[10] *See Christine Blasey Ford's Opening Statement for Senate Hearing*, NPR (Sep. 26, 2018), www .npr.org/2018/09/26/651941113/read-christine-blasey-fords-opening-statement-for-senate-hear ing. Weeks after the hearings ended, Dr. Ford continued to receive death threats. All Things Considered, *Kavanaugh Accuser Christine Blasey Ford Continues Receiving Threats, Lawyers Say*, NPR (Aug. 11, 2018), www.npr.org/2018/11/08/665407589/kavanaugh-accuser-christine-blasey-ford-continues-receiving-threats-lawyers-say.

[11] To be sure, opinion polls show that more Americans believed Ford than Kavanaugh in the days following the hearings. Daniel Bush, *More Americans Believe Ford than Kavanaugh, According to New Poll*, PBS (Oct. 3, 2018), www.pbs.org/newshour/nation/more-americans-believe-ford-than-kavanaugh-according-to-new-poll. Kavanaugh was nonetheless appointed to the Supreme Court.

[12] Judge Kavanaugh reiterated this sentiment in his now somewhat infamous opening statement to the Senate Judiciary Committee. Meg Wagner *et al.*, *Brett Kavanaugh and Christine Blasey Ford Testify on Sex Assault Allegations*, CNN (Sep. 27, 2018), www.cnn.com/politics/live-news /kavanaugh-ford-sexual-assault-hearing/h_59d94a76d6396019441a5c14bba1041b.

[13] Katie Reilly, *Here's Everything President Trump Said During an 81-Minute Press Conference about Kavanaugh, Rosenstein and More*, TIME (Sep. 27, 2018), http://time.com/5407665/presi dent-trump-press-conference-transcript/.

[14] Maggie Haberman & Peter Baker, *Trump Taunts Christine Blasey Ford at Rally*, N.Y. TIMES (Oct. 2, 2018), www.nytimes.com/2018/10/02/us/politics/trump-me-too.html. Unlike Trump, some senators seemed to want it both ways: to support both Ford and Kavanaugh. Those in this camp asserted that although they believed Dr. Ford might have been assaulted, the assailant was not Judge Kavanaugh. In other words, notwithstanding Dr. Ford's statement that she was 100 percent sure that Kavanaugh assaulted her, Dr. Ford was mistaken. Steve Benen, *Dr. Ford Is "100 Percent" Certain about Her Kavanaugh Allegation*, MSNBC (Sep. 27, 2018), www.msnbc.com/rachel-maddow-show/dr-ford-100-percent-certain-about-her-kavanaugh-allegation. This argument implies that Dr. Ford was either confused or mentally ill. Either way, she was unworthy of belief.

through" meant refusing to order the Federal Bureau of Investigation (FBI) to conduct a complete investigation, to hear corroborating witnesses, or to permit testimony from others who had accused Judge Kavanaugh of inappropriate conduct.[15]

Certainly, #MeToo and Time's Up have raised awareness of the prevalence of sexual harassment and sexual assault in the United States. Yet it is unclear whether this awareness will result in a temporary uptick in sexual harassment charges, as was the case after the Hill-Thomas hearings,[16] or lead to more convictions, discharges, and systemic reforms.[17] The thematic similarities in the nation's discourse during the Hill-Thomas and Ford-Kavanaugh hearings suggest that much work remains to be done. Indeed, a significant and powerful portion of the US population seems not to care about sexual harassment. It characterizes women who speak up as hysterical and crazy, on the one hand, or lying and crafty, on the other. Given this sustained backlash, twenty-seven years after the Hill-Thomas hearings and over forty years after Catherine MacKinnon's pathbreaking book, *Sexual Harassment of Working Women*,[18] it is not surprising that sexual harassment and sexual assault remain hugely underreported.[19]

Contemporary discourse also shows that Americans continue to filter claims of sexual assault and harassment through the lens of class and race privilege. When wealthy celebrities and upper-middle-class white women speak, they are more likely to garner attention.[20] They also are more likely to

---

[15] Associated Press, *McConnell Says Senate Will "Plow Right through" to Confirm Kavanaugh*, PBS NEWS HOUR (Sep. 21, 2018), www.pbs.org/newshour/politics/mcconnell-says-senate-will-plow-right-through-to-confirm-kavanaugh.

[16] *See* Christina Cauterucci, *Sexual Harassment Claims Spiked after the Clarence Thomas Hearings. They're Spiking Again Now*, SLATE (Oct. 9, 2018), https://slate.com/news-and-politics/2018/10/eeoc-2018-sexual-harassment-metoo-clarence-thomas-anita-hill.html.

[17] *See, e.g.*, Maya Salam, *Gender Letter: Toppled Men Are Down, but Not Necessarily Out*, N.Y. TIMES (Oct. 19, 2018), www.nytimes.com/2018/10/19/us/metoo-men-sexual-harassment.html.

[18] Catharine A. MacKinnon, SEXUAL HARASSMENT OF WORKING WOMEN: A CASE OF SEX DISCRIMINATION (1979).

[19] Rossie *et al.*, *supra* note 3, at 2 (noting that 87–94 percent of those who face sexual harassment do not report it); *Get Statistics: Sexual Assault in the United States*, NATIONAL SEXUAL VIOLENCE RESOURCE CENTER (2018), www.nsvrc.org/statistics; Cameron Kimble & Inimai M. Chettiar, *Sexual Assault Remains Dramatically Underreported*, BRENNAN CENTER FOR JUSTICE (Oct. 4, 2018), www.brennancenter.org/blog/sexual-assault-remains-dramatically-underreported. Women do not speak out because of a fear of retaliation, of social ostracization, or of loss of employment, among other things. *See* Beverly Engel, *Why Don't Victims of Sexual Harassment Come Forward Sooner?*, PSYCHOL. TODAY (Nov. 16, 2017), www.psychologytoday.com/us/blog/the-compassion-chronicles/201711/why-dont-victims-sexual-harassment-come-forward-sooner.

[20] While we should admire and support courageous women like Ford, Alyssa Milano, Ashley Judd, Gwyneth Paltrow, and others, we must not overlook or discount the historical presence of women of color as change agents in this area. Similarly, we must not forget that the experiences of wealthy white women do not represent the experiences of all women. Indeed, these

Meritor Savings Bank, FSB v. Vinson

be believed.[21] Their voices and experiences thus tend to shape discussions of harassment and sexual assault. This narrow focus obscures what happens in agricultural fields, in hotel rooms, in bars and restaurants, and in retail stores, where workers often hold low-wage jobs and are often women of color. Indeed, analysis of Equal Employment Opportunity Commission (EEOC) data shows that, between 2012 and 2016, low-wage women in the food, retail, and healthcare industries filed the highest number of sexual harassment and assault charges.[22] This same data show that Black women are disproportionately likely to experience sexual harassment at work.[23] While sexual harassment and assault occur in all workplaces and at all levels of employment, a heavy focus on high-profile celebrities obscures the experiences and the activism of poor women and women of color, making it harder to see the ways in which racism and classism render these women especially vulnerable, yet simultaneously suspicious.

All of these factors were very much at play when Mechelle Vinson sued Meritor Savings Bank for sexual harassment in 1979. In its landmark decision in *Meritor Savings Bank v. Vinson*,[24] the Supreme Court first recognized sexual harassment as a form of sex discrimination under Title VII of the Civil Rights Act of 1964.[25] While this step was monumentally significant, the Court mostly ignored the larger social context in which harassment occurs and the tremendous pressures women face to remain silent. The Court also ignored the ways in which poor women and women of color are differently situated from other women. Indeed, the opinion fails even to mention that Mechelle Vinson was economically poor and Black. By overlooking these facts, the Court has made it difficult to tackle sexual harassment effectively. By exposing some of the Court's missteps, the feminist judgment of Dean Angela

---

omissions have been major sources of criticism for #MeToo. *See* Angela Onwuachi-Willig, *What About #UsToo? The Invisibility of Race in the #MeToo Movement*, 128 YALE L.J. FORUM 105 (2018); Tarana Burke, *#MeToo Was Started for Black and Brown Women and Girls. They're Still Being Ignored*, WASH. POST (Nov. 9, 2017), www.washingtonpost.com/news/post-nation /wp/2017/11/09/the-waitress-who-works-in-the-diner-needs-to-know-that-the-issue-of-sexual-har assment-is-about-her-too/.

[21] Indeed, data show that most Americans did not believe Anita Hill's allegations against Clarence Thomas. Jane Velencia, *Americans Didn't Believe Anita Hill. How Will They Respond to Kavanaugh's Accuser?*, FIVETHIRTYEIGHT (Sep. 17, 2018) https://fivethirtyeight.com/features/ americans-didnt-believe-anita-hill-how-will-they-respond-to-kavanaughs-accuser/.

[22] Rossie *et al.*, *supra* note 3, at 16.

[23] *Id.* at 4 (noting that, out of the charges filed by women, 56 percent were by women of color, who make up only 37 percent of the workforce).

[24] 477 U.S. 57 (1986).

[25] 42 U.S.C. §2000e-2(a)(1). Title VII prohibits employers from discriminating against employees based on race, color, religion, sex, or national origin.

THE ORIGINAL OPINION

In 1974, Mechelle Vinson began working for Meritor Savings Bank as a teller-trainee. Over the next four years, the bank promoted Vinson to teller, head teller, and assistant branch manager. Shortly after her probationary period ended, Vinson alleged that Sidney Taylor, who was a vice president of the bank and the manager of one of its branches, began to harass her. Vinson testified that Taylor repeatedly demanded sexual favors, fondled her in front of other employees, exposed himself to her, and forcibly raped her on several occasions. Vinson initially refused Taylor's sexual demands, but eventually complied because she feared losing her job. Vinson testified that she had sex with Taylor between forty and fifty times over the course of her employment.[26]

Vinson also testified that Taylor touched and fondled other female bank employees, but the district court did not permit her to call supporting witnesses in her case-in-chief. In addition, Vinson testified that, because she was afraid of Taylor, she never reported his harassment to any of his supervisors and never attempted to use the bank's complaint procedures.

Taylor denied all of Vinson's allegations and maintained that Vinson's accusations were in response to a business-related dispute. The Bank also denied Vinson's allegations, asserting that "any sexual harassment by Taylor was unknown to the bank and engaged in without its consent or approval."[27]

In its groundbreaking opinion, the US Supreme Court recognized sexual harassment as a form of sex discrimination under Title VII, noting, "[w]ithout question, when a supervisor sexually harasses a subordinate because of the subordinate's sex, that supervisor 'discriminates' on the basis of sex."[28] Although the case reached the Court on a hostile environment theory, by adopting the EEOC's definition of harassment[29] the Court endorsed both *quid pro quo* and hostile environment claims. *Quid pro quo* claims involve employer demands for sexual favors in return for an employment benefit

[26] 477 U.S. 57, 60 (1986).
[27] *Id.* at 60.
[28] *Id.* at 65.
[29] At the time, the EEOC's guidelines defined prohibited harassment as "unwelcome sexual advances, requests for sexual favors, and other verbal or physical conduct of a sexual nature." *Id.* The guidelines also stated that "such sexual misconduct constitutes prohibited sexual harassment whether or not it is directly linked to the grant or denial of an economic quid pro quo, where such conduct has the purpose or effect of unreasonably interfering with an individual's work performance or creating an intimidating, hostile, or offensive working environment." *Id.*

(e.g., hiring, promotion, salary increase, time off) or to avoid an employment detriment (e.g., firing, demotion, loss of pay).[30] Hostile environment claims involve unwelcome conduct that is sufficiently severe or pervasive as to alter the terms or conditions of employment and create an abusive working environment.[31]

In addition to recognizing sexual harassment as a form of prohibited sex discrimination, the Court in *Meritor* made three important doctrinal determinations favorable to plaintiffs. First, the Court rejected the Bank's argument that psychological or environmental harm is insufficient and that a plaintiff must show "a tangible loss" of an "economic character" to state a claim.[32] In rejecting this contention, the Court noted that Title VII's language is not limited to economic or tangible discrimination; rather, the Court found that "[t]he phrase 'terms, conditions, or privileges of employment' evinces a congressional intent 'to strike at the entire spectrum of disparate treatment of men and women' in employment."[33]

Second, the Court rejected the district court's finding that any intimate or sexual relationship between Vinson and Taylor, if it existed, was voluntary. The Supreme Court clarified that the standard is "unwelcomeness," not "voluntariness," stating "the fact that sex-related conduct was voluntary in the sense that the complainant was not forced to participate against her will is not a defense to a sexual harassment suit brought under Title VII ... The correct inquiry is whether respondent by her conduct indicated that the alleged sexual advances were unwelcome ..."[34]

Third, the Court held that a plaintiff's failure to use an employer's complaint mechanism is not fatal, particularly when the employer's policies do not specify the type of behavior that is prohibited and do not provide a mechanism for a plaintiff to bypass her harasser when seeking redress.[35]

---

[30] Because the district court found that Vinson's continued employment and promotions were not conditioned upon compliance with Taylor's sexual demands, it did not treat the case as one of *quid pro quo* harassment. As Onwuachi-Willig points out in her feminist judgment, without first deciding whether and why Vinson engaged in sexual relations with Taylor, it is impossible to determine whether a viable *quid pro quo* claim existed.

[31] 477 U.S. at 67; *Harris v. Forklift Sys., Inc.*, 510 U.S. 17, 21 (1993); *Faragher v. City of Boca Raton*, 524 U.S. 775, 787 (1998).

[32] 477 U.S. at 64–65.

[33] *Id.* at 64 (citations omitted).

[34] *Id.* at 68.

[35] *Id.* at 72–73 ("Petitioner's general nondiscrimination policy did not address sexual harassment in particular, and thus did not alert employees to their employer's interest in correcting that form of discrimination. Moreover, the bank's grievance procedure apparently required an employee to complain first to her supervisor, in this case Taylor.").

While these findings arguably facilitate the bringing of sexual harassment claims, the Supreme Court reached two additional conclusions that may produce the opposite effect. First, the Court found that evidence concerning a plaintiff's dress and speech is relevant to determining whether sexual advances are unwelcome and that it is the responsibility of district courts to weigh the probative value of this evidence against its prejudicial effect in deciding whether to admit it.[36]

Second, the Court chose not to decide when employers are liable for the harassing acts of supervisors.[37] Vinson argued that employers should be strictly liable whenever a supervisor harasses an employee.[38] The Bank, however, argued for a negligence standard, maintaining that employers should be liable only when they knew or reasonably should have known of a supervisor's harassing behavior.[39] Finding the record insufficiently developed, the Supreme Court declined to issue a definitive ruling on the question and instead straddled the fence. Applying principles of agency law, the Court noted that employers are not always automatically liable for sexual harassment by supervisory personnel. However, the Court also concluded that an absence of notice would not always insulate employers from liability.[40]

THE FEMINIST JUDGMENT

Dean Angela Onwuachi-Willig, writing as Justice Onwuachi-Willig, makes several major interventions in the feminist judgment. First, and perhaps most significantly, she underscores the historical and contemporary context in which harassment occurs, highlighting the ways in which social and cultural norms and demographic characteristics shape an individual's actions and others' interpretations of these actions. While the original Supreme Court opinion omits any reference to Vinson's age, race, or economic class, Onwuachi-Willig invokes these variables immediately and intentionally in her statement of the facts, thereby affording the reader a fuller understanding of the context in which Mechelle Vinson's interactions with Sidney Taylor occurred. Importantly, Onwuachi-Willig points out that both Vinson and Taylor were Black. She notes that Vinson was nineteen years old when she met Taylor. Vinson grew up poor and was a high-school dropout with a GED.

---

[36] The Court notes that the "Court of Appeals' contrary conclusion was based upon the erroneous, categorical view that testimony about provocative dress and publicly expressed sexual fantasies 'had no place in this litigation.'" *Id.* at 69.

[37] *Id.* at 72.

[38] *Id.* at 70.

[39] *Id.*

[40] *Id.* at 72.

Prior to her employment at the bank, she had worked in lower-level, female-dominated jobs in the service industry. In contrast, Taylor was old enough to be Vinson's father. He had worked his way up the bank's hierarchy from janitor to assistant vice president. He was a father of seven, the deacon of his church, and was revered in the community.

By including these essential facts, Onwuachi-Willig exposes the power dynamics that are critical in sexual harassment cases and the ways in which race, class, and age intersect to heighten the vulnerability of women of color.[41] For example, Onwuachi-Willig reveals how Vinson's economic marginality and limited educational training likely created a sense of extreme excitement at being afforded a chance at upward mobility. This same economic marginality, however, meant that Vinson feared losing her job and therefore endured Taylor's unwanted sexual advances and assaults for years without invoking the bank's complaint mechanisms. Similarly, by revealing that Vinson was a teenager, Onwuachi-Willig shows how age, combined with Vinson's lack of social stature, likely created a sense of horror, betrayal, and helplessness when Vinson became the target of someone she viewed as a fatherly figure. Race also confounded the situation. As Onwuachi-Willig notes, stereotypes of Black women as loose, sexually promiscuous, and lacking in sexual morals are pervasive.[42] Knowing it is likely that their allegations will be viewed with deep skepticism, that their characters will be attacked, and that their harassers will walk away relatively unscathed, Black women such as Mechelle Vinson may be reluctant to report harassing behavior. As was subsequently the case with Anita Hill, intragroup views about "racial loyalty" and the appropriateness of airing the dirty laundry of sexism within the Black community may also heighten their reluctance.

Importantly, Onwuachi-Willig incorporates these insights into her doctrinal interventions, thereby showing that legal formulations can be sensitive to context. First, Onwuachi-Willig holds that harassment allegations must be evaluated from the standpoint of a reasonable victim in the plaintiff's shoes. This necessarily includes analysis of a plaintiff's sex, race, and class, among

---

[41] For additional analysis of race and class dynamics in sexual harassment cases, see Rossie *et al.*, *supra* note 3, at 4 (explaining that women of color are disproportionately more likely to experience workplace harassment); Tanya Kateri Hernandez, *"What Not to Wear": Race and Unwelcomeness in Sexual Harassment Law – The Story of* Meritor Savings Bank v. Vinson, *in* Women and the Law Stories 277–306 (Elizabeth Schneider & Stephanie Wildman eds. 2011); Leah Fessler, *The Poorest Americans Are 12 Times as Likely to Be Sexually Assaulted as the Wealthiest*, Quartz (Jan. 3, 2018), https://qz.com/1170426/the-poorest-americans-are-12-times-as-likely-to-be-sexually-assaulted/.

[42] For analysis of the pernicious consequences of these and other stereotypes, *see generally* Trina Jones & Kimberly Jade Norwood, *Aggressive Encounters and White Fragility: Deconstructing the Trope of the Angry Black Woman*, 102 Iowa L. Rev. 2017 (2017).

other things. Similar to the Ninth Circuit in *Ellison v. Brady*,[43] Onwuachi-Willig finds that the "reasonable person" standard is male-centered and ignores the ways in which groups are differently situated in society. For example, she notes that, "because of differing experiences with and distinct vulnerabilities to sexual assault and rape, women frequently hold different viewpoints from men about the same factual circumstances." Onwuachi-Willig concludes that the "reasonable person" standard perpetuates existing inequalities by failing to adjust for experiential differences.

Second, while the Supreme Court distinguished between voluntariness and unwelcomeness, Onwuachi-Willig goes one step further and rejects any requirement that a victim of harassment show that the conduct is "unwelcome." She notes that it is difficult for courts to assess welcomeness given the power differential between supervisors and their subordinates. Moreover, she asserts that "focusing on welcomeness inappropriately reinforces the notion that sexual harassment is all about sex or sexual attraction, when it is truly about power and subordination ... What is most relevant to claims of hostile environment sexual harassment is the behavior of the alleged harasser and its effects on the complainant and her workplace environment." Consistent with the focus on power and environmental effects, Onwuachi-Willig concludes that dress is never relevant to a sexual harassment determination, because it "improperly takes the focus away from the alleged harasser and places it on the complainant." While Onwuachi-Willig dismisses the notion that a woman "invites" sexual harassment or assault by dressing in a certain way, she nonetheless concludes that speech may be relevant, in some circumstances, to evaluate the effects of allegedly harassing behavior on a plaintiff. For example, she notes that if allegedly harassing behavior occurs in direct response to a plaintiff's sexually explicit speech, a court must then decide whether the complainant's speech indicates that the work environment was not hostile or whether the speech was "a means of surviving in a workplace culture permeated by masculine norms or gender inequality."

Third, unlike the Supreme Court in *Meritor*, Onwuachi-Willig does not avoid tackling the issue of employer liability for supervisory conduct. Because supervisors are agents of employers, she holds that employers are strictly liable for their acts. She also concludes that individuals need not have the power to hire, fire, or demote in order to be considered a supervisor.

Onwuachi-Willig's conclusions contrast sharply with the Supreme Court's subsequent rulings on these matters in *Faragher v. City of Boca*

---

[43] 924 F.2d 872, 878–82 (9th Cir. 1991) (explaining that a "complete understanding of the victim's view requires, among other things, an analysis of the different perspectives of men and women").

Meritor Savings Bank, FSB v. Vinson 225

Raton,[44] *Burlington Industries, Inc. v. Ellerth*,[45] and *Vance v. Ball State University*.[46] In *Ellerth* and *Faragher*, the Court held that employers are vicariously liable for the acts of their supervisors only when supervisors take a tangible employment action (e.g., to effect a significant change in employment status, such as hiring, firing, failing to promote, reassignment with significantly different responsibilities, or a decision causing a significant change in benefits). In the absence of such action, employers can avoid liability for the acts of supervisors by showing (1) that the employer exercised reasonable care to prevent and correct promptly any sexually harassing behavior, and (2) that the plaintiff unreasonably failed to take advantage of the preventive or corrective opportunities provided by the employer or to avoid harm otherwise. The Court believed that allowing this two-pronged affirmative defense would "encourag[e] forethought by employers and saving action by objecting employees."[47]

In *Vance*, in a five-to-four opinion, the Supreme Court held that only those who are empowered to take tangible employment actions against victims qualify as "supervisors" for the purposes of employer liability. The Court reasoned that the agency relation assists "most workplace tortfeasors in committing harassment and that something more was required to justify vicarious liability."[48] The Court rejected a rule that would have included those who monitor other employees' daily activities, but who lack the power to hire, fire, demote, etc., finding that "[t]he ability to direct another employee's tasks is simply not sufficient. Employees with such powers are certainly capable of creating intolerable work environments, but so are many other co-workers."[49]

Onwuachi-Willig takes a different view of these matters. She argues that because employers invest supervisors with authority by virtue of their titles and positions, employers and supervisors are one and the same. Onwuachi-Willig therefore holds that employers are strictly liable for the acts of their supervisors, regardless of whether the employers knew or should have known of the supervisor's acts. She also includes within the definition of "supervisor" those who control the day-to-day activities of a victim's work and those who have the ability to evaluate and offer input about the victim's work.[50] Onwuachi-Willig's invocation of strict liability is more protective of victim's

[44] 524 U.S. 775 (1998).
[45] 524 U.S. 742 (1998).
[46] 570 U.S. 421 (2013).
[47] 524 U.S. at 807.
[48] 570 U.S. at 439.
[49] 570 U.S. at 439.
[50] On both of these issues, Onwuachi-Willig's opinion accords with the concurring Justices in *Meritor*, who maintained that a "supervisor's responsibilities do not begin and end with the

226   Meritor Savings Bank, FSB v. Vinson

rights in that it recognizes that employers are best situated to prevent and redress discriminatory practices by supervisors, and it offers the strongest incentive for them to do so. Strict liability, without the possibility of an affirmative defense, also keeps the focus on the harasser's behavior, instead of opening up avenues to shift blame onto the victim. Onwuachi-Willig's broad definition of "supervisor" is more in tune with the real-world dynamics of workplaces. She recognizes that, even without the ability to hire, fire, or demote, those vested with authority over other employees can significantly affect these employees' conditions of employment. Moreover, these individuals may reasonably be perceived by their victims to have power, even if they do not – as was the case with Mechelle Vinson. With this approach, Onwuachi-Willig once again shows her desire to look for rules and analytical approaches that take context into consideration and keep the realities of the workplace front and center. In this way, she previews the dissent in *Vance*, where Justice Ginsburg argues that "[s]upervisors, like the workplaces they manage, come in all shapes and sizes ... One cannot know whether an employer has vested supervisory authority in an employee, and whether harassment is aided by that authority, without looking to the particular working relationship between the harasser and the victim."[51]

In essence, Onwuachi-Willig's opinion would have avoided subsequent Supreme Court cases dealing with employer liability for supervisor behavior and the definition of supervisory employees. *Faragher*, *Ellerth*, and *Vance*, as well as countless lower court cases, would not have existed.

This commentary began with the stories of two courageous women, Anita Hill and Christine Blasey-Ford, who encountered tremendous backlash when their allegations of harassment and sexual assault became public. Notably, both Hill and Ford were well educated and middle or upper-middle class. If these women found it difficult to share their experiences and to endure the resulting pushback, imagine what it is like for poor, young women who do not have Hill's and Ford's education, family support, and resources. Women who are surviving on the margins and struggling to make ends meet are especially vulnerable, yet they are largely invisible in contemporary discussions of harassment and sexual assault. In this feminist judgment, Onwuachi-Willig sees and gives voice to these women. She underscores that harassment and sexual assault are about power, not desire, and shows how race, class, and age shape women's experiences in the workplace. Moreover, through her interventions, Onwuachi-Willig shows that legal doctrine need not shy away from contextual analysis, but that

power to hire, fire, and discipline employees, or with the power to recommend such actions."
477 U.S. at 76–78 (Marshall, J., joined by Brennan, Blackmun, and Stevens, concurring).
[51] 570 U.S. at 465–66 (Ginsburg, J., dissenting).

judges can craft doctrine with sufficient flexibility to take into consideration the myriad circumstances under which sexual harassment and sexual assault occur. Mechelle Vinson was not a white, middle-aged, middle-class woman. She was Black. She was young. She was poor. These facts are essential to understanding her story and to transforming the realities of countless women like her who are abused, without the possibility of real redress, each day in America.

Meritor Savings Bank, FSB v. Vinson, 477 U.S. 57 (1986)

JUSTICE ANGELA ONWUACHI-WILLIG DELIVERED THE OPINION OF THE COURT.

This case presents important questions concerning claims of workplace "sexual harassment" brought under Title VII of the Civil Rights Act of 1964, 78 Stat. 253, as amended, 42 U.S.C. § 2000e *et seq.* These questions include (1) whether the factual record was sufficiently developed to render decisions on either a *quid pro quo* claim or a hostile environment claim, (2) whether sexual harassment leading only to psychological harm violates Title VII, (3) whether the "voluntariness" of the complainant's participation in sexual activity is pertinent in a hostile environment case, (4) whether the complainant's manner of dress or sexually provocative speech is relevant to determining whether sexual harassment occurred, (5) whether the trial court erred in excluding testimonial evidence from other women who claimed to have been harassed by the alleged wrongdoer and to have seen him harass the complainant; and (6) whether employers are automatically liable for sexual harassment by their supervisory personnel regardless of notice to the employer.

I FACTS

In September 1974, a nineteen-year-old African-American woman named Mechelle Vinson met Sidney Taylor, an African-American man who served as Assistant Vice President and Branch Manager for what is now Petitioner Meritor Savings Bank. Taylor ran into Vinson on the street and struck up a conversation with her. To Vinson, an impressionable teenager who had grown up in an impoverished environment, Taylor led an impressive life. For Vinson (and for many others), Taylor represented the American dream. Taylor had worked his way up from janitor to Assistant Vice President. He also possessed high status within his social community, serving as a church deacon. At trial, Taylor's lawyer described him as "something of an Eagle Scout."

During their initial meeting, Vinson asked Taylor about the possibility of employment at the Bank. Taylor responded by encouraging Vinson to apply for a job at his branch of the Bank. Vinson immediately followed Taylor's advice, completing and turning in her application the very next day. That same afternoon, Taylor offered Vinson a position as a teller-trainee, from which she could be promoted to teller if she performed satisfactorily. Vinson accepted the offer, becoming one of the more than 80 percent of women who worked as bank tellers nationwide. Prior to that, Vinson, a high school dropout with a GED, had worked in lower-level, female dominated jobs in the service industry, having performed the duties of a temporary employee in an exercise club, a food store, and a shoe store.

On September 9, 1974, Vinson began working at the Bank. She quickly proved to be a highly competent employee, earning promotions from teller to head teller and then to assistant branch manager. The District Court indicated that "[Vinson's] promotions were based on merit alone." *Vinson v. Taylor*, No. 78–1793, 1980 WL 100, at *1, 7 (D.D.C. Feb. 26, 1980).

During the first few months of her employment, Vinson enjoyed a pleasant, father-daughter-like relationship with Taylor, a man who was old enough to be her father. Taylor even once helped Vinson by giving her money to assist her in obtaining an apartment. Furthermore, Vinson confided in Taylor about a number of personal matters, including that she was raised in violence; had a troubled relationship with her own father; and was going through the process of separation from her then-husband, an older man who impregnated her when she was just fourteen.[52]

Ultimately, the relationship between Vinson and Taylor proved to be problematic. According to Vinson's trial testimony, by May of 1975, Taylor began to make unwelcome sexual advances toward her. Speaking about the first advance, Vinson testified that Taylor took her to dinner at a local Chinese restaurant and then suggested during dinner that they go to a motel to engage in sexual relations. Vinson contended that she initially declined Taylor's invitation, but that Taylor refused to take "no" for an answer, insisting that she owed him because he had given her a job. Vinson explained at trial, "He said just like he could hire me, he could fire me... He told me that he was my supervisor. He gave me my pay check, and I had to do what he wanted me to do." Trial Tr. vol. II, 51, 59. Vinson further declared that, despite her

---

[52] She later miscarried.

resistance, Taylor drove her to a motel and left her waiting in the car while he registered for a room. According to Vinson, Taylor then took her to the motel room and asked her to wait while he showered. Thereafter, Vinson indicated, she engaged in sexual relations with Taylor because she was afraid that she would lose her job if she did not perform sexual favors for him.

Vinson further testified that, after this incident, Taylor continued to demand sexual favors from her, usually at the Bank itself. According to Vinson, Taylor frequently forced her to engage in sexual intercourse with him inside the bank vault as well as in other rooms such as the storage area in the bank basement, both during and after work hours. Vinson estimated that, between May 1975 and 1977, she and Taylor had sexual contact somewhere between 40 to 50 times. Vinson also asserted that Taylor sexually harassed her in other ways. For example, she testified that Taylor exposed himself to her many times and groped her breasts and buttocks on the job, both in the presence of co-workers and in the women's restroom when she was there alone. Vinson also claimed that Taylor fondled other female workers and made suggestive remarks in their presence. At trial, Vinson attempted to call upon witnesses, such as Christine Malone and Mary Levarity, who could support her claims about Taylor's harassment of her and other women at the Bank. The District Court, however, excluded much of this evidence, proclaiming that Vinson could not present "wholesale evidence of a pattern and practice relating to sexual advances to other female employees in her case in chief." *Vinson*, 1980 WL 100, at *1, n. 1. Instead, the District Court advised that "she might well be able to present such evidence in rebuttal to the defendants' cases." *Vinson v. Taylor*, 753 F.2d 144 (D.C. Cir. 1985).

Most important, Vinson indicated that all of these actions by Taylor were against her will. She proclaims that Taylor often assaulted or raped her, once so brutally that she suffered serious vaginal bleeding for weeks and had to seek a doctor's care.

In 1977, Vinson began to have a steady boyfriend. At this point, she contends, Taylor stopped making sexual demands upon her, but continued to fondle, grope, and otherwise harass her at work. Vinson also testified that Taylor advised her in 1977 that she would be given her own branch managership and advised her in June 1978 that she would be promoted to a branch manager position at the company's Tacoma Park branch in December 1978. Vinson ultimately turned down this opportunity.

Taylor denies ever engaging in sexual relations with Vinson. He asserts that he never fondled Vinson, never made suggestive remarks to her, and never even asked her to have sex with him. He admits to taking Vinson to lunch, but he claims that he took her to lunch only when Christine Malone was also present and that he never took Vinson to lunch or dinner alone. He also testified that Vinson was a scorned woman who had made advances toward him, which he declined.

According to Taylor, in late summer or early September 1978, he and Vinson had a disagreement over which employee Vinson should train to become the next head teller. Taylor indicates that he instructed Vinson to begin to train Dorothy McCallam as head teller, but Vinson instead began to train Karen Kirkland. Taylor argues that Vinson has brought these charges against him because of this disagreement and his rejection of her advances toward him.

At trial, McCallam, whom Vinson refused to train, asserted that Vinson wore revealing clothing and spoke frequently about sexual fantasies in the workplace. McCallam proclaimed that Vinson "had a lot of sexual fantasies." McCallam testified, "[Vinson] talked quite a bit about sex. I guess more than half of her conversation was related to sex." She further alleged that Vinson's "dress wear was very explosive." McCallam explained that "most of the days [Vinson] would come in with, if not a third of her breasts showing, about half of her breasts showing; and some days, short dresses; or if she did wear a skirt, something that had a slit in it." Ironically, Taylor asserted during his deposition that, as a general matter, Vinson wore appropriate clothing to work and that she never did anything to suggest that she wanted to have sex with him.

Beginning on September 21, 1978, Vinson stopped reporting to work. She contends that she was forced to stop coming to work because Taylor began to tamper with her personnel records, made false complaints against her with management, denigrated her in front of other employees, entrapped her into work errors, threatened her life when she asserted she would report him, and engaged in a campaign of fault-finding against her. When Taylor contacted Vinson about her absence from the workplace, she told him that she was ill and that her absence from work would be indefinite. On November 1, 1978, the Bank informed Vinson that she was terminated due to excessive use of sick leave. On the exact same date, Vinson sent the Bank a letter indicating that she was forced to offer her "constructive resignation." J.A. 17.

Despite the fact that the Bank had a blanket policy against discrimination and a complaint procedure for reporting discrimination (though the Bank did not have any policies relating specifically to sexual harassment), Vinson never reported Taylor's actions to any of his supervisors. She never otherwise followed the Bank's complaint procedure, which mandated that an employee had to "state his grievance in writing and present it to his supervisor . . . only after oral representation has been made and it is felt that the grievance has not been fully resolved." Pl.'s Ex. 13 at 11.

Following her termination, Vinson brought this lawsuit against Taylor and the Bank, alleging that she was constantly subjected to sexual harassment by Taylor in violation of Title VII. Vinson asserts that she never reported this harassment during her employment because she was afraid of Taylor. She asserts that he had threatened to kill her and have her raped like Christine Malone, another employee of the Bank. While there is no evidence that connects Taylor to Malone's rape by an unknown assailant in 1974, Malone confided in Vinson after the rape, and Vinson recalls that a disturbed Malone was never the same after the crime. Explaining the effect of Taylor's alleged threats on her, Vinson testified, "My life was put on the line. I didn't know what might happen to me. Christine was raped. She almost lost her mind. I saw things that went on in the bank and I didn't want anything to happen to me. My life was very valuable to me." Trial Tr. vol. IV, 28. Vinson further claims that Malone and another woman, Mary Levarity, previously complained to Vice President David G. Burton about Taylor's sexually harassing behavior toward them, but that Burton took no action. Vinson further claims that, when she raised Taylor's mistreatment of women in the office to him, he said "that's my way of relaxing them, and if they didn't like it, they can get the hell out and I can get the hell out." Trial Tr. vol. III, 48.

The Bank argues that, even if the alleged sexual advances were made by Taylor, it should not be held liable because it did not know about such behavior and, as a result, could not have consented to and/or approved such activities.

II PROCEDURAL HISTORY

After a bench trial, the District Court decided the question regarding whether the Bank "received notice of the alleged sexual harassment directed against [Vinson] and allegedly other female employees" and whether the Bank should be liable for Vinson's acts. *Vinson*, 1980 WL 100, at *4–6. The court held that the Bank could not be held liable for the actions of Taylor, even assuming they were true, because neither Vinson nor any other employee notified the Bank of the alleged actions by Taylor, "the bank had a policy asserting its dedication to equal treatment and employee rights," and there was no evidence to suggest that Taylor's status as an officer in the Bank was anything more than "honorary." *Id.* at *6. The District Court noted that Taylor had no authority to hire, fire, or promote employees. Finally, after acknowledging "that sexual harassment of female employees in which they are asked or required to submit to

232   Meritor Savings Bank, FSB v. Vinson

sexual demands as a condition to obtain employment or to maintain employment or to obtain promotions falls within protection of Title VII," the District
Court determined that Vinson was not a victim of sexual harassment or sexual
discrimination. *Id.* at *8. Although the District Court issued twenty-one
factual findings, it never offered a finding as to whether sexual activity
occurred between Taylor and Vinson. Instead, it indicated the following: "If
[Vinson] and Taylor engaged in an intimate or sexual relationship during the
time of Vinson's employment ..., that relationship was a voluntary one by
[Vinson] having nothing to do with her continued employment at [the bank]
or her advancement or promotions at that institution." *Vinson*, 753 F.2d at 145.

On appeal, the D.C. Circuit began its review of the case by identifying two
different forms of sexual harassment that reflected the definitions originated by
Professor Catharine MacKinnon: (1) *quid pro quo* sexual harassment, which
occurs when a complainant is asked to perform sexual favors in order to
maintain her job or receive a promotion, and (2) hostile environment sexual
harassment, defined as "unwelcome sexual advances, requests for sexual
favors, or other verbal or physical conduct of a sexual nature ... hav[ing] the
purpose or effect of unreasonably interfering with an individual's work performance or creating an intimidating, hostile, or offensive work environment."
Id. at 145. *See also* Catharine A. MacKinnon, SEXUAL HARASSMENT OF WORKING
WOMEN 32–47 (1979). Ultimately, the D.C. Circuit reversed the District
Court's decision, concluding that the trial court's holding was inconsistent
with the intent of Title VII.

Deferring to the District Court's factual finding that Vinson "was not
required to grant Taylor ... sexual favors as a condition of either her employment or in order to obtain promotion," the D.C. Circuit left standing the
District Court's conclusion that Vinson was not a victim of *quid pro quo*
harassment. *Vinson*, 753 F.2d at 145. The D.C. Circuit concluded, however,
that the District Court failed to properly consider and evaluate whether
Vinson had been the victim of hostile environment sexual harassment and
noted the ambiguity of the District Court's finding about the existence and
nature of the sexual relationship between Vinson and Taylor. The D.C.
Circuit explained:

> This finding leaves us uncertain as to precisely what the court meant. It could
> reflect the view that there was no Title VII violation because Vinson's
> employment status was not affected, an error to which we already have
> spoken. Alternatively, the finding could indicate that because the relation-
> ship was voluntary there was no sexual harassment – no "[u]nwelcome sexual
> advances, requests for sexual favors, or other verbal or physical conduct of

Meritor Savings Bank, FSB v. Vinson

a sexual nature ... ha[ving] the purpose or effect of unreasonably interfering with an individual's work performance or creating an intimidating, hostile, or offensive working environment." *Id.* at 146.

Given this ambiguity and the District Court's failure to consider a possible hostile environment violation, the D.C. Circuit remanded the case for an examination of Vinson's hostile environment sexual harassment claim. Petitioner, Meritor Savings Bank, appeals this decision.

III CONTEXT AND BACKGROUND

Before this Court begins its review of the legal questions in this case, it first acknowledges that evaluating any particular sexual harassment claim requires an understanding of the historical and social context in which the alleged harassment occurred. The presence and persistence of sexual harassment may be influenced not only by gender dynamics in the workplace but also by racial, class, age, status hierarchy, and other relevant dynamics within the workplace. For example, this case involves an allegation of sexual harassment, including claims of rape, against an African-American man by an African-American woman. Although both parties in this case are African-American, awareness of race, and in particular, awareness of racial stereotypes and the history of racism against both African-American men and women in sexual misconduct cases are pertinent to our understanding of the claims in this lawsuit. Such stereotypes and history not only may have influenced how and why each party acted as he or she did during their workplace relationship; they also may have shaped the lens through which management and employees viewed the two parties' interactions with each other and through which the factfinder and the Court of Appeals evaluated the legal claims.

In examining the claims in this lawsuit, this Court must be cognizant of widespread and long-standing racialized tropes and stereotypes that have placed race at the center of common definitions and understandings about what rape or sexual misconduct is. Despite the fact that most sexual misconduct and rape occurs between individuals within the same racial group, the most dominant and pervasive trope regarding rape and other forms of sexual misconduct centers on an African-American male perpetrator and a white female victim. *See* Jennifer Wriggins, *Rape, Racism, and the Law*, 6 HARV. WOMEN'S L.J. 103, 105, 114 (1983); *see also* Angela Y. Davis, WOMEN, RACE, AND CLASS 173–90 (1983). Since slavery, African-American men have been cast as sexually immoral, overly aggressive predators who lack self-control when it comes to sexual urges, particularly when it comes

234   Meritor Savings Bank, FSB v. Vinson

to white women. *See, e.g.*, Susan Brownmiller, AGAINST OUR WILL: MEN, WOMEN, AND RAPE 194, 211–13 (1975). In part due to these racialized stereotypes and the lack of credibility that comes along with them, African-American men, even when the evidence against them is weak and, in fact, doubtful, have found themselves to be vulnerable and easy targets of wrongful convictions in sexual misconduct cases. One particularly disturbing example comes from the conviction of the nine young Scottsboro boys who spent many years in prison as a result of two white women who lied about being raped by them during the 1930s. *See* Davis, *supra*, at 198. Indeed, in some states, juries could consider race, or rather blackness itself, as evidence of a defendant's intent to engage in sexual crimes. *See* Wriggins, *supra*, at 111, 120. Due to the pervasiveness of the stereotype of the African-American male rapist, courts must be careful to examine sexual harassment claims with an understanding that challenged behaviors, which may be viewed as benign when performed by white men, may be read as overly sexual or aggressive when performed by African-American men. In sum, courts must evaluate claims of harassment against the backdrop of African-American men's historical and current vulnerability to false claims of rape and harassment.

Similarly, as this particular case involves an African-American female complainant, this Court must analyze this claim against the backdrop of a long history of sexual assault, rape, and harassment of African-American women as well as the history of African-American women's extreme vulnerability to sexual misconduct in the workplace and otherwise, both by white and non-white men. Historically, African-American women were viewed as so loose, sexually promiscuous, and lacking in sexual morality that they were deemed legally unrapable. In other words, for decades upon decades, the rape of African-American women was legal. *See* Davis, *supra*, at 6–12, 182–84; Beverly Smith, *Black Women's Health: Notes for a Course*, *in* ALL THE WOMEN ARE WHITE, ALL THE BLACKS ARE ME, BUT SOME OF US ARE BRAVE 110–11 (Gloria T. Hull *et al.* eds., 1982). *See also, e.g.*, Harriet Jacobs, INCIDENTS IN THE LIFE OF SLAVE GIRL (1861). In a vicious cycle of racist sexual violence, the pervasive raping of African-American women was used as evidence of their purported sexual immorality, which in turn was used to legally justify the rape and sexual assault against them. Indeed, indictments against alleged rapists were frequently dismissed for failure to allege that the victim was white. *See* Wriggins, *supra*, at 106–07. Here, Taylor's claim that Vinson is a sexually aggressive scorned woman seeking revenge for his rebuffing her invokes race and gender stereotypes that have pervaded much of rape history. In fact, such stereotypes may help to explain why no one stopped Taylor's alleged harassment of Vinson, which Vinson and others testified was open and obvious. For example, other supervisors in the workplace may have felt no need to interfere on Vinson's behalf if they had internalized stereotypes of Vinson as either a strong African American woman who needed no help or an immoral and loose African American woman who invited Taylor's attention or was simply incapable of being sexually harassed and harmed.

In places where African-American women have toiled, they have been particularly vulnerable to rape. In addition to being frequent victims of sexual assault and rape by their white masters during slavery, African-American women often worked in domestic spaces where they were continually exposed to their employers' sexual aggression. *See id.* at 118–19. Furthermore, perpetrators of crimes against African-American women have received and continue to receive less harsh punishment than perpetrators of crimes against white women. *See generally* Howard Myers, *The Effect of Sexual Stratification by Race on Arrest in Sexual Battery Cases*, 9 AMER. J. CRIM. JUST. 172 (1985). When African-American women report sexual misconduct, they are also less likely to be believed than white women. *See* Wriggins, *supra*, at 122. Not surprisingly, the result of this long history has been that African-American women are less likely to report sexual misconduct than white women are, even though they are more likely to be victims of sexual harassment and misconduct. *See id.* at 122–23 n.122 (citing a 1976 study that found that " '[w]hite rape victims were much more likely to report the crime to the police (59%) than were Black rape victims (26%)' ").

The history of African-American women and rape may shed light on why Vinson did not report Taylor's alleged raping and harassment of her to anyone in the workplace. This history of racism and sexism is further complicated by the difference in status between Taylor and Vinson. Vinson knew that Taylor was a bank vice president, a church deacon, and the father of seven while she was a high school dropout and divorcée. Moreover, bank policy required Vinson to report the harassment to her supervisor, who, in this case, was the man who was harassing her. When the context of this case is closely examined through a historical lens, it is not hard to see why Vinson failed to report Taylor's alleged assaults.

Questions about racial and gender dynamics, including that the parties were working in a predominantly white work environment, may have also shaped how they behaved. For example, African-American women can feel strong pressure not to reveal, particularly to the white community, so-called "dirty laundry" about African-American men given the subordinate status of African-American men in society. *See* bell hooks, FEMINIST THEORY: FROM

MARGIN TO CENTER 18, 68–69, 73–75 (1984). Thus, Vinson may have feared reporting Taylor because she did not want to be viewed as a traitor to her race for turning in a successful African-American man, especially given his success in a white-dominated work environment. That fear may have been further intensified by her knowledge of the historical and current injustices in the legal system against African-Americans.

Age, class, and status differences between Vinson and Taylor are also relevant to the analysis. In fact, the power dynamics connected to the status hierarchy at the Bank appear to be rooted in both gender and age differences, with young women overwhelmingly working in the subordinate and entry-level position of teller while older men dictated and governed their work as management. For example, Vinson testified that one of the reasons why she did not complain to management about Taylor's harassment was because she, a woman of limited education, feared losing the job of her dreams and because she lacked similar economic alternatives. Indeed, Vinson took legal action in this case only when her lawyer, whom she went to see about her divorce, learned of the harassment and suggested she should sue.

The basic point is that, in considering the legal questions in this lawsuit, the Court must be careful to examine all claims against historical and societal circumstances and through the various lenses that may be consciously or unconsciously affecting the behavior of the key parties.

IV THE DISTRICT COURT'S ERRORS

In this case, not only did the fact finder – here, the District Court – fail to evaluate Vinson's claims within their historical and social context, it also failed to develop a sufficient factual record. Most important, the District Court failed to provide a finding of fact as to whether sexual relations occurred between Vinson and Taylor.

The first problem with this hypothetical "factual finding" by the District Court is that it is not a factual finding at all and fails to resolve one of the most critical questions in the case. As this Court has previously held, lack of clarity or unsoundness in a material fact "sufficiently clouds the record to render the case an inappropriate vehicle" for a final determination. *Jones v. State Bd. of Educ. of Tennessee*, 397 U.S. 31, 32 (1970) (*per curiam*). Here, a determination as to whether Vinson and Taylor had sexual intercourse and whether Vinson did so to maintain her employment must occur before any court can determine the merits of a potential *quid pro quo* claim.

Indeed, factual determinations as to whether Vinson and Taylor had sexual intercourse from May 1975 to 1977, whether Taylor accosted and fondled

Vinson within the workplace, why Vinson engaged in intercourse with Taylor (if she did), and whether Taylor's actions are what pushed Vinson to take an indefinite leave from the workplace are also crucial determinations to Vinson's other potential *quid pro quo* claim based upon the link between the sexual favors and Vinson's claimed constructive discharge. Similarly, the District Court must make a factual determination regarding the existence of a sexual relationship before a decision can be made about whether the Bank violated reasonable expectations for establishing and maintaining a productive and welcoming work environment for Vinson and its other employees.

Additionally, a finding concerning sexual relations between Vinson and Taylor is an important step in determining whether Vinson was constructively discharged from the Bank. If Taylor's repeated requests for sexual favors and his retaliatory attacks on Vinson's work eventually caused Vinson's indefinite sick leave, which was the very basis for the Bank's decision to fire her, then Vinson's refusal to give in to Taylor's requests for sexual intercourse easily go to the heart of any *quid pro quo* claims. Indeed, the quintessential *quid pro quo* case involves the loss of a job because of a refusal to perform sexual acts with one's supervisor. At trial, Vinson addressed the toll that Taylor's alleged actions had on her decision to stop coming to work. She asserted, "[H]e would touch me practically every day... Whenever he felt like it... Each day was a - touching day. Each day was a mental day... I felt humiliated. I felt powerless. I was afraid of him." Trial Tr. vol. II, 66, 71, 80. Her resignation letter specifically cited the harassment as the reason for her leaving. J.A 17.

The second problem with the District Court's hypothetical "factual finding" is that it is ambiguous. As the Court of Appeals explained, the finding could mean that there was no violation under Title VII because Vinson's job position, particularly her job status, in the workplace did not change in the negative. If the District Court intended this meaning, it is incorrect as a matter of law. One, it mistakenly presumes that a negative change in job status is required to assert a *quid pro quo* claim. A demand that an employee engage in sexual relations to maintain her employment provides a sufficient basis for asserting a *quid pro quo* claim regardless of any change in status. Here, Vinson asserts that she engaged in sexual intercourse with Taylor because she feared losing her job. She explained at trial that she felt that she "had no other choice" because of lack of power and lack of viable economic alternatives. Trial Tr. vol. IV, 50. This is enough for a *quid pro quo* claim. That Vinson was a highly competent employee who earned her promotions due to her superior work performance should not defeat her claim. To hold otherwise would be to punish Vinson for being an excellent employee and reward Taylor for selecting a highly competent employee to be his victim. Taylor still may have been

238 Meritor Savings Bank, FSB v. Vinson

willing to punish Vinson, whether highly competent or not, by firing her if she refused his advances. The *quid pro quo* claim protects against the threat of retaliation and does not require that the retaliation actually occur. Here, of course, however, Vinson may have actually suffered a forced change in position as she asserts that she ultimately resigned due to Taylor's alleged harassment. Moreover, the District Court's "factual finding" about Vinson and Taylor's sexual relationship ignores Vinson's potential hostile environment claim, which this Court discusses in more detail below.

V THE SEX HARASSMENT CLAIM

Next, we address several legal questions raised by this factual record to guide the District Court on remand.

A No Limitation to Tangible and Economic Injury

The first question concerns whether a Title VII violation occurs only when sexual harassment victims suffer tangible or economic injury. The Bank argues that statutory language that prohibits discrimination with respect to "compensation, terms, conditions, or privileges" of employment indicates that Congress was concerned with injuries of an economic or tangible character only, not psychological or otherwise intangible injuries. We reject this argument.

As numerous courts have held, hostile environment sexual harassment, which tends to result in non-tangible or non-economic injury, "erects barriers to participation in the work force of the sort Congress intended to sweep away by the enactment of Title VII." *See, e.g., Katz v. Dole*, 709 F.2d 251, 254 (4th Cir. 1983). Indeed, a number of federal courts have recognized that "[s]exual harassment which creates a hostile or offensive environment for members of one sex is every bit the arbitrary barrier to sexual equality at the workplace that racial harassment is to racial equality." *Henson v. City of Dundee*, 682 F.2d 897 (11th Cir. 1982). *See also Bundy v. Jackson*, 641 F.2d 934, 934–44 (D.C. Cir 1981).

In racial harassment cases, courts have recognized that some "working environments [may be] so heavily polluted with discrimination as to destroy completely the emotional and psychological stability of minority group workers." *Rogers v. EEOC*, 454 F.2d 234, 238 (5th Cir. 1971). Similarly, this Court recognizes that certain workplaces may be so hostile to men or women based on sex and gender that workers cannot remain emotionally and psychologically stable in their jobs. For this type of hostile environment sexual harassment to be actionable, however, the challenged conduct must unreasonably interfere with the complainant's work performance, create a hostile or intimidating environment, and/or help to preserve patterns of sex segregation in employment.

In determining whether hostile environment harassment has occurred, courts must examine the allegations of harassment from the standpoint of a reasonable victim in the complainant's shoes, here a reasonable African-American woman. Examining the allegations from the perspective of a reasonable person with the complainant's identity characteristics is key because courts must be careful not to reify existing inequalities by adopting a purportedly objective perspective that simply offers the outlook of a reasonable man or a reasonable white man. For example, a male bank vice president might believe it is acceptable to tell a female subordinate that "her dress fits her body well" while a female subordinate may find such comments discomforting or offensive because they focus on her looks as opposed to her work. In fact, because of differing experiences with and distinct vulnerabilities to sexual assault and rape, women frequently hold different viewpoints from men about the same factual circumstances. Furthermore, not examining the allegations from a reasonable complainant's perspective disregards how harassers frequently target victims they know are vulnerable. For example, a male harasser may target a female subordinate of limited education or a single mother dependent on her income precisely because he knows she has fewer viable economic alternatives than a woman with more education or a married woman with other resources. In this case, Taylor knew of Vinson's vulnerabilities as a result of her impoverished upbringing, limited education, crumbling marriage, past work history in low-level service jobs, and financial burdens for her new apartment.[53] Viewed from the perspective of a victim with Vinson's background and characteristics, the evidence offered supports Vinson's claim of a hostile and intimidating work environment.

Furthermore, Taylor's actions, if true, also may have unreasonably interfered with Vinson's work performance and helped to preserve patterns of sex segregation and inequality in the workplace. First, testimony from this case describes the most severe forms of sexual misconduct. Criminal conduct involving sexual assault and rape easily satisfy the standard for proving a hostile or intimidating environment. It is difficult to imagine any actions that could more readily create an intimidating and hostile environment than

---

[53] Indeed, the record here intimates that Taylor may have harassed other women like Vinson – young, African American, poor, and "hungry for work" – by hiring them or loaning them money and then asserting that they owed him.

240   Meritor Savings Bank, FSB v. Vinson

the rape and other physical intrusions of the body, such as the fondling of private parts, that Vinson testified that she suffered at the hands of Taylor.

Vinson has also presented evidence, which if believed, could support a finding that Taylor's alleged actions unreasonably interfered with her work performance. At trial, Vinson testified that she suffered serious psychological and physical consequences, such as extreme nervousness and stress, an inability to eat or sleep, and loss of hair due to Taylor's harassment. She further indicated that, despite years of excellent job performance, she ultimately was unable to come to work to perform her job. Trial Tr. vol. II, 71, 77–80; Trial Tr. vol. III, 51, 64; Trial Tr. vol. IV, 65.

Finally, Vinson's allegations, if believed, detail behavior that would work to preserve patterns of sex segregation and inequality in the workplace. Here, Taylor's harassment and the Bank's failure to respond to it likely made harassed female subordinates feel powerless and voiceless. This dynamic can help sustain sex segregation between female tellers and male management by reinforcing the notion of the dominant and powerful man over the subordinate woman.

Therefore, Vinson's allegations, if proven, would suffice to establish a hostile environment sexual harassment.

B Voluntary Inquiry

The second remaining question concerns whether the complainant's "voluntary" participation in sexual episodes is pertinent in a hostile environment sexual harassment case. Related to that question are two more legal issues before this Court, which are (1) whether the District Court erred in excluding Vinson's evidence from alleged female victims of Taylor and witnesses of Taylor's harassment of Vinson, and (2) whether a complainant's dress or sexually provocative speech is relevant in evaluating hostile environment sexual harassment claims.

1 Unwelcomeness

Regarding the relationship between "voluntariness" and sexual harassment, the Court concludes that voluntariness is not the central inquiry in a hostile environment sexual harassment claim. The gravamen of any such claim is whether the challenged conduct unreasonably interfered with her work environment or performance, created a hostile or intimidating environment, or worked to preserve patterns of sex segregation in employment. Even if one could call Vinson's capitulation to Taylor's alleged sexual demands voluntary, that determination would not resolve the question of whether Taylor's actions constituted hostile environment sexual harassment. While the welcomeness of the advances might shed light on whether the conduct helped to create a hostile or intimidating environment or affected the complainant's work performance, as suggested by the EEOC [Equal Employment Opportunity Commission] in 29 C.F.R. § 1604.11(a) (1985), welcomeness is a digression from the heart of Title VII's purpose in addressing sex discrimination: eradicating sex segregation in jobs and arbitrary barriers to employment and advancement for people of all sexes. More so, focusing on welcomeness inappropriately reinforces the notion that sexual harassment is all about sex or sexual attraction when it is truly about power and subordination. Indeed, Vinson's testimony that Taylor's advances stopped once she had a steady boyfriend reveals how masculine power and norms about "ownership" of women were at play in this situation. Finally, parsing "unwelcomeness" or "voluntariness" in interactions between a male manager and female subordinate is problematic. For instance, sexual activity by a subordinate is hardly voluntary if the subordinate acquiesced only because she feared losing her job; in far too many instances, a subordinate may want to say "no" to a supervisor but may instead reply "yes" as a means of pleasing him to maintain her job. In the end, what is most relevant to claims of hostile environment sexual harassment is the behavior of the alleged harasser and its effects on the complainant and her workplace environment.

2 The Development of a Factual Record of Other Alleged Harassment

Relatedly, this Court holds that the District Court erred in not allowing Vinson to present all of her evidence about other employees' accounts of Taylor's harassment of Vinson during her case in chief. Witnesses Christine Malone and Mary Levarity were prepared to testify in support of Vinson's claims about Taylor's harassment of Vinson. For example, both Malone and Levarity were ready to testify about seeing Taylor sexually accost and handle Vinson, and seeing Vinson visibly become upset and repeatedly ask him to stop harassing her. Trial Tr. vol. I, 34–38, 40 (Testimony of Malone); Trial Tr. vol. VI, 25 (Testimony of Levarity). This evidence is directly relevant to whether Vinson found the environment at the Bank hostile and intimidating and whether Taylor's actions affected her work performance, and/or promoted and maintained gender inequality and segregation in the workplace.

Additionally, this Court holds that the District Court erred in not allowing Vinson to present evidence about Taylor's alleged harassment of other female employees during her case-in-chief. Both Malone and Levarity claimed Taylor sexually accosted and harassed them, too. For example, Malone stated that Taylor, "put his hands on [her] breasts and he would put his hands on [her] backside." Trial Tr. vol. I, 21. While such evidence is inadmissible to show Taylor's character or propensity for sexual harassment under Fed. R. Evid. 404, it could have been admitted as habit evidence or evidence of routine practice under Fed. R. Evid. 406. Or, it may have been helpful in assessing Vinson's testimony about why she did not report Taylor's alleged harassment to any supervisors at the Bank, as seeing a supervisor harass other women with impunity could discourage a reasonable woman from thinking any action would be taken on her complaints.

In the end, the exclusion of Malone and Levarity's testimony about Taylor's behavior deprived Vinson of the opportunity to build a factual record in support of her case. For this reason, too, we remand this case to the District Court to correct its error.

3 Dress and Speech

On the remaining issue concerning the relevancy of dress and sexually provocative speech, this Court concludes that dress is never relevant to determinations on hostile environment sexual harassment claims. It further holds that sexually provocative speech is relevant only to the extent that it can be used to discredit claims that the alleged harasser's actions either unreasonably interfered with the complainant's work environment and performance, created a hostile or intimidating environment, or worked to preserve patterns of sex segregation in the workplace.

At the outset, this Court notes that the EEOC Guidelines stress that the factfinder must evaluate the question of workplace sexual harassment in light of "the record as a whole" and the "totality of the circumstances, such as the nature of the sexual advances and the context in which the alleged incidents occurred." 29 C.F.R. § 1604.11(b) (1985). The totality of circumstances, however, does not include everything within the context, only those factors that might shed light on the central issues.

Holding that a complainant's mode of dress is relevant to a sexual harassment determination improperly takes the focus away from the alleged harasser and places it on the complainant. It allows the assumptions and interpretations that others make about the meaning of an individual's choice of clothing, even when erroneous, to dictate how that individual can be treated. Employees should feel free to select the clothing they will wear to work each day (assuming it complies with the employer's dress code) without worrying about what others may presume from it. For this reason, a complainant's clothing or dress has no probative value in workplace sexual harassment cases. Moreover, allowing such evidence may work to reinforce racial and gender stereotypes if the same type of clothing is viewed as having a different, provocative meaning when worn by women of a particular race or ethnicity or women with particular body types.

Unlike with dress, however, sexually provocative speech may sometimes have limited relevance to a determination about sexual harassment. For example, if an alleged harasser's actions are in direct response to an explicit invitation by the complainant, it would be more difficult to show that the challenged conduct created a hostile environment or affected the complainant's work performance.

We emphasize, though, that the probative value of sexually provocative speech is limited and must be evaluated with care. An alleged harasser may even respond in offensive and intimidating ways to an explicit invitation by a complainant. Moreover, a complainant may engage in sexually explicit speech as a defensive mechanism or a means to minimize gender differences, especially in sex segregated workplaces or workplaces where masculine norms and sexual banter are part of workplace culture. For example, if a complainant offered a sexually related retort in response to sexually crude language directed at her or other women in the workplace, courts would have to engage in a complex analysis evaluating whether the complainant's response revealed that she did not find the workplace hostile, or was merely a means of surviving in a workplace culture permeated by masculine norms or gender inequality.

C Employer Liability

Finally, this Court decides whether an employer is automatically liable for sexual harassment by its supervisory personnel, even if it was never notified of the complained-of conduct. The Court answers this question with an understanding of the central meaning that work holds in many individuals' lives and with an understanding of most individuals' need for paid work to survive and support themselves and their families. The Court also acknowledges that one party, the employer, best controls or directs the environment within any particular workplace. Indeed, this Court finds the following rationale by the Court of Appeals convincing:

> Instead of providing a reason for employers to remain oblivious to conditions in the workplace, we think the enlightened purpose of Title VII calls for an interpretation cultivating an incentive for employers to take a more active role in warranting to each employee that he or she will enjoy a working

Meritor Savings Bank, FSB v. Vinson

> environment free from illegal sex discrimination ... Employer responsiveness to on-the-job discrimination at the supervisory level is an essential aspect of the remedial scheme embodied in Title VII. It is the employer alone who is able promptly and effectively to halt discriminatory practices by supervisory personnel ...   *Vinson*, 753 F.2d at 151.

Given the primacy and urgency of work in many people's lives as well as the reality that employers are the ones best positioned to communicate to all employees how they must treat others in the workplace, this Court holds that an employer is strictly liable for a hostile environment created by a supervisor's conduct. The employer need not have notice of the supervisor's actions because the supervisor is an agent of the employer and, as such, his or her acts are imputed to the employer.[54]

The supervisor's actual authority to hire, fire, or promote employees is irrelevant. The ultimate question is whether the workplace environment for an employee has become so hostile or polluted with discrimination as to affect the terms and conditions of his or her employment, including his or her emotional and psychological state and performance in the workplace, and whether it preserves patterns of sex segregation in the workplace. A supervisor who controls the day-to-day aspects of an employee's work, or has the ability to evaluate or offer input about the employee's work, can alter the conditions of employment regardless of the supervisor's actual ability to hire, fire or demote.

The key point is that supervisors, by virtue of the title and position conferred on them by the employer, exercise control and authority over employees. Whether they truly have the ability to hire and fire is less important than whether their title creates the perception that they do. As long as employees believe that a supervisor has the right and power to supervise and evaluate their work, that power can allow the supervisor to abuse or otherwise terrorize employees. Because the employer has granted that authority (or perceived authority) to the supervisor by virtue of his title and position, the employer and supervisor are one and should be treated as such.

Should Vinson be able to prove the facts of her case on remand, this lawsuit is an excellent example of a supervisor and employer who are one. Here, regardless of the Bank's claim that Taylor had no authority to hire, fire, or promote employees, Vinson believed otherwise. As Vinson explained at trial, "He told me that he was my supervisor. He gave me my pay check, and I had to do what he wanted me to do." Trial Tr. vol. II, 59. In fact, everything that Vinson knew about Taylor seemed to suggest that he had the power to hire, promote, or fire her.

---

[54] We note that here, if the harassment was as open as Vinson and her witnesses indicate, the Bank certainly had constructive notice of the harassment.

Oncale v. Sundowner Offshore Services, Inc. 245

Taylor had hired Vinson or caused her to be hired. He was her direct supervisor and evaluated her, at least he evaluated her enough to know about her work performance and that her promotions were based on merit. He directed her to train certain people for other positions, and he informed her of future promotions. To deprive Vinson and other potential complainants of the possibility of redress under Title VII merely because the employer claimed to have no notice of the actions of its own supervisors would cut against the purpose of Title VII, which is to eliminate discrimination and harassment in the workplace.

VI CONCLUSION

In sum, this Court holds that that (1) the District Court failed to establish a sufficient factual record to determine the viability of either a *quid pro quo* claim or a hostile environment claim because it failed to determine whether sexual relations actually occurred between Vinson and Taylor and under what circumstances they occurred; (2) sexual harassment that results in non-economic injury or injury that is not otherwise tangible can violate Title VII; (3) the focus of the inquiry in a hostile environment claim is on the conduct of the alleged harasser and its effects on the complainant and the work environment; (4) the trial court erred in excluding testimonial evidence from other women who claimed to have been harassed by the alleged wrongdoer and to have seen him harass the complainant; (5) a complainant's manner of dress is not relevant to the inquiry of welcomeness, and a complainant's sexually provocative speech is relevant only to the extent that it helps to determine whether the challenged conduct unreasonably interfered with the complainant's work environment and performance, created a hostile or intimidating environment, or worked to preserve patterns of sex segregation in the workplace; and (6) employers are automatically liable for sexual harassment by their supervisory personnel regardless of whether they were aware of such conduct.

Commentary on *Oncale v. Sundowner Offshore Services, Inc.*

NANCY E. DOWD

INTRODUCTION

The US Supreme Court's opinion in *Oncale v. Sundowner Offshore Services, Inc.*[55] marked a landmark expansion of the scope of liability under Title VII of

---

[55] 523 U.S. 75 (1998).

246 Oncale v. Sundowner Offshore Services, Inc.

the Civil Rights Act of 1964 for sexual harassment.[56] Previously, in *Meritor Savings Bank v. Vinson*,[57] the Court had interpreted the term "discrimination" to include harassment. In *Oncale*, the Court concluded that harassment of individuals by someone of the same sex as the victim is prohibited by Title VII. The Court thus moved from a heterosexual norm and limitation to a broader understanding of "sex" that potentially extended beyond harassment to all discrimination claims. This expansion, however, was crippled by limiting language that has confused courts and litigants ever since.

In this rewritten opinion, Professor Ann McGinley, writing as Justice McGinley, reaches the same result, but renders her judgment in terms that incorporate a broad understanding of what it means to discriminate "because of sex." She incorporates a deep understanding of masculinities analysis as a lens through which to understand the conduct that occurred, as well as a framework for the analysis that is the foundation for the Court's judgment. McGinley's opinion suggests a path to broad protection against not only sexual harassment, but also all forms of sex discrimination. It also exposes male subordination within the workplace.

THE ORIGINAL OPINION

Justice Scalia's opinion for a unanimous Court in *Oncale* dramatically changed the scope of Title VII by ruling that harassment "because of sex"[58] was not limited to opposite-sex sexual harassment, but also reached same-sex sexual harassment.[59] This profoundly important expansion of the scope of Title VII and the understanding of "sex" and "discrimination" in the opinion was nevertheless coupled with language that sharply limited its reach. The opinion thus gives with one hand, while it takes away with the other. Justice Scalia sees this case as a clear issue of statutory interpretation that led simply and inevitably to the result; at the same time, his gendered lens preserves masculine privilege and norms even as it chips them away to some degree.

Justice Scalia's brief rendition of the facts is the first limitation of the opinion, justified on the basis that it is in the interests of the "dignity" of the plaintiff, Joseph Oncale, as well as a general interest in "brevity."[60] We are told that, in the course of his job, Mr. Oncale was not only subjected to "sex-related, humiliating actions" in front of the rest of the all-male work crew, but

[56] 42 U.S.C. §2000e *et seq.* (2012).
[57] 477 U.S. 616 (1987).
[58] 42 U.S.C. §2000e(a)(1).
[59] *Oncale*, 523 U.S. at 79.
[60] *Id.* at 77.

Oncale v. Sundowner Offshore Services, Inc.   247

also physically assaulted "in a sexual manner" and threatened with rape.[61] Mr. Oncale ultimately left his job because of management's failure to do anything about this harassment and out of fear for his physical safety. He alleged that the conduct directed at him not only infected his workplace environment, but also amounted to a constructive discharge when management failed to respond to his complaints.[62]

This limited recitation of the facts constructs a framework for the case suggesting that Justice Scalia is respecting the plaintiff as a man by not disclosing more precisely what actually happened (which is "unmanly"). The conduct nevertheless was severe enough and serious enough to cross the line from "roughhousing" and "teasing," which Justice Scalia later defines as not actionable harassment.[63] In light of the opinion's limitations on what conduct can be reached, the facts become incredibly important to understanding where that line is drawn.

In his analysis of the question presented by this case, Justice Scalia uses precedent to establish that Title VII prohibits all forms of sex discrimination, including sexual harassment. Moreover, although women were the primary focus and reason for including "sex" as a prohibited category of discrimination, the broad protections of Title VII extend to men as well, just as the broad protections of race discrimination extend to all races. Using race discrimination as the example, Justice Scalia notes that the statute prohibits discrimination against someone of the same racial identity, not only someone of a different racial identity. Therefore, the Court concludes, the same is true for sex discrimination: one can engage in unlawful discrimination against someone of the same sex.

But, Justice Scalia notes, this does not convert Title VII into "a general civility code for the American workplace ... Title VII does not prohibit all verbal or physical harassment in the workplace; it is directed only at 'discriminat[ion] ... because of ... sex.' "[64] Just as Title VII did not create a "civility code" for women, neither does it do so for men. This begins the process of underscoring the limitations of the interpretation rendered by the opinion. Harassment is actionable only if it constitutes discrimination, defined by Justice Scalia using the words of Justice Ginsburg: "The critical issue, Title VII's text indicates, is whether members of one sex are exposed to disadvantageous terms or conditions of employment to which members of the other sex are not exposed."[65] Thus the broad, inclusive effect of finding same-sex

---

[61] *Id.*
[62] *Id.*
[63] *Id.* at 82.
[64] *Id.* at 80.
[65] *Id.* (citing *Harris v. Forklift Systems, Inc.*, 510 U.S. 17, 25 (1993) (Ginsburg, J., concurring)).

248 Oncale v. Sundowner Offshore Services, Inc.

harassment as within the scope of Title VII is immediately walked back by articulating limitations.

Justice Scalia differentiates between proving opposite-sex and same-sex harassment. Opposite-sex harassment is "easy," because, he explains, it is usually motivated by sexual desire.[66] The same might be true, he concedes, in instances of same-sex harassment if the harasser is gay, but clearly he thinks that will be unusual. Justice Scalia adds, however, that a different motivation might drive discrimination: a "general hostility" to the same sex in the workplace.[67] So he defines harassing conduct either as motivated by desire or a totalistic negative view of one's own sex (other than oneself) in the workplace. Conspicuously missing from this analysis are the patterns of hierarchy among men, as a core component of masculinity, as well as the essential directives of preferred masculinity: don't be (or act) like a girl, and don't be gay.[68] Justice Scalia's constricted description of same-sex sexual harassment, then, misapprehends how masculinity functions in ways that foster the very "discrimination" he clearly recognizes.

But it does not stop there. Justice Scalia goes on to note more reasons why a to-be-avoided-at-all-costs "civility code" is not imposed. First, the ruling in this case does not reach "innocuous differences" between how men and women interact with each other at work.[69] Second, under prior case law, harassment must be "severe or pervasive" – objectively offensive to a sufficient degree that it affects the terms or conditions of the workplace.[70] As an example, Justice Scalia uses a gendered picture of the differences that preserve male privilege to sexually interact with women as well as sustain privilege and hierarchies among men: "We have always regarded that requirement as crucial, and as sufficient to ensure that courts and juries do not mistake ordinary socializing in the workplace – such as male-on-male horseplay or intersexual flirtation – for discriminatory 'conditions of employment.' "[71] Finally, he exhorts us to be conscious of context in applying a reasonable person standard to evaluate conduct, using another example of male hierarchy: the coach slapping the buttocks of a football player (implicitly permissible) versus the coach doing the same to his secretary (implicitly actionable discrimination).[72]

[66] *Id.* at 80.
[67] *Id.*
[68] Nancy E. Dowd, THE MAN QUESTION: MALE SUBORDINATION AND PRIVILEGE 62 (2010).
[69] *Oncale*, 523 U.S. at 81.
[70] *Id.*
[71] *Id.*
[72] *Id.*

Oncale v. Sundowner Offshore Services, Inc.   249

Thus a good deal of the opinion defends the judgment against the dreaded critique that a civility code is being imposed on the workplace.[73] In the interests of brevity, the opinion might have ended after four pages; the final three pages are solely devoted to this litany of limitations. The consequences of these limitations are several. First, they reinforce the limits of sexual harassment doctrine rather than the scope of its protection to ensure the antidiscrimination principle. Second, they misunderstand the nature of masculinities and therefore appear to limit (subject to creative interpretation of the opinion's language) the scope of subordinating, discriminatory behavior that could be reached, particularly for same-sex harassment. Third, the opinion appears to attempt to foreclose an opportunity to argue that other forms of same-sex discrimination, including discrimination on the basis of sexual orientation or transgender status, could be prohibited by the statute.

THE FEMINIST JUDGMENT

Professor Ann McGinley, writing as Justice McGinley, takes a totally different path to the same result. Her method and justification are radically different, identifying several key connections and underlying dynamics that significantly broaden the reach of this case, in contrast to the limits imposed by Justice Scalia's opinion for the unanimous Court.

First, McGinley provides more facts about the case because, as she sees it, the facts are crucial to the legal determination of discrimination, and failing to say what allegedly happened or hiding it "protects those who may have engaged in the behavior and diminishes the perceived severity of the acts." The allegations include one man using his penis to humiliate the other while the victim was physically restrained, threats of rape, and forcing a bar of soap between the victim's buttocks. These acts, McGinley concludes, clearly

---

[73] Both before and after *Oncale*, Justice Scalia was a strong critic of what he called "the culture wars." This makes his authorship of *Oncale* especially intriguing. *See, e.g., United States v. Virginia*, 518 U.S. 515, 601–03 (1996) (Scalia, J. dissenting) (defending an all-male institution and admiring the Code of Gentlemen); *Romer v Evans*, 517 U.S. 620, 636, 652 (1996) (Scalia, J. dissenting) ("The Court has mistaken a Kulturkampf for a fit of spite"; "When the Court takes sides in the culture wars, it tends to be with the knights rather than the villains – and more specifically with the Templars, reflecting the views and values of the lawyer class from which the Court's Members are drawn"); *Lawrence v Texas*, 539 U.S. 558, 590–91 (2003) (the majority had created "a massive disruption of the current social order" by striking down a Texas law barring sodomy; "State laws against bigamy, same-sex marriage, adult incest, prostitution, masturbation, adultery, fornication, bestiality, and obscenity ... [e]very single one of these laws is called into question by today's decision"); *see also*, at his most strident, *Obergefell v. Hodges*, 135 S.Ct. 2584, 2626 (2015) (Scalia, J., dissenting) ("I write separately to call attention to this Court's threat to American democracy").

250   Oncale v. Sundowner Offshore Services, Inc.

constitute sexual harassment under the statute. They also expose the gendered nature of the harassment and its play upon masculinity norms of how hierarchy is imposed upon another man, and how threats were not merely of physical violence, but of forcible sexual violence. The sense of threat was also perhaps heightened by the context of an all-male isolated workplace.

Second, while McGinley has no difficulty concluding that Title VII precedents support the conclusion that same-sex sexual harassment is covered by the statute, her articulation of what that means clearly links sexual harassment to gender discrimination and is grounded in the Court's prior decisions. The key case for her is *Price Waterhouse v. Hopkins*,[74] cited early in her decision and meriting a separate section in the opinion. She underscores the interrelation recognized in *Price Waterhouse* between sex and gender, and that discrimination based on either is prohibited. Resisting separating them, she describes them as inextricably intertwined, and she also notes that while sex might seem to be clearer and simpler than gender, in fact it is not. She reinforces the broad principle that discriminating against an individual for lack of conformity to gender roles or stereotypes is prohibited discrimination: "Title VII, then, forbids discrimination based on an individual's failure to live up to, or excessive compliance with, gendered expectations of his or her biological sex." Her embrace of the broad reach of *Price Waterhouse* and her reminder of the scope of Title VII opens the door to further consideration of claims of sexual orientation discrimination as gender discrimination, as well as to discrimination against transgender individuals as both sex and gender discrimination.

A key basis for understanding the result in this case, and the ways in which sex and gender interact, according to McGinley, is masculinities theory. This is a groundbreaking and significant use of gender scholarship that has typically been outside the scope of feminist analysis.[75] McGinley's use of this scholarship in this feminist redrafting of *Oncale* is therefore the equivalent of an academic double whammy. Sexual harassment, as a theory, owes its recognition to the pioneering work of Catherine MacKinnon and the extensive feminist scholarship that followed and continues her lead.[76] McGinley follows in this pioneering tradition by bringing the insights of masculinities theory

---

[74] 490 U.S. 228 (1989).

[75] Nancy E. Dowd, *Asking the Man Question: Masculinities Analysis and Feminist Theory*, 33 HARV. J. L. & GENDER 415 (2010); MASCULINITIES AND THE LAW: A MULTIDIMENSIONAL APPROACH (Frank Rudy Cooper & Ann C. McGinley eds., 2012).

[76] *See generally* Catharine MacKinnon, SEXUAL HARASSMENT OF WORKING WOMEN: A CASE OF SEX DISCRIMINATION (1979). For a recent retrospective of the law, *see* Joanna L. Grossman, *Moving Forward, Looking Back: A Retrospective on Sexual Harassment Law*, 95 B.U. L. REV. 1029, 1030 (2015).

into several places in her rewritten opinion. Early in the opinion, she addresses the issue of motivation with respect to sexual harassment and the understanding of harassment framed by a heterosexual lens as actions motivated by sexual desire. If limited to this lens, then the same-sex equivalent would be the homosexual desire of a gay harasser. McGinley makes it clear, however, that harassment based on desire is but one motivation. Others include preservation of one's position by excluding others of one's sex, or by policing gender by requiring conformity to stereotypes or norms. She uses masculinities scholarship to make the point that the plaintiff in *Oncale* was harassed as a man for failing to meet masculinities norms or to ensure that he knew his place at the bottom of the male hierarchy – where he would be treated like a woman, subject to sexual violence. McGinley thus uses masculinities scholarship to explain the motivation of the harassers, to identify the hierarchies among men, and to link harassment of men to harassment of women. She broadly defines motivation for harassment as sometimes based on desire, but more commonly on subordination.

A second place where McGinley very effectively uses masculinities scholarship to explain her point is with respect to how the decision in *Price Waterhouse*, defining sex discrimination as including gender stereotypes, relates to gender expectations in workplace culture, norms, and behavior. Indeed, this discussion explains and provides analysis of how workplaces are gendered, as opposed to neutral – an enduring argument of feminist theorists. One of the examples McGinley uses to describe the impact of masculinity norms is how male-on-male harassment is infused with homophobic abuse as a means to control, stigmatize, or demean the object of the harassment. The effectiveness of this weapon is directly related to dominant masculinity norms. McGinley provides this as an example of harassment prohibited by *Price Waterhouse* and by her *Oncale* opinion. By identifying the basis of such discriminatory conduct as rooted in socially constructed gender norms and expectations, McGinley enriches the understanding of what causes and underlies same-sex harassment. She also opens the door to the next logical step: the analysis of sexual harassment should apply to any act of discrimination, so that discrimination on the basis of sexual orientation or other sex-/gender-linked claims (not limited to sexual harassment) is discrimination on the basis of sex/gender and therefore prohibited under Title VII.

A final significant difference between Justice Scalia's opinion and McGinley's rewritten opinion is the response to the argument that recognizing Oncale's claim would create a "civility code" – a term meant to be disparaging and an outcome to be avoided. McGinley, like Scalia, rejects the suggestion that this is the result of her opinion, but articulates a very different, much

252   Oncale v. Sundowner Offshore Services, Inc.

broader, scope of what conduct may be reached. Like Justice Scalia, she notes the limitation imposed by *Meritor*: not all sexual harassment (assuming it has met the "because of sex" requirement) is prohibited by the statute, but only that which is so severe or pervasive as to change the conditions of the workplace. But McGinley establishes a new burden of proof: a claim of harassment that is sexual or gendered in nature raises a "rebuttable inference that the harassment occurred because of sex." Under this standard, "roughhousing" and "flirtation" would meet the "because of sex" standard as sexual or gendered, shifting the burden to the defendant to establish that they were not. While the plaintiff would still be required to meet the pervasive or severe standard, this would nevertheless bring a far broader range of conduct into play. Some of the very conduct that Justice Scalia preserves as acceptable would come under scrutiny under McGinley's rewritten judgment.

THE IMPLICATIONS OF THE REWRITTEN OPINION

The bottom line of McGinley's opinion is an affirmation of the broad scope of sex and gender harassment and the suggestion that the same broad outlines should apply to all forms of discrimination. The dynamics of discrimination outlined in the opinion certainly are not limited to harassment. Because of this rich, contextualized explanation and its use of masculinities scholarship, it would have had significant implications for the development of the law in several respects if this had been the original opinion in *Oncale*.

Most notably, it would have supported the view that Title VII, as written and interpreted, includes claims of sexual orientation and transgender discrimination. If the rewritten opinion of *Oncale* were issued in 1998, it well might have strengthened an earlier move to challenge conclusory decisions adopted in every circuit categorically denying sexual orientation discrimination and harassment claims. We are now seeing such challenges succeed in *Hively*[77] and *Zarda*,[78] holding that Title VII's prohibition of sex discrimination includes claims of sexual orientation discrimination, reversing prior circuit precedents.[79] The rationale of those cases and of the Equal Employment Opportunity Commission (EEOC) as it embraces this position[80] lies in the

---

[77] *Hively v. Ivy Tech Community College*, 853 F.3d 339 (7th Cir. 2017) (en banc). *See also Hively*, rewritten feminist judgment, this volume.

[78] *Zarda v. Altitude Express Inc.*, 883 F.3d 100 (2nd Cir. 2018) (en banc), *cert. granted* 139 S.Ct.1599 (2019).

[79] Both *Hively* and *Zarda* were *en banc* decisions reversing prior circuit precedent. Contrary precedent stands solely because of the inability of a panel to reverse circuit precedent. *Evans v. Georgia Regional Hospital*, 850 F.3d 1248 (11th Cir. 2017), *cert. denied* 138 S.Ct. 557 (2017).

[80] *Baldwin v. Foxx*, EEOC Decision No. 0120133080, 2015 WL 4397641 (July 15, 2015).

Oncale v. Sundowner Offshore Services, Inc.   253

intertwining of sex and sexual orientation (much as McGinley intertwines sex and gender), associational freedom, and stereotyping. The cases rely on statutory and constitutional decisions over time that have significantly changed the treatment of sexual orientation. *Price Waterhouse* has been the key case, accompanied by a march of constitutional cases such as *Romer v. Evans*,[81] *Lawrence v. Texas*,[82] *United States v. Windsor*,[83] and *Obergefell v. Hodges*.[84] But these recent opinions have not trumpeted *Oncale* as written as particularly significant.[85] Had the rewritten judgment of McGinley been the Court's judgment, it would have dramatically changed that dynamic and likely would have supported a course correction in interpretation that now appears to be underway.[86]

McGinley's opinion would similarly have strengthened transgender claims and the more recent move to broadly recognize those claims epitomized by the Sixth Circuit in *EEOC v. R.G. & G.R. Harris Funeral Homes*,[87] where the court held that "discrimination on the basis of transgender and transitioning status violates Title VII."[88] As the court notes, actions on the basis of transgender or transitioning status are inseparable from the person's sex – an analysis similar to that now being articulated with respect to sexual orientation.[89] Other circuits continue to avoid or refuse to recognize transgender claims.[90]

---

[81]   517 U.S. 620 (1996).

[82]   539 U.S. 558 (2003).

[83]   570 U.S. 744 (2013).

[84]   135 S.Ct. 2585 (2015).

[85]   Judge Posner perhaps suggests why in his concurrence in *Hively*. Justice Scalia's language in *Oncale*, according to Posner, might be read to support an originalist perspective on Title VII that would bind interpretation of the statute to the understanding of the drafters (who surely had not thought about sexual orientation or transgender discrimination), rather than an evolutionary perspective that reflects evolving understanding of statutory terms in light of the overarching commitment to nondiscrimination. *Hively*, 853 F.3d at 355–56 (Posner, J., concurring).

[86]   The Supreme Court granted *certiorari* on three sexual orientation/gender identity cases, with a decision expected at time of writing in June 2020. *See Zarda v. Altitude Express, Inc.*, 883 F.3d 100 (2d Cir. 2018) (holding that sexual orientation discrimination is sex discrimination under Title VII), *cert. granted* 139 S.Ct. 1599 (2019); *Bostock v. Clayton County Bd. Commissioners*, 723 Fed. Appx. 964 (11th Cir. 2018) (holding that discrimination based on sexual orientation is not prohibited by the sex discrimination provision of Title VII), *cert. granted* 139 S.Ct. 1599 (2019); *EEOC v. R.G. & G.R. Harris Funeral Homes*, 884 F.3d 560 (6th Cir. 2018) (holding that discrimination against a transgender employee is sex discrimination under Title VII), *cert. granted* 139 S.Ct. 1599 (2019).

[87]   884 F.3d 560 (6th Cir. 2018).

[88]   *Id.* at 574–75.

[89]   *Id.* at 575–76.

[90]   The Fourth Circuit Court of Appeals declined to address the coverage issue in a Title VII claim brought by a transgender employee. *Finkle v. Howard City*, 640 F. App'x 245 (4th Cir. 2016).

The full range of gender identity claims remains to be explored under Title VII.[91]

Third, the McGinley rewriting of *Oncale* would strengthen discrimination claims based on sex stereotyping and stereotyping broadly. Rather than resting solely on *Price Waterhouse*, sex-stereotyping claims would gain from the analysis in her opinion, which provides more theoretical grounding and specific examples of actions based on stereotypes, gender roles, and gender expectations. *Price Waterhouse* continues to have untapped potential, linked in part to efforts to minimize or domesticate its radical reach.[92] *Oncale* reconfigured as in McGinley's opinion would solidify the scope of the Court's clear recognition of the role of stereotyping and further permit ongoing interdisciplinary research to inform the understanding of how this constructs both individual actions and workplace culture, and thus how it underlies the persistence of structural discrimination. The enhanced and strengthened analysis of stereotyping in McGinley's opinion draws from critical race analysis, which suggests that her opinion might be used also to strengthen racial discrimination claims with expanded stereotype analysis. The original *Oncale* opinion makes use of race discrimination precedents, but McGinley's rewritten opinion more forcefully makes the connection and invites cross-pollination.

Finally, McGinley's rewriting of *Oncale* would have invited more use of masculinities scholarship to understand the nature of male discrimination and to uncover male victimization. Although available at the time, such scholarship was rarely incorporated or recognized. Closely connected to other critical theories, including critical race and queer theory, this theoretical and multidisciplinary perspective would have enhanced the understanding of discrimination dynamics. McGinley has been among a group of scholars who have called for the necessary incorporation of masculinities theories as essential to feminist and gender analysis; she has particularly advocated for multidimensional masculinities analysis, incorporating the important insights of intersectional analysis.[93] Had this thread been introduced in Supreme Court analysis at this stage and if it were used more robustly today, it would have made a significant difference by exposing more clearly how privilege functions, but

---

[91] Kris Franklin & Sarah E. Chinn, *Transsexual, Transgender, Trans: Reading Judicial Nomenclature in Title VII Cases*, 32 Berkeley J. Gender, L. & Just. 1 (2017).

[92] Stephanie Bornstein, *Unifying Antidiscrimination Law through Stereotype Theory*, 20 Lewis & Clark L. Rev. 919 (2016).

[93] *See generally* Ann C. McGinley, Masculinity at Work: Employment Discrimination through a Different Lens (2016); Cooper & McGinley, *supra* note 75 Dowd, *supra* note 68.

Oncale v. Sundowner Offshore Services, Inc.

also how those frequently assumed to never be discriminated against, men, are indeed themselves subordinated in unique ways.

Oncale v. Sundowner Offshore Services, Inc., 523 U.S. 75 (1998)[94]

JUSTICE ANN C. MCGINLEY DELIVERED THE OPINION OF THE COURT.

I INTRODUCTION

This case presents the question of whether workplace harassment violates Title VII's prohibition against "discriminat[ion] ... because of ... sex," 42 U.S.C. §2000e-2(a)(1), when the harasser and the harassed employee are of the same biological sex. We have already concluded, in *Price Waterhouse v. Hopkins*, 490 U.S. 228, 241 (1989), that Title VII's prohibition against discrimination because of sex also includes discrimination because of gender, and today we hold that discrimination against a person of the same biological sex or gender violates Title VII if the other requirements of proving illegal sex- or gender-based harassment are met.

The plaintiff, Joseph Oncale, brought suit in the United States District Court for the Eastern District of Louisiana, alleging that his employer, the defendant, Sundowner Offshore Services, Inc. (Sundowner), discriminated against him because of his sex in violation of Title VII. Specifically, the complaint alleged, and the plaintiff's affidavit and deposition avow, that Oncale's male supervisors and coworkers at Sundowner sexually harassed him at work. App. 19–22, 66–70, 76–77. The federal district court granted summary judgment to the defendant, relying on the Fifth Circuit's decision in *Garcia v. Elf Atochem North America*, 28 F.3d 446, 451–52 (1994), which held that Title VII provides no cause of action for same sex harassment. App. 106. On appeal, a panel of the Fifth Circuit concluded that *Garcia* was binding Circuit precedent and affirmed. 83 F.3d 118 (1996). We granted *certiorari*. 520 U.S. 1263 (1997).

---

[94] This opinion is reproduced from the original *Feminist Judgments* book, which was published in 2016. Accepted terminology referencing transgender and nonbinary individuals has changed rapidly over recent years. Therefore, some of the terms in this opinion would be different if I were writing the opinion today. For example, I would omit "biological" as a term applied to "sex" throughout, and I would use "nonbinary" to replace "genderqueer." Finally, I would use "intersex" rather than refer to individuals born without a defined biological sex. My intent is to be respectful of the nonbinary community and to respect the community's wishes with reference to terminology.

II FACTS

Because the District Court granted summary judgment for Respondents, we must assume the facts to be as alleged by Petitioner Joseph Oncale. While the precise details alleged by the plaintiff are disturbing, we believe it is important to relate the facts alleged. Some would argue that dignity of this Court is sacrificed by the account, but if the allegations are true, the behavior constitutes a much greater insult to Joseph Oncale than to the Court. A decision not to relate the facts alleged protects those who may have engaged in the behavior and diminishes the perceived severity of the acts. Furthermore, the facts alleged here are important to the determination of the case: when taken in the light most favorable to the plaintiff, Joseph Oncale's coworkers and supervisors engaged in serious physical and verbal harassment that emphasized their masculinity and demeaned that of Mr. Oncale.

The facts alleged are as follows: In late October 1991, Oncale was working for Respondent Sundowner Offshore Services, Inc., on a Chevron U.S.A., Inc., oil platform in the Gulf of Mexico. He was employed as a roustabout on an eight-man crew, which included Respondents John Lyons, Danny Pippen, and Brandon Johnson. Lyons, the crane operator, and Pippen, the driller, had supervisory authority. App. 41, 43, 77. On several occasions, Lyons, Pippen, and Johnson forcibly subjected Oncale to sex-related, humiliating actions against him in the presence of the rest of the crew. Pippen and Lyons also physically assaulted Oncale in a sexual manner and threatened him with rape. Specifically, the complaint alleges, among other acts, that Pippen and Johnson restrained Oncale while Lyons placed his penis on the back of Oncale's head on one occasion, and on his arm on another occasion, that Lyons and Pippen made repeated threats that they would rape Oncale, and that Lyons forced a bar of soap between Oncale's buttocks while Pippen restrained Oncale in the shower on the employer's premises, App. 66–70, 76.

The complaint further alleges and Oncale avows in his affidavit and deposition that Oncale's complaints to supervisory personnel produced no remedial action; in fact, the company's Safety Compliance Clerk, Valent Hohen, told Oncale that Lyons and Pippen "picked [on] him [Hohen] all the time too," and called Hohen "Valene, Valene the Rig Queen," a name suggesting homosexuality. App. 77. Oncale eventually quit his job because he was afraid of his coworkers and supervisors. He repeatedly asked that his pink slip reflect that he "voluntarily left due to sexual harassment and verbal abuse." App. 79. When asked at his deposition why he left Sundowner, Oncale stated: "I felt that if I didn't leave my job, that I would be raped or forced to have sex." App. 71.

III PROVING A TITLE VII CLAIM OF SEX- OR GENDER-BASED HARASSMENT

Title VII of the Civil Rights Act of 1964 provides, in relevant part, that "it shall be an unlawful employment practice for an employer ... to discriminate against any individual with respect to his compensation, terms, conditions, or privileges of employment, because of such individual's race, color, religion, sex, or national origin." 78 Stat. 255, as amended, 42 U. S. C. §2000e-2 (a)(1). We have held that this provision not only covers "terms" and "conditions" in the narrow contractual sense, but also "evinces a congressional intent to strike at the entire spectrum of disparate treatment of men and women in employment." *Meritor Savings Bank v. Vinson*, 477 U.S. 57, 64 (1986) (citations and internal quotation marks omitted). "When the workplace is permeated with discriminatory intimidation, ridicule, and insult that is sufficiently severe or pervasive to alter the conditions of the victim's employment and [to] create an abusive working environment, Title VII is violated." *Harris v. Forklift Systems, Inc.*, 510 U.S. 17, 21 (1993) (citations and internal quotation marks omitted).

We have held that Title VII's prohibition of discrimination "because of ... sex" protects men as well as women, *Newport News Ship-building & Dry Dock Co. v. EEOC*, 462 U.S. 669, 682 (1983), and in the related context of racial discrimination in the workplace we have rejected any conclusive presumption that an employer will not discriminate against members of his own race. "Because of the many facets of human motivation, it would be unwise to presume as a matter of law that human beings of one definable group will not discriminate against other members of their group." *Castaneda v. Partida*, 430 U.S. 482, 499 (1977). *See also id.* at 515–16, n. 6 (Powell, J., joined by Burger, C. J., and Rehnquist, J., dissenting). In *Johnson v. Transportation Agency*, 480 U.S. 616 (1987), a male employee claimed that his employer discriminated against him because of his sex when it preferred a female employee for promotion. Although we ultimately rejected the claim on other grounds, we did not consider it significant that the supervisor who made that decision was also a man. See *id.* at 624–25. If our precedents leave any doubt on the question, we hold today that nothing in Title VII necessarily bars a claim of discrimination "because of ... sex" merely because the plaintiff and the defendant (or the person charged with acting on behalf of the defendant) are of the same biological sex. In fact, given the evidence that biological sex is not limited to two and that persons express themselves in a number of genders, "because of ... sex" must have a much broader application.

Courts have had little trouble with the principle that persons can discriminate against others of the same biological sex in cases like *Johnson*, where an employee claims to have been passed over for a job or promotion. But when the issue arises in the context of a "hostile work environment" sexual harassment claim, the state and federal courts have taken a bewildering variety of stances. Some, like the Fifth Circuit in this case, have held that same biological sex sexual harassment claims are never cognizable under Title VII. *See also, e.g., Goluszek v. H. R. Smith*, 697 F. Supp. 1452 (N.D. Ill. 1988). Other decisions say that such claims are actionable only if the plaintiff can prove that the harasser is homosexual (and thus presumably motivated by sexual desire). *Compare McWilliams v. Fairfax County Board of Supervisors*, 72 F.3d 1191 (4th Cir. 1996), *with Wrightson v. Pizza Hut of America*, 99 F.3d 138 (4th Cir. 1996). Still others suggest that workplace harassment that is sexual in content is always actionable, regardless of the harasser's sex, sexual orientation, or motivations. *See Doe v. Belleville*, 119 F.3d 563 (7th Cir. 1997).

We see no justification in the statutory language or our precedents for a categorical rule excluding same biological sex harassment claims from the coverage of Title VII or for a limitation that would permit same biological sex harassment claims only upon proof that the alleged perpetrator is homosexual. But neither do we believe that sexual content in the workplace is always actionable under Title VII whether the behavior harasses members of a different biological sex or of the same biological sex. As some courts have observed, male-on-male sexual harassment in the workplace was assuredly not the principal evil Congress was concerned with when it enacted Title VII. But statutory prohibitions often go beyond the principal evil to cover reasonably comparable evils, and it is ultimately the provisions of our laws rather than the principal concerns of our legislators by which we are governed. Title VII prohibits "discriminat[ion] . . . because of . . . sex" in the "terms" or "conditions" of employment. Our holding in *Meritor Savings Bank v. Vinson* that this provision bans sexual harassment must extend to sexual harassment of any kind that meets the statutory requirements.

A Proof Standards

Respondents and their *amici* contend that recognizing liability for same biological sex harassment will transform Title VII into a general civility code for the American workplace. But that risk is no greater for same biological sex harassment than for different biological sex harassment, and is adequately met by careful attention to the requirements of the statute. Title VII does not prohibit all verbal or physical harassment in the workplace; it is directed only at "*discriminat[ion]* ... because of ... sex." In the context of a hostile work environment, the harassment must be sufficiently severe or pervasive to alter the terms or conditions of the plaintiff's employment. We have never held that workplace harassment, even harassment between men and women, is automatically discrimination because of sex because the words used have sexual content or connotations. Nonetheless, we believe that the presence of sexual or gendered content in the harassment is important in helping to determine whether the behavior occurred because of sex.[95] Therefore, we hold here that verbal and/or physical harassment of sexual or gendered content should raise a rebuttable inference that the harassment occurred because of sex. Once the plaintiff establishes the inference, the burden of persuasion on the issue of whether the behavior occurred because of sex shifts to the defendant.[96] Even if the defendant is unable to prove by a preponderance of the evidence that the harassment did not occur because of sex, the plaintiff must still prove by a preponderance of the evidence that the harassment was unwelcome and sufficiently severe or pervasive to alter the terms or conditions of employment. These latter requirements impose sufficient limitations on lawsuits brought under Title VII as to avoid converting Title VII into a general civility code.

B Defining "Because of ... Sex"

In harassment cases, courts and juries have found the inference of discrimination automatic in most male–female sexual harassment situations, because they interpret the challenged conduct as involving explicit or implicit proposals of sexual activity. Where the evidence suggests that the motivation of the perpetrator is sexual attraction to the victim, it may seem easy to assume that the proposals would not have been made to someone of the same sex. Of course, this assumption is based in heteronormativity – the belief that most individuals are heterosexual. The inference may be reasonable, but we note that sexuality exists along a spectrum between heterosexual and homosexual, with a number of persons either identifying as bisexual or having orientations that fall somewhere in between heterosexual and homosexual. Many

---

[95] By gendered content, we mean physical or verbal behavior that is not necessarily sexual in nature but that has the intent or effect of harming a person because of the way the individual performs gender or that generally demeans an identifiable group (i.e., a man is called "effeminate" or "macho"; a woman described as "butch" or "prissy"; or "all men are stupid," "women are terrible drivers," etc.).

[96] If there is harassment but its content lacks sexual or gendered speech or behavior, the plaintiff should retain the burden of persuasion on the "because of sex" element.

individuals who fail to identify as bisexual may adhere to heterosexual or homosexual behaviors exclusively because of societal pressures. By the same token, given that a statistical majority of persons continue to identify as heterosexual, harassing behaviors with sexual content in different sex situations can raise an inference that the behavior occurs because of sex. The same chain of inference would be available to a plaintiff alleging same biological sex harassment, if there were credible evidence that the harasser was homosexual, and that the motivation of the perpetrator is sexual attraction to the victim.

But it is important to recognize that harassing conduct need not be motivated by sexual desire to support an inference of discrimination on the basis of sex. Indeed, when the facts of the sexual harassment cases are examined closely, it appears that sexual interest may actually mask hostility rather than sexual attraction. Sex may also be used as a weapon or "technology" of sexism that is motivated by hostility. *See* Katherine M. Franke, *What's Wrong with Sexual Harassment?*, 49 STAN. L. REV. 691, 693 (1997). In the alternative, motivation that begins as sexual desire may actually convert to hostility because of the victim's rebuffs of the perpetrator's advances. There are many fact patterns that support a finding that the discrimination occurred because of sex, many of which we have no room to mention here, but we will offer a number of examples. These examples do not attempt to provide an exclusive list.

A trier of fact might reasonably find such discrimination, for example, if a female victim is harassed in such sex-specific and derogatory terms by another woman as to make it clear that the harasser is motivated by hostility to the presence of the female victim because she is a woman. Some research suggests that some women engage in discriminatory behavior against other women in order to assure their own position among men. *See generally* Robin J. Ely, *The Effects of Organizational Demographics and Social Identity on Relationships among Professional Women*, 39 ADMIN. SCI. Q. 203 (1994). Women can harass other women because of their sex if they fail to adhere to stereotypes of how female employees should dress and behave. *See generally* Karen Lee Ashcraft & Michael E. Pacanowsky, *"A Woman's Worst Enemy": Reflections on a Narrative of Organizational Life and Female Identity*, 24 J. OF APP. COMM. RES. 217 (1996). *See also* Laurie A. Rudman, *Self Promotion as a Risk-Factor for Women: The Costs and Benefits of Counterstereotypical Impression Management*, 74 J. PERSONALITY & SOC. PSYCH. 629, 642, 643 (1997). A plaintiff claiming same biological sex harassment may also, of course, offer direct comparative evidence about how the alleged harasser treated members of other sexes in a mixed-sex workplace.

Oncale v. Sundowner Offshore Services, Inc. 261

A man like Joseph Oncale in an all-male workplace may produce evidence that suggests that he was harassed because his male colleagues either considered him insufficiently masculine to perform the job and/or because they wanted to prove their own masculinity to the other members of the group and to police the masculine boundaries of the job. Behavior among men at work such as "hazing" and "roughhousing" is often gendered behavior occurring because of sex in order to establish the masculinity of the group, and to demonstrate that the newcomer is insufficiently masculine to be a member of the group, or to assure that the male newcomer adopt similar masculine behaviors to bond him to the group. A woman in a traditionally male job may encounter similar harassment by men. Her colleagues may sexually harass her to prove that a woman cannot perform the job as well as a man can and to force her out of the job or generally to demean her and all women doing a man's job. James W. Messerschmidt, MASCULINITIES AND CRIME: CRITIQUE AND RECONCEPTUALIZATION OF THEORY 130–33 (1993). Studies of masculinity demonstrate that such behavior enhances the self-worth of the male harassers and establishes gendered requirements for the job in question.

These are some means of demonstrating that the behavior occurred because of sex, but there are others. Persons of indefinable gender and/or sex may suffer from harassment because of sex because they do not conform to social norms in their dress, behavior or performed identities. Clearly, the "because of ... sex" language is broad enough to protect persons against discrimination based on their sexual orientations and gender identities, whether they fall into socially approved categories of dress and behavior or not. Of course, a finding that the behavior occurred because of sex does not automatically mean that the plaintiff will win the Title VII cause of action. The plaintiff must also prove that the behavior was unwelcome and sufficiently severe or pervasive to alter the terms or conditions of employment, requirements that will likely eliminate simple flirtation and ordinary socializing depending on the context of the situation. *Harris*, 510 U.S. at 21(citing *Meritor*, 477 U.S. at 67).

IV SEX STEREOTYPING, SEXUAL ORIENTATION, AND GENDER IDENTITY

Nearly a decade ago this Court decided *Price Waterhouse v. Hopkins*, where we held that sex stereotyping is discrimination "because of ... sex." 490 U.S. 228 (1989). In that case, Price Waterhouse refused Ann Hopkins' bid for membership in the partnership in part because of her failure to live up to female stereotypes. *Price Waterhouse*, 490 U.S. at 251. The voting partners considered Ms. Hopkins to be insufficiently feminine and too masculine. We concluded that taking an adverse employment action because a person does not adhere to gendered societal stereotypes (i.e., a woman should be feminine; a man should be masculine) is discrimination because of sex. *Id.* In other words, the term "because of . . . sex" incorporates "because of gender," which we understand to include not only the biological sex of an individual, but also the societal expectations of a person of a particular biological sex, and even the societal expectations that all individuals belong to a particular biological sex or gender. Title VII, then, forbids discrimination based on an individual's failure to live up to, or excessive compliance with, gendered expectations of his or her biological sex. Or if the person fails to identify as a particular sex or gender, as gender-queer individuals do, Title VII forbids discrimination based on this failure. Thus, had Price Waterhouse refused partnership to Ann Hopkins because she was too feminine or too good-looking or too sexy, or if it was unclear which sex and/or gender to which she belonged, it would have discriminated because of sex. Moreover, given that not all people are born with a defined biological sex and that even some who are do not identify with either male or female gender, the term "because of . . . sex" must be sufficiently broad to protect persons of all genders and neither biological sex.[97]

We understand that *Price Waterhouse*'s holding on gender combined with our ruling in this case may be interpreted as expanding the term "because of . . . sex," but separating biological sex from gender is a difficult, likely impossible, proposition that is better left to the realm of biologists and social scientists than the courts. Moreover, biological sex itself is not as easily determined as previously thought. *See generally* John Money, Gay, Straight and In-Between: The Sexology of Erotic Orientation (1988). Our decision in *Price Waterhouse* that the definition of "sex" includes the broader categories of sexual stereotypes imposed by gender expectations recognized how intertwined sex and gender are in everyday life.

Even the legislators who originally wrote Title VII in the early 1960s likely understood, either consciously or unconsciously, that the term "sex" includes aspects of gender stereotypes and expectations. Certainly, after the passage of the Act the courts interpreted the term "sex" to indicate more than biology.

---

[97] The only exception to the sex stereotyping rule would be if the employer proves that being of a particular biological sex or adherence or non-adherence to particular gendered expectations is a bona fide occupational qualification of the job ("BFOQ") under 42 U.S.C. § 2000e-2(e)(1). This is an extremely limited exception to the statute's ban on sex discrimination. The "because of . . . sex" provision of Title VII applies the same whether the discrimination alleged is failure to hire, a firing, or other adverse action because of a person's sex or gender or a sex- or gender-based hostile working environment that alters the person's terms or conditions of employment.

See, e.g., Rosenfeld v. Southern Pac Co., 444 F.2d 1219 (1971) (holding that defendant's personnel policies that forbade women from certain positions violated Title VII, and discussing approvingly an EEOC Guidance that declared it illegal to make employee assignments based on stereotypes such as men cannot do detail work or women cannot be aggressive salespersons). For example, assume that in 1965 a trucking company refused to hire a woman to do long haul trucking because "women can't be truck drivers." This refusal to hire would violate Title VII even though the reason for the employer's pronouncement did not actually reflect a woman's biological weakness. Instead, the employer's view reflected a socially constructed, stereotypical view of what women can and should do. Even in 1965, this employer could not successfully defend its case by testifying that the refusal to hire the plaintiff was not because of her sex, but rather because of her failure to adhere to societal expectations of her sex. The employer would surely have lost this argument.

In a similar vein, courts have consistently concluded that customer preferences are not a defense to a Title VII lawsuit. *See* 29 C.F.R. § 1604.2 (a)(I)(iii) (1997); *Gerdom v. Cont'l Airlines, Inc.*, 692 F.2d 602, 609 (9th Cir. 1982); *Diaz v. Pan Am. World Airways, Inc.*, 442 F.2d 385, 389 (5th Cir. 1971); *Bollenback v. Bd. of Educ. of Monroe-Woodbury Cent. Sch. Dist.*, 659 F.Supp. 1450, 1472 (S.D.N.Y. 1987). For example, an airline cannot refuse to hire female pilots because customers are more comfortable with male pilots. This rule exists to counteract societal gendered expectations and stereotypes about women. In contrast, by adopting a narrow reading of "because of ... sex," courts could have decided that an airline that succumbs to customer expectations and refuses to hire female pilots to soothe customers' nerves does not possess the necessary intent to discriminate against the female applicants because of their sex. But courts chose to interpret the statute in a broader way, because splitting hairs as to the employer's intent would not do justice to the broad purposes of the statute.

Likewise, after this case, plaintiffs will bring suits alleging that sex- or gender-based harassment in all male workplaces was motivated by the plaintiffs' failure to conform to gendered expectations. Theories of masculinity demonstrate that society pressures men and boys to live up to ideals of masculinity; this pressure leads men to engage in competitive behaviors to prove their masculinity. Because men derive their masculine self-worth in large part from the work they do, especially in all-male workplaces, men compete with one another to prove their masculinity to other men and to affirm their masculinity to themselves. A common behavior among men in traditionally male workplaces is to harass other men, sometimes in a sexual

264 Oncale v. Sundowner Offshore Services, Inc.

way. In cases where a plaintiff alleges harassment or other discriminatory treatment based on the plaintiff's failure to conform to masculine stereotypes, defendants may attempt to escape liability by arguing that the harassing behavior did not occur because of the plaintiff's failure to comply with gendered expectations, but rather because of the plaintiff's homosexual orientation or perceived homosexual orientation. In other words, defendants would attempt to distinguish between behavior that is motivated by the harassers' aversion to employees who do not meet traditional expectations of masculinity and that which is motivated by the harassers' aversion to homosexuality. Research on masculinity demonstrates, however, that concepts of masculinity and heterosexuality are so inextricably intertwined that it is virtually impossible to distinguish motivations. Michael S. Kimmel, *Masculinity as Homophobia: Fear, Shame, and Silence in the Construction of Gender Identity, in* THEORIZING MASCULINITIES 119–41 (Harry Brod & Michael Kaufman eds., 1994).

In typical workplace harassment situations, common terms for homosexuality and lack of masculinity are used in the same breath: men are accused of being limp-wristed, effeminate, "pussies" and "fags." Some of these terms appear to indicate that the harasser is motivated by homosexual orientation, either perceived or real, of the victim, but others appear to indicate the victim's failed masculinity. Especially because the most prevalent expectation about men is that they will be attracted to women, there is no space between discrimination based on sexual orientation and that based on a failure to meet gendered expectations. In fact, perhaps the most notable gendered stereotype is that members of a particular biological sex will be attracted to and have sexual relations with persons who are members of a different biological sex. Even if there were a difference between the sexual orientation and gender, it would be impossible for the courts, the juries or even the victims and perpetrators themselves to distinguish between behavior that is motivated by the victim's failure to conform to gender stereotypes and behavior motivated by the victim's sexual orientation. Asking the courts to engage in this hairsplitting would be an affront to the dignity of the courts and of the individuals Title VII was designed to protect. In essence, sexualized comments and behavior are frequently directed at individuals because they do not fit the gender norms of the workplace, which may or may not include a sexual orientation other than heterosexuality. Therefore, we conclude that an employee who suffers unwelcome severe or pervasive harassment of a sexual or gendered nature by employees of the same or different biological sex may satisfy the "because of ... sex" requirement by demonstrating that the perpetrators engaged in the harassment because of the victim's failure to adhere to masculine (or feminine) stereotypes including the real or perceived sexual orientation of the victim.

V APPLICATION TO ONCALE

In this case, Mr. Oncale is a slight man (125–135 pounds), App. 68, who complained about the harassing behavior directed at him. He can argue that he was harassed because the defendants thought him to be insufficiently masculine or because they perceived him to be homosexual. In either case, the behavior of Sundowner's employees may be explained by an interest in punishing Mr. Oncale because of his failure to meet their standards of masculinity or as a means of assuring that all members of the oil-rig conform to their masculine ideals. Or, he may explain his treatment as the homosexual desires of work colleagues to engage in sexual behavior with him. Whatever his theory of the case, Mr. Oncale has clearly set forth sufficient evidence that the behavior was sexual and/or gendered in content. Therefore, it appears that he has presented sufficient evidence to shift the burden to the defendant to prove that the behavior did not occur because of sex. The defendant should have an opportunity to present this evidence to the trial court and to move once more for summary judgment, if it desires.

Once the evidence is presented, if there is sufficient evidence for a reasonable jury to conclude that proof establishes that the behavior occurred because of biological sex or gender, and that the behavior was unwelcome to Mr. Oncale, and that the behavior was sufficiently severe or pervasive to alter Mr. Oncale's terms or conditions of employment, the defendants' motion for summary judgment should be denied.

VI CONCLUSION

Because we conclude that sex discrimination consisting of same biological sex sexual harassment is actionable under Title VII, the judgment of the Court of Appeals for the Fifth Circuit is reversed, and the case is remanded for further proceedings consistent with this opinion.

It is so ordered.

6

Sexual Orientation and Gender Identity Discrimination as Sex Discrimination

Commentary on *Etsitty v. Utah Transit Authority*

PAMELA A. WILKINS

INTRODUCTION

In *Etsitty v. Utah Transit Authority*,[1] the United States Court of Appeals for the Tenth Circuit held that discrimination against transgender persons is not sex discrimination under Title VII of the Civil Rights Act of 1964,[2] that Title VII's protection of those who fail to conform to gender stereotypes does not extend to their bathroom use,[3] and that transgender persons are not a protected class for equal protection purposes under the Equal Protection Clause of the Fourteenth Amendment to the US Constitution.[4] The feminist judgment of Professor Catherine Archibald, writing as Judge Archibald, reaches diametrically opposite conclusions.[5]

This case can be interpreted from a variety of feminist perspectives, but it is best understood through the lens of the double bind. A familiar concept within feminist thought, a double bind presents women with "situations in which options are reduced to a very few and all of them expose one to penalty, censure, or deprivation."[6]

---

[1] 502 F.3d 1215 (10th Cir. 2007).

[2] *Id.* at 1222.

[3] *Id.* at 1224.

[4] *Id.* at 1227–28.

[5] Professor Archibald's rewritten opinion draws from and builds upon her prior writings, including Catherine Archibald, *Transgender Bathroom Rights in the Time of Trump*, 6 Tenn. J. Race, Gender & Soc. Just. 241, 257–71 (2017) (arguing that transgender discrimination is sex discrimination and should be judged with heightened scrutiny), and Catherine Archibald, *Transgender Student in Maine May Use Bathroom that Matches Gender Identity: Are Co-ed Bathrooms Next?*, 83 UMKC L. Rev. 57, 63–70 (2014) (arguing that all-gender bathrooms are constitutionally required).

[6] Martha Chamallas, Introduction to Feminist Legal Theory 10 (3d ed. 2013) (quoting Marilyn Frye, The Politics of Reality: Essays in Feminist Theory 2 (1983)).

Etsitty v. Utah Transit Authority

To understand the double bind in which Krystal Etsitty's employer placed her, consider the facts of the case. Etsitty was hired as a bus operator for the Utah Transit Authority (UTA). She was good at her job; indeed, her supervisor was happy with her performance, and passengers never complained about her. But when UTA's human resources (HR) department found out that Etsitty was a transgender woman in the process of transitioning, it interrogated Etsitty about her genitalia. Upon learning that Etsitty had what the court described as "male genitalia" but was using public women's restrooms, it discharged her, citing concerns about liability.[7] The record of her termination indicated that she would be eligible for rehire upon completion of gender confirmation (also known as sex reassignment) surgery.[8] Implicit in the employer's actions was a demand that Etsitty use public men's restrooms as long as she had genitalia stereotypically associated with being male.

At first blush, UTA's implicit demand appears straightforward: use public men's restrooms along the bus route, or be terminated. However, consider Krystal Etsitty's potential responses to this demand. Her "choices" included: (1) having gender confirmation surgery and then using public women's restrooms; (2) attempting not to use restrooms at all during the workday; (3) continuing to dress and otherwise express herself as feminine, but using public men's restrooms; (4) dressing and otherwise presenting herself as masculine and using public men's restrooms; or (5) accepting termination of her employment.

Examination of these options shows the stark and gendered nature of Etsitty's *real* choice: she could dress and otherwise present as a man and use the public men's restrooms, or she could be fired. Differently put, a practical condition of her employment was that she appear masculine. All other so-called choices were untenable.

In the first instance, Etsitty did not have the money for gender confirmation surgery,[9] so that was not a realistic option.

Consider next Etsitty's option not to use the restroom at all while at work. The typical person urinates six or seven times every 24 hours; the normal range

---

[7] *Etsitty*, 502 F.3d at 1219. The term "male genitalia" that the court used is not a comfortable term for some transgender persons. *See* Elena Spivack, *What We Talk about When We Talk about Genitals*, LADY SCIENCE (Jan. 28, 2020), www.ladyscience.com/essays/what-we-talk-about-when-we-talk-about-genitals-trans-reproductive-health. For that reason, we will use the term "genitalia stereotypically associated with being male" instead.

[8] *Etsitty*, 502 F.3d at 1219. This commentary will use the term "gender confirmation surgery" for what the court called "sex reassignment surgery." Both terms describe the same surgeries, but "gender confirmation surgery" most accurately describes the experiences of transgender persons: their preexisting gender identity is confirmed through the relevant surgeries. *See* Loren S. Schechter, *"Gender Confirmation Surgery": What's in a Name?*, HUFFINGTON POST (Apr. 20, 2012), www.huffingtonpost.com/loren-s-schechter-md-facs/gender-confirmation-surgery_b_1442262.html.

[9] *See Etsitty*, 502 F.3d at 1219.

is between four and ten times.[10] Even someone at the low end of the normal range would need at least two trips to the bathroom during the workday. Add to this the nature of Etsitty's work – driving a bus – which requires regular hydration to maintain energy and focus, and it is clear that refraining from visiting a bathroom would be uncomfortable and may be impossible. Moreover, holding urine can weaken the pelvic floor muscles, resulting in an increased risk of urinary urgency, accidents, and long-term bladder incontinence.[11] In short, a choice to refrain from using the restroom would likely result in on-the-job accidents or compromised health.

Consider Etsitty's third option to continue to wear women's clothing and express herself as a woman, but use the public men's restrooms. This would put Etsitty at risk of violence, including sexual violence. For transgender women, this risk is high. For example, in 2009, transgender women comprised 50 percent of victims of fatal hate crimes against LGBTQ+ persons.[12] The 2015 US Transgender Survey reports that almost 50 percent of transgender persons have been victims of sexual violence; approximately 10 percent are victims of physical violence within any given year.[13] Concerns about hate crimes certainly exist within restrooms – enclosed, semiprivate spaces – to such a degree that almost 60 percent of transgender people report avoiding public restrooms when possible. They do so with good reason: in a period of one year, 12 percent reported being verbally harassed in a bathroom, 1 percent, physically assaulted, and another 1 percent, sexually assaulted.[14] To compound the problem, transgender women justifiably believe that they cannot rely on the police for protection.[15]

---

[10] *See, e.g.,* Jayne Leonard, *How Many Times a Day Should a Person Pee?*, MEDICAL NEWS TODAY (Apr. 11, 2018), www.medicalnewstoday.com/articles/321461.php. Frequency of bowel movements is far more variable. *See, e.g.,* Beth W. Orenstein, *Bowel Movements: What's Considered Normal?*, EVERYDAY HEALTH (Mar. 30, 2011), www.everydayhealth.com/hs/guide-to-constipation -relief/bowel-movements-whats-normal/.

[11] *See, e.g.,* Lizette Borreli, *Holding Pee for Too Long Can Weaken Pelvic Floor Muscles and Increase Risk of Bladder Problems*, MEDICAL DAILY (Oct. 12, 2016), www.medicaldaily.com /holding-pee-too-long-can-weaken-pelvic-floor-muscles-and-increase-risk-bladder-400972.

[12] National Coalition of Anti-Violence Programs, HATE VIOLENCE AGAINST LESBIAN, GAY, BISEXUAL, TRANSGENDER, AND QUEER COMMUNITIES IN THE UNITED STATES IN 2009 (2010), http://avp.org /wp-content/uploads/2017/04/2009_NCAVP_HV_Report.pdf.

[13] National Center for Transgender Equality, 2015 U.S. TRANSGENDER SURVEY: EXECUTIVE SUMMARY (Dec. 2016), https://transequality.org/sites/default/files/docs/usts/USTS-Executive-Summary-Dec17.pdf.

[14] *Id.*

[15] *Id.*

Testimonials from transgender women affected by the 2016 North Carolina bathroom bill[16] show the fear they experience when forced to use a men's restroom. One transgender woman said:

> Last year, we had 22 or 23 trans women murdered. And we've got North Carolina legislators ... having beat the drum that transgender people are perverts and have no rights. You walk into a bathroom, you've announced yourself as transgender and everyone in that bathroom has been told that you're a child-molesting, subhuman monster. Whatever compunctions they have against violence have been significantly lowered.[17]

Although transgender women may face harassment in women's restrooms, the risks of physical violence are likely far higher in men's restrooms. In the United States, men are responsible for far more violent crime than are women.[18] Masculinities theory predicts male violence against transgender women as a means of "policing" masculine identity.[19]

In short, a choice by Etsitty to use the men's restroom while appearing and acting feminine would subject her to an enhanced risk of verbal abuse and physical (including sexual) violence – even death.[20]

The fourth choice is equally fraught. Etsitty could forsake any external manifestation of her gender identity in favor of a stereotypically masculine

---

[16] The North Carolina Public Facilities Privacy and Security Act (HB2) required individuals to use public restrooms corresponding to the sex on their birth certificate. *See* H.B. 2, 2016 N.C. Sess. Laws 3. Responding to widespread boycotts of the state and litigation initiated by the US Department of Justice, the North Carolina General Assembly repealed HB2 in 2017; however, the compromise legislation that replaced the bill still prohibited municipalities from passing nondiscrimination ordinances. *See* H.B. 142, 2017 N.C. Sess. Laws 4.

[17] Nico Lang, *What It's Like to Use a Public Bathroom While Trans*, ROLLING STONE (Mar. 31, 2016), www.rollingstone.com/culture/culture-news/what-its-like-to-use-a-public-bathroom-while-trans-65793/ (quoting a transgender woman in North Carolina).

[18] For example, 2010 FBI data indicates that, where gender of offender was known, more than 90 percent of murderers were male. *See* Criminal Justice Information Services Division, United States Department of Justice FBI, *Overview: Crime in the United States 2010*, https://ucr.fbi.gov/crime-in-the-u.s/2010/crime-in-the-u.s.-2010/offenses-known-to-law-enforcement/expanded/expandhomicidemain (*last visited* Mar. 30, 2020). Similarly, in 2006, almost 80 percent of violent offenders (excluding murderers) were male. *See* Bureau of Justice Statistics, United States Department of Justice Office of Justice Programs, CRIMINAL VICTIMIZATION IN THE UNITED STATES, 2006 STATISTICAL TABLES (Aug. 2008), www.bjs.gov/content/pub/pdf/cvus0602.pdf. These years were selected for their relative temporal proximity to the *Etsitty* decision.

[19] *See, e.g.*, David S. Cohen, *Keeping Men "Men" and Women Down: Sex Segregation, Anti-Essentialism, and Masculinity*, 33 HARV. J. L. & GENDER 509, 550–51 (2010) (using masculinities theory to explain why "[m]en who do not conform to hegemonic masculinity ... are subject to harassment and violence in sex-segregated bathrooms").

[20] *See supra* notes 12–18 (describing, *inter alia*, crime rates against transgender persons and potential for victimization in bathrooms).

appearance and affect, but this is not an option for anyone ultimately seeking gender confirmation surgery (vaginoplasty, specifically). Two of the criteria for such surgery are twelve continuous months of hormone therapy and of living in a gender role congruent with one's gender identity.[21]

Etsitty's final choice was to continue to express her femininity, to use women's restrooms, and therefore to be fired.

The gendered nature of Etsitty's double bind is clear: she had to present herself as masculine, or else subject herself to compromised health or an enhanced risk of violence.

Ann Hopkins, in *Price Waterhouse v. Hopkins*,[22] experienced a similar double bind. Hopkins, an accountant at a major firm, was aggressive and unapologetically competent. Although she frequently outperformed her male peers, her application for partnership was denied. Her supervisor informed her that she could increase her chances for partnership by walking, talking, and dressing more femininely, getting her hair styled, and wearing makeup and jewelry.[23] Another male partner suggested "charm school."[24] Hopkins alleged sex discrimination under Title VII, arguing that her employer had penalized her for failing to conform to gender stereotypes. The Supreme Court found that discrimination based on gender stereotyping is sex discrimination.[25] Justice Brennan explained the role of Title VII in resolving gender-based double binds: "An employer who objects to aggressiveness in women but whose positions require this trait places women in an intolerable and impermissible catch 22: out of a job if they behave aggressively and out of a job if they do not. Title VII lifts women out of this bind."[26]

Several courts have applied the *Price Waterhouse* rationale to claims that employers discriminated against transgender women based on their failure to conform to stereotypical norms of appearance and dress for men.[27] Etsitty

---

[21] *See* World Professional Association for Transgender Health, STANDARDS OF CARE FOR THE HEALTH OF TRANSSEXUAL, TRANSGENDER, AND GENDER NONCONFORMING PEOPLE 60 (7th version, 2011), www.wpath.org/media/cms/Documents/Web%20Transfer/SOC/Standards%20of%20Care%20V7%20-%202011%20WPATH.pdf.

[22] 490 U.S. 228 (1989).

[23] *Id.* at 235.

[24] *Id.*

[25] *Id.* at 250 ("In the specific context of sex stereotyping, an employer who acts on the basis of a belief that a woman cannot be aggressive, or that she must not be, has acted on the basis of gender").

[26] *Id.* at 251.

[27] *See, e.g., Smith v. City of Salem*, 378 F.3d 566, 574 (6th Cir. 2004); *cf. Schwenk v. Hartford*, 204 F.3d 1187 (9th Cir. 2000) (analogizing to *Price Waterhouse* in finding that the Gender Motivated Violence Act protects transgender persons from attacks based on nonstereotypical gender presentation).

made a similar argument that requiring her to use the men's restrooms was discrimination based on her failure to adhere to sex stereotypes. She also claimed that discrimination against persons on the basis of their transgender status constituted sex discrimination under Title VII. Finally, she alleged that the employer's conduct violated the Equal Protection Clause by discriminating against her based on sex and transgender status.

The original Tenth Circuit judgment affirmed the district court's grant of summary judgment to UTA, but Judge Archibald's feminist judgment reverses the district court's decision and rules in favor of Etsitty. These judgments are radically different in their interpretation of the law, their attention to the realities of Etsitty's situation, and their recognition (or lack thereof) of the double bind in which Etsitty's employer placed her.

THE ORIGINAL OPINION

The original opinion begins with Etsitty's alternative argument that discrimination on the basis of transgender status is sex discrimination under Title VII. The court made short – and dismissive – work of this argument. Etsitty had claimed direct evidence of discrimination based on her transgender status, but the court dismissed this claim in a footnote, explaining that the evidence "supports only the conclusion that Etsitty was terminated because of UTA's concerns regarding her restroom usage, a motive which is not discriminatory . . ."[28]

The court then considered two arguments:

(1) that "because a person's identity as [transgender] is directly connected to the sex organs she possesses, discrimination on this basis must constitute discrimination because of sex";[29] and

(2) that Etsitty was discriminated against for failing to conform to sex stereotypes (the *Price Waterhouse* theory that was, in fact, Etsitty's principal argument).[30]

The court found that transgender persons are not a protected class under Title VII – that is, that discrimination based on transgender status is not sex discrimination.[31] In so finding, the Tenth Circuit first relied on *Ulane v. Eastern Airlines, Inc.*,[32] which interpreted Title VII as limited to

---

[28] *Etsitty*, 502 F.3d at 1220 n.1. The double-bind analysis suggests that this motive is at least indirectly discriminatory.

[29] *Id.* at 1221.

[30] *Id.*

[31] *Id.* at 1221–22.

[32] 742 F.2d 1081 (7th Cir. 1977).

"discriminat[ion] against women because they are women and men because they are men."[33] The court next pointed to Tenth Circuit precedent excluding from Title VII protection discrimination based on sexual orientation.[34] Relying on these authorities and the statutory text, the court concluded that the plain meaning of the word "sex" within Title VII is strictly binary and does not include transgender persons.[35]

The court's reliance on *Ulane* and *Medina* suggests a cramped interpretation of Title VII. *Ulane* preceded both *Price Waterhouse*, which embraced a view of Title VII as encompassing both sex and gender, and *Oncale v. Sundowner Offshore Oil Servs.*,[36] which found that Title VII's protections extend beyond the specific situations envisioned by Congress. In fact, both the Sixth and the Ninth Circuits had recognized that *Price Waterhouse* "eviscerated" the *Ulane* Court's interpretation of Title VII.[37]

Etsitty's *Price Waterhouse* claim fared no better. Although the court assumed without deciding that Etsitty had established a prima facie case of gender stereotyping, it found that UTA had offered a legitimate nondiscriminatory reason for Etsitty's termination and that Etsitty had failed to raise a genuine issue of material fact regarding whether the proffered reason was pretextual.[38]

The court's analysis of UTA's supposedly nondiscriminatory rationale for Etsitty's termination effectively condoned the gendered double bind imposed upon Etsitty by her employer, while refusing to admit that such a double bind even existed. (One is tempted to call this judicial gaslighting.[39]) The employer's proffered reason for the termination was that Etsitty, who still possessed genitalia stereotypically associated with being male, intended to use public women's restrooms along the bus route, and the employer was concerned with the possibility of liability.[40] The court accepted this as a neutral justification,

[33] *Etsitty*, 502 F.3d at 1221 (quoting *Ulane*, 742 F.2d at 1086).
[34] *Id.* at 1222 (citing *Medina v. Income Support Div.*, 413 F.3d 1131 (10th Cir. 2005)).
[35] *Etsitty*, 502 F.3d at 1222.
[36] 523 U.S. 75, 80 (1998) (concluding that Title VII prohibited sexual harassment between two men if it took place "because of sex").
[37] *Smith*, 378 F.3d at 573 (citing *Schwenk*).
[38] *Etsitty*, 502 F.3d at 1224. Under *McDonnell Douglas Corp. v. Green*, 411 U.S. 792 (1973), when plaintiffs establish a prima facie case of prohibited employment action, defendants must articulate a legitimate, nondiscriminatory reason for the action. At the summary judgment stage, the plaintiff must then establish a genuine issue of material fact that the employer's nondiscriminatory reason was pretextual. *Id.* at 802–05.
[39] The term "gaslighting" derives from *Gas Light*, a 1938 play by Patrick Hamilton. Gaslighting "describe[s] manipulative behavior used to confuse people into thinking their reactions are so far off base that they're crazy." *Gaslight*, MERRIAM WEBSTER, www.merriam-webster.com/dictionary/gaslighting (*last visited* Mar. 30, 2020) (quoting Yasher Ali).
[40] *Etsitty*, 502 F.3d at 1224.

finding that (1) "[u]se of a restroom designated for the opposite sex does not constitute a mere failure to conform to sex stereotypes,"[41] and (2) "an employer's requirement that employees use restrooms matching their biological sex does not expose biological males to disadvantageous terms and does not discriminate against employees who fail to conform to gender stereotypes."[42] Accordingly, the justification was deemed legitimate.

This reasoning ignores the double bind. A requirement that a transgender woman use a men's restroom would expose that woman to a real risk of gender-motivated violence. As a practical matter, it is almost impossible to separate a requirement that persons use a certain restroom from a requirement that their gender expression conform to gender stereotypes. The court's opinion ignored this reality, which is especially problematic given the weight accorded the employer's wholly speculative concern about liability.

In finding that the *Price Waterhouse* rationale did not encompass restroom use, the court acknowledged that "[i]t may be that use of the women's restrooms is an inherent part of one's identity as a male-to-female transsexual."[43] However, it then pivoted to its prior conclusion that Title VII does not bar discrimination on the basis of transgender status: "Etsitty may not claim protection under Title VII based on her transsexuality *per se*."[44] But the lines between gender-nonconformity and transgender status are not so easily drawn, as the Sixth Circuit recognized in *Smith*: "Yet some courts have held that this latter form of discrimination is of a different and somehow more permissible kind ... *In other words, these courts superimpose classifications such as 'transsexual' on a plaintiff, and then legitimize discrimination based on the plaintiff's gender non-conformity by formalizing the non-conformity into an ostensibly unprotected classification.*"[45]

Finally – and not surprisingly – the court found no equal protection violation, relying on Tenth Circuit precedent holding that transgender persons are not a protected class under the Equal Protection Clause.[46]

THE FEMINIST JUDGMENT

Archibald's recasting of *Etsitty* differs dramatically from the Tenth Circuit's opinion. Such differences begin with the diction and rhetoric about Etsitty herself.

[41] *Id.*
[42] *Id.* at 1225.
[43] *Id.* at 1224.
[44] *Id.*
[45] *Smith*, 378 F.3d at 574 (emphasis added).
[46] *Etsitty*, 502 F.3d at 1227–28 (citing *Brown v. Zavaras*, 63 F.3d 967, 971 (10th Cir. 1995)).

- The Tenth Circuit consistently describes Etsitty as a "transsexual"; Archibald refers to her as a "transgender woman."
- The Tenth Circuit's background facts begin with Etsitty's diagnosis of adult gender identity disorder (GID), her birth as a "biological male," and the male name she received at birth. Focusing on GID casts transgender persons as diseased – a problem to be fixed.[47] Archibald's facts begin with Etsitty's competence at her job and the absence of complaints about her performance.
- The Tenth Circuit discusses at length Etsitty's transition from male to female, including discussions of her use of female hormones and her originally presenting herself as male at work. Archibald's opinion omits these irrelevant facts.
- Only in the seventh paragraph of its opinion does the Tenth Circuit acknowledge the absence of any complaints about Etsitty (regarding her appearance, bathroom use, whatever). In contrast, this appears very early in Archibald's opinion, in the third overall paragraph and the very first paragraph describing the facts.

The differences in diction and rhetoric suggest a radically different understanding of Etsitty and of the relevant narrative of the case. Archibald accepts Etsitty's self-identification; the Tenth Circuit focuses on Etsitty's otherness. Archibald focuses on Etsitty's competent performance of her job and her employer's refusal to let her perform it, based simply on her genitalia – a trait not visible to the public. In contrast, the Tenth Circuit's facts suggest that the principal narrative concerns Etsitty's status as a "transsexual" – misunderstood as "other" – and the problem this otherness presents for her employer.

Unlike the Tenth Circuit, Archibald recognizes the double bind that Etsitty confronts, and also recognizes that the employer's requirement is irrational and its justification insubstantial. Archibald explains that the employer's implicit demand left Etsitty with poor options: using the men's bathroom, where she felt uncomfortable and unsafe, or not using a bathroom at all. Unlike the Tenth Circuit, Archibald discusses the potential ill-health effects of not using the bathroom for an entire workday. The feminist judgment also notes the speculative and shaky nature

---

[47] See, e.g., Eli Clare, *Resisting Shame: Making Our Bodies Home*, 8 SEATTLE J. Soc. JUST. 445, 459 (2010). In 2013, the American Psychiatric Association removed from its diagnostic manual the diagnosis of "gender identity disorder," a term that applied to all transgender people, and instead now lists a diagnosis of "gender dysphoria," which applies only to those transgender people who experience "significant distress" related to being transgender. *See* Am. Psychiatric Ass'n, DIAGNOSTIC AND STATISTICAL MANUAL OF MENTAL DISORDERS 451 (5th ed. 2013).

of UTA's concern about potential liability: absolutely no one had complained about Etsitty's bathroom use, and typically customer preference is not a valid justification for discriminatory treatment anyway.[48] The contrast between Etsitty's real concerns and the employer's speculative ones is well drawn.

Finally, the opinions are diametrically opposed on the law. Archibald's opinion speaks for itself, but the highlights include the following.

- Discrimination based on transgender status is sex stereotyping forbidden by Title VII. For those assigned male at birth, the "characteristics and behaviors [that] at their core denote transgender status" include "identify[ing] ... [and] [expressing] as female and intend[ing] to use the women's bathrooms while at work." Importantly, an intention or desire to have gender confirmation surgery is *not* at the core of transgender identity and is not required for Title VII protection.
- An employer's requirement that employees use restrooms based on the sex assigned them at birth rather than their gender identity is a condition of employment that adversely affects transgender employees because of sex. Unlike other employees, transgender employees are denied the opportunity to use the restroom where they are more likely to feel comfortable and safe.
- Gender is not binary.
- Transgender persons belong to a suspect class for purposes of equal protection analysis, so any state discrimination against them is subject to a strict scrutiny analysis.

However, the most radical aspect of the opinion is Archibald's dicta in section VI. Here, she questions whether public sex-segregated bathrooms comport with either Title VII or the Equal Protection Clause *at all, for anyone*. If, as Archibald says, the *Price Waterhouse* rationale requires allowing a transgender woman to use the women's restroom, then it requires the same for a cisgender man, whose use of a women's restroom also would constitute nonstereotypical conduct protected by Title VII. She points out reasons that people may not wish to use a restroom associated with the sex assigned them at birth, and she offers unisex bathroom facilities as a viable alternative to sex-segregated restrooms.

Some of Archibald's feminist judgment – especially the dicta on the constitutionality of sex-segregated bathrooms – may be forward looking

---

[48] *See, e.g., Schroer v. Billington,* 577 F.Supp.2d 293, 302 (D.D.C. 2008) ("Deference to the real or presumed biases of others is discrimination") (citing *Williams v. Trans World Airlines,* 660 F.2d 1267, 1270 (8th Cir. 1981) (rejecting employer's deference to customer's racially charged complaint against an employee)).

even for 2020. Had her feminist judgment been the original opinion, what might be different now? As it stands, the movement for transgender equality has enjoyed considerable progress (along with backlash) since 2007, despite *Etsitty*. Some progress has resulted from litigation. Notably, in March 2018, in *EEOC v. R.G. & G.R. Harris Funeral Homes*,[49] the Sixth Circuit held that an employer's discrimination based on an employee's transgender or transitioning status is *always* sex discrimination under Title VII. The Sixth Circuit's reasoning resembles that of Archibald. Likely crucial to the decision was the participation of the Equal Employment Opportunity Commission (EEOC), whose own tribunals had held in 2012 that transgender persons are protected under Title VII[50] and in 2015 that Title VII's protections extend to bathroom use.[51] Moreover, a 2014 memorandum by US Attorney General Eric Holder took the position that Title VII protects transgender persons.[52]

However, a chill wind blows. The Trump administration is trying to reverse virtually all of the legal gains realized by the transgender community during the Obama administration. In February 2017, the Education and Justice Departments jointly rescinded Obama-era Title IX guidelines directing that schools must allow transgender students to use bathrooms consistent with their gender identity.[53] In October 2017, then-Attorney General Jeff Sessions issued a memorandum[54] finding that transgender status is not protected under Title VII and that requiring transgender persons to use bathrooms corresponding to the sex assigned them at birth raises no Title VII concerns; *Etsitty* was the major authority cited. More recently, the *New York Times* has reported that the Department of Health and Human Services has drafted an internal memorandum proposing a change to Title IX policy. Specifically, the memo proposed that all agencies charged with Title IX enforcement define sex as immutable, binary (male or female), and established at or before birth; the sex on a person's birth certificate would be

---

[49] 884 F.3d 560 (6th Cir. 2018). Note, however, that the US Supreme Court granted the funeral home's petition for *certiorari*, and oral argument took place in October 2019.

[50] *See Macy v. Holder*, EOC DOC 0120120821, 2012 WL 1435995 (Apr. 20, 2012).

[51] *See Lusardi v. McHugh*, EEOC DOC 0120133395, 2015 WL 1607756 (Apr. 1, 2015).

[52] Office of the Attorney General, *Memorandum, Treatment of Transgender Employment Discrimination Claims under Title VII of the Civil Rights Act of 1964* (Dec. 14, 2014), www .justice.gov/file/188671/download.

[53] Civil Rights Division of the United States Department of Justice, & Office of Civil Rights of the United States Department of Education, *Dear Colleague Letter* (Feb. 22, 2017), www2.ed.gov /about/offices/list/ocr/letters/colleague-201702-title-ix.pdf.

[54] Office of the Attorney General, *Memorandum, Revised Treatment of Transgender Employment Discrimination Claims under Title VII of the Civil Rights Act of 1964* (Oct. 4, 2017), www .justice.gov/ag/page/file/1006981/download.

"definitive proof of a person's sex."[55] Finally, the Supreme Court granted *certiorari* in R.G. & G.R. *Harris Funeral Homes*,[56] and the Sixth Circuit's ruling stands at the precipice. A reversal would be a devastating setback for the transgender rights movement and for transgender citizens who rely on the protections of Title VII.

Would this picture have been any different had Archibald's opinion been the 2007 judgment of the Tenth Circuit? There are two possibilities. Her judgment may have come too soon, and the Supreme Court may have granted a petition for *certiorari* and issued an opinion that would have dealt a crushing blow to the transgender rights movement – notably, an opinion before social attitudes had progressed to the point we see today. Archibald's opinion probably would not have enjoyed the support of the Department of Justice (and the EEOC) or of the Solicitor General during the George W. Bush era or possibly even the early Obama era. In short, the "push" of Archibald's opinion may have generated pushback.

Another possibility, though, is that progress would have happened sooner and been more immune from reversal. Had Archibald's opinion stood within the Tenth Circuit, a slow consensus among circuits may have developed, and employers may have realized that bathroom use based on gender identity is ultimately not a big deal. Some employers may have begun establishing unisex bathrooms. This consensus would have developed at the same time that the Obama administration was providing moral leadership through its increasingly LGBTQ+-inclusive policies.[57] In this view, Archibald's opinion, including its daring dicta, may have functioned as a nudge rather than a shove.

CONCLUSION

Despite the Trump administration's recent actions, the transgender community has enjoyed tremendous progress both legally and socially since *Etsitty*. Indeed, the original opinion in *Etsitty* now seems dated, and much of Archibald's opinion reflects accepted doctrine – at least for now – in several circuits. Over time, legal and political advocacy, increased public awareness, and moral leadership by those in power will bend the arc of the universe toward justice – a justice in which others are spared the double bind experienced by Krystal Etsitty.

---

[55] Erica Green *et al.*, *"Transgender" Could Be Defined out of Existence under Trump Administration*, N.Y. Times (Oct. 21, 2018), www.nytimes.com/2018/10/21/us/politics/transgen der-trump-administration-sex-definition.html (quoting HHS memo).

[56] *See supra* note 49.

[57] *See supra* notes 50–52 and accompanying text.

Etsitty v. Utah Transit Authority,
502 F.3d 1215 (10th Cir. 2007)

JUDGE CATHERINE JEAN ARCHIBALD DELIVERED
THE OPINION OF THE COURT.

I OVERVIEW

Krystal Etsitty is a transgender woman who was fired from her job because she intended to use the women's restrooms without having gender confirmation surgery. Before her discharge, Etsitty performed her job well. She had no performance issues, no tardiness, and no absences, but her employer was concerned about her transgender status and related restroom usage. On the end-of-employment form, Etsitty's employer stated that once Etsitty had surgery, she would be eligible for rehire.

There is clear and direct evidence of sex discrimination by Utah Transit Authority (UTA). This Court therefore holds that UTA violated both Title VII of the Civil Rights Act of 1964 and the Equal Protection Clause of the Fourteenth Amendment of the US Constitution. Accordingly, we reverse the decision of the federal district court.

II FACTS

On October 24, 2001, Krystal Etsitty began training for the position of bus operator for UTA. Etsitty successfully completed her six-week training course. Immediately afterwards, Etsitty worked as a UTA bus operator for approximately two months. She was assigned the position of "extra-board" operator; thus she did not have her own regular route, but filled in for drivers who were sick or on vacation. During her two months of driving in the "extra-board" position, Etsitty drove all or part of approximately sixty different routes in the Salt Lake City area. Etsitty's immediate supervisor, Pat Chatterton, testified that Etsitty performed her job well. At no time during her employment did customers, members of the public, other UTA employees, business owners, her supervisor, or anyone else make any complaints about Etsitty's job performance, appearance, or bathroom use. Etsitty was never subject to disciplinary procedures during her time as a bus operator.

Bus operators use the public restrooms available along the different bus routes during the workday. After hearing a rumor that a male bus operator was dressing in female clothing, Chatterton's supervisor, Betty Shirley, talked to Chatterton and learned that Etsitty was transitioning. Shirley then discussed her concerns about Etsitty's restroom use with Bruce Cardon from UTA's human resources (HR) department. Shirley and Cardon "felt that there was an image issue out there for us, that we could have a problem with having someone who, even though his appearance may look female, he's still a male because he still has a penis." Soon thereafter, Shirley and Cardon met with Etsitty and asked her about her transgender status, whether she had "male genitalia," and whether she had used and intended to continue using public women's restrooms along the bus routes. At that meeting, Shirley and Cardon confirmed that Etsitty had genitalia stereotypically associated with being male. Shirley explained to Etsitty that UTA could not accommodate her restroom needs. Etsitty explained that she did not need any accommodation because she appears female, and no one using the female restrooms would know what her genitals looked like.

Three days later, Shirley fired Etsitty, stating that UTA could not accommodate her restroom needs and was concerned about liability stemming from her restroom use. On the HR form that Shirley filled out upon terminating Etsitty, Shirley stated that Etsitty would be eligible for rehire after she had sex reassignment surgery. Etsitty filed a suit against UTA and Shirley, alleging discrimination in violation of Title VII and the Equal Protection Clause.

III RULING BELOW AND SUMMARY JUDGMENT STANDARD

The district court granted UTA's motion for summary judgment and denied Etsitty's motion for partial summary judgment (which was made on the liability question only). Etsitty appeals both decisions. A court should grant summary judgment in favor of a party only if the evidence shows that there is no genuine issue of material fact and that the moving party is entitled to judgment as a matter of law. Fed. R. Civ. P. 56. All inferences should be drawn in favor of the nonmoving party. *Cortez v. McCauley*, 478 F.3d 1108, 1115 (10th Cir. 2007) (en banc). We have reviewed the grant of UTA's motion and denial of Etsitty's partial motion for summary judgment *de novo*, "applying the same standards as the district court." *Habermehl v. Potter*, 153 F.3d 1137, 1138 (10th Cir. 1998). We now reverse the lower court's order in full and remand to the lower court to enter a partial summary judgment in Etsitty's favor on the issue of liability and to reinstate the remainder of her claim, so that the factfinder may determine her remedies.

280   Etsitty v. Utah Transit Authority

IV TITLE VII

This nation has a "long and unfortunate history of sex discrimination." *United States v. Virginia*, 518 U.S. 515, 531 (1996) (quoting *Frontiero v. Richardson*, 411 U.S. 677, 684 (1973) (plurality)). Title VII seeks to remedy this history by prohibiting employers from (1) taking sex into account when making employment decisions (42 U.S.C. §2000e-2(a)(1)), and (2) classifying employees in a way that would disadvantage an individual because of sex (42 U.S.C. §2000e-2(a)(2)). Title VII is "broad remedial legislation that must be liberally construed." *Jackson v. Continental Cargo-Denver*, 183 F.3d 1186, 1189 (10th Cir. 1999). Here, UTA has violated both sections 2000e-2(a)(1) and 2000e-2(a)(2).

A *Disparate Treatment*

Title VII provides that "[i]t shall be an unlawful employment practice for an employer . . . to discharge any individual, or otherwise to discriminate against any individual with respect to his compensation, terms, conditions, or privileges of employment, because of such individual's . . . sex." 42 U.S.C. §2000e-2 (a)(1). This section forbids "disparate treatment discrimination." Disparate treatment occurs when an employer treats a "particular person less favorably than others because of the plaintiff's . . . sex." *Watson v. Fort Worth Bank & Tr.*, 487 U.S. 977, 985–86 (1988).

As one Supreme Court Justice has noted, "[T]he explicit consideration of . . . sex . . . 'was the most obvious evil Congress had in mind when it enacted Title VII.' " *Price Waterhouse v. Hopkins*, 490 U.S. 228, 275 (1989) (O'Connor, J., concurring) (quoting *Intl. Broth. of Teamsters v. U.S.*, 431 U.S. 324, 335 n.15 (1977)). Here, it is clear that UTA fired Etsitty "because of . . . sex" in violation of Title VII. First, UTA fired Etsitty because of her genitals – one characteristic at the core of an individual's sex. Second, UTA fired Etsitty because she is transgender, and transgender discrimination is discrimination because of sex.

1 Discrimination Because of One's Genitals Is Discrimination Because of Sex

UTA fired Krystal Etsitty because she had a penis. Genitalia – characterized as male, female, or intersex – are the basis on which sex is assigned at birth. Firing an employee for having one type of genitalia rather than another is therefore forbidden by the plain language of Title VII. 42 U.S.C. §2000e-2(a)(1). Title VII is violated if the employer treated the employee "in a manner which but for that person's sex would be different." *Newport News Shipbuilding and Dry*

Dock Co. v. EEOC, 462 U.S. 669, 683 (1983) (citations omitted). In the present case, UTA admitted that if Etsitty had had gender confirmation surgery, it would not have fired her for using the women's restrooms. This is direct evidence of discrimination "because of . . . sex," and UTA has therefore violated Title VII. *See Postal Serv. Bd. of Governors v. Aikens*, 460 U.S. 711, 714 n.3 (1983) ("As in any lawsuit, the [Title VII] plaintiff may prove his case by direct or circumstantial evidence"). Since there is direct evidence of sex discrimination in this case, the *McDonnell Douglas* test, used to prove discrimination through circumstantial evidence, does not apply. *See Trans World Airlines, Inc. v. Thurston*, 469 U.S. 111, 121 (1985) ("[T]he *McDonnell Douglas* test is inapplicable where the plaintiff presents direct evidence of discrimination").

Title VII's prohibition of sex discrimination includes sex discrimination that Congress may not have been aware of or may not have intended to prohibit at the time that it enacted Title VII. *Oncale v. Sundowner Offshore Oil Servs.*, 523 U.S. 75, 79 (1998). The district court below held that Title VII does not protect transgender individuals from discrimination because "Congress had a narrow view of sex in mind when it passed the Civil Rights Act" and that, by enacting Title VII, Congress meant, "[I]t is unlawful to discriminate against women because they are women and against men because they are men." *Etsitty v. Utah Transit Auth.*, No. 2:04CV616 DS, 2005 WL 1505610, at *3–4 (D. Utah June 24, 2005) (quoting *Ulane v. E. Airlines, Inc.*, 742 F.2d 1081, 1085–86 (7th Cir. 1984)). The district court erred in relying on *Ulane*, a decision that came before *Oncale*. In *Oncale*, the Supreme Court found that same-sex sexual harassment could be actionable sex discrimination under Title VII, even though "male-on-male sexual harassment in the workplace was assuredly not the principal evil Congress was concerned with when it enacted Title VII." *Oncale*, 523 U.S. at 79. The Supreme Court reasoned that "statutory prohibitions often go beyond the principal evil to cover reasonably comparable evils, and *it is ultimately the provisions of our laws rather than the principal concerns of our legislators by which we are governed.*" *Id.* (emphasis added); *see also Newport News*, 462 U.S. at 679–81 (finding that discrimination against men is prohibited by Title VII, even if Title VII was enacted principally to protect women and not men from discrimination).

2 Discrimination against Transgender Individuals Is Discrimination Because of Sex

a SEX IS A BUT-FOR CAUSE OF ETSITTY'S FIRING.   Moreover, UTA violated Title VII by firing Etsitty because she is transgender – someone assigned male at birth who identifies as a woman – and behaves in ways stereotypically associated with women. *See, e.g.*, Transgender Law Center, PEEING IN PEACE, A RESOURCE GUIDE FOR TRANSGENDER ACTIVISTS AND ALLIES (2005), https://transgenderlawcenter.org/resources/public-accommodations/peeing-in-peace (defining "transgender" as "a term ... used ... to refer to people whose gender identity or expression is different than the gender they were assigned at birth or different than the stereotypes that go with that gender"). Shirley fired Etsitty because she perceives Etsitty to be a biological male who identifies as a female, presents as female, and intended to use the women's bathrooms while at work. These characteristics and behaviors at their core denote transgender status. *Id.* Etsitty therefore lost her job because she was transgender. Discriminating against someone for being transgender is discriminating against someone for failing to conform to gender norms and sex stereotypes, which itself is forbidden by Title VII. *See Price Waterhouse v. Hopkins*, 490 U.S. 228 (1989) (holding that Title VII forbids an employer from discriminating against a woman because she fails to conform to female stereotypes).

In actuality, biological sex is not a binary of male and female. About 1 in 1,500 people are born "intersex," with some biological aspects associated with being female and others associated with being male. *See, e.g.*, Alice Domurat Dreger, *Ambiguous Sex – or Ambivalent Medicine? Ethical Issues in the Treatment of Intersexuality*, 28 HASTINGS CENTER REPORT 24 (1998), *reproduced with permission at* https://isna.org/articles/ambivalent_medicine/ (noting that doctors have long realized that some people have both male and female biological characteristics). Similarly, gender identity is also not binary, and there are more than two gender identities. *See, e.g.*, Dylan Vade, *Expanding Gender and Expanding the Law: Toward a Social and Legal Conceptualization of Gender That Is More Inclusive of Transgender People*, 11 MICH. J. GENDER & L. 253, 260 (2005) ("[M]any transgender people who do not identify as either female or male, but as a third or other gender, such [as] trans or boy-girl, just to name a few"); Transgender Law Center, *supra*, at 33 (noting that some people do not identify as either male or female).

A person who is transgender does not conform to certain gender norms or sex stereotypes. *See, e.g.*, Taylor Flynn, *Transforming the Debate: Why We Need to Include Transgender Rights in the Struggles for Sex and Sexual Orientation Equality*, 101 COLUM. L. REV. 392, 392 (2001) (transgender persons' "appearance, behavior, or other personal characteristics differ from traditional gender norms"); Ilona M. Turner, *Sex Stereotyping Per Se: Transgender Employees and Title VII*, 95 CAL. L. REV. 561, 563 (2007) ("[T]he very acts that define transgender people as transgender are those that contradict stereotypes of gender-appropriate appearance and behavior"). *Price Waterhouse* held that an individual can show sex discrimination under Title VII when they demonstrate they were discriminated against for not conforming to sex stereotypes. *Price Waterhouse v. Hopkins*, 490 U.S. 228, 251 (1989) (plurality) ("[W]e are beyond the day when an employer could evaluate employees by assuming or insisting that they matched the stereotype associated with their group"); *id.* at 259 (White, J., concurring) (agreeing that the employee had successfully shown that impermissible sex discrimination was "a substantial factor in the adverse employment action"); *id.* at 261–62 (O'Connor, J., concurring) (agreeing that Price Waterhouse had "knowingly giv[en] substantial weight to an impermissible criterion"). Discrimination against someone because they are transgender is discrimination against someone because they do not conform to gender norms, and *Price Waterhouse* held that discrimination because someone does not conform to gender norms is sex discrimination under Title VII. This Court therefore holds that discrimination against someone because they are transgender is always sex discrimination.

In addition, this Court holds that transgender individuals are protected by Title VII whether they have had, will have, or will never have gender confirmation surgery. It is a sex stereotype and not a universal truth that everyone who identifies as a woman will have genitalia stereotypically associated with being female. *See, e.g.*, Dreger, *supra* (noting that about 1 in 1,500 children are born intersex); Transgender Law Center, *supra*, at 14 (noting that, in a recent survey, fewer than 15 percent of transgender respondents had had gender confirmation surgery). In the present case, Etsitty's employer stated that Etsitty could reapply for her job once she had gender confirmation surgery. However, a transgender individual may not undergo this operation for a number of reasons. *Id.* First, medical protocol requires that they not undergo this operation until they have lived in the gender they identify with for twelve months. *See, e.g.*, Terry S. Kogan, *Transsexuals and Critical Gender Theory: The Possibility of A Restroom Labeled "Other,"* 48 HASTINGS L.J. 1223, 1227 & n.14 (1997) [hereinafter Kogan, *Transsexuals*]. Second, some transgender individuals do not desire such surgery. *See id.* Any major surgery comes with health risks. Gender confirmation surgery is no different and comes with risks of "stenosis, increased ... infections, loss of feeling, and psychological trauma." Dreger, *supra*. It is understandable then that many transgender individuals choose not to have surgery even if they are able to. Finally, even if they desire it, some transgender individuals are not able to get gender confirmation surgery because they cannot afford it. *See* Kogan, *Transsexuals*, *supra*, at 1227 & n.14 (noting that gender confirmation surgery is "extremely expensive").

This interpretation of Title VII and *Price Waterhouse* is consistent with the conclusions that several other circuits considering this issue have reached. *See*

Barnes v. City of Cincinnati, 401 F.3d 729, 737 (6th Cir. 2005) (citing Price Waterhouse in upholding the district court's finding of liability under Title VII and award of damages for a Title VII violation after a transgender employee was denied a promotion in part for not appearing and behaving sufficiently masculine); Smith v. City of Salem, 378 F.3d 566, 573 (6th Cir. 2004) (citing Price Waterhouse and finding that a transgender woman had properly stated a claim of a Title VII violation where she was suspended from her job after dressing femininely); Schwenk v. Hartford, 204 F.3d 1187, 1201–02 (9th Cir. 2000) (reasoning that Price Waterhouse meant that "[d]iscrimination because one fails to act in the way expected of a man or woman is forbidden under Title VII" and ruling that a transgender prisoner had experienced sex discrimination when she was assaulted by a guard because she was transgender"); Rosa v. Park W. Bank & Trust Co., 214 F.3d 213, 215–16 (1st Cir. 2000) (looking to Title VII case law, including Price Waterhouse, and concluding that someone assigned male at birth and denied a loan for dressing in feminine clothing could state a claim for sex discrimination under the Equal Credit Opportunity Act of 1974). Thus, UTA violated Title VII because it fired Etsitty for being transgender and/or for exhibiting core characteristics of being transgender.

b SEX IS A MOTIVATING FACTOR IN ETSITTY'S DISMISSAL. For the reasons described, UTA fired Etsitty because of her sex. However, even if a reviewing court finds that there were other legitimate reasons, not related to sex, why Etsitty was fired, at the very least sex played a substantial part of the decision to terminate Etsitty. Title VII provides that "an unlawful employment practice is established when the complaining party demonstrates that ... sex ... was a motivating factor for any employment practice, even though other factors also motivated the practice." 42 U.S.C. §2000e-2(m). Therefore, even if a court finds that discrimination based on transgender status is not sex discrimination when using the but-for test, sex is clearly a "motivating factor" when an employer discharges a transgender individual for their transgender status and/or their use of bathrooms that do not conform with their genitalia. The employer has offered no evidence that it would have taken the same action absent consideration of the plaintiff's genitalia, and hence it cannot carry its burden of proving the defense under the statute to limit its remedies. See 42 U.S.C. §2000e-5(g)(2)(B).

3 The Bona Fide Occupational Qualification (BFOQ) Exception Does Not Apply

Under Title VII, an employer can take an employee's sex into account only when "sex ... is a bona fide occupational qualification [BFOQ] reasonably necessary to the normal operation of [the employer's] particular business or enterprise." 42 U.S.C. §2000e-2(e)(1). The BFOQ is an extremely narrow exception that permits an employer to make a sex-based employment decision only when sex "affect[s] an employee's ability to do the job." *International Union, UAW v. Johnson Controls, Inc.*, 499 U.S. 187, 201 (1991). "In order to qualify as a BFOQ, a job qualification must relate to the essence . . . or to the central mission of the employer's business." *Id.* at 203 (internal quotation marks and citations omitted).

Etsitty performed her job in an exemplary manner, and her bathroom usage did not affect the "central mission of the employer's business," which was to deliver customers safely and efficiently from one point to another along bus routes in Utah. *Cf. Diaz v. Pan Am. World Airways, Inc.*, 442 F.2d 385, 388 (5th Cir. 1971) (central mission of an airline is to "transport . . . passengers safely from one point to another").

UTA stated that the reason for dismissing Etsitty was concern about potential liability for UTA if customers, coworkers, and/or the public were uncomfortable with Etsitty's use of the women's restrooms. However, customers' or other third parties' discomfort with the sex of a particular employee is not sufficient as a BFOQ unless the customer preference goes to the essence of a business. *See, e.g., Fernandez v. Wynn Oil Co.*, 653 F.2d 1273, 1274 (9th Cir. 1981) (finding that customer preference does not justify a BFOQ when the plaintiff alleged that she was not promoted because of concerns that overseas businesses would not do business with a woman); *Diaz v. Pan Am. World Airways, Inc.*, 442 F.2d 385 (5th Cir. 1971) (airline could not exclude men as cabin crew even if customers expected and preferred female flight attendants because there was no evidence that the airline's primary function of transporting passengers safely from one point to another would be compromised by having male flight attendants); *Bollenbach v. Bd. of Educ. of Monroe-Woodbury Cent. Sch. Dist.*, 659 F.Supp. 1450, 1475 (S.D.N.Y. 1987) (employer could not exclude female bus drivers even in Hasidic Jewish village where parents strongly preferred male bus drivers and male students refused to board a bus driven by a female driver); *Gerdom v. Contl. Airlines, Inc.*, 692 F.2d 602, 609 (9th Cir. 1982) ("[I]t would be totally anomalous if we were to allow the preferences and prejudices of the customers to determine whether the sex discrimination was valid. Indeed, it was . . . these very prejudices [that Title VII] was meant to overcome."); *see also* 29 C.F.R. §1604.2(a)(1)(3) (EEOC guidelines stating that "the preferences of coworkers, the employer, clients or customers" will not justify the finding of a BFOQ defense).

In fact, there is no evidence in this case that customers or other third parties put pressure on UTA to hire only cisgender individuals who use the bathrooms

286 Etsitty v. Utah Transit Authority

that match their genitalia. Even if this evidence were to exist, Title VII would require that those customer preferences not dictate company policy, because refusal to give in to discriminatory customer preferences breaks down prejudices and barriers. *See* Katharine T. Bartlett, *Only Girls Wear Barrettes: Dress and Appearance Standards, Community Norms, and Workplace Equality*, 92 MICH. L. REV. 2541, 2575 (1994) ("As a result of restricting the ability of the airlines to exploit sexually subordinating consumer preferences to its commercial ends, the courts . . . help[ed] to change those preferences. Since *Diaz* . . . the 'look' of flight crews has become more diversified and less dependent on the traditional female-object stereotype and community expectations for the appearance of flight attendants have broadened."). Indeed, the very purpose of Title VII's prohibition on sex discrimination was to break down these types of sex stereotypes and barriers to employment. *Gerdom*, 692 F.2d at 609.

Here, requiring a transgender employee to use bathrooms that do not accord with her gender identity is not a "[BFOQ] reasonably necessary to the normal operation of [the employer's] particular business or enterprise." 42 U.S.C. §2000e-2(e)(1). In the vast majority of jobs, including that at issue in this case, bus driving, an individual's reproductive anatomy and/or genitalia is simply irrelevant to the normal operation of the business, and the employer may not consider genitalia in making employment decisions. In some rare instances, an individual's reproductive organs and/or genitalia may be a BFOQ for a particular job. For example, a sperm bank may hire only individuals with testes to be sperm donors. Similarly, ovaries and/or a uterus would be a BFOQ for a surrogacy agency that hires people to be egg donors or surrogates. *See* Mary DeLano, *The Conflict between State Guaranteed Pregnancy Benefits and the Pregnancy Discrimination Act: A Statutory Analysis*, 74 GEO. L.J. 1743, 1753 n.58 (1986) ("Classic examples of acceptable [BFOQs] include requiring sperm donors to be male and wet nurses to be female"). Additionally, "businesses that trade on sex and sexuality," such as a strip club that serves those seeking a particular sexual appearance, will likely be able to establish a BFOQ for hiring only women or only men, depending on its targeted clientele. Bartlett, *supra*, at 2576.

None of these rare exceptions applies in this case. Etsitty's genitalia did not affect her ability to do her job, which was to transport customers from one location to another. This Court therefore holds that UTA has violated Title VII because UTA cannot show a BFOQ that would justify its sex discrimination against Etsitty.

B Disparate Impact

UTA has also violated Title VII by classifying its employees based on sex and requiring its employees to use sex-segregated bathrooms in accordance with the sex assigned them at birth rather than their gender identity, which is a condition of employment that adversely affects transgender employees. "It shall be an unlawful employment practice for an employer ... to limit, segregate, or classify his employees or applicants for employment in any way which would deprive or tend to deprive any individual of employment opportunities or otherwise adversely affect his status as an employee, because of such individual's ... sex." 42 U.S.C. §2000e-2(a)(2). The purpose of this section "is to achieve equality of employment opportunities for women and members of minority groups by prohibiting practices that operate as 'built in headwinds' for such people and have no relationship to job performance." *Lynch v. Freeman*, 817 F.2d 380, 388 (6th Cir. 1987) (quoting *Griggs v. Duke Power Co.*, 401 U.S. 424, 432 (1971)). An employer therefore may not use a "non-job-related barrier" to limit employment opportunities to protected persons. *Conn. v. Teal*, 457 U.S. 440, 448 (1982) (finding a violation of this section when the employer used a non-job-related test as a requirement for promotion and African American employees were disproportionately excluded from promotion opportunity as a result of the test). A finding of a violation of this part of the statute is known as a finding of "disparate impact," and discriminatory intent on the part of the employer is not required. *Griggs*, 401 U.S. at 432 (finding that 42 U.S.C. §2000e-2(a)(2) had been violated when the employer power company began requiring that its employees complete high school and obtain a certain score on an intelligence test when such requirements disproportionately harmed African Americans and were not shown to be related to successful job performance); *see also* 42 U.S.C. §2000e-2(k) (stating that disparate impact can be shown if "a complaining party demonstrates that a respondent uses a particular employment practice that causes a disparate impact on the basis of ... sex ... and the respondent fails to demonstrate that the challenged practice is job related for the position in question and consistent with business necessity"); *Wedow v. City of Kan. City*, 442 F.3d 661, 671 (8th Cir. 2006) (upholding a jury finding of violation of Title VII when female firefighters alleged inadequate clothing and bathroom facilities, and reasoning that it was reasonable for a jury to find a violation of 42 U.S.C. §2000e-2(a)(2) when female firefighters often worked a 24-hour shift and the jury found the employer failed to provide adequate bathrooms); *Lynch v. Freeman*, 817 F.2d 380, 387 (6th Cir. 1987) (finding a disparate impact on women when men and women shared unsanitary portable toilets, and when the unsanitary conditions disadvantaged women more than men because women had a higher chance of urinary tract infection and other health complications as a result of the unsanitary conditions).

Here, UTA's policy of requiring its employees to use sex-segregated restrooms in accordance with the sex assigned them at birth and not their gender identity adversely affects transgender employees because of their sex. Under this employer's policy, while cisgender[58] (nontransgender) employees may use restrooms that accord with their gender identity (i.e., use restrooms where they feel comfortable and safe), transgender employees are not given the same opportunity and thus are adversely affected by such a policy. A transgender employee will have to choose between using a bathroom that is uncomfortable and may be unsafe or not using a bathroom at all while at work. This is not a valid choice under Title VII. *Cf. Lynch*, 817 F.2d at 387 (Title VII was violated when women had to choose between a risk of health harms from using unsanitary bathrooms and a risk of health harms from not using bathrooms at all). Transgender people – especially transgender women – face high risks of harassment and violence in restrooms, especially if they are not permitted to decide which restroom is most appropriate for them to use. *See* Transgender Law Center, *supra*, at 6–7. A recent survey shows that about 50 percent of transgender respondents have been harassed or assaulted in a public bathroom. *Id.* at 3. The fact that transgender men may suffer equally to transgender women under a policy like UTA's is irrelevant, because Title VII's focus is on protecting individual employees from discrimination. *See, e.g., Conn. v. Teal*, 457 U.S. at 453 ("The principal focus of the statute is the protection of the individual employee").

To put yourself in the shoes of a transgender employee, imagine your own employer forbidding you to use the bathroom you commonly use and requiring that you use a bathroom corresponding with a gender you do not identify with as a condition of employment. Although many would choose not to use a bathroom at all in this circumstance, the adverse health effects of not using a bathroom when needed are well-documented, including urinary tract infections, bladder infections, and kidney infections. *See, e.g.*, Kathryn H. Anthony *et al.*, *Potty Parity in Perspective: Gender and Family Issues in Planning and Designing Public Restrooms*, 21 J. OF PLANNING LITERATURE 267, 276 (2007) (listing the medical risks associated with holding urination or defecation); Mark Linder & Ingrid Nygaard, VOID WHERE PROHIBITED: REST BREAKS AND THE RIGHT TO URINATE ON COMPANY TIME 45–46 (1998) (same).

---

[58] The term "cisgender" is used to refer to people whose gender identity matches the sex assigned them at birth. *See, e.g.*, Eli R. Green, *Debating Trans Inclusion in the Feminist Movement: A Trans-Positive Analysis*, 10 J. LESBIAN STUD. 231, 232 n.1 (2006).

Therefore, by classifying its employees by sex and requiring that they use sex-segregated bathrooms accordingly, UTA violated Title VII. 42 U.S.C. §2000e-2(a)(2).

V EQUAL PROTECTION CLAUSE

The Equal Protection Clause provides: "No State shall ... deny to any person within its jurisdiction the equal protection of the laws." The Utah Transit Authority is a part of the Utah state government and thus is subject to the commands of the Equal Protection Clause.

Under the Equal Protection Clause, the Supreme Court has laid out a three-tiered test for judging government action that discriminates among people in meting out duties or benefits. Most government action that discriminates need pass only the lowest tier of scrutiny, the rational basis test, which requires that the government show a rational connection between the government action and a "legitimate" government interest. *See, e.g., New Orleans v. Dukes,* 427 U.S. 297, 303 (1976) ("Unless a classification trammels fundamental personal rights or is drawn upon inherently suspect distinctions such as race, religion, or alienage, our decisions presume the constitutionality of the statutory discriminations and require only that the classification challenged be rationally related to a legitimate state interest").

However, government action that discriminates between people based on personal characteristics that have little relation to a person's ability to contribute to society must either pass the intermediate scrutiny test or the strict scrutiny test. The intermediate scrutiny test, which historically has applied to sex-based classifications, requires the government to show that its discrimination is "substantially related" to "important governmental objectives." *See, e.g., Craig v. Boren,* 429 U.S. 190, 197 (1976). The strict scrutiny test, which applies to race-based classifications, requires the government to show that its discrimination is "narrowly tailored" to a "compelling" governmental interest. *See, e.g., Adarand Constructors, Inc. v. Slater,* 528 U.S. 216, 221 (2000).

To determine whether discrimination against a certain group merits intermediate or strict scrutiny, courts look to a variety of factors, including:

(1) whether and to what extent the group has suffered from historic discrimination – *see, e.g., Bowen v. Gilliard,* 483 U.S. 587, 602 (1987);
(2) whether members of the group have "obvious, immutable, or distinguishing characteristics that define them as a discrete group" – *id.*;
(3) whether the group lacks political power – *id.*; and

290 Etsitty v. Utah Transit Authority

(4) whether the characteristic that defines the group has little relation to the ability to contribute to society. *City of Cleburne v. Cleburne Living Ctr.*, 473 U.S. 432, 440–41 (1985).

The Supreme Court has not yet considered the level of scrutiny applicable to classifications based on transgender status. At the very least, intermediate scrutiny would apply to discrimination based on transgender status because it is a type of sex discrimination, and the Supreme Court has previously held that discrimination based on sex must, at the very least, be judged using intermediate scrutiny. *See, e.g., Clark v. Jeter*, 486 U.S. 456, 461 (1988).[59] We conclude that because transgender individuals comprise a small, relatively powerless, minority group that historically has suffered and continues to suffer severe discrimination, and because transgender status is not related to an individual's ability to contribute to society, strict scrutiny should apply. In case the Supreme Court decides at a later time that intermediate scrutiny should apply to transgender discrimination, this opinion will explain why UTA's actions do not pass either strict or intermediate scrutiny.

A Discrimination Based on Transgender Status: Strict Scrutiny

Based on all of these factors, we hold that strict scrutiny applies to transgender-based classifications. First, there is no doubt that transgender individuals have suffered a long history of discrimination. *See, e.g.*, Vade, *supra*, at 257 (noting that "[t]ransgender people are discriminated against in many areas of life, from employment and housing, to health care and custody rights"). Second, transgender individuals do not identify with the sex they were assigned at birth,

---

[59] Some commentators have argued, convincingly, that after the Supreme Court's decision in *United States v. Virginia*, 518 U.S. 515 (1996), something higher than intermediate scrutiny applies to sex discrimination under the Supreme Court's Equal Protection jurisprudence. *See, e.g.*, Jason M. Skaggs, *Justifying Gender-Based Affirmative Action under* United States v. Virginia's *"Exceedingly Persuasive Justification" Standard*, 86 CAL. L. REV. 1169, 1182 (1998) (arguing that "while *Virginia* does not prescribe strict scrutiny for gender classifications, it does promote a significantly more demanding standard of review than traditional intermediate scrutiny"); Colin Callahan & Amelia Kaufman, *Constitutional Law Chapter: Equal Protection*, 5 GEO. J. GENDER & L. 17, 41–44 (2004) (noting that some commentators argue that a standard of review higher than intermediate scrutiny applies to sex discrimination after *Virginia*); *see also Virginia*, 518 U.S. at 579–96 (Scalia, J., dissenting) ("[T]he rationale of today's decision is sweeping: for sex-based classifications, a redefinition of intermediate scrutiny that makes it indistinguishable from strict scrutiny"). While this debate is ongoing, we hold that sex discrimination must meet a standard higher than intermediate scrutiny – perhaps a standard that is "indistinguishable from strict scrutiny." However, we rule that even if a reviewing court finds that the traditional intermediate scrutiny standard applies to sex-based classifications not related to transgender status, that UTA cannot meet even the traditional intermediate scrutiny standard.

Etsitty v. Utah Transit Authority

which clearly is a "distinguishing characteristic" that defines the group. Third, the group lacks political power because only a very small minority of people identify as transgender – a minority that has suffered at the hands of the majority and has been treated as societal outcasts. *Id.* Finally, the characteristic that defines the group is not relevant to its ability to contribute to society because transgender people can and do contribute to society, as Krystal Ettsity, who did her job well before she was terminated because of her transgender status, amply showed.

Strict scrutiny requires that "the classification be narrowly tailored to meet a compelling state interest." *See, e.g., Adarand Constructors, Inc. v. Pena*, 515 U.S. 200, 227 (1995). Government classifications will pass the strict scrutiny test in rare cases. *See City of Richmond v. J.A. Croson Co.*, 488 U.S. 469, 521 (1989) (Scalia, J., concurring) (only a "social emergency rising to the level of imminent danger to life and limb – for example, a prison race riot, requiring temporary segregation of inmates, ... can justify [race segregation, a type of discrimination judged by strict scrutiny]"); *see also Bernal v. Fainter*, 467 U.S. 216, 219 n.6 (1984) (citation omitted) ("Only rarely are statutes sustained in the face of strict scrutiny. As one commentator observed, strict-scrutiny review is "strict" in theory but usually 'fatal' in fact.").

Requiring employees to access bathrooms that match the sex assigned to them at birth discriminates against transgender employees because they are forced to use bathrooms that do not match their gender identity, while cisgender employees may use bathrooms that match their gender identity. This puts transgender people in a dangerous and unhealthy situation. This discrimination fails strict scrutiny because it is not narrowly tailored and there is no compelling state interest. There is no risk to Etsitty's or anyone else's life or safety if she uses the women's restroom; to the contrary, using the men's restroom would be extremely dangerous for her. Concerns about the privacy and safety of cisgender employees using the restrooms cannot meet the stringent strict scrutiny standard because there is no evidence that Etsitty and other transgender employees pose any risk to their cisgender counterparts in public restrooms.

B Discrimination Based on Sex

The Supreme Court has held that, under the Equal Protection Clause, discrimination on the basis of sex is forbidden unless there is an "exceedingly persuasive justification" for sex discrimination. *United States v. Virginia*, 518 U.S. 515, 524 (1996). There is no "exceedingly persuasive justification" here that could justify the discrimination Etsitty has faced because of her sex.

292   Etsitty v. Utah Transit Authority

For the reasons discussed, UTA's actions and policy on its transgender employees' bathroom usage is sex discrimination under Title VII. It is also sex discrimination under the Equal Protection Clause. *See, e.g., Smith v. City of Salem, Ohio*, 378 F.3d 566, 577 (6th Cir. 2004) (a showing of sex discrimination under Title VII "mirrors" what must be shown to prove sex discrimination under the Equal Protection Clause); *Back v. Hastings on Hudson Union Free Sch. Dist.*, 365 F.3d 107, 117–21 (2d Cir. 2004) (holding that the Equal Protection Clause prohibits sex-stereotyping discrimination just as *Price Waterhouse* held that Title VII prohibits sex-stereotyping discrimination).

Transgender discrimination is sex discrimination, and sex discrimination must be judged with strict scrutiny. *See supra* note 59. Because requiring employees to access bathrooms that match the sex assigned to them at birth discriminates against transgender employees and does not pass strict scrutiny, UTA has violated the Equal Protection Clause.

However, if a reviewing court finds that traditional intermediate scrutiny applies to sex discrimination, *see supra* note 59, then sex discrimination will survive constitutional scrutiny only if it "serve[s] important governmental objectives and [is] substantially related to achievement of those objectives." *Craig v. Boren*, 429 U.S. 190, 197 (1976). UTA's actions cannot pass traditional intermediate scrutiny.

Under the Equal Protection Clause, there is no important government interest in preventing a transgender woman from using the female restrooms that would justify the discrimination here. The harms UTA fears are speculative; there have been no complaints about Etsitty's use of the women's restroom. Additionally, people do not see other people's genitals in women's restrooms; thus other users of the women's restrooms would not see Etsitty's genitals. As the Eighth Circuit recently ruled, a reasonable person would not find that the presence of a transgender person in the restroom creates a hostile or abusive environment. *Cruzan v. Spec. Sch. Dist. No. 1*, 294 F.3d 981, 984 (8th Cir. 2002) (finding no violation of Title VII when a school permitted a transgender women to use the women's restrooms). Here, UTA had to ask Etsitty about her genitals to determine whether she could use the women's restrooms. This need to ask is instructive. It demonstrates that no one in the women's restrooms would be concerned with Etsitty's body parts given her feminine gender expression.

On limited occasions, the Supreme Court has upheld sex discrimination when "real differences" between men and women justify a difference in treatment under the law. *See, e.g., Rostker v. Goldberg*, 453 U.S. 57, 76, 79 (1981) (upholding application of mandatory draft laws to men, but not women, because combat exclusion of women, which was not challenged in the case, made men and women not similarly situated in ability to go to combat); *Michael M. v. Superior Court*, 450 U.S. 464, 471, 473, 478 (1981) (upholding statutory rape laws with differential ages for boys and girls because women and girls may become pregnant from statutory rape, while men and boys cannot); *Nguyen v. INS*, 533 U.S. 53, 62–63 (2001) (upholding law requiring a father who was a US citizen to apply for citizenship for his son, who was born abroad, even though a mother in the same situation would not have similar requirements because the mother is present at the child's birth and her biological connection is verifiable).[60]

In the present case, the real differences between a transgender woman with a penis and a cisgender woman with a vagina do not justify the UTA's difference in treatment. Both transgender and cisgender women need to use the bathroom several times daily. Both transgender and cisgender women use the women's bathroom in similar ways: by going into a stall, closing the door, and eliminating human waste out of sight of others. In homes across the United States, people with different genitals from one another use the same bathrooms. In contrast to *Rostker*, *Michael M.*, and *Nguyen*, where the Supreme Court found that real differences between men and women meant they were not similarly situated, here transgender and cisgender women both need to eliminate human waste and use a comfortable and safe bathroom to do so. Therefore, even assuming the continued viability of *Rostker*, *Michael M.*, and *Nguyen* where the Supreme Court found relevant "real differences" between men and women, here there is no relevant real difference between cisgender and transgender women that justifies different treatment by UTA. UTA has violated the Equal Protection Clause.

C Personal Preference Concerns Are Inadequate to Justify Discrimination

UTA's admitted reason for firing Etsitty was that other people might object to her using the women's bathrooms and then sue, subjecting UTA to liability. However, as described in section IV.A.3, customer preferences may not be taken into account under Title VII, and similarly they may not be considered under the Equal Protection Clause. Here, the concern is purely speculative, because Etsitty used women's restrooms while on the job, and no one complained. UTA certainly has not shown an "exceedingly persuasive justification" for the discrimination based on anyone's preferences. *United States*

---

[60] It is unclear whether the Supreme Court would hold the same way today in all of these cases, especially *Rostker* and *Michael M.*, which came before *Virginia* – *see supra* note 59 – but if it would not, that fact only strengthens the argument that the classification in this case would not survive either intermediate or strict scrutiny.

v. *Virginia*, 518 U.S. 515, 524 (1996). In fact, it has been Etsitty who has suffered harm: the loss of her dignity and her job, based on her former employer's speculations.

D Safety Concerns Are Inadequate to Justify Discrimination

The Supreme Court has found that, in certain circumstances, safety reasons can require a difference in treatment based on sex. *See Dothard v. Rawlinson*, 433 U.S. 321, 336 (1977) (upholding a rule forbidding women from working as guards in maximum-security men's prisons in Alabama because having women work in that position would create a real risk of violence to the women workers and the inmates themselves). The Court reasoned that the evidence showed that 20 percent of the inmates were sex offenders, that the Alabama prison system was inadequately staffed, and that the prison system itself was an "environment of violence and disorganization." *Id.* at 335. In that environment, the Court reasoned that it was highly likely that women guards would be assaulted by male prisoners and would therefore be unable to provide security to other inmates, thus increasing the risk of violence to other inmates. *Id.* at 335–36. The Court therefore concluded that there was no equal protection violation by Alabama's forbidding women to work as guards in its maximum-security prisons. *See id.* at 336–37, 334 n.20.

Here, by contrast, there is no evidence that Etsitty's use of the women's restrooms would put anyone in danger. In fact, the suggestion that Etsitty or other transgender women would create danger to other women using the women's restrooms is reminiscent of the concerns raised when bathrooms were segregated by race: that women of color would cause disease and harm to white women if they had to share a bathroom. *See, e.g.,* Jo Carol Nesset-Sale, *The Making of a Civil Rights Plaintiff: A Retrospective by the Plaintiff in* Cleveland Board of Education v. Lafleur, *a Landmark Pregnancy Discrimination Case*, 7 GEO. J. GENDER & L. 1, 5 (2006). These concerns did not materialize once bathrooms were racially integrated in 1964. There is no doubt that women are disproportionately affected by assault by cisgender men. There is no evidence, let alone "exceedingly persuasive" evidence, to suggest that transgender women disproportionately assault cisgender women. By contrast, there is plenty of evidence that transgender individuals – particular transgender women – disproportionately suffer from assault by cisgender men. *See* Transgender Law Center, *supra*, at 3. Therefore, safety concerns require that transgender women use women's bathrooms.

E Privacy Concerns Are Inadequate to Justify Discrimination

Some courts have found that, in certain circumstances, privacy reasons can permit a difference in treatment based on sex. *See, e.g., Everson v. Mich. Dep't. of Corr.*, 391 F.3d 737, 756–59 (6th Cir. 2004) (noting that, to protect the privacy interests of female inmates, courts have allowed men to be excluded from employment positions where the employees would perform pat-down searches on female inmates and/or observe female inmates showering or using the toilet).

Here, Etsitty's use of women's bathrooms does not intrude on anyone's privacy interests. Multiuser public bathrooms are, by their nature, not private because they are shared by multiple people. In the women's bathrooms, stalls provide significant privacy to both transgender and cisgender individuals using them. No one is seen by anyone else in a nude or partially nude state in the women's bathrooms. In the men's bathrooms, men wishing to avoid being seen by others in a partially nude state can use the stalls. Men wishing to avoid seeing others in a nude or partially nude state can avoid looking at any urinal section of the bathroom. Privacy concerns therefore do not preclude transgender women from using women's bathrooms.

VI THE LEGALITY OF SEX-SEGREGATED BATHROOMS: TITLE VII AND THE EQUAL PROTECTION CLAUSE

While it is not necessary to this Court's decision in this particular case to determine whether sex-segregated bathrooms are always illegal, we believe it is important to voice our educated view of the issue. It is doubtful that sex-segregated bathrooms comport with either Title VII in the workplace or, when operated by the government, the Equal Protection Clause. After all, sex-segregated bathrooms themselves classify explicitly based on sex, and racially segregated bathrooms, once commonplace, have been outlawed since the Civil Rights Act of 1964. Unisex, or all-gender, bathroom facilities are a viable alternative to sex-segregated restrooms and are used across the country in places such as universities and other places of public accommodations. Anthony, *supra*, at 282–83, 287–88 (discussing all-gender bathroom options already available at the University of New Hampshire and Kellogg Park Comfort Station at La Jolla Shores, San Diego, California). All-gender restrooms are helpful in disability and caring contexts where people may be caring for others with different genitalia from their own, as well as for men and boys who may be uncomfortable with or unable to use the men's restrooms because of the lack of privacy afforded by many. *Id.* at 276 (noting that a boy may be the target of bullying if he chooses to use a stall instead of a urinal for urination).

The district court below expressed concern that a decision in favor of Etsitty would necessarily mean that any man could use the women's restroom, and any woman could use the men's restroom. This is actually the crux of the fear for safety and loss of privacy that opponents to a finding in favor of Etsitty have. *Etsitty v. Utah Transit Auth.*, No. 2:04CV616 DS, 2005 WL 1505610, at *5 (D. Utah June 24, 2005). The decision to use the women's restrooms is behavior stereotypically associated with girls and women, and the decision to use the men's restrooms is behavior stereotypically associated with boys and men. Because, under *Price Waterhouse*, an employer is forbidden from penalizing behavior or appearance because it is typically associated with one sex but not another, then even today a nontransgender man must be permitted to use the women's restrooms, and a nontransgender woman must be permitted to use the men's restrooms. It is, however, unlikely that many nontransgender individuals will choose to use a restroom that does not correspond to the sex assigned to them at birth, whereas it is likely that most transgender individuals will do so. *See, e.g.,* Kogan, *Transsexuals, supra,* at 1223, 1227 & n.14 (1997) (noting that, for transgender individuals, the "choice of public restrooms is in fact the source of considerable anguish").

It is possible that, on occasion, a nontransgender man may choose to use a women's restroom or vice versa. Under Title VII and the Equal Protection Clause, such individuals should not be penalized. For example, a man who is uncomfortable or unable to use the men's room, perhaps because exposure to others' genitals is distressing owing to past abuse, may choose to use the women's restrooms. *See* Anthony, *supra,* at 276 (some men are unable to urinate in the viewing presence of others, and many men are uncomfortable with seeing others' genitals in the restroom). In another example, a woman who sees a long line for the women's restroom, but not the men's, and who needs the restroom immediately may choose to use the men's restroom. *See Woman is Acquitted in Trial for Using the Men's Room,* N.Y. TIMES (Nov. 3, 1990), www.nytimes.com/1990/11/03/us/woman-is-acquitted-in-trial-for-using-the-men-s-room.html (describing a woman in just that situation who was acquitted of wrongdoing at trial by a jury of her peers). There are certainly many more examples of why nontransgender individuals may choose to use restrooms that others may consider inappropriate. Of course, no one may use the restroom to harass or abuse others, and those behaviors are already forbidden by law. *See, e.g.,* Utah Code §§76-9-702.7 (forbidding voyeurism, which includes "view[ing] or attempt[ing] to view … any portion of [an] individual's body regarding which the individual has a reasonable expectation of privacy"); *id.* §76–5-102 (prohibiting assault); *id.* §76–5-405 (prohibiting sexual assault).

The problem of who belongs in what bathroom based on sex or gender identity will disappear if the courts decide in future cases that sex-segregated bathrooms violate both Title VII and the Equal Protection Clause, as this Court believes they should. This Court's remarks on the legality of sex-segregated bathrooms here are, of course, dicta, because Etsitty did not challenge the existence of sex-segregated bathrooms. Nevertheless, we discuss this matter now because when all-gender bathrooms become more wide-spread, whether through court action and/or through social change, the problems that Etsitty and other transgender and gender-nonconforming people face with bathrooms will be greatly diminished.

A *Title VII*

We have noted that Title VII provides: "It shall be an unlawful employment practice for an employer ... to limit, segregate, or classify his employees or applicants for employment in any way which would deprive or tend to deprive any individual of employment opportunities or otherwise adversely affect his status as an employee, because of such individual's ... sex." 42 U.S.C. §2000e-2 (a)(2). Classifying employees as men and as women for bathroom use tends to deprive transgender employees of employment opportunities on the basis of their sex, even if an employer permits employees to use bathrooms according to their gender identity. First, many transgender individuals do not identify as either male or female and therefore do not have a comfortable or safe bathroom to choose if the bathrooms are sex-segregated. *See, e.g.*, Transgender Law Center, *supra*, at 4; Terry S. Kogan, *Sex-Separation in Public Restrooms: Law, Architecture, and Gender*, 14 Mich. J. Gender & L. 1, 15–16, 55–56 (2007) [hereinafter Kogan, *Sex-Separation*]. Next, many transgender individuals will not be comfortable or safe in either a male or female bathroom because they do not conform to how others think they should look to access either bathroom. Transgender Law Center, *supra*, at 4. Cisgender individuals who do not conform to gender norms and sex stereotypes may also be harassed in sex-segregated bathrooms. *Id.*

The Ninth Circuit has found that some policies that differentiate based on sex do not violate Title VII unless they impose "unequal burdens" on men and women as groups. *See, e.g., Jespersen v. Harrah's Operating Co.*, 444 F.3d 1104, 1109–10 (9th Cir. 2006) (en banc) (finding no violation of Title VII when women, but not men, were required to wear makeup as part of a company dress-code and a woman was fired as a result of failing to wear makeup); *Nichols v. Azteca Restaurant Enters., Inc.*, 256 F.3d 864, 875 n.7 (9th Cir.

298 Etsitty v. Utah Transit Authority

2001) (noting that different grooming codes for men and women do not violate Title VII).[61] However, the reasoning of the Ninth Circuit in these cases does not comport with the plain language of Title VII itself, which forbids an adverse employment action or deprivation of employment opportunities "because of [an] individual's ... sex." 42 U.S.C. §2000e-2(a)(1)-(a)(2). The statute mentions an "individual" of a particular sex who is disadvantaged, not a group of people of a particular sex that is disadvantaged.

Additionally, these Ninth Circuit decisions do not comport with the logic and language of *Price Waterhouse*, which found that a woman had stated a Title VII violation when she suffered an adverse employment action because she did not wear makeup and conform to other gender norms expected for women, but not for men. *Price Waterhouse*, 490 U.S. at 272, 251 (1989) (plurality) ("[W]e are beyond the day when an employer could evaluate employees by assuming or insisting that they matched the stereotype associated with their group"). As the Sixth Circuit noted in *Smith v. City of Salem*, 378 F.3d 566, 574 (6th Cir. 2004), "After *Price Waterhouse*, an employer who discriminates against women because, for instance, they do not wear dresses or makeup, is engaging in sex discrimination because the discrimination would not occur but for the victim's sex."

The decision in *Smith* conflicts with the decision in *Jespersen*. *Smith* is the better reasoned case and the case that is true to the holding in *Price Waterhouse*. The Tenth Circuit should therefore follow *Smith* and not *Jespersen* if and when any similar case comes before it.

Individual transgender employees and gender-nonconforming employees are harmed by the existence of sex-segregated bathrooms. Many transgender employees and gender-nonconforming employees do not look as others think someone entering a particular sex-segregated bathroom should look, and as a result they may experience fear or discomfort using sex-segregated bathrooms. Requiring employees to use sex-segregated bathrooms in the workplace therefore violates Title VII because sex-segregated bathrooms result in a disparate impact on transgender and gender-nonconforming individuals because of sex.

B The Equal Protection Clause

For similar reasons to why there are no "exceedingly persuasive" reasons that would justify excluding transgender women from women's restrooms, there

---

[61] The Tenth Circuit has one similar case, *Holman v. Cody*, No. 93-6370, 1994 U.S. App. LEXIS 6500 (10th Cir. Apr. 6, 1994), where the court found no sex discrimination in a prison grooming code that allowed women, but not men, to have long hair. However, the *Holman* court was careful to note that "this order and judgment is not binding precedent," and so this Court shall not treat it as precedent.

are no "exceedingly persuasive" justifications for sex-segregated restrooms. The history of why the United States has separate bathrooms for men and women shows that the original ideology behind the practice can no longer justify it. Multiuser public bathrooms first appeared in the second half of the 1800s, when plumbing technology had advanced to the point at which such bathrooms became physically possible. Kogan, *Sex-Separation, supra*, at 15–16, 35–39. At that time, there was profound discomfort with women entering the workforce and the public sphere in general. *Id.* at 54–55. The prevailing view was that women should be kept in their own private sphere of the home, while men went out into the public world. *See, e.g.*, David E. Shi, FACING FACTS: REALISM IN AMERICAN THOUGHT AND CULTURE 1850–1920 17 (1995) ("[T]he middle-class home [was] a 'separate sphere' governed by mothers"); *see also Bradwell v. Illinois*, 83 U.S. 130, 141 (1872) (Bradley, J., concurring) (finding that a law barring women from becoming attorneys was valid because "the domestic sphere ... properly belongs to the domain and functions of womanhood").

As economic realities meant that women started joining the workforce, laws began to require the creation of separate men's and women's restrooms to keep some semblance of the "separate spheres" ideology intact. Kogan, *Sex-Separation, supra*, at 50. At the same time, libraries began to create separate "ladies' reading rooms" and trains had separate ladies' cars. *Id.* at 6–7. The first law mandating separate toilets for men and women in factories was passed in Massachusetts in 1887. *Id.* at 39. By 1920, more than forty states had passed similar laws. *Id.*

This "separate spheres" argument cannot justify a separation of the sexes now, when the Supreme Court has made it clear that men and women should not be assumed to occupy such. *See, e.g., United States v. Virginia*, 518 U.S. 515 (1996). Additionally, the "separate but equal" doctrine has long been discredited for race segregation and should be discredited for this example of sex segregation. *See, e.g., Brown v. Bd. of Educ.*, 347 U.S. 483, 495 (1954). As described earlier, anatomical differences between men and women do not justify separate bathrooms because men and women use the same bathrooms in home environments, proving that separate bathrooms are not necessary. *Cf.* Sharon M. McGowan, *The Bona Fide Body: Title VII's Last Bastion of Intentional Sex Discrimination*, 12 COLUM. J. GENDER & L. 77, 123 (2003) (noting that "[u]nisex bathrooms are fairly common in Europe"). Additionally, safety concerns that women would be attacked in bathrooms if men were allowed to enter are speculative, because it is doubtful that a sign would keep out someone intent on assault or harassment. *See* Transgender Law Center, *supra*, at 5. Additionally, restrooms may become safer for women if men knew that, at any moment, another man could enter the space. *Id.* Restrooms would certainly become safer for children if not sex-segregated because then children could always enter the same bathroom as their adult caretakers. *Id.* Elderly or disabled individuals with caretakers would also have an easier and safer time using restrooms. *Id.* Finally, transgender and other gender-nonconforming people would be safer in all-gender bathrooms because there would be no basis for anyone to be angry or upset that a person of the "wrong gender" had just entered the bathroom. *See id.* at 18 (stating that all-gender bathrooms "decrease the potential for violence by providing a multigendered environment in which transgender and gender nonconforming people do not automatically stand out simply because of their gender expression or presentation"); *see also* Patricia Leigh Brown, *A Quest for a Restroom That's Neither Men's Room nor Women's Room*, N.Y. Times A14 (Mar. 4, 2005), www.nytimes.com/2005/03/04/us/a-quest-for-a-restroom-thats-neither-mens-room-nor-womens-room.html (transgender individual assaulted when she used a women's restroom). Overall, then, safety considerations weigh in favor of having all-gender bathrooms instead of sex-segregated bathrooms.

As for the privacy issue, women's bathrooms that are converted into all-gender bathrooms would not need any changes because stalls in current women's bathrooms are designed so that no one sees another person in a state of undress. In men's bathrooms that are converted into all-gender bathrooms, where there are urinals, modifications can and should be made, such as putting stalls or curtains around urinals, which would increase privacy for everyone. New construction could improve on privacy for everyone by doing things such as making stall doors go further up to the ceiling and lower down to the floor, putting stronger locks on doors, and enclosing urinals in stalls.

VII CONCLUSION

In conclusion, the employer here, UTA, violated both Title VII and the Equal Protection Clause when it fired a transgender employee for her intent to use the women's restrooms while having "male genitalia." The district court's decision below is reversed. Partial summary judgment (on the question of liability) is granted to Etsitty.

* * *

This case is remanded to the district court for further proceedings consistent with this judgment.

It is so ordered.

Commentary on *Hively v. Ivy Tech Community College*

DANIELLE D. WEATHERBY

INTRODUCTION

Overruling decades of circuit precedent in what was heralded as a trailblazing collage of four opinions,[62] an *en banc* panel of the US Court of Appeals for the Seventh Circuit in *Hively v. Ivy Tech Community College*[63] held that Title VII's prohibition of sex discrimination necessarily encompasses discrimination based on sexual orientation. The *Hively* court engaged in a scrupulous journey of statutory interpretation, eventually rejecting the line of cases that blindly accepted the position that "Congress had nothing more than the traditional notion of 'sex' in mind when it voted to outlaw sex discrimination."[64]

The LGBTQ+ community and the public generally celebrated the *Hively* decision as a pathbreaking victory. Indeed, it was the most important legal success for LGBTQ+ litigants since *Obergefell v. Hodges*,[65] decided just two years before *Hively*. While the holding was undoubtedly historic, because it created a circuit split ripe for Supreme Court review, the *Hively* majority's narrow emphasis on statutory interpretation was detached and devoid of any deep substantive engagement with the harmful impacts of gender policing on the LGBTQ+ community. Moreover, the panel's decision to boil the issue down to one of "pure statutory interpretation" was largely divorced from values underpinning Title VII of the Civil Rights Act of 1964, and it missed a key opportunity to draw attention to the gender patrolling that is pervasive in the American workplace and in society generally. By shirking a real discussion of the ways in which gender biases unfairly disadvantage LGBTQ+ employees in the workplace, the *Hively en banc* panel's decision was a measured, textualist means to an end – perhaps necessarily so given the political climate and the composition of the Supreme Court – rather than the commentary on gender equality that it could have been. Professor Ryan H. Nelson, writing as Chief Judge Nelson, rectifies this error, rewriting the decision to directly confront the repugnant inequalities that result when sex stereotyping and LGBTQ+ animus intersect in the workplace.

---

[62] In February 2018, the Second Circuit joined the Seventh Circuit in holding that allegations of discrimination based on sexual orientation are actionable under Title VII. *See Zarda v. Altitude Express, Inc.*, 883 F.3d 100, 112 (2d Cir. 2018) (en banc), *cert. granted* 139 S.Ct.1599 (2019).

[63] 853 F.3d 339, 341 (7th Cir. 2017) (en banc).

[64] *Id.*

[65] 135 S.Ct. 2584 (2015) (securing a constitutionally protected right to marry for same-sex couples).

302 Hively v. Ivy Tech Community College

THE ORIGINAL OPINION

Hively came on the heels of *Obergefell v. Hodges,* considered the greatest and most important legal victory for the LGBTQ+ rights movement to date. The LGBTQ+ rights movement had mobilized decades before *Obergefell,* and the decision was the culmination of a systematic and nationwide effort to challenge the constitutionality of state and federal defense of marriage Acts, which defined marriage as between a man and a woman exclusively.[66] The marriage equality movement was determined to right this wrong: on June 26, 2015, almost a year after Kimberly Hively filed her initial Title VII complaint in the Northern District of Indiana, same-sex marriage became a recognized fundamental right.[67]

While the LGBTQ+ rights movement had its eye fixed on the battle to overturn pernicious DOMA laws, an equally important fight to challenge discriminatory workplace practices targeted at LGBTQ+ employees was ongoing. There were individual efforts, many supported by human rights groups, to seek application of Title VII to claims of discrimination based on sexual orientation or gender identity.[68] However, these legal fights became secondary to those aimed at securing the right to same-sex marriage and thus the guiding Title VII precedent is less evolved. After *Obergefell,* it became an unfortunate reality that a gay person could be legally married in any of the fifty states on Saturday and fired from her job because of that marriage on Monday.[69]

The *Hively* opinion is a neonate. Only a few years old, its impacts are still largely unknown. Since *Hively* was decided, at least one other circuit has followed the Seventh Circuit's lead in holding that sexual orientation discrimination falls within the ambit of sex discrimination under Title VII,[70] and there are still a number of sexual orientation discrimination cases percolating their way through the federal district courts in other circuits.[71]

---

[66] The federal Act is the Defense of Marriage Act of 1996 (DOMA).

[67] *Obergefell,* 135 S.Ct. at 2584.

[68] There were ongoing legislative attempts at both the state and national levels to legally prohibit sexual orientation discrimination. *See* Ann C. McGinley, *Erasing Boundaries: Masculinities, Sexual Minorities, and Employment Discrimination,* 43 U. MICH. J. L. REFORM 713, 728–32 (2010); *see also, e.g.,* A Bill to Prohibit Discrimination on the Basis of Sex, Gender Identity, and Sexual Orientation, S. 1006, 115th Cong. (2017); Fair and Equal Housing Act of 2017, H.R. 1447, 115th Cong. (2017). The successful state efforts created a patchwork of laws that ultimately provided a basis for interpreting Title VII's sex discrimination prohibition as protective of discrimination on the bases of sexual orientation and gender identity.

[69] G.M. Filisko, *After Obergefell: How the Supreme Court Ruling on Same-Sex Marriage Has Affected Other Areas of Law,* ABA JOURNAL (June 2016), www.abajournal.com/magazine/article/after_obergefell_how_the_supreme_court_ruling_on_same_sex_marriage_has_affe.

[70] *Zarda,* 883 F.3d at 100.

[71] *See, e.g., Somers v. Digital Realty Trust Inc.,* No. 14-cv-05180-EMC, 2018 WL 3730469, at *6–8 (N.D. Cal. Aug. 6, 2018); *Philpott v. New York,* 252 F.Supp.3d 313, 315-317 (S.D.N.Y. 2017).

Hively v. Ivy Tech Community College

In *Hively*, the Seventh Circuit initially affirmed the Northern District of Indiana's dismissal of Kimberly Hively's complaint for failure to state a claim upon which relief could be granted.[72] After granting Hively's petition for rehearing, the Seventh Circuit sitting *en banc* reconsidered whether Hively's claim that she was fired because of her sexual orientation stated a claim for "sex discrimination" under Title VII.[73] Hively, an "openly" gay woman,[74] was a part-time, adjunct professor at Ivy Tech Community College. She alleged that she was repeatedly denied consideration for full-time employment and that her part-time contract was not renewed because of her sexual orientation.[75]

The US Supreme Court has yet to consider the reach of Title VII to sexual orientation discrimination claims, leaving the *Hively* court with no controlling precedent. Although the Supreme Court had not yet spoken on the precise issue at the time of *Hively*, it had interpreted Title VII's sex discrimination prohibition to include both same-sex sexual or gender-based harassment[76] and discrimination based on a failure to conform to sex stereotypes,[77] and it had more recently recognized a constitutionally protected right to same-sex marriage.[78] Against this backdrop, the panel acknowledged the difficulty in "extricat[ing] the gender nonconformity claims from the sexual orientation claims," and noted that the guiding precedent created "bizarre results" and a "confused hodge-podge of cases."[79]

Much of the *Hively en banc* opinion, including Judge Posner's provocative concurrence, is silent with respect to the ways that gender stereotypes involving sexual orientation actually operate in the contemporary workplace. Instead of seizing the opportunity post-*Obergefell* to draw attention to the hazards of sex stereotyping that endanger the LGBTQ+ population, Chief Judge Diane Wood, writing for the majority, engaged in a rather simplistic narrative about how sex is inextricably intertwined with sexual orientation. Quipping that "[i]t would require considerable calisthenics to remove the term 'sex' from 'sexual orientation,'" the court departed from the other circuits, which had declined to recognize a claim for sexual orientation discrimination under Title VII and instead held that sexual orientation

---

[72] *Hively v. Ivy Tech Cmty. Coll.*, 830 F.3d 698, 706 (7th Cir. 2016).

[73] *Hively*, 853 F.3d at 339.

[74] Although Nelson's rewritten opinion avoids labeling her, the common understanding is that Kimberly Hively is a lesbian.

[75] *Hively*, 853 F.3d at 341.

[76] *Oncale v. Sundowner Offshore Servs., Inc.*, 523 U.S. 75, 79–80 (1998).

[77] *Price Waterhouse v. Hopkins*, 490 U.S. 228, 250–52 (1989) (plurality opinion).

[78] *Obergefell*, 135 S.Ct. at 2584.

[79] *Hively*, 853 F.3d at 342.

discrimination does fall within the ambit of Title VII.[80] In doing so, the court made no attempt to distinguish sex stereotyping and sexual orientation discrimination: an about-face from its own precedent.

Judge Wood's decision adopted two analytical approaches: the "tried-and-true comparative method" for detecting discrimination and an "associational theory." Pursuant to the comparative method, Judge Wood's analysis isolated Hively's sex, posing a counterfactual: if Hively were a man, "but everything else stayed the same: in particular, the sex or gender of the partner," would she have been treated similarly? Answering in the negative, Judge Wood found "paradigmatic sex discrimination," explaining that "Hively represents the ultimate case of failure to conform to the female stereotype (at least as understood in a place such as modern America, which views heterosexuality as the norm and other forms of sexuality as exceptional): she is not heterosexual."[81]

Tracing the "associational theory" of discrimination born from *Loving v. Virginia*[82] and its progeny,[83] Chief Judge Wood explained that "a person who is discriminated against because of the protected characteristic of one with whom she associates is actually being disadvantaged because of her own traits."[84] Hively was passed over for promotions, and her contract was not renewed because of her partner's sex; such treatment amounted to "sex" discrimination.

Without diving too deeply into the real-life manner in which social constructions of gender negatively affect the LGBTQ+ community and aid in the policing of gender norms, the Wood majority opinion attempted to set its decision within the larger, historical context. Citing the landmark decisions of *Price Waterhouse, Oncale, Romer v. Evans*,[85] and *Lawrence v. Texas*,[86] the *Hively* court echoed the Supreme Court in *Obergefell*, reminding us that "[i]t is now clear that the challenged laws burden the liberty of same-sex couples, and it must be further acknowledged that they abridge central precepts of equality."[87] This was the court's only brief foray into any meaningful "rights" talk. Ultimately, the majority boiled its holding down to a "common-sense reality that it is actually impossible to discriminate on the basis of sexual orientation

---

[80] *Id.* at 350.

[81] *Id.* at 346.

[82] 388 U.S. 1 (1967).

[83] *See Parr v. Woodmen of the World Life Ins. Co.*, 791 F.2d 888, 892 (11th Cir. 1986); *see also Holcomb v. Iona Coll.*, 521 F.3d 130, 132 (2d Cir. 2008).

[84] *Hively*, 853 F.3d at 347.

[85] 517 U.S. 620 (1996).

[86] 539 U.S. 558 (2003).

[87] *Hively*, 853 F.3d at 350.

without discriminating on the basis of sex."[88] The majority concluded by simplifying its analysis of what the plain language of Title VII's sex discrimination prohibition means in light of "the Supreme Court's authoritative interpretations, not what someone thought it meant one, ten, or twenty years ago."[89]

Judges Joel M. Flaum and Richard A. Posner wrote concurring opinions. Judge Flaum, joined by Judge Kenneth F. Ripple, argued that even in the absence of a historical trend toward increased civil liberties for LGBTQ+ litigants, the majority would have reached the same conclusion based solely on the "statute's text." Invoking Title VII's "motivating factor" language, Judge Flaum offered another route available to the majority, explaining that, to find sex discrimination, "the [only] critical inquiry ... is whether [sex] was *a factor* in the employment decision."[90]

In a separate concurrence, Judge Posner coined the term "judicial interpretive updating," whereby courts may breathe new meaning into statutes to "satisfy modern needs and understandings."[91] Emphasizing what he described as a "lengthy" passage of time since the statute's enactment, Judge Posner relied upon a "compelling social interest in protecting homosexuals" for the majority's "admittedly loose 'interpretation' " of Title VII.[92] Questioning the majority's reliance on what he characterized as an "evasive" opinion in *Loving*, "a constitutional case ... which had nothing to do with the recently enacted Title VII," Judge Posner instead urged a reliance on the "passage of time and concomitant change in attitudes toward homosexuality and other unconventional forms of sexual orientation" for the "fresh interpretation" of Title VII's prohibition of discrimination "based on sex."[93] Like the majority, Posner's concurrence evades any real substantive rights talk, but his controversial use of "judicial interpretive updating" provides plenty of fodder for legal scholars.[94]

The dissent criticized the majority's decision as judicial activism, claiming that the majority effectuated what amounted to a "statutory amendment courtesy of unelected judges."[95] Instead, the dissent posited that Congress's failure to amend Title VII to explicitly prohibit sexual orientation discrimination indicated its intent to leave it out. Rejecting this argument, the majority cited the interpretation of the Equal Employment Opportunity Commission

---

[88] *Id.* at 351.

[89] *Id.* at 350.

[90] *Id.* at 359 (Flaum, J., concurring) (emphasis original).

[91] *Id.* at 352 (Posner, J., concurring).

[92] *Id.* at 355 (Posner, J., concurring).

[93] *Id.* at 256 (Posner, J., concurring).

[94] *See, e.g.*, Brian Soucek, Hively's *Self-Induced Blindness*, 127 YALE L.J. F. 115, 126–28 (2017).

[95] *Hively*, 853 F.3d at 360 (Sykes, J., dissenting).

306 Hively v. Ivy Tech Community College

(EEOC) in 2015,[96] clarifying that Title VII's "straightforward" prohibition of sex discrimination includes sexual orientation discrimination. (A year later, the EEOC settled a landmark sexual orientation discrimination case in favor of a lesbian employee.[97]) Based on the Commission's recent interpretation, the majority argued, Congress may have believed that it was unnecessary to clarify Title VII's reach to include sexual orientation discrimination.

THE FEMINIST JUDGMENT

The feminist judgment authored by Chief Judge Nelson reaches the same conclusion the original majority opinion does: that sexual orientation discrimination falls within the protective umbrella of Title VII. The main difference between the original opinion and the feminist opinion is the road traveled, with the feminist opinion paying homage to the ways in which psychological heterosexism – an ideology that rejects nonconforming sexual orientations and identities – continues to disadvantage the LGBTQ+ minority. Nelson's revision addresses the pervasiveness of sex stereotyping and its effect on the LGBTQ+ community, while the measured *Hively* majority did not. Contextualizing the *Price Waterhouse* holding within the Court's embrace of antiessentialism empowers Nelson to describe the extent to which gender norms negatively affect LGBTQ+ individuals in the workplace and to provide a contemporary social commentary on the state of our attitudinal evolution toward nonconforming sexual orientations and gender identities.

The feminist judgment differs from the original opinion in four distinct and important ways. First, relying on contemporary periodicals and secondary sources written by mostly feminist scholars, Nelson's opinion confronts the ugly truth that, in 2017, a large swath of Americans still retains antiquated notions of sexuality and gender roles. His opinion sets a scene of shockingly antediluvian bias. The prejudices that have been unleashed especially since President Trump took office in 2016 are even more contemptible than before, becoming almost socially acceptable because of Trump's own rhetoric. Nelson's painting of the scene is raw and apt: "[T]he stereotype at issue in the case at bar is pure disdain for people who are not heterosexual." As Brian Soucek has observed, the original four opinions cited eight reputed legislation scholars and not one feminist author, LGBTQ+ advocate, or human rights

---

[96] *Baldwin v. Foxx* (EEOC 2015) No. 2012-24738; *see also Macy v. Holder* (EEOC 2012) No. 0120120821 (setting the groundwork for the *Baldwin* holding by interpreting Title VII's protections against sex discrimination to apply to a transgender employee).

[97] *EEOC v. Pallet Cos.*, No. 1:16-cv-00595-CCB (D. Md. June 28, 2016).

activist.[98] Nelson's opinion rectifies this omission, citing more than eight distinguished civil rights and gender scholars. What the original opinion lacks in contextualization, the revision corrects, acknowledging the widespread epidemic of homophobia and giving the reader a more humanistic window into the day-to-day prejudice experienced by LGBTQ+ Americans.

Second, the original opinion refuses to bring to life the correlation between sex discrimination and sex-stereotyping discrimination, describing "the line between [them] as gossamer-thin" and concluding that "it does not exist at all."[99] Nelson's feminist opinion tackles the relationship head on. Arguing that "homosexuality is the ultimate gender non-conformity, the prototypical sex stereotyping animus,"[100] Nelson relies much more heavily on *Price Waterhouse* and its progeny, reasoning that a plaintiff's nonconforming sexual orientation is the quintessential psychological heterosexism that was the transgression in *Price Waterhouse*. This reliance on Supreme Court precedent anchors Nelson's opinion and provides a more solid jurisprudential footing on which future claimants may stand.

As the original opinion's textualist approach makes much ado about the inability to extricate an individual's sexual orientation from their sex, it fails to close the loop with respect to the real relationship between the two and its impact on the sexes. The original opinion recognized that, "viewed through the lens of the gender non-conformity line of cases, Hively represents the ultimate case of failure to conform to the female stereotype (at least as understood in a place such as modern America, which views heterosexuality as the norm and other forms of sexuality as exceptional): she is not heterosexual."[101] But it stopped there, failing to examine the *reason* that finding was important to gender equality.

As many feminist scholars have observed, "[S]exual orientation discrimination has something to do with the subordination of women."[102] Early feminist scholars claimed that "contempt for lesbian women and gay men serves primarily to preserve and reinforce the social meaning attached to gender."[103] During its initial review, the *Hively* panel even signaled this

---

[98] Soucek, *supra* note 94, at 121.

[99] *Hively*, 853 F.3d at 346.

[100] Quoting *Boutillier v. Hartford Pub. Schs.*, 221 F.Supp.3d 255, 269 (D. Conn. 2016).

[101] *Hively*, 853 F.3d at 346.

[102] Soucek, *supra* note 94, at 121 (citing, *inter alia*, Sylvia A. Law, *Homosexuality and the Social Meaning of Gender*, 1988 WIS. L. REV. 187; *see also* Vicki Schultz, *Reconceptualizing Sexual Harassment*, 107 YALE L.J. 1683, 1774–89 (1998); Mary Anne Case, *What Feminists Have to Lose in Same-Sex Marriage Litigation*, 57 UCLA L. REV. 1199, 1221 (2010); McGinley, *supra* note 68).

[103] Law, *supra* note 102, at 187.

308   Hively v. Ivy Tech Community College

codependent relationship between the two: "Who is dominant and who is submissive? Who is charged with earning a living and who makes a home? Who is a father and who a mother? In this way the roots of sexual orientation discrimination and gender discrimination wrap around each other inextricably."[104] The attitudes that perpetuate sexual orientation discrimination are the very attitudes that Title VII's sex discrimination prohibition was designed to extinguish. Sexual orientation discrimination threatens feminism because it polices one of the most quintessential gender norms – that women are sexually subservient to men – keeping women in their place both in the bedroom and in the boardroom.[105]

While the rewritten opinion could have gone even further to underscore the feminist values underlying Title VII's sex discrimination ban and the connection between psychological heterosexism and feminism, Nelson intimates at the connection between the two, echoing the first *Hively* court's shrewd recognition that "[l]esbian women and gay men upend our gender paradigms by their very status – causing us to question and casting into doubt antiquated and anachronistic ideas about what roles men and women should play in their relationships."[106] Disentangling the complex web woven among sex, sexual orientation, and feminism requires a nuanced understanding of gender norms that the majority opinion lacked. Nelson's rewritten opinion gives a glimpse into how a feminist Supreme Court considering the issue might reclaim the central values of Title VII. In fact, in *Price Waterhouse*, the Court indicated its awareness of this delicate relationship between sex discrimination and sexual orientation discrimination, observing that Title VII was "intended to strike at the entire spectrum of disparate treatment of men and women resulting from sex stereotypes."[107] Long before *Price Waterhouse*, the Supreme Court had found sex discrimination in situations where women were resisting stereotypical roles.[108]

One of the foundational goals of Title VII's sex discrimination ban was to protect women from the oppressive force of employers who expected them to fit into traditional gender roles. LGBTQ+ employees push the boundaries of those norms, creating a dichotomy that threatens the social construct of gender

---

[104] *Hively*, 830 F.3d at 706.

[105] Diana T. Sanchez *et al.*, *Doing Gender in the Bedroom: Investing in Gender Norms and the Sexual Experience*, 31 PERSONALITY AND SOCIAL PSYCHOLOGY BULLETIN 10, 1445, 1446 (Oct. 2005).

[106] *Id.*

[107] *Price Waterhouse*, 490 U.S. at 251 (quoting *Los Angeles Dept. of Water and Power v. Manhart*, 435 U.S. 702, 707 (1978)).

[108] *Philips v. Martin Marietta Corp.*, 400 U.S. 542 (1971) (finding that an employer violated Title VII when it refused to hire women, but not men, with preschool-aged children).

Hively v. Ivy Tech Community College 309

and the traditional roles that women and men are supposed to assume. Recognizing this, Judge Wood stated in the *en banc* opinion that sexual orientation discrimination "polic[es] the boundaries of what ... behaviors [employers] found acceptable for a woman."[109] As other scholars have observed, it is preventing the policing of gender norms, rather than the resolution of any syntactical squabble over the reach of the word "sex" that "ties protection against sexual orientation discrimination to Title VII's goal of dismantling constraining gender roles and hierarchies, in the workplace and beyond."[110]

Third, Nelson's opinion walks the reader, in meticulous fashion, through five reasons that compel the Seventh Circuit to overrule its own precedent. By more explicitly connecting the bridge between sex discrimination and sexual orientation discrimination, the rewritten opinion impeccably pleads the sex stereotyping, but-for, and sex-plus theories of recovery. Nelson's revision builds upon the original opinion's discussion of the associational theory of discrimination, identifying it more appropriately as "relationship discrimination" and explaining that discrimination against an employee because she is in a relationship with a person of the same sex is discrimination "because of sex." Lastly, Nelson's opinion echoes Judge Flaum's concurrence, devoting a section to the application of Title VII's motivating factor test found in section 703(m). Nelson's interpretation, while innovative, however, stretches the reach of Title VII beyond its intended limit, concluding that section 703(m) prohibits the employer's consideration of *anyone's* sex – not only the plaintiff's sex – in *any* context, no matter how attenuated, when making an adverse employment decision. This interpretation fashions a limitless cause of action for an employee to challenge an employer's action for reasons that are far too remote and unconnected to the *employee's* sex. In an ideal world, employers would never base their employment decisions on sex – that of the affected employee or anyone else's. But, in reality, to regulate employers' actions according to Nelson's desired section 703(m) approach is impractical and ultimately undermines the other viable avenues of recovery under Title VII.

Finally, the feminist opinion responds to criticism that the sex-stereotyping theory cannot apply to a sexual orientation claim absent some allegation that the discrimination was predicated on the plaintiff's nonconforming appearance or *behavior* at work rather than merely her perceived *status* as gay. The Sixth Circuit Court of Appeals embraced this argument when it rejected the application of a sex-stereotyping theory to a claim of sexual orientation

---

[109] *Hively*, 853 F.3d at 346.
[110] Soucek, *supra* note 94, at 125.

310   Hively v. Ivy Tech Community College

discrimination in 2006.[111] Nelson aptly explains that "the *Price Waterhouse* plurality referenced opposition to Hopkins' behavior as a *sufficient* means of evidencing sex stereotyping, but did not go so far as to say that opposition to Hopkins' behavior is *necessary* to evidence such stereotypes." Furthermore, Nelson points out that such a reading of *Price Waterhouse* would defy logic, for "no one miraculously divines someone else's sexual orientation." Rather, the knowledge that someone identifies as gay or lesbian comes from hearing something spoken or observing some behavior. Accordingly, any rule requiring a plaintiff to allege a triggering appearance or behavior is unworkable and illogical, and Nelson's opinion lays to rest this argument once and for all.

While at first glance the feminist judgment may seem to have made only minor alterations to the original decision, its explicit attention to and compassion for the pervasive nature of gender bias pays appropriate homage to the LGBTQ+ experience, offering a more humanistic lens through which to view the legal question posed by *Hively*. Nelson's narrative stands as a testament to the reality that gender bias in the workplace, in government, in places of public accommodation, and even in essential services such as health care is widespread, and much of it is implicit.[112]

Even though the LGBTQ+ community had celebrated the momentous same-sex marriage victory only two years earlier, the *Hively* decision came later than it should have, and the law of workplace protections still lags light-years behind. In addition to creating a blueprint for future sexual orientation discrimination plaintiffs, Nelson's opinion reveals how a reenvisioned *Hively* could have taken a more humanistic route, suggesting that change was necessary not only because of statutory construction, but also because sexual orientation discrimination is rampant, creating inequities in the workplace for millions of Americans. This, Nelson suggests, is unacceptable and inconsistent with the underlying values of Title VII.

Hively was a step in the right direction, indeed. But its ignorance of the link between sexual orientation discrimination and sex discrimination foreshadows a more formalist and less substantive analysis of a legal issue that strikes at the heart of substantive rights. Nelson's reenvisioned opinion attempts to reclaim

---

[111] *Vickers v. Fairfield Med. Ctr.*, 453 F.3d 757, 763 (6th Cir. 2006).

[112] *See, e.g.*, Janice A. Sabin *et al.*, *Health Care Providers' Implicit and Explicit Attitudes Toward Lesbian Women and Gay Men*, 105 AM. J. OF PUBLIC HEALTH 1831 (2015), (finding widespread implicit bias toward lesbian women and gay men among healthcare providers); Human Rights Campaign, THE COST OF THE CLOSET (2014), www.hrc.org/resources/the-cost-of-the-closet-and-the-rewards-of-inclusion (finding that 53 percent of American LGBTQ+ employees remain closeted at work so as to avoid discrimination and harassment). *Cf.* Erin C. Westgate *et al.*, *Implicit Preferences for Straight People over Lesbian Women and Gay Men Weakened from 2006 to 2013*, COLLABRA (2015), www.collabra.org/articles/10.1525/collabra.18/.

the substance. Time will tell whether the law of workplace equality as it pertains to LGBTQ+ employees will develop as a normative discussion, consistent with Title VII's goal of eroding the policing of gender norms, or whether *Hively*'s textualist approach will predominate the judiciary's treatment of such a substantive right.

In fact, on April 22, 2019, the Supreme Court granted *certiorari* in a trilogy of cases that pose the very issue with which the *Hively* court grappled just two years before: whether Title VII's "sex" discrimination prohibition protects employees from discrimination on the basis of sexual orientation.[113] The Court's decision in these cases threatens to roll back the protections largely available to LGBTQ+ litigants through *Price Waterhouse* and its progeny's sex-stereotyping jurisprudence. Should the Court retreat to a position permitting discrimination based on a strict interpretation of the word "sex," it could devastate years of progress, eliminating one of the only accepted mechanisms for relief for LGBTQ+ employees who suffer from workplace discrimination. Such a holding could force LGBTQ+ individuals back into the closet, at least at work.

Hively v. Ivy Tech Community College,
853 F.3d 339 (7th Cir. 2017) (en banc)

CHIEF JUDGE RYAN H. NELSON DELIVERED THE OPINION OF THE COURT.

I INTRODUCTION

Appellant Kimberly Hively alleges that Appellee Ivy Tech Community College of Indiana repeatedly denied her full-time employment and promotions based on her sexual orientation despite that she had worked for Ivy Tech for fourteen years without receiving a single negative evaluation. R. at 5–6. Hively filed a charge of discrimination against Ivy Tech with the US Equal Employment Opportunity Commission (EEOC) alleging that Ivy Tech's actions constituted unlawful sex discrimination. R. at 8. At Hively's request,

---

[113] *See Zarda v. Altitude Express, Inc.*, 883 F.3d 100 (2d Cir. 2018) (holding that sexual orientation discrimination is sex discrimination under Title VII), *cert. granted* 139 S.Ct. 1599 (2019); *Bostock v. Clayton County Bd. Commissioners*, 723 Fed. Appx. 964 (11th Cir. 2018) (holding that discrimination based on sexual orientation is not prohibited by the sex discrimination provision of Title VII), *cert. granted* 139 S.Ct. 1599 (2019); *EEOC v. R.G. & G.R. Harris Funeral Homes*, 884 F.3d 560 (6th Cir. 2018) (holding that discrimination against a transgender employee is sex discrimination under Title VII), *cert. granted* 139 S.Ct. 1599 (2019).

the EEOC terminated its processing of the charge and issued Hively a notice of right to sue. R. at 7. Upon receipt, Hively timely filed a *pro se* complaint against Ivy Tech in the US District Court for the Northern District of Indiana, alleging that the defendant had discriminated against her based on sexual orientation in violation of Title VII of the Civil Rights Act of 1964 and 42 U.S.C. §1981. R. at 4–6.

Ivy Tech moved to dismiss the complaint pursuant to Fed. R. Civ. P. 12 (b)(6), arguing that the complaint failed to state a claim upon which relief could be granted because sexual orientation discrimination is not prohibited by Title VII or section 1981. R. at 61–68. The district court granted Ivy Tech's motion in its entirety and dismissed Hively's complaint with prejudice. R. at 81–89. Hively appealed the district court's grant of Ivy Tech's motion to dismiss to this Court. R. at 90–91. In her brief supporting her appeal, Hively addressed only the dismissal of her Title VII claim and not her section 1981 claim. Appellant's Opening Br. at 2. A three-judge panel of this Court affirmed the district court's dismissal of Hively's Title VII claim, accepting the forfeiture of her appeal regarding the dismissal of her section 1981 claim. *Hively v. Ivy Tech Cmty. Coll.*, 830 F.3d 698 (7th Cir. 2016). We likewise accept forfeiture of Hively's appeal regarding dismissal of her section 1981 claim for failure to sufficiently pursue her claim on appeal. Moreover, such an appeal would have been futile because section 1981 "does not provide a cause of action for sex discrimination claims." *Bratton v. Roadway Package Sys., Inc.*, 77 F.3d 168, 177 (7th Cir. 1996). We granted this rehearing *en banc* to address the propriety of the district court's granting of Ivy Tech's motion to dismiss the Title VII claim.

II STANDARD OF REVIEW

We review *de novo* a district court's granting of a Fed. R. Civ. P. 12(b)(6) motion to dismiss. *Bonto v. U.S. Bank, N.A.*, 624 F.3d 461, 463 (7th Cir. 2010). To survive a motion to dismiss, a complaint must allege facts that state a claim that is plausible on its face. *Thermal Design, Inc. v. Am. Soc'y of Heating Refrigerating & Air-Conditioning Eng., Inc.*, 755 F.3d 832, 836 (7th Cir. 2014) (citing *Bell Atl. Corp. v. Twombly*, 550 U.S. 544, 570 (2007)). In assessing whether a motion to dismiss meets this standard, we must accept as true all well-pleaded facts in determining whether those assertions plausibly give rise to an entitlement to relief. *Thermal Design*, 755 F.3d at 836 (citing *Ashcroft v. Iqbal*, 556 U.S. 662, 679 (2009)).

III PRELIMINARY MATTERS

A Hively's Complaint

Pro se complaints such as Hively's must be construed liberally, giving the plaintiff the benefit of the doubt where appropriate. *Caldwell v. Miller,* 790 F.2d 589, 595 (7th Cir. 1986). Applying that standard, Hively pleads that Ivy Tech denied her full-time employment and promotions based on sexual orientation in violation of "Title VII of the Civil Rights Act of 1964, as amended (42 U.S.C. §2000e-5)." R. at 5. Hively's EEOC charge, which she attached to her complaint as an exhibit, has the box checked for sex discrimination; there is no option to check a box for sexual orientation discrimination, although the description of the particulars of her allegations in her charge alleges that Ivy Tech discriminated against her "based on [her] sexual orientation." R. at 8. Finally, the civil cover sheet to Hively's lawsuit states "[d]iscrimination based on sex" in her brief description of the case. R. at 9.

First, we note the subtle distinction between Hively's charge and her complaint. Her charge alleges discrimination based only on *Hively's* sexual orientation, whereas her complaint broadly alleges discrimination based on sexual orientation without identifying whose sexual orientation Ivy Tech allegedly considered (e.g., Hively's sexual orientation or the sexual orientation of her romantic or sexual partner). R. at 8. Nevertheless, even if we construe Hively's complaint liberally, because "a Title VII plaintiff cannot bring claims in a lawsuit that were not included in her EEOC charge," we must limit our analysis only to the claim from Hively's EEOC charge that Ivy Tech discriminated against her based on *her own* sexual orientation. *Cheek v. W. & S. Life Ins. Co.,* 31 F.3d 497, 500 (7th Cir. 1994) (citation omitted). We therefore do not consider any allegation that Ivy Tech discriminated against Hively based on the sexual orientation of her partner.[114] We do, however, consider Hively's partner's sex in our analysis – a consideration that, for reasons we will explain in greater detail, lies fully within the ambit of Hively's allegation that Ivy Tech discriminated against her based on her own sexual orientation.

---

[114] Although Hively and her partner *may* share the same sexual orientation, not all partners do (e.g., a heterosexual man in a relationship with a bisexual woman); hence it is entirely plausible that an employer could discriminate against an employee because of that employee's partner's sexual orientation even if the employer has no issue with the *employee's* sexual orientation. However, because Hively's pleadings are limited to discrimination because of *her own* sexual orientation, we reserve to another day ruling on whether a plaintiff plausibly alleges sex discrimination under Title VII based solely on alleged discrimination against the plaintiff's *partner's* sexual orientation.

314   Hively v. Ivy Tech Community College

We also recognize that nowhere in Hively's complaint or any of its attachments does she *actually plead* that she is a woman or a lesbian or use pronouns typically associated with women in America in 2017 (e.g., she, her), although several facts outside of her pleadings suggest as much. For example, Hively's counsel on appeal cites her complaint's allegation of sexual orientation discrimination for the proposition that she is a lesbian. Appellant's Opening Br. at 5 (citing R. at 3). Hively's *pro se* response to Ivy Tech's motion to dismiss in the district court included references to "gay rights," "same sex marriage," and "those individuals who do not identify as heterosexual." R. at 72. Reporters interviewing Hively described her as a lesbian without her protest. Lambda Legal, *Hively Speaks Out After Fed Court Dismisses Discrimination Suit –* WSBT22, YouTube (Aug. 16, 2016), www.youtube.com/watch? v=Avgobv7ex1E. Ivy Tech does not dispute the contention that Hively is a woman or a lesbian. Br. of the Def.-Appellee Ivy Tech Cmty. Coll. of Ind. [hereinafter "Appellee's Br."]. Yet, even under a liberal construction, the fact remains that nowhere in the complaint does Hively actually plead that she is a woman or a lesbian. Rather than reach conclusions of fact that are not pleaded,[115] we instead note that we need not decide Hively's sex or sexual orientation. As our analysis below demonstrates, such conclusions are immaterial. Thus we decline to identify Hively's sex or sexual orientation throughout this opinion.[116]

Moreover, the complaint fails to specify the section(s) of Title VII that Hively alleges Ivy Tech has violated. Indeed, the complaint's citation to "Title VII of the Civil Rights Act of 1964, as amended (i.e., 42 U.S.C. §2000e-5)" is unclear because 42 U.S.C. §2000e-5 (i.e., §706 of Title VII) is concerned only with enforcement of the employment practices made unlawful by 42 U.S.C. §§2000e-2 and 2000e-3 (i.e., §§703 and 704 of Title VII, respectively). Accordingly, affording a liberal construction to the complaint and accepting as true all pleaded facts, we must determine whether these

---

[115] In 1984, in dicta, we cited then-existing medical research for the proposition that, "[b]iologically, sex is defined by chromosomes, internal and external genitalia, hormones, and gonads." *Ulane v. E. Airlines, Inc.*, 742 F.2d 1081, 1083 n.6 (7th Cir. 1984). While we do not endorse this definition in today's opinion, we cite it for the proposition that, when a plaintiff fails to plead her sex, as Hively has failed to do here, determining sex and any sexual orientation that may be associated with that sex (e.g., the term "lesbian," which has traditionally and exclusively been assigned to and adopted by women) requires courts to consider *at least* these factors – none of which are pleaded in Hively's complaint.

[116] Nevertheless, throughout this opinion we use pronouns that, in America in 2017, are commonly associated with women (e.g., she, her) because Hively's counsel and Ivy Tech's counsel both use such pronouns. Appellant's Opening Br. at i; Appellee's Br. at 1. We therefore assume without deciding that they are Hively's personal pronouns.

Hively v. Ivy Tech Community College 315

sections of Title VII "plausibly give rise to an entitlement to relief." *See Thermal Design*, 755 F.3d at 836 (citing *Iqbal*, 556 U.S. at 679).

Section 703(a)(1) of Title VII prohibits employers from discriminating against an individual "because of such individual's ... sex." 42 U.S.C. §2000e-2(a)(1). Section 703(m) of Title VII states that "an unlawful employment practice is established when the complaining party demonstrates that ... sex ... was a motivating factor for any employment practice, even though other factors also motivated the practice." 42 U.S.C. §2000e-2(m). Because we find that these sections of Title VII plausibly entitle Hively to relief for the reasons we will explain, we need not address any other sections of Title VII.

B Circuit Precedent

The issue before us is whether Hively's complaint alleging sexual orientation discrimination plausibly gives rise to relief under sections 703(a)(1) and/or 703 (m) of Title VII. The US Supreme Court has yet to decide this issue explicitly, so we are left to our own precedent – and our precedent is clear: sexual orientation discrimination *is not* sex discrimination under Title VII. *Hamm v. Weyauwega Milk Prods.*, 332 F.3d 1058, 1062 (7th Cir. 2003); *Spearman v. Ford Motor Co.*, 231 F.3d 1080, 1084–85 (7th Cir. 2000); *Hamner v. St. Vincent Hosp. & Health Care Ctr., Inc.*, 224 F.3d 701, 704 (7th Cir. 2000); *see also Evans v. Ga. Reg'l Hosp.*, No. 15–15234, 2017 WL 943925, at *5–16 (11th Cir. Mar. 10, 2017) (collecting cases from our sister circuits holding likewise); *Ulane v. E. Airlines, Inc.*, 742 F.2d 1081, 1084–85 (7th Cir. 1984) (holding, in dicta, that "homosexuals ... do not enjoy Title VII coverage"). Notably, neither our earlier precedent nor that of our sister circuits draws any distinction between section 703(a)(1) and 703(m) of Title VII; instead, they all flatly conclude that sexual orientation is not sex discrimination under *any provision* of Title VII.

Nonetheless, Hively urges us to overrule our precedent. Accordingly, we must review "a series of prudential and pragmatic considerations designed to test the consistency of overruling a prior decision with the ideal of the rule of law, and to gauge the respective costs of reaffirming and overruling a prior case." *Tate v. Showboat Marina Casino P'ship*, 431 F.3d 580, 583 (7th Cir. 2005) (quoting *Planned Parenthood of Se. Pa. v. Casey*, 505 U.S. 833, 854–55 (1992)). Such considerations include whether:

(1) the rule has proven to be intolerable simply in defying practical workability;
(2) the rule is subject to a kind of reliance that would lend a special hardship to the consequences of overruling and add inequity to the cost of repudiation;

316   Hively v. Ivy Tech Community College

(3) related principles of law have so far developed as to have left the old rule
    no more than a remnant of abandoned doctrine; and

(4) facts have so changed or come to be seen so differently as to have
    robbed the old rule of significant application or justification. *Id.*

In this case, there is no evidence that interested parties such as employers, employees, agencies, or the courts have relied on the law in our circuit such that revising it would subject them to any special hardship or inequity. Furthermore, no evidence suggests that any relevant facts have changed to have robbed our extant rule of its application or justification. The only two potential bases that we may invoke to justify jettisoning *stare decisis* here are considerations (3) and (1): whether the law has so far developed that our rule is no more than a remnant of an abandoned doctrine; and/or whether our rule defies practical workability.

And these are exactly the reasons for overruling our precedent. Several discrete legal arguments have arisen since we decided *Hamner* in 2000 that have convinced us unequivocally that *Hamner* and its progeny were wrongly decided – nothing more than the "remnant[s] of an abandoned doctrine." *See Tate*, 431 F.3d at 583 (internal quotations omitted). Indeed, in light of *any* of these arguments, we must conclude that Hively's allegation of sexual orientation discrimination plausibly gives rise to an entitlement to relief under sections 703(a)(1) and 703(m) of Title VII. Moreover, we find that the rule established by *Hamner* defies practical workability in light of the sex-stereotyping arguments discussed *infra*, sections IV.A.1 and IV.B.1. Our analysis of these conclusions follows, but we also note for the sake of completeness that we reject Ivy Tech's arguments with respect to waiver[117]

---

[117] Ivy Tech argues that Hively waived her right to raise certain arguments on appeal because she allegedly failed to raise them below. Appellee's Br. at 8 (quoting *Pond v. Michelin N. Am., Inc.*, 183 F.3d 592, 597 (7th Cir. 1999)). While we have held that "[a]rguments not raised in the district court are waived on appeal," we also have clarified that "this rule has narrow exceptions," including "where, in exceptional cases, justice demands more flexibility." *Pond*, 183 F.3d at 597; *Stern v. U.S. Gypsum, Inc.*, 547 F.2d 1329, 1333 (7th Cir. 1977) (citation omitted). Thus we decline to decide whether Hively sufficiently raised certain arguments in the district court because, even if she did not, justice demands that we afford her flexibility. Hively responded *pro se* to Ivy Tech's motion to dismiss, which means that we must construe her complaint liberally. R. at 74; *Caldwell*, 790 F.2d at 595. She did not have the benefit of counsel's knowledge regarding the legal arguments that have arisen in recent years surrounding the applicability of Title VII to claims of sexual orientation discrimination. Furthermore, we see no special harm to Ivy Tech in affording Hively flexibility because it has had ample opportunity to review and respond to the arguments raised on appeal. Indeed, these arguments have been debated for years, providing further support that Ivy Tech will not be harmed by our consideration of them. Thus we hold that Hively's arguments raised on appeal are not waived.

Hively v. Ivy Tech Community College

and sovereign immunity,[118] and we analyze Title VII without considering any deference that may be owed to the EEOC.[119]

IV ANALYSIS

As noted above, our task is to analyze whether sections 703(a)(1) and/or 703(m) of Title VII plausibly entitle Hively to relief. We hold that they both do.

A Section 703(a)(1)

Section 703(a)(1) of Title VII prohibits discrimination against an individual "because of *such individual's* ... sex." 42 U.S.C. §2000e-2(a)(1) (emphasis added). Thus our inquiry is focused entirely on Hively (i.e., the "individual" referenced in the statute). If discrimination against Hively because of her sexual orientation could plausibly be construed as discrimination because of

---

[118] Ivy Tech argues that, as an alleged arm of the state, it is immune from this suit under the Eleventh Amendment "[i]f protection for sexual orientation was read into [Title VII]," given that Congress allegedly abrogated the states' sovereign immunity *only* with respect to "racial and gender discrimination as opposed to sexual orientation discrimination." Appellee's Br. at 22. Yet Congress has abrogated the states' sovereign immunity with respect to all claims under Title VII. *Fitzpatrick v. Bitzer*, 427 U.S. 445, 456 (1976); *Nanda v. Bd. of Trs. of Univ. of Ill.*, 303 F.3d 817, 831 (7th Cir. 2002). As such, Ivy Tech is not immune from suit here because the judicial branch is not being called upon to enact new laws that may or may not abrogate sovereign immunity, but rather only to "say what the law is," by determining whether Hively has plausibly stated a claim under Title VII as it is currently written. *Marbury v. Madison*, 5 U.S. (1 Cranch) 137, 177 (1803); *see generally* William D. Araiza, *ENDA before it Starts: Section 5 of the Fourteenth Amendment and the Availability of Damages Awards to Gay State Employees under the Proposed Employment Non-Discrimination Act*, 22 B.C. THIRD WORLD L.J. 1 (2002). If Hively has plausibly stated such a claim, *ipso facto* Ivy Tech is not immune from her suit under the Eleventh Amendment.

[119] We recognize that the EEOC – one of the two agencies that administers Title VII, alongside the US Department of Justice (DOJ) – has concluded that allegations of sexual orientation discrimination necessarily state a claim of sex discrimination under 42 U.S.C. §2000e-16 (i.e., §717 of Title VII). *Baldwin v. Foxx*, Appeal No. 0120133080, 2015 WL 4397641 (E.E.O.C. July 16, 2015). Thus, before we analyze other sections of Title VII on a clean slate, we recognize that agency interpretations of a statute that the agency administers may be entitled to deference. *See Chevron U.S.A., Inc. v. Nat. Res. Def. Council, Inc.*, 467 U.S. 837 (1984); *Skidmore v. Swift & Co.*, 323 U.S. 134, 140 (1944). We have yet to clarify whether to afford *Chevron* deference or *Skidmore* weight to such agency interpretations. *Krzalic v. Republic Title Co.*, 314 F.3d 875, 879 (7th Cir. 2002); *see generally* Cass R. Sunstein, *Chevron Step Zero*, 92 VA. L. REV. 187 (2006). Once again, we decline to resolve this question because we would reach the same conclusion that we reach today had the EEOC never decided *Baldwin*. Indeed, determining how much deference or weight to afford *Baldwin* would be necessary *only* if we were inclined to affirm the district court but for *Baldwin* or, perhaps, if the EEOC or DOJ had interpreted Title VII as foreclosing Hively's allegation. Since those are not the facts before us, we reserve ruling on this issue.

318   Hively v. Ivy Tech Community College

Hively's sex, then we must reverse the district court. For the reasons that follow, we hold that discrimination against Hively because of her sexual orientation could plausibly be construed as discrimination because of her sex.

1 Sex Stereotyping

In *Price Waterhouse v. Hopkins*, six members of the US Supreme Court held, *inter alia*, that section 703(a)(1) of Title VII prohibits employers from treating an employee adversely because that employee does not conform to stereotypical gender roles. *Doe v. City of Belleville*, 119 F.3d 563, 580 (7th Cir. 1997) (citing *Price Waterhouse v. Hopkins*, 490 U.S. 228 (1989)), *vacated on other grounds* 523 U.S. 1001 (1998). In other words, "discrimination based on failure to conform to sex stereotypes is discrimination because of sex under Title VII." *Chapman v. City of Danville*, No. 10-CV-2159, 2011 WL 6748511, at *4 (C.D. Ill. Dec. 22, 2011) (citing *Doe*, 119 F.3d at 581) (internal quotations omitted)).

In so holding, the Court embraced antiessentialism, which "asserts that there is no 'essence' to any characteristic so that we cannot assume individuals sharing an identity trait such as ... sex ... will necessarily have in common either world view or other aspects of identity." Suzanne B. Goldberg, *On Making Anti-Essentialist and Social Constructionist Arguments in Courts*, 81 OR. L. REV. 629, 632–33 n.14 (2002) (citing Jane Wong, *The Anti-Essentialism v. Essentialism Debate in Feminist Legal Theory: The Debate and Beyond*, 5 WM. & MARY J. WOMEN & L. 273 (1999)). Indeed, *Price Waterhouse* should be read as an opinion that would "condemn decision making that is tainted by group stereotypes." Cynthia Estlund, *The Story of* Price Waterhouse v. Hopkins, *in* EMPLOYMENT DISCRIMINATION STORIES 65, 66 (Joel William Friedman ed., 2006). To Professor Estlund's point, the Court itself noted that "[w]e are beyond the day when an employer could evaluate employees by assuming or insisting that they matched the stereotype associated with their group, for '[i]n forbidding employers to discriminate against individuals because of their sex, Congress intended to strike at the entire spectrum of disparate treatment of men and women resulting from sex stereotypes.' " *Price Waterhouse*, 490 U.S. at 251 (quoting *Los Angeles Dep't of Water & Power v. Manhart*, 435 U.S. 702, 707 n.13 (1978)). Applying that precedent here, if Hively's sexual orientation could plausibly evidence her failure to conform to prescriptive sex stereotypes, then we must reverse.

In the United States in 2017, it is a truism – much more than a mere plausibility – that a commonly held prescriptive sex stereotype about individuals is that they should be sexually and romantically attracted to individuals of the opposite sex (i.e., heterosexual) as opposed to any other sexual orientation (e.g., homosexual, bisexual, pansexual, asexual). *See, e.g., United States v. Windsor*, 133 S.Ct. 2675, 2693 (2013) (the House of Representatives Report concerning the Defense of Marriage Act, §3 of which remained good law until just four years ago, expressed "moral disapproval of homosexuality" and "a moral conviction that heterosexuality better comports with traditional . . . morality"); Sean Sullivan, *Rick Perry Doesn't Back Down from Comparing Homosexuality to Alcoholism*, WASH. POST (June 16, 2014), www.washingtonpost.com/news/post-politics/wp/2014/06/16/rick-perry-does nt-back-down-from-comparing-homosexuality-to-alcoholism/ (then Texas Governor and subsequently US Secretary of Energy Rick Perry compared homosexuality to alcoholism); Amanda Terkel, *Anti-Gay Stance Still Enshrined in Majority of State GOP Platforms*, HUFFINGTON POST (May 5, 2014), www.huffingtonpost.com/2014/05/05/gop-platform_n_5242421.html (cataloguing current state Republican Party platforms, including that of Oklahoma, which "oppose[s] the promotion of homosexuality," South Carolina, which "considers homosexuality a lifestyle detrimental to the health and well-being of individuals," and Texas, which affirms "that the practice of homosexuality tears at the fabric of society"); Sara I. McClelland *et al.*, *Adapting to Injustice: Young Bisexual Women's Interpretations of Microaggressions*, 40 PSYCH. OF WOMEN Q. 532, 532 (2016) (detailing anecdotal evidence of family members and friends describing study participants' bisexuality as "disgusting");Rod Dreher, *Miley Cyrus > Donald Trump*, THE AMERICAN CONSERVATIVE (Oct. 15, 2016), www.theamericanconservative.com /dreher/miley-cyrus-greater-than-donald-trump/ (decrying Miley Cyrus's pansexuality);Dominique Mosbergen, *Battling Asexual Discrimination, Sexual Violence and "Corrective" Rape*, HUFFINGTON POST (June 20, 2013), www .huffingtonpost.com/2013/06/20/asexual-discrimination_n_3380551.html (relating the results of an empirical university study finding that "asexuals are viewed as less human").

It is vital to note that the stereotype that everyone ought to be heterosexual is *not* the same as a stereotype that individuals ought not act in a manner typically associated with nonheterosexuals (e.g., believing that individuals should act straight) or a belief regarding legal protections that nonheterosexuals should have (e.g., believing that marriage should be between one man and one woman, opposing the explicit expansion of antidiscrimination laws to protect individuals based on their sexual orientation). As these sources aptly demonstrate, the stereotype at issue in the case at bar is pure disdain for people who are not heterosexual regardless of how such people act and regardless of beliefs about the legal protections they should (or should not) have.

320   Hively v. Ivy Tech Community College

This stereotype is so pervasive in our country that it has earned its own infamous label within prominent sociological scholarship: psychological heterosexism, meaning the "individual manifestation of a cultural, ideological system that denies, denigrates, and stigmatizes any nonheterosexual form of behavior, identity, relationship, or community." Gregory M. Herek, *Psychological Heterosexism in the United States, in* LESBIAN, GAY, AND BISEXUAL IDENTITIES OVER THE LIFESPAN: PSYCHOLOGICAL PERSPECTIVES 1, 1–2 (Anthony R. D'Augelli & Charlotte J. Patterson eds., 1995) ("One of the most widespread stereotypes is that a homosexual orientation is inherently related to gender-role nonconformity, such that lesbians uniformly manifest characteristics culturally defined as 'masculine' and gay men manifest 'feminine' qualities"). Notably, psychological heterosexism, which is wielded by an *individual,* differs from cultural heterosexism, which is a *culture's* ideological system of stigmatization itself. *Price Waterhouse* does not require stereotypes to pervade our culture for such stereotypes to run afoul of Title VII. Indeed, if heterosexism were to one day disappear from our culture, an individual's ascription to it would be no less violative of Title VII.

In assessing whether Hively's complaint plausibly alleges sex stereotyping in violation of section 703(a)(1) of Title VII, we note that we would not be the first to invoke heterosexism in this context. Indeed, the EEOC, as well as several courts, have held that allegations of discrimination based on sexual orientation plausibly allege that the plaintiff failed to conform to heterosexist stereotypes. *Baldwin,* 2015 WL 4397641, at *7–8; *Terveer v. Billington,* 34 F.Supp.3d 100, 116 (D.D.C. 2014); *Boutillier v. Hartford Pub. Schs.,* 221 F.Supp.3d 255, 269 (D. Conn. 2016) ("[H]omosexuality is the ultimate gender non-conformity, the prototypical sex stereotyping animus"); *Winstead v. Lafayette Cty. Bd. of Cty. Comm'rs,* 197 F.Supp.3d 1334, 1346 (N.D. Fla. 2016), *rev'd Evans,* 850 F.3d 1248; *Isaacs v. Felder Servs., LLC,* 143 F.Supp.3d 1190, 1194 (M.D. Ala. 2015), *rev'd Evans,* 850 F.3d 1248; *Deneffe v. Skywest, Inc.,* No. 14-CV-00348, 2015 WL 2265373, at *5–6 (D. Colo. May 11, 2015); *Heller v. Columbia Edgewater Country Club,* 195 F.Supp.2d 1212, 1224 (D. Or. 2002) ("[A] jury could find that Cagle repeatedly harassed (and ultimately discharged) Heller because Heller did not conform to Cagle's stereotype of how a woman ought to behave. Heller is attracted to and dates other women, whereas Cagle believes that a woman should be attracted to and date only men."); *Centola v. Potter,* 183 F. Supp.2d 403, 410 (D. Mass. 2002) ("The gender stereotype at work here is that 'real' men should date women, and not other men").

Today, we join their chorus. Employers violate Title VII by discriminating against an employee because she failed to adhere to heterosexist stereotypes. We conclude that Hively's complaint alleging different treatment based on

Hively v. Ivy Tech Community College

sexual orientation plausibly alleges that Ivy Tech treated Hively differently because of such psychological heterosexism and, accordingly, that Ivy Tech discriminated against Hively because of her sex. As such, the district court must be reversed.

Ivy Tech and others have raised myriad counterarguments contending that allegations of sexual orientation discrimination cannot plausibly be grounds for relief under any section of Title VII. We address each of those counter-arguments in section IV.C, *infra*. However, we take this opportunity to address a counterargument not advanced by Ivy Tech but instead adopted by one of our sister circuits that concerns *only* this sex stereotyping argument. Specifically, the US Court of Appeals for the Sixth Circuit rejected applica-tion of the sex-stereotyping theory to the plaintiff's sexual orientation discri-mination claim on the basis that the plaintiff in that case had failed to plead any *appearance* or *behavior* that failed to conform with a sex stereotype, but instead had claimed only that his perceived *status* as a gay man had failed to conform with a sex stereotype (i.e., heterosexism). The Sixth Circuit con-cluded that this pleading failure was the death knell for the plaintiff's claim because *Price Waterhouse* allegedly applies only "where gender non-conformance is demonstrable through the plaintiff's *appearance* or *behavior*." *Vickers v. Fairfield Med. Ctr.*, 453 F.3d 757, 763 (6th Cir. 2006) (emphasis added); *accord Evans*, 850 F.3d at 1259–60 (Pryor, J., concurring).

We disagree. First, we note that Ann Hopkins – the plaintiff in *Price Waterhouse* – was allegedly derided for being "aggressive, unduly harsh, difficult to work with and impatient with staff"; being "macho"; using profan-ity; and behaving in nonstereotypically feminine ways (e.g., Hopkins was allegedly told to "walk more femininely, talk more femininely, dress more femininely, wear make-up, have her hair styled, and wear jewelry"). *Price Waterhouse*, 490 U.S. at 235. While some of these criticisms concern Hopkins' appearance (e.g., her failure to wear jewelry) and behavior (e.g., using profanity), others arguably concern her status (e.g., an aggressive woman). After citing these allegations, the *Price Waterhouse* plurality refer-enced opposition to Hopkins' behavior as a *sufficient* means of evidencing sex stereotyping but did not go so far as to say that opposition to Hopkins' behavior is *necessary* to evidence such stereotypes. *Id.* at 251 (emphasis added) ("An employer who objects to aggressiveness in women but whose positions require this trait places women in an intolerable and impermissible catch 22: out of a job if they *behave* aggressively and out of a job if they do not. Title VII lifts women out of this bind."). The Sixth Circuit's contrary reading of *Price Waterhouse* (i.e., that opposition to an employee's appearance or behavior is *necessary* to evidence sex stereotyping) lacks mooring in the opinion.

322 Hively v. Ivy Tech Community College

Furthermore, it strains logic if we try to draw a distinction between a plaintiff's appearance/behavior and the individual's status (e.g., an aggressive woman in *Price Waterhouse*, a perceived gay man in *Vickers*, Hively's sexual orientation) when the text of the statute itself draws none. To that end, section 703(a)(1) prohibits discrimination against an individual "because of such individual's . . . sex," regardless of how that discrimination manifests. 42 U.S.C. §2000e-2(a)(1). Moreover, such a distinction would defy practical workability because an individual's status is discernable only through appearance or behavior. Indeed, no one miraculously divines someone else's sexual orientation. Only after a person appears or behaves in a particular way (e.g., saying that she is a lesbian) can others discern that person's sexual orientation. Thus, even if the texts of *Price Waterhouse* or Title VII were not as clear as they are, we would be forced to reject the Sixth Circuit's invented distinction between appearance/behavior and status as unworkable. *See* Ann C. McGinley, *Erasing Boundaries: Masculinities, Sexual Minorities, and Employment Discrimination*, 43 U. MICH. J.L. REFORM 713, 738–39 (2010) (citing examples of courts struggling to distinguish between discrimination based on appearance- or behavior-based sex stereotypes and discrimination based on plaintiffs' nonheterosexual status). Accordingly, based on the texts of *Price Waterhouse* and Title VII itself, as well as the need for practical workability in the standard that we establish, we hold that an alleged sex stereotype targeting a plaintiff's nonheterosexual status plausibly alleges sex discrimination under Title VII.[120]

2 Differential Treatment

In *Manhart*, the US Supreme Court held that an employer violates section 703 (a)(1) of Title VII if evidence shows "treatment of a person in a manner which but for that person's sex would be different." *Manhart*, 435 U.S. at 711 (internal quotations omitted); *accord Shepherd v. Slater Steels Corp.*, 168 F.3d 998, 1009 (7th Cir. 1999) ("So long as the [male] plaintiff demonstrates in some manner that he would not have been treated in the same way had he been a woman, he has proven sex discrimination"). Applying *Manhart*, among other precedents, we concluded in *Hall v. Nalco Co.*, 534 F.3d 644, 645 (7th Cir. 2008), that Cheryl Hall's employer violated section 703(a)(1) by terminating Hall because

[120] We note that we too are guilty of propagating this false distinction between appearance/behavior and status. *Doe*, 119 F.3d at 580 ("The Supreme Court's decision in [*Price Waterhouse*], makes clear that Title VII does not permit an employee to be treated adversely because his or her *appearance or conduct* does not conform to stereotypical gender roles") (emphasis added). However, we are convinced that this language was dicta because it was immaterial to our holding in *Doe* and, in any event, we clarify today that any such distinction is meaningless.

she underwent a medical procedure to treat infertility even though infertility is a sex-neutral condition. The medical procedure at issue – surgical impregnation – was allegedly performed only on women on account of their child-bearing capacity.[121] *Id.* Therefore, we rightly decided that, even though Hall's allegations *could* have been conceptualized in a sex-neutral manner (i.e., discrimination against employees of any sex who seek infertility treatment), Hall stated a cognizable sex discrimination claim under section 703(a)(1) because her allegations also could be stated in a sex-specific manner (e.g., discrimination against *women* who seek surgical fertility treatment). *Id.* at 646–49. Both descriptions could have described what happened; we gave Hall the benefit of the doubt in finding her Title VII claim cognizable.

Applying those precedents, we see that Hively and Hall have much in common. Hively has plausibly alleged that Ivy Tech violated section 703(a)(1) because it is plausible based on Hively's complaint that Ivy Tech rejected gynephilic[122] *women* for full-time employment, but advanced gynephilic *men* to full-time employment. According to a plausible reading of Hively's complaint, but for Hively's sex (i.e., had she been a gynephilic man), she would not have been denied full-time employment and promotions. That we *could* conceptualize Hively's allegations in an allegedly sex-neutral manner (i.e., Ivy Tech prohibited Hively from full-time employment and promotions because she is homosexual, and it would have likewise prohibited a gay man from the same) is wholly irrelevant. *See Hall*, 534 F.3d at 646–49. Both descriptions could have described what Hively alleges happened; as per our precedent, we give her the benefit of the doubt in finding her claim cognizable. In doing do, we comport not only with our precedent, but also with the holdings of the EEOC and several courts. *Baldwin*, 2015 WL 4397641, at *5; *Isaacs*, 143 F.Supp.3d at 1193–94; *Heller*, 195 F.Supp.2d at 1222–23; *see also Videckis v. Pepperdine Univ.*, 150 F.Supp.3d 1151, 1161 (C.D. Cal. 2015) (dicta); *Pearce v. Mayfield School* [2001] EWCA (Civ) 1347 [7], [2002] ICR 198 (Eng.) (Baroness Brenda Marjorie Hale of Richmond, writing as a Justice on the

---

[121] Upon reflection, we now recognize that surgical impregnation is not, in fact, a medical procedure performed *only* on women. *See, e.g.*, Heather Osterman-Davis, *I'm a Cis Woman. My Husband's a Trans Man. This Is How We Made 2 Babies*, TIME (June 17, 2016), http://time .com/4259940/transgender-family/ (detailing an example of a man's surgical impregnation). While we regret our statements to the contrary in *Hall*, the actual sex-neutral nature of surgical impregnation is irrelevant in the case at bar; rather, what matters here is that we based our analysis in *Hall* on our flawed belief that surgical impregnation was sex-specific. Based on that flawed belief, we held that the description of that medical procedure in sex-neutral terms did not inoculate the employer against Hall's claims of sex discrimination. It is only that holding of *Hall* that we rely upon today.

[122] Gynephilia refers to being aroused by adult women. Anne Fausto-Sterling, SEXING THE BODY: GENDER POLITICS AND THE CONSTRUCTION OF SEXUALITY 6 (2000).

324   Hively v. Ivy Tech Community College

England and Wales Court of Appeal before she became the first woman on the Supreme Court of the United Kingdom, would have held that "[t]hose who treat homosexuals of either sex less favourably than they treat heterosexuals do so because of their sex: not because they love men (or women) but because they are men who love men (or women who love women)," but her fellow Justices disagreed).

3 Relationship Discrimination

The EEOC and several courts recognize that discrimination based on an employee's *association* with a person of a protected classification violates Title VII. *See, e.g., Baldwin,* 2015 WL 4397641, at *6 (emphasis added) ("Sexual orientation discrimination is also sex discrimination because it is *associational* discrimination on the basis of sex"); *Holcomb v. Iona Coll.,* 521 F.3d 130, 138 (2d Cir. 2008) (emphasis added) ("[A]n employer may violate Title VII if it takes action against an employee because of the employee's *association* with a person of another race"). However, *associational* discrimination is a misnomer. A more accurate way of describing this type of unlawful conduct is *relationship* discrimination, because section 703(a)(1) demands that we consider only the sex of *the employee* and not the sex of anyone else. *See, e.g., Floyd v. Amite Cty. Sch. Dist.,* 581 F.3d 244, 249 (5th Cir. 2009) ("Title VII prohibit[s] discrimination against an employee on the basis of a personal *relationship* between the employee [of a particular race] and a person of a different race"); 42 U.S.C. §2000e-2(a)(1) (emphasis added) (prohibiting discrimination "because of *such individual's* ... sex"). Thus an employer violates section 703(a)(1) if it discriminates against an employee based on the employee's sex as viewed through the lens of a sex-based relationship (e.g., a same-sex relationship). In contrast, an employee's mere association with someone of a particular sex, untethered to the sex of the employee, is irrelevant to section 703(a)(1).

Working within that framework, Professor Schwartz provides a cogent summary of such relationship discrimination as applied to claims of sexual orientation discrimination:

> Title VII protects against discrimination because of an individual's sex when viewed *in relation to others* ... After all, sexual orientation is an inherently relational concept. For example, if a female is discriminated against for being a lesbian, she is discriminated against for her sex (female) *in relation to her sexual relationships with others* (female). Therefore, her claim for discrimination on the basis of her sexual orientation is necessarily a claim that she is

being discriminated against on the basis of her sex when viewed in relation to others.

> Victoria Schwartz, *Title VII: A Shift from Sex to Relationships*, 35 HARV. J.L. & GENDER 209, 248 (2012) (emphasis added).

Indeed, several courts have held that discrimination against an employee in a relationship with someone of a different *race* as the employee constitutes discrimination "because of [the employee's] race." 42 U.S.C. §2000e-2(a)(1); *Holcomb*, 521 F.3d at 138; *Tetro v. Elliot Popham Pontiac, Oldsmobile, Buick & GMC Trucks*, 173 F.3d 988, 994 (6th Cir. 1999); *Parr v. Woodmen of the World Life Ins. Co.*, 791 F.2d 888, 892 (11th Cir. 1986); *Gresham v. Waffle House, Inc.*, 586 F.Supp. 1442, 1445 (N.D. Ga. 1984); *Holiday v. Belle's Rest.*, 409 F.Supp. 904, 908–09 (W.D. Pa. 1976); *Whitney v. Greater N.Y. Corp. of Seventh-Day Adventists*, 401 F.Supp. 1363, 1366 (S.D.N.Y. 1975).[123] It is no great leap, therefore, to similarly hold that discrimination against an employee in a relationship with someone of the same *sex* as the employee constitutes discrimination "because of [the employee's]... sex." *See Bond v. Atkinson*, 728 F.3d 690, 692 (7th Cir. 2013) ("[S]ex discrimination is treated the same [as race discrimination] under Title VII").

This conceptualization of "but for" discrimination in *Manhart* rings especially true in the case at bar. Hively alleges that Ivy Tech discriminated against her based on her sexual orientation, meaning the relationship that Hively had (real or perceived) with someone of a particular sex. That relationship is alleged to have incited Ivy Tech's discriminatory actions *only* because Hively may be a gynephilic woman and not a gynephilic man. Accordingly, we echo the sentiments of the EEOC and concur with the conclusion of several courts that discrimination based on a plaintiff's relationship with a same-sex individual constitutes sex discrimination. *Baldwin*, 2015 WL 4397641, at *6–7; *Boutillier*, 221 F.Supp.3d at 268; *see also Latta v. Otter*, 771 F.3d 456, 479–90 (9th Cir. 2014) (Berzon, J., concurring); *Baehr v. Lewin*, 852 P.2d 44, 64 (Haw. 1993), *abrogated by Obergefell v. Hodges*, 135 S.Ct. 2584 (2015).

4 "Sex Plus" Discrimination

In its *per curiam* opinion in *Phillips v. Martin Marietta Corp.*, the Supreme Court held that an employer's policy of not accepting job applications from women with preschool-age children, but accepting applications from men

---

[123] Some of these courts use the misnomer "associational" discrimination despite the fact that the discrimination at issue involves a relationship between the plaintiff and a third party.

with preschool-age children, violated section 703(a)(1) of Title VII because it unlawfully permitted "one hiring policy for women and another for men." 400 U.S. 542, 543–44 (1971); *see also Sprogis v. United Air Lines*, 444 F.2d 1194, 1198 (7th Cir. 1971) (employer policy prohibiting married female flight attendants, but allowing married male flight attendants, violated section 703(a)(1)). We have yet to determine whether *Phillips* created an independent theory of "sex plus" discrimination under Title VII, or merely provided "a heuristic . . . developed in the context of Title VII to affirm that plaintiffs can, under certain circumstances, survive summary judgment even when not all members of a disfavored class are discriminated against." *See Coffman v. Indianapolis Fire Dep't*, 578 F.3d 559, 563 (7th Cir. 2009); *Back v. Hastings on Hudson Union Free Sch. Dist.*, 365 F.3d 107, 118 (2d Cir. 2004). Again, such distinctions are immaterial here. What matters is only that employers cannot enforce one policy for women and another for men without violating section 703(a)(1).

That is precisely what Hively alleges Ivy Tech did here. Based on the allegations in the complaint, it is plausible that Ivy Tech rejected gynephilic *women* for full-time employment and promotions, but accepted gynephilic *men* for full-time employment and promotions. In the parlance of *Phillips* and other "sex plus" discrimination cases, Hively has plausibly alleged that Ivy Tech discriminated against her based on her sex, *see supra* section IV.A.2, plus her gynephilia. As we explained, that we could conceptualize Hively's allegation in an allegedly sex-neutral manner is irrelevant. *See Hall*, 534 F.3d at 646–49. As such, Hively has either pleaded an independent theory of "sex plus" discrimination under Title VII, or we have identified yet another heuristic for explaining why Hively's complaint plausibly alleges that Ivy Tech discriminated against her because of her sex. Either way we look at it, Hively has plausibly alleged a violation of section 703(a)(1).

In sum, we find that a claim of sexual orientation discrimination necessarily states a claim of sex discrimination. Our conclusion is not all that shocking given that one cannot define the term "sexual orientation" without considering sex. Am. Psychological Ass'n, DEFINITION OF TERMS: SEX, GENDER, GENDER IDENTITY, SEXUAL ORIENTATION (Feb. 2011), www.apa.org /pi/lgbt/resources/sexuality-definitions.pdf ("Sexual orientation refers to the sex of those to whom one is sexually and romantically attracted"); *see also Baldwin*, 2015 WL 4397641, at *5. Accordingly, we conclude that Hively has plausibly alleged that Ivy Tech would not have discriminated against her "but for" her sex, meaning that she has plausibly alleged a violation of section 703(a)(1).

B *Section 703(m)*

Section 703(m) of Title VII states that "an unlawful employment practice is established when the complaining party demonstrates that race, color, religion, sex, or national origin was a motivating factor for any employment practice, even though other factors also motivated the practice." 42 U.S.C. §2000e-2(m). Section 706(g)(2)(B)(ii) of Title VII limits plaintiffs' remedies if defendants prove that they would have taken the same action absent the impermissible motivating factor. *Id.*; §2000e-5(g)(2)(B)(ii). Traditionally, courts have interpreted these sections as establishing the extent of defendants' defense in such "mixed motive" claims only in situations where plaintiffs prove an unlawful employment practice under *some other* section of Title VII (e.g., §703(a)(1)). *See, e.g., Smith v. Wilson*, 705 F.3d 674, 679–80 (7th Cir. 2013); *see also Desert Palace, Inc. v. Costa*, 539 U.S. 90, 94 n.1 (2003) ("This case does not require us to decide when, if ever, [§703(m)] applies outside of the mixed-motive context").

However, we see no reason why section 703(m) cannot stand on its own as a cause of action independent of other Title VII sections. Comparing the text of section 703(m) with that of section 703(a)(1) demonstrates that, while section 703(a)(1) prohibits discrimination against an individual "because of *such individual's* ... sex," section 703(m) is broader, making unlawful any demonstration that "sex ... was a motivating factor for any employment practice." 42 U.S.C. §2000e-2(a)(1) (emphasis added); 42 U.S.C. §2000e-2 (m). Section 703(m) lacks the narrowing "such individual's" language of section 703(a)(1). Section 703(m) therefore prohibits the consideration of sex as a motivating factor in *any* capacity, whereas section 703(a)(1) prohibits only the consideration of the *plaintiff's* sex as a motivating factor. In other words, although section 703(m) certainly establishes a causation standard applicable to "mixed motive" claims brought under other sections of Title VII (e.g., §703 (a)(1)), section 703(m) can also be invoked as its own cause of action because it makes unlawful what other sections of Title VII do not: consideration of a *nonplaintiff's* sex.

As demonstrated, *supra* section IV.A.3, section 703(a)(1) prohibits not only the consideration of the plaintiff's sex in isolation (i.e., without regard to anyone else), but also the consideration of the plaintiff's sex as a component in a relationship between the plaintiff and another individual (e.g., a romantic relationship between two women). Section 703(m) goes even further than this. It prohibits any consideration of *anyone's* sex as a motivating factor for an adverse employment action. Period. Theoretically, section 703(m) would prohibit an employer from docking the pay of an employee (regardless of that employee's sex) because that employee expressed interest in voting for more women in upcoming congressional elections, even though the female candidates have no relationship with the employee. Similarly, section 703(m) would bar a manager from firing his entire department (regardless of those employees' sexes) in protest because he found out that he was going to be replaced by a woman, even though the terminated employees have no relationship with that woman. Under section 703(a)(1), these employees would not state a cognizable claim because the employers' actions were not "because of *such individual's* ... sex." Yet, section 703(m) contains no such narrowing language. In these examples, the employers considered *someone's* sex as a motivating factor in their decision-making process, so the employers violated section 703(m).

Unfortunately, we find no support for our interpretation in the legislative history of the bill that birthed section 703(m): the Civil Rights Act of 1991 (1991 CRA). Indeed, both of the House of Representatives reports summarizing the 1991 CRA make no mention of the Act's intention to broadly prohibit any consideration of sex (or the other protected classes) as a motivating factor for an adverse employment action; rather, the reports state that the intent of sections 703(m) and 706(g)(2)(B)(ii) is to overrule a portion of *Price Waterhouse*. In *Price Waterhouse*, the Court concluded that, once an employee proves that an unlawful consideration played a part in the employer's decision, the burden shifts to the employer to prove that it would have taken the same action even if it had not been motivated by that unlawful factor. Such proof would amount to a *complete* defense. In passing the 1991 Act, however, Congress designed the law to permit a plaintiff to hold an employer liable once the plaintiff proves that the illegal consideration was a motivating factor for the adverse employment action. The employer's "same action defense" merely limits the remedies a plaintiff can recover. H.R. Rep. 102–40, pt. 1, at 45–49 (1991), *as reprinted in* 1991 U.S.C.C.A.N. 549, 583–87; H.R. Rep. 102–40, pt. 2, at 2–3, 65–66 (1991), *as reprinted in* 1991 U.S.C.C.A.N. 694, 695, 751–52.

Similarly, the congressional testimony regarding the 1991 CRA failed to address whether it should be interpreted as broadly as its text plainly reads; instead, testimony echoes the substance of the House of Representatives reports. 137 Cong. Rec. E3832-01, E3833 (1991) (statement of Rep. Julian C. Dixon); 137 Cong. Rec. H9505-01, H9529 (1991) (statement of Rep. Don Edwards); 137 Cong. Rec. S15472-01, S15476 (1991) (statement of Sen. Bob Dole); 137 Cong. Rec. S15445-02, S15464 (1991) (statement of Sen. Chris Dodd); 137 Cong. Rec. S15388-01, S15395 (1991) (statement of Sen. Howell Heflin). Finally, the title of the operative section of the 1991 CRA arguably counsels against interpreting section 703(m) as its own cause of action, instead suggesting that it merely *clarifies* existing Title VII prohibitions. Civil Rights

Act of 1991, S. 1745, 102nd Cong., 105 Stat. 1071, §107 (1991) (emphasis added) ("*Clarifying* prohibition against impermissible consideration of race, color, religion, sex, or national origin in employment practices").

To this point, the US Supreme Court recently stated, in dicta and without any analysis, that section 703(m) "is not itself a substantive bar on discrimination. Rather, it is a rule that establishes the causation standard for proving a violation defined elsewhere in Title VII." *Univ. of Texas Sw. Med. Ctr. v. Nassar*, 570 U.S. 338, 355 (2013); *see also* Jessica A. Clarke, *Protected Class Gatekeeping*, 92 N.Y.U. L. REV. 101, 114 n.81 (2017) (examining a potential justification for this dicta); Sandra F. Sperino, *Justice Kennedy's Big New Idea*, 96 B.U. L. REV. 1789, 1822–23 (2016) (same). We can find no court analyzing this dictum and only one court that cited it at all, albeit in passing. *See Chavez v. Credit Nation Auto Sales, LLC*, 641 F. App'x 883, 888 (11th Cir. 2016). Significantly, no court has applied this dictum to bar an independent section 703(m) cause of action.

Respectfully, although "[t]his Court should respect *considered* Supreme Court dicta," we find the Supreme Court's dicta in *Nassar* to be a fleeting comment unsupported by any analysis, let alone detailed analysis. *Nichol v. Pullman Standard, Inc.*, 889 F.2d 115, 120 n.8 (7th Cir. 1989) (emphasis added). We are not bound to adhere to such dicta. *Tokoph v. United States*, 774 F.3d 1300, 1304 (10th Cir. 2014), *as amended on reh'g* (Jan. 26, 2015); *Lebamoff Enters., Inc. v. Huskey*, 666 F.3d 455, 467 (7th Cir. 2012) (Hamilton, J., concurring) (rejecting a "passing comment" that "does not amount to even a considered dictum"); *United States ex rel. Garibaldi v. Orleans Par. Sch. Bd.*, 397 F.3d 334, 338 (5th Cir. 2005). Moreover, we are troubled by the prospect of our interpreting section 703(m) more narrowly than its text demands based only on such dicta and the title of the operative section of a bill. Indeed, "statutory prohibitions often go beyond the principal evil [that Congress was concerned with when it enacted the statute] to cover reasonably comparable evils, and it is ultimately *the provisions of our laws* rather than the principal concerns of our legislators by which we are governed." *Oncale v. Sundowner Offshore Servs., Inc.*, 523 U.S. 75, 79 (1998) (emphasis added). In short, absent ambiguity or an unreasonable result, neither of which exists here, we are best served by following the text. Thus we hold that section 703(m) prohibits consideration of *anyone's* sex as a motivating factor for an adverse employment action.

1 Discrimination Based on Hively's Sex

Discrimination based on *anyone's* sex necessarily includes discrimination based on *the plaintiff's* sex (i.e., the sort of discrimination prohibited by

330 Hively v. Ivy Tech Community College

§703(a)(1)), meaning all cognizable section 703(a)(1) claims are necessarily cognizable and independent section 703(m) claims, as well. Turning to the case at bar, all of the grounds upon which Hively plausibly alleges a violation of section 703(a)(1) must necessarily plausibly allege a violation of section 703(m). *See supra* sections IV.A.1–4. For these additional reasons, we must reverse.

2 Discrimination Based on Hively's Partner's Sex

Hively's complaint, which alleges discrimination based on Hively's sexual orientation, plausibly invokes *Hively's partner's* sex for the same reason that it plausibly invokes *Hively's* sex. R. at 8. Indeed, identifying a plaintiff's sexual orientation requires knowledge of the sex of that plaintiff as well as the sex of another person (real or hypothetical) to whom the plaintiff may be romantically or sexually attracted. In section IV.A.2, *supra*, we demonstrated that Ivy Tech plausibly committed discrimination based on sex because Hively alleges that had she been a gynephilic man instead of a gynephilic woman (i.e., if Hively were a male employee interested in a relationship with a woman), Ivy Tech would not have denied her full-time employment and promotions. On the flip side of the same coin, Ivy Tech plausibly committed discrimination based on sex because Hively alleges that had *her partner* been a gynephilic man instead of a gynephilic woman (i.e., if Hively were a female employee interested in a relationship with a man), Ivy Tech similarly would not have denied Hively full-time employment and promotions.

Applying that logic, we conclude that Hively has plausibly alleged that Ivy Tech violated section 703(m) because "sex" (i.e., the sex of Hively's known or perceived partner) is alleged to be "a motivating factor for any employment practice." *See* 42 U.S.C. §2000e-2(m). Indeed, it is a necessary corollary of any claim of discrimination based on a plaintiff's same-sex relationship, in which the defendant necessarily is alleged to have considered the sex of a nonplaintiff as part of that relationship, that the plaintiff not only (1) has plausibly alleged discrimination based on the plaintiff's own sex under sections 703(a)(1) and 703 (m), but also (2) has plausibly alleged discrimination based on the sex of the plaintiff's real or perceived partner under section 703(m) (which prohibits discrimination based on the sex of nonplaintiffs, whereas section 703(a)(1) does not). *See supra* section IV.A.3. For this additional reason, we conclude that Hively has plausibly alleged a violation of Title VII, and we must reverse the district court.

C Counterarguments

We now turn to myriad counterarguments raised by Ivy Tech and other courts. Upon examination, none of these counterarguments convince us to affirm.

First, Ivy Tech argues that our holding today would "judicially amend Title VII" and amount to a "clear violation of separation of powers." Appellee's Br. at 9 (quoting *Schroeder v. Hamilton Sch. Dist.*, 282 F.3d 946, 951 (7th Cir. 2002)). Not so. It is our task to "say what the law is," not what the law should be. *See Marbury*, 5 U.S. at 177. We take no position on whether the other coequal branches of our government should enact a law clarifying whether claims of sexual orientation discrimination plausibly allege violations of sections 703(a) (1) and 703(m); today, we hold only that the law is already thus. In doing so, we discharge our constitutionally ordained duty as per *Marbury* and nothing more.

Second, Ivy Tech directs us to legislative history as support for its argument, as do many of our sister circuits. Ivy Tech explicitly argues that Congress has blessed its position by twice amending Title VII (i.e., with the 1991 CRA and with the Lilly Ledbetter Fair Pay Act of 2009, Pub. L. 111–2, S. 181, 111th Cong., 123 Stat. 5 (2009)) without explicitly endorsing Hively's claim, despite judicial opinions in existence in 1991 and 2009 that allegedly foreclosed Hively's contention, and by failing to enact legislation explicitly adding "sexual orientation" alongside "sex" in sections 703(a)(1) and 703(m). Appellee's Br. at 14–15. To that end, several of our sister circuits have relied, in part, on Congress's failure to enact such legislation as one reason why they reject the plausibility of relief for allegations of sexual orientation discrimination under Title VII. *See, e.g., Medina v. Income Support Div.*, 413 F.3d 1131, 1135 (10th Cir. 2005); *Bibby v. Phila. Coca Cola Bottling Co.*, 260 F.3d 257, 261 (3d Cir. 2001); *Simonton v. Runyon*, 232 F.3d 33, 35 (2nd Cir. 2000); *see also Evans*, 850 F.3d at 1259–60 (Pryor, J., concurring); *Rene v. MGM Grand Hotel, Inc.*, 305 F.3d 1061, 1076 (9th Cir. 2002) (Hug, J., dissenting).

We respectfully disagree with Ivy Tech and our sister circuits. Absent ambiguity or unreasonableness, we focus only on what Congress *has* done (i.e., the text of the statute) and not what Congress *has not* done, since "congressional silence lacks persuasive significance." *Brown v. Gardner*, 513 U.S. 115, 121 (1994) (quotations and citations omitted); *accord Pension Ben. Guar. Corp. v. LTV Corp.*, 496 U.S. 633, 650 (1990) ("Congressional inaction lacks persuasive significance because several equally tenable inferences may be drawn from such inaction, including the inference that the existing legislation already incorporated the offered change"). Applying that standard here, there is no ambiguity in the conclusion that we reach, and there is certainly no

332 Hively v. Ivy Tech Community College

argument that prohibiting such discrimination would be unreasonable. As such, we conclude that examining the legislative intent here would be inappropriate.

Yet even if we attempt to examine the legislative intent here, there is simply no *evidence* supporting Ivy Tech's contention. Indeed, we can find no congressional report or floor statement from any member of Congress from 1964, 1991, 2009, or otherwise that addresses whether an employee claiming sexual orientation discrimination plausibly alleges a violation of sections 703(a)(1) or 703(m) of Title VII. Ivy Tech assumes, *ex nihilo*, that Congress did not intend for plaintiffs alleging sexual orientation discrimination to plausibly allege such violations. Presumably, Ivy Tech reaches its conclusion based on its hypotheses – ones shared by this Court – that the majority of Americans (and thus the majority of Congress) in 1964 and 1991 (but perhaps not in 2009) *probably would have* opposed any law permitting sexual orientation discrimination claims to be cognizable under Title VII and, similarly, *probably would have* opposed prohibiting sexual orientation discrimination in the workplace. However, we decline to take the drastic measure of overturning the text of Title VII based on the presumed, but entirely undocumented, legislative intent of Congress.

Finally, even assuming for the sake of argument that we take as gospel the probable view of Congress in 1964 and 1991, we decline to interpret congressional silence, legislative inaction, or the probable American zeitgeist from bygone eras as the basis for interpreting the text of Title VII as something other than what it says. "In short, it is what Congress says, not what Congress means to say, that becomes the law of the land. Statutory interpretation is therefore an exercise best grounded in the text of the statute itself." *Bernstein v. Bankert*, 733 F.3d 190, 211 (7th Cir. 2013).

V CONCLUSION

Advocates for employment antidiscrimination protections based upon sexual orientation have adopted a rallying cry that points out the logical dissonance of our federal laws – one cited by the panel below in the instant appeal: gay and lesbian employees can be married legally and fired shortly thereafter for that very act. *See, e.g.*, Lisa Bornstein & Megan Bench, *Married on Sunday, Fired on Monday: Approaches to Federal LGBT Civil Rights Protections*, 22 WM. & MARY J. WOMEN & L. 31 (2015–16); *Hively*, 830 F.3d at 714 ("The cases as they stand do, however, create a paradoxical legal landscape in which a person can be married on Saturday and then fired on Monday for just that act"). Their argument is that a society that extends "equal dignity in the eyes of the law" to

Hively v. Ivy Tech Community College

gay and lesbian couples by permitting them to legally marry, as ours does, should extend to those couples the same equal dignity by forbidding employers from discriminating against them on account of their sexual orientation. *Obergefell*, 135 S.Ct. at 2608.

While their argument certainly has normative and emotional appeal, whether same-sex marriage is protected by the US Constitution or not, Title VII stands on its own. Had we considered the case at bar on the day before *Obergefell* was decided or even the day before we struck down Indiana's ban on same-sex marriage in *Baskin v. Bogan*, 766 F.3d 648 (7th Cir. 2014), we still would have held as we do today, as have tribunals in countries where bans on same-sex marriage persist. *Toonen v. Australia*, UN Human Rights Comm., Commc'n No. 488/1992, U.N. Doc. CCPR/C/50/D/488/1992, at ¶8.7 (1994) (the United Nations Human Rights Committee struck down Tasmania's ban on consensual sodomy, in part, by interpreting references to "sex" in Art. 2(1) and (26) of the International Covenant on Civil and Political Rights as "including sexual orientation"); *Suratt v Attorney Gen.* [2004] Trin. & Tobago C.A. (Civ) 64, [43] (the Court of Appeal of Trinidad and Tobago held that "specifically excluding a particular category of persons, on the ground of sexual orientation, from the protection afforded by [local law] to others, is to deny them a fundamental right on a basis analogous to [sex]"), *rev'd* [2007] UKPC 55.[124] Hively alleges that Ivy Tech discriminated on the basis of her sexual orientation. Her allegations plausibly entitle her to relief under sections 703(a)(1) and 703(m) of Title VII. That is the end of the matter.

* * *

We reverse the district court's grant of Ivy Tech's motion to dismiss and remand for further proceedings consistent with this opinion. We overturn our circuit precedent to the extent that it is inconsistent with this holding.

It is so ordered.

---

[124] Neither *Toonen* nor *Suratt* provides an analysis of their conclusions.

7

Systemic Claims and Gender: Proving Disparate Treatment and Impact

Commentary on *AFSCME v. State of Washington*

STEPHANIE BORNSTEIN

INTRODUCTION: THE GENDER PAY GAP, FROZEN IN AMBER

It is hard to believe that, more than half a century after federal law outlawed sex discrimination in employment,[1] there is still a significant gender pay gap in the United States. As of 2019, when comparing only those working full-time, year-round, all women earn 82 cents on the dollar to men annually; Black and Latina women earn much less, at 62 and 54 cents respectively.[2] Yet, even harder to believe, the current US gender pay gap has been stuck at this ratio *for two decades*. After narrowing from the 1960s until about 2000, improvement in the gender pay gap simply stopped.[3] Women have been averaging about 75 to 80 cents on men's dollar every year since.

There is no shortage of debate on the gender pay gap and its measurement and causes. Recent economic data, however, confirm one major source of persistent pay disparities: gender workforce segregation.[4] In the US economy, most jobs are "gendered," performed predominantly by one sex, so that they are viewed as either masculine (e.g., firefighter or truck driver) or feminine

---

[1] Title VII of the Civil Rights Act of 1964, 42 U.S.C. §2000e *et seq.*; Equal Pay Act of 1963, 29 U.S. C. §206(d).

[2] Am. Ass'n of Univ. Women, THE SIMPLE TRUTH ABOUT THE GENDER PAY GAP 1 (Fall 2019), www .aauw.org/app/uploads/2020/02/Simple-Truth-Update-2019_v2-002.pdf (analyzing data from the US Census Bureau's Current Population Survey).

[3] Elise Gould *et al.*, *What Is the Gender Pay Gap and Is It Real? The Complete Guide to How Women Are Paid Less than Men and Why it Can't Be Explained Away*, ECONOMY POLICY INSTITUTE 1 (2016), www.epi.org/publication/what-is-the-gender-pay-gap-andis-it-real/.

[4] *See generally* Stephanie Bornstein, *Equal Work*, 77 MD. L. REV. 581 (2018); Deborah L. Rhode, *Occupational Inequality*, 1988 DUKE L.J. 1207.

(e.g., teacher or nurse).[5] Data shows that "masculine" jobs are paid more than "feminine" jobs, even when the work is substantially the same.[6] As more women enter jobs predominantly held by men, the pay for those positions goes down.[7] This phenomenon reflects that gender stereotypes are built into societal structures that we perceive as "neutral," such as the "free market." It also reflects a missed opportunity: a potential course correction over thirty years ago on the issue of "comparable worth" that might have significantly reduced today's gender pay gap. The case of *AFSCME v. Washington*[8] represents the unfortunate turning point.

THE ORIGINAL OPINION: A PATH FORECLOSED

By 1985, the year of the *AFSCME* decision, the problem of the gender pay gap was already the subject of significant debate. Both the Equal Pay Act of 1963 (EPA),[9] which requires equal pay for "equal work" regardless of sex, and Title VII of the Civil Rights Act of 1964,[10] which prohibits discrimination in compensation and other terms and conditions of employment on the basis of sex and other protected classes, had long been in effect. Yet from 1960 to 1980, the pay gap showed virtually no improvement, with all women averaging between 57 and 60 cents on men's dollar annually.[11] Advocates began to argue for a new approach to reach the gender workforce segregation they believed contributed to the problem: a recognition of a theory of "comparable worth," under which employers would be required to pay the same wages for jobs that were of "equal worth or value," but predominantly filled by one sex.[12] Whether comparable worth arguments could fit within existing federal law was an open question.

Until 1981, the US Equal Employment Opportunity Commission (EEOC) – the federal agency responsible for enforcing Title VII, then led

---

[5] Women's Bureau, US Dep't. of Labor, *Occupations*, www.dol.gov/wb/stats/Occupations.htm (*last visited* Apr. 15, 2020).

[6] *See* Francine D. Blau & Lawrence M. Kahn, *The Gender Wage Gap: Extent, Trends, and Explanations*, NBER Working Paper No. 21913, 27 (Jan. 2016), www.nber.org/papers/w21913.

[7] *See* Asaf Levanon *et al.*, *Occupational Feminization and Pay: Assessing Causal Dynamics Using 1950–2000 U.S. Census Data*, 88 SOCIAL FORCES 865, 875–87 (2009).

[8] 770 F.2d 1401 (9th Cir. 1985).

[9] 29 U.S.C. §206(d).

[10] 42 U.S.C. §2000e-2.

[11] Nat'l Committee on Pay Equity, *The Wage Gap over Time: In Real Dollars, Women See a Continuing Gap*, www.pay-equity.org/info-time.html (*last visited* Oct. 15, 2018) (analyzing data from the US Census Bureau).

[12] *See* Bornstein, *supra* note 4, at 616–19; Nancy Levit & Joan Mahoney, *The Future of Comparable Worth Theory*, 56 U. COLO. L. REV. 99, 100 (1984); Paul Weiler, *The Wages of Sex: The Uses and Limits of Comparable Worth*, 99 HARV. L. REV. 1728, 1728–29 (1986).

336 AFSCME v. State of Washington

under the Carter administration by Eleanor Holmes Norton – supported a comparable worth approach.[13] President Reagan, however, described comparable worth as a "cockamamie idea," and the EEOC chair he appointed in 1982, Clarence Thomas, rejected it. In 1984, the year between the district and appellate court rulings in *AFSCME*, the US Commission on Civil Rights held a two-day hearing, featuring sixteen experts arguing both for and against comparable worth.[14] The Commission's resulting report – released one week after the *AFSCME* oral argument before the Ninth Circuit Court of Appeals – recommended that the EEOC and other federal agencies reject comparable worth.[15] "If the wage gap is in large part the result of nondiscriminatory factors [such as] familial and societal socialization," the Commission explained, "then an antidiscrimination 'remedy' imposed on employers is the wrong answer": "anti-intellectual" and "vague notions about 'societal discrimination'" were not enough to make the employer bear the remedial burden.[16]

The plaintiffs in *AFSCME* were two unions representing 15,500 employees of the state of Washington who worked in job categories filled at least 70 percent by female workers.[17] The state set pay rates based on "prevailing market rates" derived from surveys of other employers, subject to hearings and review by personnel boards; salary recommendations were then enacted through the state budget process.[18] In 1974, at the behest of one of the plaintiff unions, the state hired experts to conduct a "pay equity" study.[19] After comparing sixty-two job classifications predominantly held by women with fifty-nine classifications predominantly held by men, the experts found that women were paid 20 percent less for jobs of "comparable worth," as determined by comparable "knowledge and skills, mental demands, accountability, and working conditions."[20] The state, rightly, found this troubling: the governor acknowledged the problem at a press conference and commissioned follow-up studies in 1976 and 1980, with the express purpose of rectifying the situation.[21]

---

[13] *See* Bornstein, *supra* note 4 at 616–19; Levit & Mahoney, *supra* note 12, at 100, 104; Weiler, *supra* note 12, at 1728–29.

[14] *See* US Commission on Civil Rights, COMPARABLE WORTH: AN ANALYSIS AND RECOMMENDATIONS i, 22, 70, 72 (1985), https://files.eric.ed.gov/fulltext/ED263243.pdf.

[15] *Id.* at 70, 72.

[16] *Id.*

[17] *AFSCME v. Washington*, 770 F.2d 1401, 1403 (9th Cir. 1985), *reh'g denied* 813 F.2d 1034 (9th Cir. 1987).

[18] *Id.* at 1403.

[19] *AFSCME v. Washington*, 578 F.Supp. 846, 859–60 (W.D. Wash 1983), *rev'd* 770 F.2d 1401 (9th Cir. 1985).

[20] *Id.* at 859–63.

[21] *Id.* at 860–63.

In 1982 – after years of study, but no action – the plaintiffs filed a lawsuit alleging that the state's knowing failure to correct the pay disparity violated Title VII's prohibition against sex discrimination.[22] In a complex, double-bifurcated trial that took place over four months in 1983, the district court sided entirely with the plaintiffs.[23] The district court certified a class of employees in 70 percent or more female-occupied job classifications and held that the state's compensation system resulted in a disparate impact on the basis of sex that could not be justified by a business necessity.[24] Moreover, the district court held that the state engaged in intentional sex discrimination by continuing to operate under its existing compensation scheme. The "evidence [was] overwhelming" that the state "manifested . . . direct, overt and institutionalized discrimination" against female employees, and the state's arguments that fixing the problem would be cost-prohibitive were unavailing.[25] In the district court's opinion, while the case involved a comparable worth compensation system, it was neither remarkable nor new, but "rather a straightforward 'failure to pay' case" involving an employer's "failure to rectify an acknowledged [sex-based] disparity in pay."[26]

The state appealed and, in an opinion written by then circuit judge (later US Supreme Court Justice) Anthony Kennedy, the Ninth Circuit Court of Appeals disagreed and reversed.[27] The circuit court rejected the district court's framing of the legal issues and instead read the case as a referendum on the validity of the theory of comparable worth. It was not a case about an employer who ignored years of evidence of sex discrimination in pay; instead, the circuit court explained, its task was to "determine whether comparable worth . . . affords [plaintiffs] a basis for recovery under Title VII."[28] With the question so reframed, the circuit court made short work of the district court's ruling in favor of plaintiffs on disparate impact. The state's choice to set wages by analyzing prevailing market rates was not the type of "specific, clearly delineated employment practice applied at a single point in the . . . process" that could be subject to a disparate impact challenge, the circuit court ruled, reversing the holding on disparate impact in one tidy paragraph.[29] True, at the time of its decision, the circuit court was operating under a narrow version of the disparate impact claim, later expanded by the Civil Rights Act of 1991 to

[22] *Id.* at 850–51, 859–63.
[23] *Id.* at 851–52, 864–69.
[24] *Id.* at 852, 864–69.
[25] *Id.* at 864–71.
[26] *Id.* at 864–71.
[27] AFSCME, 770 F.2d at 1403.
[28] *Id.* at 1404.
[29] *Id.* at 1405–06.

338   AFSCME v. State of Washington

allow challenges to a wider array of employment practices.[30] Nevertheless, as the district court found, the plaintiffs could have met even the narrower test in effect at the time. The circuit court chose to frame the challenged employment practice as a vague philosophical battle between "competitive market rate" compensation and "the theory of comparable worth,"[31] rather than the actual practice the plaintiffs challenged: the state's concrete decision at three distinct points in time to ignore evidence of discrimination and maintain its biased pay structure.

More consequentially, the circuit court also reversed and rejected the plaintiffs' disparate treatment claim, enshrining the neutrality of market forces in what became the *coup de grâce* for the theory of comparable worth. To prove disparate treatment under Title VII, the circuit court explained, an employee must prove that the employer has engaged in intentional discrimination, which requires a "discriminatory motive" and "intent ... linked at least in part to culpability."[32] The plaintiffs failed to make this showing of proof, the circuit court held, because the state was merely "participat[ing] in the market system" and "did not create the market disparity."[33] Highlighting that "[w]hether comparable worth is a feasible approach to employee compensation is a matter of debate," the circuit court reasoned that the state was not to blame for what was really a problem of the "neutral" free market:

> Neither law nor logic deems the free market system a suspect enterprise ... [N]othing in ... Title VII ... indicate[s] Congress intended to abrogate fundamental economic principles such as the laws of supply and demand or to prevent employers from competing in the labor market ... Title VII does not obligate [the State] to eliminate an economic inequality that it did not create ... The State['s ...] reliance on a free market system in which employees in male-dominated jobs are compensated at a higher rate than employees in dissimilar female-dominated jobs is not in and of itself a violation of Title VII, notwithstanding that the [State's own] study deemed the positions of comparable worth. Absent a showing of discriminatory motive, ... the law does not permit the federal courts to interfere in the market-based system for the compensation of ... employees.[34]

Again, it was the circuit court's choice of frame that doomed the plaintiffs' disparate treatment claim. Because the state simply relied on the "neutral" free

---

[30] The Ninth Circuit relied on *Atonio v. Ward's Cove Packing Co.*, 768 F.2d 1120, 1130 (9th Cir. 1985), *rev'd on other grounds* 490 U.S. 642 (1989) and superseded by statute, 42 U.S.C. §2000e-2 (k)(B)(i).

[31] *AFSCME*, 770 F.2d at 1406.

[32] *Id.* at 1406–07.

[33] *Id.*

[34] *Id.* at 1407–08.

market to set wages, the circuit court reasoned, it could not have had discriminatory intent. But the plaintiffs did not challenge the principle of free market economics; they challenged the state employer's specific intentional choice to repeatedly ignore its own evidence of correctable sex discrimination in pay. That others may have also been engaging in sex discrimination should not have rendered "unintentional" the state's knowing choice to ignore clear evidence that it too was discriminating.

The AFSCME plaintiffs petitioned for a rehearing *en banc*, but the petition was later dismissed when the parties settled the case.[35] Ironically, while the circuit court could not see the problem, the Washington state legislature could. After years of the state dragging its feet and compelled by AFSCME's lawsuit, the legislature enacted a comparable worth plan for state employees.[36] Yet the enshrining of what has become known as the "market defense" to cases alleging sex discrimination in unequal pay under both Title VII and the Equal Pay Act was complete.[37] The circuit court's decision made clear that if female employees were disadvantaged by the free market economy, the employer's actions were irrelevant.

Despite scholars' and advocates' arguments that the US Supreme Court could rule differently,[38] *AFSCME v. Washington* would prove to be, in effect, the final nail in the coffin for the legal theory of comparable worth. Courts in the Seventh, Eighth, and Tenth Circuits held similarly.[39] Within a handful of

---

[35] *AFSCME v. Washington*, 813 F.2d 1034 (9th Cir. 1987).

[36] Act of June 15, 1983, ch. 75, 1983 Wash. Laws 1st Ex. Sess. 2071, later codified as Wash. Rev. Code §§41.06.160(5) and 28B.16.110. The lawsuit was filed in 1982; the bill passed in 1983, to enact comparable worth over the course of ten years. The District Court was not impressed, noting that the State failed to act on comparable worth studies in 1978, 1980, and 1982, and only acted in 1983 after the suit was filed, passing "a token appropriation of $1.5 million" over ten years. AFSCME, 578 F.Supp. at 867–68. "Title VII remedies are now," the District Court held, "It is time, *right now* for a remedy. Defendant's preoccupation with its budget constraints pales when compared with the invidiousness of the impact ongoing discrimination has upon the Plaintiffs herein." *Id.* (emphasis in original).

[37] *See, e.g.,* Nicole Buonocore Porter & Jessica R. Vartanian, *Debunking the Market Myth in Pay Discrimination Cases*, 12 GEO. J. GENDER & L. 159 (2011); Deborah Thompson Eisenberg, *Money, Sex, and Sunshine: A Market-Based Approach to Pay Discrimination*, 43 ARIZ. ST. L.J. 951 (2011); Sharon Rabin-Marglioth, *The Market Defense*, 12 U. PA. J. BUS. L. 807 (2010); Martha Chamallas, *The Market Excuse*, 68 U. CHI. L. REV. 579, 581 (2001); Robert L. Nelson & William P. Bridges, LEGALIZING GENDER INEQUALITY: COURTS, MARKETS, AND UNEQUAL PAY FOR WOMEN IN AMERICA (1999).

[38] *See, e.g.,* Nancy E. Dowd, *The Metamorphosis of Comparable Worth*, 20 SUFFOLK U.L. REV. 833 (1986); Nancy Gertner, *Thoughts on Comparable Worth Litigation and Organizational Strategies*, 20 U. MICH. J.L. REFORM 163 (1986); Martha Chamallas, *Women and Part-Time Work: The Case for Pay Equity and Equal Access*, 64 N.C. L. REV. 709 (1986).

[39] *See Spaulding v. Univ. of Wash.*, 740 F.2d 686, 705–07 (9th Cir. 1983); *American Nurses' Ass'n v. State of Ill.*, 783 F.2d 716, 720 (7th Cir. 1986); *Christensen v. Iowa*, 563 F.2d 353, 355–56 (8th

340   AFSCME v. State of Washington

years, the term "comparable worth" all but vanished from the legal lexicon, while the "market defense" became standard, washing employers clean of any wrongdoing in perpetuating discriminatory compensation plans.[40]

THE FEMINIST JUDGMENT: WHAT MIGHT HAVE BEEN

In her rewritten judgment, Professor Teresa Godwin Phelps deftly shows the road not taken. Writing as Judge Phelps, she exposes the circuit court's faulty framing of the case, using both substance and technique of feminist legal theory. Substantively, Phelps makes one key change from which her holding in favor of the plaintiffs follows: recognizing that what is assumed to be a "neutral" standard in US society is, itself, gendered masculine.[41] Drawing comparisons to historical examples long understood to be discriminatory – the separate spheres ideology of the 1870s and biological protectionism of the 1910s, which limited women's work opportunities – Phelps explains that the state's "free market" defense to pay discrimination is another "specter of neutrality in a new guise." Indeed, as she explains, "[t]he market is not 'free,' but rather is formed by historical practices and organizational behavior"; "women's [work] opportunities and ... 'choices' ... are not formed in a vacuum," but rather are "shaped by [social structures] and a long history of discrimination against them." In short, Phelps makes clear, the "free market" system "is modeled on men and their lives." By pulling back the curtain and

---

Cir.1977); *Davidson v. Bd. of Governors of State Coll. and Univ.*, 920 F.2d 441, 446 (7th Cir.1990); *Lemons v. Denver*, 620 F.2d 228, 229 (10th Cir. 1980).

[40] *See* Robert Nelson, Law, *Markets, and Gender Inequality in Pay*, 10 BERKELEY WOMEN'S L.J. 61, 62 (1995) (describing trend away from comparable worth); *see, e.g., Wernsing v. Dep't of Human Servs.*, 427 F.3d 466 (7th Cir. 2005) (holding that an employer need not ignore market wages in pay setting); *Ottaviani v. SUNY New Paltz*, 679 F.Supp. 288 (S.D.N.Y. 1988) (explaining that a market-based pay differential is allowed); *Ciardella v. Carson City Sch. Dist.*, 671 F.Supp. 699 (D. Nev. 1987) (illustrating that market-based pay differentials are considered a factor other than sex). *Cf. Leatherwood v. Anna's Linens Co.*, 384 Fed. App'x 853, 860 (11th Cir. 2010) (allowing a market defense where an employer demonstrated "a staffing shortage and the need to lure [the higher-paid male employee] away from a competitor"); *Mulhall v. Advance Sec., Inc.*, 19 F.3d 586, 596–97 (11th Cir. 1994) (denying summary judgment for an employer who suggested, but failed to prove, that "market forces demanded" paying male comparators more "to sweeten the ... deals" to purchase their businesses); *Futran v. Ring Radio Co.*, 501 F.Supp. 734, 739–40 (N.D. Ga. 1980) (rejecting an employer's "factor other than sex" defense where it "took considerably less money to attract" the female plaintiff to a job than her male comparator, "based at least in part on her inferior bargaining position as a woman," and holding that "paying a lesser rate simply because the market will bear it is impermissible under the Equal Pay Act [of 1963]").

[41] *See, e.g.,* Joan C. Williams, UNBENDING GENDER: WHY WORK AND FAMILY CONFLICT AND WHAT TO DO ABOUT IT 5 (2000) (articulating the concept of the "ideal worker" designed around male life patterns).

exposing that the "invisible hand" of the market is male, Phelps' rationale aligns with a vast body of scholarly literature on the limits of formal equality and the recognition that to prevent and correct sex discrimination in pay may require a more substantive approach.[42]

In making her substantive case, Phelps uses the feminist legal theory technique of narrative to two powerful ends. First, she gives voice to several plaintiffs' individual stories, highlighting that the state's years of studying the problem without remedying the situation had real consequences for each of the 15,500 plaintiffs in the class – women who were paid $200, $300, even $500 less per month than their jobs were worth (the equivalent of $15,000–30,000 annually today), for years on end. This links the state's failure to act to specific, concrete, personal consequences, for which the state's defense of "Don't blame us – it's just the way the world works" appears to ring hollow.

Second, and more unusually, Phelps tells the story of the mostly male state officials who, despite "good intentions" to correct a system they knew was unfairly penalizing women, failed to act out of concern that the state could not afford the cost of fixing the problem. This is a skillful choice by Phelps to reframe the problem as structural, rather than individual, which allows her to come to the right decision without having to paint the state officials as sexist "bad guys." Even though the state officials were stuck between a rock and a hard place, once they had the knowledge that their choice of pay-setting system was actively perpetuating sex discrimination, they had a duty under federal law to act to correct it. This is important because the circuit court's need to excuse the state officials from "culpability" led it to misinterpret Title VII law to require "animus."[43] Title VII doctrine does not require a plaintiff to prove discriminatory animus or hostility; proving disparate treatment requires that an employer's intentional actions constitute discrimination, which can be proven using circumstantial or stereotyping evidence.[44] To prove disparate impact, a plaintiff need not even show that the employer acted with intent.[45] With the issue now properly reframed, Phelps can hold confidently that the state's pay practices created an unjustified disparate impact by sex and that – even though state actors did not harbor sexist motivations – once the state knew

[42] *See, e.g.,* Jack M. Balkin & Reva B. Siegel, *The American Civil Rights Tradition: Anticlassification or Antisubordination?,* 58 U. Miami L. Rev. 9, 9–11 (2003); Ruth Colker, *Anti-Subordination above All: Sex, Race, and Equal Protection,* 61 N.Y.U. L. Rev. 1003, 1005 (1986); Mary Ann Mason, *Beyond Equal Opportunity: A New Vision for Women Workers,* 6 Notre Dame J.L. Ethics & Pub. Pol'y 393, 394 (1992).

[43] *AFSCME,* 770 F.2d at 1407–08.

[44] *See, e.g., Ash v. Tyson Foods, Inc.,* 546 U.S. 454, 456–58 (2006); *Price Waterhouse v. Hopkins,* 490 U.S. 228, 250–51 (1989).

[45] *See, e.g., Griggs v. Duke Power Co.,* 401 U.S. 424, 432 (1971).

342   AFSCME v. State of Washington

of the unjustified and correctable, although costly, discrimination, its intentional failure to act constituted disparate treatment.

Notably – and sadly, given what might have been – Phelps' opinion accomplishes her task using existing precedent in place at the time of the circuit court's original decision in 1985. Prior to *AFSCME v. Washington*, the US Supreme Court had decided two cases on which Phelps relies that opened the door to ruling in favor of the AFSCME plaintiffs. In 1974, in *Corning Glass Works v. Brennan*,[46] the Supreme Court held that, to make a prima facie case of sex discrimination in pay under the Equal Pay Act's requirement that male and female employees be performing "equal work," the compared jobs need not be identical so long as they were "substantially equal." In 1981, in *Washington County v. Gunther*,[47] when faced with how to interpret a section of Title VII that incorporated all defenses in the Equal Pay Act, the Supreme Court held that this did not also limit a Title VII plaintiff to only claims involving "equal work." Together, these cases meant that a plaintiff could bring a Title VII claim with evidence that a woman was being paid less than a man doing comparable work.

By framing the case as a question of whether AFSCME could use Title VII to force the state to adopt a comparable worth plan, the circuit court set up its own straw man. Once it knocked down comparable worth theory as a threat to the free market, the circuit court foreclosed the promise of *Corning Glass* and *Gunther* to root out sex stereotypes in pay. The law requires – as the district court and Phelps' rewritten opinions would have held – that once an employer discovers proof that its chosen pay system discriminates against women, it must act *in some way* to correct its own discrimination. Neither decision would have forced the state to adopt comparable worth. As courts often say, they are not super-personnel departments that can dictate how an employer should run its business. But they are required to hold employers responsible for known unlawful discrimination.[48]

In 1985, the circuit court could have chosen another route: simply upholding the district court's ruling. Had it done so, the story may have ended the same for the AFSCME plaintiffs, who settled their own case and whose efforts led to the enactment of a comparable worth compensation plan for Washington state employees. The story might have ended quite differently

---

[46] 417 U.S. 188, 234 (1974).

[47] 452 U.S. 161, 170 (1981).

[48] The circuit court expressed concern that ruling in favor of the plaintiffs might deter employers from voluntarily conducting job evaluation studies. See *AFSCME*, 770 F.2d at 1408. Again, this is a straw man argument: while, under the district court holding or Phelps' rewritten opinion, an employer could not *ignore* discrimination it uncovered, an employer would not be required to adopt a comparable worth plan.

for other women, however, and for men working in female-dominated fields in the United States today. Data on the gender pay gap in certain sectors of the economy that have, like the state of Washington, voluntarily adopted pay plans based on comparability indicate what might have been. The pay gap among unionized workers, for whom pay is often set using job evaluation studies that classify jobs and set consistent pay based on the skills and responsibilities of the position, is a third to a half the size of that of all women: unionized women earn 88 to 90 cents on the dollar to men.[49] Likewise, the pay gap among federal sector workers, whose jobs are classified into pay bands, has been cut nearly in half: female workers in the General Schedule (GS) rank system earn 89 cents on men's dollar.[50] For the rest of US workers, however, *AFSCME v. Washington* means that, unless an employer voluntarily chooses otherwise, neither Title VII nor the Equal Pay Act can protect against pay discrimination in the "free market" that is replicated and perpetuated at work.

CONCLUSION: FULL CIRCLE, FROM COMPARABLE "WORTH" TO COMPARABLE "WORK"

AFSCME v. Washington is not, however, the last word on comparable pay. While it has taken thirty years since the decision, a focus on gender workforce segregation has resurfaced in recent advocacy on equal pay. At the federal level, the issue was part of two 2017 legislative efforts to amend the Equal Pay Act: the Paycheck Fairness Act, which would allow as a defense only "bona fide" factors other than sex that are "job-related" and "consistent with business necessity," thus limiting the "market defense";[51] and the Fair Pay Act (sponsored by now Congressperson Eleanor Holmes Norton), which would require equal pay "for equivalent jobs" that are "dominated by employees of

---

[49] *See* Bornstein, *supra* note 4, at 635–39; Bureau of Labor Stat., US Dept. of Labor, *Median Weekly Earnings of Full-Time Wage and Salary Workers by Union Affiliation and Selected Characteristics* (Jan. 22, 2020), www.bls.gov/news.release/union2.t02.htm; Katherine Gallagher Robbins & Andrea Johnson, *Union Membership is Critical for Equal Pay*, NAT'L WOMEN'S LAW CTR. 1 (2016), https://nwlc.org/wp-content/uploads/2015/02/Union-Membership-is-Critical-for-Equal-Pay.pdf.

[50] *See* Bornstein, *supra* note 4, at 639–40; US Office of Personnel Mgmt., GOVERNMENT WIDE STRATEGY ON ADVANCING PAY EQUALITY IN THE FEDERAL GOVERNMENT 12 (Apr. 2014), www .opm.gov/policy-data-oversight/pay-leave/reference-materials/reports/governmentwide-strategy -on-advancing-pay-equality-in-the-federal-government.pdf. Of course, comparable worth is not a panacea, because other countries that have worked toward it still report gender pay gaps. *See, e.g.*, Sandra J. Libeson, *Reviving the Comparable Worth Debate in the United States: A Look toward the European Community*, 16 COMP. LAB. L.J. 358, 360–61 (1995).

[51] Paycheck Fairness Act, S. 819, 115th Cong. (2017), H.R. 1869, 115th Cong. (2017).

344 AFSCME v. State of Washington

a particular sex, race, or national origin."[52] And, despite federal rejection of comparable worth, nearly half of the states have enacted their own equal pay laws that go further than federal law to require equal pay for "comparable," "substantially similar," or "equivalent" work, two-thirds of which remain open to broader state court interpretation than federal law.[53] This includes the state of Washington, which now requires, under state law, equal pay for men and women who are "similarly employed."[54] Most recently, three states have enacted new laws that revive questions of comparability[55] – although with a recalibrated approach of comparable "work," not comparable "worth," which focuses on a job's tasks rather than its value.[56] Had Judge Phelps been sitting on the Ninth Circuit in 1985, able to apply critical legal theory to expose the fallacy of "neutral" law and show that comparable worth was not a threat to the economy, but rather one reasonable tool to help achieve substantive over formal pay equality, we might have arrived here a lot sooner.

American Federation of State, County,
and Municipal Employees, AFL-CIO (AFSCME) v.
State of Washington,
770 F.2d 1401 (9th Cir. 1985)

JUDGE TERESA GODWIN PHELPS DELIVERED THE JUDGMENT
OF THE COURT.

More than a century ago, a Supreme Court Justice used "neutral" principles – God, history, and nature – to deny a more-than-qualified woman an employment opportunity. *Bradwell v. Illinois*, 83 U.S. 130 (1872). In an oft-quoted concurrence, Justice Bradley agreed that the state of Illinois could deny Myra

---

[52] Fair Pay Act, H.R. 2095, 115th Cong. (2017) (defining equivalent jobs as "jobs that may be dissimilar, but whose requirements are equivalent, when viewed as a composite of skills, effort, responsibility, and working conditions").

[53] *See* Bornstein, *supra* note 4, at 611–19.

[54] *See* Wash. Rev. Code Ann. §49.12.175 (West 2008); *Hemmings v. Tidyman's Inc.*, 285 F.3d 1174, 1190–91 (9th Cir. 2002) (citing *Adams v. Univ. of Wash.*, 722 P.2d 74, 76–78 (Wash. 1986)). Cf. *Hudon v. W. Valley Sch. Dist.*, 97 P.3d 39, 43 (Wash. Ct. App. 2004) (noting more generally that "Washington's equal pay act . . . is virtually identical to its federal counterpart, 29 U.S.C. § 206 (d)," so that "[d]ecisions interpreting the federal act may . . . be helpful" in a state law case).

[55] *See* Bornstein, *supra* note 4, at 624–31; Mass. Gen. Laws ch. 149, §105A (West eff. Jan. 1, 2018); Cal. Lab. Code §1197.5 (West 2017); Or. Rev. Stat. §252 (West eff. Jan. 1, 2019).

[56] *See* Bornstein, *supra* note 4, at 624–31; Deborah Thompson Eisenberg, *Shattering the Equal Pay Act's Glass Ceiling*, 63 SMU L. REV. 17, 48 (2010) (noting that a comparable "work" statute "still require[s] proof" that there are "common similarities between the jobs," which is "a factual question about the nature of the work, not a value question about the intrinsic 'worth' of the job").

AFSCME v. State of Washington 345

Bradwell, who had otherwise qualified as a lawyer, admission to the bar. The privileges and immunities clause, he concluded, should not be interpreted to contravene the natural law and historical fact of separate spheres for women and men:

> [T]he civil law, as well as nature herself, has always recognized a wide difference in the respective spheres and destinies of man and woman. Man is, or should be, woman's protector and defender. The natural and proper timidity and delicacy which belongs to the female sex evidently unfits it for many of the occupations of civil life. The constitution of the family organization, which is founded in the divine ordinance, as well as in the nature of things, indicates the domestic sphere as that which properly belongs to the domain and functions of womanhood. *Id.* at 141.

Twenty-six years later, other "neutral" principles – this time, biology and medicine – were used to "protect" women from equal employment opportunities:

> That woman's physical structure and the performance of maternal functions place her at a disadvantage in the struggle for subsistence is obvious. This is especially true when the burdens of motherhood are upon her. Even when they are not, by abundant testimony of the medical fraternity continuance for a long time on her feet at work, repeating this from day to day, tends to injurious effects upon the body, and, as healthy mothers are essential to vigorous offspring, the physical well-being of woman becomes an object of public interest and care in order to preserve the strength and vigor of the race. *Muller v. Oregon*, 208 U.S. 412, 421 (1908).

The state of Oregon could legally prohibit women from working more than ten hours a day in laundries, although the same Court had made it clear only three years earlier that the state of New York could not limit the hours that male bakers worked: "Statutes of the nature of that under review, limiting the hours in which grown and intelligent men may labor to earn their living, are mere meddlesome interferences with the rights of the individual ..." *Lochner v. New York*, 198 U.S. 45, 61 (1905).

Today, the state of Washington raises again that specter of neutrality in a new guise – the free market – to justify paying female state employees on average 20 percent less than it pays male state employees. Although federal law now prohibits denying women employment opportunities, the state argues that it may pay women less for jobs that are deemed to be of equal worth to the state according to standard personnel evaluation methods than it pays for jobs held by men because it is using prevailing market rates to set salaries in job categories. It argues that its use of the market as a means to set wages for its approximately 45,000 employees does not violate Title VII of the Civil Rights

346 AFSCME v. State of Washington

Act of 1964. We disagree. A method that systematically results in jobs predominantly held by women being paid 20 percent less than jobs predominantly held by men cannot be neutral. If jobs are of the same or comparable worth to an employer and nonetheless the employer pays at least 20 percent less to the jobs held primarily by women, the lesser pay must be based on sex. What else is it based on? The very market rates on which the state claims to rely are set in a historical context filled with discrimination, legal and illegal, against women. We agree with the district court that the state of Washington, aware of the inequitable gendered results of its pay scale and knowing that another method is available that avoids the inequity, violated both the letter and the spirit of Title VII.

This class action charges the state of Washington with sex discrimination in employment, under both disparate treatment and disparate impact frameworks, in violation of Title VII. 42 U.S.C. §2000e. The class represented in this case comprises female and male employees of all job classifications under the jurisdiction of the state's Department of Personnel (DOP) and Higher Education Personnel Board (HEPB) that were 70 percent or more female as of November 20, 1980, or any time thereafter. The district court found that the class met all seven of the requirements for class certification. *AFSCME v. State of Washington*, 578 F.Supp. 853, 860 (1984).

The standard of review is clearly erroneous. *Texas Dept. of Community Affairs v. Burdine*, 450 U.S. 248 (1981); *McDonnell-Douglas Corp. v. Green*, 411 U.S. 792 (1973). At trial, both the plaintiff AFSCME and the defendant state presented volumes of evidence that the district court evaluated. The district court's opinion painstakingly reviews a lengthy history of memoranda from state authorities acknowledging the inequity in pay and an equally lengthy history of studies undertaken to reveal the disparity and remedy it. Nonetheless, the state did nothing to rectify the salaries. We affirm the district court's opinion that the state continues to violate Title VII and that remedies are appropriate.

I FACTS

This case involves two intersecting stories: one about the good intentions, but inaction of numerous state actors – mainly men; the other story about workers – mainly women – struggling to make ends meet.

The first story. The facts in this case, going back several decades, indicate that the state has known for some time that its wage structure has discriminatory results. The facts also show that actions that the state took in the past actually contributed to and helped to perpetuate segregation in the workforce. For example, as recently as 1973, a year after Title VII was made applicable to the state governments, the state ran ads in the "male" and "female" help wanted sections of newspapers throughout the state, thus perpetuating and even furthering a sex-segregated workforce, in which the jobs held predominantly by women were paid at least 20 percent less than jobs held predominantly by men. *AFSCME*, 578 F.Supp.at 841. The state finally ended the sex-segregated advertising practice and then Governor Daniel J. Evans vowed to "reverse the inequity" in pay. *Id.* The gender-segregated workforce still persists, however, and at the time of the filing of this class action lawsuit, filed on behalf of approximately 15,500 workers in jobs predominantly held by women (i.e., 70 percent or more women), female job categories were paid approximately 20 percent less than male job categories. *Id.* at 861.

This disparity persists despite actions taken by the state to uncover the problem and to discover solutions to it. Wages for state employees are set by the boards of two civil service systems: the HEPB and the SPB. After numerous complaints and a directive from the governor, in 1974 the two boards initiated a joint study that concluded that there were "clear indications of pay differences between classes predominately held by men and those predominately held by women within the State systems. Such differences are not due solely to job 'worth.' " *Id.* at 860–61.

Following this study, the state commissioned an outside independent study of the state wage structure in an effort to eliminate the wage discrimination. The resultant study (the Willis Study), conducted by the consulting firm of Norman Willis & Associates, stated that, "based on the measured job content of the 121 classifications evaluated as a part of this project, the tendency is for women's classes to be paid less than men's classes, for comparable job worth ... Overall, considering both systems together, the disparity is approximately 20 percent." *Id.* at 861. The Willis study used a "comparable worth" scale to evaluate the worth of a job to the employer, so that dissimilar jobs could be compared. Comparable worth was calculated by evaluating jobs in terms of four criteria: knowledge and skills, mental demands, accountability, and working conditions. A maximum number of points was allotted to each: 280 for knowledge and skills, 140 for mental demands, 160 for accountability, and 20 for working conditions. Every job was assigned a numerical value for each of the four criteria. In 1976, the state commissioned Willis & Associates to update the study and to devise a plan by which the state could use comparable worth to complement its use of prevailing market rates. *Id.* at 862. After two governors voiced concerns about pay inequity and the legislature passed several bills to address it, as of today at least the 15,500 people in this class

348   AFSCME v. State of Washington

action continue to be paid far less than their jobs are worth – because of the sex
of the majority of workers in the particular job.

The second story is about Willie May Willis, who makes $968 a month as
a food services worker at the University of Washington and whose salary
would increase to $1,208 if the state were to abandon the market and instead
use comparable worth to set her salary – an additional $240 a month. It's
about Louise Peterson, a licensed practical nurse, who makes $1,239
a month, but would make $1,795 – an additional $555 a month. It's about
Lauren Louise McNiece, a library technician at Washington State
University, who makes $1,179 a month, but would make $1,585 – an additional $406 a month. And it's about thousands of other workers, almost all
women, who are paid less than their jobs are worth because of the market –
a market formed by centuries of lack of opportunity for women and legal
discrimination against them.

Indeed, across the board in the state of Washington, male-dominated
job categories are paid significantly more than female jobs, with no
apparent rhyme or reason. For example, on average, a female clerk typist
makes a monthly salary of $612, while a male warehouse worker makes
$997 – a salary difference of $385; a female licensed practical nurse
makes $801, while a male park ranger makes $928 – a difference of
$127; a female supervisor of a secretarial pool makes $1,097, while
a male parole and probation officer makes $1,243 – a difference of $198.
In job category after job category, men are paid more with no discernible
difference in responsibility, skill, or worth to the state. *See* Gisela
E. Taber & Helen Remick, BEYOND EQUAL PAY FOR EQUAL WORK:
COMPARABLE WORTH IN THE STATE OF WASHINGTON, Papers prepared for
Conference on Equal Pay and Equal Opportunity Policy for Women in
Europe, Canada, and the United States, Center for Research on Women,
Wellesley College (May 1978).

This discriminatory pattern is reflected throughout the country. In
Wisconsin, bakers (men) make more than cooks (women) and uphol-
sterers (men), more than seamstresses (women). In Minnesota, licensed
practical nurses working for the state make less than groundskeepers. In
the City of Philadelphia's computer room, all of the technicians are
women and paid less than the men, who are computer room managers
and paid more. *See* AFSCME, BREAKING THE PATTERNS OF INJUSTICE:
AFSCME's BLUEPRINT FOR PAY EQUITY (1980). Indeed, "the more an
occupation is dominated by women, the less it pays." *See* Donald
J. Treiman & Heidi I. Hartmann, WOMEN, WORK, AND WAGES: EQUAL
PAY FOR JOBS OF EQUAL VALUE 28 (1981).

II THE FALLACY OF THE FREE MARKET

Economic behavior is embedded within social structures. The market is not "free," but rather is formed by historical practices and organizational behavior. A gender-segregated workforce is not a natural phenomenon that results from an "invisible hand" or women's choices, but rather becomes cemented in place because of past discrimination that restricted women's opportunities and present conditions that discourage women from entering jobs that are predominantly held by men.

As we can see from *Bradwell v. Illinois*, 83 U.S. 130 (1872), *Muller v. Oregon*, 208 U.S. 412 (1908), and numerous other cases where women were denied the opportunity to work or to compete freely with men in many job categories regarded as "male," women's opportunities and the subsequent "choices" they make about what jobs to train or apply for are not formed in a vacuum, but instead are shaped by a long history of discrimination against them. *See, e.g., Goessart v. Cleary*, 335 U.S. 464 (1948) (women who were not the wives or daughters of bar owners could not obtain a bartender's license because of possible "moral and social problems"); *Massachusetts v. Feeney*, 442 U.S. 256 (1979) (Massachusetts could use veterans' preference when hiring for civil service jobs although the practice had a significant discriminatory impact on women). This history includes girls' and women's educational opportunities and "choices" directed by parents and teachers. Who got what education or training was based on sex – not talent or interest. Many can recall shop class for the boys and home economics for the girls.

The male-dominated legal establishment did not fret too much about women having few job opportunities because it embraced the myth of women working only for "pin money": women and their children were fully supported by men, the breadwinners, who properly had all the job opportunities (or so the story went). In fact, the idea of women, who did not need to work, competing with men, on whose shoulders rested the financial well-being of families, was anathema. Women who "manned" the factories during the world wars quickly stepped aside when the men came home and were once again available for the jobs. Competing with men was not socially acceptable, and, in most workplaces, women were simply denied the jobs they held during the war. *See* Sheila Tobias & Lisa Anderson, WHAT REALLY HAPPENED TO ROSIE THE RIVETER? DEMOBILIZATION AND THE FEMALE LABOR FORCE, 1944–47 (1974). One sociologist, Willard Waller, went so far as to claim that "during the war women had gotten 'out of hand,' with the result that children were neglected and the very survival of the home was endangered." *See* William Henry Chafe, THE AMERICAN WOMAN: HER CHANGING SOCIAL, ECONOMIC, AND POLITICAL

350 AFSCME v. State of Washington

ROLES, 1920–1970 176 (1972). Consequently, women stayed home or in "female" jobs that did not have to pay much and in which they did not compete with men. Despite the passage of the Equal Pay Act and Title VII, which both had the lofty purpose of leveling the playing field and opening up job opportunities to women, the lingering effects of past mythologies, inadequate childcare, and outright discrimination perpetuate a sex-segregated workforce with wide discrepancies in wages.

Additionally, the long-embraced notion of "separate spheres" (men as rational and thus properly in the public sphere; women as emotional and properly in the home) relegates women to only certain kinds of jobs in which their supposed "domestic" or "nurturing" knacks are useful: school teaching, nursing, food service, and the like. Lack of educational opportunities, lack of the right to enter training programs or to join unions, sex-segregated help wanted ads: all have contributed to a gender-segregated workforce in which women may have recently acquired the technical legal right to apply for a better paying "male" job, but only a very few of the bravest would have the wherewithal to do so. *Id.*

And what happens to those few who can see beyond the iron curtain that has existed between male and female jobs? They are weeded out in job application forms and interviews by male supervisors who are looking for "male" traits or experiences – such as having played football or baseball in high school. Just as Duke Power Company used requirements that were not actually job-related, but did eliminate a disproportionate number of black applicants, everyday employment practices use activities common to the male sphere as appropriate preparation for a job regardless as to whether they are actually job-related. *See Griggs v. Duke Power*, 401 U.S. 424 (1971); Rosabeth Moss Kanter, MEN AND WOMEN OF THE CORPORATION (1977). If some women are lucky enough to actually get through the application process and get the job, what happens next? Frequently, they are so harassed by the male workers that they are driven out. *See* Catharine A. MacKinnon, SEXUAL HARASSMENT OF WORKING WOMEN (1979). Thus the sex-segregated workforce goes on and on despite legal reforms. Some mechanisms are in place to bring about change to this dynamic that keeps women in their proper place in "female" jobs, but it is slow and vigorously resisted. A gender-integrated workplace may be an aspiration, but it remains just that – an aspiration. The concept of a rational self-interested individual is based on the model of a (white) man, who has had all of the choices on which market theory is based. Women have never been and still cannot be the self-interested rational actors that market theory envisions. They simply do not have the same choices as men. The "free market" is a patriarchal construct that is modeled on men and their lives.

AFSCME v. State of Washington 351

Other basic market theory, such as supply and demand, also does not explain the disparity in wages paid in male and female job categories. For example, nurses are in short supply, but in 1981 full-time female registered nurses earned an average of only $331 a week – less than male ticket agents, vehicle dispatchers, electricians, and drafters. Male bakers make more than female cooks, and male upholsterers more than female seamstresses, and yet the supply and demand for the jobs are similar. *See Government Employee Relations Report* (May 12, 1983) (citing AFSCME, *Breaking the Pattern, supra*); *see also* Congressional Testimony of AFSCME President, Gerald W. McEntee, May 1982 ("Pay disparities of this sort are clearly not a result of swings in supply and demand. They are based on sex discrimination, which has been instituted so systematically that by now it is the system."). Supply and demand theory, like other market theory, falls short in providing any adequate explanation for the deeply intractable disparity between women's and men's wages.

III DISPARATE TREATMENT

The district court found that this case should be "characterized as a straightforward 'failure to pay' case, markedly analogous to the recently decided *County of Washington v. Gunther* case." *AFSCME*, 578 F.Supp. at 865. We agree that characterizing this action solely as a "comparable worth" case misses the mark. We do not have to go so far as to insist that the state use comparable worth to set salaries. This case is not about what the state did not do. It is about what it has done. It may not knowingly use a method to set wages that is prejudicial to female workers. The state of Washington has violated Title VII under both disparate treatment and disparate impact frameworks by paying considerably less for positions predominantly held by women, knowing that its decision to use prevailing market rates results in this gender disparity. Merely saying that it is using the "free market" does not excuse the continuance of a prohibited discriminatory employment practice. The faith-based or magical incantation of "free market" as a neutral arbiter of value masks the underlying forces that form prevailing market rates and does not excuse deliberate discrimination in pay scales.

Section 703(a) of Title VII states, in pertinent part:

It shall be an unlawful employment practice for an employer

(1) to fail or refuse to hire or to discharge any individual, or *otherwise to discriminate* against any individual with respect to his compensation,

352 AFSCME v. State of Washington

> terms, conditions, or privileges of employment because of such individual's ... sex.
>
> (2) to limit, segregate, or classify his employees or applicants for employment in any way which would deprive or tend to deprive any individual of employment opportunities ... because of such individual's ... sex ...
>
> 42 U.S.C. §2000e-2(a) (1982) (emphasis added).

In its recent decision in *Washington County v. Gunther*, 452 U.S. 161 (1981), the Court explicitly rejected the state's argument that the Bennett Amendment limits Title VII's reach to only equal jobs as defined using the standards of the Equal Pay Act (EPA).[57] The Bennett Amendment, intended to eliminate any discrepancies between the EPA and Title VII, delineated the relationship between Title VII and its predecessor, the EPA, by ensuring that wage differentials that are allowable under the EPA's affirmative defenses are not actionable under Title VII. The EPA permits differences in pay that are based on four factors: seniority, merit, quality or quantity of production, and "any other factor other than sex." Civil Rights Act of 1964, §§701 *et seq.*, 703I(1) as amended; 42 U.S.C.A. §§2000e *et seq.*, 2000e-2I(1). In *Gunther*, the Court broadly interpreted the meaning of Title VII, saying: "Title VII's prohibition of discriminatory employment practices was intended to be broadly inclusive, proscribing 'not only overt discrimination but also practices that are fair in form, but discriminatory in operation.' (citation omitted). The structure of Title VII litigation, including presumptions, burdens of proof, and defenses, has been designed to reflect this approach." *Gunther*, 452 U.S. at 170. The Court has consistently interpreted Title VII with an eye to Congress's intent "to strike at the *entire spectrum* of disparate treatment of men and women resulting from sex stereotypes." *Los Angeles Dept. of Water & Power v. Manhart*, 435 U.S 702, 707 n.13 (emphasis added).

Under disparate treatment analysis, the plaintiff is required to prove a prima facie case of sex discrimination by a preponderance of the evidence. *Furnco*

---

[57] 29 U.S.C.A §206(d) provides:

> No employer having employees subject to any provisions of this section shall discriminate, within any establishment in which such employees are employed, between employees on the basis of sex by paying wages to employees in such establishment at a rate less than the rate at which he pays wages to employees of the opposite sex in such establishment for equal work on jobs the performance of which requires equal skill, effort, and responsibility, and which are performed under similar working conditions, except where such payment is made pursuant to (i) a seniority system; (ii) a merit system; (iii) a system which measures earnings by quantity or quality of production; or (iv) a differential based on any other factor other than sex.

Construction Corp. v. Waters, 438 U.S. 567, 576 (1978); *McDonnell Douglas Corp. v. Green*, 411 U.S. 792, 802 (1973); *Spaulding v. University of Washington*, 740 F.2d 686, 700 (1984). Liability for disparate treatment and discriminatory intent may be inferred from statistical evidence. *Spaulding*, 740 F.2d at 703; *Lynn v. Regents of the University of California*, 656 F.2d 1337, 1342 (9th Cir.1981), *cert. denied* 459 U.S. 823 (1982); *accord, International Brotherhood of Teamsters v. United States*, 431 U.S. 324, 339 (1977). In *Teamsters*, the Court made clear that statistical evidence often filled an evidentiary gap because employers rarely admit that they intend to discriminate and that "experience has proved that in the absence of any other explanation [for discrepancies in the statistics] it is more likely than not that those actions were bottomed on impermissible considerations." *Id.* at 335 n.15. The district court in the present case outlined the kinds of factors that can support a case based on circumstantial evidence of intent:

> Circumstantial evidence which courts have found probative of intentional discrimination, includes the following: the historical context out of which the challenged practices arise; obstacles confronting applicants and/or employees; subjective employment practices utilized by the Defendant resulting in a pattern disfavoring females; the foreseeable adverse impact of those practices; the increase in pay to the Plaintiffs since filing of the instant suit; discriminatory treatment in other areas of employment; and, perhaps most telling, *recognition of disparate treatment by responsible State officials*. The *Burdine* Court explained that the "prima facie case" raises an inference of discrimination only because we presume these acts, if otherwise unexplained, are more likely than not based on the consideration of impermissible factors.
>
> *AFSCME*, 578 F.Supp. at 858 (emphasis added) (citations omitted).

The evidence that AFSCME submitted at trial easily met the burden of showing a prima facie case of discrimination. AFSCME presented evidence of the state's prior practices, such as sex-segregated job advertisements, which had the foreseeable result of perpetuating a sex-segregated work force. Additionally, AFSCME presented unrebutted statistical evidence regarding the state's employment and salary-setting practices. Expert testimony based on sophisticated multiple regression analyses demonstrated that predominantly female job classifications fared worse than predominantly male job classifications regardless of evaluated worth. The same results were found even when controlled for other factors, such as educational requirements. As discussed above, AFSCME also presented evidence that state officials were aware of the discriminatory results and had even promised to move toward more equity.

354 AFSCME v. State of Washington

Once a prima facie case has been shown, the burden then shifts to the state to rebut the presumption of discrimination by showing that its actions in setting pay rates were legitimate and nondiscriminatory. *Burdine*, 450 U.S. at 254. The state's evidence showed quite the opposite. At trial, AFSCME showed that the state commissioned and had available to it the Willis study, which concluded that relying on prevailing market rates resulted in large discrepancies in the pay scales in jobs held predominantly by women and those held predominantly by men. In fact, then Governor Evans admitted as much at a press conference: "[T]here is, indeed, a general relationship which results in an average of about 20 percent less for women than for males doing equivalent jobs ... I think that steps ought to be taken to rectify the imbalance which does exist." *AFSCME*, 578 F.Supp. at 861. But nothing happened. Six years later, the new governor, Dixy Lee Ray, acknowledged the unfairness and the inaction and pushed for a solution:

> [T]he only thing that we ... have done about that 1974 study, was to have it up-dated [*sic*]. The update revealed that since salary increases have been established on a percentage basis, the inequality gap between men's and women's salaries for similar work has now increased. The dollar cost of a solution will be high; it probably cannot be achieved in one action. But, the cost of perpetuating unfairness, within State government itself, is too great to put off any longer ...   *Id.* at 862.

At the time of the filing of this class action, despite the passage of several bills, the discrepancy in pay scales was substantially the same as years earlier. The cost of fairness was too high, and the state's response was to throw its collective hands up and blame the market. While the state and several *amici* argue that the state is not responsible for the preferences of the market, and an employer relying on the market to set salaries is a legitimate business practice and a "factor other than sex," the facts of this case militate against such a conclusion. Instead, they lead to the conclusion that the state, somewhat disingenuously, reverted to the "free market" when the bill got too high and purposefully continued to discriminate against workers in positions predominantly held by women. Meanwhile, Willie May Willis, Louise Peterson, and Lauren Louise McNiece continue to earn far less than their positions are worth.

IV DISPARATE IMPACT

Under the disparate impact theory, discrimination may be established by showing that a facially neutral employment practice, not justified by business

AFSCME v. State of Washington

necessity, has a disproportionately adverse impact upon members of a group protected under Title VII. *See Dothard v. Rawlinson*, 433 U.S. 321, 328–29 (1977); *Griggs*, 401 U.S. at 430–31, 91. Proof of an employer's intent to discriminate in adopting a particular practice is not required in a disparate impact case. *Teamsters*, 431 U.S. at 335 n.15; *Spaulding*, 740 F.2d at 705.[58]

At trial, AFSCME submitted evidence of multiple studies that the state conducted that showed that the state's practice of setting salaries using prevailing market rates resulted in workers in positions primarily held by women being paid on average 20 percent less than those in positions primarily held by men: "Several comparable worth studies, since 1974, found a 20% disparity in salary between predominately male and predominately female jobs which require an equivalent or lesser composite of skill, effort, responsibility and working conditions as reflected by an equal number of job evaluation points." Joint Exhibit #4. "There is a significant inverse correlation between the percentage of women in a classification and the salary for that position." Testimony of Dr. Stephen Michelson, *AFSCME*, 578 F.Supp. at 863.

Once a disparate impact has been established, the burden shifts to the employer to show that the practice that results in the disparate impact is a business necessity or, more specifically in an employment compensation case, to "demonstrate that legitimate and overriding business considerations provide justification." *Bonilla v. Oakland Scavenger Co.*, 697 F.2d 1297, 1303 (9th Cir. 1982).

Here, the state argues that using prevailing market rates to set salaries is a business necessity and is justified by business considerations. The voluminous record in this case shows quite the opposite. The state spent years and millions of dollars in taxpayer money to find out that prevailing market rates resulted in inequity and that another system – comparable worth – could be used to measure jobs and set pay scales that avoided the inequality. Using one system rather than another is a business choice, not a necessity. The evidence presented at trial also showed that the state ultimately believed that using comparable worth rather than the market was too costly. Thus, despite legislation directing the state to remedy the discrimination and use comparable worth to set salaries, at the time of the filing of the class action suit the state had not done so. Like the Court in *Gunther*, this Court is not required to substitute its assessment of the worth of the jobs for that of the employer. The employer, the state of Washington, has already done that assessment.

---

[58] Until recently, it was not clear that disparate impact analysis was available in section 703(a)(1) cases, but this court has cleared up that uncertainty, stating that it is. *Wambheim v. J.C. Penney Company, Inc.*, 705 F.2d 1492, 1493–94 (9th Cir.1983) (*per curiam*).

That the alternative, yet fair, comparable worth system costs too much is not a justification. Title VII does not contain, nor have Congress or the courts recognized, a cost justification defense in Title VII cases. *See Manhart*, 435 U.S. at 716–17. Nonetheless, when confronted with the price tag for equality, the state made a specific choice to continue to use prevailing market rates to set salaries. Such a continuance runs counter to the Supreme Court's admonishment that "practices, procedures, or tests neutral on their face, and even neutral in terms of intent, cannot be maintained if they operate to freeze the status quo of prior discriminatory employment practices." *Griggs*, 401 U.S. at 430.

Thus we affirm the district court's conclusion that the state of Washington violated Title VII by using prevailing market rates to set salaries in job categories under both disparate treatment and disparate impact frameworks.

V COMPARABLE WORTH

Although failing to use comparable worth does not itself create a cause of action, if it is shown that an employer is using a discriminatory method to set salaries, it must find a new method or modify the one it is using to mitigate the discriminatory results. Thus the state of Washington must forgo using prevailing market rates to set salaries and find another method of determining salaries that does not result in discrimination based on sex. Its own studies have shown that using a system known as "comparable worth" achieves this goal, and it thus seems prudent that the state move forward in this direction.

Comparable worth may be defined as a system for determining compensation in job categories based on the worth of the job to the employer. Under a comparable worth scheme, jobs that are not alike or even similar may be compared using worth to the employer as the criterion. Features of the job are examined such as knowledge and skills required for the job, the mental demands of the job, accountability, and working conditions. *See Spaulding*, 740 F.2d at 686. This Court is aware that comparable worth remains a contentious issue, with its critics and proponents having equal fervor. Some of its critics, my fellow judges among them, simply argue that apples and oranges cannot be compared. Others launch a more sophisticated economic argument that, over time, women will on their own move into better-paying "male" jobs and that the economic playing field will be eventually leveled without interference in the market. In fact, they say, any manipulation of the market will have a reverse effect and actually drive down wages in jobs and otherwise upset a crucial market equilibrium. Others go so far as to fear the complete downfall of the American economy, seeing comparable worth as

AFSCME v. State of Washington

"pregnant with the possibility of disrupting the entire economic system of the United States of America." *Lemons v. City and County of Denver*, 17 Fair Empl. Prac. Cas. (BNA) 906, 906 (1978).

The proponents of comparable worth argue that it provides a way of creating equality when the original playing field is far from equal. Using market principles to set wages, they argue, is:

> ... [a] simplistic vision based on laissez-faire theories of competitive markets characterized by the operation of unfettered supply and demand. These notions must be viewed with suspicion, since they apply poorly, if at all, to the market for labor as opposed to the market for products. People are not sold in the market for labor as goods are sold in the market for products ... To the extent that the "market" is nothing more than a cost justification defense for paying women, and other protected groups, the lowest wages they can be employed for, the "market" should not be allowed as a defense [to a Title VII claim].
>
> National Center for Economic Alternatives, *Amicus* Brief,
> *AFSCME v. State of Washington*, 578 F.Supp. 853 (1984).

In fact, using a comparable worth theory to set wages is not an entirely new idea: something like comparable worth was used by the National War Labor Board during World War II. *See* TERMINATION REPORT OF THE NATIONAL WAR LABOR BOARD: INDUSTRIAL DISPUTES AND WAGE STABILIZATION IN WARTIME, ch. 24 (1947–49). Additionally, American industry has long used a similar method in setting salaries. During the hearings for the EPA, corporation representatives concerned about the ramifications of federal legislation testified that the standard in American industry was to use formal, systematic job evaluation plans to set wages, assessing four separate factors to determine job value: skill, effort, responsibility, and working conditions. Under a job evaluation plan, point values are assigned to each of the subcomponents of a given job, resulting in a total point figure representing a relatively objective measure of the job's value. *See* Senate Hearings 96–104; House Hearings 232–40; *see also* House Hearings 304–05, 307–08. This job evaluation plan sounds remarkably similar to the comparable worth system used by Willis & Associates in the study that the state of Washington commissioned.

A brief history of the jurisprudential developments from the EPA through Title VII illustrates why a decision today favoring a comparable worth system is a sensible next step. The final version of the EPA was a compromise between those who wanted equal pay for identical jobs and those who wanted equal pay for comparable jobs. *See* S. Rep. No. 176, 88th Cong., 1st Sess. (1963); *see also* Susan Kelley-Claybrook, *The Comparable Worth Dilemma: Are Apples and*

358   AFSCME v. State of Washington

Oranges Ripe for Comparison?, 37 BAYLOR L. R. 227 (1985). But the standard of comparison (identical, equal, or comparable) under the EPA remained murky until the Supreme Court clarified the standard in *Corning Glass Works v. Brennan*, 417 U.S. 188 (1974). The Court looked to the impetus for the enactment of the EPA, writing:

> Congress' purpose in enacting the Equal Pay Act was to remedy what was perceived to be a serious and endemic problem of employment discrimination in private industry – the fact that the wage structure of "many segments of American industry has been based on an ancient but outmoded belief that a man, because of his role in society, should be paid more than a woman even though his duties are the same." S.Rep. No. 176, 88th Cong., 1st Sess., 1 (1963).   *Id.* at 195.

The issue in *Corning* was whether the company's practice of paying night shift inspectors, who were all men (because of state laws that had prohibited women from working at night), more than it paid day shift inspectors, largely women. Corning argued that the jobs were different and that the fourth affirmative defense – a factor "other than sex" – was the reason for the pay difference. The Court disagreed and found that the jobs, although not identical, were "substantially equal," thus creating a standard for comparison in between comparable and identical. *Id.* at 234.

Title VII expanded the protection of the EPA and prohibited a broad range of employment decisions from being based on sex, including compensation, which is seemingly redundant if it is meant only to replicate the provisions of the EPA. Instead, the passage of Title VII and subsequent interpretations embraced a much broader view of what could constitute discrimination and a much fuller understanding of the reasons for the discrimination. By the early 1970s, Congress understood this:

> In 1964, employment discrimination tended to be viewed as a series of isolated and distinguishable events, for the most part due to ill-will on the part of some identifiable individual or organization . . . Employment discrimination as viewed today is a far more complex and pervasive phenomenon. Experts familiar with the subject now generally describe the problem in terms of "systems" and "effects" rather than simply intentional wrongs, and the literature on the subject is replete with discussions of . . . the mechanics of seniority and lines of progression, perpetuation of the present effect of pre-act discriminatory practices . . .
>   S. Rep. No. 415 at 5; *accord*, H.R Rep. No. 238 92d Cong (1971).

This Court is unconvinced by the doom-and-gloom predictions of the critics of comparable worth and instead is persuaded by the arguments put forth by *amici* and others that comparable worth is a useful and equitable tool for setting salaries. It is also persuaded by the jurisprudential developments concerning Title VII over the last decade. Employment discrimination comes in many guises, and the purpose of Title VII is to eliminate it. Therefore, while this Court does not order the state of Washington to use its own extensive comparable worth studies to set salaries for state jobs, it recommends that it do so. This Court also recommends that the state vigorously implement measures to integrate the workplace so that there are fewer predominantly female- and male-dominated positions.

VI REMEDIES

Once it has been established that a Title VII violation has occurred, courts have discretion to fashion an appropriate remedy. "If the Court finds that the respondent has intentionally engaged in or is intentionally engaging in an unlawful employment practice charged in the complaint, the Court may enjoin the respondent from engaging in such unlawful employment practice, and order such affirmative action as may be appropriate ..." 42 U.S.C. §2000e–5(g). The district court ordered both injunctive relief and back pay. We affirm that decision.

The state argues against injunctive relief for a variety of reasons, but primarily because of the cost and the effect on the state budget in a time of budgetary crisis. It is a distressingly familiar excuse to treat women unfavorably in a time of financial crisis. That mythology – that women do not need the money as much as men do – cannot continue. Many of the women who are unfairly underpaid by the state are the sole support of their families. Moreover, even if women as a group may rely on men for support, an employer may not choose under the statute to discriminate against women merely because, statistically as a group, women contribute less to their families' support. If the state has a financial crisis, it must be shared by all – women and men.

The state also argues that it plans to rectify the pay discrepancies *in the future*. That is not acceptable. As the district court aptly pointed out: "It is time, *right now* for a remedy. Defendant's preoccupation with its budget constraints pales when compared with the invidiousness of the impact ongoing discrimination has upon the Plaintiffs herein." *AFSCME*, 578 F.Supp. at 868.

Finally, the district court ordered that the employees who had been subject of discrimination receive back pay to make them whole for the years of inequity in pay scales. The "make whole" purpose of Title VII is evident from its legislative history. *See Albemarle Paper Co. v. Moody*, 422 U.S. 405,

360 AFSCME v. State of Washington

419 (1975) ("The backpay provision was expressly modeled on the backpay provision of the National Labor Relations Act"). The *Albemarle* Court went on to delineate the circumstances under which back pay should be awarded and how it should be reviewed on appeal:

> [G]iven a finding of unlawful discrimination, backpay should be denied only for reasons which ... would not frustrate the central statutory purposes of eradicating discrimination throughout the economy and making persons whole for injuries suffered through past discrimination. The courts of appeals must maintain a consistent and principled application of the backpay provision, consonant with the twin statutory objectives, while at the same time recognizing that the trial court will often have the keener appreciation of those facts and circumstances peculiar to particular cases. *Id.* at 422.

Acknowledging that the district court had a much keener appreciation of the facts of this case, we affirm the district court's opinion to award back pay.

VII CONCLUSION

If the sweeping intentions of Congress in enacting Title VII are to be realized and if the groups that have been systematically barred from the best-paying jobs merely because of their group identity are to have an equal opportunity to thrive, then employers have not only a negative obligation not to discriminate, but also a positive obligation to find ways of dismantling the entrenched bias that exists in the market. The "neutral" arbiter of value in the market is a white, able-bodied male. Any so-called market equilibrium serves these men, and it comes as no surprise that so many fear a change. A world of solely white, male, able-bodied employees is not the world we live in. That is not the landscape in the employment market. This Court does not assume that fairness comes easily after centuries of discrimination. But come it must, and this is a first step.

Accordingly, this Court finds that the district court correctly found that the state of Washington violated Title VII under both disparate treatment and disparate impact theories. The district court correctly ordered a declaratory judgment against the state of Washington. It correctly ordered injunctive relief and back pay.

* * *

The opinion is affirmed in whole.
It is so ordered.

Commentary on *Equal Employment Opportunity Commission v. Sears, Roebuck & Co.*

MARIA L. ONTIVEROS

INTRODUCTION: THE SOFTER SIDE OF SEARS

When I was growing up, Sears meant two things: Craftsman tools and Kenmore appliances. Craftsman tools were known to be tough and came with a lifetime guarantee. They were a perfect gift for men and, like Sears Kenmore appliances, a staple in households across America. While lacking upscale style, they offered quality and durability at a price that wouldn't break the bank. These products, along with their Die Hard batteries and the location of Sears Auto Centers adjacent to many stores, created a retail store with a very masculine feel.

I have another memory of Sears: a television advertising campaign with a soothing melody imploring customers to "Come see the softer side of Sears." In an imaginative use of word play, images of jewelry, cosmetics, clothing, and formal wear floated across the screen as examples of hardware, paintbrushes, seat covers, and flashlights. Sears was looking to rebrand itself – reaching out to customers interested in products other than washers, dryers, screwdrivers, and drills. And it worked. The 1990s advertising campaign was wildly successful and was credited with revitalizing Sears' flagging sales revenue.[59] Sears had managed to change its gender in the eyes of American consumers.

It is not surprising that retail stores use advertising to create an image that appeals to consumers of certain demographics that they deem desirable. It may be surprising that the same retail stores, when acting as employers, create structures designed to appeal to employees of certain demographics that they deem desirable. This can result in a workplace segregated by sex. When these structures and the underlying decisions made to create them remain invisible and unexplored, the segregation is not analyzed or viewed as discriminatory. Such was the case of Sears, Roebuck & Company. When the US Equal Employment Opportunity Commission (EEOC) challenged Sears' segregated workforce, the US Court of Appeals for the Seventh Circuit could not recognize the discrimination.[60] In her reimagined opinion, Professor Leticia Saucedo, writing as Judge Saucedo, deftly explains why and how Sears did, in

---

[59] Susan Chandler, *Sears' "Softer Side" May Be Too Limp to Survive*, CHICAGO TRIBUNE (Feb. 18, 1999), www.chicagotribune.com/news/ct-xpm-1999–02-18–9902180317-story.html. The advertising campaign is unrelated to Sears' hiring practices challenged in the case.

[60] 839 F.2d 302 (7th Cir. 1988).

362   EEOC v. Sears, Roebuck & Co.

fact, engage in discriminatory practices when creating a "softer side" in its noncommissioned workforce.

THE ORIGINAL OPINION: CREDITING STORIES OVER STATISTICS

The EEOC challenged Sears' employment practices, focusing on its methods for hiring and promotion into the commissioned sales force. The EEOC offered two main types of proof of discrimination: regression analysis, to establish that there was a statistically significant disparity in the presence of women in the commissioned sales force, and a description of the subjective selection process chosen by Sears that encouraged – or, at the very least, allowed – discriminatory practices.[61] The store did not respond with statistical evidence. Instead, it offered testimony by Sears managers and officials describing the difficulty in finding women who were interested in commissioned sales positions or who were qualified. The district court gave more weight to this evidence than to the government's statistical analysis and made three key findings, which the circuit court believed were not clearly erroneous. The district court found that a commissioned sales job was significantly different from a noncommissioned sales job, that women showed a lack of interest in selling on commission, and that women were not as qualified to work in commissioned sales.[62] Based on these findings, the lower court concluded that the lack of women in commissioned sales positions was the result of lack of interest and lack of qualifications, not discrimination.

The Seventh Circuit's discussion of the lack of interest defense illustrates its basic approach to reviewing the decision of the lower court. It agreed with the district court that the most credible and convincing evidence offered was the "detailed, uncontradicted testimony of numerous men and women who were Sears store managers, personnel managers and other officials" who were unable to recruit women into commission sales.[63] Testimony established that women preferred to sell noncommissioned product lines, such as clothing, jewelry, and cosmetics, while men preferred commissioned product lines, such as automotives, roofing, and furnaces.[64] Sears managers also testified that women did not want to work on outside sales, implying that women were afraid to enter strangers' homes at night, and further that women feared or disliked the "cut-throat competition, and increased pressure and risk

[61] *Id.* at 312–13 (7th Cir. 1988).
[62] *Id.* at 319.
[63] *Id.* at 320.
[64] *Id.*

EEOC v. Sears, Roebuck & Co.   363

associated with commission sales."[65] Finally, Sears' witnesses testified that
women were attracted to noncommissioned sales work because it "was associated with more social contact and friendship, less pressure and less risk."[66]
With regard to qualifications, the court concluded that some subjectivity in
hiring is allowable and dismissed concerns that hiring managers relied on
testing manuals containing questions that would more likely be answered
correctly by men.[67]

In light of this testimony, the court found that no discrimination existed. It
harshly criticized the EEOC for its failure to come forward with even one
witness describing a specific instance of discrimination, and it concluded that
the "district court properly recognized the value of anecdotal evidence when it
determined that lack of individual victim testimony reinforced its conclusions
regarding the deficiencies in the EEOC's statistical evidence."[68]

THE FEMINIST JUDGMENT: HOLDING EMPLOYERS ACCOUNTABLE
FOR GENDERING JOBS AND COURTS ACCOUNTABLE
FOR UNDERSTANDING STATISTICS

In the rewritten opinion, Saucedo reaches a starkly different conclusion from
that of the circuit court. She overturns the district court's finding of no
discrimination, relying on three main arguments. First, she fully credits the
statistical analysis offered by the EEOC, concluding that "Dr. Siskin's analyses
exposed a statistically significant differential hiring pattern ... based on gender, even after controlling for differences based on" Sears' nondiscriminatory
sought-after characteristics, such as job applied for, age, education, job type
experience, product line experience, and commission product sales experience. Second, she rejects the district court's findings as clearly erroneous
because they are based on gendered stereotypes about the types of jobs
women will take, emphasizing that these stereotypes also include stereotypes
about class and race. Finally, she explicates the ways in which employers can –
and Sears did – structure its workplace and hiring processes to gender[69]
commissioned sales jobs as masculine. Each of these arguments offers insights

---

[65] Id.

[66] Id. at 321.

[67] Id. at 332.

[68] Id. at 311.

[69] "Gender" can be used as a verb when people or organizations affirmatively act to define
something as masculine or feminine, or try to influence the way in which masculine and
feminine identities are portrayed or understood. John Totten, On Gender as a Verb, THE GOOD
MEN PROJECT (Mar. 5, 2016), https://goodmenproject.com/featured-content/on-gender-as
-a-verb-snsw/.

364 EEOC v. Sears, Roebuck & Co.

into how the doctrine of employment discrimination law could have evolved to provide greater equality for all women in the workplace had the Saucedo opinion been issued.

The need for courts to understand and fully credit statistical analysis, especially for systemic pattern or practice discrimination claims, has become critical because less direct evidence of discriminatory conduct exists. The effects of discriminatory practices still exist, apparent in statistical analysis, even if there is no "smoking gun" evidence of discriminatory animus. Cases such as *Wal-Mart v. Dukes*[70] illustrate the need for courts to find that statistics can establish discriminatory conduct under Title VII of the Civil Rights Act of 1964. In cases involving subjective hiring practices, statistics can provide a particularly important way of proving that subjectivity allowed unconscious biases to infect the employment process. If Saucedo's approach to crediting statistical analysis, coupled with the subjective practices, had been established in 1988, it is possible that a better understanding of the nature of pattern and practice discrimination could have changed the outcome of cases such as *Wal-Mart* in 2011.

Saucedo also clearly states that courts may not rely on stereotypes based on historically and biologically inaccurate information. In 1873, the US Supreme Court, in *Bradwell v. Illinois*,[71] infamously found that Illinois' prohibition of women from the practice of law was acceptable because "Man is, or should be, women's protector and defender. The natural and proper timidity and delicacy which belongs to the female sex evidently unfits it for many of the occupations of civil life."[72] Twenty-five years later, in *Muller v. Oregon*,[73] the Supreme Court affirmed a state regulation limiting the number of hours women could work because it was "obvious" that "woman's physical structure and the performance of maternal functions place her at a disadvantage in the struggle for subsistence," and working long hours "tends to injurious effects upon the body, and, as healthy mothers are essential to vigorous offspring, the physical well-being of woman becomes an object of public interest and care in order to preserve the strength and vigor of the race."[74] Further, the Court found that women were dependent on men and that "some legislation to protect [women] seems necessary to secure a real equality of right."[75] While courts may no longer proclaim these sexist stereotypes themselves, Saucedo

[70] 564 U.S. 338 (2011) (refusing to certify what would have been the largest employment discrimination class action in history); *see also* the rewritten *Wal-Mart* opinion in this volume.

[71] 83 U.S. (16 Wall.) 130, 141 (1872).

[72] *Id.* at 141.

[73] 208 U.S. 412 (1908).

[74] *Id.* at 421.

[75] *Id.* at 422.

demonstrates how accepting arguments based on stereotypes as "facts" can be just as detrimental in perpetuating discrimination.

Saucedo highlights how the "lack of interest" defense stereotypes the kinds of work that interest women. Moreover, it perpetuates the stereotype that women seek only work in which they are interested. As Saucedo points out, the district court continually relies on stereotypically feminine traits as the reason why women are not interested in commissioned sales jobs and credits these presumed traits as facts sufficient to overcome statistical disparities. According to the court, women are not interested in commissioned jobs because women are fearful, dislike competition, and prefer certain product types (cosmetics, jewelry, and clothing). Saucedo demonstrates that there is only a difference of degree, not of kind, between the *Sears* court's reasoning and the antiquated analysis found in *Bradwell* and *Muller*. Unfortunately, the lack of interest defense has taken hold in the courts and has been used to disadvantage plaintiffs in both race and sex discrimination cases.[76]

With respect to Sears' arguments that women are not qualified to do commissioned work, Saucedo explains how Sears developed a list of traits necessary to do the job that had a definite masculine tilt, including aggressiveness, competitive drive, and dominance. In addition, she shows that training manuals and interview questions equated these traits (competitiveness and drive) with experiences most likely associated with men. Thus Sears asked applicants if they ever played football, rather than if they had ever been successful in any type of competition, which could have included anything from softball to baking or spelling bees. By ignoring the stereotypes embedded in Sears' rationale and accepting Sears' arguments over the statistical analysis offered by the EEOC, the court accepted these stereotypes as facts.

Saucedo also emphasizes that the stereotypes buttressing the lack of interest defense are based not only on sex, but also on race and class. She argues that working-class women – especially working-class women of color – enter the workplace primarily because of a need to earn income for the entire household. They are not driven to choose certain jobs out of "interest." She could have added how the court's finding that women work primarily for "social contact and friendship" is also influenced by race and class because it perpetuates the narrative of women – represented by white, middle-class women – who work for "pin money" or because they are bored and want to get out of the house. This stereotype ignores the realities of women of color and all working-class women who have always been a large presence in the labor force.

[76] Vicki Schultz & Stephen Petterson, *Race, Gender, Work and Choice: An Empirical Study of the Lack of Interest Defense in Title VII Cases Challenging Job Segregation*, 59 U. CHI. L. REV. 1073 (1992); Vicki Schultz, *Taking Sex Discrimination Seriously*, 91 DENV. L. REV. 995 (2015).

366   EEOC v. Sears, Roebuck & Co.

Finally, Saucedo highlights how Sears created the commissioned and non-commissioned job categories and then affirmatively structured them in a gendered way.[77] Importantly, drawing upon the expert testimony of Dr. Kessler-Harris, she provides historical examples of how other employers have done this in other fields, such as banking. A similar phenomenon can be found in the facts underlying *Corning Glass Works v. Brennan*.[78] In that case, prior to 1925, Corning Glass had structured its inspector job as a woman's job and hired only women as inspectors. When the company needed to add a night shift of inspectors, it was required to hire men for that shift because women were prohibited by law from working at night.[79] To attract men to what had previously been labeled a woman's job, the company was forced to pay men more.[80] In finding a violation under the Equal Pay Act of 1963, the Supreme Court emphasized that the difference in pay was not due to a shift differential (there were no other shift differentials for any other job), but because men had to be paid more to perform what had been regarded as "demeaning tasks" associated with women.[81] A more contemporary example of this phenomenon is the way in which high-tech employers structured circuit board assembly jobs in the 1980s–2000 to fit a workforce that was "small, foreign and female."[82] The employers claimed, on the one hand, that these women were better suited to the job because of their unique skills (dexterity, concentration, etc.) and, on the other, paid them less because, as immigrants, they were said to be able to survive on less income. In this way, employers not only gendered jobs, but also used race and immigrant status to their advantage.[83] Most recently, understanding how employers use a combination of policies and practices that may at first appear neutral, but which ultimately work to systematically disadvantage women has become key to challenging employment practices in glass-ceiling lawsuits, currently prevalent in law firms, the financial service sector, and big-box stores.[84]

---

[77] For a discussion of how employers shape women's work aspirations through structural and cultural features of work organizations, *see* Vicki Schultz, *Telling Stories about Women and Work: Judicial Interpretations of Sex Segregation in the Workplace in Title VII Cases Raising the Lack of Interest Defense*, 103 Harv. L. Rev. 1749 (1990).

[78] 417 U.S. 188 (1974).

[79] *Id.* at 191.

[80] *Id.* at 204–05.

[81] *Id.* at 205.

[82] Maria L. Ontiveros, *A Vision of Global Capitalism that Puts Women and People of Color at the Center*, 3 J. Small & Emerging Bus. L. 27, 35–36 (1999); Karen J. Hossfeld, *Their Logic against Them: Contradictions in Sex, Race, and Class in Silicon Valley*, in Women, Workers and Global Restructuring 149 (Kathryn Ward ed. 1990).

[83] Ontiveros, *supra* note 82; Hossfeld, *supra* note 82.

[84] *See generally* Tristin K. Green, *Targeting Workplace Context: Title VII as a Tool for Institutional Reform*, 72 Fordham L. Rev. 659 (2003).

EEOC v. Sears, Roebuck & Co. 367

As a related benefit, if Saucedo's opinion had been the original opinion, it could have established an approach for accepting social science research as a way of explaining the presence of discrimination. Her opinion highlights and fully accepts the nuances of Dr. Kessler-Harris's research, which revealed the role of both the employer and economic factors in creating a context that explains the differences in application rates. The original opinion found this expert testimony less convincing than the testimony of Sears personnel. As discrimination has become more complex and more hidden, social science research explaining the underlying constructs has become essential to understanding the nature of discrimination in pattern and practice cases, yet its acceptance is still controversial.[85] Plaintiffs have also found the use of social science research necessary in other areas of discrimination, such as cases challenging "English Only" language policies as a form of national origin discrimination due to a phenomenon known as code-switching. The social science evidence of this phenomenon has received only tentative recognition.[86] In recognizing and accepting the social science research underlying the EEOC's theory of discrimination, Saucedo's opinion provides a blueprint for how other courts could have used this type of research.

CONCLUSION: JOBS DO NOT HAVE A GENDER

When I first began practicing employment law in the San Francisco Bay Area, I was invited to attend periodic dinners hosted by Professor Bill Gould of Stanford Law School that gathered together both sides of the labor and employment bar to break bread and discuss current issues. One of these dinners featured a discussion led by EEOC attorney Jack Pemberton on the concept of the bona fide occupational qualification (BFOQ).[87] I remember that Pemberton argued that night that the only two jobs for which sex was a BFOQ were "sperm donor and wet nurse." It is hard to disagree. It is difficult to find any other job that cannot be performed by a man or a woman. However, employers continue to structure jobs and compensation in such a way to appeal primarily to men or women. When this occurs, jobs become gendered. Uncritical acceptance of these techniques and a refusal to understand

---

[85] Michael J. Zimmer, *Title VII's Last Hurrah: Can Discrimination be Plausibly Pled?*, 2014 U. Chi. Legal Forum 19, 26–33.

[86] *Pacheco v. N.Y. Presbyterian Hosp.*, 593 F.Supp.2d 599 (S.D.N.Y. 2009); Mark Colon, *Line Drawing, Code Switching, and Spanish as Second-Hand Smoke: English-Only Workplace Rules and Bilingual Employees*, 20 Yale L. & Pol'y Rev. 227, 250–57 (2002).

[87] William B. Gould, IV, *A Tribute to Professor John De J. Pemberton, Jr. at the Commencement of the Jack Pemberton Lecture on Workplace Justice*, 39 USF L. Rev. 693 (2005).

368 EEOC v. Sears, Roebuck & Co.

statistical analysis revealing these biases mean that Pemberton's vision of jobs without a gender has still not been realized.

Equal Employment Opportunity Commission v. Sears, Roebuck & Co., 839 F.2d 302 (7th Cir. 1988)

JUDGE LETICIA M. SAUCEDO DELIVERED THE OPINION OF THE COURT.

The Equal Employment Opportunity Commission (EEOC) brought this sex discrimination case against Sears, Roebuck and Co., alleging discriminatory practices in the hiring and promotion of its commissioned sales force. During a 134-day trial, the EEOC produced voluminous evidence that Sears carried out a nationwide pattern or practice of discrimination against women from March 3, 1973, to December 31, 1980. The data establishes that Sears failed to hire and promote women into commissioned sales positions at the same rate as men and paid women in "checklist"[88] positions less than it paid men in similarly situated positions. Sears challenged the evidence, but its most vigorous and concentrated defense rested on its claim that women generally were neither interested in nor qualified for work in commissioned sales.

The trial court ruled in favor of Sears on all counts. The trial court also denied the EEOC's partial summary judgment motion regarding the Sears personnel manual, which gave men, but not women, a paid day off after the birth of a child. The trial court's findings were clearly erroneous. We hold that the proffered evidence demonstrates a pattern or practice of sex discrimination stemming directly from the company's policies and practices. Sears' efforts to explain away the strong statistical evidence of discrimination are illegitimate because they are grounded in stereotypical beliefs about the types of jobs that women are willing to accept and the skills needed to qualify for commissioned salesperson positions. We reverse the trial court's findings in favor of Sears as clearly erroneous and hold that the court also erred as a matter of law when it applied a higher proof standard than is required for a pattern or practice case.

---

[88] Checklist employees are salaried management, professional, and administrative employees exempt from Fair Labor Standards Act protections. The EEOC asserted that Sears had a nationwide pattern and practice of discrimination against women in fifty-one specified checklist jobs. *EEOC v. Sears, Roebuck & Co.*, 628 F.Supp. 1264, 1328 (N.D. Ill. 1986).

EEOC v. Sears, Roebuck & Co.   369

I THE FACTS OF RECORD

We begin with a review of the evidence that the EEOC produced to show that Sears intentionally discriminated in its hiring, promotion, and wage policies.

In 1973, the EEOC filed charges against Sears, alleging that Sears had failed to hire women into higher-paid commissioned sales positions, and also that Sears paid male sales managers more than similarly situated female sales managers. Before the EEOC filed charges, few women worked in commissioned sales. After the EEOC filed its charges, Sears' numbers improved in some departments. Nevertheless, the most lucrative positions were filled disproportionately with men. These included positions in departments such as appliances and home entertainment, sporting goods, home improvements, and automotive accessories. The EEOC estimated that the men had at least twice the chance of being hired into commissioned sales positions as women. *EEOC v. Sears, Roebuck & Co.*, 628 F.Supp. 1264, 1297 (N.D. Ill. 1986). The EEOC alleged that Sears' hiring practices resulted in significant statistical aberrations that established a violation of Title VII of the Civil Rights Act of 1964. *Id.* at 1298.

A Hiring Policies

Sears controlled the hiring policies of its stores by means of directives, manuals, written policies, and common application processes. During the 1972–80 period, Sears operated 920 retail stores in five regions: Pacific Coast, Southwestern, Southern, Midwestern, and Eastern. *Id.* at 1288. Sears disseminated corporate policies, including hiring, promotion, and pay structuring, to regional and store managers. *Id.* at 1288–89. In the relevant period, retail stores had roughly fifty-five divisions. *Id.* at 1289. Salespersons were divided into noncommission and commission pay grades. *Id.* Commissioned salespersons were tasked with selling "big ticket" merchandise (e.g., major appliances); noncommissioned salespersons typically sold lower-priced items, such as paint and makeup.

Until 1977, commissioned salespersons had a "draw versus commission" system that guaranteed an amount at or below 70 percent of their average earnings. This policy changed after 1977, to a salary plus 3 percent commission plan. Noncommissioned salespersons earned an hourly rate, and they also earned a 1 percent commission on all sales until January 1979. *Id.* at 1289. Both types of sales, in other words, involved commissions in one way or another. During the relevant period, however, both full-time and part-time commissioned salespersons earned significantly more than their noncommissioned counterparts. *Id.*

370   EEOC v. Sears, Roebuck & Co.

Applicants for a sales position at Sears did not, for the most part, self-select. The application form did not have a checkbox to indicate interest in a commissioned sales position. *Id.* at 1301. Before 1974, the application asked the applicant to list the type of work sought in a blank space on the form. Between 1974 and 1980, the applicant could indicate the type of work she sought by placing a check mark next to any of the five categories listed: sales, office, mechanical, warehouse, or other. For the "other" category, the applicant could specify the type of work sought in a blank space. At all times, the application asked whether the applicant sought part-time or full-time work, permanent or temporary employment, and the hours available for work. *Id.* at 1291 n.10.

To guide interviewers in the application process, Sears disseminated a document entitled "Psychological Tests for Use in Sears Retail Stores," which outlined desired personality traits for commissioned salespersons. *Id.* at 1290. The desired qualities for these positions included a sharper intellect, a more powerful personality than other retail personnel, ample drive and physical vigor, social dominance, outgoingness, quick reactions to customers' verbal suggestions, and the ability to approach strangers. *Id.*

One part of the application process, in particular, deserves mention. Sears included a "vigor" scale test as part of the process that it claimed measures traits related to job performance. The test included questions such as, "Have you played on a football team?," "Do you have a low-pitched voice?," "Do you swear often?," and "Have you ever done any hunting?" *Id.* at 1300 n.29. Sears' test, derived from standardized tests such as the Thurstone Temperament Schedule, produced a score that accompanied the application as it moved through the process. *Id.* at 1292.

Guided by these hiring policies and practices, Sears managers sought candidates who displayed certain traits during interview, such as aggressiveness, competitive drive, effective communication skills, persuasiveness, extroversion, confidence, dominance, desire to earn a high income, resilience against rejection, enthusiasm and motivation to work, personal appearance, and maturity. *Id.* at 1290. One need not look into a crystal ball to see where these hiring practices would lead.

B Statistical Evidence

The results of Sears' hiring efforts are stark. In 1973, women comprised 73.5 percent of the full-time noncommissioned sales positions, but only 15.4 percent of the full-time commissioned sales positions. Plaintiffs' Proposed Findings of Fact and Conclusions of Law, 9, *EEOC v. Sears,*

EEOC v. Sears, Roebuck & Co.   371

Roebuck & Co., 628 F.Supp. 1264 (1986). The numbers were not much different in 1980, the end of the EEOC challenge period. Between 1973 and 1980, for example, women constituted 61 percent of all full-time sales applicants at Sears, but only 27 percent of the newly hired full-time commission sales force. In contrast, women made up approximately 75 percent of Sears' noncommission sales force. Brief of Equal Employment Opportunity Comm'n as Appellant at 7.

In determining the significance of differential hiring patterns, experts measure the standard deviation to estimate the likelihood that a difference occurred by chance. A standard deviation of 2 indicates approximately 5 percent probability that the observed results occur by chance. Courts generally accept standard deviations of 2 or 3 as significant if the results also demonstrate practical significance. *Castaneda v. Partida*, 430 U.S. 482, 496 n. 17 (1977); *Hazelwood School Dist. v. United States*, 433 U.S. 299, 308 (1977). The EEOC's expert, Dr. Bernard Siskin, concluded that the standard deviations in his analyses had both statistical and practical significance.

Dr. Siskin performed several types of statistical analyses that controlled for any differences between the male and female sales applicants on various characteristics that may have influenced their selection into commission sales, including age, education, job applied for, job type experience, product line experience, and expanded commission sales experience. *Sears*, 629 F.Supp. at 1296–98. Without going into the details of the numbers, it suffices to say that Dr. Siskin's analyses exposed a statistically significant differential hiring pattern into commissioned sales positions based on gender, even after controlling for differences based on these characteristics. *Id.*

Dr. Siskin calculated "z" values, which he used to explain the standard deviation between the expected hiring results and the actual results for hiring into commissioned sales. *Id.* at 1296. He compared those women who checked sales on their application form against those who were hired into commissioned sales positions. *Id.* at 1295. He asserted that, absent discrimination, roughly the same percentage of female applicants in the pool of applications would be hired into commissioned sales positions. *Id.* By contrast, the "z" values in his tables ranged from 11.9 to 45.1, indicating large disparities between the actual and expected percent of female commissioned salespersons on a national level for the period 1973–80. *Id.* at 1295–96. In addition, when Dr. Siskin adjusted the original pool of applicants to account for skill, interest, and experience, he still found a statistically significant discrepancy between the expected and actual hires. *Id.* at 1299–1300. He found similar discrepancies when he calculated the expected promotions for women using the proportion of women in the noncommissioned pool for each year, which he compared to the proportion of women actually hired into commissioned sales. *Id.*

In addition, Dr. Siskin calculated "T" values to measure the deviation for the compensation analysis to test the claim that women checklist cashiers were paid less than similarly situated males in fifty-one checklist positions. *Id.* at 1287. Again, Dr. Siskin's analysis revealed a statistically significant wage disparity in thirty-two of the fifty-one positions. *Id.* at 1340.

In response to the damning statistical evidence, Sears argued that the disparities were the result of women's failure to seek the higher-paid commissioned sales jobs because they were not interested in them. Sears contended that, even though most applicants did not indicate whether they were applying for commissioned or noncommissioned jobs, 75 percent of those who did express a preference for commissioned sales were men. *Id.* at 1301. In other words, it was the fault of the women themselves that Sears did not have gender balance in its commissioned sales force. Sears' evidence included the testimony of managers that women and men expressed different interests and that their efforts to convince women to take commissioned sales jobs had failed. *Id.* at 1306. In response, the EEOC produced several witnesses who shared their experiences with the Sears hiring process. Alice Howland and Lura Nader both testified that they applied to Sears and expressed their interest in commissioned sales positions. Written Testimony of Lura Nader at 1, *Sears*, 628 F.Supp. 1264; written Testimony of Alice Howland at 4, *Sears*, 628 F.Supp. 1264. Neither was hired. The EEOC introduced their testimony as direct evidence of discriminatory intent, but also to refute Sears' position that women simply were not interested in commissioned sales positions. The testimony properly supported the EEOC's case, which rested on a theory of a pattern or practice of discrimination. Both Howland and Nader testified that they felt they were discriminated against in the hiring process.

The trial court embraced Sears' explanation for the statistical aberrations based on stereotypical assumptions about women's interests and choices. In short, the court accepted Sears' argument that women had individually made choices that resulted in the general lack of opportunities for women. We address the rest of our opinion to the trial court's assumptions, which skewed its interpretation of the facts and data. Because the trial court relied on assumptions that were based on gender, class, and race stereotypes about the types of jobs women will take, its findings were clearly erroneous.

C The Historical Context for Women's Interest in Commission Sales

Sears introduced an expert on the history of work to buttress its claim that women had less interest in, and fewer qualifications for, commissioned sales

EEOC v. Sears, Roebuck & Co.

jobs. Dr. Rosalind Rosenberg testified, in essence, that societal pressures contributed to women's lack of interest in jobs that were traditionally dominated by males. Dr. Rosenberg testified that women generally prefer social and cooperative aspects of the workplace, avoid competition, and prefer the certainty in noncommissioned sales positions. *Id.* at 1308. Dr. Rosenberg testified that women tend to enter the workplace to find friendships and social contact and that they prefer jobs with less stress. *Id.* at 1308. It should come as no surprise that Dr. Rosenberg offered little empirical evidence to support her sweeping generalizations that women's desires and interests were predetermined before they entered the labor market. Importantly, Dr. Rosenberg's testimony failed to address how race, class, national origin, immigration status, or even geography may affect what employees seek in the workplace. Most importantly, her testimony did not address the role of employers in establishing gendered preferences for certain jobs and creating job requirements based on stereotypical preconceptions – a failure that, given the comprehensive testimony of the plaintiff's expert on the issue, proves to be a fatal mistake.

The EEOC presented a rebuttal expert, Dr. Alice Kessler-Harris, who testified that Sears' "interest defense" was not well grounded in history. She provided numerous examples of women who accepted a job because of the opportunity for increased income, regardless of the demands of the job. Dr. Kessler-Harris provided evidence in her testimony of the socially contingent nature of "women's" and "men's" jobs, noting that contextual factors such as the availability of men to do the work at a given price strongly influenced the gendered character of a position. She described several occupations that varied by gender depending on the region. Weavers in New England were largely women, for example, until employers moved mills to the South, where men were available to take those jobs because of local economics. Several other examples demonstrate how gender has less to do with the character of a job than the pool of people available to take the job. As she concluded, "[T]he sexual division of labor is a malleable concept." Kessler-Harris Written Testimony, at 4, Plaintiffs' Exhibit Kessler-Harris 1, *Sears*, 628 F.Supp. 1264.

Moreover, Dr. Kessler-Harris emphasized that employer preferences play a large role in perpetuating gendered workplaces. The historical patterns of women's participation in the workplace led her to conclude that, "[i]n an industrial society, a major part of the cycle of reinforcement is played by employers whose hiring policies significantly influence women's self-perception, their assessment of reasonable aspirations, and their announced goals. What appear to be women's choices, and what are characterized as

374 EEOC v. Sears, Roebuck & Co.

women's 'interests' are, in fact, heavily influenced by the opportunities for work made available to them." *Id.* at 2.

Kessler-Harris provided the following illustration to buttress her testimony that employers can shape the demand for certain positions by emphasizing aspects of the job that are stereotypically masculine or feminine:

> [I]n 1917, the banking community, faced with a shortage of labor, attracted women into clerical and lower-level managerial jobs by arguing that "women are exceptionally fitted for work of this character – their neatness, deft handling of money and papers, tact and a certain intuitive judgment all being qualifications that count in their favor." In the early 1930s, when men became available for work due to the depression, the industry changed its mind and argued that it could not hire women, even as tellers, because they were poor at figures, and because the public would not accept the notion of handing over their money to women. Between 1941 and 1944, faced again with male labor shortages, banks relented and began to hire women as tellers. Industry journals then argued that women would make ideal tellers because they were good at dealing with the public. *Id.* at 3.

This pattern or practice case rests on the facts. But facts have significance and meaning only in context. The central issue in this case can be stated plainly: can this Court accept as "facts" certain behaviors and assumptions that are grounded in stereotyped notions of men's and women's roles in the workplace that were reinforced or introduced by the employer? The trial court erroneously concluded that it should not look behind the manner in which Sears attempted to frame the facts. Despite extensive and credible statistical evidence presented by the EEOC demonstrating the disparities between the percentages of men and women hired into and promoted to commissioned sales positions (even when controlling for interest), the trial judge refused to accept the plaintiff's statistical proof, ignored Sears' failure to present its own statistics to rebut the EEOC's demonstration, and accepted Sears' framing of its own "facts" as a *complete explanation* for the statistical disparities. The trial judge credited the underlying assumptions made by Sears, and, in so doing, the court perpetuated the notion that women's feminine traits lead them to prefer noncommissioned sales positions. Working from the assumption that the lack of women in commissioned sales positions resulted from societal expectations, women's interests, and their qualifications, the court failed to acknowledge that Sears had perpetuated and encouraged these expectations, interests, and qualifications. The district court's findings of fact were therefore clearly erroneous.

EEOC v. Sears, Roebuck & Co.   375

II THE STANDARD OF REVIEW

We may reverse the trial court only if it makes a legal error or its judgment is based on findings of fact that are clearly erroneous. The trial court made both types of errors in this case. A trial court's findings are clearly erroneous if "the trial judge's interpretation of the facts is implausible, illogical, internally inconsistent or contradicted by documentary or other extrinsic evidence." *Ratliff v. City of Milwaukee*, 795 F.2d 612, 617 (7th Cir. 1986). By ignoring the statistical evidence and the expert testimony in the plaintiff's favor and accepting the defendant's illogical factual allegations, which were based on stereotypical assumptions about men and women in the workplace, the court's findings of fact are clearly erroneous. Under Title VII, employment decisions based on stereotypes of how men or women should or do behave constitute discriminatory treatment. See *Phillips v. Martin Marietta Corp.*, 400 U.S. 542 (1971) (a policy of hiring men with small children, but not women with small children, was based on discriminatory stereotypes about women); *Los Angeles Dept. of Water and Power v. Manhart*, 435 U.S. 702 (1978) (decisions based on the ascription of group-based stereotypical assumptions on an individual were held to be discriminatory); see also *Price Waterhouse v. Hopkins*, 825 F.2d 458 (D.C. Cir. 1987) (decisions based on sex-stereotyped preconceptions of appropriate behavior are discriminatory). Legal errors occur when the trial court applies a different legal standard than the one required. As we describe below, the trial court erred when it imposed a higher standard of proof than is required in a pattern or practice case.

III THE BURDEN OF PROOF

The parties agree that the EEOC has the burden of proving a prima facie case of disparate treatment discrimination under section 703(a)(1) of Title VII. 42 U.S.C. §2000e-2(a)(1). The EEOC must demonstrate by a preponderance of the evidence that Sears carried out a "pattern or practice" of discrimination against female employees. *Bazemore v. Friday*, 478 U.S. 385, 398 (1986). The plaintiff may prove its case by direct or circumstantial evidence. In this case, the EEOC chose to prove intentional discrimination by demonstrating through statistical analysis that the proportion of women in commissioned sales positions lagged far behind the proportion of women in the relevant labor market (here, the applicants for sales positions at Sears). The EEOC's evidence of disparity was statistically significant, establishing the EEOC's prima facie case.

376 EEOC v. Sears, Roebuck & Co.

The burden then shifted to Sears to demonstrate that the EEOC's evidence was inaccurate or insignificant, or to otherwise show a nondiscriminatory reason for the disparity. *International Brotherhood of Teamsters v. United States*, 431 U.S. 324, 360 (1977). It is at this juncture that Sears argued that women were choosing not to be selected for the higher-paying jobs – a position that is grounded in class- and gender-stereotypical views of what it takes to succeed as a commissioned salesperson and of the choices that women employees freely make. In addition, the district court erred by placing the burden on the EEOC to show that male and female applicants had equal interest in the commissioned sales positions. In other words, in addition to proving a statistically significant disparity, as is required in a pattern or practice case, the court required the EEOC to prove that the relevant pool included women who were actually interested in the jobs. This proof standard is unprecedented in pattern or practice litigation. We reject the district court's attempt to add this requirement to the plaintiff's prima facie case and find that the trial court erred as a matter of law in attempting to impose it.

IV ANALYSIS

A *The EEOC's Prima Facie Case*

Without belaboring the details of the voluminous statistical evidence the EEOC produced to show that Sears failed to hire women in commissioned sales positions, we accept that the EEOC proved its case. Sears failed to produce statistical evidence to rebut the EEOC's numbers or to bring forth evidence to discredit the EEOC's evidence. For example, Sears argued that the EEOC's statistical evidence, which the district court found to be statistically significant, was based on an overinclusive pool of applicants. The EEOC's pool included everyone who applied for all sales positions. Sears attempted to limit the pool of applicants to interested and qualified candidates. This construction of the pool excludes people who have been discouraged from applying for one reason or another, including those excluded because of biased understandings of who makes a good salesperson.[89] For the sake of argument, however, even when it controlled for so-called differences in applicant interest, the EEOC found significant disparities between expected

[89] Sears argues that we must defer to the district court's findings on the significance of the EEOC's statistical evidence. The trial courts weighed statistical evidence proffered by experts on both sides of the litigation, Drs. Bernard Siskin and Joan Haworth. To the extent that the trial based its conclusions on explanations of statistical evidence steeped in stereotypes, however, we cannot accept the court's findings.

and actual percentages of female commissioned sales hires. *Sears*, 628 F.Supp. at 1299–3000.

The district court also erred in accepting Sears' argument that the EEOC had to prove not only its statistical case, but also that men and women had an equal interest in commissioned sales jobs. The trial court accepted this mischaracterization of the EEOC's burden and then credited Dr. Rosenberg's testimony that inherent gender differences explained the absence of women in commissioned sales positions. Requiring the plaintiff to prove equal interest at the liability stage is unprecedented in a pattern or practice case. In *Teamsters*, the Supreme Court determined that a plaintiff can establish its prima facie case through statistical evidence showing a disparity in targeted positions. *Teamsters*, 432 U.S. at 339. The Court reasoned that disparity itself is probative evidence of discrimination. *Id.* The burden then shifts to the employer to show reasons other than discrimination for the disparity. *Id.* at 360. The Court articulated the extent of a pattern or practice case at its liability stage in *Teamsters*:

> At the initial, "liability" stage of a "pattern or practice" suit the Government is not required to offer evidence that each person for whom it will ultimately seek relief was a victim of the employer's discriminatory policy. Its burden is to establish a prima facie case that such a policy existed. The burden then shifts to the employer to defeat the prima facie showing of a pattern or practice by demonstrating that the Government's proof is either inaccurate or insignificant. *Id.*

By placing an additional requirement on the EEOC to show that all sales applicants were equally interested in commissioned sales positions, the trial court failed to shift the burden to the employer to prove its own assertions that women were not interested. Sears, in fact, failed to bring forth witnesses who were not interested in sales positions and instead relied on managers who asserted that they could not find women to fill these jobs.

Sears argues that the district court correctly questioned the absence of direct victims of discrimination in this case. However, the EEOC was not required to produce individual testimony to establish discrimination by Sears at the liability stage of litigation. *Bazemore, supra; Teamsters, supra; Hazelwood School District v. United States*, 433 U.S. 299 (1977). Although individual testimony might bring "the cold hard numbers to life," the Supreme Court has never required a party to prove individual instances of discrimination in a pattern or practice case, and this Court will not start here. *Teamsters*, 431 U.S. at 339. At the liability stage, the EEOC need only establish the pattern or practice of discrimination. Once that stage is complete, the EEOC may produce individual victims at a later hearing on remedies. *Id.* at 361. This Court declines to raise the standard of proof for the plaintiff by requiring the direct testimony of victims at the liability stage. The EEOC's evidence clearly demonstrated, through the large volume of applications, the very obvious lack of women in commissioned sales positions. Bringing forward a parade of women to testify that they applied for and did not get a job would add nothing to the broad picture of discrimination the EEOC had already painted, and it would, perversely, give credence to the argument that women's interests somehow determine job composition for which employers should not be responsible. Nonetheless, the EEOC did produce the testimony of several witnesses, including Alice Howland and Lura Nader, who testified they were interested in and applied for commissioned sales positions and were rejected. The district court therefore erred in assuming that Sears somehow rebutted the EEOC's evidence of women's underrepresentation in commissioned sales.

B Rebutting Sears' Interest and Qualifications Defense

With respect to Sears' affirmative defense, the district court accepted Sears' arguments that women either were not interested in or not qualified for these jobs, concluding that the mountain of evidence that the EEOC produced had no probative weight in the face of women's lack of interest or qualifications in commissioned sales.

There are several problems with the district court's (and Sears') assumptions. First, they are based in historically and biologically inaccurate evidence. Second, they ignore the extent to which their assumptions are based on an outdated white, upper middle-class narrative about entry into the workplace, which is different from the reality of these jobs as held by working-class women. Third, they ignore the extent to which Sears, as the employer, structured commissioned jobs to reflect behaviors associated with males. All of these assumptions lead to a conclusion that is unsupported because of its gender bias.

First, the assumptions behind Sears' interest defense are historically inaccurate. Although Dr. Rosenberg's broad categorizations may have fit normative understandings of men and women in the workplace, it failed to explain, without falling into stereotypical characterizations, the nuances that the EEOC's statistical evidence revealed. In contrast, the EEOC's expert, Dr. Kessler-Harris, provided a more accurate and nonbiased picture of the interaction between women and the workplace. Her testimony accounts for the varied intersectional experiences of men and women in the workplace, as well as the role of the employer in creating workplace expectations, hopes, and dreams. Contrary to Sears' narrative of gendered interests reflecting the natural order, the EEOC's theory and Dr. Kessler-Harris's testimony reveal a complex interaction between the employer's preferences and the systems the employer uses to attract employees to the positions it creates. There is no monolithic gender-based inherent trait controlling one's interest in a particular job. Instead, jobs have historically shifted based on the economy, the market, labor needs and supply, and personal characteristics such as race, national origin, and immigration status. Alice Kessler-Harris, OUT TO WORK: A HISTORY OF WAGE-EARNING WOMEN IN THE UNITED STATES 128 (1982).

Professor Kessler-Harris's concept of malleability demonstrates the role of employer narratives in the development of gendered jobs. Dr. Kessler-Harris's example of the role of employers in moving women into banking clerk positions is instructive. When banks faced a labor shortage at the turn of the century, they created preferences for female workers in clerk positions by associating the positions with stereotypically feminine qualities. The idea that certain jobs are intrinsically appealing to women is a cover for discriminatory shaping of the job market.

Second, by accepting Sears' interest defense, the district court ignores the lived experiences of working-class women, regardless of their race or national origin, who seek the opportunity for better-paying jobs. It compounds its error by not acknowledging the intersectional identities of women and the ways in which some jobs are tracked not only as female jobs, but also as jobs for women of color. *See, e.g.,* J. Jones, LABOR OF LOVER, LABOR OF SORROW: BLACK WOMEN, WORK, AND THE FAMILY FROM SLAVERY TO THE PRESENT (1985); Patricia Zavella, WOMEN'S WORK AND CHICANO FAMILIES: CANNERY WORKERS OF THE SANTA CLARA VALLEY (1987); Evelyn Nakano Glenn, *Racial Ethnic Women's Labor: The Intersection of Race, Gender and Class Oppression, in* HIDDEN ASPECTS OF WOMEN'S WORK (C. Bose *et al.* eds.,1987). Ultimately, women who need to earn an income to sustain a household are as motivated to enter the workplace as men, and their motivations are as aspirational as men's. Kessler-Harris, *supra*, at 123, 301. They do not have the choice to stay home, as evidenced by the long history of African American, Latina, immigrant, and low-income women entering the wage labor market in large numbers despite overt discrimination. *Id.* A finding that women simply are not interested in higher-paying jobs or jobs with better working conditions is one that relegates all working-class women to the bottom of the economic ladder.

Third, by accepting Sears' argument that women's interests govern their choice of work, the district court ignores the employer's role in structuring its jobs. As Dr. Kessler-Harris noted, women's choices are heavily influenced by the opportunities for work that employers make available. One purpose of Title VII is to target the ways in which employers perpetuate societal views of what types of jobs are appropriate for women. To the extent that Sears attributed "manly" characteristics to the commissioned sales jobs in its stores, it reinforced the very gendered stereotypes that Title VII set out to eliminate from the workplace. For example, Sears' interview questions virtually predetermined that men would be the most desirable candidates for the commissioned sales jobs.

Sears' application questions demonstrate its attitude toward success in commissioned sales. *See supra* section I.A. Notwithstanding the questionable relationship between "vigor" and a successful sales career, the questions themselves are disturbingly reflective of stereotypically male activities.[90] It is clear from the questions that Sears equated eligibility for commissioned sales positions with traits, interests, and signals of male behavior. None of these gendered traits, interests, or behaviors are – or should be – requirements for the job of commissioned salesperson.

Even if the test had little impact on ultimate decisions to hire or even if decision-makers had adjusted test scores for women, the fact that Sears' headquarters would suggest these questions indicates that Sears expected men to hold the commissioned sales positions. Sears claims it had a process for adjusting scores for women. This practice does nothing to eliminate the discriminatory effects of the test itself, especially if the expected outcome was more men than women in commissioned sales. *Teal v. Connecticut*, 457 U.S. 440 (1982).

Sears created the commissioned and noncommissioned job categories, then tracked women into the lower-paid positions through gendered assumptions and practices. The evidence shows that applicants applied for sales positions. They did not apply for commissioned or noncommissioned sales positions. Recall that the application included a section of questions such as, "Have you played on a football team?," "Do you have a low-pitched voice?," "Do you swear often?," and "Have you ever done any hunting?" It stands to reason that if these questions conflated job requirements with stereotypically male qualities, more men than women would end up in the interview pool. In fact, 75 percent of those who specifically expressed interest in the commissioned sales positions were male. The numbers may reflect the extent to which Sears' hiring process conflated traditionally masculine behaviors with success in commissioned sales.

---

[90] For example, one part of Sears' vigor scale, which purportedly tests for traits related to job performance, asks whether the applicant swears often. How is swearing related to success in selling goods?

The district court clearly erred when it accepted Sears' interest defense, rather than question the role of the employer in creating jobs that required stereotypically manly traits that were unrelated to successful performance in the jobs. Moreover, the evidence shows that Sears structured those same jobs to include after-work hours, in-home visits, competitive and pressured sales environments, and risky pay structures. After shaping these jobs to be unattractive to many women, in part because of their family obligations, Sears then blamed women for not filling them. Interestingly, Sears itself provided evidence of the effect of changes in the structure of the position on women's interest in those positions. Once Sears restructured commissioned sales jobs to include part-time work, a salary plus commissions, availability of day care, and a critical mass of female commissioned sales clerk role models, women quickly filled these positions. This evidence contradicts the district court's finding that applicant interest was primarily at play in the segregated sales positions at Sears.

The district court completely ignored uncontested evidence, including the testimony of a Sears official that Sears measured success in commissioned sales with characteristics that "on average more men possess than women." *Sears*, 628 F.Supp. at 1321. Moreover, the evidence in the record fails to show a difference in qualifications inherent in gender. Instead, the evidence clearly demonstrates that Sears' search for qualified candidates was itself embedded in stereotypically gendered and masculinized notions of qualifications and expertise.

C *Wage Discrimination*

The EEOC contends that the district court erred in applying the proof standards of the Equal Pay Act of 1963 to its Title VII wage discrimination claim. The Title VII sex discrimination standard requires that male and female salespersons doing similarly situated work be paid the same. Contrary to the trial court's characterization, the EEOC's claim was not a comparable worth claim; rather, the EEOC claimed that Sears intentionally discriminated by paying women less based on their gender. The trial court misconstrued the import of Sears' wage evaluation study in ways that make its finding clearly erroneous. It was not that Sears failed to implement a compensation program after its study, but rather that Sears used the information in the study to determine how it would treat its female workers. This is the import of *Gunther* and the line of Title VII cases that distinguish sex discrimination in wages from a comparable worth theory of discrimination. *County of Washington v. Gunther*, 452 U.S. 161 (1981). Sears intentionally created wage structures for men and women in the general job category of salesperson and denominated them as commissioned or noncommissioned based on gender.

382   EEOC v. Sears, Roebuck & Co.

The wage evaluation study demonstrated to Sears that its female and male salespeople were paid differently. Sears had control over how it structured its sales positions. It should not be allowed to structure wages differently and then argue that the jobs were not similarly situated. The trial court erred in failing to apply the Title VII disparate treatment standard in this case.

D Day's Leave with Pay Provision

The EEOC argues that the district court erred in finding that the Sears manual was not discriminatory on its face. We review this issue *de novo*. On summary judgment, we must determine whether there are genuine issues of material fact that preclude judgment as a matter of law. *Adickes v. S.H. Kress & Co.*, 398 U.S. 144, 157 (1970); Fed. R. Civ. P. 56(c). Until 1974, the Sears personnel manual allowed male employees a day off with pay when their wives gave birth, but did not afford the same to female employees giving birth. The district court held that the EEOC failed to meet its burden because it did not establish a prima facie case that the provision amounted to an enforced discriminatory policy. The district court required the EEOC to show that the written policy was actually enforced. The district court erred in refusing to accept the manual as evidence of the employer's practice or policy. The EEOC made its prima facie case by introducing the manual as evidence of Sears' policy. The existence of the policy and its wide distribution is itself evidence that the policy was "standard operating procedure, the regular not the unusual practice." *Teamsters*, 431 U.S. at 336. Sears' contention that the discriminatory policy should not count if there is a possibility that employees may not read it or know about it is specious. Sears' response that "[m]en were not required to utilize this provision, and in many instances would have fulfilled their domestic obligations when they were not scheduled for work or rearranged their work schedules so that time off was not necessary," misses the point of the policy. The policy itself reflects the outdated and stereotypical attitudes of Sears' decision-makers toward the responsibilities of men and women in the home. Women are expected to "figure it out," while men are rewarded with the possibility of time off when they have a child.

The court found an issue of material fact when it wondered whether the policy was enforced. Its interpretation misses the point. The written policy sends a message to the women at Sears that their time is not valued or that it need not be compensated. Pregnancy is seen as a detriment to mothers who work at Sears and a cause for reward for fathers who work at Sears. Clearly, the reward system is based on gender, in violation of Title VII, which prohibits sex discrimination on the basis of pregnancy, childbirth, or related medical conditions. 42 U.S.C. §2000e(k).

Ricci v. DeStefano

V CONCLUSION

The trial court's judgment is reversed because it relies on clearly erroneous factual findings that are based on stereotypical views of men's and women's interests and qualifications in the workplace. Workplace preferences are the product of feedback mechanisms between employers and employees that govern working conditions, wages, and ultimately, the opportunities for the development of future preferences. We should be skeptical when an employer argues that women are uninterested in certain jobs without a critical analysis of the working conditions and work culture that the employer offers. Hiring criteria, training programs, wages, and the parameters of the job will all have an effect on women's interests. Women do not have predetermined interests, but rather their preferences are a response to the structures the employers create. As long as courts accept the interest argument, they free employers of responsibility for their gender discrimination. Sears failed to provide us with persuasive reasons for accepting this line of reasoning. We therefore find that the trial court clearly erred.

* * *

We reverse and remand this case to the district court to determine the remedial phase of litigation.

It is so ordered.

Commentary on *Ricci v. DeStefano*[*]

REBECCA K. LEE

INTRODUCTION: EXCLUSION IN THE FIELD OF FIREFIGHTING

Fire departments in various municipalities nationwide had long kept racial minorities and women out through discriminatory hiring and promotion practices.[91] As a result, firefighting has traditionally been performed by

---

[*] *Editors' note*: *Ricci* is not a sex discrimination case, but we chose to rewrite this opinion because the original opinion may have a devastating effect on the disparate impact cause of action, which is extremely important to sex discrimination, as well as race discrimination, cases. For further explanation of the importance of rewriting *Ricci*, see Chapter 1.

[91] *See, e.g.*, Ann C. McGinley, Ricci v. DeStefano: *Diluting Disparate Impact and Redefining Disparate Treatment*, 12 Nev. L.J. 626, 626 (2012) (noting that white men, primarily of Irish, Italian, and German descent, historically filled the ranks of fire departments countrywide); Mark S. Brodin, Ricci v. DeStefano: *The New Haven Firefighters Case and The Triumph of White Privilege*, 20 S. Cal. Rev. L. & Soc. Just. 161, 196 (2011) (stating that, in the 1960s and 1970s, as a greater number of African Americans sought to join the ranks of departments, "[r]acism in both hiring and promotion was rampant"); Susan T. Epstein, *Women in the Firehouse: The Second Circuit Upholds a Gender-Biased Firefighters' Examination*, 54 Brook. L. Rev. 511, 511 (1988) (noting that firefighting has historically been a man's job and that,

384 Ricci v. DeStefano

a racially homogeneous workforce.[92] The firefighting field also has traditionally been a nearly all-male environment.[93] To address the discrimination that was commonplace in public sector employment, in 1972 Congress expanded Title VII of the Civil Rights Act of 1964,[94] which until then had applied only to private employers. Recognizing the gap this created, Congress broadened the statute to also cover discrimination by state and local employers.[95] Thus the protective arm of Title VII was extended to fire departments operated by municipalities. Despite this, there remains little diversity in firefighting today.[96] White firefighters currently make up 87.1 percent of firefighters nationally, while 8.9 percent are black, 7.4 percent Hispanic or Latino, and 1.1 percent Asian American.[97] In terms of gender, women currently make up only 5.1 percent of all firefighters.[98]

The lack of racial and gender representation continues despite efforts by some municipalities to integrate their firefighting workforces.[99] New Haven, Connecticut, is an example of a city that tried to make racial progress in its fire department, taking action that gave rise to the issues litigated in *Ricci v. DeStefano*.[100]

THE ORIGINAL OPINION: CREATING CONFLICT BETWEEN TITLE VII'S ANTIDISCRIMINATORY PROVISIONS

Ricci concerned the promotion of firefighter candidates to command positions in the New Haven Fire Department. At the time the case went to federal district court,[101] the City of New Haven's fire department was far from demographically diverse, with black firefighters making up only 5.8 percent of

---

    for example, women historically had been barred from working in the New York City Fire Department.)

[92] *See, e.g.*, Cheryl I. Harris & Kimberly West-Faulcon, *Reading* Ricci: *Whitening Discrimination, Racing Test Fairness*, 58 UCLA L. REV. 73, 75 (2010).

[93] *See id.*

[94] 42 U.S.C. §2000e *et seq.*

[95] US Equal Employment Opportunity Comm'n, *Equal Employment Opportunity Act of 1972*, www.eeoc.gov/eeoc/history/35th/thelaw/index.html (*last visited* Sep. 18, 2019) (stating that "[s]tate and local governments are no longer exempt from Title VII").

[96] Bureau of Labor Statistics, *Employed Persons by Detailed Occupation, Sex, Race, and Hispanics or Latino Ethnicity, Force Statistics from the Current Population Survey* (Jan. 22, 2020), www.bls.gov/cps/cpsaat11.htm.

[97] *Id.*

[98] *Id.*

[99] *See, e.g.*, Corinne Bendersky, *Making U.S. Fire Departments More Diverse and Inclusive*, HARV. BUS. REV. (Dec. 7, 2018), https://hbr.org/2018/12/making-u-s-fire-departments-more-diverse-and-inclusive.

[100] 557 U.S. 557 (2009).

[101] *Ricci v. DeStefano*, 554 F.Supp.2d 142, 144 (2006).

first-line supervisors.[102] The plaintiffs in *Ricci* were a group of seventeen white and one Latino firefighters in New Haven who had taken the exams administered in 2003 for promotion to either lieutenant or captain and who, because of their high scores, had a good chance of being promoted.[103] The plaintiffs were not able to move forward in the promotion process because New Haven's Civil Service Board (CSB) did not certify the exam results.[104]

In preparing to administer these promotion exams, the City had put out a request for proposals and ultimately had hired Industrial/Organizational Solutions (IOS), a company with expertise in designing exams for fire departments.[105] For promotion to captain, forty-one applicants took the corresponding exam: twenty-five white, eight black, and eight Latino.[106] Of this total group, twenty-two passed: sixteen white, three black, and three Latino.[107] The department at that time had seven openings at the captain level.[108] Using the City Charter's "rule of three," which required a civil service vacancy to be given to one of the three top-scoring individuals on the exam, the nine highest-scoring candidates turned out to be seven white and two Latino, meaning that no black and two Latino candidates at most were on the list eligible for promotion.[109]

For promotion to lieutenant, seventy-seven applicants took the corresponding exam: forty-three white, nineteen black, and fifteen Latino.[110] Of this total group, thirty-four passed: twenty-five white, six black, and three Latino candidates.[111] There were eight openings for lieutenant, but the ten highest scorers were all white, and thus no black or Latino candidates were eligible for promotion.[112]

The City's corporation counsel, Thomas Ude, raised concerns to the CSB about the significant disparate impact of both the captain and lieutenant exam results, and he ultimately recommended that the CSB not certify the results.[113]

---

[102] Brief for International Association of Black Professional Fire Fighters *et al.* as *Amici Curiae* Supporting Respondents at 6, 27, *Ricci v. DeStefano*, 557 U.S. 557 (2009) (No. 07–1428) (citing US Department of Labor Bureau of Labor Statistics).

[103] *Ricci*, 554 F.Supp.2d at 144 (decided by Judge Janet Bond Arterton); *Ricci v. DeStefano*, 557 U.S. 557, 562–63 (2009).

[104] *Ricci*, 554 F.Supp.2d at 144.

[105] *Id.* at 145.

[106] *Id.*

[107] *Id.*

[108] *Id.*

[109] *Id.*

[110] *Id.*

[111] *Id.*

[112] *Id.*

[113] *Id.* at 145–46, 150.

386   Ricci v. DeStefano

The results showed the scores by race and gender, but did not include any names, and so the applicants did not know how they ranked.[114] To obtain more information on the question of whether to certify, the CSB conducted a series of hearings.[115] Several of the applicants spoke at the hearings in support of certifying the results, arguing that the exams were fair and contained relevant and valid questions.[116] Other firefighters spoke against certification, asserting that the exams were unfair and contained irrelevant questions.[117]

The CSB also heard testimony from Chad Legel, IOS's vice president, who oversaw the development of the exams.[118] He explained that the exams were developed based on interviews with a random sample of current New Haven Fire Department lieutenants, captains, and battalion chiefs, all of whom provided information about the department, the tasks involved in each position, and training materials.[119] Using this information, IOS created a written job analysis questionnaire for the incumbent firefighters at the rank of lieutenant or captain and used the questionnaire answers to determine which tasks would be tested in the written and oral parts of the exam.[120] A syllabus listing the study materials was handed out with the promotion applications, and all of the exam questions came from the study materials.[121] Two independent reviewers from outside Connecticut checked the written and oral exam questions for substance and consistency with the source material; IOS was not allowed to use a reviewer from Connecticut because the City had concerns that using an internal reviewer could result in cheating on the test.[122] For the oral section of the exam, IOS brought in evaluators from fire departments outside Connecticut to serve as oral exam panelists.[123] IOS focused on making these oral exam panels racially diverse, with each panel except for one comprising one black, one Latino, and one white member.[124] The panelists were trained on how to assess the oral exam scenarios so that their scoring would be consistent.[125]

The CSB also took statements from Christopher Hornick, Ph.D., an industrial and organizational psychologist with a company that competed with

[114] *Id.* at 146.
[115] *Id.* at 145.
[116] *Id.* at 146.
[117] *Id.*
[118] *Id.* at 147.
[119] *Id.*
[120] *Id.*
[121] *Id.*
[122] *Id.*
[123] *Id.*
[124] *Id.*
[125] *Id.*

IOS.[126] In looking at the statistics given to him by the City (although he had not carefully reviewed the exam), he stated that the tests showed "significant adverse impact," similar to the overall data indicating that white candidates do better than ethnic minorities on standardized testing procedures, but that the results also seemed worse than those he generally saw on tests in the firefighting field.[127] Dr. Hornick was not certain of the reason for this, but he pointed to the 60:40 weighting of the written and oral parts of the exam (which was required by the collective bargaining agreement between the firefighters union and the department) as a possible explanation.[128] He knew from his research that a written exam is less valid than other existing testing processes.[129] He also commented that other types of testing mechanisms may be more effective in selecting the most qualified individuals for these posts, such as using an assessment center, which would allow applicants to demonstrate how they would tackle a given problem rather than simply to state the answer or select the correct choice on a written exam.[130]

At the close of the hearings, Ude urged the CSB to refrain from certifying the results because certification would run afoul of Title VII, and said that if a disparate impact lawsuit were brought, the CSB would have to justify its decision to use the exams.[131] The Mayor's Office also issued a statement advising against certification given the discriminatory outcomes that would result.[132] The four members of the CSB voted and tied, leading to the test results not getting certified.[133]

A group of firefighter candidates who had taken the exams sued the City of New Haven, city officials, and the two CSB members who voted not to certify the test results.[134] The plaintiffs argued that the defendants violated their rights under several federal laws: Title VII of the Civil Rights Act of 1964, the Equal Protection Clause of the Fourteenth Amendment, the First Amendment, and 42 U.S.C. §1985.[135] The parties each moved for summary judgment concerning the Title VII and equal protection claims, and the defendants further requested summary judgment on the plaintiffs' remaining claims.[136]

---

[126] *Id.* at 148.
[127] *Id.*
[128] *Id.*
[129] *Id.*
[130] *Id.* at 149.
[131] *Id.* at 150.
[132] *Id.*
[133] *Id.*
[134] *Id.* at 144.
[135] *Id.*
[136] *Id.* at 144–45.

388   Ricci v. DeStefano

The plaintiffs – one Latino and seventeen white – alleged that the defendants intentionally discriminated against them based on race and violated and conspired to violate their federal rights by voting or arguing against certifying the exam results.[137] They also contended that the defendants had political motivations in arguing against certification because they sought to appease minority constituents who wanted to promote racial diversity in the fire department.[138] In response, the defendants asserted that they had a good faith belief that certifying the results would have violated Title VII's disparate impact provision and that there should be no liability for trying to comply with this provision.[139] Moreover, they asserted that the plaintiffs did not have standing to bring their equal protection claim and that, even if they did, the claim was meritless, since all of the candidates were treated equally in that no one was promoted using those test results.[140] The plaintiffs counterargued that having a "good faith belief" that certification would violate Title VII is not a proper defense.[141]

The federal district court applied the *McDonnell Douglas* burden-shifting framework to the plaintiffs' intentional discrimination claim.[142] It concluded that the plaintiffs satisfied the first three elements in making a prima facie case of racial discrimination by proving that: (1) they were members of a protected class; (2) they were qualified for the position; and (3) they had suffered an adverse employment action.[143] To satisfy the fourth element, they had to prove that the action occurred under circumstances giving rise to an inference of discrimination.[144] Although the defendants posited that there could be no inference of discrimination because all of the candidates were treated equally, the court noted that the prima facie burden is *de minimis*, and a jury could infer that the defendants were motivated by racial considerations in advocating against certification and ultimately refusing to certify the test results because of the disparate impact of the test results.[145] The court thus assumed *arguendo* that the fourth prong of the prima facie case was satisfied.[146] The burden then shifted to the defendants to assert a legitimate, nondiscriminatory reason for taking the adverse employment action.[147] The defendants met this burden of

[137] *Id.* at 151.
[138] *Id.* at 150.
[139] *Id.* at 151.
[140] *Id.*
[141] *Id.*
[142] *Id.* at 151–52 (citing *McDonnell Douglas Corp. v. Green*, 411 U.S. 792 (1973)).
[143] *Id.* at 151–52.
[144] *Id.*
[145] *Id.* at 152.
[146] *Id.*
[147] *Id.*

Ricci v. DeStefano

production by relying on their good faith belief that, to comply with Title VII's disparate impact provision, they would have to discard the exams.[148] The burden then shifted back to the plaintiffs to show that the employer's stated reason was pretextual.[149] Here, the plaintiffs contended that the defendants sought not to uphold Title VII, but instead to respond to the interests of black firefighters and the mayor's minority supporters.[150]

As the district court explained, this case was atypical in that the plaintiffs were not arguing that the defendants used allegedly discriminatory test results, but that the defendants discriminated by refusing to use the test results.[151] To assess the level of disparate impact the tests created, the court applied the four-fifths rule set out by the Equal Employment Opportunity Commission (EEOC).[152] Under this rule, if an employer uses a selection method where the pass rate for a racial group is less than four-fifths or 80 percent of the pass rate for the racial group with the highest rate, this will generally be seen as evidence of adverse impact.[153] Regarding the lieutenant exam, the pass rate was 60.5 percent for white candidates, 31.6 percent for black, and 20 percent for Latino.[154] Thus the pass rate for black candidates was 52 percent of the pass rate for white – well below the four-fifths or 80 percent threshold – and the pass rate for Latino candidates was 33 percent of the pass rate for white candidates – also well below the four-fifths rule of thumb.[155] On the captain exam, the pass rate for white candidates was 88 percent, and despite a dispute between the parties as to the exact pass rate for black and Latino candidates on this exam, using either party's numbers the pass rate for each again fell far below the four-fifths bar.[156] Indeed, the plaintiffs did not disagree that the results demonstrated a racially adverse impact on black applicants on both the lieutenant and captain exams.[157]

---

[148] *Id.*

[149] *Id.* at 152–53.

[150] *Id.* at 153.

[151] *Id.*

[152] *Id.* at 153–54. This rule states that an employer's decision that yields a "selection rate for any race, sex, or ethnic group which is less than four-fifths (4/5) (or eighty percent) of the rate for the group with the highest rate will generally be regarded by the Federal enforcement agencies as evidence of adverse impact, while a greater than four-fifths rate will generally not be regarded by Federal enforcement agencies as evidence of adverse impact." 29 C.F.R. §1607.4(D).

[153] 29 C.F.R. §1607.4(D).

[154] *Ricci*, 554 F.Supp.2d at 153.

[155] *See id.*

[156] *Id.* at 153–54.

[157] *Id.* at 153.

390 Ricci v. DeStefano

The exam pass rate, however, is not the same as the promotion rate, as the district court correctly noted, since, under the required rule of three, only the three highest-scoring candidates could be eligible for each open position.[158] Thus it mattered how the minority candidates placed in terms of their test scores.[159] Based on the number of captain vacancies in 2003, a maximum of two Latino and zero black applicants would have been eligible for promotion.[160] Based on the number of lieutenant vacancies in 2003, no racial minorities would have been eligible for promotion.[161]

The plaintiffs argued that the defendants' rejection of the exams, without first completing a validation study to determine if the exams were sufficiently job-related, supported a showing of pretext.[162] The district court, however, disagreed.[163] Because the defendants decided against using the selection process at issue, the court found that they were not mandated to conduct a validation study under the EEOC guidelines.[164]

The plaintiffs theorized that the City wanted to diversify the fire department and thus threw out the test results, thereby engaging in reverse discrimination.[165] In addressing this claim, the court cited several Second Circuit cases showing that an employer's race-conscious actions regarding the use of exams in public safety departments to lessen adverse impact did not amount to reverse discrimination against white candidates.[166] Because there was a prima facie showing of disparate impact discrimination in *Ricci* using the EEOC's four-fifths rule, the defendants were justified in taking race-conscious steps and avoiding promotion procedures that would adversely impact black and Latino candidates.[167] The court explained that while race was an important factor in the CSB's decision not to certify the results, since the employer decided to do away with the test results completely, the outcome

[158] *Id.* at 154.
[159] *Id.*
[160] *Id.*
[161] *Id.*
[162] *Id.*
[163] *Id.* at 154–55.
[164] *Id.*
[165] *Id.* at 156–57.
[166] *Id.* at 157–59 (citing *Hayden v. County of Nassau*, 180 F.3d 42 (2d Cir. 1999), *Kirkland v. New York State Dept. of Correctional Svcs.*, 711 F.2d 1117 (2d Cir. 1983), and *Bushey v. New York State Civil Service Comm.*, 733 F.2d 220 (2d Cir. 1984)). Although two of the cases involved the race-norming or altering of the selection results based on race, a practice now prohibited under the 1991 amendments to Title VII, the district court explained that this was not an issue in *Ricci* in any event, and that the reasoning and holding of these cases still stand in allowing for an employer's race-conscious actions with respect to the use of selection procedures. *Ricci*, 554 F.Supp.2d at 159 n.9.
[167] *Ricci*, 554 F.Supp.2d at 158–59.

was race-neutral in that no one was promoted, and all candidates, regardless of race, would have to reapply using another selection process to be eligible for promotion.[168] As the court articulated, in focusing on avoiding disparate impact based on race, the CSB did not show discriminatory animus toward the plaintiffs and did not show an intent to discriminate against them.[169]

The district court also explained that the plaintiffs were not, as they put it, "deprived of promotions."[170] The plaintiffs were not guaranteed any promotion under the application of the rule of three, which at most would give the highest-scoring candidates a chance at promotion, depending on the number of open positions.[171]

While the court held that the plaintiffs had standing to bring the equal protection claim,[172] it concluded that the constitutional claim was without merit.[173] The court rejected the plaintiffs' claims that the CSB used racial classifications with respect to the exams, given that each exam was given and scored in the same way for every applicant, and because exam results for all applicants were thrown out so that no promotions resulted.[174] For the same reasons, the court further rejected the plaintiffs' claim that the test was facially neutral, but employed in a discriminatory fashion.[175] Although the plaintiffs tried to advance their equal protection claim by contending that they did well on the tests and therefore were differently situated than the minority candidates who did not perform as well, the court again noted that getting promoted was not guaranteed, even for the highest-scoring applicants.[176] The plaintiffs also failed to show that the defendants had an intent to discriminate due to the lack of evidence demonstrating any discriminatory animus.[177]

In its opinion, the district court rightly distinguished between race-conscious actions and race-discriminatory actions taken by an employer. The court understood that the kind of race-conscious action taken here was to prevent an unintentional, but harmful, disparate impact on minority and underrepresented groups, so that the selection process is fair. As the court concluded, this is not the same as a race-discriminatory decision, which

---

[168] *Id.* at 158.
[169] *Id.* at 158–60.
[170] *Id.* at 159–60.
[171] *Id.*
[172] *Id.* at 160–61.
[173] *Id.* at 161.
[174] *Id.*
[175] *Id.*
[176] *Id.*
[177] *Id.* at 161–62.

392　Ricci v. DeStefano

intentionally harms and disadvantages a racial group by undermining fairness in the selection process.

The plaintiffs appealed, and the Second Circuit affirmed in a very brief *per curiam* opinion, stating that it agreed with the "thorough, thoughtful, and well-reasoned opinion of the court below."[178] The court of appeals noted the plaintiffs' frustrated efforts and made particular reference to Frank Ricci's efforts as a candidate with dyslexia.[179] But because the CSB's actions were not prohibited under Title VII, the plaintiffs could not succeed on their claims.[180] The appellate court voted against rehearing *en banc*.[181]

The plaintiffs appealed to the US Supreme Court.[182] In a five-to-four opinion, Justice Kennedy wrote for the majority, joined by Chief Justice Roberts and Justices Scalia, Thomas, and Alito.[183] The Court departed from the lower-court opinions and sided with the plaintiffs.[184] At the beginning of its opinion, the Court conveyed its sympathy for the firefighters who wanted the results certified, stating that the candidates had spent significant time and money in preparing for the exams, as several plaintiffs had testified at the hearings before the CSB.[185] The Court recounted the testimony of Frank Ricci, who, to compensate for learning disabilities, studied for many hours a day and spent more than $1,000 on study materials and to have the information recorded on tape.[186] Even though the minority firefighters faced their own hardships in getting access to the materials,[187] Justice Kennedy did not engage

---

[178] *Ricci v. DeStefano*, 530 F.3d 87 (2d Cir. 2008) (decided by Judges Pooler, Sack, and Sotomayor).

[179] *Id.*

[180] *Id.*

[181] *Ricci v. DeStefano*, 530 F.3d 88 (2d Cir. 2008).

[182] *Ricci v. DeStefano*, 557 U.S. 557 (2009).

[183] In addition to Justice Kennedy's majority opinion, Justice Scalia wrote a concurring opinion, and Justice Alito wrote a concurring opinion that was joined by Justices Scalia and Thomas. Justice Ginsburg wrote the dissent, joined by Justices Stevens, Souter, and Breyer.

[184] *See Ricci*, 557 U.S. 557 (2009).

[185] *See id.* at 562.

[186] *Id.* at 567–68.

[187] *Ricci*, 554 F.Supp.2d at 146:

> During the first hearing, the CSB also took statements from several New Haven firefighters who complained that some of the questions were not relevant to knowledge or skills necessary for the positions (*see, e.g.,* Statement of James Watson ... ("I think this test was unfair. We don't use a lot of things that were on that test ...")), or that the study materials were difficult to obtain (*see* Testimony of Gary Kinney ... ("The only books that most of us had in front of us in the fire houses were Essentials of Fire Fighting ... .[T]hese books [on the syllabus] were never in the fire houses.")).

Ricci v. DeStefano 393

with the same level of personal detail or understanding about their experiences in trying to prepare for the exams.[188]

The Court saw the plaintiffs as having had their opportunity to be promoted taken away,[189] but the Court neglected to see it the same way for the minority candidates. Yet, because of the exams' disparate impact, the minority firefighters largely had no chance for promotion.

Through one-sided storytelling and empathizing, the Court favored the white candidates over the minority candidates,[190] further entrenching the deep foothold that white firefighters have historically benefited from in the City's fire department. Unfortunately, despite the City's efforts to comply with Title VII and remove a discriminatory obstacle for racial minorities seeking positions in the department's command positions, the Court weakened the statute's disparate impact provision. Disparate impact discrimination aims to deal with unintentional discrimination – that is, indirect discrimination caused by neutral policies or practices that yield numerically large differences in the hiring or promotion rates of members of protected classes. These differences are an all-too-common phenomenon in occupations where racial and ethnic minorities and women are significantly underrepresented.

In addressing the plaintiffs' disparate treatment claim under Title VII and the defendants' disparate impact defense, the Supreme Court acknowledged, as it had to, that Title VII prohibits both disparate treatment and disparate impact discrimination.[191] The Court began with the presumption that the CSB's actions would contravene Title VII's disparate treatment provision if it did not have a recognized defense.[192] Although the City declined to certify the exam results because of the disparate impact on minority candidates, the Court nevertheless viewed this as the kind of "express, race-based" action that Title VII prohibits.[193] The Court acknowledged that the City discarded the test results so as not to incur disparate impact liability and yet still characterized the City's action as intentionally "based on race" because the

---

[188] *See Ricci*, 557 U.S. 557 (2009); Rebecca K. Lee, *Judging Judges: Empathy as the Litmus Test for Impartiality*, 82 U. Cin. L. Rev. 145, 192–94 (2013) (arguing that the *Ricci* Court "more easily empathized with the white firefighters ... [who were] more familiar and similar to the Justices in terms of race – but did not demonstrate the same degree of empathy for the minority firefighters, with whom the majority of the Justices did not readily identify," resulting in a decision that demonstrates a failure of judicial impartiality.)

[189] *Ricci*, 557 U.S. at 574.

[190] Lee, *supra* note 188.

[191] *Ricci*, 557 U.S. at 577.

[192] *Id.* at 579.

[193] *Id.*

394   Ricci v. DeStefano

higher scorers were white.[194] Justice Kennedy narrowly looked at the consequences for the white applicants only, rather than fully assessing the City's
action within the larger context of seeking to abide by Title VII's disparate
impact provision and avoiding discrimination against the minority applicants.

The promotion exams resulted in significant disparate impact on minority
test takers, giving minority applicants strong reason to view the exams as unfair
and illegitimate, and yet Justice Kennedy still referred to the exams as "creat-
[ing] legitimate expectations on the part of those who took the tests."[195] He
went on to reiterate the time, expense, and personal dedication that some of
the firefighters put into studying for the exams, and stated that "the firefighters
saw their efforts invalidated by the City in sole reliance upon race-based
statistics."[196] Again, it is unclear why he did not also give serious weight to
the situation of the minority applicants: regardless of their efforts, the exams
disproportionately gave white applicants a greater chance of getting promoted.
Justice Kennedy failed to explain why a test that was found to have racially
disparate impact results does not upset minority candidates' legitimate expectations of a fair, unbiased assessment.

Finding that the City's action constituted unlawful disparate treatment
discrimination, the Court then examined whether the City's aim in averting
disparate impact liability could justify its actions.[197] In granting that Congress
intended employers to engage in voluntary compliance in satisfying Title VII,
the Court did not require that employers know with certainty that their
conduct would amount to disparate impact discrimination before seeking to
comply with the statute.[198] But the Court chipped away at the protections
against disparate impact in order to prioritize the statute's prohibition against
intentional discrimination. The Court characterized intentional discrimination as the "original, foundational prohibition of Title VII,"[199] and it noted
that, although Congress amended Title VII to include the disparate impact
prohibition, Congress did not eliminate protection against disparate treatment
liability when an employer acts in good faith to comply with the disparate
impact provision.[200] The Court expressed concern that permitting employers

---

[194] *Id.* at 579–80 (referring to the City's objective in avoiding disparate-impact liability, the Court
    directs that the "City's conduct in the name of reaching that objective" should not be over-
    looked, and that "[w]hatever the City's ultimate aim – however well intentioned or benevolent
    it might have seemed – the City made its employment decision because of race. The City
    rejected the test results solely because the higher scoring candidates were white.")
[195] *Id.* at 583.
[196] *Id.*
[197] *Id.* at 580.
[198] *Id.*
[199] *Id.* at 581.
[200] *Id.*

to take race-conscious actions if they have a good faith belief that they otherwise would be engaging in disparate impact discrimination could cause them to take such action based on the smallest showing of disparate impact.[201] Oddly, the Court ignored the purpose of the EEOC's four-fifths rule in providing clear guidance on how much disparate impact would demonstrate significant and actionable disparate impact. This rule could, however, be used to support an employer's good faith belief that it could not proceed with the practice causing the disparate impact.

Justice Kennedy, in diverging from Title VII's purposes and aims as he laid out the Court's reasoning, adopted a new standard, which would allow an employer to violate a provision under Title VII only when the employer had a "strong basis in evidence" that the employer's policies or practices resulted in an illegal disparate impact.[202] The Court adopted this standard from its constitutional cases under the Equal Protection Clause and applied this constitutional standard to Title VII statutory law.[203]

Departing from the reasoning of the lower courts, Justice Kennedy agreed with the plaintiffs that since Title VII does not allow the rescoring of a test based on race, then Title VII also must not allow discarding the results of a test to attain a better racial distribution of candidates eligible to be promoted (unless there is a strong basis in evidence that disparate impact liability would result).[204] He did not explain, however, why rescoring a test and discarding a test are the same thing, given that each leads to different consequences for the test-takers, as the district court had fully explained.

The Supreme Court ultimately held that the defendants did not satisfy the strong basis-in-evidence standard in seeking to comply with Title VII's disparate impact provision.[205] Although the pass rates for the minority candidates on both promotion exams were far below the EEOC's 80 percent standard, this established only a prima facie case of disparate impact discrimination, the Court said, and more would be needed for the City to be liable for such discrimination.[206] Specifically, the exams would have had to fail the test for job-relatedness and business necessity, or there would have had to be an alternative selection tool that was less discriminatory and equally valid.[207] The Court found that the exams here were job-related and consistent with

[201] Id.
[202] Id. at 582–83.
[203] See id.
[204] Id. at 584.
[205] Id. at 585–93.
[206] Id. at 585–87.
[207] Id. at 587.

business necessity.[208] Moreover, according to the Court, there was not a strong basis in evidence that a less discriminatory and equally valid alternative selection tool was available that the City rejected using.[209]

The Court disagreed with the defendants' various arguments that an alternative existed. First, a different weighting of the written and oral parts of the exam (e.g., using a 30:70 weighting instead of the 60:40 that was used) was not an equally valid substitute that the City could have used because there was a lack of evidence that the weighting used was arbitrary.[210] Second, the City could not have applied the City Charter's rule of three differently after seeing the test results because Title VII bars adjusting test results based on race.[211] Third, there was insufficient evidence that another testing tool, such as an assessment center, was an available selection procedure in 2003 and that using a different tool would have yielded less discriminatory results.[212] The Court found that there was no genuine issue of material fact that the respondents did not have a strong basis in evidence and held that the City's action violated Title VII, reversing the lower court and granting summary judgment for the plaintiffs on their disparate treatment claim.[213] Because answering the Title VII question resolved the plaintiffs' grievance, the Court did not reach the Equal Protection Clause issue.[214]

The Court ended its opinion by reemphasizing the plight of the white candidates who had sacrificed in preparing for the exams, once again referring to their "justified" expectations that the exam results would not be thrown out and suggesting that, as a result, their "injury caused by the City's reliance on raw racial statistics at the end of the process was all the more severe."[215] It is hard to miss the Court's repeated mentions of the hardship and cost to the white candidates, reminding the reader of the majority group candidates' difficulties as individuals trying to succeed on a promotion exam. By describing what was at stake for the other candidates as simply "raw racial statistics," however, the Court impersonalized and dismissed the difficulties and injured expectations of the minority candidates who, as individuals, also wanted to succeed.

The Court heard the grievances of the white male plaintiffs more vividly and ultimately empathized with their asserted injury in not getting promoted.

[208] *Id.*
[209] *Id.* at 589–92.
[210] *Id.* at 589–90.
[211] *Id.* at 590.
[212] *Id.* at 591–92.
[213] *Id.* at 592–93.
[214] *Id.* at 593.
[215] *Id.*

The white male candidates' stories took precedence over the stories of the minority male candidates, following a pattern in which the stories of women and other marginalized individuals are overlooked.

THE REWRITTEN OPINION: RESTORING THE FULL PROMISE AND PURPOSE OF TITLE VII

Professor Marley S. Weiss, writing as Justice Weiss in her rewritten opinion, demonstrates why the majority of the Supreme Court got it wrong and rules in favor of the defendants. She upholds the purpose of Title VII by laying out what the disparate treatment and disparate impact provisions are each meant to address. Her opinion allows these provisions to coexist as equally important, rather than pitting them against each other. In her opinion, Weiss better ensures that Title VII can continue to rein in employer practices that constitute intentional discrimination or unintentionally result in significant disparities based on a protected trait, including race and gender.

Addressing the plaintiffs' core claim, Weiss differentiates between an employer's consideration of race in statistical outcomes and an employer's classifications directly based on race, and she concludes that the former does not amount to direct or intentional discrimination. As she states:

> [V]erbally treating the City's decision-making as though it were directly based on the race of the affected employees, thus categorizing black candidates and white candidates differently, does not transform the plaintiffs' allegations into claims of actual facial discrimination under our precedents. The City indirectly took aggregate racial outcomes into account in a policy-making decision, as opposed to directly classifying individual employees for different treatment based on their race.

Consistent with the Supreme Court's precedents, including on workplace affirmative action under Title VII and the Equal Protection Clause, Weiss shows that taking into account race or gender as part of an employment policy is not the same as a policy that directly distinguishes on the basis of race or gender.

Weiss also gives more credence to the City's disparate impact defense, characterizing the City's actions as "diagnosing and preventing a present violation." In light of this, she recasts the question before the Court as "whether there was sufficient evidence that certifying the test results would likely have led to an actionable disparate impact claim brought by black and Latino candidates against the City." Like the appellate and district courts, Weiss reasons that because the CSB did not certify the test results, their action was facially neutral in that none of the candidates – white, black, or Latino – were promoted. The CSB's action did not result in facially discriminatory classifications. In evaluating whether the plaintiffs could prove their disparate treatment claim, Weiss appropriately places the burden on them to prove that the CSB threw out the test results "because of the race of the most successful candidates, rather than because it wished to avoid violating the Title VII disparate impact provisions."

Weiss rejects the defendants' proposed "good faith" defense to a Title VII claim in this situation and adopts the somewhat stricter "actual and reasonable belief" defense. Because the Court's "firm" and "strong basis in evidence" standards used in the context of the Equal Protection Clause apply when the alleged government action involves direct affirmative action classifications based on race or gender, Weiss concludes that these standards are too stringent to use for the facially neutral action by the employer in this case. Given that the City in *Ricci* did not use an affirmative action plan, using a less strict evidentiary standard, as Weiss does, seems appropriate here.

Looking at the evidence that the employer had at the time it took its challenged actions, Weiss asserts that the CSB met its burden of production in setting forth its legitimate nondiscriminatory reason by producing evidence that it discarded the test results to prevent a Title VII violation. If the employer demonstrated as a matter of law that it had an actual and reasonable belief in light of the evidence available to it at the time it made the decision, then the employer would prevail on summary judgment. If, however, the plaintiffs could raise a factual question as to whether the employer's stated motive was actually pretextual, the defendant would not be entitled to summary judgment. In a case like this one involving an allegation of reverse discrimination, Weiss switches the burdens. As she explains:

> If reverse discrimination plaintiffs wish to contend that the selection process is defensible, on the basis that it meets the job-relatedness and business necessity criteria, that burden of persuasion belongs to the plaintiffs. They must show that the evidence before the employer at the time of the challenged employment decision sufficiently established job-relatedness and business necessity such that a reasonable employer would not have feared Title VII disparate impact liability.

If the plaintiffs can show this, then it would raise a question of material fact concerning whether the employer had an actual and reasonable belief that its selection process was causing a disparate impact in violation of Title VII. Moreover, Weiss explains that the employer in a reverse discrimination suit "will also have the burden of production as to the existence of a less discriminatory alternative, should it choose to rely on it."

Accordingly, Weiss examines the evidence available to the CSB when it decided to throw out the test results. As the data showed, there were uncontested and significant disparate impact outcomes on both the lieutenant and captain exams on the basis of race far worse than the allowable limit under the four-fifths rule established by the EEOC. The black and Latino candidates who were adversely affected thus clearly would have been able to set forth a prima facie claim of disparate impact. In light of the changed burdens in this reverse discrimination case, Weiss assesses whether the plaintiffs could prove that the promotion exams met the requirements for job-relatedness and business necessity, using the evidence the CSB had when it made its decision to discard the results. She also examines whether they could prove that there were no less-discriminatory alternatives that would be equally effective. This proof, however, was hard to come by, given that a number of alternatives existed, such as reformulating the 60:40 ratio for the written and oral test components, using assessment centers, and changing the application of the "rule of three." Although the plaintiffs tried to undermine the CSB's fear of liability by positing that the tests were valid or could have been shown to be valid, Weiss thoroughly exposes the flaws in their argument. In doing so, she concludes that "[i]t suffices that there is no dispute of material fact that the CSB had an actual and reasonably based belief that the process and its components had neither been validated nor likely could have been."

Because Weiss finds that the plaintiffs failed to present sufficient evidence that the exams were job-related and satisfied business necessity, they failed to meet their burden. Moreover, Weiss points out that there was substantial evidence before the CSB of less-discriminatory alternatives. Given this, Weiss holds that there is no dispute of material fact that the defendants had an actual and reasonable belief that the black and Latino candidates would have had a disparate impact case against the City had the City refused to throw out the test results. As a result, the City had a valid defense under Title VII.

Weiss further states that the CSB's total rejection of the test results does not violate Title VII's ban on race-norming. Although the plaintiffs argued otherwise, Weiss does not find support for their proposition under the relevant statutory language and legislative history. She clearly notes that discarding all of the test results is a facially neutral action and not a facially race-based classification. Since this facially neutral action was not motivated by discriminatory intent and did not cause a disparate impact, it was a permissible employer action. It was in line with Congress's interest in allowing employers

400 Ricci v. DeStefano

to exercise discretion when implementing their selection processes so long as they do not run afoul of Title VII.

Finally, with respect to the plaintiffs' equal protection claim, Weiss finds against the plaintiffs for the same reasons articulated in addressing their Title VII claim. As she explains, "The determination that an employment practice has caused or is likely to cause a race-based disparate impact does not, on its own, directly classify individuals based on race for either benefits or burdens. It therefore does not trigger strict scrutiny, and it easily survives rational basis analysis." Because the evidence was insufficient to show discriminatory intent on the part of the CSB, its acting to prevent disparate impact liability satisfies rational basis review.

In reinterpreting Title VII accurately in her rewritten opinion and thereby ruling for the defendants, Weiss recognizes the full purpose of Title VII and keeps alive its full promise. She takes a feminist approach in deciding the case by giving important weight to the harms of disparate impact discrimination and the way in which it undermines the job opportunities of historically excluded groups such as racial minorities and women. To more explicitly describe through a feminist lens the obstacles that such groups face, the opinion could have told the stories of the individual firefighters as they tried to prepare for the exams. Fully understanding the stakes in the case requires looking at the full picture of the firefighters involved. Yet, as earlier described, Justice Kennedy gives only one side of the story. Having the other side of the story – that of the individual minority fire-fighters trying to advance in New Haven's Fire Department – would have provided further context for the kind of injury that Title VII's disparate impact provision seeks to address. Weiss does not get into such facts in her rewritten opinion, but if she had, her judgment would have been that much richer.[216] Legal analysis certainly matters, but the facts are what makes a case compelling.

CONCLUSION: A CALL TO OVERTURN RICCI

If a majority of the Supreme Court justices in *Ricci* had fully taken into account the harms of disparate impact discrimination and properly understood that an employer's effort to avoid disparate impact is distinguishable from race-based discrimination, in the way that Weiss does in her rewritten opinion, then traditionally segregated occupations might have seen more integration in terms of race and gender over the last ten years. Minorities and women would not find themselves further excluded from occupations and positions that they

---

[216] *Editors' note*: Although we agree with Professor Lee's analysis, the author of the rewritten opinion (Professor Marley Weiss) was constrained by strict word limits. Because this case is so complicated, the rewritten opinion was already very long, and it therefore would have been difficult for Professor Weiss to delve into the stories of the minority firefighters.

Ricci v. DeStefano   401

historically did not have access to, but seek to enter. If *Ricci* had been
decided differently, an employer with an actual and reasonable evidence-
based belief that its selection process for hiring and promotion had created
a disparate impact based on race or gender would be able to abandon the
discriminatory process without worry of a disparate treatment lawsuit.
Because *Ricci* renders Title VII's disparate impact provision largely ineffec-
tual, restoring the statute's full strength requires overturning *Ricci*. Given
the current makeup of the Supreme Court, our best hope is for Congress to
heed the call.

Ricci v. DeStefano, 557 U.S. 557 (2009)

JUSTICE MARLEY S. WEISS DELIVERED THE OPINION OF THE COURT.

The City of New Haven relied on sharp racial differences in the outcomes of
its firefighter officer promotion selection system in determining that it had
apparently caused a racially disparate impact. This led the New Haven Civil
Service Board (CSB) to refuse to base promotions on the results of the
selection process. The plaintiffs, who believed they would have been promoted under the selection system, sued the City.

The plaintiffs claim that consideration of race in analyzing the selection
system's statistical outcomes itself constitutes unlawful, intentional racial
discrimination. The plaintiffs' reasoning would set the prohibition of disparate impact discrimination under Title VII of the Civil Rights Act of 1964
at odds with the prohibition of disparate treatment and intentional discrimination under both Title VII and the Equal Protection Clause of the
Fourteenth Amendment. Because the plaintiffs' claims raised innovative
theories of discrimination, alongside a novel characterization of "racial
classification" and "race-based disparate treatment," this Court granted
certiorari.

We hold that there is no inconsistency between the disparate impact provisions
of Title VII and the prohibition against intentional discrimination of Title VII and
the Equal Protection Clause. In cases such as this one, where the employer
defends claims of intentional discrimination based on its alleged efforts to avoid
causing an unlawful disparate impact, it is sufficient to support summary judgment in favor of the employer if it proves that it had an actual and reasonable
belief that absent a change in its existing employment practices, a prohibited
disparate impact would have resulted. Such evidence negates discriminatory
intent under both Title VII and the Equal Protection Clause. In light of this

402   Ricci v. DeStefano

test, we find that the district court was correct in concluding that there were no genuine issues of material fact that New Haven did not engage in intentional discrimination. We therefore affirm the judgment of the courts below.

I FACTUAL BACKGROUND

A *The Promotional Selection Process*

As the district court noted, although the parties dispute the inferences to be drawn from some of the facts, as well as their legal significance, there was little dispute as to the material facts themselves. *Ricci v. DeStefano*, 554 F.Supp.2d 142, 145 (D. Conn. 2006).

In 2003, the New Haven Fire Department determined that it needed additional supervisory firefighter officers, both lieutenants and captains. The City retained Industrial/Organizational Solutions, Inc. (IOS) to develop new multiple-choice written and oral examinations. Joint Appendix (JA) 49. Under the rules in the City Charter, the promotional list resulting from an examination was to be in effect for two years. *Ricci*, 554 F.Supp.2d at 145.

Article XXX of the New Haven City Charter dictated many of the rules regarding promotions for civil service positions. Openings had to be filled on the basis of competitive examinations. Under Article XXX(160), only those with a passing score of 70 percent or better could be considered. Those who passed were to be placed on a list in order of their test scores. For each vacancy, a "rule of three" required that the selection be made from among the three highest-scoring applicants on the list at that time. Additional selection criteria – that there be both a written test and an oral test, and that the combined score be weighted 60 percent to the written test and 40 percent to the oral test – were specified by the collective bargaining agreement (CBA) between the City and Local 825, International Association of Fire Fighters. JA 107, 183; *Ricci*, 554 F. Supp.2d at 145, 154. The CBA provision dated back to the mid-1980s. JA 107. The written exam was used to test for memorized technical and administrative knowledge, while the oral examination tested for skills. Pet. App. 648a–650a.

The pass/fail results of the 2003 examinations, applying the 70 percent cutoff score as well as the 60:40 weighting of exam components, were as follows: seventy-seven candidates took the full lieutenant exam, including forty-three white, nineteen African American, and fifteen Latino candidates.[217] Thirty-four candidates passed, twenty-five of whom were white, compared to six

[217] All candidates completing both components of either set of promotional examinations were men. Two women were among those who commenced the selection process, but they dropped out before completing the tests.

African American and three Latino candidates. Forty-one candidates took the captain exam, including twenty-one white, eight African American, and eight Latino candidates. Sixteen white candidates passed. Three African American and three Latino candidates passed.

At the time the 2003 examinations were administered, there were eight vacancies for lieutenant. Applying the rule of three, only the top ten scorers on the lieutenant exam would be considered for promotion. The African American candidates ranked 14, 15, 16, 20, 22, and 24; the Latino candidates ranked 27, 28, and 31. No African American and no Latino candidates ranked highly enough to be considered. *Ricci*, 554 F.Supp.2d at 145, 154.

At the time of the 2003 examinations, there were seven vacancies for captain. Applying the rule of three, only the nine top-ranked candidates would be considered for promotion. The Latino candidates ranked 7, 8, and 13 on this exam; the African American candidates ranked 16, 19, and 22. *Id.* at 145 & n.2.[218] Applying the rule of three, no African American candidates would be considered for promotion to captain, while one or perhaps two Latino candidates would be.[219] *Id.* at 145, 154.

B *The CSB Hearings and Decision*

Faced with these results, Thomas Ude, corporation counsel for the City of New Haven, advised the CSB to consider not certifying the results of the examinations. *Id.* at 145–46. The CSB is an independent organ of the City government that is charged with administering the civil service system, including reviewing the results of the examinations before certifying rank-order lists of eligible candidates. Pet. App. 74a–77a. In response, the CSB held a series of five hearings, on January 22, February 5, February 11, March 11, and March 18, 2004. JA 22, 54, 78, 84, 134; *Ricci*, 554 F.Supp.2d at 145.

At one of the CSB hearings, Ude advised the CSB that "the case law does not require that the City find that the test is indefensible in order to take action that it believes is appropriate to remedy ... disparate impact from the examination." He informed the CSB that "federal law does not require that you make a finding that this test ... was not job-related, which is another way of saying it wasn't fair. A test can be job-related and have a disparate impact on an ethnic group and still be rejected because there are less discriminatory alternatives for the selection process." *Id.* at 145–56.

---

[218] The rank order numbers found by the district court are not entirely consistent with those presented by the City administration to the CSB, but none of the discrepancies are material.

[219] Whether only one or both of the highest-ranked Latino candidates would be considered would depend on the selections among the top three candidates in each of the preceding selections.

404 Ricci v. DeStefano

The CSB also heard presentations by counsel for the eventual plaintiffs in this lawsuit, by the firefighters' union, and by the African American firefighters' association. Court of Appeals Joint Appendix (CAJA) 816–17, 838. In addition, it heard testimony from individual firefighters, some supporting and some opposing certification of the test results. At that time, the racial composition of the test results had been made public, but individual scores had remained undisclosed. *Ricci*, 554 F.Supp.2d at 146–47.

Patrick Egan, president of the New Haven firefighters' local union, urged the CSB to have a proper validation study performed. Donald Day and Ronald Mackey, representatives of the International Association of Black Professional Firefighters, who worked in nearby Bridgeport, Connecticut, urged that the exam results be thrown out as biased or adjusted to ensure that a proportionate number of minority candidates were promoted, although they also supported the firefighters' union's proposal that a validation study should be conducted. *Id.* Some African American firefighters threatened to sue if the examination results were certified and promotions were based on them. A group of white firefighters also threatened to sue if the results of the examination were not certified and promotions were not based on them. CAJA 814–17, 838.

Chad Legel, vice president of the test development company, IOS, testified before the CSB about the careful process by which the written and oral examinations had been developed. *Ricci*, 554 F.Supp.2d at 147–48. Three witnesses testified regarding the content and possible validation of the tests utilized in New Haven, as well as testing methodology and alternative selection practices. The first was Christopher Hornick, Ph.D., an industrial psychologist who headed up a competing test development firm; the second was Vincent M. Lewis, an African American retired fire captain who had since become a consultant with the US Department of Homeland Security regarding arson; the third was Janet Helms, Ph.D., a professor specializing in the psychology of race and culture. *Id.* at 148–49.[220]

After concluding its hearings, four members of the CSB voted on whether to certify the lists resulting from the examinations. JA 160–69. The fifth, the only African American member, had recused herself because her brother had been a candidate on one of the two exams. CAJA 812–14, 875; *Ricci*, 554 F.Supp.2d at 150 & n.5. Under the City Charter, the CSB as an entity had final authority to act on behalf of the City. The CSB vote was tied, thereby failing to certify the examination scores. JA 168–69; *Ricci*, 554 F.Supp.2d. at 150.

---

[220] Further details regarding analysis of the views of the experts on disparate impact, validation of the selection process, and alternative selection practices will be discussed *infra* section II.C.

Ricci v. DeStefano

One of the two CSB members who voted against certification, Malcolm Webber, stated on the record that his initial intent had been to vote for certification of the test results, but the hearings had changed his mind. He now had "great doubts about the test itself." JA 166. The other, Zelma Tirado, said she had concluded that "the test was flawed" and the entire selection "process was flawed." JA 167. Both of these CSB members subsequently filed affidavits in this litigation attesting that they had voted against certification because of concern that certifying the examination results would place the City in violation of Title VII. CAJA 1604, 1610.

After the CSB decision, a group of disappointed white and one Latino firefighter promotion candidates commenced the instant lawsuit.[221] JA 180, 184. They named as defendants the City of New Haven, along with seven individuals, including the two CSB members who had voted against certification of the test results. JA 178–80. The plaintiffs exhausted their remedies with the Equal Employment Opportunity Commission (EEOC). JA 196.

C Procedural Background

In the district court, the plaintiffs alleged, among other claims, discrimination based on race in violation of Title VII and the Fourteenth Amendment to the US Constitution. JA 176–77, 194–97. The gravamen of their claims was discriminatory "denial of promotion, denial of fair consideration for promotion and denial of opportunities for promotion." JA 197. The parties completed discovery and filed cross-motions for summary judgment. On September 28, 2006, the district court granted the defendants' motion for summary judgment, reported at 554 F.Supp.2d 142.

On appeal, the Second Circuit initially affirmed in an unpublished summary order. 264 Fed. Appx. 106 (2008). The panel subsequently withdrew its order and issued a formal *per curiam* opinion, adopting by reference the opinion of the district court. 530 F.3d 87 (2d Cir. 2008). In the meantime, one judge on the circuit court had urged that the court of appeals grant rehearing *en banc*. Three days after the reissuance of the panel decision, the full circuit court denied rehearing *en banc* by a vote of seven to six, over written dissents and concurring opinions by several of the court's members. 530 F.3d 88 (2d Cir. 2008). The plaintiffs petitioned for *certiorari*, which this Court granted. 555 U.S. 1091 (2009).

---

[221] At the time of the district court's decision, there were seventeen white and one Latino firefighter plaintiffs. *Ricci*, 554 F.Supp.2d at 144.

406   Ricci v. DeStefano

II THE PLAINTIFFS' TITLE VII DISPARATE TREATMENT CLAIM

The plaintiffs have claimed disparate treatment because of race under Title VII and intentional racial discrimination under the Equal Protection Clause. In accordance with our usual practice, we consider the statutory questions before those arising under the Constitution. *New York City Transit Authority v. Beazer*, 440 U.S. 568, 582 (1979).

The defendants claim that the reason they refused to certify the test results – which would have led to the promotion of some, if not all, of the plaintiffs – was the need to avoid violating Title VII because of the disparate impact caused by the promotion process. *Ricci*, 554 F.Supp.2d at 152–53. In claiming intentional race discrimination, plaintiffs argue that the mere failure to certify a test, based on its disparate impact on black and Latino candidates constitutes intentional discrimination based on race against the most successful test takers, nearly all of whom were white.

A Consideration of Racial Statistical Outcomes as Opposed to Race-Based Classifications

At the heart of their argument, the plaintiffs contend that, in acting voluntarily to avoid disparate impact liability, the defendants took account of the race-based statistical results that made up the prima facie case and hence based their decision on race. The plaintiffs characterize this as a "race-based refusal to promote plaintiffs," a set of "overtly race-based determinations," "self-initiated race-based deprivations," and engaging in "intentional race-based disparate treatment." Pet. Br. 27; *id.* at 3; *id.* at 54; *id.* at 57. They contend that the disparate impact basis for liability under Title VII is itself both unconstitutional and inconsistent with the prohibitions against intentional discrimination in Title VII itself. Pet. Rep. Br. 9, 14. In the plaintiffs' view, disparate impact doctrine inevitably requires statistical consideration of race and hence requires classification based on race, as well as prohibited race-based or at least race-conscious decision-making. The plaintiffs also reason that the disparate treatment provisions of Title VII trump the disparate impact provisions in the event of conflict. Pet. Br. at 49.

However, verbally treating the City's decision-making as though it were directly based on the race of the affected employees, thus categorizing black and white candidates differently, does not transform the plaintiffs' allegations into claims of actual facial discrimination under our precedents. The City indirectly took aggregate racial outcomes into account in a policy-making decision, as opposed to directly classifying individual employees for different treatment based on their race. *Cf. Parents Involved in Community Schools v. Seattle School Dist. No. 1*, 551 U.S. 701, 789–90 (2007) (Kennedy, J., concurring in part and concurring in judgment).

The plaintiffs' contentions deviate from precedent in two dimensions at once.[222] First, they conflate indirect with direct reliance on race or gender; second, they treat consideration of race or sex in formulating an employment policy as equivalent to a policy that itself differentiates directly and intentionally based on race or gender. This Court has never equated consideration of racial or gender statistics in formulating an employment policy with a directly race-based or sex-based classification nor with refusing to hire a particular individual because of that individual's race or gender. *See id.* at 789 (Kennedy, J., concurring in part and concurring in judgment). This is to confuse the ends and the means – the predicate for decision-making and the decision itself – and would break down the distinction between disparate treatment and disparate impact. Cases have labeled "race-based" or "facially discriminatory" only those selection criteria involving direct reliance, whether complete or partial, upon the prohibited characteristic. The "color-blind Constitution" theory has not been adopted by a majority of this Court. *See Parents Involved*, 551 U.S. at 783, 788–89 (Kennedy, J., concurring in part and concurring in judgment); *id.* at 830 (Breyer, J., dissenting). Even if it were, it would reach means, but not ends. *But see id.* at 748, 752, 772–73, 780 (Thomas, J., concurring) (embracing the "color-blind constitution" theory and rejecting reliance of any sort on race); *Grutter v. Bolinger*, 539 U.S. 306, 353–54 (2008) (Thomas, J., concurring in part and dissenting in part) (same).

For example, in the affirmative action cases under both Title VII and the Equal Protection Clause, the issue was how strong a race- or gender-based statistical predicate – the purpose or end – was necessary to support various degrees of direct racial or sexual preference. The calculation of the statistical predicate, whether labeled "conspicuous imbalance in traditionally segregated job categories," or "underrepresentation" of women in jobs from which they had historically been excluded, or "a statistical prima facie case against the employer," all require that the employer engage in racial or gender

---

[222] Because nearly all of our affirmative action cases that take race into account have been decided under the Equal Protection Clause of the Fourteenth Amendment, we rely on this precedent to analyze the Title VII as well as the Fourteenth Amendment claims. Under Title VII, we have decided *United Steelworkers of America, AFL-CIO-CLC v. Weber*, 443 U.S. 193 (1979) and *Johnson v. Transportation Agency*, 480 U.S. 616 (1987), affirmative action cases addressing, respectively, racial and gender-based preferences. We will also refer to these cases in our analysis of the Title VII claim here. We recognize that the case before this Court does not deal with an affirmative action plan, but we view the affirmative action cases as analogous to the present case.

408 Ricci v. DeStefano

head-counting among the relevant portion of its workforce. *Weber*, 443 U.S. 193, 209 (1979); *Johnson v. Transportation Agency*, 480 U.S. 616, 631–32 (1987) (plurality opinion); *id.* at 649 (O'Connor, J., concurring in part and concurring in judgment),

Pattern or practice claims of discrimination likewise depend on proof requiring racial identification of workers. Whether the underlying theory of prior discrimination is systemic disparate treatment or disparate impact, the prima facie case depends on similar race- or gender-based identification of applicants and a comparison of the race or gender composition of those selected during the employer's processes with those who applied or were available to be hired. *Compare Hazelwood Sch. Dist. v. United States*, 433 U.S. 299 (1977) and *Teamsters v. United States*, 431 U.S. 324 (1977) *with, e.g., Connecticut v. Teal*, 457 U.S. 440 (1982).

The concerns raised about direct reliance on race or gender in allocating employment burdens or benefits do not apply when diagnosing workplace problems rather than devising solutions. This Court's cases have repeatedly accepted either past or present unlawful discrimination by employers or unions, with or without a judicial finding, as sufficient to support even directly race- or gender-based remedial preferences. *See, e.g., United States v Paradise*, 480 U.S. 149, 167 (1987) (plurality opinion) (past discrimination); *Sheet Metal Workers v. EEOC*, 478 U.S. 421, 480 (1986) (plurality opinion) (present discrimination); *id.* at 486 (Powell, J., concurring in part and concurring in judgment) (same); *Wygant v. Jackson Board of Educ.*, 476 U.S. 267, 290, 291 (1986) (O'Connor, J., concurring in part and concurring in judgment) (past or present discrimination; with or without a judicial finding).

Here, the defendants argue that they threw out the test results because the test caused a disparate impact against black and Latino candidates. This is the equivalent of diagnosing and preventing a present violation. The question before us, then, is whether there was sufficient evidence that certifying the test results would likely have led to an actionable disparate impact claim brought by black and Latino candidates against the City. To answer this question, we must first determine the allocation of burdens of proof, as well as the standard that the City would have to meet regarding its contention that its refusal to use the test results was lawfully motivated.

Preliminarily, it is important to note that, here, unlike the affirmative action cases discussed above, the means – that is, the remedial solution adopted by the CSB, the noncertification of the test results – was facially neutral. It did not directly differentiate based on race, even though the statistical results of the selection process were known and hence the racial impact of refusing to certify

Ricci v. DeStefano 409

the list could be fairly accurately predicted. White, African American, and Latino candidates who had passed the tests all equally had their hopes of promotion deferred.

Our decision in *Personnel Administrator v. Feeney*, 442 U.S. 256 (1979), establishes that even the known, severe disparate impact of a facially neutral employment practice or decision is not equivalent to a facially discriminatory classification. *See also, e.g., Washington v. Davis*, 426 U.S. 229 (1976); *Arlington Heights v. Metropolitan Housing Dev. Corp.*, 429 U.S. 252 (1977). In *Feeney*, the Commonwealth of Massachusetts combined a heavy veterans' preference with civil service test scores in selecting among applicants. At the time, 98 percent of eligible veterans in the state were men, because nearly all military service roles had been limited to men; over one-quarter of the state's population were veterans. *Feeney*, 442 U.S. at 270. The foreseeable, indeed inevitable, result was that almost no women could attain the more desirable jobs. *Id.* at 271. Nevertheless, the Court held that these effects were insufficient to support a finding of intentional discrimination. " 'Discriminatory purpose' ... implies more than intent as volition or intent as awareness of consequences. It implies that the decisionmaker, ... selected or reaffirmed a particular course of action at least in part 'because of,' not merely 'in spite of,' its adverse effects upon an identifiable group." *Id.* at 279. *See also, e.g., Pullman-Standard v. Swint*, 456 U.S. 273, 277 (1982) ("[A]ny challenge to a seniority system under [§703(h) of] Title VII will require a trial on the issue of discriminatory intent: [w]as the system adopted because of its racially discriminatory impact?"); *Hazen Paper Co. v. Biggins*, 507 U.S. 604, 608–09, 611 (1993) (a positive correlation between increasing age and ten-year pension vesting rule did not render the pension rule facially discriminatory based on age and was insufficient to establish age-based discriminatory intent in violation of the Age Discrimination in Employment Act of 1967).

The plaintiffs' burden in proving disparate treatment in violation of Title VII, therefore, is to prove that the CSB refused to certify the test results because of the race of the most successful candidates, rather than because it wished to avoid violating the Title VII disparate impact provisions. The plaintiffs at all times bear the burden of persuasion that the City's "real" reason was intentional discrimination – that is, that the City's intent was to prefer African American candidates over white, or to exclude white candidates from the promotions. *See, e.g., Texas Dep't of Community Affairs v. Burdine*, 450 U.S. 248, 253, 256 (1981); *St. Mary's Honor Ctr. v. Hicks*, 509 U.S. 502, 507–08, 511, 514–15 (1993).

410   Ricci v. DeStefano

B Allocation of Evidentiary Burdens

We now turn to the question of what standard an employer must meet to support summary judgment in its favor based on the employer's contention that its employment decision or change in an employment practice was motivated by the desire to comply with the law – that is, Title VII's disparate impact provisions – rather than by intentional race discrimination. Under our disparate treatment precedents, assuming that the plaintiffs establish the four-prong prima facie case, the employer needs merely to articulate a legitimate nondiscriminatory reason. *See, e.g., McDonnell Douglas Corp. v. Green*, 411 U.S. 792, 802 (1973); *Burdine*, 450 U.S. at 254. Here, on cross-motions for summary judgment in the district court, the employer did not contest the first three prongs of the prima facie case: that the plaintiffs were members of a protected class, had applied for and were qualified for promotion to an officer position, and were denied the positions. *Ricci*, 554 F.Supp.2d at 151–52. The district court assumed that the plaintiffs met the fourth prong – which, under circuit precedent, was that the adverse employment action occurred under circumstances giving rise to an inference of discriminatory intent. *Id.* at 152.[223] The legitimate nondiscriminatory reason that the employer asserted was that the CSB decision was required by law, or at least was based on a good faith belief that certifying the results would violate Title VII's disparate impact provisions. *Id.* at 151–53. Basing the employment decision on avoiding a real and significant risk of a present violation of the law constitutes a legitimate nondiscriminatory reason; it would suffice for the constitutional claim[224] as well:

> The Court is in agreement that, whatever the [level of constitutional scrutiny] employed, remedying past or present racial discrimination by a state actor is a sufficiently weighty state interest to warrant the remedial use of a carefully constructed affirmative action program. This remedial purpose need not be accompanied by contemporaneous findings of actual discrimination to be accepted as legitimate as long as the public actor has a firm basis for believing that remedial action is required.
>
>   *Wygant v. Jackson Board of Educ.*, 476 U.S. 267, 286 (1986)
>   (O'Connor, J., concurring in part and concurring in judgment).

In this case, after the defendant has articulated a legitimate nondiscriminatory reason – that is, its desire to avoid breaking the law – the burden of production shifts back to the plaintiffs to prove pretext and merges with their

---

[223] This Court takes no position on the propriety of the Second Circuit's modified version of the *McDonnell Douglas* four-prong test.

[224] The Equal Protection Clause claim is discussed *infra* section III.

ultimate burden of persuasion. The plaintiffs can satisfy this requirement either by showing that the employer's supposed concern with a disparate impact violation was not real, because such a claim against the City lacked substance, or that the true reason was racial preference for African American candidates or antipathy toward white candidates. To support summary judgment in its favor, the employer would have to show that no reasonable fact finder could conclude that the CSB had declined to certify the test results because of the race of the successful candidates, as opposed to because of the risk of disparate impact liability. The plaintiffs in fact attempted to litigate both forms of pretext evidence. First, they argued that the tests were plainly valid and hence presented no liability exposure. They contended that, even assuming *arguendo* a viable disparate impact prima facie case by minority candidates against New Haven, the City would have an iron-clad job-relatedness and business necessity defense. They further asserted that the City knew that the tests were valid and legally defensible. Alternatively, the plaintiffs argued that the City did not really care about compliance with the law, but that the mayor wanted to curry favor with his African American political allies and that promoting more African American candidates was a means to accomplish that goal. The plaintiffs' pretext argument is discussed *infra* section II.D.

Turning back to the employer's legitimate nondiscriminatory reason, our affirmative action precedents shed light on the question of how to treat an employer's assertion of legal compliance with the Title VII disparate impact provisions as the basis for a challenged employment decision. In *Johnson v. Transportation Agency*, 480 U.S. 616 (1987), the predicate for affirmative action was either conspicuous imbalance in traditionally segregated job categories (majority view) or a statistical prima facie case of discrimination (Justice O'Connor's concurrence). In *Wygant*, an Equal Protection Clause decision, Justice O'Connor would have required the employer to have a "firm basis in evidence" that a systemic disparate impact or disparate treatment claim loomed; she would have applied the same standard under Title VII in her concurring opinion in *Johnson*. *Johnson*, 480 U.S. at 650–51 (citing *Wygant*, 476 U.S. at 292–93). Our more recent constitutional cases, however, have required governments to show a "strong basis in evidence." Because both of these standards (firm basis and strong basis in evidence) are predicates to support directly race- or gender-based affirmative action classifications, the standard they set is too high for the currently challenged, facially neutral employment decision to refuse to certify the test results for all promotion applicants. This is not a case of justifying an affirmative action plan, but rather one in which the defendants argue that they were attempting to comply with the law and avoid illegal discrimination.

412   Ricci v. DeStefano

The City, on the other hand, has advocated that proof of its "good faith belief" in a potential disparate impact violation is a sufficient legitimate nondiscriminatory reason to support summary judgment in its favor. *Ricci*, 554 F.Supp.2d at 152–53. However, "good faith" alone is normally not a defense to a Title VII action. *See Albermarle Paper Co. v. Moody*, 422 U.S. at 423 & n.17 (the statute only recognizes a very narrow "good faith" defense, in 42 U.S.C. §2000e-12(b), for actions undertaken in "good faith, . . . and in reliance on any written interpretation or opinion of the [EEOC]. It is not for the courts to upset this legislative choice to recognize only a narrowly defined 'good faith' defense."). We therefore require the employer to support summary judgment in its favor with proof that it had an actual and reasonable belief that, absent a change in its employment practices, a statutorily prohibited disparate impact would have resulted. This proof must be sufficiently strong that no reasonable jury could find that the employer lacked such belief. We now turn to the evidence of a disparate impact claim to assess whether the defendants' evidence is sufficiently strong that a reasonable jury could not conclude that the defendants lacked an actual and reasonable belief that they should throw out the test results to avoid liability.

In a traditional disparate impact case, (1) the plaintiff must show that a selection system "causes" a disparate impact. Title VII §703(k)(1)(A)(i). At that point, (2) the defendant employer must demonstrate that the selection process is job-related and consistent with business necessity, or it will lose the case. *Id.* Assuming that the employer establishes this affirmative defense, the plaintiff (3) has the opportunity to prove that a less-discriminatory alternative – an equally valid selection process with a less-discriminatory impact – exists and that the defendant refused to adopt it. Title VII §703(k)(1)(A)(ii), 703(k)(1)(C). Each of these three steps involves a shift in the burden of persuasion, not merely the burden of production, because the statute uses the word "demonstrates" for each, which section 701(m) defines as "meets the burdens of production and persuasion." *See also Desert Palace v. Costa*, 539 U.S. 90 (2003).

The plaintiffs here urge that the Court require the employer to make a showing of a statistical prima facie case and either to prove the negative, that the selection system is invalid, or to demonstrate that an alternative practice that is equally valid with a less adverse impact exists. This would treat the statute as though, in a traditional disparate impact case, it imposed all of the burdens of persuasion on the plaintiff, contrary to both the text of section 703(k) and *Griggs* and its progeny. Moreover, it would assume the validity of the evidentiary burden allocation urged in Justice O'Connor's plurality opinion in *Watson v. Fort Worth Bank & Trust*, 487 U.S. 977 (1988), and adopted

Ricci v. DeStefano 413

by the majority in *Wards Cove Packing Co. v. Atonio*, 490 U.S 642 (1989). Congress rejected this allocation of evidentiary burdens when it amended Title VII by inserting section 703(k)(1)(A)(i) as part of the 1991 Civil Rights Act; hence this Court must do so as well. Because the core issue in this case is whether the CSB was motivated by racially discriminatory intent in its decision not to certify the selection process results, as opposed to motivated by the desire to ensure legal compliance, it would be especially inappropriate to use such a stringent standard.

We have accepted a statistical prima facie case alone as a sufficient predicate for race- and sex-based affirmative action. *Johnson*, 480 U.S. 616 (1987). No higher standard should be imposed when an employer takes race-neutral action, rather than facially race-based action, in response to a disparate impact in its selection process. When, as here, the employer claims that the reason for its employment action is to avoid causing a potentially unlawful, racial disparate impact, the employer bears merely a burden of production, not persuasion, in articulating this as its legitimate nondiscriminatory reason.

If reverse discrimination plaintiffs wish to contend that the selection process is defensible on the basis that it meets the job-relatedness and business necessity criteria, that burden of persuasion belongs to the plaintiffs. They must show that the evidence before the employer at the time of the challenged employment decision sufficiently established job-relatedness and business necessity such that a reasonable employer would not have feared Title VII disparate impact liability. This would tend to disprove that the employer actually had based its challenged employment decision upon its supposed desire to avoid causing a disparate impact violation. This would create a dispute of material fact as to the actuality and reasonableness of the employer's alleged belief that its selection system was causing an unlawful disparate impact. Should the plaintiffs meet that burden at trial, the fact finder may (but would not be required to) infer that intentional racial discrimination was the employer's true reason for its decision. *See Reeves v. Sanderson Plumbing Prods.*, 530 U.S. 133, 146–48 (2000). The employer in a reverse discrimination case, as here, will also have the burden of production as to the existence of a less-discriminatory alternative, should it choose to rely on it, either in the alternative or exclusively if the selection process is deemed to be demonstrably valid based on the evidence before the employer at the time it made its decision. At trial, this burden of production does not alter the rule that the plaintiffs must at all times bear the burden of persuasion of discriminatory intent; in a motion for summary judgment by the employer, however, the plaintiff would merely have to create a dispute of material fact as to the alternative

414   Ricci v. DeStefano

employment practice. This allocation of evidentiary burdens comports with the thrust of section 703(k); moreover, it also implements the long-standing rule of *McDonnell Douglas Corp. v. Green*, 411 U.S. 792 (1973) and its progeny that the burden of proving intentional discrimination remains at all times on the plaintiff.

This allocation of evidentiary burdens is also supported by the centrality of voluntary compliance by employers to the proper functioning of the Title VII scheme. "In pursuing the goal of 'bring[ing] employment discrimination to an end,' Congress chose '[c]ooperation and voluntary compliance' as its 'preferred means.'" *Ford Motor Co. v. EEOC*, 458 U.S. 219, 228 (1982) (quoting *Alexander v. Gardner-Denver Co.*, 415 U.S. 36, 44 (1974)). Courts should avoid placing employers between a rock and a hard place, between Scylla and Charybdis. *Weber*, 443 U.S. at 210 (Blackmun, J., concurring). The procedural scheme of the statute itself directly requires the EEOC to "endeavor to eliminate [an] alleged unlawful employment practice by informal methods of conference, conciliation, and persuasion." 42 U.S.C. §2000e-5(b). As we held in the sexual harassment context, the employer has an "affirmative obligation to prevent violations and [our case law gives] credit . . . to employers who make reasonable efforts to discharge their duty." *Faragher v. City of Boca Raton*, 524 U.S. 775 (1998). Title VII aims to encourage "forethought by employers" to voluntarily correct potentially discriminatory employment actions to bring themselves into compliance. *Id.* at 807; *Burlington Indus. v. Ellerth*, 524 U.S. 742, 764 (1998); *see also Local No. 93, International Ass'n of Firefighters v. City of Cleveland*, 478 U.S. 501, 517–18 (1986). Imposing any heavier a burden on employers would disrupt this core congressional objective.

The district court in this case correctly held that an employer cannot be required to actually prove either the statistical prima facie case against itself or, assuming that the question is reached, the actual existence of a less-discriminatory alternative. That is because the underlying issue is the employer's intent in adopting or changing its employment practice. An actual good faith belief is not enough. However, combined with a reasonable basis in the evidence before the employer at the time it made the challenged employment decision, it is sufficient to support summary judgment for the employer unless the plaintiffs present enough evidence to allow a reasonable fact finder to conclude that the employer's asserted motive (preventing disparate impact liability) is pretextual.

The presence or absence of the potential unlawful disparate impact must exclusively be based on the evidence before the employer at the time it made its challenged employment decision, since the central issue remains the employer's motivation at that time. *See, e.g., McKennon v. Nashville*, 513 U.S. 352, 360 (1995) (evidence of employee wrongdoing that the employer acquired after the termination of the worker's employment has no relevance as to proof of intentionally discriminatory motive in the termination). Here, only evidence considered by the decision-maker, the CSB, in reaching its decision is relevant as to the employer's motive. The employer should produce enough evidence that a reasonable fact finder would have to conclude that the employer actually and reasonably believed that a statistical disparate impact prima facie case existed and *either* that the selection system was not job-related *or* that a less-discriminatory alternative employment practice existed. However, the burden should not be on the employer to show that these facts were actually true as opposed to that it actually and reasonably believed them to be true when it made the challenged employment decision.

C The New Haven Selection Process

To properly evaluate the CSB's motive in failing to certify the 2003 examination results, we start with the situation as understood by the CSB when it made the challenged employment decision. *See, e.g., McKennon, supra; Little v. Ill. Dep't of Revenue*, 369 F.3d 1007, 1015 (4th Cir. 2004) (analysis of motive should be based on decision-maker's knowledge at the time of the decision). The CSB was the decision-maker as to the challenged employment action, since it and only it had the legal authority to withhold certification of the promotion lists. The issue here, therefore, is why that body took the action it did. Within that body, the motives of the two members who voted against certification must be regarded as decisive, since their votes caused the lists' rejection. Those two CSB members expressly stated at an open CSB proceeding that they found the examinations and the process as a whole flawed, which is why they voted not to certify the examination results. Absent sufficient evidence to permit a reasonable fact finder to conclude that these statements were pretextual, discussed *infra* section II.D, the summary judgment for the City must be affirmed.

1 The Minority Candidates' Counterfactual Disparate Impact Prima Facie Case

At the time of the CSB decision, it was expected that all eight promotions to lieutenant would go to white firefighters and that at least five of the seven promotions to captain would go to white, nonminority lieutenants, with one or

416   Ricci v. DeStefano

two remaining captain positions going to Latino candidates. No African American candidates would have been promoted. The fact that additional openings developed thereafter was unexpected and could not have been taken into account by the CSB in making its decision; hence it is irrelevant in assessing the legality of its decision.

The Uniform Guidelines for Employee Selection Procedures (UGESP), 43 Fed. Reg. 38295, Aug. 25, 1978, 29 C.F.R. Part 1607, "apply to tests and other selection procedures which are used as a basis for any employment decision," including promotions. *Id.* §1707.2(B). *See Griggs v. Duke Power Co.*, 401 U.S. 424, 434 (1971) (following predecessor EEOC guidelines); *Albemarle Paper Co. v. Moody*, 422 U.S. 405, 430–31 (1975) (same). The four-fifths (80 percent) rule of thumb, established under the UGESP, presumes disparate impact when the pass rate of a racial minority group is less than 80 percent of the pass rate of the highest-scoring racial group. 29 C.F.R. §1607.4(D) (2008). *See, e.g., Watson v. Fort Worth Bank & Trust*, 487 U.S. 977, 995–96 n.3 (1988) (plurality opinion). The ratio calculated by dividing the pass rate of the affected minority group by the pass rate of the highest-scoring racial group may be referred to as the adverse impact ratio (AIR). *See Ricci*, 554 F.Supp.2d at 153.

New Haven's selection process for both lieutenants and captain is composed of: (1) a written test; (2) an oral test; (3) computation of a combined score for the two components weighting the written test at 60 percent and the oral test at 40 percent; (4) a 70 percent cutoff score to pass the two test components combined in the 60:40 weighting; (5) a rank ordering of those whose score was at least 70 percent; (6) and selection permitting consideration only of the top three in the rank-ordered list. The statistical results of the 2003 selection system for both lieutenant and captain positions constituted a prima facie case of racially discriminatory impact at several stages of the process, as well as cumulatively.

The 70 percent cutoff score, combined with the 60:40 weighting of the written and oral test results, without regard to the effects of rank ordering, produced a statistically significant disparate impact. The overall results of the New Haven selection process were extremely adverse as to both African American and Latino candidates. The selection rate for lieutenant promotions of white candidates would have been 19 percent; that of both African American and Latino candidates would have been zero. JA 223–24. Zero is, mathematically, as far as one can get from 80 percent.

The comparative bottom-line selection rate for promotion to captain was just as adverse with respect to African American candidates, although impact was uncertain with regard to Latino candidates. The white selection rate would have been at least five and perhaps six out of twenty-five applicants – a 20 percent or

Ricci v. DeStefano 417

24 percent selection rate. The African American rate would have been zero out of eight – again a zero percent rate and a zero percent AIR, compared to the 80 percent threshold. The Latino selection rate, however, would have been either one out of eight or two out of eight – that is, either a 12.5 percent or a 25 percent rate – yielding a much milder disparity in the first case or none at all in the second. JA 223–24.

Disparate impact is also reflected in the comparative pass rates on the two sets of exams. There was an overall pass rate of 44 percent (34/77). The pass rate on the lieutenant exam among white candidates was 58 percent (25/43); among African American candidates, it was 31.6 percent (6/19); among Latino candidates, it was 20 percent (3/15). The AIR for African American lieutenant candidates was 54 percent (31.6/58). The AIR for Latino lieutenant applicants compared to white was 34 percent (20/58). The pass rate of white candidates on the lieutenant exam thus was nearly twice that of African American and almost three times that of Latino candidates.

The combination of the contents of the tests, the 60:40 ratio in producing the combined score, and the application of the 70 percent cutoff as to the captains' examination produced an overall pass rate of 54 percent (22/41). The pass rate among white candidates was 64 percent (16/25); among African American candidates, it was 37.5 percent (3/8); among Latino candidates, it was 37.5 percent (3/8).[225] The AIR comparing African American captain applicants to white applicants was 58.6 percent (37.5/64). The AIR comparing Latino captain applicants to white applicants likewise was 58.6 percent. The disparities are the result of the combined effect of the examinations together with the 70 percent passing score dictated by the City Charter.

Each of these disparities was far in excess of those permitted under EEOC's four-fifths rule, including the AIRs for promotion both to lieutenant and to captain, and those for Latino, as well as for African American, candidates. Under our precedents, this is enough for African American and Latino applicants who had failed the tests to establish a prima facie claim of disparate impact.[226] *See, e.g., Dothard v. Rawlinson*, 433 U.S. 321, 329 (1977) ("[T]o establish a prima facie case ..., a plaintiff need only show that the facially neutral standards in question select applicants ... in a significantly

[225] In the district court, plaintiffs claimed that 32 percent of the African American candidates passed the captains' examination. *Ricci*, 554 F.Supp.2d at 153 & n.7. This opinion will use the higher percentage figure, which reduces the disparate impact and hence would favor the plaintiffs, although in light of the lack of dispute regarding the raw numbers of those passing the exams, it may be that the plaintiffs' figure is a typographical error.

[226] Although the numbers may not be as large as preferable for statistical analysis, in light of the large deviation from 80 percent, a more sophisticated statistical analysis most likely would yield similar results.

418   Ricci v. DeStefano

discriminatory pattern"). Moreover, Dr. Hornick – the only statistical expert who testified before the CSB – stated that he had utilized more sophisticated measures of statistical significance to confirm that "there is adverse impact in the test." JA 103, 106.

2 Job-Relatedness/Business Necessity in the Counterfactual Disparate Impact Case

In an ordinary disparate impact lawsuit, once the plaintiff proves that a disparate impact exists, the burden shifts to the defendant to prove that the policy, test, or procedure causing the disparate impact is job-related and consistent with business necessity. Here, we have inverted the burdens because the plaintiffs are trying to prove intentional discrimination against white candidates in the jettisoning of the selection process results. Thus the plaintiffs have the burden of proving that the evidence before the CSB when it made its decision showed that the selection process was job related and consistent with business necessity. The plaintiffs in the instant case contend that the examinations were valid or could have been validated; hence the defendants' risk of liability was not real or substantial. Pet. Br. at i, 51–52.[227] The plaintiffs label the employer's burden to prove job-relatedness and business necessity in the ordinary disparate impact case as "slight," and they contend that a prima facie statistical case of disparate impact against the employer "only creates an easily rebuttable presumption." Pet. Rep. Br. at 16.

However, under *Griggs, Albemarle*, and section 703(k), that statistical prima facie case has far more weight than the readily rebuttable presumption created by the prima facie case in individual disparate treatment cases. The result of a statistical prima facie case in typical disparate impact litigation, unless the statistical basis itself can be rebutted, is that the plaintiff wins unless the employer "demonstrates" (i.e., "meets the burden of production and persuasion") under section 701(k) that the employment practice meets two criteria: that it is job-related and consistent with business necessity. *Desert Palace v. Costa*, 539 U.S. 90, 99 (2003). As to a selection system like the one here, unless the employer (in an ordinary disparate impact case) can present a sound and persuasive validation study, the plaintiff will prevail. In the context of

[227] The plaintiffs also alleged that, in the district court, the defendants took the position that its defense did not require it to prove that the exams were not valid or not possible to validate and hence that the defendants had conceded the validity of the tests. However, in the district court, the plaintiffs also asserted that it was the duty of the defendants to conduct a validation study, i.e., to attempt to validate the tests. *Ricci*, 554 F.Supp.2d at 154. The plaintiffs thereby, in effect, admitted that the test had *not* at that point been validated. The contention of the plaintiffs that the defendants had conceded the validity of the selection process must therefore be rejected.

Ricci v. DeStefano 419

a reverse discrimination case such as this, it is the plaintiffs who must show job-relatedness and business necessity.

Under the UGESP, there is no assumption of validity of a selection mechanism. 29 C.F.R. §1607.9. No formal validation study was ever conducted utilizing the examinations, either before or after they were administered in 2003. "When a formal and scored selection procedure is used which has an adverse impact, the validation techniques contemplated by these guidelines usually should be followed if technically feasible." 29 C.F.R. §1607.6(B)(2).

The plaintiffs in this case contend that the selection process was valid, based on the job analysis performed at the outset by IOS and its utilization as the basis for selecting test questions. Because the information content tested, in their view, was valid, they claim that the tests were subject to "content validity." Content validation, however, is only proper for tests "when content closely approximates tasks to be performed on the job by the applicant." *Washington v. Davis*, 426 U.S. 229, 247 n.13 (1976). These tests were never properly validated, on their own or in conjunction with the 60:40 weighting and the 70 percent cutoff score, by comparing results under the selection system with actual performance on the job. It would have been improper to attempt to use content validation methodology to validate them. Content validation is a methodology used only when the test taker is required to perform a sample of the regularly required job performance, such as a typist taking a test of typing speed and accuracy. The multiple-choice written exam could not possibly have tested an actual sample of job performance for fire-fighter supervisors. Firefighter captains and lieutenants do not stand around in emergencies, competitively regurgitating their pertinent knowledge. They lead those under their command, making difficult, time-critical judgments about risks (and methods of managing or minimizing them) to building inhabitants, neighboring buildings and their residents, passersby, and the firefighters themselves.

Legel, vice president of IOS, did not testify that the design of the tests sufficiently accurately measured key job *performance* (as opposed to knowledge) components to be valid under industrial psychology testing principles, as incorporated into the Title VII selection procedure guidelines. *Ricci*, 554 F.Supp.2d, at 148–49. Legel instead told the CSB that any "lay person could look at the tests and tell whether they were biased." CAJA 996–97. Such testimony fails to establish that the tests were designed to accurately measure key elements of job performance apart from informational knowledge. The tests did not minimize disparate impact. Pet. App. 685a-686a, 698a.

Dr. Hornick, in addition, explained to the CSB his fundamental methodological problem with the multiple-choice and other testing methods used in the 2003 examinations: "I've spoken to at least 10,000 ... firefighters in group settings in my consulting practice and I have never ... had anyone in the fire service say to me, 'Well, the person who gets the highest score on a written job knowledge, multiple guess test makes the best company officer.'" JA 96–97. "I think a person's leadership skills, their command presence, their interpersonal skills, their management skills, their tactical skills," Dr. Hornick added, "could have been identified and evaluated in a much more appropriate way that would have tested their real skills and not necessarily their ability to in two and a half-minutes describe" in the oral test. JA 105.

In addition to the methodological problem with using multiple-choice tests to select officers, the other elements of the selection process were predetermined by the City Charter or CBA and never validated at all. IOS claimed that it had calibrated the exams so that "minimally qualified job performance equated to the 70% composite cutoff score," mandated by the City Charter. Pet. App.77a, 330a. Legel conceded, however, that IOS had failed to use the process it had originally proposed to establish a "legally defensible cutoff score," but instead had simply used the 70 percent score required by the City Charter. Pet. App. 321; Pet. App. 77a, 698a. IOS admitted that the 70 percent cutoff score "isn't very meaningful when you are trying to find ... the cutoff score that defines minimally competent or minimally qualified, which is ultimately what you are looking to do in a situation like this." Pet. App. 697a. A test cutoff score set too high unnecessarily screens out applicants capable of successfully performing the job and thus is invalid. 29 C.F.R. §1607.5(H). *See also McDonnell Douglas v. Green*, 411 U.S. at 806.

In addition, there was a total lack of any attempt to validate the 60:40 weighting of the written to oral tests, dictated by the CBA, separately or together with the 70 percent cutoff score mandated by the City Charter. Without a valid cutoff score, IOS admitted, it had resorted to designing more difficult tests, even though "more difficult tests tend to have greater levels of adverse impact." Pet. App. 698a–99a; Pet. App. 698a. The combined effect of the 60:40 ratio and the 70 percent cutoff, together with the test questions themselves and their written multiple-choice versus oral format produced deep disparities in pass rates and selection probabilities on the lieutenants' and captains' promotion exams.

Finally, the rank-ordering system, as well, was not validated nor was there any evidence that it could be:

> Evidence which may be sufficient to support the use of a selection procedure on a pass/fail (screening) basis may be insufficient to support the use of the

same procedure on a ranking basis under these guidelines. Thus, if a user decides to use a selection procedure on a ranking basis, and that method of use has a greater adverse impact than use on an appropriate pass/fail basis . . ., the user should have sufficient evidence of validity and utility to support the use on a ranking basis. 29 C.F.R. §1607.5(G).

Faced with the threat of African American promotion candidates filing suit, had the City attempted to validate its selection system, the chances of successful validation of rank ordering among examination scores differing by a fraction of a point would be miniscule. To validate a rank-ordering selection system, each incremental test score would have to be demonstrably correlated with better performance on the job. 29 C.F.R. §1607.15(C)(7). Legel did not contend that the higher the examination score, the better the performance on the job predicted for the candidate. There is nothing in the record to suggest that the rank ordering based on fractions of a point and selection based on a rule of three from among the top three candidates on the rank-ordered list was valid.

None of the aspects of the selection process had been validated at the time the CSB voted not to proceed with the selection list. It is highly improbable that any, much less each, of these selection system elements could have been validated after the fact.

The City's burden here is not to show that there is no dispute of material fact over the validation of any or combined elements of the City's selection process. It suffices that there is no dispute of material fact that the CSB had an actual and reasonably based belief that the process and its components had neither been validated nor likely could have been.

3 Less Discriminatory Alternatives in the Counterfactual Disparate Impact Case

In disparate impact suits, ordinarily it is the plaintiffs' burden to respond to the employer's proof of job-relatedness and business necessity by proving that a less-discriminatory alternative exists and that the employer refused to adopt it. Here, because we are inverting the burdens, at trial it would be the employer's burden to produce evidence that a less-discriminatory alternative existed, but only once the plaintiff has proven that there was sufficient evidence to require the employer to conclude that the tests were defensible as job-related and consistent with business necessity. As discussed above, the plaintiffs have failed to show a dispute of material fact as to the City's actual and reasonable belief that its selection process would have caused an unlawful disparate impact and could not have been validated. Alternatively, however, summary judgment in the employer's favor could likewise be supported by evidence eliminating any dispute of material fact as to the City's actual and reasonable belief in the existence of a less-discriminatory alternative selection process and its adequacy to meet the employer's business needs. It should be noted that, because the minority firefighters' disparate impact claim is a counterfactual, the prevention of which allegedly motivated the City's employment decision, the City is not required to produce evidence that it would not have adopted the less-discriminatory alternative. Such proof would entail a doubly hypothetical evidentiary presentation. Nevertheless, in effect, the City has done so here.

There are two types of alternate selection systems with less adverse impact that the employer could have adopted in place of the existing system. First, it could have removed elements from the system that had been shown to cause an impact without contributing to prediction of better performance on the job; second, there were alternate testing methodologies that the employer could have adopted. As to the second, Dr. Hornick testified before the CSB about the availability of alternative testing procedures that would better identify the most capable candidates with the requisite skills, including the use of assessment centers rather than written and oral tests. JA 96, 102–05. As to the first, built into the composition of the then-existing selection system was the possibility of lessening the disparate impact by eliminating one or more of the elements. If the 2003 tests were unchanged, the 60:40 weighting ratio were to remain unchanged, and the 70 percent cutoff score were still utilized, but no rank order list or rule of three were applied, random selection from among those achieving the 70 percent cutoff score would substantially reduce the disparity for both African American and Latino candidates in promotion to lieutenant, and as to African American candidates' promotions to captain as well.

These changes could have equally well served the employer's interest in having knowledgeable and capable captains and lieutenants, while attaining a significant reduction in the disparate impact of the exams themselves. Rank ordering and the rule of three have never been validated in New Haven. In earlier rounds of promotional testing, broader bands for scoring had been used. The broader bands had resulted in a much weaker racially disparate impact. To validate the more stringent version of rank ordering would have required the City to show that each incremental increase in score – sometimes less than a point – was correlated with better job performance as a lieutenant or captain. However, there is no evidence that those promoted in previous testing rounds failed to perform properly in their positions. The rank ordering and rule of three have played no demonstrated role in improving on-the-job outcomes; hence their elimination would not have diminished the employer's interest in job performance, while it would have reduced the disparate impact.

These computations are without even taking into account the very disproportionate success rates of white compared to African American candidates on both the captain and lieutenant exams, an amalgam of the composition of the tests themselves, the 60:40 weighting ratio of the written and oral components, and the 70 percent cutoff score for passing the exam. Had this case gone to trial, the City may well have attempted to show that, were the cutoff score lowered or the 60:40 weighting ratio altered, a significantly higher percentage of African American candidates and Latino candidates would have been promoted, while maintaining a sufficiently high cutoff score to ensure that those promoted had the requisite minimum of knowledge of technical details pertinent to the lieutenant and captain positions.

The plaintiffs appear to regard the elements of the selection process dictated by the City Charter or CBA as immune from challenge under Title VII. Our precedents make it clear that this position is incorrect. In *Dothard v. Rawlinson*, 433 U.S. at 332, state statutory minimum height and weight requirements for prison guards that had a disparate impact prohibited by Title VII were held to be unlawful. This Court held that the statutorily determined job qualifications were entitled to no "greater deference than is typically given private employer-established job qualifications." Even state legislative practices that cause a disparate impact "must be shown to be necessary to safe and efficient job performance to survive a Title VII challenge." *Id.* at 331–32 n.14. The language of section 708 of Title VII establishes that Title VII preempts state laws that conflict with its prohibitions, including both disparate impact and disparate treatment. 42 U.S.C. §2000e-7. *See, e.g., California Federal Sav. & Loan Ass'n v. Guerra*, 479 U.S. 272, 281–82 (1987); *id.* at 292 (Scalia, J., concurring); *Shaw v. Delta Air Lines*, 463 U.S. 85, 101 (1983).

The argument for privileged treatment of the 60:40 written to oral test weighting stands on even shakier ground. Except as to elements of a bona fide seniority system, the fact that a selection criterion is contained in a CBA provides it with no protection from the prohibition against employment practices causing a disparate impact. *See, e.g., California Brewers Ass'n v. Bryant*, 444 U.S. 598, 600, 608–09 (1980).

It is true that the City might not have been able to simply drop the rank ordering and rule of three without obtaining a termination of a state court injunction. *See Kelly v. City of New Haven*, 881 A.2d 978 (Conn. 2005). Similarly, as to the 60:40 written to oral test component ratio, "[a]bsent

424   Ricci v. DeStefano

a judicial determination, ... the [employer] ... cannot alter the collective bargaining agreement without the Union's consent." W. R. Grace & Co. v. Rubber Workers, 461 U.S. 757, 771 (1983). Cf. NLRA §§8(a)(5), 8(d); 29 U.S.C. §§158(a)(5), 8(d). However, the City's inability to easily change these elements of its selection system bolsters, rather than undermines, the City's defense based on the existence of an alternative employment practice that would reduce or eliminate the disparate impact. Whether established under the City Charter or under the CBA, the limitations on the City's ability to unilaterally modify its selection system components establishes as a matter of law that it would have refused to adopt each of these less-discriminatory alternatives.

In short, the CSB had a reasonable basis in the evidence presented to it for believing its selection process to be both unvalidated and not susceptible to validation, and this was the belief of those members who voted against certifying the test results. The CSB also had significant evidence that there existed several possible alterations to the process that would have reduced its disparate impact that the City would not have adopted. None of the plaintiffs' evidence creates a dispute of material fact as to the minority candidates' potential disparate impact case against the City had the CSB certified the lists resulting from the selection process. This suffices to establish the City's defense under Title VII.

D Pretext Based on Evidence of Pro-Black or Anti-White Bias

The plaintiffs argue that, beyond a wholly defensible promotional selection process, their evidence established, or at least created a dispute of material fact, that the City was not motivated by a desire to avoid violating Title VII. They contend that the City's motive was instead to maximize promotions of African American candidates or minimize promotions of white candidates. Their theory was not that the leadership of the City or the CSB was biased against white firefighters or harbored stereotypes about their job performance. The plaintiffs argued instead that influential African American political leaders had successfully pressured the mayor and his administration to increase minority officer representation by refusing to use the 2003 test results.

First, it should be noted that New Haven is a racially diverse city, with no racial or ethnic group constituting a majority. We are not presented with a case where a majority African American electorate is attempting to utilize tactics historically used by the dominant white majority to reserve the plum jobs for its own members. The 2000 Census found that, out of a total population of 123,626, 53,723 (43.5 percent) of the City's residents were white, 46,181

Ricci v. DeStefano

(37 percent) were African American, 25,384 (20.5 percent) were Latino, and 5,433 (4 percent) were other races, while 4,829 (4 percent) characterized themselves as being of two or more races. The population was almost exactly evenly divided on the basis of gender.

Second, the plaintiffs presented virtually no evidence of any political influence, either by the mayor or by African American leaders, upon the decision-making of the CSB. What evidence there was had no connection to the CSB's decision-making process, and hence is the type of "stray remarks" and comments by non-decision-makers to which our disparate treatment cases routinely give little weight. *See, e.g., Price Waterhouse v. Hopkins*, 490 U.S. 228, 277 (1989) (O'Connor, J., concurring in judgment).

Third, the plaintiffs argue that the City had previously certified tests with similar levels of disparate impact against minority candidates, but only now took action to prevent implementation; hence the stated aim to avoid causing a violation of the disparate impact provisions must be pretextual. However, the combined adverse impact of the components of the test had never before been so severe. The plaintiffs themselves presented this evidence. The rank ordering and application of the rule of three had changed as a result of a state court decision in early January 2004, which had altered the City's prior interpretation of these components. Previously, the City had rounded test scores to the nearest integer, with each rounded score treated as constituting a "rank." Several candidates with fractionally different scores would be banded at one rank, with seniority used to break ties within the rank. The City had applied the rule of three to each "rank," rather than to each candidate, based on a prior change in the Charter's wording to refer to "score." This had permitted the fire department to sometimes promote from among a considerably larger grouping of closely ranked candidates. The state court had issued an injunction prohibiting the rounding of scores, forcing the City to rank each candidate individually before applying the rule of three. Pet. App. 443-44a. *See Kelly v. City of New Haven*, 881 A.2d at 993–95. Moreover, the injunctive order precluding the rounding off of fractional scores was issued in early January 2004, after the administration in November and December of the 2003 examinations, but before the list was finalized. CAJA 700–01.

This means that none of the candidates could have relied on the altered rule of three at the time when they took the examinations. At the same time, it provides a wholly legitimate explanation for why the CSB rejected these selection system results when it had not done so in previous rounds of examination: the bottom-line outcome would have been considerably more disparate than in previous years. It cannot provide a basis to infer intent to discriminate against white candidates or in favor of African

426   Ricci v. DeStefano

American candidates. This evidence further supports the City's contention that it took action to avoid causing a disparate impact against minority promotion candidates.

E Refusing to Certify Selection Process Results Is Not Race-Norming

The plaintiffs further contend that any change in the selection system once the tests have been administered would violate section 703(l) of Title VII. This provision states in pertinent part: "It shall be an unlawful employment practice for a respondent, in connection with the selection... of candidates for ... promotion, to adjust the scores of, use different cutoff scores for, or otherwise alter the results of, employment related tests on the basis of race, color, religion, sex, or national origin."

Under this so-called anti-race-norming provision, examination results cannot be separately scored or adjusted for each race to eliminate any disparate impact. Congress squarely aimed this provision at a practice that had been judicially ordered as a remedy in several disparate impact cases and had been voluntarily adopted by employers in other instances to avoid causing a racial disparate impact. See, e.g., Bushey v. New York State Civil Service Comm'n, 733 F.2d 220 (2d Cir. 1984), cert. denied 469 U.S. 1117 (1985); Kirkland v. New York State Dep't of Correctional Servs., 711 F.2d 1117 (2d Cir. 1983). See also Bushey, 469 U.S. 1117 (1985) (Rehnquist, J., dissenting from denial of certiorari).

The plaintiffs assert that this provision also means that test results cannot be rejected in their entirety once they have been computed. Neither the language nor the legislative history of this provision, added as part of the Civil Rights Act of 1991, supports the plaintiffs' construction. Employers generally maintain their selection processes at will, absent contractual or statutory requirements. Most employers under Title VII are private actors, with every right to alter their employment practices so long as the change is not motivated by prohibited discriminatory intent and so long as the subsequently adopted practice does not cause a disparate impact prohibited under Title VII. Our precedents have emphasized Congress's desire to interfere as little as possible with employer prerogatives under Title VII. See, e.g., Burdine, 450 U.S. at 259; Weber, 443 U.S. 193, 205–07 (1979). It would require a far clearer expression of congressional intent than the wording of section 703(l) to overcome the presumption of employer freedom to make changes in employment practices, up to and including wholly rejecting the results of a selection process, even after it has been administered.

The plaintiffs' argument here, like their argument that considering the statistical outcomes of a selection process is equivalent to directly race-based decision-making, depends on ignoring the differences between facially race-based classifications and facially neutral decisions that are based in part on recognition of statistical outcomes. Section 703(l) is aimed at facially race-based classifications in altering test results to score them differently for different races or to use different cutoff scores for each race, or to validate the test separately for each race and achieve equivalent validity by separate analysis for candidates of each race. All of these entail directly race-based classifications, unlike throwing out a set of test results entirely or modifying a selection system, which are facially neutral.

III THE PLAINTIFFS' EQUAL PROTECTION CLAUSE CLAIM

In addition to challenging the CSB's noncertification decision under Title VII, the plaintiffs contend that it violated their rights under the Fourteenth Amendment. This claim can largely be disposed of on the basis of the same reasoning as that applied to the Title VII disparate treatment claim.

The plaintiffs' suggestion that disparate impact doctrine itself violates the Equal Protection Clause prohibition against intentional racial discrimination suffers from the same confusion about aggregate consideration of race in determining ends, as opposed to consideration of the race of individuals in devising means to allocate benefits or burdens. The determination that an employment practice has caused or is likely to cause a race-based disparate impact does not, on its own, directly classify individuals based on race for either benefits or burdens. It therefore does not trigger strict scrutiny, and it easily survives rational basis analysis.

This Court itself interpreted section 703(a) of Title VII, as originally enacted, to encompass disparate impact as well as disparate treatment claims. *Griggs v. Duke Power Co.*, 401 U.S. 424 (1971). An unbroken line of cases accepted this interpretation. *See Albemarle Paper Co. v. Moody*, 422 U.S. 405 (1975); *Dothard v. Rawlinson*, 433 U.S. 321 (1977); *New York City Transit Auth. v. Beazer*, 440 U.S. 568 (1979); *Connecticut v. Teal*, 457 U.S. 440 (1982); *Watson v. Fort Worth Bank & Trust*, 487 U.S. 977 (1988) (plurality opinion of O'Connor, J.); *Wards Cove Packing Co. v. Atonio*, 490 U.S. 642 (1989). Neither the *Wards Cove* majority nor the *Watson* plurality hinted that disparate impact doctrine under Title VII violated the Equal Protection Clause.[228] These decisions simply expressed concern that employers might be incentivized to take voluntary action to avoid disparate impact liability that

---

[228] The plaintiffs here have also alleged that the disparate impact provisions in Title VII "violate" its disparate treatment prohibition. This contention is legally incoherent. Two components of a single statute, even if in tension with each other, must be construed on the assumption that

428 Ricci v. DeStefano

might sometimes involve intentional reverse discrimination. Congress has now squarely rejected the reasoning of the portion of *Wards Cove* and Justice O'Connor's plurality opinion in *Watson* that would have altered the *Griggs/Albemarle* allocation of evidentiary burdens in disparate impact cases in section 703(k) of Title VII. This legislative action reconfirms Congress's exercise of its "broad" enforcement powers under section 5 of the Fourteenth Amendment – powers that include remedying, preventing, and deterring racial discrimination. *See, e.g., Hibbs*, 538 U.S. at 728. Congress has determined that any risk that disparate impact liability will encourage employers to prefer women or minority candidates over men or white candidates can be addressed, just as other forms of direct, gender- or race-based disparate treatment are addressed, through the channel of ordinary litigation. This conclusion deserves our respect, as does the congressional restoration of the *Griggs/Albemarle* allocation of burdens of proof and persuasion.

There remains the plaintiffs' contention that the action the City took – in this case, the CSB decision to refuse to certify the results of the selection process – intentionally denied them promotions on the basis of their race. As already discussed, however, the decision to withhold certification – and hence, in effect, to change the officer promotion selection system – was a facially neutral one. The plaintiffs were not individually singled out by the CSB action. Members of all races were equally deprived of their results in the existing selection process and made to await the development of a new one before trying again. Absent proof of discriminatory intent, the City need only justify its decision on a rational basis. Avoidance of incurring liability under Title VII certainly would satisfy this requirement.

"When facially neutral [policy-making] is subjected to equal protection attack, an inquiry into intent is necessary to determine whether the [employment practice] in some sense was designed to accord disparate treatment on the basis of racial considerations." *Washington v. Seattle School Dist.*, 458 U.S. 457, 484–85 (1982). "[M]echanisms [that] are race conscious but do not lead to different treatment based on a classification that tells each [individual] he or she is to be defined by race, . . . [are] unlikely . . . to demand strict scrutiny to be found permissible." *Parents Involved*, 551 U.S. at 789 (Kennedy, J., concurring in part and concurring in judgment). "Strict scrutiny does not apply merely because redistricting is performed with consciousness of race" so long as lines are not drawn based explicitly on race. *Bush v. Vera*, 517 U.S. 952, 958 (1996)

> both were intended by Congress and, if at all possible, in a manner that gives full effect to both. In addition, the argument based on intentional discrimination under Title VII is indistinguishable from that arising under the Equal Protection Clause and hence is rejected on the same basis.

(plurality opinion) (quoting *Adarand Constructors v. Pena*, 515 US. 200, 213 (1995)).

Absent proof of racially discriminatory intent in the adoption of the change in policy, strict scrutiny does not apply. *See Seattle School Dist.*, 458 U.S. at 484–85. As Justice Kennedy explained in his concurring opinion in *Parents Involved*, "Executive and legislative branches which for generations now have considered these types of policies and procedures, should be permitted to employ them with candor and with confidence that a constitutional violation does not occur whenever a decisionmaker considers the impact a given approach might have on [persons] of different races." *Parents Involved*, 551 U.S. at 789. The "presumptive invalidity of a State's use of racial classification to differentiate its treatment of individuals" – that is, the utilization of "individual racial classifications" – does not apply when a facially neutral action is taken. *Id.* at 793, 795. The state "must seek alternatives to the classification and differential treatment of individuals by race," as Justice Kennedy explained in *Parents Involved*, because racial classification of individuals for benefits or burdens presents "dangers ... that are not as pressing when the same ends are achieved by more indirect means." *Id.* at 796, 797. In fact, such facially neutral means "first must be exhausted." *Id.* at 797. That is precisely what the CSB did here, in declining to certify the results of the selection process, no matter the race of the candidate.

"[D]etermining whether invidious discriminatory purpose was a motivating factor [in the adoption of the policy change] demands a sensitive inquiry into such circumstantial and direct evidence of intent as may be available." *Arlington Heights*, 429 U.S. at 266. "The legislative or administrative history may be highly relevant, especially where there are contemporary statements by members of the decisionmaking body, minutes of its meetings, or reports." *Id.* at 268. The administrative historical background of the CSB decision has been thoroughly discussed in the context of the Title VII disparate treatment claim. Other factors that the *Arlington Heights* decision indicated might be pertinent include the degree of disproportionate racial effect, if any, of the policy and the justification, or lack thereof, for any disproportionate racial effect that may exist. *Id.* at 266–68. These factors here are the same as those regarding the Title VII claim: the City's effort to avoid violating Title VII's disparate impact provision as justification for any disproportionate racial effect in the CSB decision. The district court's conclusion that there was insufficient evidence of discriminatory intent in the CSB decision-making process to preclude summary judgment for the employer under Title VII has been sustained. That suffices as to the equal protection issue as well.

IV CONCLUSION

The United States is headed for an overall majority minority labor force and ever-increasing occupational integration of the genders as well as races, both horizontal and vertical. The fundamental goal of Title VII, to achieve true equality of opportunity, is glimmering on the horizon. This Court, in *Griggs* and its progeny, and Congress, in enacting both the 1972 amendments extending Title VII to public employers and section 703(k) in the 1991 Civil Rights Act, have recognized that eliminating facially neutral employment practices that operate disproportionately to exclude or marginalize women and minority group members is essential to the accomplishment of that goal. The alternative is to move into a world in which women and nonwhite workers remain disproportionately isolated in predominantly lower-paid, lower-status occupations and industries, with white men continuing to hold the great majority of higher-paid, higher-status executive positions. It is inconceivable that this result is compatible with either Title VII or the Fourteenth Amendment, let alone that it could be required by the Equal Protection Clause.

$$* * *$$

The decision below is affirmed.

It is so ordered.

Commentary on *Wal-Mart Stores, Inc. v. Dukes*

CHARLES A. SULLIVAN

INTRODUCTION

As decided by the Supreme Court, *Wal-Mart Stores, Inc. v. Dukes*[229] posed a triple threat to the effective enforcement of Title VII of the Civil Rights Act of 1964. Its most well-known holding – that plaintiffs' proposed class did not possess sufficient "commonality" to be certified under Rule 23(a) of the Federal Rules of Civil Procedure – necessarily meant that private enforcement of systemic claims would be dramatically more difficult. That would largely relegate systemic cases to public enforcement, with the obvious problems of limited Equal Employment Opportunity Commission (EEOC) resources and risk of political capture.

---

[229] 564 U.S. 338 (2011).

Its second holding – that recovery of monetary damages required certification under Rule 23(b)(3) and not (2)[230] – was less noted, but also devastating. It not only raised the specter of class actions failing the Rule 23(b)(3) tests for predominance of class claim and superiority in resolving the dispute, but also triggered the requirement to provide notice and opt-out rights for class members. In short, this aspect of the Court's opinion erected another major obstacle to fortunate plaintiffs who survived the Supreme Court's commonality screen.

But perhaps most important, if less clearly a reframing of substantive doctrine, was the strong implication that systemic disparate treatment – one of the two systemic theories that had been core to Title VII since the 1970s – was radically less powerful than conventional wisdom held. Although the systemic disparate impact theory remained untouched by *Wal-Mart*, systemic disparate treatment, a theory that traced back to the mid-1970s, seemed less viable in the wake of the decision, perhaps even in suits brought by the EEOC.[231]

Wal-Mart has proven less eviscerating than many feared when it was handed down,[232] but it remains a major setback for the antidiscrimination project.

THE ORIGINAL OPINION

Betty Dukes and other named plaintiffs brought what the Court described as "one of the most expansive class actions ever,"[233] and it largely survived the journey through the district court and the *en banc* Ninth Circuit. However, the Supreme Court, in an opinion written by Justice Scalia, found that the putative class of approximately 1.5 million current and former Wal-Mart female employees did not adduce "significant proof" that the company operated under a general policy of discrimination and therefore did not satisfy the Rule 23(a) "commonality" requirement. Given the overlap between the procedural commonality question and the merits question of whether there was

---

[230] *See* text beginning *infra* note 248. A certification under Rule 23(b)(2) neither requires notice to class members nor accords them the right to opt out of the class. Both requirements attach to a Rule 23(b)(3) certification, as does the further requirement that class issues "predominate."

[231] The EEOC may sue on behalf of a class of employees without meeting the requirements of Rule 23, but, of course, can proceed only to the extent of the substantive law. *EEOC v. Waffle House, Inc.*, 534 U.S. 279 (2002).

[232] *See, e.g., Chi. Teachers Union, Local No. 1 v. Bd. of Educ. of Chi.*, 797 F.3d 426 (7th Cir. 2015) (certifying a class reaching ten schools because one set of criteria was employed for all); *Brown v. Nucor Corp.*, 785 F.3d 895, 898 (4th Cir. 2015) (2-1) (decertification of a class challenging plantwide discrimination was an abuse of discretion). *See generally* Michael C. Harper, *Class-Based Adjudication of Title VII Claims in the Age of the Roberts Court*, 95 B.U. L. REV. 1099, 1101 (2015); Michael Selmi & Sylvia Tsakos, *Employment Discrimination Class Actions after* Wal-Mart v. Dukes, 48 AKRON L. REV. 803 (2015).

[233] *Wal-Mart*, 564 U.S. at 342.

432   Wal-Mart Stores, Inc. v. Dukes et al.

discrimination to begin with,[234] *Wal-Mart* has important implications not only for private class actions, but also for government pattern and practice suits.

To be certified as a class action, any suit under Title VII must satisfy two sets of requirements under Rule 23. The first set is found in Rule 23(a), which establishes threshold standards for possible class treatment.[235] While that paragraph lists four factors, the focus of *Wal-Mart* was on "commonality": the apparently straightforward requirement of Rule 23(a)(2) that "there are questions of law or fact common to the class." Although the Supreme Court had earlier recognized that "suits alleging racial or ethnic discrimination are by their very nature class suits, involving class wide wrongs," such that "[c]ommon questions of law or fact are typically present," it had also required a showing that the more specific claims by the class representative parallel the claims of the class she sought to represent.[236] And *General Telephone Co. of Southwest v. Falcon*,[237] upon which Justice Scalia's majority opinion in *Wal-Mart* heavily relied, refined the commonality inquiry by listing two possibilities for finding commonality. The first, the employer's use of "a biased testing procedure," could be challenged by "a class action on behalf of every applicant or employee who might have been prejudiced" by it.[238] This would embrace the typical disparate impact claim, and *Wal-Mart* left this possibility untouched for class actions as far as commonality is concerned.

The second framework in *Falcon* was deemed applicable to the case at bar: if the plaintiffs could establish that the defendant operated under "a general policy of discrimination" that manifested itself in the pay and promotion practices of the company, then certification of the class would be possible.[239] Applying this standard, however, the *Wal-Mart* majority found such proof

---

[234] *Id.* at 351.

[235] Rule 23(a) provides:

Prerequisites. One or more members of a class may sue or be sued as representative parties on behalf of all members only if:

    (1) the class is so numerous that joinder of all members is impracticable;

    (2) there are questions of law or fact common to the class;

    (3) the claims or defenses of the representative parties are typical of the claims or defenses of the class; and

    (4) the representative parties will fairly and adequately protect the interests of the class.

[236] *East Tex. Motor Freight Sys., Inc. v. Rodriguez*, 431 U.S. 395, 405 (1977).

[237] 457 U.S. 147 (1982).

[238] *Id.* at 159 n.15.

[239] *Wal-Mart*, 564 U.S. at 353.

"entirely absent."[240] Wal-Mart (not surprisingly!) had no formal policy of discriminating against women; indeed, the majority stressed that its policies emphasized equal opportunity.[241] Absent that, the plaintiffs relied on three kinds of proof to satisfy the "policy" requirement. The first was the expert testimony of Dr. William T. Bielby, whose "social framework" analysis supported the conclusion that Wal-Mart's devolution of largely unstructured decision-making to local managers enabled bias at that level.[242] The second kind of proof consisted of two statistical studies, one internal to Wal-Mart[243] and another a comparison of Wal-Mart to competitor "big box" retailers,[244] both revealing statistically significant disparities in promotion and pay for women at Wal-Mart.

Neither variety of proof was sufficient to find the "policy" necessary to support a finding of commonality. In fact, Wal-Mart's according discretion to local managers seemed, to the majority, to be the diametric opposite of a uniform employment discrimination practice: in a company the size of Wal-Mart, it is "quite unbelievable" that "all managers would exercise their discretion in a common way without a common direction."[245] Even if plaintiffs had established a pattern of pay and promotions that differed from the nationwide figures or regional figures in all of Wal-Mart's 3,400 stores, the Court continued, this still would not have demonstrated that commonality of issue existed.[246] Presumably, that would have shown only a lot of individual cases of violations, not a policy to discriminate.

Nor was the Court impressed with the third kind of proof offered: 120 declarations setting out instances of discrimination by current and former employees. Such anecdotal evidence was too weak to raise an inference that hundreds of thousands of individual, discretionary personnel decisions were discriminatory.[247] And, given the Court's approach to statistical evidence, maybe even showing thousands of instances would not amount to proof of a "policy."

While commonality is the most noted aspect of *Wal-Mart*, the Court did not stop there, but went on to make it harder for any plaintiffs who manage to survive the Rule 23(a) analysis to have suits certified under Rule 23(b). That

---

[240] *Id.*
[241] *Id.*
[242] *Id.* at 354–55.
[243] *Id.* at 356.
[244] *Id.*
[245] *Id.*
[246] *Id.* at 357.
[247] *Id.* at 356.

434 Wal-Mart Stores, Inc. v. Dukes et al.

paragraph typically requires a choice between (b)(2) and (b)(3), which requires a determination that:

(2) the party opposing the class has acted or refused to act on grounds that apply generally to the class, so that final injunctive relief or corresponding declaratory relief is appropriate respecting the class as a whole; or

(3) the court finds that the questions of law or fact common to the members of the class predominate over any questions affecting only individual members, and that a class action is superior to other available methods for the fair and efficient adjudication of the controversy ...

The language of Rule 23(b)(2) focusing on injunctive and declaratory relief sparked a long-running split in the circuits over whether class actions seeking monetary relief could ever be certified under the provision. In an effort to make it more likely that their class could be certified under paragraph (b)(2) in light of this problem, the *Wal-Mart* plaintiffs had not made any claims for compensatory damages for class members, limiting the monetary relief sought to back pay, an equitable remedy.[248] But the *Wal-Mart* Court rejected any such bifurcation of monetary relief for certification purposes. Although there was a dissent on the issue of commonality, the justices were unanimous that Rule 23(b)(2) was inapplicable when monetary relief was more than incidental to equitable relief, regardless of whether the monetary relief was framed as legal (damages) or equitable (back pay). There was even a question as to whether "incidental" monetary relief would be appropriate when a class is certified under paragraph (b)(2).[249]

This means that, for all practical purposes, employment discrimination suits will now have to be brought under Rule 23(b)(3) and thus must satisfy its "predominance" and "superiority" inquiries – and the latter could prove fatal to many class actions. The problem largely lies with the relationship between a successful class action and individual relief. Although proof of the existence of a pattern or practice of discrimination is sufficient to shift a burden to the employer of proving that any given individual was unaffected (in the sense that the same decision would have been reached anyway[250]), the potential need for hundreds of thousands of individual determinations could easily render

---

[248] *Id.* at 364. The plaintiffs did, however, seek punitive damages. *See id.* at 342.

[249] *Id.* at 360.

[250] *See Franks v. Bowman Transportation Co.*, 424 U.S. 747 (1976); *Int'l Bro. of Teamsters v. United States*, 431 U.S. 324 (1977).

individual claims predominant and the class action an inferior way of resolving the dispute.

The Ninth Circuit had found to the contrary by suggesting what the Supreme Court called "Trial by Formula," under which a sample set of the class members would be selected and Wal-Mart's back pay liability to that set would be determined in proceedings supervised by a master. The percentage of claims determined to be valid would then be applied to the entire remaining class, and the number of (presumptively) valid claims thus derived would be multiplied by the average back pay award in the sample set to arrive at the entire class recovery – without further individualized proceedings.[251] This approach was substantially different from what the district court likely had in mind when it certified the class, but in any event the majority "disapprove[d of] that novel project," because such an approach would deprive Wal-Mart of its right to "litigate its statutory defenses to individual claims," which in turn would violate the Rules Enabling Act of 1934, which "forbids interpreting Rule 23 to 'abridge, enlarge or modify any substantive right.' "[252]

Even assuming that these requirements can be satisfied, Rule 23(b)(3) certification also requires the class representatives to provide notice and the right to opt out to class members. The costs of notice may be prohibitive for very large class actions such as *Wal-Mart* and will often be a challenge even where much smaller employers are involved. And any substantial invocation of opt-out rights by individuals will reduce the settlement leverage of the class.

In short, *Wal-Mart* created a series of obstacles – some apparently insurmountable at least for large-scale suits – to private enforcement of Title VII by class actions.

THE FEMINIST JUDGMENT

Professor Tristin Green, writing as Justice Green, takes the opportunity of deciding a procedural question of class certification not only to reaffirm conventional views of systemic disparate treatment, but also to expand them. She signals her goal early in the opinion when she says that "the petitioner misunderstands the nature of the substantive law of employment discrimination." The point is that a systemic claim is not just a collection of individual claims, but an "independent violation." It is the practice itself, not any supposed "policy" underlying it, which is the violation.

---

[251] *Wal-Mart*, 564 U.S. at 367.

[252] *Id.* Subsequent to *Wal-Mart*, the Supreme Court's decision in *Tyson Foods, Inc. v. Bouaphakeo*, 136 S.Ct. 1036 (2016), seemed to retreat somewhat from this position, albeit not in the Title VII context.

436 Wal-Mart Stores, Inc. v. Dukes et al.

In section I, she elucidates the point, and the departure from Justice Scalia's opinion in *Wal-Mart* could not be starker. In looking for the "glue" that binds a class together, he required an employer's "general policy" of discrimination and rejected looking to employer practices that could not be said to be in furtherance of such a policy. While there is some textual basis for Justice Scalia's interpretation in the seminal systemic disparate treatment cases *Teamsters* and *Hazelwood*[253] (which Green deals with later in her feminist judgment), Green establishes that the main thrust of those opinions is to allow plaintiffs to prevail simply by showing that discrimination is a company's "standard operating procedure." And such a showing allows the court "to infer that the employer as an entity is responsible for that discrimination and must take measures to correct it." In other words, an employer that allows its decision-makers to make biased decisions is responsible for those decisions, regardless of whether or not it has a "policy" of discriminating.

Green then explains how statistical proof can be used to detect the existence of such a pattern and grounds her argument in the observation made in *Teamsters* that, "absent explanation, it is ordinarily to be expected that non-discriminatory hiring practices will in time result in a work force more or less representative of the racial and ethnic [and gender] composition of the population in the community from which employees are hired."[254] While "gross statistical disparities" may alone establish a prima facie case, the inference that bias is the cause of such disparities (rather than, say, some innocent explanation correlated with the protected class in question) can be bolstered in a variety of ways, which Green explores.

To this point, the feminist judgment breaks little new ground since it mostly corrects the Scalia opinion's departure from conventional wisdom about the reach of systemic disparate treatment. However, Green then proceeds to widen the lens: while *Teamsters* and *Hazelwood* focused on the binary hire/do not hire decision, Green stresses that discrimination arises not only at these major decision points, but also in "day-to-day judgments" such as an employer's changing "work cultures, job structures, and decision-making systems."

It is only after this discussion that Green states – perhaps overstates slightly – that "[t]his is how we have laid down the law." Her exegesis is a logical development of *Teamsters* and *Hazelwood*, and her various examples have support in at least lower court authority. But the "we" suggests a robust Supreme Court support for, say, changing "work cultures" which (except for sexual harassment) goes beyond what the Court had previously held. Indeed,

---

[253] *Int'l Bro. of Teamsters v. United States*, 431 U.S. 324 (1977); *Hazelwood Sch. Dist. v. United States*, 433 U.S. 299 (1977).
[254] *Teamsters*, 431 U.S. at 340 n.20.

Wal-Mart Stores, Inc. v. Dukes et al. 437

Wal-Mart itself was the Court's opportunity to make this clear, and it is Green's feminist judgment, not the Scalia opinion, that does so. Were hers the governing opinion, liability for discriminatory employment outcomes would have the salutary effect of incentivizing employers to address aspects of work culture that contribute to this result.

Having established the essential framework, Green deals with two objections. She asserts first that "[t]here is nothing inherently discriminatory about subjective decision-making," which is obviously an attempt to allay fears about the consequences of defining systemic disparate treatment so broadly. But any comfort some skeptics might take from this concession is immediately dispelled when she notes that such processes "can both serve as a cover for discriminatory decisions and can also provide space for biased decisions to occur." Presumably, the "space" point refers to processes that render decisions "vulnerable" to discrimination. In any event, she stresses that the critical factor is "disparities in employment outcomes" rather than the particular mechanisms that cause them. Indeed, plaintiff need not "isolate a specific practice" to bring a (disparate treatment) pattern or practice case. In short, an employer with "bad numbers" had better do something to identify and address the problem.

The second objection is the claim that systemic disparate treatment precedent requires a finding of a motive or purpose at the top levels of an organization. This is a real sticking point for any attempt to situate the feminist judgment as an application, rather than a modification, of systemic disparate treatment authority. Green does a nice job of explaining why the facts of *Hazelwood* do not support such an interpretation. But she does not really grapple directly with the recurrent use in *Teamsters* of the term "policy," which is the strongest textual basis for requiring a finding of intent by high-level decision-makers.[255] Instead, she argues that taking that term literally would put systemic disparate treatment "out of sync" with individual disparate treatment. One could argue the opposite: that requiring a finding of intent by the decision-maker in each setting synchronizes the two theories. But Green effectively deploys *Staub v. Proctor Hospital*[256] to make the point that, even in the disparate treatment context, the decision-maker need not be biased if the challenged decision was proximately caused by someone with the prohibited motivation. Presumably, something similar could be said of a pattern of biased decision-making uncontrolled by upper management. She also suggests that requiring a "policy" would create a gap between the disparate impact and

---

[255] I am not so sure that a firm's continuing practices that it knows enable discrimination by its decision-makers cannot be said to constitute a policy of discrimination.

[256] *Staub v. Proctor Hosp.*, 562 U.S. 411 (2011).

438   Wal-Mart Stores, Inc. v. Dukes et al.

systemic disparate treatment theories, but I am not sure I understand why any gulf is not the natural result of requiring intent for a violation under the latter theory – a requirement that is absent under the former.

Having so defined the substantive law of Title VII in section I, in section II Green turns to the application of that law to the class certification commonality question in *Wal-Mart* itself. Not surprisingly, the opinion finds common questions. As a first step, Green "rein[s] in the creep post-*Falcon*" of requiring proof of a "policy." Under the feminist judgment's view, *Falcon* held only that a named plaintiff cannot "represent a class substantially differently situated"; in the case itself, the Mexican American plaintiff claimed discrimination against him in promotions, but sought to represent a class of Mexican American applicants denied employment. While the national origins matched, there was no showing that practices that affected current workers also affected potential employees.

In the process of demonstrating the limits of the *Falcon* holding, the feminist judgment reproduces that portion of the opinion on which Justice Scalia relied to show the absence of a common question. Green deftly avoids the bifurcated choice that *Falcon* posed for Scalia by simply reading the passage as stating two illustrative avenues of proof, not exhausting the possibilities for plaintiffs – that is, the language in that case reflected the facts before the Court, not the universe available to plaintiffs. While proof that an employer "operated under a general policy of discrimination" is one method of establishing commonality, it is not the only way. Another, applicable to *Wal-Mart* itself, was proof that individual plaintiffs were "subjected to the same relevant practices ... as the members of the class they sought to represent."

That provides the segue to the feminist judgment's application of this principle to the facts of the case, and Green leads off with the two statistical studies showing lower pay and promotions for women, both within Wal-Mart and as compared with competitors. The former "suggest that discrimination against women may be occurring throughout Wal-Mart, perhaps not in every supervisory decision, but as the regular, rather than the unusual, practice across the organization."

In addition, the plaintiffs adduced evidence of Wal-Mart's uniform practice of giving its managers "substantial discretion in their pay and promotion decisions" (which seems not to have been disputed). They presented evidence "of a strong corporate culture at Wal-Mart and evidence of gender stereotyping." Viewed by itself, this passage might be the weakest part of the feminist judgment: Green looks to the declarations, which – numerous though they were – represented a tiny fraction of Wal-Mart stores and an infinitesimal fraction of the members of the class. All could be taken at face value without agreeing that they established pervasive gender stereotyping across the company.

But Green then bolsters the declarations with the expert opinion of Dr. William Bielby, who attested that Wal-Mart's devolution of largely unstructured decision-making to managers, given social science research on bias and stereotyping, rendered Wal-Mart "vulnerable to gender bias." That testimony was "helpful" at the class certification stage because it suggests that the discrepancies identified by the statistical studies are the result of discrimination, not some unidentified random factor. Added to the statistical disparities between male and female employees' salaries and promotions and the declarations, Bielby's testimony should have been sufficient to certify the class.

The second section of the feminist judgment concludes by stating that the named plaintiffs and the class share "the common issue of whether Wal-Mart engaged in a pattern or practice of discrimination nationwide." And the large size of the resulting class cannot be allowed to operate an "arbitrary, nonhistoric" limitation on Rule 23.

The feminist judgment now turns from Rule 23(a) to Rule 23(b). It starts off by rejecting the argument that Title VII accords Wal-Mart a right to an individualized hearing on every class member's claim (which would necessarily result in a finding that individual issues predominate over class issues and bar certification under Rule 23(b)(3)). This requires dealing with relevant statutory language, which seems to say exactly that.[257] Green's argument tries to confine the relevant provision to a different application of Title VII (the mixed-motive setting), but the feminist judgment does not develop the textual analysis necessary for a powerful rebuttal of the argument.

More persuasively, and without developing in detail the correct "statistical modeling" of remedies if a pattern or practice violation is proven, Green cleverly argues that using such modeling "does not require a court to order a defendant to pay an individual who was not discriminated against" and therefore does not violate the statutory command. Green views this approach as simply determining a lump-sum liability that the court will then allocate to individuals. She also correctly notes that the Ninth Circuit's suggested approach was only one "conceivable" way of dealing with class remedies and

[257] 42 U.S.C §2000e-5(2)(A) provides:

> No order of the court shall require the admission or reinstatement of an individual as a member of a union, or the hiring, reinstatement, or promotion of an individual as an employee, or the payment to him of any back pay, if such individual was refused admission, suspended, or expelled, or was refused employment or advancement or was suspended or discharged for any reason other than discrimination on account of race, color, religion, sex, or national origin or in violation of section 704(a).

440   Wal-Mart Stores, Inc. v. Dukes et al.

that the lower courts have used other approaches. Having dismantled the juridical bar the defendant tried to erect, the feminist judgment addresses the argument that statistical modeling was also unfair to class members. It "may serve only rough justice" for such individuals, "but without it we also fear that there will be no justice at all as employers will continue to discriminate with little to dissuade them from doing so." Green will return to the "rough justice" theme at the end of the opinion.

Although rejection of the individualized trials would have opened the door to Rule 23(b)(3) certification, plaintiffs typically prefer Rule 23(b)(2) certification because there is neither a requirement of a duty to notify class members nor a right to opt out and because such certification avoids the potentially fatal inquiry into predominance.[258] The feminist judgment declares such certification to be appropriate, at least when plaintiffs do not seek "individualized compensatory damages," but (as in *Wal-Mart* itself) "injunctive and other equitable relief, which includes back pay." This neatly opted for the more permissive side of the circuit split, which would allow for Rule 23(b)(2) certification where legal relief did not "predominate." But there is a rub: the plaintiff class did seek punitive damages – clearly a legal remedy. For that reason, the Ninth Circuit had found it an abuse of discretion for the district court to certify this aspect of the case without making a predominance determination.

The feminist judgment then, without explicitly rejecting the predominance rule, states, "That the [punitive damages] award might be large does not mean that monetary damages will 'predominate' such that Rule 23(b)(2) certification is inappropriate." Green's point may be that the punitive damages determination will be relatively simple once liability is established such that it does not "predominate" even if it is multiples of any back pay award. I do not know if I agree, but, in any event, I am not sure it renders the Ninth Circuit's holding wrong: should not the district court have determined the relationship of the equitable and legal remedies before certifying, given the predominance rule? (How it might have done so is more than a little complicated!)

At this point, somewhat surprisingly, the feminist judgment shifts gears and notes that, even under a Rule 23(b)(2) certification, a district court may order notice and opt-out rights for the class members. Green notes that the court below "did not consider whether notice and opportunity to opt out might also be wise, even mandated by due process, for the back pay portion of the

---

[258] Rule 23(b)(3) provides in part that certification is appropriate if "the court finds that the questions of law or fact common to class members predominate over any questions affecting only individual members, and that a class action is superior to other available methods for fairly and efficiently adjudicating the controversy." Fed. R. Civ. P. 23 (2015).

Wal-Mart Stores, Inc. v. Dukes et al.   441

plaintiffs' claim," and that it was error not to do so. This is surprising – maybe shocking – for a feminist judgment, which to this point has been uniformly plaintiff-friendly. Even in the days of electronic communication, notifying 1 million or more class members (most of whom are probably no longer employed by Wal-Mart and whose contact information has likely changed) is a herculean and expensive task. Green's concern here is for the "class members losing their rights to seek individualized monetary awards, including back pay." While Green argues that due process requirements are flexible enough to make this manageable, I have my doubts – although maybe if someone who wrote this feminist judgment could be counted on to write the due process opinions, it might not be the problem I am imagining. Absent that, I doubt whether the (arguably) marginal improvements in "rough justice" in this regard is worth the risks to pattern and practice enforcement that the feminist judgment so eloquently urges.

I guess feminists can differ on that point.

Wal-Mart Stores, Inc. v. Dukes et al., 564 U.S. 338 (2011)

JUSTICE TRISTIN K. GREEN DELIVERED THE OPINION OF THE COURT.

This case gives us an opportunity to clarify the requirements for systemic employment discrimination cases brought under Title VII of the Civil Rights Act of 1964 to proceed as private class actions under Rule 23 of the Federal Rules of Civil Procedure. Clarification is long overdue. For years now, lower courts have distorted the substantive law of Title VII and misinterpreted our opinion in *General Telephone Co. of Southwest v. Falcon*, 457 U.S. 147 (1982), wreaking havoc on private plaintiffs' efforts to use the preeminent federal Civil Rights Act to combat discrimination in employment. We correct the path today.

Petitioner Wal-Mart is the defendant in an employment discrimination suit filed in 2001 by seven named plaintiffs, all women who worked or are working for Wal-Mart, holding a variety of positions. Betty Dukes, a named plaintiff, for example, is an African American woman who started working for Wal-Mart in 1994 in its Pittsburgh, California, store as a part-time cashier earning $5 an hour. She later worked as a customer service manager and a greeter. Deborah Gunter, another named plaintiff, is a white woman who was hired by Wal-Mart in 1996 as a photo lab clerk at a store in Riverside, California. She later worked as a night stocker and a service clerk in the tire lube express

442 Wal-Mart Stores, Inc. v. Dukes et al.

department. These and the other named plaintiffs (respondents) allege that Wal-Mart has engaged in and continues to engage in sex discrimination in violation of Title VII, 78 Stat. 253, as amended, 42 U.S.C. §2000e-1 *et seq.* Specifically, they allege that women employed in Wal-Mart stores are paid less than men in comparable positions, despite the women having higher performance ratings and greater seniority, and that women receive fewer – and wait longer for – promotions to in-store management positions than men. The women seek declaratory and injunctive relief, back pay, and punitive damages, but not traditional compensatory damages.

On April 28, 2003, the respondents filed a motion to certify a nationwide class consisting of women employed in a range of positions, from hourly positions to salaried managerial positions. The respondents proposed that the trial judge certify pursuant to Rule 23 a class of "women employed at any Wal-Mart domestic retail store at any time since December 26, 1998, who have been or may be subjected to Wal-Mart's challenged pay and management track promotions policies and practices." *Dukes v. Wal-Mart Stores, Inc.*, 222 F. R.D. 137, 141–42 (N.D. Cal. 2004). Wal-Mart is the largest employer in the world, and this, together with the time elapsed since filing and high employee turnover, makes for a potentially very large class.

The parties conducted extensive discovery and filed briefs and documentary and testimonial evidence regarding class certification. Judge Martin Jenkins held several hours of oral argument, and, on June 21, 2004, he issued an eighty-four-page order granting in part and denying in part the respondents' motion. *Id.* Judge Jenkins granted the respondents' motion and certified the proposed class for the claims involving pay discrimination. He also certified a class for promotion claims seeking declaratory and injunctive relief and punitive damages, but declined to certify a promotion claim seeking back pay. Both parties appealed. A divided *en banc* court for the Court of Appeals for the Ninth Circuit substantially affirmed. *Wal-Mart Stores, Inc. v. Dukes*, 603 F.3d 571 (9th Cir. 2010) (en banc). We granted *certiorari* to consider whether Judge Jenkins' certification of the plaintiff class is consistent with Rule 23(a) and (b).

We make three initial key points regarding the petitioner's arguments in this case.

(1) The petitioner misunderstands the nature of the substantive law of employment discrimination on which the respondents sue. The systemic pattern or practice theory is not a mere amassing of many individualized claims; rather, it presents an independent violation of Title VII for which the employer is directly liable. In the seminal case, *Teamsters v. United States*, 431 U.S. 324 (1977), we held that plaintiffs

Wal-Mart Stores, Inc. v. Dukes et al. 443

must prove that discrimination was the regular rather than the unusual practice within the employer's workplace to establish a "pattern or practice" of discrimination in violation of Title VII. This standard has not changed in the years since *Teamsters*, and we see no reason for it to change simply because a system of highly subjective decision-making serves as one piece of the respondents' case.

(2) The petitioner misreads our decision in *General Tel. Co. of the SW v. Falcon*, 457 U.S. 147 (1982), to require that the plaintiffs present significant proof of a policy of discrimination at Wal-Mart in order to satisfy commonality for class certification. We held no such thing in *Falcon*. Instead, in order for the proposed nationwide class to satisfy the requirements of Rule 23(a), the plaintiffs must simply show that members of the class share a common issue of fact or law. That common issue can be whether women employees at Wal-Mart were discriminated against on the basis of their sex in pay and/or promotion decisions. Mere allegation of this, of course, is not enough to show a common issue, but statistical and other evidence that tends to show that sex-based discrimination is occurring across the class is sufficient.

(3) The petitioner misunderstands the role of Rule 23(b) as well as its own perceived right to individualized defenses under Title VII. The categories delineated under Rule 23(b) are meant to guide judges in their decisions about how much notice to provide to absent class members and when to provide an opportunity for those absent members to opt out of a class. Rule 23(b) was not intended as a straightjacket to prevent civil rights claims like those presented by the respondents. Moreover, the petitioner has no right to individualized defenses to a systemic claim under Title VII, and therefore the trial court did not abuse its discretion when it decided it could, upon finding of liability for a pattern or practice of discrimination, compute money owed by the petitioner using a formula, thereby rendering the claims suitable to Rule 23(b)(2) certification.

I TITLE VII AND SYSTEMIC DISCRIMINATION

It is crucial to see from the start that the respondents allege systemic discrimination in their complaint, not merely claims of individual discrimination. This case, in other words, is not like a mass tort, where many individuals come together wholly out of efficiency to sue en masse. The substantive law of Title VII presents plaintiffs with another option. Plaintiffs suing under Title VII can

444   Wal-Mart Stores, Inc. v. Dukes et al.

allege a pattern or practice of discrimination, as the respondents did here, which invokes an independent theory of entity liability for discrimination.[259]

To hold an employer liable for a pattern or practice of discrimination, as we stated in *Teamsters*, plaintiffs must prove that discrimination is the regular rather than the unusual practice within the employer's workplace. *Teamsters*, 431 U.S. at 336. If an employer has a facially discriminatory policy or even a neutral one designed with express purpose to discriminate, that employer will, of course, be held liable for systemic discrimination. But the pattern or practice theory allows plaintiffs to establish employer liability without showing that the employer has adopted a policy of discrimination. Rather, plaintiffs can show that discrimination is the regular rather than the unusual practice – the standard operating procedure – within the company. *Id.* From there, we have been willing to infer that the employer as an entity is responsible for that discrimination and must take measures to correct it. *See also Hazelwood School District v. United States*, 433 U.S. 299 (1977).

We have also said that plaintiffs may use statistics to prove a pattern or practice of discrimination under Title VII. Statistical analyses comparing what is observed in a workplace and what one would expect to observe, given the relevant labor pool, can serve as evidence that discrimination is operating within an organization.[260] Stark disparities in this comparison, in other words, can support an inference that the employer is engaging in a pattern or practice of discrimination.[261] This is because, as we said in the hiring context, "absent explanation, it is ordinarily to be expected that nondiscriminatory hiring practices will in time result in a work force more or less representative of the racial and ethnic [and gender] composition of the population in the community from which employees are hired." *Teamsters*, 431 U.S. at 340 n.20. Indeed,

---

[259] The respondents also invoked the systemic disparate impact theory, but we see their pattern or practice claim, alleging systemic disparate treatment, as the principal theory on which they rely and on which the trial judge certified the class. Because we find certification proper for the systemic disparate treatment claim, we decline to address the disparate impact claim separately.

[260] The respondents in this case also presented statistics benchmarking Wal-Mart against other big-box retailers. These statistics showed, for example, that while the proportion of female hourly workers at Wal-Mart and its top competitors is similar, Wal-Mart's store management is roughly one-third women, whereas at its top competitors women comprise over half of management employees. *See* Dr. Mark Bendick Report in Support of Plaintiffs' Motion for Class Certification. This type of statistical comparison may be useful in proving a pattern or practice case, but it is not essential. After all, it would do no justice to require that plaintiffs prove that their employer was worse than the rest of the nation's employers if other employers are also discriminating.

[261] In *Hazelwood*, we identified 2–3 standard deviations as sufficient to render a disparity suspect and thereby to infer discrimination, unless the disparity is otherwise explained. *Hazelwood*, 433 U.S. at 308 n.14.

"[w]here gross statistical disparities can be shown, they alone may in a proper case constitute prima facie proof of a pattern or practice of discrimination." *Hazelwood*, 433 U.S. at 307–08 (citing *Teamsters*, 431 U.S. at 339). Statistics, as an important source of proof, are not limited to the hiring context, but extend equally to promotion and pay, as alleged by the respondents. We have also extended our approval of statistical analyses in proving systemic discrimination to a variety of statistical models, including multiple regression analysis. *Bazemore v. Friday*, 478 U.S. 385 (1986).

Plaintiffs, however, will rarely rely on statistics and statistical analyses alone. In early cases, plaintiffs often presented anecdotal evidence – testimony of individual instances of discrimination involving overtly biased statements by supervisors, for example – to "bolster" their statistical proof. *Teamsters, supra.* This and other anecdotal testimony can bolster the statistical evidence by providing more reason to believe that discrimination within the organization rather than some nondiscriminatory cause or cause external to the organization explains the observed disparity. Plaintiffs have also presented testimony (sometimes by social scientists) to the effect that the particular structures, systems, or cultures in place at the defendant organization are likely to result in regular, widespread bias in employment decisions. *See, e.g., Butler v. Home Depot, Inc.*, 984 F.Supp. 1257, 1260–62 (N.D. Cal. 1997). A system of highly subjective decision-making may be among these systems. Or plaintiffs can present other evidence, such as evidence that stereotyping or similar biases are widespread within the company or that they emanate from top leaders down to the rank-and-file. All of this evidence is aimed at convincing the fact finder that the employer engages in a pattern or practice of discrimination and that "discrimination is the regular rather than the unusual practice within the employer's workplace." *Teamsters*, 431 U.S. at 336.

Depending on the specifics of the case, defendants can rebut plaintiffs' evidence of a pattern or practice of discrimination by adequately challenging the plaintiffs' statistical data, analyses, or other evidence. *Id.* at 340 (noting that "statistics . . ., like any other kind of evidence, may be rebutted"). Or defendants can provide their own showing of an alternative and more plausible reason for observed disparities. If the court believes that no reasonable fact finder can infer from the plaintiffs' evidence that the employer engaged in a pattern or practice of discrimination, or if the case proceeds to trial and a jury finds that a pattern or practice of discrimination has not been proven, there will be no finding of liability on a systemic disparate treatment claim.

This pattern or practice theory is essential to the efficacy of Title VII as a tool for reducing employment discrimination today. Women continue to suffer discrimination in employment. *See* Robert Nelson & William Bridges, Legalizing Gender Inequality (1999) (providing an in-depth account of

446 Wal-Mart Stores, Inc. v. Dukes et al.

how sex-based discrimination can operate within institutions). Nor are racial and national origin discrimination a thing of the past. *See* Marianne Bertrand & Sendhil Mullainathan, *Are Emily and Greg More Employable Than Lakisha and Jamal? A Field Experiment on Labor Market Discrimination*, 94 AM. ECON. ASSOC. 991 (2004). This is not to say that we should find every employer liable for discrimination simply because we know that discrimination remains prevalent. It is to say, however, that we see no reason to diverge from our prior precedent. We know from the social sciences that employment discrimination often operates in day-to-day judgments in addition to key moments of decision, such as pay and promotion. *See* Barbara F. Reskin, *The Proximate Causes of Employment Discrimination*, 29 CONTEMP. SOCIOL. 319 (2000). Indeed, a vast and growing body of research tells us that organizations influence these judgments and decisions in myriad ways. *See* Tristin K. Green & Alexandra Kalev, *Discrimination-Reducing Measures at the Relational Level*, 59 HASTINGS L.J. 1435 (2008). Organizations are not mere bystanders to the discrimination of their employees; they are active participants in discrimination with measures at their disposal to minimize it. These measures go beyond the policing of individual bad actors to include organizational changes, such as changes in work cultures, job structures, and decision-making systems. Statistical disparities that are unlikely due to chance and that are not otherwise explained – together, in some cases, with other evidence tending to show that discrimination within the organization explains the disparities – can support an inference that an employer is engaging in a pattern or practice of discrimination that must be remedied.

Without the pattern or practice theory, Title VII would miss much of the discrimination that can take place on a day-to-day basis in a workplace, but that may not be immediately actionable or pinpointed as discriminatory. Individual discrimination claims simply cannot do the same job. Pattern or practice, systemic disparate treatment theory provides plaintiffs with a way of capturing discrimination in the aggregate, when it results in significant group disparities in outcomes such as hiring or pay or promotion. And it thereby puts pressure on employers to take discrimination seriously and to build their structures and systems and cultures in ways that will not facilitate or incite it.

Nothing we have said so far should come as a surprise. This is how we have laid down the law since *Teamsters* and *Hazelwood*. Contrary to the petitioner's insistence, there is nothing "new" in the respondents' effort to rely on this theory.[262] Our improved knowledge from the research in the social sciences on

---

[262] The respondents rely heavily on a law review article describing plaintiffs as relying on a "bold new theory" of discrimination in this and similar cases. Richard A. Nagareda, *Class Certification in the Age of Aggregate Proof*, 84 N.Y.U. L. REV. 97 (2009). Professor Nagareda

Wal-Mart Stores, Inc. v. Dukes et al. 447

how discrimination operates within workplaces does not require that we create a new legal theory to address discrimination. Nor, as the petitioner claims, does a trial judge's decision to certify a class determine whether plaintiffs can use the pattern or practice, systemic disparate treatment theory, relying in part on statistical evidence to prove their claim. To hold otherwise would put Rule 23 certification at the helm of the substantive law, which would surely violate the Rules Enabling Act, 28 U.S.C. §2072(b) (forbidding interpretation of Rule 23 to "abridge, enlarge or modify any substantive right"), if not the US Constitution.[263]

A few words are in order about subjective decision-making, given its rise in prominence in this and other cases. There is nothing inherently discriminatory about subjective decision-making on its own; the petitioner is right about that. However, we have long known that highly subjective decision-making can be a mechanism for discrimination. An employer's use of a highly subjective decision-making system, as we explained earlier, can be evidence, depending on the case, that points to discrimination within the organization rather than to some other explanation for observed statistical disparities. This has always been so. *Hazelwood*, for example, involved hiring decisions that were based on interviews conducted typically by the principal at the school where the teaching vacancy existed. As we relayed the facts there on appeal:

> Although those conducting the interviews did fill out forms rating the applicants in a number of respects, it is undisputed that each school principal possessed virtually unlimited discretion in hiring teachers for his school. The only general guidance given to the principals was to hire the "most competent" person available, and such intangibles as "personality, disposition, appearance, poise, voice, articulation, and ability to deal with people" counted heavily. The principal's choice was routinely honored by Hazelwood's Superintendent and the Board of Education.
>
> Hazelwood, 433 U.S. at 302.[264]

A highly subjective decision-making system like this one, or like that allegedly adopted by Wal-Mart for its supervisors in making decisions about pay and training programs and promotions, is evidence in a pattern or practice

---

was mistaken. The pattern or practice theory of discrimination has been around for decades. *Teamsters, supra.*

[263] We are particularly concerned about this possibility. *See infra* section II.

[264] *Teamsters*, too, involved subjective decisions by lower-level managers. *See Teamsters*, 431 U.S. at 338, n.19 (describing testimony that one manager told an applicant "I don't feel the company is ready for this right now" and that a personnel officer told another that he had one mark against him because "You're a Chicano, and as far as we know, there isn't a Chicano driver in the system.").

448   Wal-Mart Stores, Inc. v. Dukes et al.

case because we know that highly subjective decision-making can both serve as a cover for discriminatory decisions and provide space for biased decisions to occur.[265] *See* M. E. Heilman & M. C. Haynes, *Subjectivity in the Appraisal Process: A Facilitator of Gender Bias in Work Settings, in* BEYOND COMMON SENSE: PSYCHOLOGICAL SCIENCE IN THE COURTROOM 128 (E. Borgida & S. Fiske eds., 2008). A highly subjective decision-making system is but one of any number of an employer's practices, systems, or work cultures that can result in significant disparities in employment outcomes, and in many cases we would expect it to operate together with other practices. It is important to remember that plaintiffs in a pattern or practice case need not isolate a specific practice, but, as we have said, will instead seek to use the evidence of practices and cultures to support an inference that discrimination rather than something else explains observed disparities.

The matter of purpose or intent in systemic disparate treatment theory also calls for some clarification. The systemic disparate treatment, pattern or practice theory of liability under Title VII imposes liability for intentional discrimination, and we have used the language of purpose or intent along these lines. *See Teamsters*, 431 U.S. at 339 n.20 (stating that "statistics showing racial or ethnic imbalance are probative ... because such imbalance is often a telltale sign of purposeful discrimination"); *Hazelwood*, 433 U.S. at 306 n. 12 (describing the government's case in terms of "purpose" and "deliberately continued employment policies"). This language should not be taken to mean, however, that plaintiffs must prove purpose or motivation on the part of high-level decision-makers within an entity in order to establish Title VII liability. In some cases, the evidence will suggest as much – for example, when the chief executive has expressed a desire to keep women in particular positions, or when high-level decision-makers are made aware of pervasive harassment or discrimination and do nothing about it – but such evidence is not required to prove a violation of Title VII.[266] Instead, we see our cases as standing for the proposition that plaintiffs can prove a pattern or practice of discrimination by using statistics and other evidence showing that discrimination, treating employees differently on the basis of a protected category, such as sex or race, is widespread within the employer's workplace, and that it is the

[265] We have held, of course, that a subjective decision-making system can be challenged using disparate impact theory. *Watson v. Fort Worth Bank & Trust*, 487 U.S. 977 (1988). We do not disturb that holding today; we simply note that a highly subjective decision-making system may also be evidence of illegal discrimination in a pattern or practice case.

[266] Given the era in which our earlier cases were decided – a time when blatant discrimination and resistance to civil rights was commonplace – we may have expected purpose or intent by high-level decision-makers in the cases that came before us, but it would be a mistake to hold that our expectation in those cases translated to a legal requirement for all cases.

Wal-Mart Stores, Inc. v. Dukes et al.

"regular rather than the unusual practice." *Teamsters, supra.* In *Hazelwood*, for example, our discussion of the ways in which Hazelwood could rebut the government's prima facie case did not include mere protestations that the Hazelwood School District or its leaders lacked intent or purpose to discriminate. *Hazelwood*, 433 U.S. at 309 (quoting *Teamsters, supra*) (noting that the employer must be given an opportunity to show that "the claimed discriminatory pattern is a product of pre-Act hiring rather than unlawful post-Act discrimination"). Pointing to "its own officially promulgated policy 'to hire all teachers on the basis of training, preparation and recommendations, regardless of race, color or creed' " was not sufficient. *Hazelwood*, 433 U.S at 303–04.

Lower courts in recent years have adopted something of a "we didn't mean it" defense by holding that evidence showing professed commitment to diversity by high-level decision-makers or evidence that such decision-makers made "sincere attempts to achieve greater diversity" can rebut evidence of a pattern or practice of discrimination, such as evidence of a gendered work culture biased against women and resulting in significant disparities. *See Serrano v. Cintas Co.*, No. C04-40132 (E.D. Mich. 2009) (denying the plaintiffs' motion for class certification). To be clear, this cannot stand in light of our understanding of the law. Nor can an employer defeat a pattern or practice case by merely pointing to its official nondiscrimination policy, as Wal-Mart seeks to do here or as the Hazelwood School District sought to do in that case. Such evidence can surely be admitted in a pattern or practice case, but without some inquiry into how that policy is implemented and whether it is effective, the evidence alone cannot rebut a prima facie case of a pattern or practice of discrimination.

We add only that, beyond this textual read of our earlier cases, as a practical matter it makes little sense to require proof of intent or motive on the part of individuals at the highest levels of an organization to establish a pattern or practice of discrimination. Only in very rare cases will plaintiffs have evidence of biased statements on the part of the highest-level decision-makers – and in those cases inferring an organizational role from statistics may not even be necessary. The pattern or practice theory was meant to provide plaintiffs with another route to employer liability, one that rests on pervasive or widespread discrimination within an employer's organization and thereby on the confidence that something within that organization and within the control of the employer is causing the discrimination, regardless of the states of mind of the highest level of decision-makers.[267] The intent for pattern or practice liability

---

[267] The state of mind of those decision-makers may come in at the determination of punitive damages, if sought. *See* 42 U.S.C. §1981a (allowing for punitive damages upon finding that the employer engaged in discrimination "with malice or reckless indifference to the federally

450   Wal-Mart Stores, Inc. v. Dukes et al.

can be found in the disparate treatment itself and by inference to the organization (the employer) as entity, not to the individuals who lead it.

To hold otherwise would put systemic disparate treatment theory out of sync
with individual disparate treatment theory, where we have rightly focused on
causation over the ultimate decision-maker's specific state of mind. *See Staub
v. Proctor Hospital*, 562 U.S. 411 (2011) (rejecting the defendant's argument that
there could be no disparate treatment if the ultimate decision-maker exercised
no bias, even if earlier decision-makers did). Moreover, it would leave
a vacuous gulf between our theory of disparate impact – where plaintiffs
identify a specific practice that causes a disparate impact on members of
a group, regardless of whether members of the group are being treated
differently than other groups within the organization – and our theory of
pattern or practice, systemic disparate treatment – where plaintiffs seek to
prove that discrimination is the regular rather than the unusual practice within
the organization. *Griggs v. Duke Power Co.*, 401 U.S. 424 (1971). We see no
reason to open that gulf, which, for reasons discussed above, would largely
relegate to the dustbin Title VII as a tool for effectuating meaningful change.

II CLASS ACTION CERTIFICATION RULE 23(a)

We turn now to applying the requirements of Rule 23(a) to systemic discrimination cases. Today, we rein in the creep post-*Falcon*, which was premised on
the misunderstanding that *Falcon* requires plaintiffs alleging systemic discrimination to provide significant proof of a policy of discrimination to satisfy the
Rule 23(a) requirement of commonality.[268] In *Falcon*, we cautioned that "[a]

---

protected rights of [the members of the class]"). *See, e.g., Velez v. Novartis Pharmaceutical
Corp.*, No. CV04-09194 (S.D.N.Y. 2010) (describing jury award of punitive damages following
a trial involving evidence that the defendant "tolerated a culture of discrimination in pay and
promotion, tolerated a culture of sexism, a boy's club atmosphere").

[268] Class certification is governed by Rule 23. Under Rule 23(a), the party seeking certification
must demonstrate that:

    (1) the class is so numerous that joinder of all members is impracticable;
    (2) there are questions of law or fact common to the class;
    (3) the claims or defenses of the representative parties are typical of the claims or defenses
        of the class; and
    (4) the representative parties will fairly and adequately protect the interests of the class.

The proposed class must also satisfy the requirements of at least one of the categories listed in
Rule 23(b). The respondents rely on, and the trial court certified the class under, Rule 23(b)(2),
which applies when "the party opposing the class has acted or refused to act on grounds that
apply generally to the class, so that final injunctive relief or corresponding declaratory relief is
appropriate respecting the class as a whole." Fed. R. Civ. Pro. 23(b)(2).

Title VII class action, like any other class action, may only be certified if the trial court is satisfied, after a rigorous analysis, that the prerequisites of Rule 23 (a) have been satisfied." *Falcon*, 457 U.S. at 161. The plaintiff in that case brought a claim of individual discrimination involving his denial of promotion, alleging that the denial was made based on his national origin, Mexican American. He additionally sought to assert a pattern or practice claim and specifically to represent a class of Mexican American applicants who had been denied employment. The trial judge did not hold an evidentiary hearing on the class certification question, and the plaintiff made no presentation identifying the questions of law or fact that were common to his individual claim and the systemic claim, which included himself and the members of the class he sought to represent. In reversing the trial judge's certification of the class, we noted that "[i]f one allegation of specific discriminatory treatment were sufficient to support an across-the-board attack, every Title VII case would be a potential companywide class action." *Id.* at 159.

Our holding in *Falcon* means that plaintiffs cannot allege an individual claim and then seek to represent a class substantially differently situated, such as an applicant class when the individual claim is one of a current employee. Instead, the plaintiff must identify a common issue of law or fact between his own experience and that of the class members he seeks to represent – a common issue other than merely being a member of a protected class employed by the same employer. In a footnote in *Falcon*, we provided several examples of ways in which an employee who had been denied a promotion might share issues in common with applicants who had been denied employment. Because this footnote has gone on to cause great mischief, we lay it out in full. We stated:

> If petitioner used a biased testing procedure to evaluate both applicants for employment and incumbent employees, a class action on behalf of every applicant or employee who might have been prejudiced by the test clearly would satisfy the commonality and typicality requirements of Rule 23(a). Significant proof that an employer operated under a general policy of discrimination conceivably could justify a class of both applicants and employees if the discrimination manifested itself in hiring and promotion practices in the same general fashion, such as through entirely subjective decisionmaking processes. In this regard, it is noteworthy that Title VII prohibits discriminatory employment *practices*, not an abstract policy of discrimination. The mere fact that an aggrieved private plaintiff is a member of an identifiable class of persons of the same race or national origin is insufficient to establish his standing to litigate on their behalf all possible claims of discrimination against a common employer. *Id.* at 159 n.15 (emphasis in original).

452 Wal-Mart Stores, Inc. v. Dukes et al.

Some judges, including the dissenting judges in the *en banc* court of appeals decision below, have taken this footnote to mean that in order to satisfy commonality required for certification, employment discrimination plaintiffs must always (at least if they cannot point to a biased testing procedure applied to all) provide "significant proof that [the] employer operated under a general policy of discrimination." *Wal-Mart*, 603 F.3d at 631. This takes *Falcon* too far. By providing examples, *Falcon* did not exhaust the possibilities for all plaintiffs in employment discrimination cases seeking class certification. Because we were addressing Falcon's case, which involved a plaintiff seeking to represent a class that included applicants and employees based on stated allegations of a general policy, we spoke in terms of proof of a general policy. Had Falcon provided significant proof of such a policy of discrimination at the top of the company, then commonality would have been satisfied.

Staying true to our long-standing view that, even in Title VII cases, the prerequisites of Rule 23(a) must be satisfied,[269] we hold that plaintiffs pursuing a pattern or practice claim need not present significant proof that the employer operated under a general policy of discrimination. That is one way of establishing commonality that will be useful in some cases, but there are certainly others. For example, relevant to this case, plaintiffs can also meet the commonality required by Rule 23(a) if they present evidence that they are or were subjected to the same relevant practices (practices that allegedly resulted in observed disparities, for example) as the members of the group whom they seek to represent.[270] At the class certification stage, plaintiffs need not prove that they were subjected to the same practices; they need merely submit evidence tending to show as much – evidence that, in the trial judge's discretion, satisfies the prerequisites of 23(a). We did not use the term "significant proof" in *Falcon* to ratchet up what Rule 23 requires of employment discrimination plaintiffs beyond what it requires of any plaintiff seeking certification of a class under Rule 23.

In the present case, each of the named plaintiffs alleges discrimination in pay and/or promotions.[271] They seek to represent in a systemic discrimination case employees and former employees of Wal-Mart who allegedly were subjected to the same discriminatory practices that resulted in substantial

---

[269] Private plaintiffs must meet the Rule 23 requirements; the EEOC, however, is not required to do so. *General Tel. Co. of the NW, Inc. v. EEOC*, 446 U.S. 318 (1980).

[270] We do not decide whether and, if so, when statistics alone covering all members of the class might be sufficient to establish commonality.

[271] Again, to be clear, the named plaintiffs alleged systemic discrimination, not individual claims of discrimination. However, they did relay their individual experiences of discrimination, including presentation of evidence of such, to aid in the trial judge's class certification decision.

Wal-Mart Stores, Inc. v. Dukes et al. 453

disparities in pay and promotion for women in the company nationwide. The respondents did not rely on mere allegations in support of their motion for class certification; they submitted copious evidence to support their motion, evidence that the trial judge considered together with the evidence and argument submitted by the petitioner in opposition.

Specifically, the respondents presented evidence that included statistical analyses of pay and promotions across Wal-Mart typical of what one would expect in a pattern or practice case. A statistical multiple regression analysis conducted by Dr. Richard Drogin on a regional level concluded that gender was a statistically significant variable in accounting for salary differentials between men and women, and also identified statistically significant disparities in the number of women promoted to management, given the relevant labor pools. These statistical analyses suggest that discrimination against women may be occurring throughout Wal-Mart, perhaps not in every supervisory decision, but as the regular rather than the unusual practice across the organization.[272] Further, the descriptive statistics showed that disparities in promotions and pay were widespread across regions of Wal-Mart.[273] A second statistical analysis conducted by Dr. Marc Bendick compared promotions at Wal-Mart and those at twenty of Wal-Mart's competitors and concluded that Wal-Mart promotes a lower percentage of women than its retail counterparts.

In addition to the statistical evidence, the respondents presented evidence of Wal-Mart's nationwide practice of giving substantial discretion to managers in their pay and promotion decisions, a practice that applied uniformly across regions of the company, like many of Wal-Mart's practices. Moreover, they presented evidence of a strong corporate culture at Wal-Mart and evidence of gender stereotyping. The evidence included testimony that some senior managers called female store managers "little Janie Qs" and "girls," and that a company newsletter featured an executive sitting in a giant, leopard-skin, stiletto-shaped chair surrounded by dancing women. Plaintiffs' Motion for

[272] The petitioner challenged Dr. Drogin's decision to conduct his analysis at a regional level rather than store by store. As the court of appeals correctly pointed out, however, whether workforce statistics should be viewed at the macro (regional) or micro (store or substore) level depends largely on the similarity of the employment practices across stores and regions. *Wal-Mart*, 603 F.3d at 605. We see no reason to believe that the district court abused its discretion in rejecting the petitioner's objection at the class certification stage.

[273] Dr. Drogin analyzed Wal-Mart's payroll and personnel data and found that, on average, women in hourly positions made $1,100 less annually than men. In salaried management positions, the annual pay gap between men and women was $14,500. Wal-Mart has a strong policy of promoting from within, yet women comprised 67 percent of hourly workers and 78 percent of hourly department managers and only 35.7 percent of assistant managers, 14.3 percent of store managers, and 9.8 percent of district managers. Declaration of Dr. Drogin in Support of Plaintiffs' Motion for Class Certification.

454   Wal-Mart Stores, Inc. v. Dukes et al.

Class Certification in No. 3:01-cv-02252-CRB (N.D. Cal.), Doc. 99, at 10, 13 (internal quotation marks omitted). The plaintiffs in the case submitted declarations reciting multiple incidents of expressed biases and stereotyping, including declarations that a male manager told an employee, "Men are here to make a career and women aren't," and "[R]etail is for housewives who just need to earn extra money." *Dukes*, 222 F.R.D. at 166. Other testimony stated that male managers responded to women's requests for transfers to departments such as hardware or guns with sex-stereotyped refusals and statements such as "You're a girl, why do you want to be in hardware?" and "You don't want to work with guns," and that male managers would hold company management meetings at Hooters restaurants and strip clubs. Plaintiffs' Motion for Class Certification; Brief for Respondents at 19. This additional evidence need not meet a specific numerical hurdle to serve as evidence that sex-based discrimination rather than some other reason explains the observed statistical disparities. Indeed, evidence consisting of incidents of gender stereotyping like those included by the respondents in this case can be evidence of widespread discrimination because together they suggest that gender stereotyping may be pervasive within the company, likely resulting not only in bias in specific managerial pay and promotion decisions, but also in an overall culture that can affect day-to-day expectations of women's competence and value in the workplace and thereby dampen the trajectory of women's careers even before pay and promotion decisions are made.

Finally, the respondents presented evidence in the form of expert testimony of Dr. William Bielby, a sociologist specializing in organizational behavior. Dr. Bielby examined the organizational features of Wal-Mart in light of existing social science research on bias and stereotyping. Dr. Bielby identified a highly subjective decision-making system, lack of accountability, lack of consistent job posting, and lack of clarity in relocation requirements as some of the organizational features of Wal-Mart's workplace nationwide that together made employment decisions regarding pay and promotion at Wal-Mart "vulnerable to gender bias." Declaration of William T. Bielby in Support of Plaintiffs' Motion for Class Certification. Bielby appropriately framed his task as: "to look at distinctive features of the firm's policies and practices and to evaluate them against what social science research shows to be factors that create and sustain bias and those than minimize bias." *Id.* There has been some effort to undermine the utility of such testimony. *See* John Monahan *et al.*, *Contextual Evidence of Gender Discrimination*, 94 VA. L. REV. 1715 (2008) (arguing that, for their testimony to be admissible, social scientists should be required to undertake audit studies or other objective observational studies of conditions within an organization). But that effort falls short given the scope of Dr. Bielby's task. Dr. Bielby's testimony is helpful at the class certification stage principally because it buttresses a finding that organizational features of Wal-Mart make bias likely to operate in its employment decisions nationwide. The question of whether bias is operating at Wal-Mart to deprive women of equal pay and promotion opportunities is a common one for the class. Of course, the testimony would also be helpful at the substantive stage as evidence that discrimination within the company rather than some other explanation is the more likely cause of observed disparities, thereby supporting an inference that discrimination is the regular rather than the unusual practice. This is so even if Dr. Bielby cannot properly testify directly on the issue of causation or specify a percentage of decisions likely attributable to bias without undertaking a controlled experiment or observational study.

Whether this and other evidence is sufficient to prove a pattern or practice of discrimination to warrant liability for Wal-Mart is yet to be determined in a trial on the merits. Taken together, however, the evidence presented by the respondents in support of their motion for class certification is more than sufficient to satisfy the commonality and typicality requirements of Rule 23(a). The named plaintiffs share with proposed class members the common issue of whether Wal-Mart engaged in a pattern or practice of discrimination nationwide. Evidence of the practices and disparities across the company serves to take the respondents from mere allegations of this common issue for all members of the proposed class to a showing of the common issue. That the named plaintiffs claim to have experienced this sex-based discrimination in their own working lives at Wal-Mart renders them typical of the class members in this case as well. We do not say that plaintiffs must always present the same amount of evidence that the respondents presented here to satisfy the prerequisites of Rule 23(a); only that the plaintiffs in this case presented sufficient evidence from which the trial judge could, in his discretion, determine that the prerequisites of Rule 23 were satisfied.

The petitioner marks the historic size of the potential class in this case as reason for declining certification. As we mentioned, this is likely to be an unusually large class, but so is Wal-Mart an unusually large employer. We see no reason to limit Title VII classes to an arbitrary, nonhistoric number or to allow employers to evade Title VII by becoming too big to sue. If, however, plaintiffs could not point to practices that operate across the proposed class, then such a broad class would not be warranted. That is not the case here.

We mark instead today the historic need for private class enforcement of Title VII, particularly for systemic claims like that of a pattern or practice of discrimination. Some courts have held that individual plaintiffs cannot bring a pattern or practice claim without class certification. *See, e.g., Davis v. Coca-*

456   Wal-Mart Stores, Inc. v. Dukes et al.

Cola Bottling Co., 516 F.3d 955, 965–69 (11th Cir. 2008); *Bacon v. Honda of Am. Mfg. Inc.*, 370 F.3d 565 (7th Cir. 2004). Others have declined class certification on lack of numerosity grounds, and then prevented the named plaintiff from asserting a pattern or practice claim. *See, e.g., Watson v. Fort Worth Bank & Trust*, 798 F.2d 791, 794 (5th Cir. 1986) (describing the trial judge's decisions), *vacated by* 487 U.S. 977 (1988).[274] Pattern or practice systemic discrimination claims should not be allowed to slip through the cracks by procedural wrenching in this way.

III CLASS ACTION CERTIFICATION RULE 23(b)

The petitioner claims a statutory right to individualized hearings regarding each class member's relief in this case, which it argues would render the case unmanageable for class treatment. Nothing in Title VII or our cases confers such a right. The petitioners point to section 706(g)(2)(A) of the Act, which directs that "[n]o order of the court shall require the ... payment to [an individual] of any back pay if such individual [suffered an adverse action] for any reason other than discrimination ..." 42 U.S.C. §2000e-5(g)(2)(A). This provision is found in the "Enforcement Provisions" of the statute. The language of the provision itself directs toward the court, rather than toward the rights of parties to the suit. It provides no right to defendants to individualized hearings. The only case of ours to have faced similar argument held to the contrary. *See Local 28 of Sheet Metal Workers Int'l Ass'n v. EEOC*, 478 U.S. 421 (1986) (involving a court's affirmative action remedies).[275]

Using statistical modeling to determine a lump sum owed by a defendant does not require a court to order a defendant to pay an individual who was not discriminated against. The court order will determine liability on the pattern or practice claim, and, if liability is imposed, it will direct Wal-Mart to pay a lump-sum amount. Allocation of that class-wide recovery to individuals will be handled separately by the court. For possible approaches, see *McClain v. Lufkin Indus. Inc.*, 519 F.3d 264 (5th Cir. 2008); *Domingo v. New Eng. Fish Co.*, 727 F.2d 1429 (9th Cir. 1984); *Pettaway v. Am. Cast Iron Pipe Co.*, 494 F.2d

---

[274] Although we leave resolution of the question for another day, we are inclined to think that even individuals should be permitted to use systemic disparate treatment theory in the first instance. The scope of their statistics and proof of disparate treatment would inform the judge regarding how to treat the case, including whether to solicit briefing on propriety of class treatment. Mere small numbers of plaintiffs in an employment discrimination suit involving systemic claims should not destroy class certification.

[275] Nor does section 706(g)(2)(B), which the petitioner also points to, provide a right to individualized arguments in a systemic discrimination case. That section is tied specifically to individual claims brought under section 703(m). 42 U.S.C. §2000e-5(g)(2)(B).

Wal-Mart Stores, Inc. v. Dukes et al. 457

211, 260–63 (5th Cir. 1974). Defendants have a right to argue and present evidence to rebut the systemic discrimination case put forward by plaintiffs. This they can do, for example, by attacking the plaintiffs' statistical or other evidence of a pattern or practice of discrimination or by presenting their own showing of an alternative and more plausible reason for observed disparities. Defendants do not, however, have a right to individualized hearings.[276]

Nor does our decision in *Teamsters* block the use of statistical modeling for remedial determinations in Title VII cases. We stated there that "[w]hen the plaintiff seeks individual relief such as reinstatement or backpay after establishing a pattern or practice of discrimination, a district court must usually conduct additional proceedings ... to determine the scope of individual relief." *Teamsters*, 431 U.S. at 361. But we also emphasized the importance of district court flexibility in fashioning the remedial phase of pattern and practice litigation to satisfy the goals of Title VII. We noted that "a primary objective of Title VII is prophylactic: to achieve equal employment opportunity and to remove the barriers that have operated to favor white male employees over other employees," and that "[t]he prospect of retroactive relief for victims of discrimination serves this purpose by providing the 'spur or catalyst which causes employers ... to self-examine and to self-evaluate their employment practices and to endeavor to eliminate, as much as possible, the last vestiges' of their discriminatory practices." *Id.* at 364 (internal citation omitted).

Statistical modeling in pattern or practice cases can be both fair and accurate, and judges have accordingly relied on it now for decades. *See, e.g., Segar v. Smith*, 738 F.2d 1249 (D.C. Cir. 1984) (affirming the trial court's use of statistical modeling at the remedial stage); *Shipes v. Trinity Ind.*, 987 F.2d 311, 318 (5th Cir. 1993); *Pettaway*, 494 F.2d at 260–63.[277] If we were to adopt the

---

[276] While the defendant is not entitled to individualized hearings, it could reduce the total sum owed by reducing the scope of the class. Depending on the circumstances of the case, it might, for example, show that a defined group of people are unlikely to have suffered discrimination and therefore should be excluded from the class and thereby excluded for purposes of determining the lump sum owed.

[277] In its opinion, the Ninth Circuit referred to a sampling method used by some courts whereby a random sample of individual cases are first tried and then results from that sample are extrapolated across the class. *See, e.g., Hilao v. Estate of Ferdinand Marcos*, 103 F.3d 767 (9th Cir. 1996). We point out that the court was right to note that this is not the "only conceivable" way of determining relief through statistical modeling nor is it the only way that courts have proceeded. *Segar, supra; Shipes, supra; Pettaway, supra; see also Catlett v. Missouri Highway & Transp. Comm'n*, 828 F.2d 1260 (8th Cir. 1987); *Domingo v. New England Fish Co.*, 727 F.2d 1429, 1444 (9th Cir. 1984). In some cases, courts have held no individualized hearings and have instead computed back pay across the class using available statistics. It may be that this latter method will be preferred in cases involving highly subjective decision-making where

458 Wal-Mart Stores, Inc. v. Dukes et al.

petitioner's suggested position that "the second stage of a *Teamsters*-bifurcated proceeding may be dispensed with only on the consent of both parties," we would render pattern or practice cases merely a tool for defendants at settlement. Brief for Petitioner at 42. This is something that we are not willing to do. Requiring individualized hearings in a case involving a potentially very large class like this one, as the petitioner knows, would render the case much more difficult for a court to administer, thereby making class certification less likely. Class certification facilitates the bringing of private pattern or practice, systemic discrimination claims, and, as we have said, these claims are an important lever of Title VII. Statistical modeling to determine scope of monetary liability may serve only rough justice for individuals who are members of the class, this we understand, but without it we also fear that there will be no justice at all as employers will continue to discriminate with little to dissuade them from doing so.

There remains the question of Rule 23(b)(2) certification in this case. Understanding that it was not error for the trial judge to imagine a system in which statistical modeling would be used to determine a remedial amount, we nonetheless must ask whether certification of the class is consistent with Rule 23(b)(2). We start here with a reminder that the categories of Rule 23(b) are guides, not straightjackets. Rule 23 states that a class action may be maintained under Rule 23(b)(2) if "the party opposing the class has acted or refused to act on grounds that apply generally to the class, so that final injunctive and corresponding declaratory relief is appropriate respecting the class as a whole." The circuits have long held that back pay can be awarded to a Rule 23(b)(2) employment discrimination class. *See, e.g., Reeb v. Ohio Dep't of Rehab. & Corr.*, 435 F.3d 639, 650 (6th Cir. 2006); *Cooper v. S. Co.*, 390 F.3d 695, 720 (11th Cir. 2004), *overruled on other grounds by Ash v. Tyson Foods Inc.*, 546 U.S. 454, 457 (2006) (*per curiam*); *Jefferson v. Ingersoll Int'l Inc.*, 195 F.3d 894, 896 (7th Cir. 1999); *Pettaway*, 494 F.2d at 257–58; *Robinson v. Lorillard Corp.*, 444 F.2d 791, 802 (4th Cir. 1971). The plaintiffs in this case do not seek individualized compensatory damages, but rather injunctive and other equitable relief, which includes back pay.

The plaintiffs do, however, seek punitive damages. The Civil Rights Act of 1991 made punitive and compensatory damages available for private Title VII

---

identifying the precise moment of bias in decisions against each individual can be particularly difficult or in cases otherwise involving circumstances under which individualized hearings would merely "drag the court into a quagmire of hypothetical judgments." *Segar*, 738 F.2d at 1289–90. Indeed, it is this "formula" method that the district court seems to have had in mind in this case. *Dukes v. Wal-Mart Stores, Inc.*, 222 F.3d 137, 176–83 (relying primarily on *Domingo, supra*, as an example).

plaintiffs upon a showing that the employer engaged in a discriminatory practice or practices "with malice or reckless indifference to the federally protected rights of [the members of the class]." 42 U.S.C. §1981a. The petitioner contends that a class seeking punitive damages can never be certified under Rule 23(b)(2). The district court considered and rejected this argument, finding that the equitable relief sought by the plaintiffs predominated over their claim for punitive damages, thereby rendering the suit proper for certification under Rule 23(b)(2). *Dukes*, 222 F.R.D. at 170–73. The court of appeals held that the district court abused its discretion in certifying the punitive damages portion of the plaintiffs' claim under Rule 23(b)(2) without undertaking a sufficiently "comprehensive analysis," including consideration of the potential size of the punitive damages award. *Wal-Mart*, 603 F.3d at 622.

The position of the petitioner (and to some extent that of the court of appeals) again rests on a misunderstanding of the nature of the pattern or practice claim and the relationship of a punitive damages inquiry to that claim. By asking whether discrimination is widespread within the organization, whether it is the regular rather than the unusual practice, a pattern or practice claim necessarily focuses on a group rather than on individuals. As we have discussed, the total amount of back pay due is tied to individual harm in theory. With a pattern or practice case, however, it is not necessarily tied to each individual's specific harm in practice, such that there must be an individualized factual determination at the stage of calculating amount due. For the same reason, punitive damages in a systemic case like that brought by the respondents are differently situated than punitive damages sought in an individual case, or even in a case involving many individual claims merely coming together for efficiency, as with a mass tort. In both types of cases, the ultimate statutory standard for punitive damages liability is the same: malice or reckless indifference to federal rights.[278] But in the systemic case the malice or reckless indifference is to the class as a whole, not to specific individuals. That the monetary award might be large does not mean that monetary damages will "predominate" such that Rule 23(b)(2) certification is inappropriate. We held

---

[278] *Kolstad* involved a case of individual discrimination in which the plaintiff sought punitive damages. There, we held that "an employer may not be vicariously liable for the discriminatory employment decisions of managerial agents where these decisions are contrary to the employer's 'good-faith efforts to comply with Title VII.' " *Kolstad v. Am. Dental Assoc. Inc.*, 527 U.S. 526, 545 (1999). The two-layered inquiry in *Kolstad* – first at the level of the specific employment decision, then at the level of the employer – rested on the fact that the plaintiff's claim was an individual one that involved vicarious liability of the employer. Because in pattern or practice cases the employer is held directly liable for discrimination, the inquiry will always be at the entity level: did the employer engage in a pattern or practice of discrimination, and did it engage in that discrimination "with malice or reckless indifference to the federally protected rights of [the members of the class]"? 42 U.S.C. §1981a.

in *State Farm Mut. Automobile Ins. v. Campbell*, 538 U.S. 408 (2003), that punitive awards must correspond to the plaintiffs who filed suit in the case, and we stand by that holding today, but *State Farm* does not mean that all punitive damage determinations must turn on individualized hearings. The district court did not abuse its discretion in deciding that the punitive damages claim in this case was secondary to the claim for equitable relief and thereby appropriate for Rule 23(b)(2) certification.[279]

We come then to the matter of notice and opportunity to opt out. Rule 23 gives district courts discretion to order notice and opt-out rights when certifying a Rule 23(b)(2) class, which the trial court did here for the punitive damages portion of the plaintiffs' claim. The 2003 amendments to Rule 23 (c)(2) confirmed a court's authority to order notice in Rule 23(b)(1) and (2) actions. The Notes explain that the amendment "call[s] attention to the court's authority – already established in part by Rule 23(d)(2) – to direct notice of certification to a Rule 23(b)(1) or (b)(2) class." Fed. R. Civ. P. 23 Advisory Committee's Note (2003). Nonetheless, Judge Jenkins did not consider whether notice and opportunity to opt out might also be wise, even mandated by due process, for the back pay portion of the plaintiffs' claim. It was error for him to decline to do so. Certification under Rule 23(b)(2) may be proper, but notice and opportunity to opt out still be required. This determination we know can involve a difficult balance of considerations, including feasibility and the importance of collective action, and also concern about class members losing their rights to seek individualized monetary awards, including back pay or compensatory damages now available under the 1991 Act. *Morrissey v. Brewer*, 408 U.S. 471, 481 (1972) ("It has been said so often by this Court . . . that due process is flexible and calls for such procedural protections as the particular situation demands"). Our due process jurisprudence counsels against rigid notice requirements that can be overly costly and thereby undermine collective actions. *See Mullane v. Central Hanover Bank & Trust Co.*, 339 U.S. 306, 317 (1950) (noting that "the Court has not hesitated to approve of resort to publication as a customary substitute in another class of cases where it is not reasonably possible or practicable to give more adequate warning"). We have held that a plaintiff class loss on a pattern or practice, systemic discrimination claim does not bar a class member from pursuing an individual claim.

---

[279] We think it important to reiterate that Rule 23(b)(2) was designed for civil rights cases, including employment discrimination cases. This does not mean that all employment discrimination cases will be properly certified under Rule 23(b)(2), but to move employment discrimination cases to Rule 23(b)(3) merely because monetary damages are sought is ill-advised. Rule 23(b)(3) imposes additional requirements that were fashioned for mass torts involving many individual claims, not for employment discrimination claims proceeding under systemic theories.

Wal-Mart Stores, Inc. v. Dukes et al.

Cooper v. Federal Reserve Bank of Richmond, 467 U.S. 867 (1984). But, as we have acknowledged above, a plaintiff class win on a systemic discrimination claim can result in rough rather than individualized justice for monetary claims, even in equitable ones like those for back pay. A female employee at Wal-Mart, for example, may be awarded an amount based on the court's statistical modeling applied to her objective circumstances, while if the same individual were to proceed with an individual claim (depending on the strength of her evidence and her individual circumstances), she might be able to obtain a substantially larger amount. With this reality in mind, the district court may decide that plaintiffs should be permitted to opt out of the class and pursue their monetary relief through individual claims, even if it is not practical for them to opt out of the portion of the claim pertaining to injunctive or declaratory relief.

We therefore substantially affirm, remanding to the district court for consideration of whether an opportunity to opt out should be provided in this case on the request for back pay, given all of the circumstances of the case and possible due process concerns.

We close with a final note of the importance of pattern or practice, systemic disparate treatment claims for the future of Title VII and its goal of reducing discrimination in employment in the American workplace. We may have come a long way, but there is a long way yet to go.

* * *

It is so ordered.

8

Retaliation

Commentary on *Clark County School District v. Breeden*

REBECCA HANNER WHITE

INTRODUCTION

Clark County School District v. Breeden,[1] to my mind, has always been a sleeper case. A *per curiam* opinion, it takes up no more than five pages in the US reports, yet when I taught this case to my employment discrimination students, we often would spend a full class period – and sometimes more – on it. Why? Because it presents virtually every issue that can crop up under section 704 of Title VII of the Civil Rights Act of 1964,[2] the statute's antiretaliation provision.

Section 704 has two clauses: an opposition clause[3] and a participation[4] clause. *Breeden* involves claims under both, thus allowing exploration of the different standards of "protected conduct" that have emerged under each.[5] *Breeden* raises the question of what constitutes an "adverse action" for purposes of section 704 – an issue that the Court ultimately addressed several years later in *Burlington Northern and Santa Fe Railway Co v. White*.[6] It also allows

---

[1] 532 U.S. 268 (2001).

[2] 42 U.S.C. §2000e-3(a).

[3] The statute protects opposing unlawful discrimination in ways that go beyond making use of the statutory machinery; internal complaints to the employer, for example, are considered opposition conduct.

[4] Participation clause claims are sometimes referred to as "free exercise" claims and involve retaliation resulting from use of the statute's mechanisms, such as filing a charge with the Equal Employment Opportunity Commission (EEOC), filing a lawsuit, or testifying.

[5] As explored more fully later in the commentary, opposition clause conduct has been deemed protected by the lower courts if based on a reasonable, good faith belief that the conduct being opposed is unlawful under Title VII; participation clause protection, generally speaking, is absolute.

[6] 548 U.S. 53 (2006). The Court found it unnecessary to discuss the issue in *Breeden* because it rejected the claims on other grounds.

462

exploration of the causation requirement in retaliation cases – particularly the question of temporal proximity. But the most important aspect of *Breeden*, at least to my mind, is that its resolution presented a clear conflict with the Court's decisions a few years earlier in *Burlington Industries, Inc. v. Ellerth*[7] and *Faragher v. City of Boca Raton*[8] – a conflict that the Court failed to acknowledge and one that has significantly influenced not only the law of retaliation under Title VII, but also the law of sexual harassment.

Curiously, other than the question of temporal proximity, *not one* of these issues is explored by the Court in its opinion in *Breeden*. Rather, the Court unanimously gave short shrift to Shirley Breeden's claims, brushing them aside as simply too trivial to merit the attention of busy federal courts.

Breeden's claims, however, were far more serious than the Court appeared to recognize. So too is the impact of the *Breeden* case. Taken together with *Ellerth* and *Faragher*, the bottom line is this. If plaintiffs fail to report harassment when it occurs, the employer can often claim an affirmative defense to a sexual harassment claim. But if plaintiffs speak up too soon, before the conduct complained of is sufficiently egregious to be legally actionable, then they can be demoted, reassigned, or even fired for their internal complaints. This catch-22 created by the *Breeden* Court for sexual harassment victims, most of whom are women, has no doubt contributed to the underreporting of workplace harassment that the recent #MeToo movement has spotlighted.[9]

The feminist judgment by Professor Michael Green, writing as Justice Green, eliminates this conflict, harmonizing *Breeden* with the Court's previous decisions in *Ellerth* and *Faragher*. Importantly, it recognizes and avoids the catch-22 created by the actual opinion. It also expressly adopts a "reasonable, good faith belief" standard for opposition claims, and it more fully explores the temporal proximity issues surrounding the participation clause claim. Finally, Green's *Breeden* opinion adopts the "mixed motive" framework for retaliation claims: a move that would have precluded the Court's subsequent decision in *University of Texas Southwest Medical Center v. Nassar*.[10] In summary, Green's fully developed opinion, unlike the

---

[7] 524. U.S. 742 (1998).

[8] 524 U.S. 775 (1998).

[9] The #MeToo movement has captured significant attention in the news media and has begun generating academic commentary as well. For an overview of Title VII and #MeToo, see Rebecca Hanner White, *Title VII and the #MeToo Movement*, 68 EMORY L.J. ONLINE 1014 (2018). For academic pieces on the #MeToo movement and its broader implications, see the joint online symposium on the #MeToo movement at www.stanfordlawreview.org/online/type/symposium-metoo/ and www.yalelawjournal.org/collection/MeToo.

[10] 133 S.Ct. 2517 (2013).

464   *Clark County School District v. Breeden*

per curiam one of the Court, uses the *Breeden* case to establish a broad and remedially focused reading of Title VII's section 704 – one that would have protected those complaining of workplace discrimination, particularly those complaining of hostile work environment harassment, in a manner that complements the Court's sexual harassment jurisprudence.

THE ORIGINAL OPINION

The facts of the case are stated in abbreviated fashion. Breeden, her male supervisor, and another male employee were reviewing job applicant files, one of which made reference to an off-color remark one job applicant had made to a coworker: "I hear making love to you is like making love to the Grand Canyon." The male supervisor read the comment aloud and said to Breeden, "I don't know what that means." The other employee said, "Well, I'll tell you later," and both men chuckled. Breeden complained about this exchange to the supervisor himself, to his supervisor, and to an assistant superintendent. As the Court put it, Breeden claimed that she was "punished" for these complaints, although the Court does not specify in what way she suffered harm.[11]

Title VII prohibits discrimination against an employee because she has opposed practices made unlawful by Title VII.[12] The Court noted that the Ninth Circuit, in its opinion below, had protected employee opposition not only to practices that are in fact unlawful under Title VII, but also to those that could reasonably and in good faith be considered unlawful: "We have no occasion to rule on the propriety of that interpretation, because *even assuming it is correct*, no one could reasonably believe that the incident recounted above violated Title VII."[13] Because the conduct Breeden complained of was so far below the level of severity or pervasiveness required to state an actionable claim of sexual harassment,[14] she could not, reasoned the Court, have reasonably believed that Title VII had been violated. Thus she had no opposition clause claim.

---

[11] Whether the "punishment" Breeden received was sufficiently adverse to state a claim was not discussed by the Court.

[12] 42 U.S.C. §2000e-3(a).

[13] *Breeden*, 532 U.S. at 270 (emphasis added).

[14] The Court has repeatedly held that to state a claim for a hostile work environment, the conduct complained of must be "so severe or pervasive as to alter the conditions of employment and create an abusive working environment." *Meritor Savings Bank v. Vinson*, 477 U.S. 57, 67 (1986). As the Court has stated, "[A] recurring point in [our] opinions is that simple teasing, offhand comments, and isolated instances (unless extremely serious) will not amount to discriminatory changes in the 'terms and conditions' of employment." *Faragher*, 524 U.S. at 788 (quoted by the Court in *Breeden*).

Clark County School District v. Breeden 465

In addition to making her internal complaints, Breeden also filed charges with the Nevada Equal Rights Commission and with the Equal Employment Opportunity Commission (EEOC), and she ultimately brought the lawsuit that ended up before the Court. This was her participation clause claim: she alleged she had been transferred to an inferior position for filing the charges and the lawsuit.[15] Without determining whether the transfer complained of was in fact sufficiently adverse, the Court rejected her participation clause claim on causation grounds: "The cases that accept mere temporal proximity between an employer's knowledge of protected activity and an adverse employment action as sufficient evidence of causality to make a prima facie case uniformly hold that the temporal proximity must be 'very close' ..." Finding no evidence that the defendant was aware of the lawsuit when the discussion about transferring the plaintiff occurred, the Court found no evidence of causation arising from the lawsuit's filing. Thus Breeden had no retaliation claim under either the opposition clause or the participation clause.

THE IMPACT OF BREEDEN

The Court's perfunctory – dare I say dismissive? – treatment of Shirley Breeden's claims was intended to deliver a message: busy federal court dockets should not be clogged with every slight or unpleasantness that occurs in the workplace. The only facts laid out in full were a description of the remark that triggered the internal complaints, EEOC charge, and lawsuit; in laying these out, the Court seemed to be saying, "See? There was nothing here for any reasonable person to complain about." To this extent, the Court's dismissal of Breeden's opposition claim is similar to its treatment of workplace harassment that is not sufficiently severe or pervasive: the Court views Title VII as expecting workers to tolerate discriminatory conduct so long as it is not sufficiently egregious.[16]

---

[15] Note that the Court, in evaluating the participation clause claim, implicitly recognizes that when someone has been retaliated against for filing an EEOC charge and/or lawsuit, it does not matter whether or not the underlying conduct that triggered the filings was based on a reasonable belief the statute had been violated. Adverse actions that result from the use of statutory machinery receive absolute protection under section 704.

[16] See Rebecca Hanner White, *De Minimis Discrimination*, 47 EMORY L.J. 1121 (1998). Essentially, the lower courts require that discrimination must be "materially adverse" to be actionable, although what constitutes material adversity under section 703 is unclear. One commentator has suggested that the "adverse action" requirement may no longer exist in the wake of *Texas Dept. of Housing & Comm. Affairs v. Inclusive Cmtys. Project, Inc.*, 135 S.Ct. 2507 (2015), but the lower courts to date have continued to require an adverse action. *See* Sandra Sperino, *Justice Kennedy's Big New Idea*, 96 B.U.L. REV. 1789, 1791–92 (2017). For retaliation claims, the Court has held that material adversity must exist, but defined materially adverse to mean conduct that

466 *Clark County School District v. Breeden*

If Breeden's had been a hostile work environment claim, the Court's rejection of it would have been in keeping with its precedent in *Meritor Savings Bank, FSB v. Vinson, Harris v. Forklift Sys. Inc., Ellerth,* and *Faragher.*[17] The single incident, standing alone, would not have been viewed as sufficiently severe or pervasive to support a claim of sexual harassment.[18]

But the claim before the Court was not a sexual harassment claim; rather, it was a claim alleging retaliation.[19] The lower courts, before and after *Breeden,* have reasoned that even if the conduct being opposed is not in fact unlawful, the protections of section 704 encompass those who oppose what they reasonably and in good faith believe to be unlawful conduct. In *Breeden,* the Court questioned this approach, wondering whether the conduct being opposed must in fact be unlawful, not only reasonably appear to be so, but it did not resolve this issue. However, the Court's flagging of the issue is a reason for concern. Were plaintiffs forced to assume the risk of being wrong about conduct's lawfulness, the chilling effect would be enormous – particularly in areas such as hostile work environment claims, where the line between lawful and unlawful is anything but bright.[20] In any event, the lower courts have not taken the bait to date and still assess opposition conduct under the "reasonable, good faith belief" test.

Was Shirley Breeden reasonable in making her internal complaints? The Court said she was not: no reasonable person could have considered the remark to constitute actionable sexual harassment. But when juxtaposed with the Court's decisions two years earlier in *Ellerth* and *Faragher,* this result is quite troubling.[21] In *Ellerth* and *Faragher,* the Court had crafted an affirmative defense to hostile work environment claims. If an employer could show that it had taken steps to prevent and to correct harassment, and if the plaintiff had unreasonably failed to avail herself of those steps, then no liability for

---

would dissuade a reasonable worker from complaining about discrimination. *See Burlington Northern,* 548 U.S. at 68.

[17] *Meritor,* 477 U.S. 57 (1986); *Harris,* 510 U.S. 17 (1993); *Ellerth,* 524 U.S. 742 (1998); *Faragher,* 524 U.S. 775 (1998).

[18] *See supra* note 14 and accompanying text.

[19] Breeden had originally brought a sexual harassment claim, but that claim had been abandoned at the district court level.

[20] Even under a reasonable, good faith standard, there is a significant disparity between the number of women who experience harassment and the number who report it. *See* Nicole Buonocore Porter, *Ending Harassment by Starting with Retaliation,* 71 STAN. L. REV. ONLINE 49 (2018), www.stanfordlawreview.org/online/ending-harassment-by-starting-with-retaliation/ (describing the low incidence of reporting of sexual harassment and citing sources attributing this lack of reporting to women's fears of retaliation for lodging a complaint).

[21] *See, e.g.,* Deborah L. Brake, *Retaliation in an EEO World,* 89 IND. L.J. 115, 117–18 (2014); Ernest F. Lidge, *The Necessity of Expanding Protection from Retaliation to Employees Who Complain about Sexual Harassment,* 53 U. LOUISVILLE L. REV. 39, 85–86 (2014).

Clark County School District v. Breeden   467

sexual harassment would attach.[22] The affirmative defense was aimed at preventing harassment from rising to the level of severity or pervasiveness required to state an actionable sexual harassment claim. Workers, the Court reasoned, want workplaces free of harassment, not lawsuits, and the affirmative defense furthers that goal.[23] In the wake of *Ellerth* and *Faragher*, employers have crafted policies aimed at preventing harassment and encouraging workers to make internal complaints, so that claims may be investigated and misconduct corrected before it becomes sufficiently severe or pervasive.[24]

But what about Shirley Breeden, who reports a sexually suggestive remark (as the Supreme Court's *Ellerth* and *Faragher* opinions would have encouraged a worker to do[25]) and is punished for doing so?[26] The Ninth Circuit had held that the "reasonable belief" standard was "very low," in keeping with the remedial nature of the statute. That standard would also be in keeping with the *Ellerth* and *Faragher* affirmative defense. After all, if complaining about conduct that falls significantly short of the severe or pervasive requirement can lead to the unemployment line, then employers' antiharassment policies are likely to be little more than a bait and switch.

Speaking up when faced with harassment is already difficult.[27] *Breeden* compounded that problem enormously. Moreover, its questioning and application of the "reasonable, good faith belief" standard and its treatment of the temporal proximity issue substantially weakened section 704's protections across the board.

Despite *Breeden*, retaliation claims in recent years have been viewed as a bright spot for plaintiffs in employment discrimination cases.[28] And when compared to how plaintiffs have fared in section 703 claims, they are. But the

---

[22] *Ellerth*, 524 U.S. at 765; *Faragher*, 524 U.S. at 807.

[23] *Faragher*, 524 U.S. at 807–08.

[24] The efficacy of these policies, however, has been questioned. *See, e.g.*, Susan Bisom-Rapp, *An Ounce of Prevention Is a Poor Substitute for a Pound of Cure: Confronting the Developing Jurisprudence of Education and Prevention in Employment Discrimination Law*, 22 BERKELEY J. EMP. & LAB. L. 1 (2001); Linda Hamilton Krieger *et al.*, *When "Best Practices" Win, Employees Lose: Symbolic Compliance and Judicial Inference in Federal Equal Employment Opportunity Cases*, 40 LAW & SOC. INQUIRY 843 (2015).

[25] Although Breeden's internal complaint was made before the Court's decisions in *Ellerth* and *Faragher*, her employer had regulations in place that defined sexual harassment as including "uninvited teasing, jokes, remarks, and questions," 2000 U.S. App. LEXIS 17564, at *4–5.

[26] Because the case was decided on summary judgment, the allegation that Breeden was stripped of her supervisory authority and assigned lower-level duties because of her complaint must be assumed.

[27] This is a point significantly relied upon by Green in his rewritten opinion, citing to numerous sources documenting women's reluctance to speak up when harassed on the job.

[28] Michael J. Zimmer, *A Pro-Employee Supreme Court? The Retaliation Decisions*, 60 S. CAROLINA L. REV. 917 (2009).

468 *Clark County School District v. Breeden*

sad fact remains that – particularly for those complaining of workplace harassment – *Breeden* has been a significant and troubling contributor to the
persistence of sexual harassment in the workplace.

THE FEMINIST JUDGMENT

Professor Michael Z. Green, writing as Justice Green, reverses the outcome in *Breeden*. The rewritten opinion uses the case as a vehicle not
only to reinforce the remedial nature of section 704, but also as a means
to harmonize section 704 with the affirmative defense created in *Ellerth*
and *Faragher*.

Green begins his analysis of the opposition claim by adopting the "reasonable, good faith belief" standard employed by the court below. The Ninth
Circuit had rejected a literal reading of the statute, noting that the circuit courts
had not uniformly read the opposition clause as requiring that an "opposed"
practice in fact violate Title VII, but instead required only an objectively
reasonable and good faith belief that the antidiscrimination statute has been
violated. Green's opinion agrees with this approach, finding "that this interpretation is consistent with the remedial objectives of Title VII's antiretaliation
provision." Thus the feminist judgment, unlike the original opinion, accepts the
reasonable, good faith belief standard for opposition clause claims.[29]

Green then turns to the difficult question of whether Breeden had an
objectively reasonable, good faith belief. Good faith was never in question, so
the issue was whether her belief was reasonable. Sexual harassment is actionable
under Title VII only if the challenged conduct is either severe or pervasive, and
the incident at issue here was neither, as the Ninth Circuit, the original opinion,
and Green's opinion all acknowledge, nor was the question even close on that
point. Only in the most egregious of cases will a single incident, standing alone,
be deemed sufficiently severe to constitute sexual harassment. So how, then,
could Breeden's belief that the statute had been violated be reasonable?

Here, Green addresses the issue in a way that appreciates section 704's
distinctive role: "[W]e find that any complaint involving a single act of
unwelcome harassment can be objectively reasonable if such behavior
would, if repeated, culminate in an actionable claim of severe or pervasive
harassment." The opinion elaborates:

---

[29] As noted earlier, lower courts to date have not pursued the Court's suggestion that a reasonable,
good faith belief may not be sufficient. *See supra* note 20 and accompanying text. The
possibility remains, however, that the Court – particularly with its changed membership and
in light of the statutory language – will require, when it gets the opportunity to do so, that the
conduct opposed actually be unlawful.

Clark County School District v. Breeden

[A] standard that requires harassment to be "very close" to being actionable underestimates the incentive an employee has under *Ellerth and Faragher* to report all incidences of harassment before they reach the level of severe or pervasive ... If an employee's internal complaint were not protected in this situation, an employee would face a catch-22: Either complain to the employer about the offensive conduct experienced or witnessed before it becomes severe or pervasive (and risk losing a retaliation claim if her employer retaliates against her for complaining); or wait to complain until the harassment is so severe or pervasive that she is certain she will be protected from retaliation (and risk losing her harassment complaint if the court finds she failed to take advantage of preventative or corrective opportunities).

Thus, if a complaint involves a single act, the question is: if that act were repeated, *could it become* sufficiently severe or pervasive? If so, it meets the test of objective reasonableness.

Relying on feminist writings, Green recognizes the difficulties women experience in speaking up about harassment. He also uses such scholarship to put Breeden's experience into context. The two men in the room "chuckling" about a sexual remark at Breeden's expense "could represent the type of microaggression that many women and other vulnerable employees face in the workplace. Breeden's experience was undoubtedly made worse by the fact that the two men present were her supervisor and subordinate, who likely appeared to be teaming up to make her uncomfortable." And given the research indicating that a passive response from vulnerable workers is more likely than not to such behavior, "when a woman or any vulnerable worker does bravely report as Breeden has done in this case, that report should be presumed reasonable and protected from retaliation to achieve the broad remedial goals of Title VII." This approach to the underlying incident – an approach girded in a feminist understanding of dynamics that diminish and devalue women in the workplace – puts a very different spin on what Breeden encountered. The remark suddenly seems far less innocuous and Breeden's being "punished" for complaining about it far more serious. Providing a remedy under section 704 for complaints such as Breeden's is understood as necessary to stop workplace harassment: an approach that complements the affirmative defense created in *Ellerth* and *Faragher*.

Green's opinion also addresses the issue of causation for retaliation claims. The feminist judgment holds that "but for" causation need not be shown; instead, "motivating factor" analysis is embraced for section 704 claims. As Green states:

This principle follows from an earlier case from this Court, *Price Waterhouse v. Hopkins*, 490 U.S. 228 (1989), and an ensuing statutory amendment by

470   *Clark County School District v. Breeden*

Congress ... While the 1991 Act did not address specifically retaliation claims brought under section 704(a) of Title VII, Congress endorsed the general plurality approach in *Price Waterhouse* by making clear that the language "because of" used in section 703(a) meant that an employee has to show only that discrimination was a motivating factor in the employer's decision to take the adverse employment action.

Green's opinion thus appears to apply *Price Waterhouse* to section 704 claims rather than to hold that section 703(m) itself, added by the 1991 Act, applies to retaliation claims.[30] Either way, the feminist judgment rejects "but for" as the causation standard for retaliation claims. This approach would have pre-empted the Court's subsequent decision in *University of Texas Southwest Medical Center v. Nassar*,[31] holding that but-for causation is required under section 704. Rejecting "but for" causation for retaliation claims, as Green does, makes clear that Congress intends retaliation claims to be taken just as seriously as discrimination claims; no higher level of causation is needed. Having the same causation standards for claims under sections 703 and 704 has the benefit of avoiding unnecessary confusion for juries, who are often tasked with deciding claims under each of the statutory provisions.

Additionally, with regard to the participation clause claim, Green's rewritten opinion, unlike the original opinion, finds that factual questions exist on the question of causation. The transfer had been under consideration after the right to sue notice was received; the final decision was made after the lawsuit's filing, and "[R]easonable jurors could conclude that [the supervisor] decided to retaliate against Breeden for filing the lawsuit by settling on and finalizing the transfer after learning of the lawsuit." This, coupled with evidence that the reasons put forward for the transfer were pretextual, meant that the case should be remanded to the district court. This is a straightforward and much more appropriate approach to what essentially is a fact-based inquiry.

Moreover, unlike the original Court, which had found twenty months too great a time difference to support an inference based on temporal proximity, Green refuses to identify a fixed time period within which such inferences may be drawn: "Such an inquiry is a fact-specific exercise, and the significance of any timing regarding a given act of retaliation will often depend upon the

[30] The difference is this: section 703(m) establishes liability once the plaintiff proves that discrimination was a motivating factor. The defendant may avoid remedies by proving that it would have made the same decision anyway. Under *Price Waterhouse*, once plaintiff proves that discrimination was a motivating factor, the burden of proof passes to the defendant to prove it would have made the same decision anyway, and carrying that burden relieves it of liability.

[31] 133 S.Ct. 2517 (2013). The *Nassar* decision, a five-to-four opinion of the Court, rejected not only the application of section 703(m) to section 704 claims, but also refused to apply *Price Waterhouse* to retaliation claims.

Clark County School District v. Breeden

471

particular circumstances." Furthermore, exact time limits would encourage employers to bide their time and wait to retaliate against the employee "until a time strategically placed outside that arbitrary window." This, too, marks a significant change. While temporal proximity can support an inference of discrimination under *Breeden*, only relatively short time periods have generally sufficed in a post-*Breeden* world. Green's opinion, in refusing to draw a hard-and-fast line, allows exploration of context in determining whether temporal proximity is sufficient to support an inference of unlawful motive.

CONCLUSION

Justice Green's feminist approach in *Breeden* is important on many fronts. It establishes "reasonable, good faith belief" as the operative standard in opposition clause claims under section 704 of Title VII. It establishes that an internal complaint regarding sexual misconduct that, standing alone, is far below the bar needed for severity or pervasiveness may yet be reasonable if the misconduct, if repeated or ongoing, would be sufficiently close to the level needed for severe or pervasive. In so doing, it harmonizes the law governing retaliation claims arising out of internal workplace complaints with the affirmative defense the Court had created in its sexual harassment jurisprudence. The feminist judgment establishes the need for a broad look at questions of causation – one that eschews any strict time limit in determining whether temporal proximity is sufficient to support an inference of causation. And it endorses motivating factor analysis as the standard plaintiffs must meet to establish causation.

Any of these holdings alone would have strengthened the protections of section 704. Taken together, they would have provided those claiming discrimination under Title VII – particularly, though not exclusively, those complaining of workplace harassment – strong and effective safeguards against employer retaliation.

Clark County School District v. Breeden,
532 U.S. 268 (2001)

JUSTICE MICHAEL Z. GREEN DELIVERED THE OPINION
OF THE COURT.

This case presents important questions concerning claims of workplace retaliation under Title VII of the Civil Rights Act of 1964, section 704(a), when an

472 Clark County School District v. Breeden

employee's underlying claim of a single incident of harassment has not yet become actionable. Those questions include:

(1) whether an employee may bring a successful retaliation claim when the incident she opposed is not in fact unlawful, but she has a reasonable, good faith belief that a violation of Title VII had occurred;

(2) whether an employee can have a reasonable, good faith belief that a violation of Title VII occurred when a single incident of harassment might represent a link in a chain establishing an overall pattern for a hostile environment claim that her employer's harassment policy requires her to report;

(3) whether the level of overall proof that must be established to demonstrate causation requires only that retaliation be a motivating factor in the employer's adverse employment actions; and

(4) whether a few months between the protected activity and the retaliatory action can represent sufficient temporal proximity for causation.

We answer yes to all these questions, as explained below.

Section 704(a), Title VII's antiretaliation provision, has two clauses making it "an unlawful employment practice for an employer to discriminate against any of his employees ... [1] because [the employee] has opposed any practice made an unlawful employment practice by [Title VII], or [2] because [the employee] has made a charge, testified, assisted, or participated in any manner in an investigation, proceeding, or hearing under [Title VII]." *Id.* The first one is known as the "opposition clause"; the second, as the "participation clause." We address both clauses in this case.

In addition to filing a claim of sexual harassment under Title VII, the respondent, Shirley Breeden, accused the petitioner, Clark County School District, of responding to that sexual harassment claim by retaliating against her in violation of both clauses of section 704(a). The district court granted summary judgment on all claims to the School District, No. CV–S–97–365–DWH(RJJ) (D. Nev., Feb. 9, 1999), but a panel of the Court of Appeals for the Ninth Circuit reversed the grant of summary judgment on the retaliation claim and remanded over the dissent of Judge Fernandez, No. 99–15522, 2000 WL 991821 (July 19, 2000) *per curiam* (unpublished), judgt. order reported at 232 F.3d 893. We granted the writ of *certiorari*, and, for the reasons that follow, we now affirm.

I STANDARD OF REVIEW

Because the district court granted summary judgment for the petitioner, we must determine whether the petitioner had demonstrated that there is "no

Clark County School District v. Breeden

genuine issue as to any material fact" and that it is "entitled to judgment as a matter of law." Fed. Rule Civ. Proc. 56(c). In a *de novo* review, we have held that summary judgment is appropriate only when a court determines that, given the substantive legal and evidentiary standards that apply to the case, there exists no genuine issue of material fact. *Anderson v. Liberty Lobby, Inc.*, 477 U.S. 242, 255 (1986). In ruling on a motion for summary judgment, a court does not sit as a fact finder. *Id.* The evidence of the nonmoving party must be believed at the summary judgment stage, and all justifiable inferences must be drawn in the nonmoving party's favor. *Id.* A disputed issue of fact is "genuine" if the evidence is such that a reasonable fact finder could find in favor of the nonmoving party. *Celotex v. Catrett*, 477 U.S. 317, 322–23 (1986). As a result, we assume the facts to be as alleged by the respondent.

II BREEDEN'S RETALIATION CLAIMS

Breeden began working for the School District in 1984 as an administrator in the human resources (HR) department. App. to Pet. for Cert. 9. In the fall of 1994, while in the supervisory position of director of support staff services in the HR department, her duties included overseeing the hiring process for school police officers. As part of those duties, she reviewed psychological evaluation reports regarding job applicants. *Id.* Breeden and the staff that she supervised did background checks, reviewed reports from the Federal Bureau of Investigation (FBI), handled leave requests and unemployment claims, and helped to place injured workers back in work.

A *Opposition Activity*

On October 21, 1994, Breeden's immediate (male) supervisor, Don Eldfrick, the personnel manager, met with her and another male employee, Jim McIntosh, who reported to Breeden. The purpose of their meeting was to review the psychological evaluation reports of four job applicants for police officer positions with the School District. The report for one of the applicants disclosed that the applicant had once made a sexual remark to a coworker, "I hear making love to you is like making love to the Grand Canyon." Brief in Opposition at 3. At the meeting, Eldfrick read the comment aloud, looked at Breeden, and stated, "I don't know what that means." *Id.* The other male employee at the meeting, McIntosh, said, "Well, I'll tell you later," and both men chuckled. *Id.*

Breeden testified that she was embarrassed and offended by this remark and by Eldfrick's overall behavior at the meeting. That afternoon, Breeden

474 Clark County School District v. Breeden

spoke to her friend and an administrator in another department, Dr. Edward Goldman, assistant superintendent. Breeden complained specifically about the conduct of her immediate supervisor, Eldfrick, at the meeting. Goldman told her she had three options: (1) file a sexual harassment complaint; (2) talk directly to Eldfrick; or (3) do nothing. App. to Pet. for Cert. at 10. Breeden then spoke to Eldfrick later that day, informing him that she was not pleased by his conduct during the meeting and that he had offended her. Breeden testified that Eldfrick's attitude and conduct toward her changed, and he addressed her in a hostile tone for the next two weeks. App. to Pet. for Cert. at 11.

After two weeks of being uncomfortable with Eldfrick's behavior, Breeden complained to Eldfrick's immediate (female) supervisor, George Ann Rice, the assistant superintendent in charge of HR. Breeden informed Rice about Eldfrick's behavior at the October 21, 1994 meeting, as well as Eldfrick's treatment of her after complaining about his conduct at that meeting. Breeden's claim of opposition retaliation asserts that she was punished by Rice for these complaints and that Rice did nothing to respond to her complaints other than asking Breeden, "What are you going to do to bring harmony back into the department?" *Id.* Less than a month after Breeden complained to Rice about Eldfrick's behavior, Rice revised several of Breeden's duties and gave Eldfrick more of Breeden's responsibilities.

B Participation Activity

On August 23, 1995, Breeden filed a charge with the Equal Employment Opportunity Commission (EEOC) and the Nevada Equal Rights Commission, alleging that her interaction with Eldfrick and changes in her job responsibilities after the October 1994 staff meeting constituted harassment and retaliation for her objection to Eldfrick's behavior related to the "Grand Canyon" remark. Because both Title VII and its implementing regulations require that an employer be given notice within ten days of a charge filling, it is assumed that the School District had knowledge of Breeden's filing with the EEOC shortly after the charge was filed in August 1995. 42 U.S.C. §§2000e–5(b), (e)(1); 29 C.F.R. §1601.14 (2000).

On January 13, 1997, the EEOC issued a right-to-sue letter notifying Breeden and the School District that Breeden had ninety days from receipt to file a claim in court related to her charge. Thus, by operation of simple mathematics, the School District must have been aware that Breeden would have to file the lawsuit at some time in early April 1997. On April 1, 1997,

Breeden filed the lawsuit in this case charging the School District with sexual harassment and retaliation based on her opposition activity related to the October 21, 1994 meeting. On April 10, 1997, Rice mentioned to a union representative that she was contemplating transferring Breeden. The School District argued to the trial court that Rice could not have been aware of Breeden's lawsuit when she spoke to the union representative because the School District was not officially served and put on notice until April 11, 1997. However, disputed facts suggest that, regardless of when she first contemplated Breeden's transfer, Rice made the final decision to reassign Breeden a little less than one month after the School District learned that Breeden had filed a lawsuit. App. to Pet. for Cert. at 7. Furthermore, the transfer was not implemented until July 1997 – only about three months after the School District became aware of Breeden's lawsuit.

Breeden alleged that the School District retaliated against her for filing the lawsuit when it transferred her to the position of director of professional development education at the District's North Ninth office in July 1997. *Id.* at 6. According to Breeden, this new position had been previously performed by someone three levels below Breeden in the organization. *Id.* In addition, the transfer required her to relocate from the School District's main building to a trailer 9 miles away from where she had previously worked as a member of the HR department. *Id.* at 20–21. Although her salary did not change, Breeden also alleged that this July 1997 transfer changed her duties from supervisory to primarily clerical, with her overall responsibilities and prospects for promotion greatly reduced. *Id.* at 6. As a result, Breeden amended her complaint to also allege a claim of participation retaliation, asserting that she had been punished for participating in the processes protected by Title VII by filing a charge with the EEOC and for bringing a lawsuit in federal court pursuing these complaints.

III BREEDEN'S OPPOSITION RETALIATION CLAIM
SURVIVES SUMMARY JUDGMENT

A *A Reasonable and Good-Faith Belief Standard Applies to Opposition Retaliation Claims*

To establish her opposition retaliation claim, Breeden need not prove that her supervisor's conduct was actually unlawful under Title VII; "Rather, con-cerned that a literal reading would chill use of informal means to resolve claims by employees lacking the sophistication to interpret Title VII or predict law, the Circuits construe [section 704(a)] as requiring [a] plaintiff to have

476   Clark County School District v. Breeden

only an 'objectively reasonable' and 'good faith' belief that the complained of conduct violated the anti-discrimination provisions of Title VII." Pet. for Cert. at 23–24. The Court of Appeals for the Ninth Circuit has determined that this objectively reasonable and good faith belief standard applies to section 704(a) opposition claims. *Trent v. Valley Electric Assn. Inc.*, 41 F.3d 524, 526 (9th Cir. 1994). We agree and find that this interpretation is consistent with the remedial objectives of Title VII's retaliation provision.

B Opposing a Single Nonactionable Incident of Harassment Can Be Objectively Reasonable

Now, we must determine whether Breeden had both a reasonable and a good faith belief that the single incident of alleged harassment that occurred in this case violated the law. It is clear that Breeden's opposition to the interaction with Eldfrick and McIntosh and their comments made during the meeting on October 21, 1994, was in good faith. The parties do not dispute this. The more difficult question is whether her belief that the conduct complained of violated Title VII was reasonable. Title VII forbids actions taken on the basis of sex that "discriminate against any individual with respect to his compensation, terms, conditions, or privileges of employment." 42 U.S.C. §2000e–2(a)(1) [section 703(a)]. Just three terms ago, we reiterated what was plain from our previous decisions: that sexual harassment is actionable under Title VII only if it is "so 'severe or pervasive' as to 'alter the conditions of [the victim's] employment and create an abusive working environment.' " *Faragher v. Boca Raton*, 524 U.S. 775, 786 (1998) (quoting *Meritor Savings Bank, FSB v. Vinson*, 477 U.S. 57, 67 (1986) (some internal quotation marks omitted)). *See also Burlington Industries, Inc. v. Ellerth*, 524 U.S. 742, 752 (1998) (finding that only harassing conduct that is "severe or pervasive" can produce a "constructive alteratio[n] in the terms or conditions of employment"); *Oncale v. Sundowner Offshore Services, Inc.*, 523 U.S. 75, 81 (1998) (Title VII "forbids only behavior so objectively offensive as to alter the 'conditions' of the victim's employment").

Workplace conduct is not measured in isolation; instead, "whether an environment is sufficiently hostile or abusive" must be judged "by 'looking at all the circumstances,' including the 'frequency of the discriminatory conduct; its severity; whether it is physically threatening or humiliating, or a mere offensive utterance; and whether it unreasonably interferes with an employee's work performance.' " *Faragher*, 524 U.S. at 787–88 (quoting *Harris v. Forklift Systems, Inc.*, 510 U.S. 17, 23 (1993)). Thus, "[a] recurring point in [our] opinions is that simple teasing, offhand comments, and isolated

Clark County School District v. Breeden

incidents (unless extremely serious) will not amount to discriminatory changes in the 'terms and conditions of employment.' " *Faragher*, 524 U.S. at 788 (citation and internal quotation marks omitted). Breeden did not challenge the district court's finding that she had failed to establish that the incident occurring on October 21, 1994 with Eldfrick exhibited sufficient severity or pervasiveness to effectuate discriminatory changes in terms or conditions of employment to represent an actionable sexual harassment hostile environment claim. Pet. for Cert. at 3.

Nevertheless, we must now ask whether a reasonable person in Breeden's situation could have believed that the single incident recounted above violated Title VII's standard. The ordinary terms and conditions of the respondent's job required her to review the sexually explicit statement in the course of screening job applicants. Her coworkers who participated in the hiring process were subject to the same requirement, and indeed, in the district court, Breeden "conceded that it did not bother or upset her" to read the statement in the file. App. to Pet. for Cert. at 15 (district court opinion). Her supervisor's comment – made at a meeting to review the application – that he did not know what the statement meant, her coworker's responding comment, and the chuckling of both are at worst an "isolated inciden[t]" that cannot remotely be considered "extremely serious," as our cases require. *Faragher*, 524 U.S. at 788. One could then stop at this point, as the dissenting opinion in the Ninth Circuit suggested, and find that "Breeden has unreasonably built a whole edifice of alleged harassment and retaliation upon the shaky foundation of a single comment at a single meeting." App. to Pet. for Cert. at 8.

However, the Ninth Circuit dissent and the School District conflate the proof necessary for establishing a claim of sexual harassment with the proof necessary to establish the objective reasonableness of an opposition retaliation claim. The objective reasonableness standard must be broad enough to address a Title VII complaint involving actions that do not violate the law, but which could eventually do so if repeated. We have found no case issued by this Court that offers support for the School District's argument that a complaint of a single incident of harassment, albeit not actionable within the context of Title VII hostile environment analysis, can never be protected opposition activity for a retaliation claim under Title VII. If we were to join the analysis required for establishing a hostile environment claim with opposition retaliation analysis in the way in which the employer argues we should, we would overlook viable opposition retaliation claims.

We reject this stilted approach, which would allow an employee to prevail in opposition retaliation claims only if the underlying complaint had resulted in actionable harassment or had somehow become "close enough" or very

478 Clark County School District v. Breeden

"close to being unlawful 'sexual harassment' or any violation of Title VII." Pet. for Cert. at 27–28 (citing *Clover v. Total System Services, Inc.*, 176 F.3d 1346, 1351 (11th Cir. 1991)). Such a narrow reading of opposition retaliation would result in just the type of chilling effect on the use of informal means to resolve claims by employees lacking the sophistication to interpret Title VII that motivated us to find in this case that a reasonable, good faith belief standard should apply. Specifically, the argument that the underlying harassment must be close to being actionable in order to meet the reasonable belief standard is unconvincing.

We also think a standard that requires harassment to be "very close" to being actionable underestimates the incentive an employee has under *Ellerth* and *Faragher* to report all incidences of harassment before they reach the level of severe or pervasive. This approach of encouraging early reporting follows directly from our decisions in *Ellerth* and *Faragher*, where we held that "[a]n employer ... is subject to vicarious liability to a victimized employee for an actionable hostile environment created by a supervisor with ... authority over the employee." *Ellerth*, 524 U.S. at 765; *Faragher*, 524 U.S. at 807. Although the employer is strictly liable and has no affirmative defense if the hostile environment "culminates in a tangible employment action" against the employee, an employer does have a defense "[w]hen no tangible employment action is taken" if it "exercised reasonable care to prevent and correct promptly any" discriminatory conduct, and "the plaintiff employee unreasonably failed to take advantage of any preventive or corrective opportunities provided by the employer or to avoid harm otherwise." *Ellerth*, 524 U.S. at 765. As a result, if an employer has a policy and a reporting system for harassing behavior and if the employee fails to promptly report the behavior, the employer is not liable. Lower courts have held in favor of employers on the second prong of the affirmative defense when plaintiffs have delayed reporting the first incident of harassment. *See, e.g., Jackson v. Arkansas Dept. of Educ.*, 272 F.3d 1020, 1026 (8th Cir. 2001) (failure to report for more than nine months); *Montero v. AGCO Corp.*, 192 F.3d 856, 863 (9th Cir. 1999) (failure to report for almost two years); *Scrivner v. Socorro Indep. Sch. Dist.*, 169 F.3d 969, 971 (5th Cir. 1999) (failure to complain for several months). Although we do not decide today whether these opinions are appropriate interpretations of the second prong of the affirmative defense we announced in *Faragher* and *Ellerth*, they do demonstrate the strong incentive employees have to report harassing conduct early.

Under *Faragher* and *Ellerth*, the victim is incentivized to report the harassment misconduct, not to investigate, gather evidence, and then approach company officials. *Faragher*, 524 U.S. at 807; *Ellerth*, 524 U.S. at 765. If an

Clark County School District v. Breeden

479

employee's internal complaint were not protected in this situation, an employee would face a catch-22: Either complain to the employer about offensive conduct experienced or witnessed before it becomes severe or pervasive (and risk losing a retaliation claim if her employer retaliates against her for complaining); or wait to complain until the harassment is so severe or pervasive that she is certain she will be protected from retaliation (and risk losing her harassment complaint if the court finds she failed to take advantage of preventive or corrective opportunities). In this case, if Breeden had waited until Eldfrick had repeatedly harassed her, the School District would have argued that she had not promptly reported the prior acts and that therefore it should win on the affirmative defense. This not only hurts Breeden, but also harms the employer, who benefits from correcting harassing behavior before it becomes severe or pervasive.

The incentive to report harassing behavior promptly flows from *Ellerth* and *Faragher* and leads us to conclude that Breeden's opposition was reasonable. If we adopt the approach of the Ninth Circuit dissent and the employer in this case, an employee would face an inevitable Goldilocks problem in reporting harassing behavior: Report too soon and lose the retaliation claim; report too late and lose the harassment claim because of the *Ellerth* and *Faragher* affirmative defense. Such a result would leave an employee with only one realistic option: report harassing conduct at just the perfect time, when it has reached a sufficiently hostile or abusive level to be actionable or very close to being actionable, but had not passed the point at which the plaintiff would be deemed unreasonable in not reporting earlier. Furthermore, such a ruling would give an employer *carte blanche* to take retaliatory actions. Employers, in anticipation of defeating a retaliation claim, could take adverse employment actions with impunity before a viable underlying harassment claim occurs (i.e., before repetitive harassing behavior becomes sufficiently severe or pervasive).

We believe that Title VII's remedial provisions do not support such a reading of how to interpret when a plaintiff has a reasonable belief that unlawful harassment has occurred. *See Robinson v. Shell Oil Co.*, 519 U.S. 337, 346 (1997) ("a primary purpose of antiretaliation provisions . . . [is] [m]aintaining unfettered access to statutory remedial mechanisms," and the Court should look for an "interpretation . . . more consistent with the broader context of Title VII and the purpose of . . . [section] 704(a)"). Instead, we find that any complaint involving a single act of unwelcome harassment can be objectively reasonable if such harassment would, if repeated, culminate in an actionable claim of severe or pervasive harassment. Or, put another way, single-incident complaints should be considered valid "protected activity" under section

480   Clark County School District v. Breeden

704(a) even if the single incident has not yet become an actionable (or close to actionable) harassment claim.

Applying that standard to this case, it seems to us clear that Breeden's opposition was objectively reasonable. We hold that a reasonable jury could conclude that Breeden reasonably believed that even the single incident involving the conduct of her male supervisor and her male subordinate at the October 21, 1994 meeting constituted sexual harassment under Title VII because: (1) It represented a microaggression – a type of everyday indignity and dismissive behavior that women and other vulnerable workers face based on hostility to their presence in the workplace; and (2) it involved behavior aimed at undermining her and demonstrating that she was inferior to men in the workplace, including her subordinate.

Well-established resources suggest that a male supervisor's dismissive approach and hostile treatment of a female employee can be seen as a form of gendered microaggressive behavior. *See* Peggy C. Davis, *Law as Microaggression*, 98 YALE L.J. 1559, 1576 (1989) ("automatic acts of disregard" for concerns of those who are vulnerable represents microaggression); *see also* Francisco Valdes, *Beyond Sexual Orientation in Queer Legal Theory: Majoritarianism, Multidisciplinary, and Responsibility in Social Justice*, 75 DENVER U. L. REV. 1409, 1428 n.77 (1998) (referring to microaggressions as "everyday social slights that represent and replicate larger structures of subordination"). Professor Marc Poirer has explained that "cognitive distortions" can lead to microaggression in the workplace based upon gender. *See* Marc R. Poirier, *Gender Stereotypes at Work*, 65 BROOKLYN L. REV. 1073, 1073–74 & n.3 (1999) (referring to how "women are disadvantaged through myriad small, often unconscious, judgments, decisions, and evaluations that occur systematically over the course of months and years of social interactions").

A single act such as the one in this case of reading a comment of a sexual nature in front of the only woman in the room, who is then faced with the two men present "chuckling," could represent the type of microaggression that many women and other vulnerable employees face in the workplace. Breeden's experience was undoubtedly made worse by the fact that the two men present were her supervisor and subordinate, who likely appeared to her to be teaming up to make her uncomfortable. The men's microaggressions, even in a single interaction, can become part of an overall pattern if not reported and stopped before they are repeated.

Furthermore, the message being sent to Breeden by the events at that meeting was that she, as a woman, could not understand something the men easily had understood or that, even if she did understand it, she could not explain this comment of a sexual nature to them, because they are men.

Instead, her male subordinate would "explain it later" to her boss, when the men had time to devote to it, while chuckling at her lack of a response. The sum of this interaction reasonably indicates an attempt to make the only woman in the room feel uncomfortable.

Professor Vicki Schultz has also noted that the gendered undermining of competence via "[h]armful acts of hazing and harassment frequently fall[s] between the cracks of legal analysis" because, alone, such acts appear not to be pervasive enough for hostile environment liability and to be too remote to a tangible job benefit to represent disparate treatment. *See* Vicki Schultz, *Conceptualizing Sexual Harassment*, 107 YALE L.J. 1683, 1721, 1767 (1998) (discussing how much of the sex-based discrimination women experience in the workplace is the result of small interactions driven by the perception that women are inferior to men – not acts of overt harassment, but "alienation acts that undermine their confidence and sense of belonging"). Schultz has also explained how these gendered workplace acts against women involving "nonsexualized forms of harassment that are geared toward undermining their competence" can come from male supervisors and subordinates who feel threatened by the presence of women in traditionally male-dominated jobs. *Id.* at 1700, 1767. This research supports our conclusion that gendered allegations of alienation (similar to what happened to Breeden) can constitute a reasonable belief that harassment occurred. *Id.* at 1700 (referring to how sexual harassment can be understood to exist in nonsexualized terms, as more about "attempts ... to wear down, frustrate, or get a reaction from another," and how for "those who have made it ... [h]arassment is a mechanism for achieving exclusion and protection of privilege"). As discussed earlier, the reasonable belief standard should not be limited to allegations that actually meet or closely meet the legal definition of harassment and should encompass a broader understanding of how vulnerable workers perceive harassment in the workplace.

Finally, in developing an understanding of reasonable belief about harassment as a violation of Title VII, research indicates that vulnerable workers are more likely to engage in passive responses to the microaggressions and competence-undermining behavior present in this case. *See* Denise H. Lach & Patricia A. Gwartney-Gibbs, *Sociological Perspectives on Sexual Harassment and Workplace Dispute Resolution*, 42 J. OF VOCATIONAL BEHAVIOR 102, 110 (1993) (describing studies of how women are willing to confront a workplace harasser only when the harassment is more serious, because they prefer not to report "because they perceive that their complaints may not be taken seriously by their superiors" and that "the organization cannot protect them from retaliation"). This research supports our finding in this case that, when a woman or any vulnerable worker does bravely report, as Breeden has done in this case, that

482   Clark County School District v. Breeden

report should be presumed reasonable and protected from retaliation to achieve the broad remedial goals of Title VII. When Breeden came forward and reported harassing behavior not only to the male supervisor involved, Eldfrick, but also to *his* supervisor, Rice, we presume that Breeden reasonably believed that the conduct was serious enough to become a violation of Title VII. *Id.* The microaggressions and competence-undermining that occurred at the October 1994 meeting, if repeated, would create a severe or pervasive hostile environment under Title VII. As a result, we find that Breeden had a good faith, reasonable belief that the harassment she was reporting was unlawful.

Of course, the presumption we establish here can be rebutted because there are some single-incident harassment allegations that no reasonable person would believe could ever become a link in an overall chain of events leading to actionable hostile environment. We have no need to identify such allegations in this case, because they are not present. The facts here demonstrate that the underlying event leading to Breeden's complaint reasonably could be part of an overall chain of sexual harassment even if it was not sufficient, by itself, to be actionable harassment.

IV BREEDEN ESTABLISHED SUFFICIENT EVIDENCE OF CAUSATION FOR HER PARTICIPATION RETALIATION CLAIM TO SURVIVE SUMMARY JUDGMENT

A *Plaintiffs in Section 704(a) Claims Need Prove Only That Retaliation Was a Motivating Factor in the Adverse Employment Decision*

The employee's burden to address the issue of causation under a section 703(a) claim has been established clearly by the Civil Rights Act of 1991. 105 Stat. 1071. An employee who alleges status-based discrimination under section 703(a) of Title VII need not show that the causal link between injury and wrong is so close that the injury would not have occurred "but for" the act. So-called but-for causation is not the test. It suffices instead to show that the motive to discriminate was one of the employer's motives, even if the employer also had other lawful motives that influenced its decision.

Similar to the 1991 Act's section 703(m) clarification on causation for section 703(a) status-based discrimination claims, we hold that but-for causation is not the test for a section 704(a) retaliation claim as well. This principle follows from an earlier case of this Court, *Price Waterhouse v. Hopkins*, 490 U.S. 228 (1989), and an ensuing statutory amendment by Congress in the 1991 Act that codified in part and abrogated in part the holding in *Price Waterhouse*. 1991 Act, 42 U.S.C. §§2000e–2(m), 2000e–5(g)(2)(B). In *Price Waterhouse*, a plurality of this Court held that section 703(a) requires a plaintiff to prove only that discrimination was "a motivating factor" for an adverse employment action. *Price Waterhouse*, 490 U.S. at 268–69. While the 1991 Act did not address specifically retaliation claims brought under section 704(a) of Title VII, Congress endorsed the general plurality approach in *Price Waterhouse* by making clear that the language "because of" used in section 703(a) meant that an employee has to show only that discrimination was a motivating factor in the employer's decision to take the adverse employment action.

Accordingly, Congress clearly rejected the notion that the term "because of" in Title VII meant but-for causation: an argument that the dissenters in *Price Waterhouse* had asserted. *Id.* at 281–86 (dissenting opinion by Justice Kennedy joined by Justice Thomas). Instead, Congress made it clear in section 703(m) that it agreed with the plurality in *Price Waterhouse* that "because of" required only that plaintiffs show that their protected class was a motivating factor in order to establish causation. The only other time we have addressed the meaning of the "because of" language in a provision of Title VII was in *Price Waterhouse*. With our plurality decision in that case and further approval of that reasoning by Congress in the 1991 Act for section 703(a) claims, we are convinced that but-for causation should also not be the standard for a retaliation claim under Title VII. Based on the plurality's analysis in *Price Waterhouse*, we find that the very similar "because" language in the retaliation provision, section 704(a), requires only proof that retaliation was a motivating factor for the employer's adverse action.

B A Jury Must Resolve Several Issues of Fact Regarding Causation

We have no reason to disturb the Ninth Circuit's finding that changing Breeden's duties and transferring her in response to her opposition and participation activity were adverse employment actions. *See also Ray v. Henderson*, 217 F.3d 1234, 1241 (9th Cir. 2000) (broadly defining adverse employment actions to focus on the remedial effects intended by Title VII's retaliation provision). With respect to the timing of the participation retaliation claim, the School District asserted that Rice contemplated transferring Breeden in early April 1997 before the lawsuit was served later that month. As a result, the School District argued that summary judgment on the participation claim was appropriate because, when Rice made her decision to transfer Breeden, she could not have been retaliating for Breeden's filing of a lawsuit that Rice did not know had been filed. However, the Ninth Circuit concluded that there was sufficient evidence in the record that the School District received Breeden's right-to-sue letter in January 1997 indicating that

484 Clark County School District v. Breeden

Breeden had ninety days in which to file a lawsuit. This right-to-sue letter informed the School District that the EEOC charge Breeden filed in 1995 was not only unresolved, but also could be continued in court if filed before the expiration date, which would occur in April 1997. Moreover, the record contains conflicting information on the timing of Rice's decision to transfer Breeden. Rice wrote a memorandum on April 20, 1997, about the need for reorganization, which suggests that the decision to transfer Breeden did not occur until after Breeden filed the lawsuit on April 1, 1997, and after the School District was served with the suit on April 11, 1997. *See* Pet. for Rehearing at 3. Although the School District has argued that Rice could not have known about the lawsuit when she first contemplated transferring Breeden, this is a genuine issue of material fact that must be construed in Breeden's favor.

The Ninth Circuit also noted that the record suggests that Rice did not make the final decision to transfer Breeden until May 1997, certainly after Rice received notice of the filed lawsuit on April 11, 1997. App. to Pet. for Cert. at 7. Regardless of whether Rice might have contemplated the transfer decision before knowing about the lawsuit filing, a reasonable jury could find that she did not make a definitive decision to implement the transfer until May 1997. Further, there is uncontradicted evidence that the transfer did not become effective until July 1997 – three months after Breeden filed the lawsuit in this case.

Whether contemplated earlier or not, reasonable jurors could conclude that Rice decided to retaliate against Breeden for filing the lawsuit by settling on and finalizing the adverse transfer after learning of the lawsuit. Pet. for Rehearing at 2–3. The one-month span between the filing of the lawsuit and the finalized decision to transfer Breeden, or even the three-month span between the lawsuit's filing and the implemented transfer, are both of sufficiently close temporal proximity to justify reversing the district court's grant of summary judgment and remanding for further proceedings.

Further, the record indicates that Rice's purported reasons for transferring Breeden could be pretextual in that she stated that part of the reason for the transfer was that Breeden could focus on unemployment and leave claims in the transferred position. However, the handling of those duties was transferred back to Eldfrick shortly after Breeden started in the new position in July 1997. App. to Pet. for Cert. at 5–7.

With respect to whether Breeden could establish causation through temporal proximity, the School District has suggested that we identify a specific time frame for sufficient proximity to establish a causal link. App. to Pet. for Cert. at 6–7 (citing *Nidds v. Schindler Elevator Corp.*, 113 F.3d 912, 919 (9th Cir. 1997) (holding that four months between protected activity and adverse

Clark County School District v. Breeden

action was sufficient proximity)). We decline to identify a fixed time frame for inferring discriminatory motives based upon temporal proximity as a measure of establishing causation in a retaliation action. Such an inquiry is a fact-specific exercise, and the significance of any timing regarding a given act of retaliation will often depend upon the particular circumstances.

Given the broad statutory text and the variety of workplace contexts in which retaliation may occur, Title VII's antiretaliation provision is simply not reducible to a comprehensive set of clear rules. Furthermore, if we were to create an exact limit on temporal proximity, it would encourage employers to wait until a time strategically placed outside that arbitrary window before they retaliate against their employees. Viewing a summary judgment motion in the light most favorable to the plaintiff, Breeden must be given the opportunity to establish her retaliation claim by demonstrating causation that could convince a reasonable juror.

We now apply the motivating factor standard we have adopted for causation in this case. The School District asserted that the motivation for the changes in Breeden's duties in December 1994 and her transfer in July 1997 were the result of an overall restructuring of the HR department. Pet. for Cert. App. at 11. However, a reasonable juror could conclude that the change in Breeden's job duties and the later transfer were motivated at least in part by retaliation, because Rice never acted upon Breeden's complaints about Eldfrick, and the adverse employment actions occurred within reasonable temporal proximity after Breeden's protected activity. As a result, we conclude that there are sufficient material facts in dispute that a reasonable juror could find causation using the motivating factor standard we have adopted today.

* * *

The judgment of the court of appeals is affirmed, and the case is remanded for proceedings consistent with this decision.

It is so ordered.

Index

abortions/abortion rights, 106–7

accommodations, 198–202

Adarand Constructors, Inc. v. Slater (10th Cir. 2000), 140, 289, 291

Adickes v. S.H. Kress & Co. (1970), 382

Adiele, Laura, 169

ADR Tr. Corp. v. Carr (1st Cir. 1993), 140

affirmative action claims, 359, 397–98, 407–8, 410

affirmative defenses, 16, 20, 48, 54, 466–69, 478–79, *see also* bona fide occupational qualification (BFOQ)

African American Women/African descendants, *see* Black women

AFSCME v. State of Washington (9th Cir. 1985), 334–60
  comparable worth theory, 355–59
  conclusion, 360
  disparate impact, 354–56
  disparate treatment, 351–54
  facts, 346–48
  feminist judgment, 68–87, 340–60
  free market fallacy, 349–51
  original opinion, 335–40
  overview, 13–14
  pay gap, 334–35
  remedies, 359–60
  strengthening litigation tools, 18

Age Discrimination in Employment Act (ADEA), 25–27, 77, 79

Albemarle Paper Co. v. Moody (1975), 360, 412, 416, 418, 427–28

Alexander, Leigh: *Do Google's "Unprofessional Hair" Results Show It Is Racist?*, 174

Ali, Muhammad, 181

Alito, Samuel, 92, 392

Allen, Wynter: *Johnson Controls* feminist judgment, 8, 58–68

Am. Psychological Ass'n, *Definition of Terms: Sex, Gender, Gender Identity, Sexual Orientation*, 326

American Bar Ass'n: *Model Rules of Professional Conduct*, 127

Americans with Disabilities Act (ADA), pregnancy and, 24–25, 88–89, 93, 95, 115–17

Americans with Disabilities Act Amendments Act (ADAAA), 95, 115–17

Anderson v. Liberty Lobby, Inc. (1986), 132, 473

Anthony, Kathryn H. *et. al.: Potty Parity in Perspective: Gender and Family Issues in Planning and Designing Public Restrooms*, 288, 295–96

anti-race-norming provision, Title VII, 399–400, 426–27

appearances, intersectional approaches to, 119–214, *see also EEOC v. Catastrophe Management Solutions* (11th Cir. 2016), *Jespersen v. Harrah's Operating Co* (9th Cir. 2006)

Araújo, Tais, 167–68

Archibald, Catherine: *Etsitty* feminist judgment, 12, 266, 273–300

Areheart, Bradley: *Young* feminist judgment, 8, 87–96

Arlington Heights v. Metropolitan Housing Dev. Corp. (1977), 409, 429

Ash v. Tyson Foods Inc. (2006), 458

Index

Ashcraft, Karen Lee and Michael E. Pacanowsky: *"A Woman's Worst Enemy": Reflections on a Narrative of Organizational Life and Female Identity*, 260

Ashcroft v. Iqbal (2009), 162

#AskHerMore campaign, 127

associational theory of discrimination, 304

Aziz, Sahar: *Webb* feminist judgment, 10, 180–91

Back v. Hastings on Hudson Union Free Sch. Dist. (2d Cir. 2004), 292, 326

Bacon v. Honda of Am. Mfg. Inc. (7th Cir. 2004), 456

Baehr v. Lewin (Haw. 1993), 325

Baker v. California Land Title Co. (9th Cir. 1974), 132–33

Baldwin v. Foxx (EEOC 2015), 320, 323–25

Barnes v. City of Cincinnati (6th Cir. 2005), 284

Barrett, Elisabeth M.: *The Effect of State Maximum-Hours Laws on the Employment of Women*, 80

Barrett, Nancy S.: *Obstacles to Economic Parity for Women*, 80

Bartlett, Katharine T., 138

Only Girls Wear Barrettes: Dress and Appearance Standards, Community Norms, and Workplace Equality, 286

Bartol, Kathryn M.: *Female Managers and Quality of Working Life: The Impact of Sex-Role Stereotypes*, 80

Baskin v. Bogan (7th Cir. 2014), 333

Batali, Mario, 215

bathrooms

bathroom bills, 268–69

sex-segregated, 275, 295–300

transgender persons use of, *see Etsitty v. Utah Transit Authority* (10th Cir. 2007)

Bawa, Jesse: *Catastrophe Mgmt.* feminist judgment, 9, 146–56

Bazemore v. Friday (1986), 375, 377, 445

Becker, Mary E.: *From Muller v. Oregon to Fetal Vulnerability Policies*, 81, 83, 84, 85

Bell Atl. Corp. v. Twombly (2007), 162

Bell, Roxana: *Jespersen* feminist judgment, 9, 119–28

Benard, Stephen et al.: *Cognitive Bias and the Motherhood Penalty*, 99

Bendick, Marc, 453

Bennett Amendment, 352

Benson, Sara R.: *Hacking the Gender Binary Myth: Recognizing Fundamental Rights for the Intersexed*, 136

Berger, Linda L.: *Feminist Judgments: Rewritten Opinions of the Supreme Court*, 2

Bernal v. Fainter (1984), 291

Bernstein v. Bankert (7th Cir. 2013), 332

Bertrand, Marianne and Sendhil Mullainathan: *Are Emily and Greg More Employable than Lakisha and Jamal? A Field Experiment on Labor Market Discrimination*, 446

biases, implicit and explicit, 4, 55–56

Bibby v. Phila. Coca Cola Bottling Co. (3d Cir. 2001), 331

Bielby, William, 439, 454–55

Black women, 127–28, *see also* intersectionality

Black hair, regulation of, 151–52, 154–55, 161, 162–70

CROWN Act (Cal. 2019), 127–28

hair and makeup requirements, *see* hair and makeup requirements, *Jespersen v. Harrah's Operating Co* (9th Cir. 2006)

immutability doctrine and, 177–79, *see also* immutable characteristics

Islam, intersection with, 180–214, *see also Webb v. City of Philadelphia* (3d Cir. 2009)

natural hair, 134, 151–52, 162–70

sexual harassment and, 233–36

straight hair mandate and unequal burdens, 175–76

Blasi, Gary: *Advocacy against the Stereotype: Lessons from Cognitive and Social Psychology*, 51

Bollenbach v. Bd. of Educ. of Monroe-Woodbury Cent. Sch. Dist. (S.D.N.Y. 1987), 263, 285

bona fide occupational qualification (BFOQ)

employer's purpose and, 76

fetuses as third parties, 78–79

in *Etsitty*, 284–86

in *Jespersen*, 137–39

in *Johnson Controls*, 82

occupational, defined, 77

pregnant women, 8, 59, 60–61

provisions in ADEA and Title VII, 77

safety exception, 61, 62–64, 77–82

sex-differentiated standards, 125

Bond v. Atkinson (7th Cir. 2013), 325

488 *Index*

Bonilla v. Oakland Scavenger Co. (9th Cir. 1982), 355

Bonto v. U.S. Bank, N.A. (7th Cir. 2010), 312

Bornstein, Lisa and Megan Bench: *Married on Sunday, Fired on Monday: Approaches to Federal LGBT Civil Rights Protections*, 332

Bornstein, Stephanie
 AFSCME feminist judgment, 13–14, 334–44
 Poor, Pregnant, and Fired, 99

Boutillier v. Hartford Pub. Schs. (D. Conn. 2016), 320, 325

Bowen v. Georgetown University Hospital (1988), 113

Bowen v. Gilliard (1987), 289

Bowen v. Massachusetts (1988), 117

Bradley, Joseph P., 344–45

Bradwell v. Illinois (1872), 299, 344–45, 349, 364

Bratton v. Roadway Package Sys., Inc. (7th Cir. 1996), 312

Breaking the Patterns of Injustice: AFSCME's Blueprint for Pay Equity, 348

Breeden, *see Clark County School District v. Breeden* (2001)

Brennan, William, 106, 110, 270–71

Breyer, Stephen, 92

Bridgeman v. Ford, Bacon & Davis (8th Cir. 1947), 140

Brown v. Bd. of Educ. (1954), 299

Brown v. D.C. Transit Sys., Inc. (D.C. Cir. 1975), 133

Brown v. Gardner (1994), 331

Brown v. General Motors Corp. (8th Cir. 1979), 198

Brown v. Henderson (2d Cir. 2001), 142

Brown, Patricia Leigh: *A Quest for a Restroom That's Neither Men's Room Nor Women's Room*, 300

Brownmiller, Susan: *Against Our Will: Men, Women, and Rape*, 234

Bundy v. Jackson (D.C. Cir. 1981), 238

burden of production of evidence, 398–99, 410–15

Bureau of Labor Statistics, Dep't of Labor: *Women in the Labor Force: A Databook*, 99

Burlington Industries, Inc. v. Ellerth (1998), 10, 20, 21, 224–26, 414, 463, 465–69, 476

Burlington Northern and Santa Fe Railway Co v. White (2006), 462

Burwell v. Eastern Air Lines, Inc. (4th Cir. 1980), 78–79

Bush v. Vera (1996), 428

Bush, George W., 277

Bushey v. New York State Civil Service Comm'n (2d Cir. 1984), 426

business necessity test, 61, 76, 418–21

Butler v. Home Depot, Inc. (N.D. Cal. 1997), 445

Byrd, Ayana and Lori Tharps: *Hair Story: Untangling the Roots of Black Hair in America*, 167

Cainkar, Louise and Sunaine Malra: *Targeting Arab/Muslim/South Asian Americans: Criminalization and Cultural Citizenship*, 212

Caldwell v. Miller (7th Cir. 1986), 313

Caldwell, Paulette M.: *A Hair Piece: Perspectives on the Intersection of Race and Gender*, 163–64

California Brewers Ass'n v. Bryant (1980), 423

California Fed'l Sav. & Loan Assoc. v. Guerra (1987), 107–9, 114, 115, 423

Carroll v. Talman Fed. Sav. & Loan Ass'n of Chicago (7th Cir. 1979), 135, 144

Carter v. Three Springs Residential Treatment (11th Cir. 1998), 55

Castaneda v. Partida (1977), 257, 371

Catastrophe Management, see EEOC v. Catastrophe Management Solutions (11th Cir. 2016)

Census Bureau, 84

Centola v. Potter (D. Mass. 2002), 320

Chamallas, Martha: *Deepening the Legal Understanding of Bias: On Devaluation and Biased Prototypes*, 51

Chapman v. City of Danville (C.D. Ill. 2011), 318

Chavez v. Credit Nation Auto Sales, LLC (11th Cir. 2016), 329

Chavkin, Wendy: Walking a Tightrope: Pregnancy, Parenting, and Work, 81

Cheek v. W. & S. Life Ins. Co. (7th Cir. 1994), 313

Chevron, USA v. NRDC (1984), 105, 109

circumstantial evidence in disparate treatment cases, 32–34, 39, 48–52

City of Cleburne v. Cleburne Living Ctr. (1985), 290

Index

489

City of Los Angeles Dep't of Water & Power v. Manhart (1978), 78, 86
City of Richmond v. J.A. Croson Co. (1989), 291
Civil Rights Act of 1964, *see* Title VII, Civil Rights Act of 1964
Civil Rights Act of 1991, *see also* Title VII, Civil Rights Act of 1964
  causation, issue of, 482
  disparate impact claims, 337
  punitive damages under, 458–61
  reason, 426
  retaliation claims, 469–70
civility code, Title VII and, 247–49, 251–52, 258–59
C.K., Louis, 215
Clark v. Jeter (1988), 290
Clark County School District v. Breeden (2001), 16, 462–85
  affirmative defense to hostile work environment claims, 466–69, 478–79
  causation, issues of, 483–85
  feminist judgment, 468–85
  impact of, 465–68
  introduction, 462–64
  issues addressed, 471–72
  opposition retaliation claim, 473–74, 475–82
  participation retaliation claims, 470, 474–75, 482–85
  reasonable, good faith belief standard, 466, 468–69, 475–82
  retaliation claims, 469–71, 473–75
  standard of review, 472–73
  temporal proximity determination, 470–71, 479–80, 484–85
Clarke, Jessica A.: *Protected Class Gatekeeping*, 329
class actions, 432
  common issue of law or fact, 430, 438–39, 451–52, *see also Wal-Mart Stores, Inc. v. Dukes* (2011)
  FRCP Rule 23(a), 450–56
  FRCP Rule 23(b), 456–61
  individual hearings, compared, 439–40, 451
  notice and-opt out rights, 440–41, 460–61
  predominance rule, 434–35, 440
  systemic discrimination, *see* systemic discrimination claims
clothing, relevance in sexual harassment cases, 242–43

Cobble, Dorothy Sue: *The Other Women's Movement: Workplace Justice and Social Rights in Modern America*, 105
Coffman v. Indianapolis Fire Dep't (7th Cir. 2009), 326
color-blind Constitution theory, 407
commission sales, historical context for women's interest in, 372–74, *see also EEOC v. Sears, Roebuck & Co.* (7th Cir. 1988)
commonality requirement for class actions, 430, 438–39, 451–52, *see also Wal-Mart Stores, Inc. v. Dukes* (2011)
comparable worth theory, 334–68, *see also AFSCME v. State of Washington* (9th Cir. 1985)
Condit v. United Air Lines, Inc. (4th Cir. 1977), 79
Congressional Research Service, 182
Connecticut v. Teal (1982), 287–88, 408, 427
Connecticut Nat. Bank v. Germain (1992), 48
Constitution, US, *see* First Amendment, US Constitution
content validation, 419
Cooper v. Federal Reserve Bank of Richmond (1984), 461
Cooper v. S. Co. (11th Cir. 2004), 458
Corning Glass Works v. Brennan (1974), 342, 366
Cortez v. McCauley (10th Cir. 2007), 279
Cosby, Bill, 215
Council on American Islamic Relations (CAIR): *Presumption of Guilt: The Status of Muslim Civil Rights in the United States*, 211–12
County of Washington v. Gunther (1981), 381
Cox, Jeannette: *Pregnancy as Disability and the Amended Americans with Disabilities Act*, 116
Craig v. Boren (1976), 289
Crawford, Bridget J.: *Feminist Judgments: Rewritten Opinions of the Supreme Court*, 2
credibility of witnesses, 37–38, 41, 216–18
Crenshaw, Kimberlé: *Demarginalizing the Intersection of Race and Sex: A Black Feminist Critique of Antidiscrimination Doctrine, Feminist Theory, and Antiracist Politics*, 163
Criswell case, *see Western Air Lines, Inc. v. Criswell* (1985)

490   *Index*

critical race theory, 212–13, 254
CROWN Act (Cal. 2019), 84–85
Cruzan v. Spec. Sch. Dist, No. 1 (8th Cir. 2002), 292
Cudahy, Richard, 77
cultural heterosexism, 320
Cummins v. Parker Seal Co. (6th Cir 1975), 197

Daniels v. City of Arlington (5th Cir. 2001), 186
Davis v. Coca-Cola Bottling Co. (11th Cir. 2008), 456
Davis, Angela Y.: *Women, Race, and Class*, 233–34
Davis, Peggy C.: *Law as Microaggression*, 480
Day, Phyllis J.: *Sex-Role Stereotypes and Public Assistance*, 84
Defense of Marriage Acts (DOMA), 302
DeLano, Mary: *The Conflict Between State Guaranteed Pregnancy Benefits and the Pregnancy Discrimination Act: A Statutory Analysis*, 286
Deneffe v. Skywest, Inc. (D. Colo. May 11, 2015), 320
de novo review, 131, *see also* standards of review
Dep't of Defense, 204
Dep't of Health and Human Servs.: *Births, Final Data for 2009.*, 99
Desert Palace, Inc. v. Costa (2003), 30–57, 327
    background facts, 23, 43–47
    commentary on, 30–43
    disparate impact, 412, *see also* disparate impact claims
    feminist judgment, 43–57
    narrative technique and, 17
    original opinion, 30–34
    rewritten decision, implications of, 41–43
    summary, 7
    Title VII, § 703(m), 418, *see also* Title VII, Civil Rights Act of 1964:§ 703(m)
Devitt, Edward J. and Charles B. Blackmar, *Federal Jury Practice and Instructions* § 15.02, 52
Diaz v. Pan American World Airways (5th Cir. 1971), 201, 263, 285
diction and rhetoric, 273–74
direct evidence standard in disparate treatment cases, 32–34, 37–39, 42, 43, 48–57
discrimination, *see also* gender identity discrimination, pregnancy discrimination, retaliation claims, sex discrimination,

sexual orientation discrimination, stereotypes, transgender discrimination
    associational theory of, 304
    because of one's genitals, 280–81
    discriminatory on its face, 61, 75–76
    discriminatory reasons for employer's actions, 30–34
    intent to, 51
    pattern or practice of, 444–47
    personal preferences and, 293–94
    privacy concerns and, 295
    relationship, 324–25
    reverse, 390–91
    safety concerns, discrimination and, 294
    sex of plaintiff, 329–30
    sex of plaintiff's partner, 330
    sex plus, 325–26
    sex stereotyping and sex discrimination, 307–10
    subjective decision making and, 447–48
    systemic, *see* systemic discrimination claims
    under PDA, 75–76
    victims of, 34–36, 37–38
    wage discrimination, 381, *see also* Equal Pay Act (EPA)
disparate impact claims, 334–461, *see also* AFSCME v. State of Washington (9th Cir. 1985), disparate treatment claims, EEOC v. Sears, Roebuck & Co. (7th Cir. 1988), Ricci v. DeStefano (2009), Wal-Mart Stores, Inc. v. Dukes (2011)
    in *AFSCME*, 336–39, 354–56
    in *Etsitty*, 286–89
    in *Ricci*, 389, 396–98
    job-relatedness/business necessity defense, 61, 76, 418–21
    less-discriminatory alternatives, 421–24
    minority candidate's counterfactual case in *Ricci*, 415–18
    systemic claims, 13
disparate treatment claims, *see also* AFSCME v. State of Washington (9th Cir. 1985), disparate impact claims, EEOC v. Sears, Roebuck & Co. (7th Cir. 1988), Ricci v. DeStefano (2009), Wal-Mart Stores, Inc. v. Dukes (2011)
    evidence for, 32–34
    genitals, discrimination based on, 280–89
    in *AFSCME*, 338–39, 351–54
    makeup requirements, 132–46
    mixed motives, 30–34

Index

491

pregnant employees and, 104
reverse discrimination and, 393–95, 406–27
sex discrimination, 280–89
statistical outcomes vs. classifications, 406–9
systemic claims, 13–16
systemic discrimination, 334–461
Doe v. City of Belleville (7th Cir. 1997), 318
DOMA (Defense of Marriage Acts), 302
Domingo v. New Eng. Fish Co. (9th Cir. 1984), 456
Dothard v. Rawlinson (1977), 62–63, 77–79, 81, 138, 294, 355, 417, 423
double bind, 18, 120, 145, 266–71, 274
Dowd, Nancy: *Oncale* feminist judgment, 11, 245–55
Draper v. U.S. Pipe & Foundry Co. (6th Cir. 1975), 200–1
dreadlocks, *see* Black women: Black hair, regulation of, *EEOC v. Catastrophe Management Solutions* (11th Cir. 2016)
Dreger, Alice Domurat: *Ambiguous Sex – or Ambivalent Medicine? Ethical Issues in the Treatment of Intersexuality*, 282–83
Dreher, Rod: *Miley Cyrus > Donald Trump*, 319
dress, relevance in sexual harassment cases, 242–43
Drogin, Richard, 453
Due Process Clause, 440–41, 460–61

Easterbrook, Frank H., 82
Eatman v. United Parcel Serv. (S.D.N.Y. 2002), 163
economic harm, 199
EEOC, *see* Equal Employment Opportunity Commission (EEOC)
EEOC v. Catastrophe Management Solutions (11th Cir. 2016), 9, 146–80
Black women's hair, regulation of, 162–70, 172–74
factual background, 158–59
feminist judgment, 150–80
immutability doctrine, 147–48, 150–51, 153–55, 159–61, 177–79
intersectionality, Black and female, 147, 151–52, 162–70
legal analysis, 170–79
legal standard, 162
original opinion, 147–50
other communities of color, implications for, 155–56

procedural history, 159–62
straight hair mandate and unequal burdens on Black women, 175–76
Title VII, protections and purposes, 170–72
EEOC v. R.G. &. G.R. Harris Funeral Homes (6th Cir. 2018), 253, 276–77
EEOC v. Reads, Inc. (E.D. Pa. 1991), 197
EEOC v. Sears, Roebuck & Co. (7th Cir. 1988), 361–83
analysis, 376–82
burden of proof, 375–76
commission sales, historical context for women's interest in, 372–74
conclusion, 383
day's leave with pay provision, 382
EEOC's prima facie case, 376–78
facts of record, 369–74
feminist judgment, 18, 363–83
introduction, 361–62
jobs do not have gender, 367–68
lack of interest defense, 362–63, 365
Sears hiring policies, 369–70
Sears' interest and qualifications defense, 378–81
statistical analysis, 363–64, 370–72, 376–79
stereotypes, 364–65
summary, 13
wage discrimination, 381–82
Ellerth case, *see Burlington Industries, Inc. v. Ellerth* (1998)
Ellison v. Brady (9th Cir. 1991), 224
Ely, Robin J.: *The Effects of Organizational Demographics and Social Identity on Relationships among Professional Women*, 260
employers
actions, accountability for, 36–37
actions, motivations for, 30–34
BFOQ and purpose, 76
credibility of, 37–38
liability for supervisory conduct, 224–26, 243–45
liability under Title VII, 53–54
employment discrimination
appearances, intersectional approaches, 119–214, *see also EEOC v. Catastrophe Management Solutions* (11th Cir. 2016), *Jespersen v. Harrah's Operating Co.* (9th Cir. 2006)

Index

employment discrimination (cont.)
  gender identity discrimination, 266–300, *see also Etsitty v. Utah Transit Authority* (10th Cir. 2007)
  gender narratives, Supreme Court and, 30–57, *see also Desert Palace, Inc. v. Costa* (2003)
  introduction, 1–29
  pregnancy discrimination, 58–118, *see also International Union, UAW v. Johnson Controls* (1991), pregnancy discrimination, Pregnancy Discrimination Act (PDA)
  retaliation, 462–85, *see also Clark County School District v. Breeden* (2001), retaliation claims
  sexual harassment, 215–65, *see also Meritor Savings Bank, FSB v. Vinson* (1986), *Oncale v. Sundowner Services* (1998), sexual harassment
  sexual orientation discrimination, 301–33, *see also Hively v. Ivy Tech Community College* (7th Cir. 2017)
  systemic claims, proving disparate treatment and impact, 334–461, *see also AFSCME v. State of Washington* (9th Cir. 1985), disparate impact claims, disparate treatment claims, *EEOC v. Sears, Roebuck & Co.* (7th Cir. 1988), *Ricci v. DeStefano* (2009), *Wal-Mart Stores, Inc. v. Dukes* (2011)
employment practices under Title VII
  in private sector, 48
  in public sector, 383–430, *see also Ricci v. DeStefano* (2009)
English Only policies, 367
Ensley-Gaines v. Runyon (6th Cir. 1996), 116
Environmental Protection Agency, 85
EPA, *see* Equal Pay Act (EPA)
equal burdens test, 122–25, 136–44, 175
Equal Employment Opportunity Commission (EEOC), 76, 98–99
  comparable worth theory, 334–60
  Compliance Manual on Religious Discrimination, 200
  EEOC Pregnancy Guidance (2014), 110–12
  four-fifths rule, 389–91, 416–18
  PDA, interpretation of, 109–14
  prima facie case, 376–78
  Questions and Answers document (1979), 111
  Race and Color Discrimination, 210

race, definition of, 149
  sex discrimination guidelines, 105–6
  temporary disabilities regulations, 115
  undue hardship, guidelines on, 198
  workplace sexual harassment, guidelines for, 242
Equal Pay Act (EPA), 335, 342, 352, 357–58, 366, 381–82
Equal Protection Clause, 289–95
  affirmative action claims, *see* affirmative action claims
  discriminatory intent requirement, 400
  Etsitty claim under, 273
  intermediate scrutiny test, 289, 290, 292
  personal preference concerns, discrimination and, 293–94
  privacy concerns, discrimination and, 295
  rational basis test, 289
  Ricci claim under, 391, 427–29
  safety concerns, discrimination and, 294
  sex-based discrimination, 271, 291–93
  sex-segregated bathrooms and, 275, 298–300
  strict scrutiny test, 289–92
  Title VII, sex-segregated bathrooms and, 295–300
  transgender discrimination and, 290–91
Espinoza, Leslie and Angela P. Harris: *Embracing the Tar-Baby: LatCrit Theory and the Sticky Mess of Race*, 134
Estlund, Cynthia: *The Story of Price Waterhouse v. Hopkins*, 318
Etsitty v. Utah Transit Authority (10th Cir. 2007), 11–12, 18–19, 295
  BFOQ exception, 284–86
  diction and rhetoric, 273–74
  discrimination because of one's genitals, 280–81
  disparate impact, 286–89
  disparate treatment, 280–86
  double bind, 266–71, 273, 274
  Equal Protection Clause, 289, 298–300
  facts, 266–68, 278–79
  feminist judgment, 273–300
  introduction, 266–71
  original opinion, 271–73
  personal preference concerns, discrimination and, 293–94
  ruling below and summary judgment standard, 279
  safety concerns and, 294
  sex as "but for" cause of firing, 281–84

Index

sex as motivating factor in dismissal, 284

sex-based discrimination, 291–93

sex-segregated bathrooms, legality of, 295–300

strict scrutiny test for transgender discrimination, 290–91

Title VII, sex-segregated bathrooms and, 297–98

transgender discrimination as sex discrimination, 281–84

Evans v. Ga. Reg'l Hosp. (11th Cir. 2017), 315, 331

Evans, Daniel J., 347

Everson v. Mich. Dep't of Corr. (6th Cir. 2004), 295

evidence

default rules in civil cases, 49, 54

in disparate treatment cases, 32–34, 37–39, 48–52

explicit biases, 4, 55–56

facially discriminatory, 61, 75–76

Fagan v. National Cash Register Co. (D.C. Cir. 1973), 138

Fair Pay Act, 343

Family and Medical Leave Act (FMLA), 101

Faragher v. City of Boca Raton (1998), 11, 20, 21, 224–26, 414, 463, 465–67, 476–79

Febres v. Challenger Caribbean Corp. (1st Cir. 2000), 55

Federal Arbitration Act (FAA), 26–27

Federal Exp. Corp. v. Holowecki (2008), 110

Federal Rules of Civil Procedure (FRCP)

Rule 12(b)(6), 157, 159

Rule 23, 432, 439–43, 459–61, *see also* *Wal-Mart Stores, Inc. v. Dukes* (2011)

Rule 23(a), 15, 432, 450–56

Rule 23(b), 456–61

Rule 56(c), 382, 473

Feldman v. Allegheny Airlines, Inc. (2d Cir. 1975), 140

Feminist Judgments project (U.K.), 2

Feminist Judgments: Rewritten Opinions of the Supreme Court (Stanchi, Berger, and Crawford) – 34,

feminist legal theory

antiessentialism vs. essentialism debate, 318

double bind, 120, *see also* double bind

narrative technique, 17, 341–42, *see also* *Desert Palace, Inc. v. Costa* (2003)

social framework analysis, 433

Fernandes v. Costa Bros. Masonry, Inc. (1st Cir. 1999), 50, 54–55

Fernandez v. Wynn Oil Co. (9th Cir. 1981), 138, 285

fetal protection policies, 58–60, *see also* *International Union, UAW v. Johnson Controls* (1991)

fetus as third party for BFOQ, 77–82

impact on families, 65–67

safety concerns for entire workforce, 67

Fields v. New York State Office of Mental Retardation and Developmental Disabilities (2d Cir. 1997), 54

Fifty-Six Women Officers Are the First to Patrol Philadelphia's Streets, 213

firefighting, discriminatory hiring and promotion practices, 383–84, *see also* *Ricci v. DeStefano* (2009)

First Amendment, 214

Flaum, Joel M., 305

Floyd v. Amite Cty. Sch. Dist. (5th Cir. 2009), 324

Flynn, Taylor: *Transforming the Debate: Why We Need to Include Transgender Rights in the Struggles for Sex and Sexual Orientation Equality*, 282

Ford, Christine Blasey, 216–18, 226

Ford Motor Co. v. EEOC (1982), 414

four-fifths rule, 389–91, 399, 416–18

Fourteenth Amendment, 180, 214, *see also* Equal Protection Clause

Frank v. United Airlines, Inc. (9th Cir. 2000), 122, 133, 135

Franke, Katherine M.: *What's Wrong with Sexual Harassment?*, 260

Fraternal Order of Police Newark Lodge No. 12 v. City of Newark (3d Cir. 1999), 186–87, 194

FRCP, *see* Federal Rules of Civil Procedure

free market

defense to unequal pay claims, 339–41, 345–46

free market fallacy, 349–51

Fudge, Marcia, 170

Furnco Construction Corp. v. Waters (1978), 353

Gagnon v. Sprint Corp. (8th Cir. 2002), 55

Gagnon, Louise: *Community Partnerships Connect Hair Loss Patients with Dermatologists*, 176

494 *Index*

Garcia v. Elf Atochem North America
  (1994), 255
Garcia v. Gloor (5th Cir. 1980), 160
gender
  gender-based harassment, 19–20, 257–61
  gender bias, 50, 378–81
  gender binary, *see also* equal burdens test,
    stereotypes
  gender binary, equal burdens test and,
    136–37
  gender narratives, 7, 30–57, *see also Desert
    Palace, Inc. v. Costa* (2003)
  gender nonconforming individuals, 136, *see
    also Etsitty v. Utah Transit Authority* (10th
    Cir. 2007)
  gender-segregated workforce, 334–35,
    349–50, 361–83, *see also EEOC v. Sears,
    Roebuck & Co.* (7th Cir. 1988)
  indirect vs. direct reliance on, 407–8
  stereotyping, *see* stereotypes
gender identity discrimination, 11–13, *see also
    Etsitty v. Utah Transit Authority* (10th Cir.
    2007), *Hively v. Ivy Tech Community
    College* (7th Cir. 2017)
  as sex discrimination, 266–333
  paradigms for understanding, 39
  sex stereotyping and gender identity, 261–65
General Electric Co. v. Gilbert (1976), 92, 93,
    102–3, 106–8, 110
General Telephone Co. of Southwest v. Falcon
    (1982), 432, 438, 441, 443, 450–52
Gerdom v. Cont'l Airlines, Inc. (9th Cir. 1982),
    122, 263, 285–86
Gilbert case, *see General Electric Co. v. Gilbert*
    (1976)
Gilmer v. Interstate/Johnson Lane Corp. (1991),
    26–27
Ginsburg, Ruth Bader, 226, 247
Glynn, Sarah Jane: *The New Breadwinners:
    2010 Update*, 99
Goessart v. Cleary (1948), 349
Goldberg, Suzanne B.: *On Making Anti-
    essentialist and Social Constructionist
    Arguments in Courts*, 318
Goldilocks problem, 479, *see also* temporal
    proximity determination
Goldman v. Weinberger (1986), 185, 202, 204
Goluszek v. H. R. Smith (N.D. Ill. 1988), 258
good faith defense, 198, 387–89, 394–95, 398,
    411–12, *see also* reasonable, good faith
    belief standard

Gould, Bill, 367
Government Employee Relations Report,
    May 12, 351
Green, Michael Z.: *Breeden* feminist
    judgment, 16, 463, 468–85
Green, Tristin
  *Discrimination-Reducing Measures at the
    Relational Level* (with Alexandra
    Kalev), 446
  Wal-Mart feminist judgment, 15, 435–61
Greene, D. Wendy: *Catastrophe Mgmt.*
    feminist judgment, 9, 147, 148, 150–80
Greenwald, Anthony G. et al: *Measuring
    Individual Differences in Implicit
    Cognition: The Implicit Association
    Test*, 51
Greeson v. Imperial Irr. Dist. (9th Cir. 1932), 139
Gregory, Ted: *Sexual Harassment Suits Put
    Casinos in Spotlight*, 141
Gresham v. Waffle House, Inc. (N.D. Ga.
    1984), 325
Griggs v. Duke Power Co. (1971), 287, 350, 355,
    412, 416, 418, 427–28, 430, 450
Gross v. FBL Financial Services, Inc. (2009), 25
Grutter v. Bolinger (2008), 407

Habermehl v. Potter (10th Cir. 1998), 279
Hagel, Chuck, 170
hair and makeup requirements, 119–46, *see also
    Jespersen v. Harrah's Operating Co* (9th
    Cir. 2006)
  costs of, 139–40, 142–43
  diversity and, 18
  equal burdens test, 139–44
  psychological costs, 141
  religious exceptions, 152, 155–56
  time required for, 140–41
Hall v. Nalco Co. (7th Cir. 2008), 322–23, 326
Hallett, Karen, 50
Hamm v. Weyauwega Milk Prods. (7th Cir.
    2003), 315
*Hamner v. St. Vincent Hosp. & Health Care
    Ctr., Inc.* (7th Cir. 2000), 315–16
harassment, because of sex, *see* sexual
    harassment
*Hardison, see Trans World Airlines, Inc.
    v. Hardison* (1977)
Harris v. Forklift Systems, Inc. (1993), 257,
    261, 466
Harriss v. Pan Am. World Airways, Inc. (9th
    Cir. 1980), 78, 138

Hayes v. Shelby Mem. Hosp. (11th Cir. 1984), 75
Hazelwood School Dist. v. United States (1977),
   371, 377, 408, 436–37, 444–49
Hazen Paper Co. v. Biggins (1993), 409
Heilman, M. E. and M. C. Haynes:
   *Subjectivity in the Appraisal Process:
   A Facilitator of Gender Bias in Work
   Settings*, 448
Heller v. Columbia Edgewater Country Club
   (D. Or. 2002), 320, 323
Henson v. City of Dundee (11th Cir. 1982), 238
Herek, Gregory M.: *Psychological
   Heterosexism in the United States*, 320
Hermer, Laura: *Paradigms Revised: Intersex
   Children, Bioethics and the Law*, 136
heterosexism, 306–8, 318–22
heterosexuality, 259, 263–65
Hill, Anita, 38, 223, 226
   Speaking Truth to Power, 216
Hively v. Ivy Tech Community College (7th Cir.
   2017), 301–33
   analysis, 317–32
   analytical approaches in, 304
   as 7th Cir. precedent, 315–17
   background, 311–12
   counterarguments, 331–32
   differential treatment, 322–24
   discrimination based on Hively's partner's
      sex, 330
   discrimination based on Hively's sex, 329–30
   feminist judgment, 306–33
   Hively's complaint, 313–15
   original opinion, 302–6
   relationship discrimination, 324–25
   sex plus discrimination, 325–26
   sex stereotyping, 318–22
   sexual orientation discrimination claim,
      313–26
   standard of review, 312
   summary, 12–13
   Title VII, § 703(a)(1), 314–15, 317–26
   Title VII, § 703(m), 316–17, 327–30
   transgender discrimination and, 19, 252
Holcomb v. Iona Coll. (2d Cir. 2008), 324–25
Holder, Eric, 276
Holiday v. Belle's Rest. (W.D. Pa. 1976), 325
Holland v. U.S. (1954), 52
Hollins v. Atl. Co. (6th Cir. 1999), 163
homosexuality, 259, 264–65, *see also* gender
   identity discrimination, *Hively v. Ivy Tech
   Community College* (7th Cir. 2017)

hooks, bell: *Feminist Theory: From Margin to
   Center*, 236
Hornick, Christopher, 386
*Hosanna-Tabor Evangelical Lutheran Church
   & School v. EEOC* (2012), 25–26
hostile work environment claims, 238–40, 258,
   464, 466–67, 478–79
Huber v. Taylor (3d Cir. 2006), 196
Hudgins v. Wrights (Va. 1806), 152, 165, 177
Hughes, Mark Alan: *Poverty in Cities*, 84
Human Rights Watch: *Failing Its Families:
   Lack of Paid Leave and Work-Family
   Supports in the U.S.*, 101

immutable characteristics, 121, 125, 133–36,
   150–55, 159–62, 177–80
impact, 394–95
impermissible/discriminatory reasons for
   employer actions, 30–34
implicit biases, 4, 13–16, 21, 39, 42, 55–56
In re Nat'l Airlines, Inc. (S.D. Fla. 1977), 79
   BFOQ defense, 132
intent to discriminate, 51
intermediate scrutiny test, 289–92
*International Brotherhood of Teamsters
   v. United States* (1977), 353, 355, 375–78,
   408, 436–37, 442, 444–49, 457
International Union, UAW v. Johnson Controls
   (1991), 58–87
   background, 59–60
   BFOQ defense, 62–64, 75–83, 138, 285
   facially discriminatory policy, 61–62
   feminist judgment, 64–65
   fetal protection policy, impact of, 65–67,
      68–69
   Johnson Controls' policies, 69–71
   original opinion, 58–59
   proceedings below, 71–74
   societal context, 83–86
   summary, 7–8
   Supreme Court analysis, 61
   workforce safety concerns, disregard for, 67
intersectionality
   appearances and, 119–214, *see also EEOC
      v. Catastrophe Management Solutions*
      (11th Cir. 2016), *Jespersen v. Harrah's
      Operating Co* (9th Cir. 2006), *Webb
      v. City of Philadelphia* (3d Cir. 2009)
   Black and female, 151–52, 162–70, 172–74
   complexity of facts and, 36
   feminist judgments and, 20–21

intersectionality (cont.)
   Islam, Blackness and gender, 180–214, *see also Webb v. City of Philadelphia* (3d Cir. 2009)
   sex and gender, 250–51
   sex stereotyping and LGBTQ+, 301
intersexuality, 282, *see also* transgender discrimination
Investment Co. Institute v. Camp (1971), 113
Isaacs v. Felder Servs., LLC (M.D. Ala. 2015), 320, 323
Islam, stereotyping of, 180–214, *see also* Muslims, stereotyping of, *Webb v. City of Philadelphia* (3d Cir. 2009)

Jackson v. Arkansas Dep't. of Educ. (8th Cir. 2001), 478
Jackson v. Continental Cargo-Denver (10th Cir. 1999), 280
Jacobs, Harriet: *Incidents in the Life of Slave Girl*, 234
Jefferson v. Ingersoll Int'l Inc. (7th Cir. 1999), 458
Jeffries v. Harris County Comty. Action Comm'n (5th Cir. 1980), 210
Jenkins v. Blue Cross Blue Mut. Hosp. Ins., Inc. (7th Cir. 1976), 161
Jespersen v. Harrah's Operating Co. (9th Cir. 2006), 119–46
   amicus curiae brief, 137, 141
   background, 129–31
   BFOQ defense, 132–33, 137–39
   disparate treatment under Title VII, 132–46
   double bind in, 18
   equal burdens test, 136–44, 175, 297–98
   facts, 119–20
   feminist judgment, 128–46
   feminist judgment, implications of, 124–28
   intentional sex discrimination, 172
   mutability/immutability distinction, 133–36, 178
   original opinion, 120–22
   sex stereotyping, 123–24
   standard of review, 131–32
   summary, 9
job-relatedness/business necessity test, 61, 76, 418–21
Johnson v. Transportation Agency (1987), 257–58, 407, 413
Johnson, Maude: *Caring for African American Hair*, 134

Johnson, Paulette M. Johnson: *A Hair Piece: Perspectives on the Intersection of Race and Gender*, 134
Johnson Controls, see International Union, UAW v. Johnson Controls (1991)
Jones v. State Bd. of Educ. of Tennessee (1970), 236
Jones, Jasmine, 169–70
Jones, Trina: *Meritor* feminist judgment, 10, 215–27
judicial deference, 202–4

Kanter, Rosabeth Moss: *Men and Women of the Corporation*, 350
Katz v. Dole (4th Cir. 1983), 238
Kavanaugh, Brett, 216–18
Keillor, Garrison, 215
Kelley v. Johnson (1976), 185, 202–3, 204
Kelley-Claybrook, Susan: *The Comparable Worth Dilemma: Are Apples and Oranges Ripe for Comparison?*, 358
Kelly v. City of New Haven (Conn. 2005), 423
Kennedy, Anthony, 337, 392–95, 400, 429
Kershaw, Jeila Martin: *Tignon of Colonial Louisiana*, 166
Kessler-Harris, Alice
   expert testimony, *EEOC v. Sears*, 366–67, 373–74, 378–80
   Out to Work, 80
Kim, Clare: *Florida School Threatens to Expel Student over "Natural Hair,"*168
Kimmel, Michael S.: *Masculinity as Homophobia: Fear, Shame, and Silence in the Construction of Gender Identity in Theorizing Masculinities*, 264
Kirkland v. New York State Dep't of Correctional Servs. (2d Cir. 1983), 426
Kogan, Terry S.
   Sex-Separation in Public Restrooms: Law, Architecture, and Gender, 297, 299
   *Transsexuals and Critical Gender Theory: The Possibility of a Restroom Labeled "Other,"*283, 296
Koontz, Elizabeth Duncan: *Childbirth and Child-Rearing Leave: Job-Related Benefits*, 105
Kozinski, Alex, 215

Lach, Denise H. and Patricia A. Gwartney-Gibbs: *Sociological*

Index

Perspectives on Sexual Harassment and Workplace Dispute Resolution, 481
lack of interest defense, 362–63, 365, 378–81
Laderach v. U-Haul of Northwestern Ohio, et al. (6th Cir. 2000), 55
Lam v. University of Hawai'i (9th Cir. 1994), 210
Lambda Legal: *Hively Speaks out after Fed Court Dismisses Discrimination Suit*, 314
Landgraf v. USI Film Products (1994), 53
Latta v. Otter (9th Cir. 2014), 325
Lauer, Matt, 215
Lawrence v. Texas (2003), 253, 304
lead exposure, *see International Union, UAW v. Johnson Controls* (1991)
Lebamoff Enters., Inc. v. Huskey (7th Cir. 2012), 329
Lee, Rebecca K.: *Ricci* feminist judgment, 14, 384–401
legitimate reasons for employer actions, 30–34
Lemons v. City and County of Denver (Fair Empl. Prac. Cas. 1978), 357
LGBTQ+ rights, 18–19, 301, *see also* gender identity discrimination, intersectionality, transgender discrimination
Linder, Mark and Ingrid Nygaard: *Void Where Prohibited: Rest Breaks and the Right to Urinate on Company Time*, 288
Little v. Ill. Dep't of Revenue (2004), 415
Local 28 of Sheet Metal Workers Int'l Ass'n v. EEOC (1986), 456
Local No. 93, International Ass'n of Firefighters v. City of Cleveland (1986), 414
Lochner v. New York (1905), 345
locs. *See* Black women: Black hair, regulation of, *EEOC v. Catastrophe Management Solutions* (11th Cir. 2016)
Loftin, Tiffany Dena, 128
Lopez, Ian F. Haney: *The Social Construction of Race: Some Observations on Illusion, Fabrication, and Choice*, 177
Lorde, Audre, 56
Los Angeles Dep't. of Water & Power v. Manhart (1978), 76, 322–23, 325, 352, 356, 375
Loving v. Virginia (1967), 304–5
Lusardi, Annamaria et al.: *Financially Fragile Households: Evidence and Implications*, 101

Lynch v. Freeman (6th Cir. 1987), 287–88
Lynn v. Regents of the University of California (1981), 353

MacKinnon, Catharine A., 250
Sexual Harassment of Working Women, 218, 350
Madu, Pamela and Roopal Kundu: *Follicular and Scarring Disorders in Skin of Color: Presentation and Management*, 176
makeup, employer policy requiring, *see Jespersen v. Harrah's Operating Co* (9th Cir. 2006)
male discrimination, 254, *see also Oncale v. Sundowner Services* (1998)
Mann, Naomi: *Desert Palace* feminist judgment, 7, 30–43
Marbury v. Madison (1803), 331
Marino v. Indus. Crating Co. (3d Cir. 2004), 196
market defense to unequal pay claims, 339–41, 343, 349–51
Marshall, Thurgood, 106, 110
Martin Marietta case, *see Phillips v. Martin Marietta Corp.* (1971)
masculinities theory, 250–51, 263–65
Massachusetts v. Feeney (1979), 349
McClain v. Lufkin Indus. Inc. (5th Cir. 2008), 456
McClelland, Sara I. et al: *Adapting to Injustice: Young Bisexual Women's Interpretations of Microaggressions*, 319
McConnell, Mitch, 28, 217
McCormick, Marcia: *Johnson* feminist judgment, 8, 58, 64–87
McDonnell Douglas Corp. v. Green (1973)
burden-shifting framework, 23–25, 91, 94, 353, 388–89
circumstantial evidence, 281
disparate impact, 103, 410
disparate treatment analysis, 420
mixed motives, 31
standard of review, 346, 414
McEntee, Gerald W.: *Congressional Testimony of AFSCME President, Gerald W. McEntee, May 1982*, 351
McGinley, Ann C.
Erasing Boundaries: Masculinities, Sexual Minorities, and Employment Discrimination, 322
introduction, xxv

498 Index

McGinley, Ann C (cont.)
Oncale feminist judgment, 11, 246, 249–65
¡Viva la Evoluciòn! Recognizing Unconscious Motive in Title VII, 50
McGowan, Sharon M.: The Bona Fide Body: Title VII's Last Bastion of Intentional Sex Discrimination, 299
McKellips v. Franciscan Health Sys. (W.D. Wash. 2013), 116
McKennon v. Nashville (1995), 414–15
McWilliams v. Fairfax County Board of Supervisors (4th Cir. 1996), 258
Medina v. Income Support Div. (10th Cir. 2005), 272, 331
Meritor Savings Bank, FSB v. Vinson (1986), 215–45
background, 215–20, 233–36
district court's errors, 236–38
employer liability for sexual harassment, 243–45
facts, 222–23, 227–31
feminist opinion, 2
harassment defined, 246
injury, tangible and economic, 238–40
original opinion, 220–22
other alleged harassment, 241–42
preventing sex and gender-based harassment, 19–20
procedural history, 231–33
sexual harassment claim, 238–45, 257–58
strict liability for illegal harassment, 16
summary, 10–11
unwelcomeness standard, 240
voluntary participation inquiry, 240–43
Messerschmidt, James W.: Masculinities and Crime: Critique and Reconceptualization of Theory, 261
#MeToo movement, 27, 35, 37, 42, 215–18
Metropolitan Life Ins. Co., Statistical Bulletin 9, 86
Michael M. v. Superior Court (1981), 293
microaggressive behavior, 480
military policies, US, 169–70, 189–90, 201–2
Miller v. Fed. Land Bank of Spokane (9th Cir. 1978), 139
Minow, Martha: Making All the Difference: Inclusion, Exclusion, and American Law, 89–90
Miró, Esteban, 166–67
Mitchell, Holly, 127–28

Mitchell, Stephen: Testimony to ERISA Advisory Council (2012), 100
mixed-motive cases, 30–31, 47–48, 53–54, 326–27, 439
Mokoena, Hlonipha: From Slavery to Colonialism and School Rules: A History of Myths about Black Hair, 168–69
Monahan, John et al.: Contextual Evidence of Gender Discrimination, 454
Money, John: Gay, Straight and In-Between: The Sexology of Erotic Orientation, 262
Montero v. AGCO Corp. (9th Cir. 1999), 478
Moore, Roy, 215
Morris, Madeline, 80
Morrissey v. Brewer (1972), 460
Morton v. Mancari (1974), 117
Mosbergen, Dominique: Battling Asexual Discrimination, Sexual Violence and "Corrective" Rape, 319
Mullane v. Central Hanover Bank & Trust Co. (1950), 460
Muller v. Oregon (1908), 79, 345, 349, 364
Mullins, Anne: Desert Palace feminist judgment, 7, 17, 30, 34–57
Muslims, stereotyping of, 152, 155, 180–214, see also Webb v. City of Philadelphia (3d Cir. 2009)
mutable characteristics, 121, 125, 133–36, 178
Myers, Howard: The Effect of Sexual Stratification by Race on Arrest in Sexual Battery Cases, 235

NAACP, 154
narrative technique, 17, 30–57, 341–42, see also Desert Palace, Inc. v. Costa (2003)
Nathan, Richard P. and Charles F. Adams, Jr.: Four Perspectives on Urban Hardship, 84
National Ctr. for Children in Poverty, Columbia Univ.: Five Million Children: A Statistical Profile of Our Poorest Young Citizens, 85
National Ctr. for Economic Alternatives: amicus curiae brief, AFSCME v. State of Washington, 357
National Ctr. of Lesbian Rights, 137
National War Labor Board: Termination Report: Industrial Disputes and Wage Stabilization in Wartime, 357
natural hairstyles, see Black women: Black hair, regulation of

Index

499

Nelson, Robert and William Bridges: *Legalizing Gender Inequality*, 445

Nelson, Ryan H.: *Hively* feminist judgment, 12, 301, 306–33

Nesset-Sale, Jo Carol: *The Making of a Civil Rights Plaintiff: A Retrospective by the Plaintiff in Cleveland Board of Education v. Lafleur, a Landmark Pregnancy Discrimination Case*, 294

Nevada Dep't of Human Res. v. Hibbs (2003), 109, 428

Nev-Cal Elec. Securities Co. v. Imperial Irr. Dist (9th Cir. 1936), 141

New Orleans v. Dukes (1976), 289

New York City Commission on Human Rights, 154–55

New York City Transit Authority v. Beazer (1979), 406

Newport News Shipbuilding & Dry Dock Co. v. EEOC (1983), 76, 103, 108, 257, 280–81

Nguyen v. INS (2001), 293

Nichol v. Pullman Standard, Inc. (7th Cir. 1989), 329

Nichols v. Azteca Rest. Enters., Inc. (9th Cir. 2001), 144, 298

noneconomic harm, 199

Norton, Eleanor Holmes, 336

O'Connor, Sandra Day, 31, 53–54, 55, 412, 428

O'Hanlan, Kevin: *City Settles Suit with Woman Who Was Told to Remove Muslim Garb*, 211

O'Reilly, Bill, 215

Obama, Barack, 170, 277

Obergefell v. Hodges (2015), 153–55, 253, 301–2, 304, 325, 332–33

occupational, defined, 77

Occupational Safety and Health Administration (OSHA), 60, 67, 70–71, 82

Oncale v. Sundowner Services (1998), 2, 19–20, 33, 245–65, 272, 304
civility code, 247–49, 251–52, 258–59
defining "because of sex," 259–61
facts, 246–47, 249–50, 256, 476
feminist judgment, 11, 249–65
feminist opinion, impact on subsequent law, 252–55
LGBTQ+ rights, 329
masculinities theory, 250–51
original opinion, 246–49

proving claim of sex- or gender-based harassment, 257–61
same-sex sexual harassment, 250, 304
sex stereotyping, sexual orientation, and gender identity, 261–65
summary, 281
Title VII protections, 258–59, 272, 281, 329, 476

Ontiveros, Maria: *Sears* feminist judgment, 13, 361–68

Onwuachi-Willig, Angela
Another Hair Piece: Exploring New Strands of Analysis under Title VII, 175
Jespersen feminist judgment, 9, 119, 124–46
Meritor feminist judgment, 9–10, 222–45
opposition retaliation claims, 473–74, 475–82

Ostapowicz v. Johnson Bronze Co. (3d Cir. 1976), 209

Ostrowski v. Atlantic Mut. Ins. Cos. (2d Cir. 1992), 51

Parents Involved in Community Schools v. Seattle School Dist. No. 1 (2007), 407, 428–29

Parr v. Woodmen of the World Life Ins. Co. (11th Cir. 1986), 325

participation clause claims, 463–65, 470, 474–75, 482–85

pattern or practice claims, 368, 372–78, 408, 439–40, 442–61

Patton, Tracey Owens: *Hey Girl, Am I More Than My Hair? African American Women and Their Struggles with Beauty, Body Image, and Hair*, 134

Paul, Maureen, et al.: *Corporate Response to Reproductive Hazards in the Workplace: Results of the Family, Work, and Health Survey*, 85

pay gap, 334–35, 342–43

Paycheck Fairness Act, 343

Pearce v. Mayfield School [2002] (Eng.), 323

Pemberton, Jack, 367

Pennsylvania Religious Freedom Protection Act (RFPA), 195

Pension Ben. Guar. Corp. v. LTV Corp. (1990), 331

Perception Institute: *The Good Hair Study*, 175–76

personal preferences, discrimination and, 293–94

Personnel Administrator v. Feeney (1979), 409

Pettaway v. Am. Cast Iron Pipe Co. (5th Cir. 1974), 456–58
Phelps, Teresa Godwin: AFSCME feminist judgment, 14, 340–60
Philips v. Perry (9th Cir. 1997), 201
Phillips v. Martin Marietta Corp. (1971), 75–76, 325–26, 375
Pitts v. Wild Adventures (M.D. Ga. 2008), 163
Plair v. E.J. Brach & Sons, Inc. (7th Cir. 1997), 55
Poirier, Marc R.: *Gender Stereotypes at Work*, 480
police uniform regulations, 181–214, *see also Webb v. City of Philadelphia* (3d Cir. 2009)
Porter, Nicole Buonocore: introduction, xxv
Posner, Richard, 77, 303–5
Postal Service Bd. of Governors v. Aikens (1983), 49, 281
predominance rule, 434–35, 440
pregnancy discrimination, 58–118, *see also* fetal protection policies, *International Union, UAW v. Johnson Controls* (1991), Pregnancy Discrimination Act (PDA), *Young v. United Parcel Service, Inc.* (2015)
    bona fide occupational qualification (BFOQ), 8, 59, 60–61
    dilemma of difference, 89–90
    disparate treatment, 54–55, 72–73
    double bind, 18
    EEOC Pregnancy Guidance (2014), 110–12
    summary of rewritten opinions, 7–8
Pregnancy Discrimination Act (PDA), 59, 62, 79–82
    ADAAA and, 116–17
    BFOQ standard, 63–64, 80–81
    discrimination defined under, 75–76
    EEOC's interpretation of, 109–14
    history and purpose, 105–9
    legislative history, 65–67, 81–82, 107–8, 117
    leveling-up mandate, 114–18
    other persons, interpretation of, 93–94
    pregnancy-neutral accommodation rules and, 94
    rights under, 88
    statutory mandate, 102–5
prenatal care, 84–85
prevention of sex-and gender-based harassment, 19–20
Price Waterhouse v. Hopkins (1989)
    disparate treatment claims, 34, 280, 425

employers' liability under Title VII, 53–54
gender narratives, 30–31
immutable characteristics, 307–11
in original *Feminist Judgments*, 23
intersectional stereotypes, 153, 250–51, 253–54, 261–62, 275
retaliation claims and, 255
sex stereotyping, 178, 318
social constructions, 304
standard of review, 375
stereotypes and discrimination, 78, 82, 121, 124, 136–37, 144–46, 272–73, 282–84, 296, 469–70, 482–83
Title VII violation, 173, 298, 321–22, 328
Prince, Althea: *The Politics of Black Women's Hair*, 165
privacy concerns and discrimination, 295
proof methodologies, 4
Protos v. Volkswagen of America (3d Cir. 1986), 196–97
psychological heterosexism, 319–20
public sector employment practices, 383–430, *see also Ricci v. DeStefano* (2009)
Pullman-Standard v. Swint (1982), 409

queer theory, 254
quid pro quo claims, 237–38
race
    definition of, 149–50
    direct vs. indirect reliance on, 407–9
    race-norming ban, Title VII, 399–400, 426–27
    racial statistical outcomes opposed to race-based classifications, 406–9
    sexual harassment and, 233–36, *see also* intersectionality
    rape, sexual harassment
    corroboration requirements, 37
    definitions and understandings, 233–35
    status, differences in, 235

Rastafarians, 155
rational basis test, 289, 400, 427–28
Ratliff v. City of Milwaukee (7th Cir. 1986), 375
Ray v. Henderson (9th Cir. 2000), 483
Reagan, Ronald, 336
reasonable, good faith belief standard, 463, 466–68, 475–82, *see also* good faith defense
reasonable person standard, 224
recovery, theories of, 4

Index

501

Reeb v. Ohio Dep't of Rehab. & Corr. (6th Cir. 2006), 458
Reeves v. Sanderson Plumbing Products, Inc. (2000), 49, 413
Reeves v. Swift Transp. Co. (6th Cir.2006), 103, 115
relationship discrimination, 324–25
religion
  Rastafarians, 155
  religious accommodations, 156, 187–88
  religious discrimination, 197, 200, 210–12
  religious garb, 18
  religious neutrality defense, 205–7
  religious stereotyping, Islam, 180–214, *see also* Muslims, stereotyping of, *Webb v. City of Philadelphia* (3d Cir. 2009)
  Sikhism, 152, 155
Religious Apparel Amendment, 203
Religious Garb Statute (Pa.), 205
remedies for sex-and gender-based harassment, 19–20
Rene v. MGM Grand Hotel, Inc. (9th Cir. 2002), 331
Reskin, Barbara F.
  Supervisors as Gatekeepers: Male Supervisors' Response to Women's Integration in Plant Jobs (with Irene Padavic), 84
  The Proximate Causes of Employment Discrimination, 446
retaliation claims, 462–85, *see also Clark County School District v. Breeden* (2001)
  Breeden feminist judgment, 473–85
  causation, issue of, 469–71
  opposition activity, 473
  overview, 16
  participation claims, 474–75, 482–85
  retaliation as motivating factor, 482–83
reverse discrimination, 390–91, 393–95, *see also Ricci v. DeStefano* (2009)
Rhodan, Maya: *U.S. Military Rolls back Restrictions on Black Hairstyles*, 169–70
Ricci v. DeStefano (2009), 383–430
  burden of production of evidence, 398–99
  call to overturn, 400–1
  CSB hearings and decision, 403–5
  disparate impact claim, 389, 397–98
  disparate treatment claim, 393–96, 406–27
  equal protection claim, 391, 400, 427–29
  evidentiary burdens, 410–15
  factual background, 402–5

feminist judgment, 397–430
firefighting, discriminatory hiring and promotion practices, 383–84
four-fifths rule, 399, 416–18
good faith defense, 387–89, 398
job-relatedness/business necessity defense, 418–21
less discriminatory alternatives, 421–24
minority candidates' counterfactual dispute, 415–18
New Haven selection process, 415–24
original opinion, 384–97
pro-black/anti-white bias, evidence of, 424–26
procedural background, 405
promotional selection process, 402–3
race-norming ban, Title VII, 399–400, 426–27
reverse discrimination, 390–91
strengthening litigation tools, 18
summary, 14–15
Title VII, purpose of, 397–400, 430
Richards, Bill: *Face-off on Hazardous Jobs: Women's Rights, Fetus Safety*, 83
Ripple, Kenneth F., 305
Roberts, John, 392
Robinson v. Lorillard Corp. (4th Cir. 1971), 458
Robinson v. Shell Oil Co. (1997), 479
Robinson, Lori S.: *The Politics of Hair*, 143
Rogers v. American Airlines (S.D.N.Y. 1981), 148, 161, 177, 179–80
Rogers v. EEOC (5th Cir. 1971), 238
Rogers v. Missouri Pacific R. Co. (1957)., 52
Romer v. Evans (1996), 304
Rosa v. Park W. Bank & Trust Co. (1st Cir. 2000), 284
Rosado, Sybil Dione: *No Nubian Knots or Nappy Locks: Discussing the Politics of Hair among Women of African Descent in the Diaspora*, 143
Rose, Charlie, 215
Rosenberg, Rosalind, 372–73, 377, 378
Rosenfeld v. Southern Pac Co. (1971), 263
Rostker v. Goldberg (1981), 292–93
Rudman, Laurie A.: *Self-Promotion as a Risk Factor for Women: The Costs and Benefits of Counterstereotypical Impression Management*, 260
Rudov, Melvin H. and Nancy Santangelo: *Health Status of Minorities and Low-Income Groups*, 86

Index

Rules Enabling Act, 435, 447
Rush, David: *Socioeconomic Status and Perinatal Outcome*, 84–85
Russell, Constance Dionne: *Styling Civil Rights: The Effect of § 1981 and the Public Accommodations Act on Black Women's Access to White Stylists and Salons*, 167

safety concerns, discrimination and, 294
San Francisco Human Rights Commission, 137
Saucedo, Leticia: *Sears* feminist judgment, 13, 361, 363–83
Sbraga, Tamara Penix and William O'Donohue: *Sexual Harassment*, 141
Scalia, Antonin, 11, 246–48, 392, 431–32, 436, 438
Schultz, Vicki: *Reconceptualizing Sexual Harassment*, 50, 481
Schwartz, Kevin S.: *Equalizing Pregnancy: The Birth of a Super Statute*, 107
Schwartz, Victoria: *Title VII: A Shift from Sex to Relationships*, 324–25
Scrivner v. Socorro Indep. Sch. Dist. (5th Cir. 1999), 478
Sears case, *see EEOC v. Sears, Roebuck & Co.* (7th Cir. 1988)
Segar v. Smith (D.C. Cir. 1984), 457
separate but equal doctrine, 299
Serednyj v. Beverly Healthcare, LLC (7th Cir.2011), 103
Serrano v. Cintas Co. (E.D. Mich. 2009), 449
Sessions, Jeff, 276
sex-based animus, 50
sex discrimination
    comparable worth theory, 334–68, *see also AFSCME v. State of Washington* (9th Cir. 1985)
    conscious intent and, 51
    defining "because of sex,"259–61
    discrimination because of one's genitals, 280–81
    disparate treatment, 280–89
    EEOC guidelines, 105–6
    Equal Protection Clause and, 291–93
    in *Webb*, 209–13
    intermediate scrutiny, 290
    PDA and, 88
    safety exception, 62
    sex plus discrimination, 325–26
    sexual harassment as form of, 220–21

sexual orientation and gender identity discrimination as, 266–333, *see also Etsitty v. Utah Transit Authority* (10th Cir. 2007), *Hively v. Ivy Tech Community College* (7th Cir. 2017)
    sexuality, spectrum of, 259
    transgender discrimination as, 281–84, 291–93, *see also* transgender discrimination
sex-segregated bathrooms, legality of, 266–333, *see also Etsitty v. Utah Transit Authority* (10th Cir. 2007)
    Equal Protection Clause, 298–300
    Title VII, 297–98
sex-stereotyping discrimination, *see* stereotypes
sexual harassment, 215–65, *see also Clark County School District v. Breeden* (2001), *Meritor Savings Bank, FSB v. Vinson* (1986), *Oncale v. Sundowner Services* (1998)
    affirmative defense to, 466–69, 478–79
    age, class, and status differences, 236
    "because of sex" defined, 259–61
    dress and speech, relevance of, 242–43
    EEOC guidelines for, 242
    employer liability for, 243–45
    factual records of other alleged harassment, 241–42
    historical and social context, 233–36
    hostile environment sexual harassment, 238–40, 257–58
    in *Meritor*, 238–45
    injury, tangible and economic, 238–40
    motivation for, 260–61
    overview, 10–11
    prevention of, 19–20
    proving claims of, 257–61
    retaliation claims, *see* retaliation claims
    same-sex harassment, 245–65
    sexual misconduct, 233–36
    temporal proximity determination, 470–71, 479–80, 484–85
    unwelcomeness standard, 221, 224, 240–41
    verbal and/or physical, 259
    voluntary participation inquiry, 240–43
sexual orientation discrimination, *see also Etsitty v. Utah Transit Authority* (10th Cir. 2007), *Hively v. Ivy Tech Community College* (7th Cir. 2017)
    as sex discrimination, 266–333
    feminist scholars on, 307–10

immutable characteristics, 155
  in *Hively*, 313–15
  overview, 11–13
  sex stereotyping and gender identity, 261–65
  Title VIIs coverage of, 301–33
Shakespeare, William, 216
Shauffler, Allen: *TSA to Woman: We're Going to Have to Search Your Hair*, 169
Shaw v. Delta Air Lines (1983), 423
Sheet Metal Workers v. EEOC (1986), 408
Shelton v. Univ. of Med. and Dentistry of N.J. (3d Cir. 2000), 196
Shepherd v. Slater Steels Corp. (7th Cir. 1999), 322
Shi, David E.: *Facing Facts: Realism in American Thought and Culture 1850–1920*, 299
Shipes v. Trinity Ind. (5th Cir. 1993), 457
Shorter v. ICG Holdings, Inc. (10th Cir. 1999), 55
Sikhism, 152, 155
Simmons, Russell, 215
Simonton v. Runyon (2nd Cir. 2000), 331
Siskin, Bernard, 371–72
Skidmore v. Swift & Co. (1944), 105, 109–10, 113
Smith v. City of Salem, Ohio (6th Cir. 2004), 144, 273, 284, 292
Smith v. Wilson (7th Cir. 2013), 327
Smith, Beverly: *Black Women's Health: Notes for a Course*, 234
social framework analysis, 433
social norms, 125–26, 132, 261
Solarz, Steve, 203
Soucek, Brian: *Hively's Self-Induced Blindness*, 306
Spaulding v. University of Washington (1984), 353, 356
Spearman v. Ford Motor Co. (7th Cir. 2000), 315
speech, sexually provocative, 242–43
Sperino, Sandra F.: *Justice Kennedy's Big New Idea*, 329
Spivey v. Beverly Enter., Inc. (11th Cir. 1999), 103
Sprogis v. United Air Lines (7th Cir. 1971), 326
Sreeram v. Louisiana State Medical Center-Shreveport (5th Cir. 1999), 54
St. Mary's Honor Ctr. v. Hicks (1993), 409
Stanchi, Kathryn M.: *Feminist Judgments: Rewritten Opinions of the Supreme Court*, 2

standards of review, 131, 196, *see also* summary judgments: standard of review
stare decisis, 315–17
State Farm Mut. Automobile Ins. v. Campbell (2003), 460
statistics
  statistical analysis, 363–64, 370–72, 376–79
  statistical modeling, 439, 456–58
  statistical outcomes vs. race-based classifications, 406–9
  statistical studies in *Wal-Mart*, 433, 438, 444, 453–55
statutory interpretation
  ambiguous language, 105, 109–14
  legislative text, focus on, 32
  of Title VII, 48–52
  statutory construction, rules of, 102–3
Staub v. Proctor Hospital (2011), 437, 450
stereotypes
  bathroom use and, 296–97
  gender-based, 79–80, 120, 364–65, 438–39
  genitalia and, 283
  heterosexism, 318–21
  implicit biases, 21
  in disparate treatment claims, 34, 39–41
  job performance and, 136–37
  LGBTQ+ community, effect on, 306
  pregnancy and, 109
  race and gender, 234–35
  religious stereotyping, Islam, 180–214, *see also Webb v. City of Philadelphia* (3d Cir. 2009)
  sex, sexual orientation and gender identity, 261–65
  sex stereotyping, 144–46, 254, 318–22
  sex-stereotyping discrimination, 307, 318–19
  sexuality, spectrum of, 259
  social norms and, 125–26
Stevens, John Paul, 106
straight hair mandate, 175–76
strict liability for illegal harassment, 16
strict scrutiny test, 289–91
structural inequalities, 37
Sullivan, Charles: *Wal-Mart* feminist judgment, 16, 430–41
Sullivan, Sean: *Rick Perry Doesn't Back Down from Comparing Homosexuality to Alcoholism*, 319
summary judgments
  evidentiary burden, 401–2, 410–15, 483–85

summary judgments (cont.)
standard of review, 97, 131–32, 184, 196, 207–8, 279, 472–73
supply and demand market theory, 351
Suratt v. Attorney Gen. [2004] (Trin. & Tobago), 333
Sweeny, JoAnne, 9, 120, 124–46
Jespersen feminist judgment, 128–46
systemic discrimination claims, 13–16, 334–461, see also AFSCME v. State of Washington (9th Cir. 1985), class actions, EEOC v. Sears, Roebuck & Co. (7th Cir. 1988), Ricci v. DeStefano (2009), Wal-Mart Stores, Inc. v. Dukes (2011)
systemic disparate treatment, 431, 435–38, 448–50, see also AFSCME v. State of Washington (9th Cir. 1985), EEOC v. Sears, Roebuck & Co. (7th Cir. 1988), Ricci v. DeStefano (2009), Wal-Mart Stores, Inc. v. Dukes (2011)

Taber, Gisela E. and Helen Remick: *Beyond Equal Pay for Equal Work: Comparable Worth in the State of Washington*, 348
Tate v. Showboat Marina Casino P'ship (7th Cir. 2005), 315–16
Tavora v. N.Y. Mercantile Exch. (2d Cir. 1996), 132
Teal v. Connecticut (1982), 380
temporal proximity determination, 470–71, 479–80, 484–85
Terkel, Amanda: *Anti-Gay Stance Still Enshrined in Majority of State GOP Platforms*, 319
Terveer v. Billington (D.D.C. 2014), 320
Tetro v. Elliot Popham Pontiac, Oldsmobile, Buick & GMC Trucks (6th Cir. 1999), 325
Texas Dep't of Community Affairs v. Burdine (1981), 346, 409–10, 426
Thermal Design, Inc. v. Am. Soc'y of Heating Refrigerating & Air-Conditioning Eng., Inc. (7th Cir. 2014), 312
Thomas v. Natl. Football League Players Ass'n (D.C. Cir. 1997), 55
Thomas, Clarence, 32, 216, 336, 392
Thomasson v. Perry (4th Cir. 1996), 202
Tignon Law, 166
Time's Up movement, 42, 215–18
Title VII, Civil Rights Act of 1964,
§ 701, 205, 346, 382
§ 701(k), 418

§ 703, 48, 298
§ 703(a), 75, 351, 427, 476, 482–83
§ 703(a)(1), 53, 194, 196, 255, 280, 285, 317–26, 332–33
§ 703(a)(2), 287
§ 703(e), 77, 159
§ 703(k), 412–13, 418, 428, 430
§ 703(l), 426–27
§ 703(m), 30, 316–17, 327–30, 332–33, 482–83
§ 704, 314, 462–85, see also Clark County School District v. Breeden (2001)
§ 704(a), 471, 482
§ 706, 48, 314
§ 706(g), 456
§ 708, 423
affirmative action claims, see affirmative action claims
amendments to (1991), 31–32
animus/hostility and, 341
antiretaliation provision, 462–85, see also Clark County School District v. Breeden (2001)
BFOQ provision, 77, see also bona fide occupational qualification (BFOQ)
civility code not created by, 247–49, 251–52, 258–59
class certification vs. individual hearings, 439–40
conflict between antidiscriminatory provisions, 384–97
direct evidence requirement, 33–34
discrimination based on plaintiff's partner's sex, 330
discrimination based on plaintiff's sex, 329–30
disparate impact, 286–89, 354–56, 389, 393–96, see also disparate impact claims
disparate treatment under, see disparate treatment claims
employer liability under, 53–54
enforcement provisions, 456
EPA and, 358
equal pay for equal work, 335
hostile work environment claims, 466–67
in Etsitty, 280–89
inclusion mandate, 205–6
legislative history, 331–32
mixed-motive disparate treatment, see mixed-motive cases
Oncale rewritten, impact on, 252–53

Index

participation clause, 463–65, 470, 474–75, 482–85

pattern or practice claims, 368, 372–78, 408

proving claim of sex-or gender-based harassment, 257–61

public sector, coverage of, 384

punitive damages, 458–61

purpose and principles of, 49–50, 83, 170–72, 187, 308–9, 397–400, 430, 457

race-norming ban, 399–400, 426–27

reasonable, good faith belief standard, 463, 468, 475–82

relationship discrimination, 324–25

religious discrimination, 196–208

retaliation claims, *see* retaliation claims

same-sex sexual harassment, 246, *see also* *Oncale v. Sundowner Services* (1998)

sex as "but for" cause of firing, 281–84

sex as motivating factor for dismissal, 284

sex-segregated bathrooms, 275

sex stereotyping, 144–46, 318–22

statutory interpretation of, 48–52

subjective decision making, 447–48

systemic discrimination and, 443–50

transgender discrimination, 281–84

transgender persons and, 276

violations, remedies for, 359–60

voluntary compliance, 414

Title IX guidelines, 276–77

Tobias, Sheila and Lisa Anderson: *What Really Happened to Rosie the Riveter? Demobilization and the Female Labor Force, 1944–47*, 349

Tokoph v. United States (10th Cir. 2014), 329

Toledo v. Nobel-Sysco, Inc. (10th Cir. 1989), 198

Tooley v. Martin Marietta Corp. (9th Cir. 1981), 198

Toonen v. Australia (U.N. Human Rights Comm. 1994), 333

Trans World Airlines, Inc. v. Hardison (1977), 196–97

Trans World Airlines, Inc. v. Thurston (1985), 77, 281

transgender discrimination, 253–54, 266–300, *see also* *Etsitty v. Utah Transit Authority* (10th Cir. 2007), gender identity discrimination

as sex discrimination, 281–84

double bind, 18, 266–71, 273, 274

strict scrutiny test under Equal Protection Clause, 290–91

under Title VII, 271

Transgender Law Center: *Peeing in Peace: A Resource Guide for Transgender Activists and Allies*, 137, 282, 288, 294, 297, 299

Treiman, Donald J. and Heidi I. Hartmann: *Women, Work, and Wages: Equal Pay for Jobs of Equal Value*, 348

trial by formula, 435

Trump, Donald, 28, 217, 276–77, 306

TRW Inc. v. Andrews (2001), 102

Turner, Ilona M.: *Sex Stereotyping per se: Transgender Employees and Title VII*, 282

Turner, Michelle L.: *The Braided Uproar: A Defense of My Sister's Hair and a Contemporary Indictment of Rogers v. American Airlines*, 144

Tyler v. Bethlehem Steel Corp. (2d Cir. 1992)., 52

Ude, Thomas, 385–87

Ulane v. Eastern Airlines, Inc. (7th Cir. 1977), 271–72, 281, 315

unconscious bias, 50–51

undue hardship defense, 197–202

unequal burdens analysis, 122–25, 136–39, 175–76

unequal pay claims, 339–41, 345–46

Uniform Guidelines for Employee Selection Procedures (UGESP), 416, 419

United States v. Board of Education of Philadelphia (3d Cir. 1990), 198, 205

United States v. Mead Corp. (2001), 110

United States v Paradise (1987), 408

United States v. Philadelphia (E.D. Pa. 1980), 213

United States v. Ricciardi (2d Cir. 1966), 140

United States v. Ritchie (9th Cir. 2003), 139

United States v. Virginia (1996), 201, 280, 291, 294, 299

United States v. Windsor (2013), 253, 319

United States Code, 42 U.S.C. §2000e-1 *et seq.*, *see* Title VII, Civil Rights Act of 1964

United States ex rel. Garibaldi v. Orleans Par. Sch. Bd. (5th Cir. 2005), 329

United Steelworkers of America, AFL-CIO-CLC v. Weber (1979), 407, 414, 426

Univ. of Texas Sw. Med. Ctr. v. Nassar (2013), 21, 329, 463, 470

unwelcomeness standard, 221, 224, 240–41

506 *Index*

Urbano v. Cont'l. Airlines, Inc. (5th Cir.1998), 103, 115
US Census Bureau, US Dep't of Commerce: *Maternity Leave and Employment Patterns of First-Time Mothers 1961–2008*, 99
US Coast Guard
 Office of Civil Rights Newsletter, 204
 Religious Apparel Requirement Law, 189
US Commission on Civil Rights, 336
US Constitution, *see* Equal Protection Clause, First Amendment, Fourteenth Amendment
 Due Process Clause, 440–41, 460–61
 First Amendment, 214
 Fourteenth Amendment, 180, 214
US Dep't of Air Force: *Dress and Personal Appearance of Air Force Personnel*, 204
US Dep't of the Army: *Wear and Appearance of Army Uniforms and Insignia*, 204
US Merit Sys. Protection Bd.
 Sexual Harassment in the Federal Government: An Update, 50
 Sexual Harassment in the Federal Workplace: Is It a Problem?, 50

Vade, Dylan: *Expanding Gender and Expanding the Law: Toward a Social and Legal Conceptualization of Gender that Is More Inclusive of Transgender People*, 282, 290
Valdes, Francisco: *Beyond Sexual Orientation in Queer Legal Theory: Majoritarianism, Multidisciplinary, and Responsibility in Social Justice*, 480
Vance v. Ball State University (2013), 11, 21, 225–26
Vickers v. Fairfield Med. Ctr (6th Cir. 2006), 321
Videckis v. Pepperdine Univ. (C.D. Cal. 2015), 323
Villiarimo v. Aloha Island Air, Inc. (9th Cir. 2002), 131
Vinson v. Taylor (D.C. Cir. 1985), 243–44, *see also Meritor Savings Bank, FSB v. Vinson* (1986)
Vojdik, Valorie K.
 Beyond Stereotyping in Equal Protection: Reframing the Exclusion of Women from Combat, 201

Gender Outlaws: Challenging Masculinity in Traditionally Male Institutions, 213
 Webb feminist judgment, 10, 183, 187–214
voluntariness standard, 221–24, 227, 240–41

wage discrimination, 381–82, *see also* Equal Pay Act (EPA)
Wagner v. Dillard Dep't Stores, Inc. (4th Cir. 2001), 54
Waller, Willard, 349
Wal-Mart Stores, Inc. v. Dukes (2011), 430–61
 class actions, notice and opt-out rights, 440–41, 460–61
 class certification commonality question, 438–39
 class certification vs. individual hearings, 439–40
 facts, 441–42
 feminist judgment, 435–61
 FRCP Rule 23, 430–35, 439–41, 443
 FRCP Rule 23(a), 450–56
 FRCP Rule 23(b), 456–61
 key points in feminist judgment, 442–43
 litigation tools in feminist judgment, 18
 original opinion, 431–35
 pattern or practice of discrimination, 444–47
 predominance rule, 440
 purpose or intent in systemic disparate treatment, 448–50
 statistical studies, 364
 subjective decision-making, 447
 summary, 15–16
 systemic discrimination and Title VII, 443–50
Wards Cove Packing Co. v. Atonio (1989), 413, 427–28
Washington v. Davis (1976), 409, 419
Washington v. Seattle School Dist (1982), 428–29
Washington County v. Gunther (1981), 342, 352
Watson v. Fort Worth Bank & Tr. (1988), 280, 412, 416, 427
Watson v. Fort Worth Bank & Tr. (5th Cir. 1986), 456
Watson v. Southwestern Pa. Transp. Auth. (3d Cir. 2000), 54
Weatherby, Danielle: *Hively* feminist judgment, 12, 301–11
Webb v. City of Philadelphia (3d Cir. 2009), 180–214
 background, 180–87, 191–93

Index

constitutional claims, 214
facts, 193–94
feminist judgment, 187–214
good faith efforts to accommodate, 198–202
intersection of race, gender, and religion, 188
judicial deference unwarranted, 202–4
objectification of women's bodies, 188
original opinion, 183–87
police uniform regulations, 202–4
procedural history, 194–96
religious accommodations, 187–88
religious discrimination, 196–208
religious neutrality defense, 205–7
sex discrimination, 209–13
summary, 9–10
summary judgment, genuine disputes of fact and, 207–8
undue hardship defense, 197–202
Wedow v. City of Kan. City (8th Cir. 2006), 287
Weeks v. Southern Bell Tel. & Tel. Co. (5th Cir. 1969), 82
Weinstein, Harvey, 215
Weiss, Marley: *Ricci* feminist judgment, 14, 397–430
welcomeness standard, 240–41
Western Air Lines, Inc. v. Criswell (1985), 77, 79, 81
White v. Cmty. Care, Inc. (W.D. Pa. Dec. 11, 2008), 201
White, Byron, 53
White, Rebecca Hanner: *Breeden* feminist judgment, 16, 462–71
White, Shane and Graham White: *Slave Hair and African American Culture in the Eighteenth and Nineteenth Centuries*, 165–66
Whitman v. Walt Disney Productions, Inc. (9th Cir. 1958), 139
Whitney v. Greater N.Y. Corp. of Seventh-Day Adventists (S.D.N.Y. 1975), 325
Widiss, Deborah: *Young* feminist judgment, 8, 93–118
Wilkins, Pamela: *Etsitty* feminist judgment, 12, 266–77
William Chafe, Henry: *The American Woman: Her Changing Social, Economic, and Political Roles*, 349–50
Williams, Christine L.: *Gender Differences at Work, Women and Men in Non-traditional Occupations* 4, 204

Williams, Joan C. et al.: *A Sip of Cool Water*, 116
Williams, Wendy W.: *Firing the Woman to Protect the Fetus*, 84, 86
Willingham v. Macon Telephone Publishing Co. (5th Cir. 1975), 147–50, 159
Willis study, 347–48, 354
Wilson, William Julius: *The Truly Disadvantaged: The Inner City, the Underclass, and Public Policy*, 84
Wing, Adrien Katherine and Monica Nigh Smith: *Critical Race Feminism Lifts the Veil? Muslim Women, France, and the Headscarf Ban*, 212
Winstead v. Lafayette Cty. Bd. of Cty. Comm'rs (N.D. Fla. 2016), 320
Wise, Lauren A. et al.: *Hair Relaxer Use and Risk of Uterine Leiomyomata in African-American Women*, 176
Witherspoon, Reese, 127
women of color, *see also* Black women
beauty stereotypes and, 146–80, *see also* EEOC *v. Catastrophe Management Solutions* (11th Cir. 2016)
hair and makeup requirements, 126, 142–43
Women's Research and Educ. Inst.: *The American Woman*, 84
Wood, Diane, 303–5
workplace accommodations, 99–102
W. R. Grace & Co. v. Rubber Workers (1983), 424
Wriggins, Jennifer: *Rape, Racism, and the Law*, 233–35
Wright v. Olin Corp. (4th Cir. 1982)., 75
Wrightson v. Pizza Hut of America (4th Cir. 1996), 258
Wygant v. Jackson Board of Educ. (1986), 408, 410

X., Malcolm, 181

Young v. United Parcel Service, Inc. (2015), 24, 87–118
amicus curiae briefs, 100–2, 107, 112–13, 115
double bind in, 18
EEOC's interpretation of PDA, 109–14
factual background, 97–99
feminist judgment, 92–95
original opinion, 90–92
PDA history and purpose, 105–9

508 Index

Young v. United Parcel Service (cont.)
  PDA's leveling-up mandate, 114–18
  PDA's statutory mandate, 102–5
  pregnant women's needs for workplace
    accommodations, 99–102
  rewritten opinion, 96–118
  summary, 8–9

Young v. UPS (4th Cir. 2013), 115
Yuval-Davis, Nira, 212

Zarda v. Altitude Express Inc. (2019), 252, 253
Zinn, Maxine Baca and Bonnie Thornton
    Dill: *Theorizing Difference from
    Multiracial Feminism*, 134

For EU product safety concerns, contact us at Calle de José Abascal, 56–1°, 28003 Madrid, Spain or eugpsr@cambridge.org.

www.ingramcontent.com/pod-product-compliance
Ingram Content Group UK Ltd.
Pitfield, Milton Keynes, MK11 3LW, UK
UKHW020407060825
461487UK00009B/845